Genealogical and Historical

NOTES ON

CULPEPER COUNTY, VIRGINIA.

Embracing a Revised and Enlarged Edition of

DR. PHILIP SLAUGHTER'S

HISTORY OF

ST. MARK'S PARISH.

COMPILED AND PUBLISHED
—BY—
RALEIGH TRAVERS GREEN.
CULPEPER, VA.
1900.

Notice

In many older books, foxing (or discoloration) occurs and, in some instances, print lightens with wear and age. Reprinted books, such as this, often duplicate these flaws, notwithstanding efforts to reduce or eliminate them. The pages of this reprint have been digitally enhanced and, where possible, the flaws eliminated in order to provide clarity of content and a pleasant reading experience.

Copyright © 1900, Raleigh Travers Green

Originally Published:
Culpeper, Virginia
1900

Reprinted by:

Janaway Publishing, Inc.
732 Kelsey Ct.
Santa Maria, California 93454
(805) 925-1038
www.janawaygenealogy.com

2012

ISBN: 978-1-59641-270-5

Made in the United States of America

PREFACE.

———:ooo:———

When the publication of this book was commenced, the undersigned little dreamed of the magnitude of the task he had undertaken. Our intention at first was to reprint Dr. Philip Slaughter's History of St. Mark's Parish, together with as much revised and supplemental matter as we could gather together. Consequently, we had expected to have a book of one hundred and fifty pages, instead of three hundred.

We have endeavored to advertise, as extensively as possible, the proposed publication of the work, in order that all might have the opportunity of making additions and revisions to the genealogical part of the publication. Quite a number availed themselves of the invitation, and to them we are much indebted.

In a work of this kind, mistakes, in the way of omission, and some misstatements, are bound to occur. A work on genealogy, without such, is an impossibility.

We have, for a number of years, contemplated the re-publication of Dr. Slaughter's book, but have waited, hoping to become better equipped for the undertaking. However, thinking that a wait for such improvement, would be in vain, we decided not to delay the publication, but to present to the public the best that we were able to do with our present mechanical equipment, the printing of the book being done in the Exponent office at Culpeper, a Richmond firm doing the binding.

For much valuable assistance we received in our work acknowledgement is made, and thanks therefor returned to Mr. Warren E. Coons, Clerk of the Culpeper courts, Judge Daniel A. Grimsley, of Culpeper, Mr. Thomas Towles Slaughter, of Culpeper, Mr. George Dabney Gray, of Culpeper, Mr. John Strode Barbour, of Culpeper, Major H. C. Burrows, of Culpeper, Rev. E. W. Winfrey, Pastor of the Culpeper Baptist Church, Mr. George M. Williams, of Culpeper, Rev. F. G. Ribble, Rector of St. Stephen's Episcopal Church, of Culpeper, Dr. A. G. Grinnan, of Madison, Mrs. Mary Dunnica Micou, of the Theological Seminary, Virginia, Mr. Joseph Wilmer, of Culpeper, Mrs. John B. Sparrow, of Martinsville, Virginia, Mr. John S. Carpenter, of Louisville, Kentucky, Judge John W. Jones, of Culpeper, formerly of Kentucky, Mr. Willis M. Kemper, of Cincinnati, Ohio, Dr. John A. Fitzhugh, of Amesbury, Massachusetts, Maj. B. S. Thompson, of Huntington, West Virginia, Mr. James M. Rice, of Peoria, Illinois, and Mr. William F. Boogher, of Washington, District of Columbia.

RALEIGH TRAVERS GREEN,

November, 1900.   Culpeper, Va.

TABLE OF CONTENTS.

	Part First.	Part Second.
ASHBY FAMILY,		80.
BALL FAMILY,		79.
BAPTISTS OF CULPEPER, THE,		38.
BARBOUR FAMILY,	52.	135.
BRANDY RIFLES, THE,		35.
BRANDY STATION, BATTLE OF,		34.
BRICK MAKING IN VIRGINIA,	112.	
BROADDUS FAMILY,	84.	146.
BROMFIELD PARISH,	35.	
BROWN FAMILY,	111.	83.
BROWNING FAMILY,		151.
BRYAN-LILLARD FAMILY,		150.
CALVARY CHURCH REBUILT,	118.	
CARTER FAMILY,	53.	
CATALPA,		6.
CAVE FAMILY,	54.	
CEDAR RUN, BATTLE OF,		33.
CHURCH, ORGANIZATION OF IN VIRGINIA,	19.	
CHURCHES OF ST. MARK'S PARISH.	31.	

	Part First.	Part Second.
CLAYTON FAMILY,	55.	
CLAYTON, MAJ. PHILIP,		6.
COLE, REV. JOHN,	27.	
COLE, REV. JOHN, SUCCESSORS OF,	30.	
COLEMAN FAMILY,	56.	
COMPANY B, 6TH. VA. CAVALRY,		35.
COMPANY B, 13TH. VA. INFANTRY,		21.
COMPANY C, 7TH. VA. INFANTRY,		19.
COMPANY E, 7TH. VA. INFANTRY,		21.
CONWAY FAMILY,	57.	
COOKE FAMILY,		79.
COUNTY COURT OF CULPEPER, THE FIRST,		160.
CULPEPER AS A BATTLE GROUND,		97.
CULPEPER COMMITTEE OF SAFETY,		5.
CULPEPER, COUNTY OF	11.	
CULPEPER COUNTY, HISTORY,		1.
CULPEPER COUNTY, ENGAGEMENTS IN		32.
CULPEPER, FREEHOLDERS OF, MEETING OF.	120.	
CULPEPER IN THE CIVIL WAR,		18.
CULPEPER IN THE REVOLUTION,		2.
CULPEPER MINUTE MEN,		12.
CULPEPER OF TO-DAY,		11, 160.
CULPEPER, PRESENT LIMITS OF,		2.
CULPEPER'S PROTEST AGAINST STAMP ACT,		131.
CULPEPER, TOWNS IN,	112.	11.
CUPEPER, TOWN OF, LAID OUT,		160.
FAIRFAX LODGE, A. F. & A. M.		6.
FAMILY GENEALOGIES,	51.	75, 132.
FIELD FAMILY,	57.	
FONTAINE, JNO., DIARY OF,	39.	
FRY FAMILY,	58.	
GARNETT FAMILY,	59.	

	Part First.	Part Second.
GENEALOGISTS, NOTES FOR,		45.
GERMANNA SETTLEMENT,	4, 42.	2, 159.
GLASSELL FAMILY,	60.	
GREEN, COL. JOHN,	68.	
GREEN FAMILY,	61.	
GRINNAN FAMILY,		79.
HENRY-WINSTON FAMILY,	75.	
HILL FAMILY,		85.
HILL, GEN. A. P.	111.	94.
HISTORICAL EXCURSIONS,	36.	
JONES FAMILY,		89.
KNIGHTS OF THE GOLDEN HORSE SHOE,	36.	
LA FAYETTE IN CULPEPER,		156.
LAMON, REV. A. H.,	25, 118.	
LAWYERS IN CULPEPER BEFORE REVOLUTION,	112.	
LILLARD-BRYAN FAMILY		150.
LITTLEPAGE, LEWIS,	48.	
MADISON FAMILY,	71.	
MARRIAGE RECORD,		56.
MARRIAGE RECORD, INDEX TO,		161.
MASON FAMILY,		79.
MEDICAL MEN IN CULPEPER BEFORE REVOLUTION,	111.	
MICOU FAMILY,		75.
MISCELLANEOUS ENLISTMENTS,		23.
PENDLETON, EDMUND,	105.	
PENDLETON FAMILY,	95, 119.	
REVOLUTION, PENSIONERS OF,		128.
RICE FAMILY,		132.
SLAUGHTER, CAPT. PHILIP, DAIRY OF	46.	
SLAUGHTER FAMILY,	85.	
SOLDIERS IN FRENCH AND INDIAN WAR,	14.	
SOLDIERS IN WAR OF 1812,		130.

	Part First.	Part Second.
SOMERVILLE FAMILY,		79.
SPOTSWOOD FAMILY,	72.	
SPOTSWOOD, SIR ALEXANDER,	1.	
STEVENS, GEN. EDWARD,		5.
STEVENSON, REV. JAMES,	20, 73.	
ST. MARK'S PARISH, ADDENDA,	114.	
ST. MARK'S PARISH, FIRST MINISTER OF,	7.	
ST. MARK'S PARISH HISTORY CONTINUED,	114.	
ST. MARK'S PARISH, NOTES ON,	118.	
ST. MARK'S PARISH, ORGANIZATION OF,	3.	
ST. MARK'S PARISH, VESTRYMEN OF,	113, 117.	
STROTHER FAMILY,	83.	
ST. THOMAS' PARISH,	32.	
TAYLOR FAMILY,	74.	
THOM FAMILY,		84.
THOMAS FAMILY,		155.
THOMPSON FAMILY,	79.	86.
THOMPSON, REV. JOHN,	8.	
THOMPSON, RICHARD W.,		87.
TOBACCO PLANT, THE,	50.	
WAR OF 1812, CULPEPER COMPANY,		130.
WASHINGTON, GEORGE, SURVEYOR,		5.
WILL RECORDS OF CULPEPER,		45.
WILLIAMS FAMILY,	108.	
WINSTON-HENRY FAMILY,	75.	
WOODVILLE, REV. JOHN,	21, 79.	
YANCEY FAMILY,		81.

PART FIRST.

Rev. PHILIP SLAUGHTER, D. D.

REV. PHILIP SLAUGHTER, D. D.

———:ooo:———

Stretching from the foot hills of the Blue Ridge mountains eastward, some thirty miles, and taking in the valleys of the Rapidan, Robertson and Rappahannock rivers, lies an extensive plain. It is broken here and there by several small mountains—miniature models of the great range to the west. This constituted the colonial parish of St. Mark's, which was established in 1731, with Robert and Francis Slaughter as its first church wardens.

The Slaughters owned large landed estates in this parish and west of Slaughter's mountain, at the old homestead of "Springfield," was born in 1808, Philip Slaughter, destined, many years later, to be the chronicler of this parish and many others, as well as historiographer of the Diocese of Virginia.

His grandfather and father were both soldiers, the former commanding a regiment at the battle of Great Bridge, the latter serving gallantly throughout the war of independence as captain in the 8th continental regiment, and going through the terrible campaign of Valley Forge with John Marshall, afterwards chief justice of the United States, as his lieutenant and mess mate.

Thus was blended in the young Philip Slaughter the qualities of his great-grandfather and uncle—the first church wardens—and those of his grandfather and father—the soldiers—and no one who ever saw him rise to speak, could doubt that the soldier of the Cross would have been as valiant a soldier of the State, if such service had been his. His tall, spare figure, with a manner which combined great personal dignity with the utmost courtesy and kindliness, made him noticeable in any assemblage, and when he spoke, a voice, whose wonderful modulations even advancing years could not affect, never failed to fix the attention of his hearers.

Trained by the best tutors of the day, and at one of the first classical schools, young Slaughter learned, not only to avail himself of the thoughts of others, but to think for himself. He entered the University of Virginia the first year of its existence, and formed one of a class of notable men, many of them afterwards distinguished in the service of the State.

He was admitted to the bar, but in a few years entered the Theological Seminary of Virginia, and was ordained deacon in 1834, and priest in 1835. For some fourteen years he did most effective work in some of the important parishes in Virginia and elsewhere. Failing health caused him to go abroad for a time in the years 1848 and 1849. On his return he devoted his energies to the cause of African colonization; with wise foresight anticipating and trying thus to avert the dreadful catastrophe he lived to witness.

Five years were given to this task, and to general evangelistic work. He then returned to Slaughter's mountain, where he built a chapel on his own land, and ministered to his neighbors and their dependents, giving his services as a free will offering. Here he lived up to the outbreak of the war between the States, occupying a unique position. A staunch churchman in the midst of members of other Christian bodies, he provoked no antagonism from those who differed with him, and by his wise and affectionate counsel and sympathy, probably did more than any man in the State to win the respect, and often the allegiance of men of every class to the church of his forefathers.

He was a man of rare gifts. Of a poetic temperament, he was fond of literature, and master of the best writers in the English language. As a pulpit orator he was unsurpassed in his day, and his personal magnetism was such that he swayed his audience "whithersoever he listed."

The "mission" of the present day with its week of continuous services and preaching was not unknown fifty years ago. Dr. Slaughter had great power as a missioner, and hosts of the careless and indifferent were brought by him into the "way of righteousness."

In his own community and beyond, he was the trusted friend and adviser, as well as the pastor, the adjuster of variances, and the ultimate court of arbitration.

An exile from home, during the four years of war, he ministered whenever opportunity offered to those among whom his lot was cast. In hospital and camp his kindly presence carried help and solace to many a stricken body, and many a weary soul.

And when the war was over, he came back to his devastated home—the scene of one of its bloodiest battles—and took up his work with the strength that was left, meeting the privations and trials of his lot with the courage of a soldier and the loyalty of a patriot, in uncomplaining toil, as an humble parish minister, setting a noble example of the old Roman tradition "Fortuna non mutat genus." And so the end nobly crowned his work after a life spent in the service of his master in the land, and among the people he loved so well, in the home of his childhood and of his ripened years, he was, in the month of June, 1890, "gathered unto his Father's, having the testimony of a good conscience, in the confidence of a certain faith, and in favor with God and man."

W.

A HISTORY

—OF—

ST. MARK'S PARISH,

CULPEPER COUNTY, VIRGINIA,

WITH NOTES OF

✦ OLD CHURCHES AND OLD FAMILIES ✦

AND ILLUSTRATIONS OF THE

MANNERS AND CUSTOMS OF THE OLDEN TIME.

—BY—

REV. PHILIP SLAUGHTER, D. D.

Rector of Emmanuel Church, Culpeper Co., Va.

AUTHOR OF THE HISTORIES OF ST. GEORGE'S AND BRISTOL PARISHES, VA.

THE AUTHOR'S PREFACE.
——:oo:——

The author believes that he was the first person who conceived the idea of writing a history of the old parishes in Virginia upon the basis of the old vestry-books and registers. Thirty years ago he published the History of Bristol Parish (Petersburg), of which he was then rector. In 1849 he published the History of St. George's Parish, in Spotsylvania. His labors were then suspended by ill-health, and he went abroad, never expecting to resume them. This personal evil resulted in the general good. Bishop Meade, the most competent of all men for this special task, was induced to take up the subject, and the result was the valuable work, "The Old Churches and Families of Virginia," in which the author's histories of St. George and Bristol Parishes, and some other materials which he had gathered, were incorporated. The author, in his old age, returns to his first love, and submits to the public a history of his native parish of St. Mark's. The reader will please bear in mind that this is not a general history of the civil and social institutions within the bounds of this parish, and yet he will find in it many incidental illustrations of these subjects. He must also be reminded that it does not purport to be a history of Christianity in its varied forms and polities within in the lines of St Mark's. That would open a large field, which the author has not time or strength now to traverse. He means, therefore, no disrespect to other Christian polities and peoples (among whom are numbered many valued friends and relatives) in omitting all reference to them. In this respect he has followed the example of the parish records, which are the basis of this history, and in which there is not one word about Christians of other names, from the first organization of St. Mark's Parish, in 1731, to the present moment. The vestry abstained in like manner from political allusion; for while keeping up its organization and records during the whole of the American Revolution, the only allusion to an event which so absorbed men's minds is the following entry:—"Capt. Richard Yancey is appointed a vestryman in place of Major John Green, in Continental service."

Church history in Virginia may be distributed into several eras, the observation of which will make it more intelligible. The first is the Era of the Church of England in the Colony and Dominion of Virginia. This covers the whole period from the first plantation of Jamestown to the American Revolution. During this period the Church was in bondage to the State, which never allowed it to organize. For political reasons it was not permitted to have a bishop; and there were no ordinations or confirmations during the whole colonial term. Candidates for orders had to make the then costly, protracted and perilous voyage across the sea. Some of them could not pay the expense, and others were lost at sea, while some died of the small-pox in London, which was very fatal before the use of vaccination. The Church was not only denied an executive head, but it had no legislature. It had no authority to pass a law, enact a canon, or inflict a penalty, not even for the discipline of its own ministers and members; and it never performed one of these functions.

The second Era may be called the Transition Age, during which the ties that bound it to the State were one by one severed; and this lasted from 1776 to the first organization of the Protestant Episcopal Church of Virginia, in 1785, when it became free, although its organization was not perfected until the election of its first bishop (Madison).

The next era may be called the Era of Decline, when the Episcopal Church was staggering under the odium of having been an established church, which lasted until William Meade, William Wilmer, William Hawley, Oliver Norris, and such like, came upon the stage, and elected Richard Channing Moore, of New York, to be their leader. Then began the Era of Revival; after a torpid winter, an awakening spring followed by a fruitful summer. To this season we may apply the words of Shakspeare, but in a higher sense:—

> "Now is the winter of our discontent
> Made glorious summer by this son of YORK;
> And all the clouds that lowered upon our house,
> In the deep bosom of the ocean buried"—

While we recognize and rejoice in the good that has been done by other Christian ministers outside of our fold, we too may be permitted to rejoice that our Virginia Episcopal Roll is "without a blemish"; and that their hands have been upheld by a goodly and growing company of preachers, who have rekindled the fires upon many an old altar where the sparrow had found her an house, and the swallow a nest for herself, even thine altars, O Lord God of Hosts! my King and my God.

SUGGESTIONS TO OUR READERS.

In such an almost countless number of names and dates as occur in this book, it must needs be that errors of the pen or of the press will creep in. If those who detect them will kindly communicate them to the author, he will gladly correct them in a new edition; the proposed first edition having been ordered in anticipation of publication. If the reader will bear in mind the following facts it will facilitate his understanding of this history. In 1720 Spotsylvania County was taken from Essex, King and Queen and King William, whose jurisdiction hitherto extended to the great mountains. St. George's Parish, coterminous with Spotsylvania, was formed by the same act. In 1731 St. Mark's was taken from St. George. In 1734 Orange was formed from

Spotsylvania. In 1740 St. Thomas was taken from St. Mark's. In 1748 Culpeper was formed from Orange. In 1752 Bromfield Parish was taken from St. Mark's. In 1792 Madison County was taken from Culpeper. In 1831 Rappahannock County was formed from Culpeper, and in 1838 the County of Greene was taken from the County of Orange.

ACKNOWLEDGMENTS,

Besides the acknowledgments made in the body of this work, the author is under obligations to Isaac Winston, Jr., for volunteering to transcribe his entire manuscript into a fair hand—a task almost as difficult as the interpretation of hieroglyphical characters by Oriental scholars. I am indebted for a like favor to Rev. Dr. Randolph, of Emmanuel Church, Baltimore, for volunteering to read the proof-sheets as they passed through the press; and to the Rev. Dr. Dalrymple, the Hon. Hugh Blair Grigsby, Mr. R. A. Brock, of the Virginia Historical Society, Dr. Andrew Grinnan, of Madison, Mr. George Mason Williams, of Culpeper, Col. Edward McDonald, of Louisville, to the gentlemen of the press, and to many correspondents too numerous to be named, for aid and sympathy in his work.

ST. MARK'S PARISH.

SIR ALEXANDER SPOTSWOOD,
Lieutenant-Governor of Virginia.

HIS ANCESTRY, BIRTH, MARRIAGE, ADMINISTRATION, DEATH, BURIAL, DESCENDANTS, AND RELATION TO ST. MARK'S PARISH.

A history of St. Mark's Parish in which Gov. Spotswood did not have a prominent place, would be like a portrait with the most prominent feature left out. Not only was he a sagacious statesman, a gallant cavalier, a brave and dashing soldier; but he was also a devout Church of England man, ready to enter the lists as her champion against all comers, not excepting the vestries, who were the advocates of the people's rights, and the miniature Parliaments in which the leading statesmen of the American Revolution were trained. He was the largest landed proprietor within the bounds of the parish; he founded the first town (Germanna), he developed the first mines, and erected the first iron furnace in America. He erected, chiefly at his own expense, the first parish church, and organized and equipped, at Germanna, "The Knights of the Golden Horseshoe," who first passed the Blue Ridge, and blazed the way to the Valley of Virginia, and whose whole course was within the limits of the original parish of St. Mark's.

Governor Spotswood was the great-grandson of John Spotswood, Archbishop of St. Andrew's and author of the History of the Church of Scotland. His grandfather was Robert Spotswood, Lord President of the College of Justice, and author of the "Practicks of the Laws of Scotland," who was one of the eight eminent lawyers executed by the Parliament of Scotland, which (according to Sir Walter Scott) consisted wholly of Covenanters. While he was at private prayer on the scaffold (says Sir Walter) he was interrupted by the Presbyterian minister in attendance, who asked if he did not desire his prayers and those of the people. Sir Robert replied that he earnestly desired the prayers of the people but not those of the preacher; for that, in his opinion, God had expressed his displeasure against Scotland by sending a lying spirit into the mouths of the prophets. The father of Governor Spotswood was Dr. Robert Spotswood, physician to the Governor of Tangiers in Africa, and his mother had been Mrs. Catherine Elliott. Dr. Spotswood died in Tangiers in 1688, leaving one son, the subject of this notice, who was born in 1676. Governor Spotswood, "who had been bred in the army," was aide to the Duke of Marlborough, and was badly wounded in the breast at the battle of Blenheim.

His arrival in Virginia, says Campbell, was greeted with joy, because he brought with him the right of Habeas Corpus—a right guaranteed to every Englishman by Magna Charta, but hitherto denied to Virginians. Spotswood entered upon his duties as Governor in 1710, and the two Houses of the General Assembly,severally, returned thanks for their relief from long imprisonment, and appropriated more than two thousand pounds for completing the Governor's palace. Although he was, in accordance with the dominant doctrines of his day, a strenuous advocate of the Royal prerogative in Church and State, yet he was one of the most energetic, patriotic and farseeing statesmen that ever ruled Virginia. He first suggested a chain of forts from the Lakes to the Mississippi (beyond the Alleghanies) to check the encroachments of the French; but many years elapsed before his suggestion and policy were adopted. It was he who conceived the idea of making tobacco notes a circulating medium. His military genius and experience enabled him to wield the militia with great effect against the hostile Indians; but he was no less zealous in the conception and execution of measures for their civilization and convertion to Christianity, as the Indian school at Christanna on the Meherin river, and the fund of £1000 for instructing their children at William and Mary College, attest. In 1739 he was made Deputy Postmaster-General for the Colonies; and it was he (says Campbell) who promoted Benjamin Franklin to be postmaster for the province of Pennsylvania.

Governor Spotswood died at Annapolis, on his way to command the army against Carthagena, and was buried at Temple Farm, one of his old country seats near Yorktown, so named from a house in the garden erected by Governor Spotswood as a cemetery. Dr. Shield, who bought the farm in 1834, says, "the walls of the temple were then only several feet high: within them I found heaps of broken tombstones, and on putting the fragments together, I found the name of Governor Spotswood."

It was in the Temple Farm mansion that Lord Cornwallis met Washington and signed the articles of capitulation which secured American independence.

There is some verbal discrepancy between the authorities about the name of the lady whom Governor Spotswood married. Bishop Meade, upon the authority of a daughter of General Alexander Spotswood, says that her name was Jane Butler, sister of the Duke of Ormond. Charles Campbell, our painstaking historian, says her name was Butler Bryan (pronounced Brain), daughter of Richard Bryan, of Westminster, and her Christian name was after Jas. Butler, Duke of Ormond, her godfather. On the other hand, several of her lineal descendants have informed the present writer that Mrs. Spotswood was the daughter of Richard Brayne, "whose letters to his daughter show him to have been a man of culture." The name of Butler Brayne has been perpetuated in this branch of the family to this day, which raises a strong presumption that it is the true orthography.

Since the above was written I have procured, through the medium of Judge Barton and Capt. George Minor, of Fredericksburg, documentary proof which settles the vexed question, in the form of a letter written by Judge Edmond Pendleton for his client John Benger, the son of Dorothea (Col. Byrd's Miss Thecky) Brayne, sister of Lady Spotswood. The letter is dated Virginia, Sept. 8th, 1762, and is addressed to Capt.Wm. Fox, and is signed by John Benger and Edmond Pendleton, and in it is the following paragraph:—"Richard Brayne and his wife are dead, and Mrs. Brayne's issue was four daughters, Anne, Diana, Dorothy,and Butler. Dorothy intermarried with Elliot Benger, gentleman, and, with her husband, is since dead, and I am her son and heir. Butler intermarried with Major-General Alexander Spotswood, and afterwards married John Thompson (Clerk). She is dead, and Alexander

Spotswood, infant, is her grandson and heir, and is now in England. Anne and Diana remained in England and never married."

Governor Spotswood had four children, John, Robert Anne. Catherine, and Dorothea. John married in 1745, Mary, daughter of Capt. Dandridge, of the British army and had two sons, General Alexander and Capt. John, both officers of the Revolution; and two daughters, Mary and Ann. John, son of John, and grandson of the Governor, married Mary Rousee of Essex, and had many children. General Alexander Spotswood, grandson of the Governor married Elizabeth, daughter of Augustine and niece of General Washington. Robert, second son of the Governor, was an officer under Washington in 1755, and was killed by the Indians. Anne Catherine (Kate) married Bernard Moore, of Chelsea in King William; and their daughter married Charles Carter of Shirley, and was the grandmother of our Chevalier Bayard (sans peur et sans reproche), General Robert Edward Lee, named after two of his uncles, Robert and Edward Carter.

Kate Spotswood, Mrs. B. Moore, was a great beauty. The late Mrs. Dunbar of Falmouth, had seen her, and was so impressed by the vision, that, with true womanly instinct, she remembered, after the lapse of many years, the details of her dress, which we reproduce for the benefit of our lady readers. It was a fawn-colored satin, square in the neck, over a blue satin petticoat, with satin shoes and buckles to match, on very small and beautifully shaped feet. A granddaughter of Kate, now living in a green old age, says that when she was a little girl she saw Kate sitting up in her bed at Chelsea, combing her white and silken hair, with a servant holding up a looking-glass before her.

There is a portrait of Governor Spotswood at Chelsea, and there was another at Sedley Lodge in Orange (now in the State Library at Richmond), which the author of this historical tract had daguerreotyped. It represents him in full dress, scarlet velvet—graceful and commanding in face and figure—antique model of the cavalier,—the old English and the old Virginia gentleman, who are as much alike as father and son. What a genealogical tree!—with General Sir Alexander Spotswood its root in Virginia, and Robert Edward Lee its bright, consummate flower.

ORGANIZATION OF ST. MARK'S PARISH.

The Register of St. Mark's Parish, which lies before me, is the oldest manuscript record in the county of Culpeper. The parish is older than the county by eighteen years, the former having been established by Act of Assemby in 1730, and the latter in 1748. It is curious to note the progress of population, and parishes and counties, from their original seats on tidewater towards the mountains. The people went before, the parishes followed after, and the counties completed the organization, according to the uniform policy of the British Government to keep the Church and State in union.

In 1634 the colony of Virginia was divided by the House of Burgesses into eight counties, or shires, as they were then called. In 1692 the old county of Rappahannock was extinguished, and its territory distributed into the counties of Richmond on the north, and Essex on the south, side of the Rappahannock River. The movement of the growing population was along the banks of the rivers, on account of the greater productiveness of the soil, and the facilities of transportation, in the absence of roads in the intervening wilderness. Thus early in the eighteenth century the settlement had passed the Falls of the Rappahannock and reached the Rapid Ann River, where a colony of Germans had seated themselves, and Lieutenant-Governor Spotswood had established a furnace and built a "castle," in which he occasionally resided.

Over the new settlement a new county and a new parish were erected in 1720. The preamble to the Act of Assembly declares that "the frontiers towards the high mountains, being exposed to dangers from the Indians and the French settlements towards the west, a new county is established, bordering upon Snow Creek up to the Mill thence by a southwest course to the North Anna, thence up the said river as far as convenient, and thence by a line over the high mountains to the river Shenandoah, so as to include the North Pass through said mountains; thence down said river till it comes against the head of Rappahannock River, and down that river to the mouth of Snow Creek; which tract of land shall be come a county by the name of Spotsylvania, and the whole county shall be one parish, by the name of St. George."

The Act also appropriated five hundred pounds for a church, courthouse, pillory and stocks, where the Governor shall appoint. Another clause appropriates one thousand pounds for arms and ammunition, to such "Christian tithables" as shall go to seat this county. The county of Brunswick was established by the same law. The inhabitants were made free of levies for ten years. The same privilege is extended to Germans and other foreign Protestants, "who may not understand English readily," if they will entertain a minister of their own.

It will be observed that the movement of counties, parishes and people, by way of Spotsylvania and Brunswick, was towards the northern and southern passes through the "high mountains" to transcend which and see what lay beyond was the great problem of the day.

The Rev. Hugh Jones, one of the Colonial clergy, in his "Present State of Virginia," published about 1724, says:—"Beyond Governor Spotswood's furnace, within view of the vast mountains, he has founded a town called Germanna, from some Germans sent over by Queen Ann, who are *now removed up further*. Here he has servants and workmen of most handicraft trades, and he is building a church, courthouse, and dwelling-house for himself, and with his servants and negroes he has cleared plantations about it, proposing great encouragement for people to come and settle in that uninhabited part of the world, lately divided into a county."

Colonel Byrd, of Westover, on James River, an accomplished gentleman, an adventurous traveller, and inimitable humorists, visited Colonel Spotswood in 1732, and indites the following pleasant gossip on the occasion.

"The famous town of Germanna consists of Colonel Spotswood's enchanted castle on one side, and a baker's dozen of ruinous tenements on the other where so many German families had dwelt some years ago, but are now removed ten miles higher, in the Fork of the Rappahannock, to land of their own. There had also been a chapel about a bow shot from the Colonel's house, at the end of an avenue of cherry trees, but some pious people had lately burnt it down, with intent to get another built nearer their own homes. Here I arrived abour three o'clock, and found only Mrs. Spotswood at home, who received her old acquaintance with many a gracious smile. I was carried into a room elegantly set off with pier glasses, the largest of which came soon after to an odd misfortune. Among other favorite animals which cheered this lady's solitude, a brace of tame deer ran familiarly about the house, and one of them came to stare at me as a stranger, but unluckily spying his own figure in the glass, he made a spring over the tea-table that stood under it, and shattered the glass to pieces, and falling back upon the tea table made, a terrible fracas among the china. This exploit was so sudden, and accompanied by such noise, that it surprised me and perfectly frightened Mrs. Spotswood. But it was worth all the damage to show the moderation and good humor with which she bore the disaster. In the evening the noble Colonel came from his mines, who saluted me very civilly; and Mrs. Spotswood's sister Miss Thecky, who had been to meet him, en cavalier, was so kind, too, as to bid me welcome. We talked over a legend of old stories, supped about nine, and then prattled with the ladies till it was time for a traveller to retire. In the meantime I observed my old friend to be very uxorious and exceedingly fond of his children. This was so opposite to the maxims he used to preach up before he was married, that I could not forbear rubbing up the memory of them. But he gave a very good-natured turn to his change of sentiments, by alleging that whoever brings a poor gentlewoman into so solitary a place, from all her friends and acquaintances, would be ungrateful not to use her and all that belongs to her with all possible tenderness. We all kept snug in our several apartments till nine, except Miss Thecky, who was the housewife of the family. At that hour we met over a pot of coffee, which was not strong enough to give us the palsy. After breakfast, the Colonel and I left the ladies to their domestic affairs, and took a turn in the garden, which has nothing beautiful in it but three terrace walks, that fall in slopes one below another. I let him understand that, besides the pleasure of paying him a visit, I came to be instructed by so great a master in the mystery of making iron, wherein he led the way, and was the Tubal Cain of Virginia. He corrected me a little there, saying that he was not only the first in his country, but the first in North America who had erected a regular furnace; that they ran altogether on bloomeries in New England and Pennsylvania till his example had made them attempt greater works. He said that the four furnaces now at work in Virginia circulated a great sum of money for provisions, &c., in the adjacent counties. He told me that he had iron in several parts of his tract of forty-five thousand acres of land, but that the mine he was at work upon was thirteen miles below Germanna. He raised the ore a mile from the furnace, and carted the iron, when made, fifteen miles to his plantation on Massaponax. He said that during his absence in England he had lost eighty slaves, his furnace was still the greater part of the time, and all his plantations ran to ruin. But he was rightly served for trusting his affairs to a mathematician (Mr. Graeme), whose thoughts were always 'among the stars.' The afternoon was devoted to the ladies who conducted me through a shady lane to the river, and by the way made me drink some very fine water that issued from a marble fountain. Just behind it was a covered bench, where Miss Thecky often sat and bewailed her virginity. The river is about fifty yards wide, and so rapid that the ferry-boat is towed over by a chain, and therefore called the Rapidan." The Miss Thecky above mentioned was evidently the sister of Mrs. Spotswood, who married Mr. Benger, a cousin of the Governor, and from whom some of the Minors and Frenchs of Spotsylvania are descended.

Governor Spotswood, after whom Spotsylvania was called, fixed the seat of justice at Germanna, which was named after the German settlement. The history of these Germans deserves further investigation. In 1717 they consisted of one hundred and thirty persons, in twenty nine families, and anticipated a large accession to their number. In a petition to the Bishop of London and the English society for the propagation of the Gospel in foreign lands, they described themselves as very desirous of having the ministers of religion in their own tongue, " not understanding English well." They invoke the aid of the Bishops in England to procure for them and ordain a young German minister, to assist and to succeed their old pastor (Haeger), now seventy-five years of age, and to send with him the Liturgy of the Church of England translated into High Dutch, which they are desirous to use in public worship. They were exempted by the General Assembly from the payment of parish levies. Dr. Hawks says that the parish of St. George was created for them. This is clearly a mistake. Colonel Byrd, in the passage quoted above, says he saw in 1732 "the ruinous tenements" which they had occupied at Germanna, and adds that they had moved higher up to the Fork of the Rappahannock, to land of their own, which must mean the juncture of the Rapid Ann (often called the Rappahannock in those times) and the Robinson, which is now in the county of Madison. I believe I was the first to suggest that there was the nucleus of the German population in Madison county (see my history of St. George's Parish, 1747). Bishop Meade adopts this suggestion, and refers to an old gentleman in Culpeper who had told him that in his boyhood he had often seen the Lutherans from Madison, when they had no minister of their own, come to Buck Run Church, in Culpeper, to receive the Holy Communion. That old gentleman was the venerable vestryman and watchful warden, the late Samuel Slaughter, of Western View, in St. Mark's Parish. I have initiated inquiries which I hope will throw some light on this obscurity.

In May, 1730, the General Assembly, in view of the inconveniences arising to the parishioners of St. George's Parish by reason of the great length thereof, divided it by a line running "from the mouth of the Rapid Ann to the mouth of the Wilderness Run; thence up the said run to the bridge, and thence southward to the Pamunky River. All of the territory above that line to be called and known as St. Mark's Parish." The same Act directs the freeholders and housekeepers of the new parish to meet at the new church in Germanna, on the first day of the following January, and elect twelve of the most able and discreet persons of the parish to be vestrymen of said parish. In pursuance of this Act, the freeholders and housekeepers did meet at Germanna on the 1st day of January, 1731, and elected Goodrich Lightfoot, Henry Field, Francis Kirtly (not Huntley as in Bishop Meade's "Old Churches, &c."), William Peyton, James Barbour, Robert Slaughter, Thomas Staunton, Benjamin Cave, Robert Green, Jno. Finlason and Samuel Ball. Robert Slaughter and Francis Slaughter were the first church wardens, and William Peyton first clerk.

These antique vestrymen were the fruitful germs of geneological trees which have scatterd their prolific seeds from New York to Florida, and from Virginia to California. This is not a rhetorical flourish, but is literally true, and could be easily demonstrated, were "the play worth the candle." The progress of this narrative will furnish some suggestive illustrations of this truth.

1731. St. Mark's Parish now begins its independent career at Germanna, without a shepherd to seek after the flock scattered in the wilderness bounded by the Blue Mountains, which look so enchanting in the distance, when their summits are lighted by the setting sun. There were three churches in the new parish—one of them at Germanna, one in the Little Fork, and one in the S. W. Mountain. in the neighborhood of Messrs. James Barbour and Benjamin Cave, vestrymen. For the several years in which they had no pastor the vestry employed occasionally the Rev. Mr. DeButts and the Rev. Mr. Purit, two adventurers who were seeking parishes, and paid them three hundred pounds of tobacco per sermon.

In the absence of regular ministers, the churches and chapels were served by Lay readers, or clerks, as they were then called, whom the vestries seem to have preferred to inefficient clergymen. The vestry went vigorously to work, by ordering the churches to be repaired and vestry-houses built ; buying two hundred acres of land for a glebe, of Wm. Ashley; contracting for a glebe-house, with all the appurtenances of barns, stables, meat houses, dairies &c. William Peyton was made Lay Reader at the Little Fork; John McMurth had the double office of clerk and sexton at Germanna ; and William Phillips and Dave Cave, alternating clerks at the Southwest Mountain Chapel. The churchwardens settled with the old vestry of St. George's and bought parish books. The parish lines were surveyed. Zachery Lewis was chosen as their attorney. Robert Turner was made collector of tithes. A. Chambers was engaged to keep the church clean at Germanna; John Carder to do the same office at the Fork, and William Stevenson at the Mountain Chapel. Col. Waller was employed to bring up a copy of the oaths of allegiance to the British Crown, and of conformity to the Church of England, and the test oath against Popery—all of which the vestry had to take. Some idea may be formed of the state of the country, from the fact that Augustine Smith, Jr., was paid 200 pounds of tobacco for PILOTING the minister to the Mountain Chapel, which was not far from Cave's Ford in Orange.

The vestry seem too, to have been animated by a laudable spirit of church extension. Within two years (1732-1733) two churches and two chapels were projected. The first church was seated on what is now the road from Germanna to Stevensburg, " convenient to the springs above Major Finlason's path." This church, or one on the same site, was standing within the memory of men now living, and was used by the venerable Mr. Woodville. It is called, in the vestrybook, the Lower or Great Fork Church. Mr. Spotswood, of Orange Grove, now in his 77th year, says he remembers when the Spotswoods, Gordons, Grymes, and Thorntons, near Germanna, used to attend this church. The other churches were built " convenient to the Southwest Mountain road, on the first run below the chapel;" and John Lightfoot and John Rucker were ordered " to pitch on the place near to some good spring." This was the old church near Ruckersville, in the county of Greene. Its age is left uncertain in Rev. Mr. Ernest's interesting article on St. Thomas's Parish in Bishop Meade's " Old Churches, &c." The old minister who first preached in this church, and whom Mr. Ernest could not identity, was either De Butts or Becket; both of whom were discharged by the vestry of St. Mark's. The first place of worship on the Southwest Mountain was a chapel, which James Barbour and Benjamin Cave undertook " to have kept clean." At the chapel, De Butts preached until 1732, at which date I find this entry in the vestry book—"Ordered, that the Rev. Mr. De Butts be paid 9000 pounds of tobacco for thirty sermons." In December, 1733, a new chapel was ordered, only twenty feet square, at Batley's, or Bradley's Quarter, "convenient to the best spring that Benjamin Cave can find," Rev. Mr. De Butts, who had been employed BY THE SERMON, was now discharged, and St. Mark's had its first elected minister in the Rev. John Becket.

FIRST MINISTER OF ST. MARK'S.

May 11, 1733, "ordered, the Rev. J. Becket, being recommended by the Governor and Commissary, be entertained as Minister of the Parish; and that he receive the glebe and what is on it, and the house when finished, and be paid as the law directs; and that he preach at the Southwest Chapel every other Sunday until further orders." At the next vestry (1733) it was ordered that the churchwardens offer the Hon. Col Alexander Spotswood the choice of a seat for himself and family in the church on the G rmanna road. In 1730, Major G. Lightfoot was ordered to wait on Major John Taliaferro, to bring up the surplice for Germanna Church. It was also ordered that the church be painted and tarred, and that S. Wright put four barrels of tar on the roof of the glebe-house. 1735 it was ordered that "a chapel of ease" be erected and built between Shaw's Mountain and the Devil's Run and the river; and that Francis Slaughter, Robert Green, and Henry Field, gentlemen, "pitch on the place most convenient to the best spring that they can find, on one of the branches of the run or river." Our fathers kept as close to the rivers as if they had been amphibious,and kept as sharp a look-out for a good cool spring as Arabs do in the desert. They had ladles chained to the church-springs, and were careful to have good framed horse-blocks and bridle-hooks for those who went to church EN CAVALIER.

Up to 1734-5, St. Mark's Parish was in Spotsylvania. At that date Spotsylvania was divided by the line between St. George's and St. Mark's Parishes. Spotsylvania was limited to St. George's Parish. All above that line, bounded southerly by old Hanover county, and to the north by the Lord Fairfax grant (the Rappahannock river), and westerly by the utmost limits of Virginia, was made the county of Orange. In 1738 John Catlett was added to the vestry in the place of Goodrich Lightfoot deceased. The Rev. J. Becket now came to grief for some scandalous conduct, and was discharged. In 1739 the churchwardens were instructed to agree with Mr. McDaniel to serve the parish, or with some other minister, EXCEPT MR. BECKET. In 1738, Augusta and Frederick counties and parishes were separated from Orange and St. Mark's, by a line from the head-spring of Hedgeman's river to the head-spring of the Potomac, to take effect when there were people enough in the Valley for erecting courts of justice; and in the meantime, the people there were exempted from levies by Orange and St. Mark's. In 1740, St. Mark's was divided by a line from the Wilderness bridge up the mountain road, to the head of Russel Run; thence down the said run to the river Rapidan; thence up the Rapidan to the Robinson river; thence along the ridge, between the Robinson and Rapidan, to the top of the Blue Ridge. All north of said line to retain the name of St. Mark's, and all south of said bounds to be the new Parish of St. Thomas. This division threw the Southwest Mountain Church and Chapel into St. Thomas; and with them Messrs. James Barbour and Benjamin Cave vestrymen. William Triplett and William Russell were elected to fill the vacancies. We now reach the incumbence of the first respectable minister in St. Mark's Parish.

REV. JOHN THOMPSON.

June 10th, 1740. Under this date is the following entry in the Register:— "At a vestry in the vestry house at the Fork: it is ordered, that the Rev. John Thompson, being recommended by the Governor and Commissary, we do entertain him as Minister of our parish; and that he be paid as the law directs." Mr. Thompson was a Master of Arts of the University of Edinburgh. He had been ordained Deacon by the Bishop of St. David's in the year of 1734, at Westminster; and Priest in November of the same year, in the Chapel Royal of St. James. It must have been very pleasant to the gentlemen of the vestry and of the parish,to have exchanged the former disreputable incumbent for the accomplished gentleman. It seems also to have been agreeable to one the ladies of the parish(if one may venture to say so, after all parties have been so long dead); for the new minister was not only a scholar and a literary gentleman, but he was a very handsome man. The vestry testified their pleasure by ordering a study to be added to the glebe-house and the widow of Governor Spotswood presented a velvet cloth and cushion to the church in 1741; and on the 9th of November, 1742, she vowed to obey and to serve him in the holy estate of matrimony. Governor Spotswood's castle at Germanna, with its fair commander, did not surrender to the consummate address of the clerical beseiger without a severe struggle, as the following letter will testify.

I procured the original of this letter from Mrs. Murray Forbes of Falmouth, a lineal descendant of Mr. and Mrs. Thompson, and published it for the first time in my history of St. George's Parish, from whence it was copied by Bishop Meade in his "Old Churches and Families." Mrs. Spotswood's children and connections were so opposed to the match that she begged to be released from her engagement, and was answered thus:

MADAM.—

By diligently perusing your letter, I see that there is a material argument, which I ought to have answered, upon which your strongest objection to completing my happiness seems to depend, viz.: That you would incur ye censures of ye world for marrying a person of my station: by which I understand that you think it a diminution of your honour and ye dignity of your family to marry a person in the station of a clergyman. Now, if I can make it appear that the ministerial office is an employment in its nature ye most honorable, and in its effects ye most beneficial to mankind, I hope your objections will immediately vanish, y' you will keep me no longer in suspense and misery, but consummate my happiness. I make no doubt, Madam, but y' you will readily grant y' no man can be employed in any work more honorable than what immediately relates to the King of kings and Lord of lords, and to ye salvation of souls immortal in their nature and redeemed by ye blood of the Son of God. The powers committed to their care cannot be exercised by ye greatest princes of earth, and it is ye same work in kind and ye same in ye design of it with y' of the blessed angels, who are ministering spirits for those who shall be heirs of salvation. It is ye same business y' ye Son of God discharged when he condescended to dwell among men, which engages men in ye greatest acts of doing good in turning sinners from the errors of their way, and by all wise and prudent means in gaining souls unto God. And the faithful and diligent discharge of this holy function gives a title to ye highest degree of glory in the next world; for they y' be wise shall shine as ye brightness of ye firmament, and they y' turn many to righteousness as the stars forever.

All nations, whether learned or ignorant, whether civil or barbarous, have agreed to this, as a dictate of natural reason, to express their reverence for the Deity and their affection for religion, by bestowing extraordinary privileges of honour upon such as administer in holy things, and by providing liberally for their maintenance. And that ye honour due to the holy function flows from ye law of nature appears from hence, y' in the earliest times the civil and sacred authority were united in ye same person. Thus Melchisedech was King and Priest of Salem, and among ye Egyptians ye priesthood was joined with ye crown. The Greeks acccounted the priesthood with equal dignity with kingship, which is taken notice of by Aristotle in several places of his Politicks. Among the Latins we have a testimony from Virgil y' at ye same time Æneas was both Priest and King. Nay, Moses, who was Prince of Israel before Aaron was consecrated, officiated as Priest in ye solemn sacrifice by which ye covenant with Israel was confirmed. And ye primitive Christians always expressed a mighty value and esteem for their clergy, as plainly appears, from ecclesiastical history. And even in our days, as bad as ye world is, those of ye clergy who lived up to ye dignity of their profession are generally reverenced and esteemed by all religious and well-disposed men. From all which it evidently appears y' in all ages and nations of ye world, whether Jews, Heathens or Christians, great honour and dignity have always been conferred upon the clergy. And therefore, dear Madam, from hence you may infer how absurd and ridiculous those gentlemen's notions are who would fain persuade you y' marrying with ye clergy ye would derogate from ye honour and dignity of your family, whereas, in strict reasoning, the contrary thereof would appear, and y' it would very much tend to support the honour and dignity of it. Of this I hope you will be better convinced when you consider the titles of honour and respect that are given to those who are invested with ye ministerial functions, as are amply displayed in ye Scriptures. Those invested with that character are called the ministers of Christ, ye stewards of the mysteries of God, to whom they have committed the word of reconciliation—ye glory of Christ, ambassadors of Christ in Christ's stead, co-workers with him, Angels of the churches. And then it is moreover declared that whosoever despiseth them despiseth not man, but God. All which titles shew that upon many accounts they stand called, appropriated to God himself. And therefore if a gentleman of this sacred and honorable character should be married to a lady though of ye greatest extraction and most excellent personal quality (which I am sensible you are endowed with), it can be no disgrace to her nor her family, nor draw ye censures of ye world upon them, for such an action. And, therefore, dear Madam, your argument being refuted, you can no longer consistently refuse to consummate my happiness.

JOHN THOMPSON.

May, 1742.

A reconciliation was effected between Mr. Thompson and Mrs. Spottswood's family some years afterwards, by the kind offices of that remarkable man, Rev. R. Rose, who was one of Governor Spottswood's executors, and had much to do with his estate, and with his widow and children after Governor Spotswood's death, which happened in 1740, at Annapolis, on his way to command the army against Carthagena. Mr. Rose, in his journal speaks of having visited Mr. Thompson in Culpeper, as he seems to have done every other man of note in the colony. Mr. Rose's journal, a great desideratum to antiquaries, and which was supposed to have been lost, was seen by Bishop Meade in the possession of Mr. Henry Carter of Caroline, and is now in possession of Mr. Brock, of Richmond.*

[*Since writing the above I have been permitted by the kindness of Mr. Brock to make the following extract from Mr. Rose's journal:]

"1746. Feb. 18, I set out for Germanna, called at Capt. Taliaferro's, lodged at New Post.

"19th, went in the rain towards Germanna; met Mrs. Spottswood Dandridge and Isaac Campbell, who waited for us at the Bridge quarter; got to Germanna at night. 20th, spent in settling sundry accounts. 21st, went at night to Major Finlason's. 22d, went to church, heard Mr. Thompson preach on the words, "Your life is hid with Christ in God;" went to the Glebe. 23d, settled I hope all differences in the family, and laid a plan for preventing any. 24th, came early to Germanna, where found Col. B. Moore and his lady; settled Mr. Thompson's account with some others. 26th, went from New Post to see Mr. Benger's plantation."

The next few years are rather barren of known incidents. The following small items from the parish register serve to fill the gap. (1741) Goodrich Lightfoot came into the vestry, took the oath of allegiance, signed the test, and subscribed to be conformed to the doctrine and discipline of the Church of England, in the place of Thomas Stanton, deceased. (1742) Ordered, that notice be given in church and chapel that a vestry will meet first Monday in March, to place a church convenient to the inhabitants of the upper part of the parish, and that workmen come and agree for building the same. At a vestry held in Tenant's old field, a contract was made with J. Kincaid to build a church fifty-eight by twenty-four feet. Benjamin Roberts is chosen vestryman in place of Captain William Triplett, removed. Robert Slaughter places a dial at the church door. (1743) Vestry contracted with J. Eve for an addition to Little Fork Church. (1744) "Ordered, that the Rev. J. Thompson erect, fabricate, and build (*sic*) divers additions to the Glebe house." William Peyton is directed to view the church three times. (1745) Captain Abraham Field chosen vestryman, in place of F. Kirtley, removed, and Philip Clayton in place of John Catlett, deceased. (1746) B. Roberts and Coleman Brown are lay readers at the two churches, James Pendleton at the chapel, and Thomas Dillard at the Little Fork (1747) Robert Slaughter vestryman, in place of Major Finlason, deceased. Dr. James Gibbs is paid "for doing his best to cure the widow George." (1748) At this date Orange was divided, and the county of Culpeper (comprising what is now Madison, Rappahannock and Culpeper) was formed. It was named after one of the proprietors of the Northern Neck, Lord Culpeper, from whom it descended to Lord Fairfax, who married his daughter. The original county of Culpeper covered all the "debatable land" between the

Crown of England and Lord Fairfax east of the Blue Ridge, and was for a long time the subject of a very curious controversy, a synopsis of which will be found in the next chapter.

CULPEPER COUNTY.

1748. Culpeper county begins its career on historical ground. Its territory originally embracing what is now Culpeper, Madison and Rappahannock, was the subject of a protracted controversy, involving the title to several million acres of land. The entire tract of land "within the heads of the rivers Tappahannock, alias Rappahannock, and Quirough, or Potomac, the courses of those rivers, and the Bay of Chesapayoak, &c.," was granted at different times, by Kings Charles I. and II., to Lord Hopton, the Earl of St. Albans, and others, and subsequently by King James to Lord Culpeper, who had purchased the rights of the other parties. Lord Fairfax, who married the daughter of Lord Culpeper, became the proprietor of this princely domain, commonly known as the Northern Neck. In 1705 Governor Nott, of Virginia, in the name of the King, granted 1920 acres of land to Henry Beverly, in the forks of the North and South branches of the Rappahannock River. Robert Carter, commonly known as King Carter, who was Fairfax's agent, objected to the grant, as being within the limits of Lord Fairfax's grant. The question then arose whether the South (the Rapidan) or the North branch of the Rappahannock was the chief stream. The Rapidan, named after the English Queen, contested the supremacy of the Indian Rappahannock. The Governor and Council of Virginia appointed commissioners to meet those of Fairfax, and survey the said rivers. The joint commission reported in 1706 that the streams seemed to be of equal magnitude. In 1733 Lord Fairfax complained to the King that patents had been granted, in the name of the Crown, in the disputed territory. Mr. Carter himself, the agent of Fairfax, had taken grants from the Crown, to two tracts within the forks of the Rappahannock River. The King in council, ordered the Governor of Virginia to appoint another commission. On the part of the Crown he appointed William Byrd, of Westover, John Robinson, of Piscataway, Essex county, and John Grymes, of Brandon, Middlesex county, Virginia. The commissioners of Fairfax were Charles Carter, William Berkley and William Fairfax. Omitting the survey of the Potomac, as outside of our subject, we confine ourselves to the survey of the Rapidan. Mr. Graeme, with Mr. Hume as assistant, was commissioned on the part of the Crown, and Mr. Thomas on the part of Lord Fairfax, "to survey and measure the South Branch of the Rappahannock (the Rapidan,) from the fork to the head spring, and return an exact map of the same, and describe all the runs and creeks that run into it." Colonel Byrd says:—"While we stayed at Fredericksburg we lodged at Colonel Henry Willis's, but kept a magnificent table at the ordinary, and entertained all gentlemen who came to visit us, which were many. We then went to the fork of the river, and found the North branch to be wider by three poles and nine links, though it was objected by my Lord's Commissioners that the South was made narrower by an island that runs along the south shore. We carried a surloin of beef from Colonel Carter's, and picked it as clean as a pack of wolves would those of a wounded deer. The same gentleman furnished us with strong beer, but forgot to bring a vessel to drink it from. However, we supplied that want with the shell of a poor terrapin, which we destroyed, as Henry VIII. did Cardinal Wolsey, for the sake of his house. We then proceeded to Germantown, where Governor Spotswood received us very courteously, and lest we should have forgotten the battles of Marlborough, he fought them all over again, for the nine-and-fortieth time. There we took the depositions of Taliaferro, Thornton, and Russell, as follows:—John Taliaferro, gentleman, aged forty-nine years, being summoned, saith:—"About the year 1707 he came to live where he now lives, above Snow Creek, nine miles below the falls, and there were then but three settlements above his house, on the south side of the river. He had been acquainted with the fork of the river above twenty-four years, and that one of the forks was called South River until Governor Spottswood, about twenty years ago, named the south branch Rapidan, and it has ever since been so called." Francis Thornton, of Caroline, gentleman, aged fifty-three years and upwards, being sworn, declared:—"About thirty years ago he came to dwell where he now lives, on the lower side of Snow Creek, and there were but two settlements above his house, the uppermost of which was about four miles below the Falls. He had been acquainted with the forks of the river about twenty-seven years, and that one was called the South and the other the North Branch." William Russel, aged fifty-six years, being sworn saith:- "He has known the Great Fork of the Rappahannock River thirty-five years as a hunter, and one of the branches was always called South River until he heard Governor Spotswood name South River Rapidan, and the other river has been called Rappahannock; that the uppermost settlement thirty years ago was Montjoy's tobacco house, now Colonel Carter's quarter, on the north side of the river; that he saw some posts of the house on Mott's land, three or four miles above the Falls, which was said to have been burned by the Indians near thirty years ago."

On the 3d of August, 1736, the King's Commissioners met at Williamsburg. Major Mayo attended with an elegant map, delineating clearly the branches of the Rappahannock up to their sources, and with copies of their field-notes. The commissioners of the King made their report. Lord Fairfax took the report of his commissioners to England with him, and got the matter referred to the Lords of Trade, to report all the facts and their opinion to the Lords of the Committee of Council. All the reports and papers were laid before the latter. The question was argued by able counsel; and without going into further details, let it suffice to say, that it was finally decided in favor of Lord Fairfax: making that branch of the Rapidan, called the Conway, the headstream of the Rappahannock River, and the southern boundary of the Northern Neck; and thus adding the original county of Culpeper to the princely plantation of Lord Fairfax. The Rapidan, named after an English Queen, prevailed over the Indian Rappahannock. Queen Ann's name and reign are perpetuated in Rapidan, North and South Anna, Fluvanna, Rivanna, Germanna, &c. Authorities differ as to the orthography of the name of the river in question. Many spell it Rapid Ann; and yet in the proceedings of the commissioners for settling the boundaries of the Northern Neck, and throughout Henning's Statutes at large, it always has the form Rapiddan or Rapidan. The decision referred to was ratified by the formal assent of the General Assembly, and by the authority of the highest judicial tribunals.

1749. William Green is chosen vestryman in the place of Capt. Robert Green, deceased. The county of Culpeper was now honored by the presence and services of George Washington in the humble office of County Surveyor. The marriage of his brother Lawrence with Miss Fairfax made him known to the proprietor of the Northern Neck, who gave him the appointment of Surveyor. In 1748 he was employed in the valley of the Shenandoah. His compensation was a doubloon ($7.20) a day. In the following year he was made a public surveyor by the President of William and Mary College; and in the County Court of Culpeper we find the following record:

July 20th, 1749. "George Washington, gentleman, produced a commission from the President of William and Mary College, appointing him Surveyor of this county, which was received; and thereupon took the usual oaths to his Majesty's person and government; and took and subscribed the abjuration oath and test, and then took the oath of surveyor, according to law."

Washington was now in his seventeenth year, and continued in office three years. As no one had the sagacity to see the undeveloped germs of greatness which lay hid in this unfledged youth, his daily life passed without special observation. Had it been otherwise, we should in all probability have found, in our old parish register, the record that he was the surveyor who laid off our glebes and sites of churches, and ran some of our parish lines.

1750. A "chapel of ease" was ordered at the Little Fork, and the vestry agreed to meet at or near the old muster-field at the forks of the road, to choose the site, and contract with Thomas Brown to undertake it.

1751. Thomas Slaughter is chosen vestryman in place of Robert Slaughter, Jr., removed from the parish; and James Pendleton in place of Capt. Ball, deceased. Gabriel Jones is paid 200 pounds tobacco for attorney's fees, Dr. Thomas Howison 1000 pounds tobacco for medical attendance on the poor, and Wm. Peyton 200 pounds tobacco for processioning lands.

1752. St. Mark's Parish is again divided by the Meander or Crooked Run, falling into the Robinson River, up to Col. John Spottswood's corner on that run, thence by his line, north 28 degrees east to Bloodsworth's road, then by a straight line to Crooked Run, a branch of the north fork of the Gourdvine River, where the main road called Duncan's, crosses the said run, thence by said run up to the head thereof; thence to the head of White Oak Run, thence by that run down to the North River. All below that line except so much as lies in the county of Orange, to be one distinct parish, and retain the name of St. Mark's; and all above said bounds, together with so much of St. Thomas as lies in Culpeper, which is hereby added to and made part of the same, by another distinct parish, and called Bromfield (see 6th Henning 256.) As this division threw Tennant's Church into the Parish of Bromfield, the church wardens were ordered to provide benches or seats in the court-house for the accommodation of so much of that congregation as remained in St. Mark's. This gives the date of the first church services held at Culpeper Courthouse. The churchwardens were also ordered to apply to the surveyor to run the lines between the parishes, and Henry Field and Philip Clayton were directed to attend the surveyor when running these lines. Mr. Brown was also ordered to remove the materials for the intended chapel in the Little Fork, and to erect a church, instead of a chapel, with them, on a ridge between Freeman's [This Freeman was the grandfather of Mrs. Waller Yager. His father and Major Eastham came from Gloucester county, and were among the early settlers in what is now Culpeper. Mrs. Yager's father was one of the first members of Little Fork Church. His father owned a large body of land there. He died in the 96th year of his age, leaving five sons and four daughters.] Mill Run and the river, in the edge of Freeman's old field—the church to be ceiled with plank instead of clapboards, and to have wainscot instead of plain pews, in the best manner. A new church was also ordered upon Col. Spotswood's land, near the cool spring above John Leavell's, on or near Buck Run. The present writer well remembers to have seen, in his boyhood, the relics of the burying-ground of this old church, which stood in a grove upon the hill, above and across Buck Run from the dwelling where old Capt. Moore then resided, and Capt. John Strother now lives.

1753 to 1757. Some of the leaves of the vestry book have been torn out, leaving a gap in the record from 1753 to 1757, which Bishop Meade has passed over. I propose to fill that gap from the folio, which is entire, and with inevitable inferences from other known facts. One of these inferences is, that there was a church at Mount Pony. The ground of this inference is the fact that an appropriation had been made for a church at that place in 1752; and one of Mr. Thompson's manuscript sermons (still extant) is endorsed as having been preached at Mount Poney Church some years after.

The names of the following persons appear in a record before me as having served in a campaign against the French and Indians about this date, viz., Col. Robert Slaughter, Lieut.-Col. Wm. Russell, Capt. Wm. Brown, Capt. Jno. Strother, Lieut. John Field, Lieut. Wm. Slaughter, Martin Nalle, Wm. Nalle, Charles Yancey, Wm. Lightfoot, Reuben Long, Thomas Slaughter, William Robertson, Wm. Yager, Henry Gaines, Henry Stringfellow, and Wm. Roberts. All these names have their representatives still in Culpeper, and they are reproduced as items of interest to their descendants. Robert Slaughter, Robert Coleman, Daniel Brown, Philip Rootes, Reuben Long, and Wm. Williams, are spoken of as being neighbors. Dr. Michael Wallace presented an account to the vestry for 800 pounds of tobacco, for curing Eliza Maddox. Daniel Brown, James Spillman, and Henry Field, are credited with services rendered; and C. Hutchens is allowed 100 pounds tobacco for grubbing the churchyard at Little Fork.

1757. The vestry met at the vestry-house, and the following gentlemen were present:—Rev. Mr. Thompson, minister; Wm. Lightfoot, Robert Green, Goodrich Lightfoot, Wm. Green, Jas. Pendleton, Francis Slaughter, Robert Slaughter, Philip Clayton, Benj. Roberts and Henry Field. James Pendleton was continued as Clerk (Lay Reader) of Little Fork Church; Nat. Pendleton, Clerk of the Lower Church, Richard Young, Clerk of Buck Run Church, and Wm. Peyton, Clerk of the Vestry. The churchwardens were directed to provide two new surplices and two prayer-books for the use of the parish. Col. Wm. Green and Col. Wm. Russell were made church wardens for the ensuing year, and Robert Eastham vestryman, in place of Thomas Stubblefield, deceased. Divers poor and infirm persons were exempted from paying parish levy, and appropriations were made for the support of all poor and disabled people. Last Monday in November, 1757, vestry met at the new church on Buck Run. H. Field reported that he had paid the quit-rents for the glebe and church for 1755-56. Thomas Covington was paid for tarring the church, grubbing the yard, and making the horse-block at Buck Run.

1758. Dec. 1st. Robert Eastham and Robert Green churchwardens for the ensuing year. Thos. Slaughter and Anthony Garnett made vestrymen, in place of Wm. Stubblefield, deceased, and Wm. Lightfoot, removed out of the parish. James Pendleton, Sheriff gave bond and security as collector of parish levy.

1759. In February, Act of the General Assembly established the town of Fairfax, on a "high and pleasant situation in the county of Culpeper, where the courthouse now stands;" and set apart thirty acres of Robert Coleman's land, to be laid off into lots and streets by the trustees, Thomas Slaughter, Wm. Green, Philip Clayton, Nat Pendleton, and Wm. Williams. This land was held by Benjamin Davis, lessee of Coleman, who was permitted to hold his houses, and have one fifth of his rent deducted. Hence the name of Davis and Coleman Streets. Nov. 26th, 1759, payments were made to William Russell, R. D. Parks, J. M. Tackett, Charles Morgan, and J. Carnager, R. Wright and Joseph Newman, for providing for certain poor persons. Thomas Slaughter and Anthony Garnett made churchwardens for ensuing year.

1761. Sept. 1st, an addition to Little Fork Church, 32 feet long and 22 feet wide, was ordered. Thos. Covington, with Lewis Davis Yancey as his security, gave his bond to build it for 100 pounds. Nov. 1761, the usual annual appropriations for the poor were made. 1500 pounds tobacco were ordered to be sold out of the depositum for cash, to pay 100 pounds to Covington for additions to Little Fork Church. Goodrich Lightfoot and Wm. Williams were chosen churchwardens for the ensuing year, and John Green collector.

1762. Sept. 1st, Wm. Pollard was elected clerk of the Lower Church. An order of Bromfield Parish being exhibited by Ambrose Powell and Martin Nalle, gentlemen of the vestry of said parish, to join them in the division of the two parishes, it is ordered that the same lie for the further consideration of the vestry. From this entry it would seem that although the two parishes had been separated for ten years, the parish lines had not been run. Dec. 18th, 1762, at a vestry at Little Fork Church the usual routine business was gone through, and Henry Field and Benjamin Roberts made churchwardens for the ensuing year.

1763. April 8th, Wm. Ball was chosen vestryman in the room of James Pendleton, deceased, and Henry Field, Jr., in the place of Henry Field, Sr., resigned. Philip Clayton was chosen to succeed Henry Field as churchwarden.

Dec. 19th, "Wm. Ball and Henry Field, Jr., having in the court of Culpeper taken the oath to his Majesty, and subscribed the test, and in the vestry subscribed to be conformable to the doctrine and discipline of the Church of England as by law established, took their places as vestrymen accordingly." The above entry is more circumstantial than usual, but it only describes in detail what always took place when a new vestryman was qualified. Wm. Ball and Henry Field made churchwardens for the ensuing year. 5500 lbs. of tobacco were set apart for repairing the Lower Church, and 3000 lbs. for paying allowances to the poor.

1764. Nov. 19th, appropriated to Thos. Covington, in full satisfaction for repairing the church, vestry-house, dial-post, stand and six benches, 700 lbs. of tobacco, he having already received 3500 lbs.

The Rev. Mr. Thompson having represented to the vestry that the glebeland of this parish is insufficient to furnish timber, fire-wood and fences, the vestry do order that a petition be presented to the General Assembly for an act enabling the vestry to sell the glebe and purchase another in lieu thereof. Mr. Thompson having asked for leave to build a gallery in Lower Church for the use of his family, the vestry consent, provided the lower part of the gallery be above the windows and not inconvenient to any part of the church, except the back pew, in which the stairs are to be carried up. John Green and Robert Green are appointed churchwardens.

1765. Nov. 26th, the usual routine business being dispatched, the vestry adjourned to meet at Frederick Zimmerman's on the 17th December.

Dec. 17th, ordered, that the churchwardens agree with workmen to build a house at Buck Run Church, and another at the Fork Church, each 12 feet wide and 16 feet long, well framed and covered with shingles free from sap, weather-boarded with feather-edged plank, underpinned with brick or stone 18 inches from the surface of the earth, a brick or stone chimney to each, sash windows to each with eight lights of glass 8 by 10 inches, with a plank floor above and below. We give the style of these houses in detail because they are specimens of the vestry-houses of that day, and illustrate some other points. James Slaughter and James Pendleton were elected vestrymen in the room of Francis Slaughter, gentleman, deceased, and Thos. Slaughter, who had removed from the parish. Goodrich Lightfoot and William Williams churchwardens for next year.

1766. Nov. 17, Samuel Clayton chosen vestryman in room of Major Philip Clayton. Benjamin Roberts and James Pendleton made churchwardens for next year, and appropriations for current expenses.

1767. Nov. 24th, James Slaughter and Samuel Clayton churchwardens. Samuel Clayton, Jr., in behalf of the congregation of Buck Run Church, moved that R. Young be removed from being reader at said church, and said Young is ordered to answer the complaint on the 18th of December. Mr. Young soon after came into the vestry and resigned. The cause of complaint is not stated.

1768. February 23d, an addition to Buck Run Church, twenty-eight feet wide and three feet long, sills, sleepers, posts and braces all of oak, and underpinned with brick or stone, is ordered: and Captain William Brown being the lowest bidder at 11,500 lbs. of tobacco, it is let to him upon his entering into bond with security that it be done in a workman-like manner, and finished by October of the ensuing year.

November 23d, James Pendleton and G. Lightfoot churchwardens for the ensuing year, and Cadwallader Slaughter appointed vestryman in place of Robert Slaughter, deceased.

1770. Leave is given to Samuel Henning to build a gallery in Buck Run Church at his own expense. The wardens are instructed to advertise the glebe for sale in the Virginia Gazette, and to buy a more convenient site for a glebe. The glebe was sold to Samuel Henning for one hundred and ninety-nine pounds current money. Goodrich Lightfoot and others report that they had viewed several tracts of land, and that Francis Slaughter's or George Catlett's was the most convenient for a glebe. The vestry adjourned to meet at Lawrence Catlett's and decide upon the site. John Green vestryman in the room of William Green, deceased.

November, the vestry this day bought three hundred acres of the tract on which Francis Slaughter lives (Francis Slaughter owned a large tract of land, including the old glebe tract, near what is now called Brandy Station,) and adjoining the land of Reuben Slaughter and Cadwallader Slaughter, gentlemen, for 199 pounds in money and 10,000 pounds of tobacco. An overseer's house, a quarter, a barn and a corn-house are ordered to be built on the glebe immediately.

1771. At a vestry at Buck Run Church, French Strother, gentleman, and John Gray, gentleman, are made vestrymen, in place of Goodrich Lightfoot and Henry Field, gentlemen, removed from the parish. Philip Pendleton is made clerk of the vestry in place of William Peyton, deceased. Mr. Peyton had served the vestry as clerk for forty years continuously. An addition is ordered to the south side of Little Fork Church, to correspond to the other addition. These enlargements of the church, new galleries and extra benches, would seem to show that Mr. Thompson's ministry was attended by large and growing congregations. Mr. Waugh chosen a vestryman in 1772. Colonel James Slaughter, gentleman, agreed to have the glebe-house built for 35,900 pounds of tobacco. The plans and specifications are minutely detailed in the vestry book. This was the glebe-house so long occupied by the reverend and venerable John Woodville, and afterwards by Messrs. Glassell and Wager. The original glebe-house was burned; perhaps some of the outbuildings may be standing.

The glebe-house, the plan of which is described in the last chapter, was built for the Rev. John Thompson; but man proposes and God disposes. Before this earthly tabernacle was finished, Mr. Thompson was called to "a house not made with hands, eternal in the heavens." After a laborious and fruitful ministry of more than thirty years, the brave soldier of the cross laid aside his armor and put on his crown. He was buried at the brick house near Stevensburg so long tenanted by the Hansbroughs, and now owned and occupied by Dr. Grayson. By his first wife (Lady Spotswood) he had two children, viz: Anne, who in her fifteenth year married Francis Thornton, of Fall Hill, near Fredericksburg. Mr. Thompson also had a son by Mrs. Spootswood, named William, who married Miss Sallie Carter, of Cleve. Among their descendants were Commodore Thompson of the U. S. Navy, and many of the Thompsons of Kentucky.

After the death of his first wife, the Rev. John Thompson married Miss Rootes. One of their children was the Hon. Phillip Rootes Thompson, who once represented the district of Fauquier and Culpeper in Congress, and then moved to the county of Kanhawa, where his family was the nucleus around which was gathered the Episcopal Church and Parish at the mouth of Coal, one of the tributaries of the Kanhawa River.

The second wife of the Hon. P. R. Thompson was a daughter of the old patriarchal vestryman, Robert Slaughter, of Culpeper. Bishop Meade said of her, "She was esteemed and loved by all who knew her, as one of the humblest and most devoted members of the church in Virginia I have always (he adds) felt my own sense of the Divine power and excellency of religion strengthened by every visit to her abode. She exchanged it some years since for a better one above."

After the death of Mr. Thompson, the Rev. Charles Woodmason was employed to do some service in the parish. This is all that seems to have been known by our historians of this person; but I have found in "Perry's Collection," a memorial to the Bishop of London signed by him, in which he says,— "Through much sickness, brought on by fatigue in traversing the back part of Carolina, I had accepted for my health the Parish of Bromfield in Culpeper county. Being delayed so long in waiting for a successor, Bromfield was granted away, fearing its lapse to the Governor, while I was on my way. I might have gotten some other parish, had not the Virginians entered into resolves NOT TO ELECT ANY MAN FOR THEIR MINISTER BUT A NATIVE OF AMERICA." This explains the whole matter, and shows the patriotic spirit of the vestry of St. Mark's, among whom were some persons who soon became conspicuous in the war of the Revolution. November, 1772, the vestry proceeded to consider of a proper person to recommend to the Governor as minister of the parish, when the Rev. Edward Jones, of Caroline, was unanimously nominated. James Slaughter and John Gray were chosen churchwardens. January 6th, 1773, the Rev. Edward Jones produced his induction from the Governor, appointing him minister of this parish, agreeable to a presentation of a former vestry, and took his seat in vestry accordingly. April 21st, 1773, the vestry met to fix on a site for the mansion on the glebe, and finding no place where water was convenient, agreed with Mr. Francis Slaughter for 100 acres of land adjoining the former purchase, for the sum of 150 lbs. current money. October 26th, 1773, the church in the Little Fork having been burned, the vestry met on the ground, and concluded to erect one of wood, sixty feet long and forty feet wide, on Robort Freeman's or Peter Bowman's land. It was also ordered that William Williams, John Green, James Slaughter and Cadwallader Slaughter have James Pendleton's tobacco-house repaired for Divine worship until the church be finished. December, 1773, the vestry reconsidered their former order and resolved to build a church of brick, eighty feet long and thirty feet wide in the clear, with twenty feet pitch, to be finished completely in best manner by first day of November, 1776. Thirty thousand pounds of tobacco to be paid next summer, and the balance to be paid in three equal annual payments.

This is the old brick church in the Little Fork which has stood for one hundred years, the mute memorial of other times and other men. The walls of this centennial church once resounded with the voices of sires, some of whose sons now pass by on the other side, or look coldly at the shrine where their fathers worshipped, and speak lightly of the anthems they sung in days of auld lang syne.

> And rudely sighs the wandering wind,
>   Where oft, in years gone by,
> Prayer rose from many hearts to Him,
>   The Highest of the High.
> The tramp of many a busy foot
>   That sought thy aisles is o'er,
> And many a weary heart around
>   Is stilled forever more.
>
> Oh! could we call the many back
>   Who've gathered here in vain,
> Who careless roved where we do now,
>   Who'll never meet again,
> How would our souls be stirred
>   To meet the earnest gaze
> Of the lovely and the beautiful,—
>   The light of other days.

The churchwardens are ordered to let the following buildings on the glebe-land, viz.:—A kitchen thirty-two by sixteen feet, with an inside brick chimney with two fire-places, covered with good shingles, and boarded with feather-edged plank. A quarter, twenty by sixteen feet covered with long shingles, and boarded with good oak-boards,, and an inside wooden chimney. Also, a dairy and meat-house twelve feet square, each to be done in the best manner; a stable twenty feet square, of sawed logs, covered with long shingles; also, seven hundred feet of sawed paling, five feet long, with sawed rails three square. The wardens are also ordered to let the building of a gallery in the Lower Church. John Green and James Pendleton are ordered to agree with Peter Bowman for two other acres of his land, for the use of the church.

1774. Benjamin Roberts and John Green are appointed churchwardens for the ensuing year.

1775. The vestry met to lay the parish levy, but the inspecting law ceasing, they are in doubt what method will be pursued through this colony for levying and collecting the same, and conclude to await the opinion of the General Convention.

1776. The vestry met and proceeded to lay the levy. Robert Gaines was made clerk of the Lower Church, in place of John Hume. It is ordered that Peter Bowman be paid two pounds for one and a half acres of land for the use of the brick church, and that Edmund Vass be paid five pounds for two plans for the brick church. The collector is ordered to pay Samuel Clayton three pounds seven shillings and sixpence for laying off the brick church lot, and Mr. Ball and James Pendleton are made churchwardens for the ensuing year. Richard Yancey is chosen vestryman in the place of John Green, IN CONTINENTAL SER-

VICE. (This is the only allusion to the Revolutionary War in the vestry-book. The vestry seem to have limited themselves rigidly to their duties, and never to have invaded the political sphere, although several of them were officers of the army, and all sympathized with the American cause. Culpeper county was conspicuous for the services of her sons in the old Revolution, having contributed eight companies of eighty-four men each to the army. Those companies were raised by the following captains, viz.: John Green, John Thornton, George Slaughter, Gabriel Long, Gabriel Jones, John Gillison, Captain McClanahan (a Baptist preacher), and Abraham Buford. In the notes and illustrations at the end of this volume will be found some interesting details upon this point. We return to the acts of the vestry.)

1777. Ordered, that the churchwardens advertise the vacancy of this parish and the renting of the glebe. As Mr. Jones had not resigned, this looks like a broad hint that his resignation would be accepted.

1778. The General Assembly having suspended the salaries of clergymen, the vestry met to fix on some method of paying the salaries of the officers of the church, and recommended subscriptions for that purpose. The recommendation is signed by French Strother, James Slaughter, William Gray, Robert Green, Robert Yancey, Benjamin Roberts, Cad. Slaughter and James Pendleton. Burkett Davenport is made vestryman in place of Wm. Williams, deceased.

1780. February 21st, the Rev. Edward Jones this day came into the vestry and resigned the charge of this parish. In March the vestry met at Capt. Bradley's, and ordered that the Sheriff collect of each tithe in the parish five pounds tobacco, or in money at the rate of twenty-five per hundred. Robert Pollard and Lawrence Slaughter are appointed vestrymen to fill the vacancies. In the ensuing April the vestry met at the glebe, and agreed to receive the Rev. James Stevenson as minister of their parish, according to law, and Thomas Stanton was made lay-reader at the Little Fork Church, in the room of Philip Pendleton, resigned. The vestry met again in December of this year, and ordered certain payments to be made to John Jameson, clerk of the county, Henry Field, Reuben Long, Robert Latham William Terrill, and Michael Sloane, for the benefit of the poor of the parish. Lawrence Slaughter and Robert Pollard churchwardens for the ensuing year.

1771. Robert Coleman made collector, and ordered to collect of 1957-tithes seven pounds of tobacco each, for the clothing, feeding, and providing medical attention for the poor distributed among the farmers.

1782. Ordered, that the churchwardens inform the poor claimants of this parish three months before meeting that they attend the vestry (if able) and let their situation be known.

1783. Bowles Armstead appointed vestryman in the room of Benjamin Roberts, deceased.

1784. Resolved, That the churchwardens provide the goods for the poor on the best terms they can and report the result. James Jett is appointed clerk of the vestry, and Samuel Clayton and Robert Yancy churchwardens.

This is the last meeting of the vestry recorded in the old register, which began in 1730. This gap in the record of the parish can only be filled with a general outline of its history, which must be gathered from many scattered sources. Rev. James Stevenson probably continued to be the minister of St. Mark's Parish until he exchanged places with Mr. Woodville, the former going to Fredericksburg and the latter coming to Culpeper.

THE ORGANIZATION OF THE CHURCH IN VIRGINIA.

1785. The Episcopal Church in Virginia had its first legislative council.

For 175 years it had been in bondage to the Crown and Parliament of Great Britain. For political reasons it was not allowed to have a Bishop, nor to make a law for its own government, or for the discipline of its ministers and members. One of its first acts after becoming free, was to meet in convention and frame a constitution and code of discipline. Mr. Stevenson, with James Pendleton, lay deputy, represented St. Mark's in the Convention of 1785. One of the first acts of the Church, when free, was to divide the State into districts, the ministers in each district forming a "Presbytery." To supply, in some measure, the place of a Bishop, a clergyman was appointed to visit each district and to preside in its presbytery. Mr. Stevenson was made visitor of the district composed of the parishes of St. Mark's, St. George's, Bromfield, and Berkley. In 1786 St. Mark's was represented only by Robert Slaughter, lay delegate. Mr. Stevenson was the minister of Berkley Parish, Spotsylvania, in the interval between 1768, when he was licensed for Virginia, and 1780, when he took charge of St. Mark's Parish. Col. Taylor, of Orange, in his diary of 1787, says:—"I went to James Taylor's to the marriage of Thomas Barbour and Jane Taylor by the REV. JAMES STEVENSON," and in 1788 he says:—"Thomas Barbour's son was baptized and named James Taylor."

In January, 1794, he was elected by the unanimous vote of the people assembled at the market-house in Fredericksburg. It was during his charge of St. George's that those two institutions which have done so much good, the male and female charity schools, were instituted.

In 1799 Mr. Stevenson preached the annual sermon in behalf of these schools, whose pupils were required to go to church and be catechised by the minister, for which the teachers were bound to prepare them. In 1802 he preached an appropriate discourse on the anniversary of St. John the Evangelist, before the Masons of Fredericksburg. Soon after he was confined by a protracted illness in Culpeper, from which he never sufficiently recovered to resume his ministry. The following correspondence will explain the occasion of his resignation:

FREDERICKSBURG, JULY 25TH, 1805.
DEAR SIR:
In conformity to a resolution of the trustees of your church, at a meeting on the 24th inst., we beg leave to express the just sense entertained of your past services, and the sincere regret that your indisposition has so long deprived us of their continuance. It has been intimated that you had expressed yourself doubtful of your health's enabling you to perform those clerical duties, so justly appreciated; though from motives of personal consideration, the trustees feel a repugnance in the discharge of this duty, yet the welfare of this church requiring every attention that can promote it, and well knowing your unremitting zeal for its interest, we flatter ourselves that you will excuse the request we now make, of being informed of your intention of continuing in the office of your present appointment.

With sentiments of affectionate regard, we are, very repectfully, dear sir, your obedient servants, WILLIAM TAYLOR,
JAMES BROWN,
CHURCH WARDENS.

[ANSWER.]

CULPEPER, JULY 29TH, 1805.
GENTLEMEN:
Your letter of the 25th current came to hand yesterday; and I am requested by my husband to make his acknowledgements for the sentiments therein contained, both in regard to his past services and health. As to the latter, he has but little hope of its being established so far as to enable him to perform the duties of a parish; but he begs you will believe, that the zeal he has hitherto manifested towards your church is still alive, and to hear of its welfare will ever be grateful to him. He therefore recommends it to the trustees to provide a minister as soon as they can, and that he may be one every way suitable is his sincere wish.

With much respect and esteem, I am, gentlemen, yours. &c..
FRANCES STEVENSON.

Mr. Stevenson married Miss Littlepage, a lady of fine intelligence and culture. The Hon. Andrew Stevenson, who was Speaker of the House of Representatives and Minister of England, and the late Carter Stevenson, were his sons. The Hon. J. White Stevenson, late Governor, and present Senator in Congress from Kentucky, is his grandson. Mr. Stevenson survived his resignation of St. George's several years, and departed this life June, 1809. The following brief item from the VIRGINIA ARGUS furnished the only intelligence we have of the event: "Died on Friday in Culpeper after a tedious illness, the Rev. James Stevenson, a gentleman much and deservedly esteemed by an extensive acquaintance."

Since the foregoing pages were written we have received from Dr. Payne, of Tennessee, some valuable illustrations of the lives of his grandfather Woodville and his great-grandfather Stevenson. Of the latter he says he was an invalid in his last days, having been stricken by paralysis, and was the guest of Mr. Woodville at St. Mark's glebe. Your father, he adds, Capt. P. Slaughter, was one of his vestrymen, and gave me many interesting incidents of his private life. His last family residence was Hopewell, near Fredericksburg, where the Hopewell nursery now is. His library was bought for a mere trifle by a gentleman of Fauquier, who designed returning it to the family, but died before fulfilling his purpose. The following is a copy of his letters of ordination (now before us,) engrossed on parchment:

Be it known unto all men by the presents, that we, Richard, by Divine permission, Bishop of London, holding by the assistance of Almighty God a special ordination on Thursday, 29th of September, in the year of our Lord 1768, being the feast of St. Michael the Archangle, in the chapel of our Palace in Fulham in Middlesex, did admit our beloved in Christ, James Stevenson, (of whose virtuous and pious life and conversation, and competent knowledge and learning in the Holy Scriptures, we were well assured) into the Holy Order of Priests, according to the manner and form prescribed and used by the church of England; and him, the said James Stevenson, did then and there rightly and canonically ordain a Priest. He having first in our presence and in the form of law taken the oaths appointed by law to be taken for and instead of the oath of supremacy, and he likewise having freely and voluntarily subscribed to the 39 articles of religion, and to the three articles, contained in the 36 canon.

In testimony whereof, we have caused our Episcopal seal to be hereunto affixed. Dated the day and the year above written, and in the fifth year of our translation.

MARK HOLMAN,
LONDON.   DEP. REG.

On the mitred seal appended is inscribed the seal of Richard Terrick, Bishop of London, 1764.

Among the documents sent by Dr. Payne is an original Thanksgiving sermon preached by Mr. Stevenson at Mattapony Church, Berkley Parish, Spotsylvania, on Thursday, 13th of November, 1777, on the occasion of the surrender of Burgoyne's army. In outward form the sermon is a curious relic of bygone days. It is about four inches long and six inches wide. It consists of nineteen pages, with only nine lines on each page. In point of sentiment and literary execution it is excellent, and gives us a pleasing illustration of the piety and patriotism of one of our old colonial ministers.

REV. JOHN WOODVILLE.

In the progress of our narrative we have reached in Mr. Woodville a link between the two centuries, overlapping several generations. There are those now living who remember his antique face and form. Patriarchs who were once his pupils still linger on the horizon. Many survive upon whose brows he poured the water of holy baptism; some whom he visited in sickness, and to whom he administered the holy communion; and there are hundreds for whose fathers and mothers, grandfathers and grandmothers, he performed all these offices, consigning them at last to the tomb in the burning words of our grand old burial-service. His official advisers, those venerable vestrymen, Robert Slaughter, of "The Grange"; Peter Hansbrough, of "Coal Hill"; Champ Carter, of "Farley"; John Jameson, Clerk of the County; William Broadus; Samuel Slaughter, of "Western View"; John Thom, of "Berry Hill"; Isaac and Walter Winston, of Auburn, with whom he took counsel and walked to the house of God in company, are all gone. The parish register, in which were recorded his official acts, and which, like the old register we have been following, would have been such a fruitful source of information for the illustration of the history of the parish and county, cannot be found. We are therefore limited to the few facts scattered through the extant journals, and the memories of living men, for materials to construct a meagre skeleton of his administration.

Mr. Woodville having been a teacher, with a boarding school under his charge, could not always attend the conventions, which were held in Richmond, the horse being almost the only mode of locomotion in those days. Mr. Woodville, who married a daughter of the Rev. James Stevenson, succeeded him as minister of St. Mark's. Mr. Woodville, like Mr Stevenson, was elected minister of St. George's Parish by a vote of the people assembled in the market-house in Fredericksburg. The vote was ninety-six for Mr. Woodville and thirty-four for Rev. Thomas Davis, whereupon Mr. Woodville was proclaimed by the senior warden, Mr. Day, to be duly elected. In the Virginia Herald of that date we find two brief notices of him. In June, 1792, he preached a well-adopted discourse before the Masons. In a poem of the day, written by a minister apologizing for levity of conversation with which he had been reproached, occur these lines:

"Deny him not those aids within his reach;
But let me laugh, and modest Woodville preach."

Mr. Woodville was Professor of the Humanities in the Fredericksburg Academy when Gilbert Harrow was Professor of Mathematics. These gentlemen were required to be examined by Bishop Madison in the classics and in the sciences. It is probable that Mr. Woodville spent some years in teaching before he was chosen as minister of St. George's Parish, as I find in the diary of Colonel Frank Taylor, of Orange, under the date of 1789, the following entry: "Mr. Woodville preached to a large congregation on Sunday at Orange C. H., and he preached to a much larger one on the Sunday before at Pine Stake Church, near Raccoon Ford."

In 1791 St. Mark's was represented in Convention by David Jameson as lay delegate, in 1796 by Mr. Woodville and Robert Slaughter; in 1797 by J. Woodville and John Jameson; in 1805 by William Broadus; in 1812 by J. Woodville and Robert Slaughter; in 1814 by William Broadus. The Convention appointed Robert Slaughter, Peter Hansbrough and Garland Thompson to collect funds in Culpeper for resuscitation of the church. In 1815 J. Woodville represented St. Mark's Parish, and the Rev. William Hawley and Samuel Slaughter represented St. Stephen's Church, which is the first appearance of the latter upon the record.

And now a new era begins to dawn on the church in Virginia. The black cloud of despair is spanned by the bow of hope. The Good providence of God sent Bishop Moore to lead the "forlorn hope," and never was there a man better fitted for the special crisis. Baptized with the Holy Ghost and with fire, his heart was a gushing spring of emotion, which overflowed his eyes, and streaming from his eloquent tongue and trembling hands, melted his hearers to tears. He wept over the ruins of the old churches and the scattered sheep without a shepherd, like the lamentation of Jeremiah over the desolation of Zion.

In St. Mark's Parish the first fruit of this new movement was St. Stephen's Church at Culpeper C. H., and its first heralds were Rev. Wm. Hawley and Mr. Samuel Slaughter, all making their first appearance on the record in 1815. There is no record that I can find of the building or consecration of St. Stephen's Church. It connects itself with history at this point, but when and how it came into being has eluded all my researches in print and in the memories of living men.

Bishop Moore reported having visited Culpeper during the past year, and confirmed sixty persons: This was the first and the largest confirmation ever held in the parish. In August of this year Bishop Moore preached in four places in Culpeper, and confirmed eighteen. He also reports having ordained Mr. Hawley to the priesthood. Mr. Hawley was elected a delegate to the General Convention. He extended his labors to Orange C. H., and after a ministry of two years he was called to St. John's Church, Washington, where he spent the remainder of his days, beloved by all men. Of his ministry in Culpeper and Orange, Bishop Meade said he "preached and labored with much effect." And Rev. Mr. Earnest, in his sketch of St. Thomas, Orange, says:—When Mr. Hawley began his labors in Orange the Episcopal Church had wellnigh died out. But three or four communicants remained. Under his ministry there began to dawn a brighter day for the Church. Some of the communicants added by him still remain. During Mr. Hawley's administration Bishop Moore made his first Episcopal visit to Orange, and preached with great effect, and administered the rite of confirmation to a goodly number. It was the first confirmation ever held in St. Thomas's Parish. Among the goodly number was the aged mother of President Madison, who had never before had an opportunity of ratifying her baptismal vows. The ministry of Rev. Mr. Hawley was evidently blessed in this parish; but having been called to a larger field, he took charge of St. John's Church, Washington, which soon became a centre of much influence. In the course of Mr. Hawley's ministry there he numbered among his parishioners many Presidents of the United States, and other persons of the highest social and political position, before whom he went in and out for more than a quarter of a century, "an Israelite indeed in whom is no guile." He was among the originators and most earnest supporters of our Education Society, and of the measures which led to the establishment of our Theological Seminary. Of the tributes to his memory by Dr. Tyng and others, one of the most loving was by the Rev. Dr. Lawrie, of the Presbyterian Church between whom and Mr. Hawley there prevailed an intimacy like that between Bishop Johns and Dr. Hodge, of Princeton, and between the Episcopal Buchannon and the Presbyterian Blair, of Richmond. When the prayers for the sick were read at the bedside of Mr. Buchannon, he said, with childlike simplicity, "Pray for Blair, too." There is an anecdote of Mr. Hawley among the traditions current in Culpeper which, whether true or not, is too good to be lost. The story is that Mr. Hawley wore ruffles on his shirt-bosom, as was common among gentlemen of that day, and that some ladies asked him to have them removed, as they were thought not becoming a clergyman. To this he gracefully assented. But he wore whiskers also, and was told that these were an offence to the weak brethren. To this he is said to have replied, with a gleam of mischievous good-humor playing on his face, "Oh no! ladies. I must keep my whiskers to save my ears."

In 1817 St. Mark's Parish was represented by the Rev. Mr. Woodville and Wm. Broadus, and St. Stephen's Church by Samuel Slaughter and Isaac Winston. In 1818, the same lay delegates, St. Stephen's is reported without a minister, notwithstanding most strenuous efforts to get one. In 1819 St. Mark's was represented by Col. John Thom, who reported twenty-five baptisms, four marriages, nine funerals, and forty-five communicants, five of whom were additions since the last convention. In 1820 the Rev. Herbert Marshall came to Culpeper and took charge of the school at Capt. Philip Slaughter's, of which John Robertson, the father of Judge Robertson of Charlottesville, and the Rev. Samuel Hoge, father of Dr. Moses Hoge of Richmond, had been masters. Mr. Marshall was ordained Priest by Bishop Moore at Walker's Church in Albemarle, and officiated very acceptably for several years as pastor of St. Stephen's Church. His name only occurs in 1822 in the Journals of the convention, with Wm. M. Thompson, father of present Secretary of the Navy, as lay delegate. His wife was the sister of the present venerable presiding Bishop. His brief and promising ministry was cut short by ill-health and a premature death. He, like Mr. Hawley, officiated at Orange C. H.

Mr. Woodville continued his modest ministry as rector of St. Mark's, officiating chiefly at the Lower Church and at the Little Fork, and occasionally at Stevensburg and the Courthouse; but St. Stephen's Church seems to have been in a state of suspended animation, until it was revived by the coming of the Rev. G. A. Smith in 1826. Mr. Smith having been in charge of Christ Church, Norfolk, and finding it a too heavy burden for his delicate health, came to rusticate and to renew his strength in this Piedmont parish. His name appears in the convention journal as representing, with Samuel Slaughter, St. Stephen's Church, and with Peter Hansbrough as delegate from St. Mark's Parish in 1827. From that time till 1830 Mr. Smith officiating alternately at St. Stephen's Church and at Orange C. H., with occasional ministrations at Stevensburg and elsewhere. He established a Bible class, and societies in aid of mission and other Church charities. He gave an onward impetus to the church, reporting an accession of nine members by confirmations in 1828; and Bishop Meade reports eleven confirmations, in 1830, when Mr. Smith, from physical infirmities, resigned his charge, an event deeply deplored in the report of the lay delegate, Dr. Winston, to the next convention.

Mr. Smith is one of those mysterious instances, so trying to our faith, of a man thoroughly furnished for the work of the ministry, and with an eye so single to the glory of God, and yet, for the want of organs through which to reveal the light that is in him, has passed much of his life in the shade, comparatively unknown and unsung, while men of far feebler powers and scantier furniture, but with stronger physique and more self-assertion, have worn the mitre and yielded the sceptre of influence. But he has not lived in vain. As editor of the Episcopal Recorder and of the Southern Churchman, and master of the school at Clarens, he has make his mark and will leave his impression upon many minds. He still lives, the patriarch of our alumni, and the fitting president of their society. May Providence prolong his years: that though his voice be hushed, the graces of his daily life, like angels trumpet-tongned, may plead the cause he loved so well. In this brief tribute I have departed from a rule laid down by Bishop Meade, and which I have prescribed to myself, not to sound the praises of living men, leaving that to those who may come after them and see their end. But as the case is unique, this single exception must prove the rule; which by the way, Bishop Meade did not always follow himself.

In 1831-32, Isaac Winston and P. Slaughter, Jr., represented St. Stephen's Church. Mr. Woodville, though ot present, reported St. Mark's Parish as gradually improving, the congregations as visibly increasing, and there being in many persons a greater anxiety to encourage "pure and undefiled religion." In June, 1832, the Rev. A. H. Lamon took charge of St. Stephen's Church in connection with Madison C. H.; and in 1833 he reported an accession of eight communicants to St. Stephen's, and twenty four at Madison, to the six whom he found there. In reference to the revival at Madison, Bishop Meade said:— "We had services four times a day for three days. It was a joyful season for the church at Madison. Fifteen months before, I scarcely knew a place which promised less to to the labors of a minister of our church. At this visit I confirmed twenty-three warm-hearted disciples of Christ, and saw a new brick edifice rising for their place of worship. God had signally blessed the preaching of his word by ministers of different denominations. He had sent to our communion an humble and faithful man, who, going from house to house, in season and out of season, was the instrument of gathering an interesting little band, with whom I spent some of the happiest days of my ministry. I also admitted their minister Mr. Lamon to Priest's orders."

In 1834 Mr. Lamon reports the addition of eight persons to the communion of St. Stephen's, the establishment of the scholarship in the seminary, and measures for the purchase of a parsonage, and the permanent establishment of a minister among them. Bishop Meade, in his report of 1834, said:—"On the 4th September, 1834, I preached to a large congregation, and confirmed eight persons at the Little Fork in Culpeper. The congregation was then, and had been for a long time, under the care of the Rev. Mr. Woodville. At this place he most conscientiously and patiently met with his people for many years; here had I often met him in my travels during the last twenty-two years, and here it was that I saw him on the occasion just mentioned for the last time. Providence has removed him from a scene of sincere obedience on earth to one of glorious enjoyment in heaven. He has left an affectionate family to mourn the loss of a kind husband and tender father, and many friends to cherish, with sincere respect, the memory of a conscientious Christian." Such was the tribute of the evangelical Wm. Meade to the childlike John Woodville, and it does as much honor to the author as it does to the subject of his praise. It is too common in these days of cant to disparage these old-time Christians, because their religion was not in our style. Such censures are as irrational as it would be to find fault with an antique statue because it is not arrayed in modern fashionable costume, or to disparage St. James because he did not give the same prominence to the doctrine of justification by faith as did St. Paul, but presented chiefly the moral phase of the gospel—there being in truth, no more incongruity between the doctrines and the morals of Christianity than there is between the root of a tree and its fruit.

Mr. Woodville left a son, the Rev. J. Walker Woodville, who for some years followed in the footsteps of his father. He was a good and guileless man. His other son, James, was a lawyer in Botetourt, and Woodville Parish perpetuates the name. Of his wife and daughters, Fanny and Sarah, Bishop Meade said, " I do not expect to meet purer spirits on this side of heaven." The sainted women, I learn from their relative, Senator Stevenson, of Kentucky, both died in Columbus, Mississippi. Dr. J. W. Payne, a prominent citizen of Tennessee, a grandson of Rev. John Woodville, and a great-grandson of the Rev. Mr. Stevenson, is probably the owner of the family relics and traditionary mementoes of his ancestors of St. Mark's. Mr. Woodville was buried at Fredericksburg, with the service of the church and of his brother Masons, on the 10th of May, 1834. He desired, says Dr. Hugh Hamilton, to be laid near the body of Mr. Littlepage.

Dr. Payne has also furnished me with some very pleasant reminiscences of his grandfather Woodville, and enables me to supply what was wanting in the foregoing sketch of Mr. Woodville. Dr. Payne was born at St. Mark's glebe, and educated and fitted for college by his grandfather. In his boyhood he used to attend him in his visitations, " carrying the communion service in his saddle-bags," after the death of Mr. Woodville's body-servant, "Uncle Jim." He speaks plaintively of the old churches in the Little Fork & Big Fork(Lower Church.)Of the latter he says it was a plain structure of wood. The gallery (called Lady Spotswood's gallery) was in ruins. The only thing of taste about the church was a marble baptismal font, the gift, he thinks, of Mrs. Spotswood, and the monument of Mr. Dowman. He had seen the communion administered by Mr. Woodville to old Robert Slaughter and old "Uncle Jim," and perhaps sometimes to one other servant belonging to some Episcopal family. On such occasions he sometimes omitted the sermon, but never a word of the service. Of the old brick church in the Little Fork, he says the long, square, high-backed pews, the sounding-board, the pulpit, reading desk and clerk's stand, its transverse aisles, its chancel in the east, the Lord's Prayer and Ten Commandments elegantly painted upon the communion table, carried you back to a past generation. The congregations here were generally large; and there were many Episcopal families in the neighborhood—Gen. M. Green, the Porters, Picketts, Farishes, Wiggintons, Freemans, Spilmans, Withers, Paynes, &c. But you had to see it filled, when the Bishops came, to conceive what it was in days of old. " I hope," he adds, "it was spared during the war, for I saw at that time in the newspapers that a sermon was found beneath the pulpit, preached near fifty years ago by Mr. Woodville, ' whose classic elegance,' &c., surprised its captors."

From the same authority we learn that Mr. Woodville was born at White Haven, Cumberland County, England, in 1763, came to America in 1787, lived as tutor in the family of Rev. J. Stevenson, who sent him with commendatory credentials, and a letter from the Rev. Mr. Scott, Principal of St. Beno School, and testimonials countersigned by the Bishop of Chester, to the Bishop White who ordained him Deacon on the 13th, and Priest on the 25th of May, 1788, in Christ Church, Philadelphia. He took charge of the Academy in Fredericksburg in 1791, and of the church in 1792, became Rector of St. Mark's in 1794, and spent the remainder of his life at the glebe. He was a great sufferer in his last years from dropsy of the chest, but never murmured. He spoke of his death with perfect composure, saying that his only reliance for salvation was upon the merits and righteousness of Christ; often saying in his last illness, I DIE HAPPY. His last words were " God bless you all." (See obituary in Episcopal Recorder, January 25, 1834.)

On the fly-leaf of his wife's devotional manual are the following lines:

His mind was of no common order, and under the immediate and habitual influence of the strongest religious principles; such was my dear and ever lamented husband. SARAH WOODVILLE.
GLEBE, March 8th, 1834.

The following is the inscription on his tombstone:—" Underneath, the body of John Woodville, a true believer in the Holy Scriptures, an earnest minister of the Protestant Episcopal Church, a diligent and faithful teacher of youth, a meek, contented sojourner on earth, a pious probationer and humble candidate for heaven, In Anglia natus die Martii undecimo MDCCLXIII; obiit Virginia undecimo die Januarii MDCCCXXXIV."

His wife, Mrs. S. S. Woodville, died at Buchanan, Va., April 6th, 1849, calm in mind and pure in heart, meekly resigned to the will of heaven, at peace with God, and in charity with the world.

Thus lived and died the last Rector of St. Mark's Parish. Other churches with other pastors, had sprung up and flourished within his cure. He bade them all " God speed" but we note that in his private diary he called them all chapels.

Among the many early pupils of Mr. Woodville were the Hon. Andrew Stevenson and the Rev. George Hatley Norton, Sr. Of the latter, Mrs. Woodville was often heard to say, " He was the best boy ever in the school." He was a Virginian, but lived most of his life, and died in Geneva, New York. He was the father of Dr. Norton, the great church-worker of Louisville, Kentucky, and of Dr. George H. Norton, the able and efficient Rector of St. Paul's Church Alexandria.

REV. JOHN COLE.

Mr. Cole was born in Wilmington, Delaware. He conceived the idea of studying for the ministry in 1822, and after concluding his course in the Theological Seminary of Virginia, was ordained by Bishop Moore, in Petersburg, on the 18th of May, 1828. He preached his first sermon at the Lower Church, in Surry county, Virginia, on the 23rd of May of the same year. He spent the first two years of his ministry in missionary work in Surry and Prince George, endeavoring to revive the fires upon the altars of the old churches, which had nearly gone out. From a diary of his ministry I infer that he was diligent in preaching the Gospel in the pulpit and from house to house, in establishing Sunday schools, and such like good works. He preached his last sermon in this county, January 16, 1830, at Cabin Point. Soon afterwards he took charge of Abingdon and Ware Parishes, in the county of Gloucester, where he ministered usefully until 1836, when, with a view of seeking a more bracing climate he resigned his charge.

The author of this history, being then rector of Christ Church, Georgetown, D. C., was visited by Mr. Cole, and advised him of the vacancy of St. Stephen's Church, Culpeper. I being about to go to Culpeper to solemnize several marriages, introduced Mr. Cole to the people of St. Stephen's, by whom he was invited to fill the vacancy. He accepted the invitation, and took charge of St. Stephen's in conjunction with two churches in Madison county. In 1838 he made his first report on his new field of labor, reporting at St. Stephen's thirty female and five male communicants, at Madison Courthouse twelve communicants, and at Trinity twelve. Of the last he says quaintly :—" This church is significantly called a free church, which, in country parlance, means free to everybody and everything, for winter and summer, snow and storm, heat and cold." His services, he adds, in these parishes, including Standardsville, are twelve sermons a month, besides a Bible class, a lecture, and prayer meeetings weekly. Rev. J. Walker Woodville, in the same year, reported seventeen communicants of St. Mark's Parish.

In 1840 Mr. Cole resigned the churches in Madison to Rev. Mr. Brown, and took charge of the new congregation of St. James, Culpeper. In 1841 the St. James congregation applied for admission into the Convention. The Convention reported against the application, as not being in conformity with the requisitions of the canon. The report was recommitted to an enlarged committee, and Dr. Winston and Dr. Hamilton came before them and testified that " St. Mark's for several years had not been in an organized state, but had gone into decay, and that the canon could not be complied with." Upon this testimony St. James was admitted as a separate congregation. Mr. Cole reported thirty communicants at St. Stephen's and eleven at St. James, with a neat and comfortable church ready for consecration. In 1842 St. James was reported as having been consecrated by Bishop Meade, who had also confirmed twelve persons. The communion at St. Stephen's, after rising to fifty-three in 1845, fell to thirty-one in 1847; while at St. James it arose from fifteen in 1843 to twenty-seven in 1848. In 1849 Rev. Walker Woodville reports St. Mark's with regular services at Little Fork, Flat Run, and the Germanna woolen factory, which probably were the only Episcopal services at Germanna for one hundred years. In 1850 Mr. Cole reports the completion of the " Lime Church " (St. Paul's), at a cost of only about $1000.

In 1859 Mr. Cole resigned St. James Church, that it might be united with a new church in Fauquier. In 1850 the communicants at St. Stephen's had risen to fifty-three, and those at St. Paul's to twenty-seven. In 1869 R. H. Cunningham, lay delegate, represented St. James, and reported a parsonage as being in progress there. In July of the same year Mr Mortimer a student at the seminary, began lay reading at St. James. S. S. Bradford represented St. Stephen's and P. P. Nalle St. Paul's, which latter applied for admission into the Convention as a separate congregation for the third time, as they allege. Mr. D. Conrad, for the committee questioned the constitutionality of establishing separate congregations in one parish, with the power to elect lay delegates, as destroying the equilibrium between the clergy and laity in Convention; but having been assured by Mr. C. and the petitioners that the congregation be admitted as a parish, and intended so to make application, the committee recommend that the said separate and petitioning congregation be admitted as a parish, to be called St. Paul's Parish, in the county of Culpeper, according to the boundaries set forth in said petition. This report does not seem to have been voted upon, and is not found in the record ; yet in 1861 Mr. Cole reports St. Paul's Church in ST. PAUL'S PARISH. In 1862-3 there were no Conventions. In 1864 none of the Culpeper churches were represented. In 1865 Mr. Cole reports St. Stephen's and St. Paul's churches in ST. MARK'S PARISH.¹ [In 1866 St. Paul's is reported as having been destroyed ; but in 1868, the last year of Mr. Cole's life, he again reports St. Paul's Church in ST. PAUL'S PARISH, as having been rebuilt by the generosity of a Virginian by birth (Mr.John T. Farish),but residing in New York. The new St.Paul's was consecrated by Bishop Whittle Nov. 8th, 1833. It is impossible now to unravel this tangled skein of facts. In 1869 there is no report, and in 1870 St. Paul's Church reappears in ST. MARK'S PARISH, and we hear no more of ST. PAUL'S PARISH.

But we have anticipated the chronological order of our narrative, and must return to 1861, when Mr. Mortimer reports St. James Church, St. Mark's Parish, with twenty-eight communicants and the contribution of $3000 for a parsonage. Mr. Cole reports in the same year the enlargement of St. Stephen's church edifice, with a steeple of fine proportions, and a fine-toned bell, at a cost of $2500, nearly the whole of which was raised within the congregation.

And now the " war-clouds rolling dun " over-shadowed the land. The peaceful parish became an intrenched camp, and a highway for the marching and counter-marching of grand armies. The churches, so lately resonant with anthems of praise, are torn down or converted into barracks and hospitals and stables, and the roar of artillery and the blast of the bugle supercede the songs of the sanctuary. Mr. Cole in his report of 1865-66, tells the tale with bleeding heart and bated breath. He says: " Since my last report of 1861 cruel war has raged. Pen cannot write or words utter the trials of mind and heart, and the privations endured. All the Episcopal churches in this county, and every other place of worship within the lines of the Federal army (except the Baptist and Episcopal churches at the Court-house), were utterly destroyed by it during the winter of 1863-64. The whole country is a wide spread desolation. The people, peeled and poor, are struggling for a living. During the occupation by the Federal army we were not permitted to use our church. We worshipped God, like the primitive Christians, in private houses, and never did the services of the Church seem sweeter or more comforting. I visited the sick and wounded, and buried the dead of both armies alike—the number of funerals being 490. It is a record for the great day, and not for the Convention. There were twenty churches of denominations destroyed within a comparatively small area. Among these in this parish were St. Paul's and St. James, and Calvary Church, under the care of Rev. P. Slaughter, at the foot of Slaughter's (Cedar) Mountain. The last named church was built by Mr. Slaughter on his own place when by ill-health he was constrained to retire to the country. This church was consecrated by Bishop Johns in June, 1860, and Mr. S. officiated for the benefit of his neighbors and servants, without fee or reward, other than that arising from the consciousness of trying to do some good, under the burden of many infirmities. That only relic of this church is a beautiful stained window, which was spared at the intercession of a young lady, who kept it under her bed till the war was over. The window now lights a chancel in Mr. Slaughter's dwelling, which also contains a desk, the only relic of another of his old churches which was burned. The chancel, with its relics has in it the seeds of an unwritten poem, whose melody is only heard in the heart."

Mr. Slaughter in his report to the Convention in 1865, says—" Since the destruction of my church and the desecration of my home by Federal soldiers, I have spent my time in the army and in the hospitals, and in editing the Army and Navy Messenger,' a religious journal for our soldiers and sailors." The despoiled church at Culpeper has been restored by the aid of friends ; St. Paul's has been rebuilt by the kindness of Mr. Farish ; St. James has risen from the ashes at the bidding of Miss Wheatley and others ; but a few stones and a little grove of evergreens of second growth are all that mark the spot where once stood a consecrated fane at the foot of Slaughter's Mountain. The wailing winds play requiems upon the evergreen harps of pine, and the birds singing sweetly among the branches, with responsive echoes, are now the only choir which chants anthems, where once young men and maidens, old men, and children, praised the name of the Lord. It is proper to say that Mr. Slaughter has declined contributions for rebuilding this church, in favor of other churches where the field promised a better harvest.

Whether this church shall rise again God only knows. His will be done ! If a sparrow cannot fall to the ground without his notice, much less can a church perish by violence. If it rise not, then let the wailing winds still play its requiem, and the plaintive dove chant its funeral dirge.

After officiating on Christmas day, 1868, Mr. Cole was stricken by paralysis, and in a few days finished his career of forty years' service in the ministry, thirty-two of which were spent in St. Mark's Parish. Dr. Dalrymple, in his address at the Semi-Centenary of the Seminary, calls special attention to our obligations to Mr. Cole for his successful labors in adding to our emolument fund, and for his agency in procuring the charter for our Theological Seminary. He also records the following interesting incident, which we had heard from Mr. Cole's own lips:—At a convention many years ago, when the clergy and laity were assembled around the chancel at the close of the services on Sunday night, Bishop Moore called on Mr. Cole to raise a hymn. He obeyed by commencing:

> The voice of free grace
> Cries, escape to the mountain.

It was caught up by Bishop, priest and people, singing jubilant at that solemn hour of night. Such was the origin of this time-honored custom of the Convention of Virginia.

Rev. Mr. Cole married first, April 10th, 1855, Fanny E., daughter of John Thompson, of Culpeper,—children Fanny Meade, John Thompson, Thomas Willoughby and Carter Stanard : and married, second, Mrs. Conway, daughter of Wm. Foushee. His second wife soon followed her husband to the tomb, dying without issue.

After what has been already said, Mr. Cole may be characterized in a few words. In all the relations of life he was a true man transparent as Dryden's ideal man, whose thoughts were as visible as the figured hours through the crystal of a clock. He was not what is called a popular preacher (a questionable compliment, since it too often implies the arts of the demagogue), and he had a true English hatred of all shams. He was a faithful and brave soldier of the Cross, not ashamed of the faith of Christ Crucified, but manfully fought under his banner unto his life's end. A fitting inscription upon his tomb would be these words: " He feared God—he had no other fear."

THE SUCCESSORS OF THE REV. MR. COLE.

Having now taken leave of the dead past, we stand in the presence of the living. We must be wary of our words, not only because (as Dr. Hawks said of Bishop Moore in his lifetime) we would not "shock the delicacy of living worth;" but because it will be the office of those who come after them and see after them and see their end, to mark their place in history. The only exception to this rule we have already noted, we have no more active field-work to do.

The Rev. George W. Peterkin, who had been assisting his father at Richmond, took charge of St. Stephen's Church in June, 1869. In 1870 he reported an addition of 26 to the communion of 1868, which he found there at his coming. Sunday School more than doubled; sermons and addresses during the year 140, and 40 public catechisings. The Rev. Chas. Yancey Steptoe, who had been recently ordained, and had recently taken charge of Christ and St. Paul's churches, reported an accession of 18 to the communion, with 110 Sunday School teachers and scholars. Bishop Johns, in 1869, had consecrated Christ's Church, "which (he said) from its position supplied the place of two churches destroyed during the war. For this beautiful building we are indebted to the Christian sympathy of Miss E. A. Wheatley, formerly of Culpeper, now of Brooklyn, New York. She provided the funds and furnished the plan. It stands in full view of the railroad, a pleasing memorial of the pious devotion of a lady who loved her people and built them a christian synagogue."

In 1871 Mr. Peterkin reported a handsome brick building at a cost of $1,669.40, raised on the credit of the vestry, and the organization of a church school for girls, under the charge of Mr. K. S. Nelson. Mr. Steptoe reports an addition of 21 to the communion of Christ and St. Paul's churches, and a contribution of $1215.23. In 1872 Mr. Peterkin reports an addition of 44 to the communion of St. Stephen's, a Sunday School of 200, and 3 teachers and 27 scholars in church school. "During the past year (he says) the school has sustained itself, and become a recognized power in the parish. An important part of my work (he adds) during two years past, has been the restoration of an old colonial church, about twelve miles from Culpeper, in the Little Fork. $250 have been spent in necessary repairs, of which $100 was from the Bruce Fund. Congregations large, and 8 communicants at the old church." Mr. Steptoe reports the building of a rectory near Brandy Station for the use of Christ and St. Paul's Churches, at a cost of $2150, of which Christ's Church contributes $1005; St. Paul's, $450; Piedmont Convocation, $180; Miss Wheatley, $415, and Mr. Suter, of New York, $100. A steeple, bell, and other improve- have been added to Christ Church by our kind friend Miss Wheatley. In 1873 Mr. Peterkin reports 137 communicants, a Sunday school of 280, of whom 35 are colored children, 3 teachers and 39 scholars in the church school, which, he says, is so established and governed as to enabled the church to extend the blessing of Christian education among her people. Mr. Steptoe reports a church at Rapidan Station as nearly finished by our own efforts and the aid of friendly communicants at Christ and St. Paul's churches.

1874. Rev. James G. Minnegerode having succeeded Mr. Peterkin (who had taken charge of Memorial Church, Baltimore,) reports 145 communicants and a Sunday school of 282. Mr. Steptoe, for Christ, St. Paul's, and Emmanuel churches, reports 96 communicants and Sunday schools of 86, contributions $1545.11, the consecration of Emmanuel Church by Bishop Johns on the 10th of December, 1873. "I officiated (he says) at Emmanuel's two Sundays in the month, in the afternoon, until we were so fortunate as to secure the services of the Rev. Dr. Slaughter, as long as his health shall hold out. By the aid of Mr. J. Wilmer, Jr., as Lay Reader, he has been able to officiate on Sunday mornings." Dr. Slaughter himself says he has been much aided by the sympathy and co-operation of Mr. Steptoe and of the Bishop of Louisiana, who spends some of the summer months here, and is always ready to help us with good words and works.

1876. PRESENT STATUS OF THE CHURCHES IN ST. MARK'S PARISH.

St. Stephen's Church, Rev. J. G. Minnegerode, Rector:—Communicants 170, Sunday school teachers and scholars 200, of whom 50 are colored.

Christ and St. Paul's Churches, Rev. C. Y. Steptoe, Rector:—Communicants; after substracting those transferred, 80.

The present writer officiates at Emmanuel Church. Of his work there it does not become him to speak, except to say, that he deems it a privilege at this eleventh hour of his ministry to be permitted to do even a day's work in the vineyard. Communicants 36, the number having just trebled since the institution of regular services.

At the last Convention St. Mark's was again divided, and Ridley Parish taken out of its eastern side, by a line beginning at Jameson's Mill, on Muddy Run, with that Run to Hazel (Eastham's) River, thence with that river to the Rappahannock river, with Rappahannock to the mouth of the Rapidan, up the Rapidan to the mouth of the Robinson, up the Robinson to Crooked Run, up that run to Wayland's Mill, thence to the top of Mount Poney, thence to the beginning. The new parish includes Christ's, St. Paul's, and Emmanuel churches, and leaves to the now mutilated St. Mark's only St. Stephen's Church at Culpeper, and the old Centennial Brick Church in the Little Fork, the only representative in this parish of the Church of England in the "Colony and Dominion" of Virginia.

We have said in the text that we had not been able to fix the precise date of the building of St. Stephen's Church, Culpeper C. H. General Edward Stevens (the Revolutionary hero), who lived in the house now occupied by Mrs. Lightfoot in his will, recorded in August, 1820, "confirms his promise to give one acre of land in Fairfax" for an Episcopal church, one acre adjoining the village for a Presbyterian church, and one acre to Free Masons' Lodge of Fairfax adjoinging his family burying-ground for a cemetery. St. Stephen's was built between 1820 and 1823.

ST. THOMAS PARISH, ORANGE COUNTY.

This parish was cut off from St. Mark's in 1740, carrying James Barbour and Benjamin Cave, vestrymen, along with it. Before the separation St. Mark's had built a church, since known as the old Orange church, near Ruckersville, and a chapel where Robert Brooken now lives. There was also a chapel ordered at Bradley's or Batley's quarter, whose site was to have been fixed by Benjamin Cave. After the separation, St. Thomas' vestry built the Pine Stake Church, near Raccoon Ford, on land originally patented by Francis Taliaferro; and a middle church below Orange C. H.. on land now owned by Erasmus Taylor. All trace of the Pine Stake Church is gone. The writer remembers in his boyhood to have been at a barbecue at the church spring. The middle church was of brick, and was well preserved as late as 1806. Some years later it shared the fate of many other old churches, which were assumed to be common property, and were torn down and carried off piece by piece. The gilt altar-piece, with other ornaments of the chancel, were attached to household furniture. The old communion service, engraved with the name of the parish, given by the grandmother of President Madison and other good women, has been recovered and is now in use.

Unhappily the old records of St. Thomas Parish have been lost, so that it is no longer possible to reproduce the chief early actors in it. The Rev. Mungo Marshall was minister in 1753. There was once a tombstone over his grave, but that too was appropriated, and was used in a tannery to dress hides upon. In 1760 he was succeeded by the Rev. Wm. Giberne. In 1761 the Rev. James Marye followed, and his first official act was the funeral sermon of the paternal grandmother of President Madison. In the family record it is said, "her funeral sermon was preached by Rev. J. Marye, jr., from Rev. 14 ch. 13 verse." In 1767-8 the Rev. Thomas Martin succeeded. He was a tutor of President Madison, and lived for a time in the family at Montpelier. He was a brother of Gov. Martin of North Carolina. A letter from Mr. Madison to him expressing a great respect and affection for his preceptor, may be seen in "Reves' Life and Times of Madison." Rev. John Burnett succeeded Martin about 1770, and was followed by Rev. John Wingate, the last of the colonial clergy, who being suspected of want of loyalty to Virginia, soon took his leave. The disloyal odor this man left behind him may have been the reason why the vestry, who were very patriotic (James Madison, the vestryman, was chairman of the Orange committee,) did not have another minister for twenty-three years, contenting themselves with occasional services by the Rev. Matthew Maury of Albemarle. The old churchwarden, Major Moore buried the dead with the church service, and the Rev. Mr. Belmaine, while paying his court to Miss Lucy Taylor, and on his visits after his marriage, officiated. The Rev. Henry Fry (Methodist) was sometimes called upon to preach, always preceding his sermons with the old church service (says Col. Frank Taylor in his diary.) In 1780 the vestry engaged the blind Presbyterian minister Mr. Waddell (whose eloquence has been so glorified and transfigured by the genius of Mr. Wirt) to officiate for them once a month in the Brick (Middle) Church, and gave him 60 pounds. Mr. O'Neil was the minister from 1790 to about 1800. In 1809-11 the Rev. Hugh C. Boggs officiated at Orange C. H. and the Pine Stake Church, which was standing as late as 1813.

This brings us to the time when the minister from Culpeper began services in Orange, of which an account will be found in the body of this work. The church at Orange C. H. is modern, having been built in 1833-34. The history of the services of the Messrs. Jones, Earnest, Davis, Carson, and Hansbrough, are within the knowledge of those now living, and need not be reproduced here; it not being within the scope of this book to give more than a brief sketch of Bromfield and St. Thomas, as having been originally within the bounds of St. Mark's Parish.

Col. Frank Taylor's diary enables one to form a life-like conception on the animated social circle of which Orange C. H. was the centre from 1786 to 1799. The circle embraced Montpelier, Coleman's Springs, Clark's Mountain, and parts of Culpeper and Madison counties. The persons who figured in it were Col. Frank Taylor, James Taylor (Clerk of the County,) Dr. Ch. Taylor, the family physician, and Erasmus, Robert, John, and other Taylors, whose name is legion. Col. Thomas Barbour and his brother James, James Barbour, Jr., Dr. Thomas Barbour, Richard Barbour—Ambrose, Gabriel, Philip, son of Thomas; Philip, son of Ambrose; and another Philip Barbour. Major Moore, Robert, John, and William Moore, and many more. Col. James Madison, Sr., Col. Jas., Jr., (President), Ambrose, William, Catlett, and other Madisons. Crump, Charles, Ben and Abner Porter. William and R. B. Morton, Andrew Shepherd, Sr. & Jr. John and Alexander Shepherd. A whole chime of Bells— John, William, Thomas, and Charles. Col. Lawrence, Hay, Frank, and William Taliaferro. Capt. Catlett, Frank, John Catlett, Jr., and Henry Conway. Col. James Pendleton, Nat., Henry, John, Bowie, Philip, and countless other Pendletons, chiefly from Culpeper. Capt. William and Francis Dade. Andrew and John Glassell, Reuben Smith, James and John Walker, Zachary, Robert, and John Burnley, and Isaac and John Williams, and Samuel Slaughter. Divers Alcockes, Lees, and Gibsons, &c., &c. Among the young Ladies were Lucy, Sally, and Fanny Barbour; Nancy, Sally, Betsy, Patsy, Lucy, and Polly Taylor; Franky Alexander, Milly and Polly Glassell, Hanna Watkins, Lucy Gaines; Mary, Betsy, Sally, and Suky Conway; Fanny, Elizabeth, Joanna, and two Katies Pendleton; Sally, Betsy, and Judy Burnley; Sally, Nelly, Elizabeth, and Frances Madison; Fanny and Polly Moore, the Misses Gilbert, Sally Throgmorton, the Misses Chew, &c., &c. And then there was an almost continuous influx of visitors, chiefly from Spotsylvania, Caroline, and Culpeper, and a stream of travellers to and from Kentucky by way of Culpeper, Winchester, and Red Stone in Monongalia.

These people seem to have had a gay time—dining parties of twenty-five to thirty from house to house; quilting parties, winding up with a dance ; balls at Sanford's, Bell's, and Alcocke's hotels in the winter, varied with hare, fox, and wolf-hunting, especially when Major Willis and Hay Taliaferro came up with twenty hounds. In the summer they had fish-fries and barbecues at Dade's Mill, Waugh's Ford, Wood's Spring, Leathers' Spring, and Herndon's Spring. Col. Taylor seems never to have missed an election ; he always records the names of the candidates for office and the number of votes for each. He brings before us Mr. Madison as candidate for Congress, Assembly and Convention, addressing the people in defence of the Constitution, to which the ignorant were opposed. He is said to have spoken from the steps of the old Lutheran Church, now in Madison, with the people standing in the snow, and the cold so intense that the orator's ears were frost-bitten. He records the votes for General Stevens of Culpeper as Presidential Elector, for French Strother for Senator, and for Tom Barbour and C. Porter for Assemby. He tells us about vestry meetings which elected Tom Barbour and William Moore deputies to the Convention ; of Col. Oliver Towles, Wm. Wirt, Robert Taylor, &c., pleading at the bar. We see the ladies shopping at Lee's, and Shepherd's, and Taylor's, and Wilson's stores, and the men playing at the five batteries. Weddings too seem to have been more common than now. Under the date of January 1786 he says: Wm. Madison and the ladies have just returned from the marriage of Mordecai Barbour and Miss Strode. 27th March, 1787, large company at J. Taylor's, at the marriage of Tom Barbour and Mary Taylor, by Rev. Mr. Stevenson. July 1st, at the marriage of John Bell and Judy Burnley, and then he varies the scene by saying: "Went to church 2d Dec., and Mr. Waddell told the people that he had heard that it would be agreeable to them for him not to attend here again till March, and he would not." 1788, 24th March, election for Convention:—James Madison 202 votes, James Gordon 187, C. Porter 34. Madison's election gave great satisfaction. May 14th, 1788, James Madison, Jr , at Goodlet's school examining the boys. The next marriage, Nov. 10th, 1789, Archy Tutt to Caty Pendleton, of Culpeper; Dec. 8th. John Stevens married to Polly Williams of Culpeper; 1790, then comes the marriage of Thos. Macon and Sally Madison, and on the 5th of Sept., R. Williamson and Caty Pendleton, Oct. 10th, John Harrison and Sally Barbour; Dec. 11th, Henry Bell and Betsy Alcocke. 1791, Ch. Porter died. April 27th, James Blair and Nelly Shepherd. 29th, July, John Bell, of Culpeper, died. B. Wood married Miss Porter. May 3d, Henry Fitzhugh and Betsy Conway. Nov., Wm. Dade and Mrs. Sarah Dade. Nov. 29th, Joshua Fry married Kitty Walker. 1794, James Madison married Mrs. Todd. · July 19th, Erasmus Taylor died, eighty-three years old. 29th, Col. Thomas Barbour's wife died. 1795, May 18th, Mrs. Sarah Thomas died, eighty-four years of age. James Barbour, Jr., married Lucy Johnson. Dec., James Bell married Hannah Gwatkin. 22d, James Taylor, Jr., married Fanny C. Moore. Thos. Bell (Courthouse) married Sally Burnley. John Walker (son of James) married Lucy Wood, of Madison. 1796, Feb. 5th, Fortunatus Winslow married Polly Alcocke. D. Turner married Miss E. Pendleton, of Caroline. March 2d, James Coleman (Springs) and Thos. Bell died. 5th, Henry Pendleton married Elizabeth Pendleton, of Culpeper. 22d, Col. Richard Barbour married Polly Moore. 23d, Thos. Scott, of Madison, died. 26th, Col. T. Moore died. Mrs. Alcocke, formerly Mrs. Dr. Walker, died. Nov. 16th, Adam Darby married Betsy Shepherd. Dec. 3d, Reuben Smith married Milly Glassell. 19th, Anthony Buck married Mary Shepherd. 1797, March 14th, Baldwin Taliaferro married Ann Spotswood, of New Post. 16th, Hay Taliaferro married Suckey Conway, and my son and daughter went to the wedding—the horses ran away and they did not get back. Nov. 19th, Ambrose Macon married Miss Thomas. Dec. 7th, Champ Porter married a daughter of John Alcocke. Wm. Mallory married Mary Gibson. 1798, March 12th, Rev. Mr. O'Neil and Phil. Barbour (son of Thomas) came here this morning. Mr. O'Neil had been to Tom Barbour's to marry T. Newman and Lucy Barbour, 1799, Jan. 8th, large company at James Taylor's, at the marriage of Thomas Crutchfield, and Col. James Barbour came home with me. G. Terrill had petition to Assembly for bridge at Barnett's Ford.

The churches in St. Thomas Parish are St. Thomas, Orange Courthouse, Rev. John S. Hansbrough, Rector, who reported in 1876 eighty-six communicants.

Christ Church, Gordonsville, Rev. F. G. Scott, Rector, communicants (1876) forty-six.

BROMFIELD PARISH.

Bromfield was cut off from St. Mark's by Act of Assembly in 1752. The dividing line has been marked in the body of this work. Its western boundary starts from John Spotswood's corner on Crooked Run (near Wayland's Mill) and runs north by east to the junction of White Oak Run with the Rappahannock River: thus including what is now Madison and Rappahannock Counties, and a small section of Culpeper. Bromfield, after this date, had its ministers, vestries, and records, of which there is now scarcely a trace. In the absence of such registers, I can only reconstruct the history of this parish with the few materials gleaned from different and distinct sources. The very name has been recently and unconsciously changed into Bloomfield, in which form it appears on the Journals of Convention ever since 1833, except in 1839 when it was represented by Jno. F. Conway, who restored the right name. After this one effort to recover its historical name, it relapsed into Bloomfield, and has been so called ever since. Even Bishop Meade calls it "Old Bloomfield Parish." The word is Saxon, and means Broomfield. Perhaps this is the origin of what we call in Virginia a broom-straw or broom sedge field. However applicable the term may have been to the lower part of the parish (the Piney Woods), BLOOMFIELD is more descriptive of the Piedmont portion, which had not then been developed. Let us hope that the lost name may be restored for history's sake.

We know the names of at least two of the old vestrymen of Bromfield. Martin Nalle and Ambrose Powell, who in 1754 negotiated with the vestry of St. Mark's about running the dividing line between the old and the new parish. Henry Field and Philip Clayton had been ordered in 1752 to attend the surveyor in running these lines. The courses threw "Tennant's Church" and the church in the Fork of Devil's Run and to Hazel River into Bromfield Parish. Later in the century there was a church at F. T., so called from the initials of Frank Thornton being cut on an oak tree near the spring, that being a corner in his survey. There was also a church not far from the present site of Washington, near where Frank Slaughter now lives.

The first minister of Bromfield probably was the Rev. Adam Menzies, who had been a respectable schoolmaster, for I find in the "Fulham MSS." that he was licensed for Virginia, and his name is set down in 1754-5 as minister of Bromfield. There was also a James Herdman (1775), some of whose books are now in my possession (Sherlock's, Secker's, and Atterbury's sermons), which were bought in Rappahannock as the remnant of an old English parson's library. The late Samuel Slaughter, who died about 1857, in his 90th year, said that he, in his boyhood, went to school to a Rev. Mr. Harrison, minister of Bromfield. Thomas, great-grandson of Burr Harrison, of Chippawamsic (who was baptized at Westminster in December, 1637, and was the first of the family in Virginia), was the father of the late Philip Harrison of Richmond, and of Mrs. Freeman, mother of Mrs. McCoy, of Culpeper. In 1790 there was a minister named Iredell who officiated at the South Church, four miles below Madison C. H. He was followed by O'Neil, an athletic Irishman, who believed in what Hudibras calls "Apostolic blows and knocks" more than in the Apostolic succession. He was a disciple of Soloman and never "spoiled the child by sparing the rod." He suspended them upon a stout negro's back when he administered the flagellations. He taught school near the Pine Stake Church, in the family of Colonel Taliaferro, and also in Madison

The late Judge Barbour and the Hon. Jere and Dr. Geo. Morton were among his pupils, and retained a lively recollection of his discipline. The memory of that mother in Israel. Mrs. Sarah Lewis, already referred to went back to O'Neil's time. The Rev. J. Woodville made occasional excursions to these churches, when vacant, and the Lutheran minister, Mr. Carpenter, baptized and buried the Episcopalians when without a pastor.

The leading Episcopal families who adhered to the church of their fathers through evil as well as good report, were, the Lewises, Burtons, Vawters, Caves, Gibbs, Strothers, Thorntons, Barbours, Conways, Gibsons, Pannills, Gaines and Beales. The last name reminds me that Reuben Beale was a Lay Delegate to the first Convention in 1789 and 1793. After the revival of the church in the Rev. Mr. Lamon's time (1834-5), when there were large accessions to its communion, the ministers have been the Rev. A. H. Lamon, deceased, Wm. T. Leavell, John Cole, deceased, R. T. Brown of Maryland, Joseph Earnest deceased, Rev. Dr. Shield, of Louisville, Ky., Wm. H. Pendleton, deceased, J. G. Minnegerode, of Culpeper, Rev. Mr. Wroth of Baltimore, with occasional services by other clergymen. There is a church at Madison C. H., which in 1834, had forty communicants, whose names are now before me, a church at Woodville, and one at Washington. These churches have been so depleted by emigration to the south and west and by infrequent and intermittent services, that they are hardly able to stand alone, and are now (Dec. 1876) like sheep scattered on the mountains, without a shepherd.

HISTORICAL EXCURSIONS.

THE KNIGHTS OF THE GOLDEN HORSESHOE.

SIC JUVAT TRANSCENDERE MONTES.

Governor Spotswood's expedition over the great mountains, as he called it, is one of the most romantic passages in the history of Virginia. Indeed, it has been happily chosen as the theme of a romance by Dr. Caruthers, entitled "The Knights of the Horseshoe," a traditionary tale of the cocked hat gentry in the Old Dominion. The author seems to have used due diligence in gathering the fugitive traditions of this adventure which lingered dimly in the minds of his generation. The popular idea of this expedition seems to have been derived from the "traditionary tale," as the author fitly calls it. One is reluctant to unmask a popular idol by substituting facts for fancies and showing the historical basis upon which it stands. Until the publication of John Fontaine's journal, the facts known about this expedition were but few. Robert Beverly, one of the party, in his Preface to the History of Virginia, 1722, merely said, "I was with the present Governor at the head-spring of both of these rivers (York and Rappahannock), and their fountains are in the highest ridge of mountains." The Rev. Hugh Jones, Chaplain to the House of Burgesses, in his Present State of Virginia (1724), says:—"Governor Spotswood when he undertook the great discovery of a passage over the mountains, attended with a sufficient guard of pioneers and gentlemen, with a supply of provisions, passed these mountains and cut his Majesty's name upon a rock upon the highest of them, naming it Mt. George, and in complaisance to him the gentlemen called the mountain next to it Mt. Alexander. For this expedition they were obliged to provide a great quantity of horseshoes, things seldom used in the eastern part of Virginia, where there are no stones. Upon which account the Governor, upon his return, presented each of his companions with a golden horseshoe, some of which I have seen covered with valuable stones resembling heads of nails, with the inscription on one side, 'Sic juvat transcendere Montes.' This he intended to encourage gentlemen to venture backward and make discoveries and settlements; any gentleman being entitled to wear this golden shoe who could prove that he had drunk his Majesty's health on Mt. George."

It has always been assumed that Gov. Spotswood communicated an account of his expedition to the home government, and it tends to confirm this assertion that Chalmers in his "Annals" says the British Government penuriously refused to pay the cost of golden horseshoes. But nothing has yet been produced from Spotswood on this subject. The present writer has recently gone through the Spotswood manuscripts recovered from England, whither they had been carried by Feathershaugh, and which are now the property of the Historical Society of Virginia. We only discovered one allusion to the subject in these papers. In a letter to the Board of Trade, 1718, Spotswood says: —"The chief aim of my expedition over the great mountains in 1716 was to satisfy myself whether it was practicable to come at the lakes. Having found an easy passage over that great ridge of mountains hitherto deemed unpassable, I discovered from the relations of Indians which frequent these parts, that from the pass where I was it was but three days' march to a great nation of Indians, living on a river which discharges itself into Lake Erie; and that from the west side of the small mountain that I saw that lake is very visible. The mountains on the other side of the great ridge being smaller than those I passed, shows how easy a matter it is to gain possession of these lakes." To account for these crude notions of the geography of the country it must be remembered that all west of Germanna was at that time a vast unexplored wilderness, covered by a dense forest, never trodden by the foot of the white man, except the flying rangers who hovered upon the frontiers of population to watch the Indians.

John Fontaine, son of Rev. James Fontaine (Huguenot), and brother of the Rev. Peter Fontaine and of the Rev. James Fontaine, clergymen of the Church of England in Virginia, was an ensign in the British army. He came to Virginia in 1713, for the purpose of exploring the country and choosing lands for the settlement of the family when they should come over. He made the acquaintance of Gov. Spotswood at Williamsburg, and under his auspices visited the new settlement at Germanna, and accompanied Spotswood to his Indian school at Christanna, on the Meherrin River, and also on his expedition over the great mountains. He kept a journal of his daily doings, which furnishes the only authentic account we have of this stirring adventure. His plain, unvarnished tale dispels the mist which the popular fancy had peopled with hostile Indians haunting the march, assassins stealing into camp at dead of night, and committing murder, perpetrating massacres, and doing battle in the mountain passes. The recent publication of this journal rescues the facts from traditional perversions and restores them to their true historical proportions. From him (an eye-witness) we learn that Gov. Spotswood came from Williamsburg by way of Chelsea (King William) and Robert Beverly's (Middlesex), where the Governor left his chaise, and bringing Beverly along came on horseback to Germanna, where, on the 26th August, 1716, they were met by other gentlemen, four Meherrin Indians, and two small companies of rangers. The names of the gentlemen of the party, deduced in part from the camps which were called after them. were: Gov. Spotswood, John Fontaine, Robert Beverly, the historian; Col. Robertson, Dr. Robertson, Taylor Todd, Mason, Captains, Clonder, and Smith, and Brooke, the ancestor of the late Judge Brooke. Campbell says;—"The whole company was about fifty persons. They had a large number of riding and pack-horses, an abundant supply of provisions, and an extraordinary variety of liquors."

There have been divers opinions about the route which this gay company of young bloods pursued, and the gap at which they passed the mountains. The starting point (Germanna) is fixed, and the terminus, we think, by the light of Fontaine's Journal, is just as certain. We have seen that Beverly (of the party) says "he was with Governor Spotswood at the head-springs of the York and Rappahannock Rivers." We shall presently see that Fontaine says "we passed from the head-waters of the Rappahannock to the head-waters of the James in a few hours." Now as Swift Run Gap is the only "pass" which the head-waters of York, James, and Rappahannock rivers approximate, and as Swift Run, a branch of the James, flows down the eastern gorge of the gap from a spring whose present site, description, and relations to another spring flowing down the western declivity correspond with Fontaine's account of them we are shut up to the conclusion that Swift Run Gap is the historical pass. As to the intermediate course between these fixed points nothing is certainly known, except the first stages, viz. Expedition (Big Russell) Run, Mine Run, Mountain Run (the last two still retaining the names given them by these cavaliers), and Rapidan River at or near Somerville's Ford. So far the route seems plain. Our theory is that, encountering Clarke's Mountain at this point, they crossed the river, which demonstrably then ran nearer the mountain than now, and proceeding up the flats until they had flanked the mountain, recrossed to the highlands, and passing through Jones', Holladay's, Bresee's, &c., encamped beyond Barnett's Ford, at a point where they had a fine view of the Appalachian Mountains, as they called them. Persons may well differ as to the precise line of travel, and maintain their theories by plausible arguments. All the points cannot now be settled with absolute certainty, and are not material; the main point being the general course of travel between Germanna and Swift Run Gap. The theory of the map is that they continued their journey on the south side of the Rapidan through the beautiful bottoms of the forks of Poplar, Blue and Marsh Runs, striking and crossing the river again where it is very small. That they returned this way is confirmed by the fact that when they reached a certain point on the Rapidan, Mr. Beverly was so pleased with the land that he said he would take out a patent for it. Mr. B. Johnson Barbour's title to his beautiful river-farm goes back to Beverly's patent. A map was kindly and gratuitously constructed for us by Capt. Joseph J. Halsey, a lawyer, versed in the lore of old land patents and surveys, and a competent topographer, after a patient study of all the materials we could gather. The sketches of the country about Germanna were made by Rev. J. C. Willis, of Indiantown, from his own surveys, and an outline map of Mr. Brooking of the upper part of the route, and upon Capt. Halsey's own surveys, supplemented by his knowledge of the country, and aided by the suggestions of Mr. Stevens of Stannardsville, and other persons of the vicinage. Messrs. Halsey, Willis and Brooking are all practical surveyors, and represent the beginning, middle and end of the route.

But we must not detain the reader longer from Fontaine's Journal, from which he can deduce his own conclusions. Those who have never read it will find it a lively picture of the first company of gentlemen whose trumpet first waked the echoes of our hill, and lifted the blue veil which hid from the eyes of the white man the fair face of nature in the Valley of Virginia.

JOURNAL OF MR. FONTAINE.

August 27th.—Got our tents in order and our horses shod.

29th.—In the morning got all things in readiness, and about one we left the German-town, to set out on our intended journey. At five in the afternoon the Governor gave orders to encamp near a small river three miles from Germanna, which we call Expedition Run, and here we lay all night. The first encampment was called Beverly Camp, in honor of one of the gentlemen of our party. We made great fires, and supped, and drank good punch. By ten of the clock I had taken all of my ounce of Jesuit's bark, but my head was much out of order.

30th.—In the morning about seven of the clock the trumpet sounded to awake all the company, and we got up. One Austin Smith, one of the gentlemen with us, having a fever, returned home. We had lain upon the ground under cover of our tents, and we found by the pains in our bones that we had not had good beds to lie upon. At nine in the morning we sent our servants and baggage forward, and we remained because two of the Governor's horses had strayed. At half-past two we got the horses, at three we mounted, and at half an hour after four we came up with our baggage at a small river three miles on the way, which we call Mine River, because there was an appearance of a silver mine by it. We made about three miles more, and came to another small river, which is at the foot of a small mountain, so we encamped here and called it Mountain Run, and our camp we called Todd's Camp. We had good pasturage for our horses, and venison in abundance for ourselves, which we roasted before the fire on wooden forks, and so we went to bed in our tents. We made six miles this day.

31st.—At eight in the morning we set out from Mountain Run, and after going five miles we came upon the upper part of Rappahannock River. One of the gentlemen and I, we kept out on one side of the company about a mile, to have the better hunting. I saw a deer and shot him from my horse, but the horse threw me a terrible fall and ran away, we ran after him, and with a great deal of difficulty got him again; but we could not find the deer I had shot, and we lost ourselves, and it was two hours before we could come upon the track of our company. About five miles farther we crossed the same river again, and two miles farther we met with a large bear, which one of our company shot and I got the skin. We killed several deer, and about two miles from the place where we killed the bear we encamped, upon the Rappahannock River. From our encampment we could see the Appalachian Hills very plain. We made large fires, pitched our tents, and cut boughs to lie upon, had good liquor, and at ten we went to sleep. We always kept a sentry at the Governor's door. We called this Smith's Camp. Made this day fourteen miles.

1st.—September.—At eight we mounted our horses and made the first five miles of our way through a very pleasant plain, which lies where Rappahannock River forks. I saw there the largest timber, the finest and deepest mould, and the best grass that I ever did see. We had some of our baggage put out of order and our company dismounted by hornets stinging the horses. This was some hindrance and did a little damage, but afforded a great deal of diversion. We killed three bears this day, which exercised the horses as well as the men. We saw two foxes, but did not pursue them; we killed several deer. About five of the clock we came to a run of water at the foot of a hill where we pitched our tents. We called the encampment Dr. Robinson's Camp, and the river Blind Run. We had good pasturage for our horses and every one was cook for himself. We made our beds with bushes as before. This day we made thirteen miles.

2d.—At nine we were all on horseback, and after riding about five miles we crossed the Rappahannock River almost at the head, where it is very small. We had a rugged way; we passed over a great many small runs of water, some of which were very deep and others very miry. Several of our company were dismounted some were down with their horses, and some thrown off. We saw a bear running down a tree, but it being Sunday we did not endeavor to kill anything. We encamped at five by a small river we called White Oak River; and called our camp Taylor's Camp.

3d.—About eight we were on horseback, and about ten we came to a thicket so tightly laced together that we had a great deal of trouble to get through. Our baggage was injured, our clothes torn all to rags, and the saddles and holsters also torn. About five of the clock we encamped almost at the head of James River, just below the great mountain. We called this camp Col. Robertson's camp. We made all this day but eight miles.

4th.—We had two of our men sick with the measles and one of our horses poisoned with a rattle-snake. We took the heaviest of our baggage, our tired horses, and the sick men, and made as convenient a lodge for them as we could, and left people to guard them and hunt for them. We had finished this work by twelve, and so we set out. The sides of the mountains were so full of vines and briers that we were forced to clear most of the way before us. We crossed one of the small mountains on this side the Appalachian, and from the top of it we had a fine view of the plains below. We were obliged to walk up the most of the way, there being abundance of loose stones on the side of the hill. I killed a large rattlesnake here, and the other people killed three more. We made about four miles, and so came to the side of James River where a man may jump over it, and there we pitched our tents. As the people were lighting the fire there came out of a large log of wood a prodigious snake, which they killed, so this camp was called Rattlesnake Camp, but otherwise it was called Brooke's Camp.

5th.—A fair day. At five we were mounted. We were obliged to have axemen to clear the way in some places. We followed the windings of James River, observing that it came from the very top of the mountains. We killed two rattlesnakes during our ascent. In some places it was very steep, in others it was so that we could ride up. About one of the clock we got to the top of the mountains; about four miles and a half and we came to the very head-spring of James River, where it runs no bigger than a man's arm from under a big stone. We drank King George's health and all the royal family's at the very top of the Appalachian mountains. About a musket-shot from the spring there is another, which rises and runs down to the other side. It goes westward, and we thought we could go down that way, but we met with such prodigious precipices that we were obliged to return to the top again. We found some trees which had been formerly marked, I suppose by the Northern Indians, and following these trees we found a good, safe descent. Several of the company were for returning, but the Governor persuaded them to continue on. About five we were down on the other side, and continued our way until seven miles further, when we came to a large river, by the side of which we encamped. We made this day fourteen miles. I, being somewhat more curious than the rest, went on a high rock on the top of the mountain to see fine prospects, and I lost my gun. We saw when we were over the mountain the footing of elk and buffaloes and their beds. We saw a vine which bore a sort of wild cucumber, and a shrub with a fruit like unto a currant. We ate very good wild grapes. We called this place Spotswood's Camp, after our Governor.

6th.—We crossed the river, which we called Euphrates. It is very deep; the main course of the water is north; it is fourscore yards wide in the narrowest part. We drank some healths on the other side and returned, after which I went swimming in it. We could not find any fordable place except the one by which we crossed, and it was deep in several places. I got some grasshoppers and fished, and another and I we catched a dish of fish, some perch and a kind of fish they called chub. The others went a-hunting, and killed deer and turkeys. The Governor had graving irons, but could not grave anything, the stone was so hard. I graved my name on a tree by the river side, and the Governor buried a bottle with a paper enclosed, on which he writ that he took possession of this place in the name and for King George First of England. We had a good dinner, and after it we got the men together and loaded all their arms, and we drank the King's health in champagne and fired a volley, the Princess's health in Burgundy and fired a volley, and all the rest of the royal family in claret and a volley. We drank the Governor's health and fired another volley. We had several sorts of liquors, viz., Virginia red wine and white wine, Irish usquebaugh, brandy, shrub, two sorts of rum, champagne, canary, cherry punch, water, cider, &c. I sent two of the rangers to look for my gun which I dropped in the mountain; they found it and brought it to me at night, and I gave them a pistol for their trouble. We called the highest mountain Mount George, and the one we crossed over Mount Spotswood.

7th.—At seven in the morning we mounted our horses and parted with the rangers, who were to go farther on, and we returned homewards. We repassed the mountains, and at five in the afternoon we came to Hospital Camp, where we left our sick men and heavy baggage, and we found all things well and safe. We encamped here and called it Captain Clonder's Camp.

8th.—At nine we were all on horseback. We saw several bears and deer, and killed some wild turkey. We encamped at the side of a run and called the place Mason's Camp We had good forage for our horses, and we lay as usual. Made twenty miles this day.

9th.—We set out at nine of the clock, and before twelve we saw several bears, and killed three. One of them attacked one of our men that was riding after him and narrowly missed him; he tore his things that he had behind him from off his horse, and would have destroyed him had he not had immediate help from the other men and our dogs. Some of the dogs suffered severely in this engagement. At two we crossed one of the branches of the Rappahannock River; and at five we encamped on the side of the Rapid Ann, on a tract of land that Mr. Beverly hath design to take up. We made this day twenty-three miles, and called this Captain Smith's Camp. We ate part of one of the bears, which tasted very well, and would be good and might pass for veal if one did not know what it was. We were very merry, and diverted ourselves with our adventures.

10th.—At eight we were on horseback, and about ten, as we were going up a small hill, Mr. Beverly and his horse fell down, and they both rolled to the bottom; but there were no bones broken on either side. At twelve as we were crossing a run of water, Mr. Clonder fell in, so we called this place Clonder's Run. At one we arrived at a large spring, where we dined and drank a bowl of punch. We called this Fontaine's Spring. About two we got on horseback, and at four we reached Germanna.

Spotswood instituted what he called the Tramontane Order, in commemoration of the expedition, each gentleman being entitled to wear the golden horseshoe who could prove that he had drunk his Majesty's health on Mt. George. The golden horse-shoes decended as heirlooms in several families. Judge Brooke, in his autobiography, speaks of one in the possession of Edmund Brooke, whose ancestor was of the party. This gentleman died in Georgetown, D. C., and we had hoped to find the relic in his daughter's possession, but it had been lost. Campbell speaks of the late Mrs. Bott, of Petersburg, a descendant of Spotswood, having seen the miniature horseshoe belonging to Spotswood, and that it was small enough to be worn on a watch-chain. Spotswood probably had more than one of them, as we find it said in the Byrd manuscripts that when Spotswood made a treaty with the five nations of Indians at Albany, in 1722, in which they bound themselves not to pass the Potomac or the Blue Ridge, the Governor told the Indians that they must take particular notice of their speaker, and gave him a golden horseshoe which he wore at his breast, and bade the interpreter tell him that there was an inscription on it which signified that it would help him to pass the mountains, and that when any of their people should come to Virginia they must bring that with them. These things are like dreams to us now. With a population which has not only transcended the Blue Ridge, but the Alleghany and Rocky Mountains, and reached the Golden Gate of California, it is hard to realize that only 160 years ago Germanna was a frontier post, and the great West an unknown world, except to the wild Indian, whose tribes have melted away before the pale faces like snow before the sun, and whose barque, like that of the crew of the fabled phantom ship, " rides on and on, and anchored ne'er shall be."

GERMANNA.

Salve Posteritas!
Posteritas Germano-politana.

The German people is a potent element in American civilization. The number of Germantowns in the United States is curious and suggestive. The oldest of these is the one in Pennsylvania, which was the scene of the battle of Germantown in the old Revolution, in which so many of the men of St. Mark's figured. It was established in 1683, under the auspices of Pastorius, to provide, as he said, a " pellace " or refuge from the judgements impending over the old world, and to Christianize the naked-going savages. He composed a noble Latin ode on the occasion, beginning—

Salve Posteritas !
Posteritas Germano-politana,

which Whittier has put beautifully into English verse thus :

Hail to Posterity !
Hail, future men of Germanopolis!
Let the young generation, yet to be,

>   Look kindly upon this;
>   Think how our fathers left their native land—
>   Dear German land ! O sacred hearts and homes !—
>   And where the wild beast roams,
>   In patience planned
>   New forest homes, beyond the mighty sea,
>   There undisturbed and free,
>   To live as brothers of one family,
>   What pains and cares befel,
>   What trials and what fears,
>   Remember, and whenever we have done well,
>   Follow our footsteps, men of coming years.
>   Where we have failed to do
>   Aught, or wisely live
>   Be warned by us, the better way pursue,
>   And knowing we were human, even as you,
>   Pity us and forgive.
>   Farewell, Posterity !
>   Farewell, dear Germany!
>   Forevermore farewell !

(See Memorial Thomas Potts, Jr., by Mrs. James.)

Our Germanna was settled under the auspices of Governor Spotswood in 1714, on a peninsula of 400 acres of land on the banks of the Rapidan. These Germans came directly from Oldensburg, or were a remnant of a settlement planted under the auspices of the Baron de Graffenried in North Carolina, many of whom were massacred by the Tuscarora Indians, as related by Governor Spotswood in a letter of October 1711, which is published in Perry's Collections from the archives of Fulham and Lambeth. Spotswood, says he had demanded the release of De Graffenried, the Chief of the Palatines and Swiss, who had been taken prisoner, and was, he feared, reserved for torture by fire. That these Germans might have been the survivors of the massacre in North Carolina is a mere conjecture, suggested by the fact that De Graffenried was the leader of both parties. I have just found in the Spotswood MSS. the following paragraph in a letter of Governor Spotswood to the Commissioners of Trade in England, dated May 1714:—" I continue to settle our tributary Indians, and in order to supply that part which was to have been covered by the Tuscarora Indians, I have placed there a number of Protestant Germans, built them a fort, furnished it with two pieces of cannon and some ammunition, which will awe the straggling parties of Northern Indians and be a good barrier to all that part of the country. These Germans were invited over some years ago by the Baron De Graffenreid, who had her Majesty's letter to the Governor to furnish them with land after their arrival. They are generally such as have been employed in their own country in mines, and say they are satisfied; there are divers kinds of minerals where they are settled, and even a good appearance of silver ; but it is impossible to know whether those mines will turn to account without digging some depth—a liberty I shall not give them until I hear from your Lordships."

The Germans landed at Tappahannock, and a dispute arose between them and the captain of the ship in which they sailed, about the money for their passage. The captain refused to deliver their effects until his demand was satisfied. Governor Spotswood being present, proposed that if the Germans would settle on his land and remain long enough to instruct some of his young men in mechanical trades, he would pay the bill. They consented, and hence the settlement at Germanna. In 1714. John Fontaine and JohnClayton of Williamsburg visited Germanna, and described it as follows:—" We went to the German minister's house (they say), and finding nothing to eat lived upon our own provisions and lay upon straw. Our beds not being easy, we got up at break of day, and in a hard rain walked about the town, which is palisaded with stakes stuck in the ground close to each other, and of substance to resist musket-shot. There are but nine families, and nine houses in all in a line; and before every house, twenty feet distant, they have sheds for their hogs and their hens; so that hog-stys on one side and dwellings on the other make a street. The place paled in is a pentagon, regularly laid out; and in the centre is a block-house with five sides, answering to the five sides of the great enclosure. There are loop-holes in it, from which you may see all the inside of the enclosure. This is intended for a retreat in case of their not being able to defend the palisades from the Indians. They use the block-house for Divine service. They go to prayers once a day and have two services Sunday. We went to hear them perform their services, which is done in their own language, which we did not understand, but they seem very devout and sing the psalms very well. This settlement is (1714) thirty miles from any inhabitant. They live very miserably. For want of provisions we were obliged to go. We got from the minister a bit of smoked beef and cabbage, and gave him thirty shillings and took our leave. In less than three hours on our way we saw nineteen deer; and we lodged at Mr. Smith's, at the Falls of the Rappahannock."

We must now let the Germans speak for themselves. In the archives of the English society for propagating the Gospel in foreign parts is the following memorial:—" The case of thirty-two Protestant German families settled in Virginia humbly sheweth, that twelve Protestant German families, consisting of about fifty persons, arrived April 1714, in Virginia, and were there settled near Rappahannock River. That in 1717, twenty Protestant German familes, consist of about four-score persons, came and settled down near their countrymen. And many more Germans and Swiss are likely to come. For the ministries of religion there will be a necessity for a small church and for a minister, who shall catechise and perform Divine offices among them in the German tongue, which is the only language they do yet understand. That there came indeed over with the first twelve German families a minister, named Henry Haeger—a very sober, honest man, about seventy-five years old; but he being likely soon to be past service, we have empowered Mr. J. C. Zollicoffer, of St. Gall, Switzerland, to go to Europe and obtain subscriptions from pious Christians towards building a church, and bringing over with him a young German minister to assist Mr. Haeger, and to succeed him when he shall die; to get him ordained in England by the Right Rev. Bishop of London, and to bring over with him the Liturgy of the Church of England, translated into High Dutch, which they are desirous to use in public worship. But this settlement consisting of only mean (poor) persons, utterly unable to build a church and support an assistant minister, they humbly implore the countenance, &c., of the Bishop of London and other Bishops, and the venerable society for propagating the Gospel in foreign parts, that they would take the case under their pious consideration and grant their usual allowance for the support of a minister, and if it may be so subscribe something towards the building of their church, and they shall ever pray that the Lord may reward their beneficence here and hereafter." The above petition was sent in 1719.

In the year 1720 Spotsylvania was cut off from Essex, and the Parish of St. George, coterminous with the county, was erected in 1721. Governor Spotswood fixed the seat of justice at Germanna, and the first court, composed of John Taliaferro and others, was holden 1st August, 1722. An appropriation was made by the General Assembly of £500 for a church, a prison, a pillory and stocks. The Act of Assembly contains this clause, doubtless for the benefit of the Germans: " Because foreign Protestants may not understand English readily, if any such shall entertain a minister of their own, they and their tithables shall be free from taxes for ten years."

By the help of Governor Spotswood a church was built, and Spotsylvania County, named after Spotswood, and St. George's Parish began their career at Germanna, named from the Germans and Queen Anne. Governor Spotswood, soon after made his home at Germanna. The Rev. Hugh Jones, in his "Present State of Virginia," published about 1724, thus describes Germanna: "Beyond Governor Spotswood's furnace, within view of the vast mountains, he has founded a town called Germanna, from the Germans sent over by Queen Anne, who are now removed up further. Here Spotswood has servants and workmen of most handicraft trades; and he is building a church, court house, and dwelling-house for himself, and has cleared plantations about it, encouraging people to come and settle in that uninhabited part of the country, lately erected into a county. Beyond this (continues Jones) is seated the colony of the Germans Palatine."

These Germans Palatine were probably the founders of Germantown in Fauquier. However this may be it is certain that the records of Fauquier develop the fact that in 1718 Jacob Spilman, John Hoffman, John and Herman Fishback, Peter Hitt, Jacob Holtzclaw, and William Weaver, not finding room at Germanna, moved to Germantown. Only three of these (Hoffman, Fishback and Weaver) having been naturalized, they were sent to enter lands at Germantown. The title was in these three, and they were to make leases for ninety-nine years. The patent was issued in 1724. Copies of the leases are on record. Tillman Weaver, in his last will (1754, Dec. 14th), devises property to Tillman W., to Ann, wife of Jno Kemper, and Mary, wife of Herman Hitt, Eva, wife of Samuel Porter, Jacob, Elizabeth, Catharine, &c. Peter Hitt in his will, 1771, devises to John, Jos., Herman, Peter, and to Mary, wife of Jacob Rector. Peter Hitt married Sarah James, and Jos. Hitt married Mary Coons. Several of these persons have their representatives in Fauquier, Culpeper and Madison counties.

Colonel Byrd, already quoted, said that in 1732, while on a visit to Colonel Spotswood, he saw the ruinous tenements which they, the Germans, had occupied at Germanna, and adds that they had moved higher up to the forks of the Rappannock (the Rapidan) to lands of their own, which must mean what is now the County of Madison, which lies within that fork. From the testimony of these witnesses the Germans must have migrated to Madison before 1724. The tradition is that they were disgusted with the poverty of the soil and the harsh treatment of their overseers in the mines; and resolved to seek their fortunes on the banks of the Robinson River; and from them has descended the very thrifty German element in the population of Madison County. What was the fate of their petition to London for a minister is not known. Had it succeeded we might have had a flourishing German Episcopal church in Virginia. The Church of England being subject to the State, and the British Ministry being generally governed in their policy to the Church by considerations of political expediency, may not have acted in the premises. However that may have been, the tradition is that our German friends procured subscriptions in Europe for building a Lutheran church, which was erected about 1740, near the junction of White Oak Run and and the Robinson River, and still stands in good condition. It is in the form of a Maltese cross. Money was also raised in Europe to buy a pipe-organ of good size, which I believe is still in use. Subscriptions were taken in Sweden too, perhaps for a communion service and other purposes, and the King of Sweden was said to have been one of the subscribers. General Banks of Madison, we are told, had seen one of these subscription papers. The church was endowed, held a glebe, and has money at interest. By the kindness of Governor Kemper I have a copy of the deed from William Carpenter to Michael Cook and Michael Smith, wardens and trustees of the German church, and people inhabiting the fork of Rappahannock river, in St. Mark's Parish and County of Spotsylvania, and their successors, for a glebe for the use of the minister of the said German people and his successors, a tract of land in the first fork of the Rapidan River, containing one hundred and ninety-three acres, more or less, &c. The deed is dated 1733, and signed, sealed and delivered by William Carpenter in the presence of Jno. Waller, Robert Turner, Ed. Broughton, Jas. King and William Henderson. This Michael Cook was no doubt the same who, with George Woots, was appointed by the vestry in 1729 to count all the tobacco plants from the mouth of the Robinson River up to the Great Mountains, including Mark Jones's plantation. The services in this church were originally in German, then once a month in English, and subsequently entirely in the English tongue.

Our interest in the history of this church is enhanced by the interchange of courtesies between the Lutherans and Episcopalians. The late Samuel Slaughter of this county remembered to have seen these Lutherans, when they had no minister of their own, came to Buck Run Episcopal church in Culpeper to receive the holy communion; and the late venerable Mrs. Sarah Lewis, the great-grandmother of Mrs. Dr Robert Lewis, of Culpeper, remembered when the Lutheran minister, Mr. Carpenter, used to baptize and perform other ministerial offices for the Episcopalians of Madison when they had no minister. Many of the first grist-mills on the Robinson River and its tributaries were built by German mechanics. The first German settlers are said to have suffered occasionally from the incursions of the Indians. There is a tradition that the last person killed by the Indians in this region was murdered near what is now New Hope Church. There are some large Old German Bibles extant which have descended as heirlooms from the primitive Germans. We are indebted to the venerable John Spotswood of Orange Grove, and to Dr. Andrew Grinnan of Madison, for some of the traditions referred to in the above chapter.

EXTRACT FROM THE DIARY OF CAPTAIN PHILIP SLAUGHTER,

BEGINNING IN 1775 AND CONTINUED TO 1849.

December 4th, 1849.—I am this day 91 years old. I was born in 1758 at my grandfather's, Major Philip Clayton's, who lived at Catalpa, where the Hon. J. S. Barbour now lives. My father, Col. James Slaughter, then lived on the Rappahannock River where Jones Green now lives. I went to school to John Wigginton, a first-rate English teacher in the Little Fork. My father sold this farm to Gavin Lawson, and bought another of his brother, Col. Francis Slaughter, near Culpeper C. H., where Samuel Rixey now lives. When we moved to the latter place, I went to write in the clerk's office with my grandfather, Major Clayton, who did the duties of that office for Roger Dixon, the clerk, whose home was in the lower country. After Dixon's death, John Jameson, who had served a regular apprenticeship in the clerk's office, was made clerk of the county. After several years' service in the office with Clayton and Jameson, my father withdrew me and sent me to a "Grammar School" of which Adam Goodlet (a Scotchman) was master, and which was the first public school in which Latin and Greek were taught in Culpeper County. [Adam Goodlet afterwards taught school in the Taylor Settlement in Orange. Col. F. Taylor often speaks of him in his diary, and mentions James Madison, Jr., (the future President) examining Goodlet's scholars.]

After going to school to Goodlet 18 months, the American Revolution began, and I, not yet 17 years old, entered in Capt. John Jameson's company of minute-men. Culpeper, Fauquier, and Orange having agreed to raise a regiment, with Lawrence Taliaferro of Orange as Colonel, Edward Stevens of Culpeper as Lieutenant-Colonel, and Thomas Marshall of Fauquier as Major, the regiment met in Major Clayton's old field, near Culpeper C. H., to drill, in strong brown linen hunting-shirts, dyed with leaves, and the words "Liberty or Death" worked in large white letters on the breast, bucktails in each hat, and a leather belt about the shoulders with tomahawk and scalping-knife. In a few days an express came from Patrick Henry, commander of the First Virginia Continental Regiment, saying that Dunmore had attempted to carry the military stores from the magazine at Williamsburg to the ships, &c. We marched immediately, and in a few days were in Williamsburg. The people hearing that we came from the backwoods, and seeing our savage-looking equipments, seemed as much afraid of us as if we had been Indians. We took pride in demeaning ourselves as patriots and gentlemen, and the people soon treated us with respect and great kindness. Most of us had only fowling-pieces and squirrel-guns. Dunmore having gone on board of a British man-of-war, half of the minute-men were discharged.

My father, Col. James Slaughter, with Col. Marshall and others, had the honor of being in the first battle (the Great Bridge) fought in Virginia. I was sent home to school. In the spring of 1776 I again left school and entered in Col. John Jameson's troop of cavalry for three years. But before we marched I was appointed by the Committee of Safety of Culpeper a Lieutenant in Capt. Gabriel Long's company of riflemen, and we marched to join the army under Washington in New York. In 1777 we were attached to the 11th Continental Regiment, commanded by Daniel Morgan.

Lt. Slaughter was promoted to a captaincy in 1778, and served during the war, being in the battles of Brandywine, Germantown, &c. He was one of the sufferers at Valley Forge. His messmates were the two Porterfields, Johnson, and Lt. John (Chief Justice) Marshall. They were reduced sometimes to a single shirt, having to wrap themselves in a blanket when that was washed; not one soldier in five had a blanket. The snow was knee deep all the winter, and stained with the blood from the naked feet of the soldiers. From the body of their shirts the officers had collars and wrist-bands made to appear on parade.

Capt. Slaughter kept a diary of his campaigns, which was lost in the wreck of so many fine libraries in the late war. Among the many anecdotes with which it abounded was the following concerning the late Chief Justice Marshall, at a camp on a night or two before the battle of Brandywine:—"At ten in the night we were aroused from sleep. Lt. Marshall had raked up some leaves to sleep on; he had pulled off one of his stockings in the night (the only pair of silk stockings in the regiment), and not being able to find it in the dark, he set fire to the leaves, and before he saw it a large hole had been burnt in it. He pulled it on so, and away we went," &c.

Capt. Slaughter's diary after the Revolution is preserved to 1849, when he died and was buried in Richmond.

LEWIS LITTLEPAGE.

As was said in the text of this history, the Rev. J. Stevenson married Fanny, the sister of Lewis Littlepage. This gentleman was born in Hanover county, Va., on 19th December, 1762, and died in Fredericksburg, July 19th, 1802. His career was brief, brilliant and unique; and yet there are but few who seem to have heard of the battles, sieges, fortunes he had passed, the many accidents by flood and field, his hair-breadth 'scapes, &c. His name has nearly lapsed from history, or rather he never had a niche in our temple of fame; for Europe and not America, was the theatre on which he played his part. I am indebted to Dr. Payne, the great-grandson of Mr. Stevenson, for an original letter, in which he narrates to his family the story of his life from 1785 to 1798. From the Memoirs of Elkanah Watson I am able to supply some incidents of his life up to the time when the narrative in his own letter begins.

Mr. Watson says:—"During my residence at Nantes I became intimately acquainted with Lewis Littlepage, one of the most remarkable characters of the age. He arrived in Nantes during the winter of 1779-80 on his way to Madrid, under the patronage of Mr. Jay, our stern and able minister to the court of Spain. He was then a mere youth, of fine manly figure, with a dark, penetrating black eye, and a physiognomy peculiar and striking. At that early period he was regarded as a prodigy of genius and acquirements. When I again heard of him he had separated from Mr. Jay's family, and entered as a volunteer aide to the Duke de Cuillon at the siege of Minorca. At the attack of Gibraltar he was on one of the floating batteries, and was blown up, but saved. He participated in a conspicuous manner in the thrilling incidents of that memorable siege. After his catastophe in the floating battery he got a situation on the Spanish Admiral's ship, and in one of the engagements he stood upon the quarter-deck during the battle and sketched the various pontoons of the fleet. On the return of the Spanish fleet to Cadiz he was sent with an officer to Madrid with dispatches, and exhibited to the minister a curious and scientific view of the battle, and was received with great applause and distinction at the court of Madrid. In the April following the close of the war I dined with him at Dr. Franklin's, in Passy, and saw the sketch. At Paris and Versailles he moved in the first circles and attracted marked attention. In June he made a visit to my bachelor hall in Berkeley Square, London. I never saw him again. He made the tour of Europe and established himself at Warsaw, and became in effect, Prime Minister, went to St. Petersburg as ambassador from Poland, acquitted himself with distinguished ability, and became one of the favorites of the Empress Catherine," &c.

The following letter of Lewis Littlepage to Lewis Holliday takes up the story of his life where Watson's narrative ends, and completes the account of his eventful career in Europe.

ALTONA, 9TH JANUARY, 1801.

DEAR SIR:—

I have this day received your letter of the 22nd August, 1800 . . . Since my existence is called in question, I give you, for the satisfaction of my family and friends, a short account of all that has happened to me in Europe since 1785. On the 2nd March 1786, I was sworn into the King of Poland's Cabinet as his first confidential secretary, with the rank of Chamberlain In February, 1787, I was sent to negotiate a treaty with the Empress of Russia at Kiovia, which I effected. The same year I was sent as secret and special envoy to the court of France to assist in the negotiations for the grand Quadruple Alliance, which failed. In 1788 I was recalled, and sent to Prince Potemkin's army in the Turkish war, where I commanded a division, acting at the same time in a political character. In 1789 I was compelled to leave Poland and travel to Italy. Shortly after I received orders to repair to Madrid upon a high political mission. in which I completely succeeded. In 1790 I was recalled from Spain and ordered to wait ultimate instructions at Paris. I afterwards received orders to repair by the way of Berlin to Warsaw for the revolution of the 3d May 1791. In 1792, 120,000 Russians invaded Poland. I was nominated Aide-de-camp-general to the King, with the rank of Major General. He signed the confederation of Fargowitz, and in April, 1793, sent me once more as his special envoy to Petersburg to prevent the division of Poland. I was stopped by the Russian Government on the road, and the division took place. In 1794 Kosciusko and Madalinski began another revolution in Poland. On 17th April the garrison and inhabitants of Warsaw rose in arms against the Russians; to save the life of my unfortunate friend and king I was obliged to take part with Poland, and that dreadful battle ended in the slaughter of 10,000 Russians. The Empress Catherine II. never forgave me my conduct upon that occasion. She was more irritated against me by hearing that I had consented to accept as commander-in-chief under the revolutionary government, although I was destined to act against Russia. My having assisted in repelling the Russian armies in their attempt to storm Willna, gave also offence. In short, I had gone so far in the revolution that I should have gone much farther had I not been defeated with my friend Prince Joseph Poniatoski, the King's nephew, by the late King of Russia on the 26th August, 1794. That event lost me all my popularity. It was very near getting me hanged, for I was regarded as the acting person, although upon my honor, Prince Poniatoski acted that day against my advice. The King of Russia attacked us with about three times our force, both in men and artillery, and Kosciusko afforded us no support until we were beaten beyond redemption, although neither his left or centre were engaged the whole day otherwise than in cannonading.

After the battle of 26th August 1 took no further part in military affairs until the storming of Prague, which cost the lives of 22,000 Polanders. On the 7th January, 1795, the King of Poland was taken from Warsaw by the Russians to be conveyed to Grodno. I was separated from him by express orders of the Empress, and it was hinted to be that nothing less than my former services in the Turkish war could have saved me from sharing the fate of the other chiefs of the revolution of 1794. After the departure of the King I set out for Vienna, but was immediately ordered to leave that metropolis, which produced a public altercation between me and the Austrian ministry, but which ended to my satisfaction, as Russia came forward and did me justice. The King of Prussia, Frederick William II., afterwards allowed me to return to Warsaw, then under his dominion, where I remained until the death of the Empress Catherine II. I was then invited to go to Petersburg with the King of Poland, but refused unless reparation was made to me for the treatment I had recently experienced. The Emperor said that "all that regarded his mother; as he had given no offence, he should make no reparation." I perhaps might have gone at last to Russia, but was prevented by the sudden death of my friend, my master, my more than father. Stanislaus Augustus, King of Poland, who expired at Petersburg 12th Feb'y., 1798. After that melancholy event a long correspondence took place between the Emperor of Russia and myself, which ended in his paying me in a very noble manner the sum assigned me by the King of Poland as a reward of my long and dangerous services.

I arrived in Hamburg in October last. My intention was to go either to France or England, but I found myself strangely embroiled with both these governments. I have settled matters in France, but not yet in England. The ministers there persist in believing me to be sent upon a secret envoy from the Emperor of Russia, who is now at variance with England. God knows I am sick of European politics. I intended to have spent the winter in Hamburg, but was driven from that sink of iniquity by a most atrocious plot against my life and fortune. The latter is in safety, and should I perish even here under the hospitable government of Denmark, I shall leave nine or ten thousand pounds sterling so disposed of that my assassins cannot prevent its coming to my family. That sum is all I have saved from the wreck of my fortunes in Poland. In the spring I shall proceed to America, either by the way of France or directly from hence, provided I escape the daggers and poison with which I am threatened here.

My duty and affection to my mother, and kindest remembrance to all relations and friends.

Ever yours, my dear Sir.
LEWIS LITTLEPAGE.

Lewis Holliday.

If the adventurous career of Lewis Littlepage needed confirmation, incidental proof and illustration of it will be found in the personal souvenirs devised by him to Waller Holladay and inherited by Col. Alexander Holladay, by whom they were kindly shown to the author:

1. The original patent conferring the position of Chamberlain upon Lewis Littlepage upon his entrance into the Polish Cabinet, 1787, signed by the King.
2. The original patent of Knighthood of the Order of St. Stanislaus, 1790, signed by the King.
3. The letter from the Prince of Nassau requesting the Marshal de Ligne to give Lewis Littlepage a captaincy in the regiment Royale l'Allemande, reciting Littlepage's distinguished service at Port Mahon and Gibraltar.
4. The letter of the Duque de Cuillon assigning Lewis Littlepage to his staff.
5. The letter of Court Florda Blanca recommending Lewis Littlepage.
6. The passport of Lewis Littlepage for his mission to France.
7. Lewis Littlepage's gold-hilted rapier presented to him by the Queen of Spain.
8. Lewis Littlepage's gold key, his badge as chamberlain to the King of Poland.
9. The portrait of the King of Poland presented to Lewis Littlepage by the King on their final parting at Grodno.

Dr. Payne has too the insignia of Littlepage's knighthood, the Star of the order of Stanislaus. In the centre is a convex silver plate, on which, formed of small ruby sets, are the initials S. A. R., Stanislaus Augustus Rex; surrounding this, wrought with gold thread, is the motto, Incitat Proemiando. Around this is a brilliant green border with gilt leaves. The rays of the star are silver spangles.

THE TOBACCO PLANT.

A very curious article might be written on the literature of tobacco, involving its relation to the church and the State, and its influence on the individual mind and body, on manners and habits, and the general wealth and happiness of the world. Such an article might be illustrated by the authority of statesmen, lawyers, medical men, merchants, farmers and political economists, and adorned with gems of wisdom and of wit from nearly all the English scholars and poets, from King James' "Counterblast" to Charles Lamb's "Farewell to Tobacco," in which praises and curses alternate with amusing felicity. It is interwoven with the history of Virginia at every stage of its progress. In colonial times many Acts of Assembly were passed regulating its culture, and one office of the early vestries was to appoint reputable freeholders to count tobacco plants in each parish. Thus, as early as 1728, Goodrich Lightfoot and Robert Slaughter counted the plants from the mouth of Mountain Run (in what is now Culpeper) up to Joseph Howe's Plantation, and across to the mouth of the Robinson River; Robert Green and Francis Kirtley on the other side of Mountain Run to the North River; George Woots and Michael Cook from the mouth of the Robinson River up to the Great Mountains. The salaries of ministers and civil officers were paid in tobacco, and it, or notes representing it in the warehouse, were the currency of the country. Some of these notes are now before us. Parishes too were known as "Orinoco" and "Sweet-scented" parishes, according to the kind of tobacco grown in them. The salary of a minister was 16,000 lbs. of tobacco, the value of which varied from £40 to £80 in money. A sweet-scented parish was worth much more than an Orinoco parish. There was a deduction of 8 per cent. for cash, and tobacco was sometimes as low as six shillings current money. A minister's tobacco was worth less than other like bulks of tobacco, because it was so mixed. Many flourishing towns, as Dumfries and Falmouth, &c., where Scotch merchants grew rich in this trade, sprang up in Virginia. In Glasgow there is now a "Virginia Street," and that city received a great impulse from becoming the entrepot whence the farmers-general of France derived their supplies of tobacco from Virginia.

THE PINE TREE AND ITS FRUITS—SALARIES PAID IN TAR.

These two were subjects of legislation. Tar was once in great demand for tarring the roofs of public and private buildings. Special instructions were given by the General Assembly of Virginia for preparing pine-trees by stripping the bark from the trunk of the trees, eight feet from the root, leaving a small slip to keep the tree alive, when in a short time, it was said, the sun would draw the turpentine to the surface, and the whole trunk would become light-wood.

It may not generally be known that towards the North Carolina line, where little or no tobacco was grown, the minister was paid in tar, pitch and pork; so says the Rev. Mr. Bagg in his report (1724) to the Bishop of London.

GENEALOGIES

OF SOME OF THE OLD VESTRYMEN AND COMMUNICANTS OF ST. MARK'S PARISH.

Many of these family-trees had their roots in Great Britain ages ago; but it would take too much space to trace them there. As a general rule, we limit ourselves to the branches which were transplanted in Virginia. If our notices of some of the families are more extended than those of others, it is because the former were better known to us. Our design in printing these genealogies is to gratify a natural desire, which most persons feel, to know something of their forefathers, and to show how family-trees in a few generations interlock their branches. It is more creditable to transmit an honorable name to one's children than it is to derive it from one's ancestors, and to be descended from good and true men than from a long line of unworthy forefathers, even though it be a line of kings and queens. But it seems to be unnatural and irrational to attach more value to the pedigrees of horses and herds than to the pedigrees of men and women. One end of history is to reproduce the past for the gratification and instruction of the present; and it is surely (at least) an innocent curiosity to look back at those who in the past century cleared the land which we now till, and who laid the foundation of the institutions under which we live.

Explanations of the abbreviations to be found in the genealogies:—m. means married; ch., child or children; dau., daughter, and d. s. p., died without offspring.

THE BARBOUR FAMILY.

This family is of Scotch origin. There was a John Barbour who was Archdeacon of Old Aberdeen as early as 1357. He was the author of the historical poem of the Life and Actions of King Robert Bruce. Whether he was the root in Scotland of the branches of the family in Virginia, the writer does not know. Our relations are with James Barbour, the first of the name in what is now Culpeper. He was one of the first vestry men of St. Mark's Parish at its organization at Germanna in 1731, and served in that office until the division of the parish in 1740, which threw him into the new parish of St. Thomas in Orange County where he lived. If the old register of St. Thomas Parish had been preserved, we should doubtless have found his name as vestryman there. Among his children were 1st James, who represented Culpeper in the House of Burgesses in 1764. He was the father of Mordecai Barbour, who married a daughter of John Strode of Fleetwood in Culpeper, and of Thomas, Richard and Gabriel, of whom the last three migrated to Kentucky. The Hon. John S. Barbour, M. C., brilliant at the bar and in the legislative halls, was the son of Mordecai and Miss Strode. He married Miss Beirne of Petersburg, and their children are, 1st John S. Barbour, President of the Virginia Midland Railroad, who married a daughter of Henry Dangerfield of Alexandria; 2d. James, member of Assembly and Convention, who married Miss Beckham; 3d. Alfred, deceased; 4th. Dr. Edwin Barbour; 5th. Sally; 6th, Eliza (Mrs. George Thompson.)

Thomas, son of James 1st, represented Orange in the Assembly in 1775, and St. Thomas Parish in the Convention in 1785–86–90. He married Isabella Thomas, daughter of Philip Pendleton. There children were, 1st. Dr. Richard, and 2d. Thomas, who died in their youth; 3d. Hon. Philip P. Barbour, Speaker of Congress, and of the Convention of 1829–30, and Justice of the Supreme Court U. S. He married Frances Todd, daughter of Benjamin Johnson of Orange. His children were: 1st. Philippa, who married Judge Field of Culpeper; 2d. Elizabeth, who married John J. Ambler of Jacquelin Hall, Madison County; 3d. Thomas, M. D., who married Catherine Strother of Rappahannock County; he died in St. Louis of cholera in 1849; 4th. Edmund Pendleton who married Harriet, daughter of Col. John Stuart of King George, and died in 1851; 5th. Quintus, who married Mary, daughter of James Somerville of Culpeper; 6th. Sextus, died in St. Louis; 7th. Septimus, died in infancy. The Hon. P. P. Barbour died in Washington, attending the Supreme Court February, 1841 His widow died April, 1872, aged 85.

4th. James, son of Thomas and grandson of James 1st, was born June 10th, 1775. He was Governor of Virginia, Senator of U. S., Minister to England, Secretary of War, &c. Besides their other qualities, the two brothers had a wondrous faculty of speech in conversation and in the forum. James married, October 29th, 1792, Lucy, daughter of Benjamin Johnson. Their children were: –1st. Benjamin Johnson Barbour, who died in 1820 in the 20th year of his age; 2d. James, who died November 7th, 1857: 3d. Benjamin Johnson Barbour, born June 14th, 1821, and married November 17th, 1844, Caroline Homoesel, daughter of the late eminent Dr. George Watson of Richmond. Mr. Barbour inherits the genius of his father, informed by rare culture, but he follows the example of his great-grandfather, and is content to be warden of the church. He was elected to Congress in 1865; but the representatives of Virginia of that year were not admitted to their seats. 4th. Lucy, daughter of Governor Barbour, married (1822) John Seymour Taliaferro, who was unhappily drowned in 1830; 5th. Frances Cornelia Barbour married William Handy Collins, a distinguished lawyer of Baltimore.

Among the daughters of Col. Thomas Barbour were: 1st. Lucy, who married Thomas Newman and had three daughters, Mrs. Macon, Mrs. Welch and Wilhelmina, and one son, James Barbour Newman. 2. Nelly, married Martin Nalle of Culpeper, father of P. P. Nalle, warden of St. Paul's Church, who married first Miss Wallace, and second Miss Zimmerman, and is the father of Mrs. Steptoe, wife of the Rector of St. Paul's. Cordelia Nalle married Joseph Hiden of Orange, father of Rev. J. C. Hiden (Baptist), Greenville, S. C. Edmonia Nalle married William Major, Esq., of Culpeper: Fanny Nalle married John C. Hansbrough (lawyer); Martinette Nalle married Blucher Hansbrough of Culpeper; Lucetta Nalle married George Booton of Madison; Jane Nalle married George Clark of Washington, D. C.; Thos. Nalle married Miss Hooe of Fredericksburg; Benjamin Johnson Nalle died unmarried; Sarah Ellen Nalle married Col. Garrett Scott, father of Rev. F. G. Scott of Christ Church, Gordonsville, Va.; and Mary Nalle m. Richard H. Willis. Sally, daughter of Thomas Barbour, married Gabriel Gray, and had daughters, Mrs. S. F. Leake, Mrs. William Anderson, Mrs. R. W. Anderson, and Mrs. Cowles. Mary, daughter of Thos. Barbour, married Daniel Bryan—children, Mrs. Lathrop, Mrs. Judge Wylie, Mrs. Brown, and two sons, B. Bryan and Wm. Bryan.

James Barbour the head of the foregoing family, took out a patent for land on the Rapidan in 1734.

On the farm of Col. Garrett Scott in Orange is a granite tombstone just as old as St. Mark's Parish. The inscription is as follows: Here lyeth the body of Jane, wife of John Scott, who was born ye 28th Dec., 1699, and departed this life ye 28th April, 1731. This farm is in direct lineal descent to the present owner from a grant known as the "Todd Grant," from the Crown of England.

Note: In the Barbour genealogy page 52, the second paragraph should read that Thos. son of James 1st. m. Mary dau. of Richard Thomas and Isabella Pendleton Thomas.

THE CARTER FAMILY.

The first of this name in Virginia was Jno. Carter of Corotoman, who died in 1669. A chart of his descendants would fill this book. I limit this notice to those known to the writer in St. Mark's Parish. Robert, called King Carter, was the son of John 1st, by his wife Sarah Ludlowe. Robert m. (1688) Judith Armstead, and among their children was John, who (1723) m. Eliza Hill of Shirley, and their third son Edward of Blenheim m. Sarah Champe and their dau. Eliza, m. William Stanard of Roxbury, Spotsylvania, who was the grandfather of Virginia Stanard, who m. Samuel Slaughter, the old churchwarden of St. Mark's, and was the mother of Mrs. William Green of Richmond, of Mrs. Dr. Daniel Green, of Sally C., wife of Rev. William Lockwood of Md., of Marcia (Mrs. John B. Stanard). Elizabeth Stanard m. Jno. Thompson. father of Fanny, wife of Rev. John Cole, of Miss Eliza Thompson, and of Mrs. Buffington. Jane, daughter of Edward of Blenheim m. Major Bradford of the British army, father of Samuel K. Bradford of the Revolution, whose son, Samuel K. Bradford. vestryman of St. Mark's m. Emily, daughter of Samuel Slaughter (churchwarden of St. Mark's), and was the father of S. S. Bradford, present churchwarden; of Mrs. Gen. Wright, U. S. army ; of Mrs. Professor Nairne of Columbia College, New York; of Dr. Robert B. Bradford, and of Mrs. Van Schaik of New York City. William Champe Carter of Farley, Culpeper County, sixth son of Edward of Blenheim, m. Maria Farley, and their daughter Eliza Hill m. Col. Samuel Storrow, the father of Mrs. Judge Bell, of Mrs. Dr. Wm. Thompson, of Mrs. Weston, of Mrs. Green, of Samuel and Farley. Charles Carter of Cleve, son of King Carter by his second wife Mary Landon, had a daughter Sarah who m. William a son of Rev. John Thompson of St. Mark's, who was the father of Commodore Charles Carter Byrd Thompson, U. S. navy, of Gilliss and of William Thompson.

THE CAVE FAMILY.

Among the members of the first vestry of St. Mark's in 1731 was Benjamin Cave. I have in my possession the original patent for 1000 acres of land on the Rappidan (sic) River, to Abraham Bledsoe and Benjamin Cave, "to be held in free and common socage, and not in capite or knight service, by paying yearly the free rent of one shilling for every fifty acres, on the feast of St. Michael the Archangel"; signed by William Gooch, Lieut.-Governor and Commander-in-Chief of the Colony and Dominion of Virginia. Done at Williamsburg, under the seal of the Colony, 28th September, 1728.

Benjamin Cave was vestryman of St. Mark's until 1740, when St. Thomas Parish was cut off from St. Mark's; and he and David Cave, who was Lay Reader at the old Orange Church near Ruckersville, became members of the new parish (St. Thomas) in Orange County, where they lived The records of St. Thomas being lost, their relation to it cannot be traced. It is known, however, that the family adhered to the Church of their fathers; and one of the old ministers, about 1740, lived with Benjamin Cave, Sr., whose residence was within reach of the first chapel (near Brooking's) and the old Orange Church.

I have in my possession some original poems in MS., entitled "Spiritual Songs," written by a sister of Benjamin Cave, Sr., endorsed 1767. It is very pleasant to find one of these old-time church people, who some modern people think had no religion, giving utterance to her pious emotions in songs which are evidently the outpourings of a truly devotional spirit. It is said that Benjamin Cave used to repeat the church service from memory, chanting the psalms.

The first Benjamin Cave lived for a time at what is now known as Rhodes in Orange, and then moved to land on the Upper Rapidan near Cave's Ford, which derives its name from him.

Benjamin Cave represented Orange in the House of Burgesses in 1756. He m. Hannah, dau. of Wm. and sister of Abraham Bledsoe; ch. David, John, Wm., Richard (who moved to Kentucky), Ann (to North Carolina); Sally m. a Strother, Hannah m. Capt. Mallory; ch. Elizabeth m. Oliver Welch. Another daughter m. Capt. Robert Terrill, the father of Mrs. Robert Lovell. Another daughter m. Oliver Terrill, the father of Dr. Uriel Terrill, Delegate from Orange. Another daughter m. Welch. William Mallory m. Miss Gibson, and was the father of Robert Mallory, late M. C. from Kentucky. Uriel Mallory was the father of Mrs. John Taliaferro. Phil. Mallory lived near Raccoon Ford. Elizabeth, dau. of Benjamin Cave m. Col. Wm. Johnson; ch. 1. Valentine m. Elizabeth Cave, ch. Belfield m. Miss Dickerson. 2. Fontaine m. Miss Duke. 3. Lucy m. Mr. Suggett. 4. Sally m. Mr. Dickerson. 5. Benjamin m. Miss Barbour (see Barbour genealogy). 6. Col. Robert m. Miss Suggett; ch. 1.

Richard M., Vice-President and hero of the "Thames"; 2. J. T. Johnson (M. C.); 3. James; 4. Benjamin. Benjamin Cave, son of first Benjamin, m. a dau. of Dr. John Belfield of Richmond County; ch. Belfield, m. Miss Christy; ch. Belfield, Clerk of Madison County, m. Miss Jones, and was the father of Mrs. Governor Kemper. Emily m. Col. Cave; Sally m. Shackelford; Hudson was Professor at Chapel Hill, N. C.; Benjamin m. Miss Glassell (father of Mrs. John Gray, Jr., of Traveller's Rest.) Benjamin, son of Benjamin and Elizabeth, m. Miss White; ch. William, Belfield, John and Margaret, all settled in Kentucky. Sarah, dau. of Benjamin, m. Wm. Cassine; ch. Mary, who m. Mr. Taliaferro. William, son of Benjamin and Elizabeth Cave, m. Miss Smith; ch. John, Wm. and Hudson, settled in Kentucky. Elizabeth m. John Bell, father of Nelson H. Bell of Baltimore, who m. Hannah Cave. Another dau. m. Mr. Irvine. Richard Cave m. Miss Porter; ch. Thomas, Capt. William (father of Mrs. Cornelia Thompson), Felix, Elizabeth, Mary, Cornelia. Anne, and Hannah.

I am indebted to Mrs. Thompson for contributions to the above notice.

THE CLAYTONS.

The first person of this name who appears in the history of Virginia was the Rev. John Clayton, who had been Rector of Crofton in Yorkshire. In 16-83 he addressed to the Royal Society in England, at their request, several letters giving an account of what he calls "Several Observables" in Virginia. These letters discuss the soil, climate, natural history and agriculture of the colony of that day. They display great acuteness of observation, fullness of learning, and practical suggestions. He seems to have been the first to point out the value of marl and muck as fertilizers, and suggest to the planters the advantage of draining the tidewater swamps. And when his opinion was laughed at and rejected by the overseers, he went to work and put them to shame by laying dry a pond of water, bringing to the light of the sun inexhaustible soil.

The next man of mark of this name was the Rev. David Clayton, minister of Blissland Parish, New Kent Co., Virginia, from 1704 to 1724. In his parochial reports to the Bishop of London he says (1724) that his parish was sixty miles long, that he had under his charge 136 families and about seventy communicants.

There is John Clayton at Williamsburg, Attorney General, and a friend of Spotswood, who accompanied Mr. Fontaine in the first trip to Germanna in 1714. There was also a Clayton a vestryman and justice in Essex Co. The family tradition is that Major Philip Clayton came to Culpeper from New Kent through Essex. What was his precise relation to the foregoing clergymen is not certainly known. His name first appears in our church records in the year 1741, when he was chosen vestryman of St. Mark's, and a patent for land from Lord Fairfax to John Brown (now before us) is endorsed as having been surveyed by Phillip Clayton, 1749. He was the deputy, doing all the duties of the office for Roger Dixon, Clerk of Culpeper, who lived in the lower country. He married Ann, sister of Robert Coleman, on whose land the courthouse was built. He had one son, Samuel (his successor in the vestry), who married his cousin Ann Coleman, and among their children were Major Philip Clayton the second, an officer of the Revolution, whose daughter Sarah Ann married Dr. James B. Wallace.

Nancy, sister of the last Philip, and daughter of Samuel, married Jeremiah Strother, and was the grandmother of the Rev. J. S. Hansbrough, and Mrs. Judge Williams of Orange C. H., Colonel Woodson Hansbrough, and Mrs. Waldridge.

Lucy, dau. of the first Philip, married William Williams (vestryman), and their children were Major John, General James, both officers in the Revolution, Philip of Woodstock, William Clayton of Richmond, Mrs. Stevens and Mrs. Green. (See Williams genealogy.)

Susan, another daughter of the first Philip, married Colonel James Slaughter, father of Captain Philip Slaughter. (See Slaughter genealogy).

Another daughter married Nathaniel Pendleton, brother of Judge Edmund Pendleton, President of the Court of Appeals (see Pendleton genealogy). Another daughter married a Crittenden, and was the mother (I believe) of Senator Crittenden of Kentucky.

Major Philip Clayton the elder lived at Catalpa, so named from a Catalpa tree he transplanted from Essex, the first of its kind in the county.

Philip Clayton went from Virginia to Georgia, where he died, and was buried at Sand Hills, near the city of Augusta. His children were first, George Roots of Milledgeville, cashier of State Bank and treasurer of the State, highly honored and esteemed. 2. Augustine Smith Clayton, of Athens, graduated at Franklin College, distinguished at the bar, Judge of the Western Circuit, and member of Congress, where he won a national reputation. He was an able statesman, jurist and man of letters, and left his impress upon the policy and literature of the State. He died a Christian, on 1st of June, 1839, in the 56th year of his age, leaving nine children, viz. George Roots, Augustine Smith, Wm. Wirt, Cashier Merchants Bank, Atlanta; Philip, consul at Callao, and churchwarden, St. Paul's, Greensboro, died 1877; Almyra; Dallas; Edward P., cotton factor and commission merchant of Augusta, and churchwarden of St. Paul's; Julia; Claudia, and Augusta.

THE COLEMANS.

Robert Coleman, 1st of the name in Culpeper, m. Sarah Ann Saunders. The town of Fairfax (Culpeper) was founded on fifty acres of his land in 1759.

He had one son, Robert, who emigrated to Kentucky and m. Mrs. Thompson, a sister of Major Philip Lightfoot.

Gilly, dau. of the 1st Robert and Miss Saunders, m. General Edward Stevens, the Revolutionary hero and elector, who cast the vote of the district for Washington, and whose son John m. Polly, dau. of the first William Williams.

Ann, 2d dau. of 1st. Robert, m. Samuel Clayton, (See Clayton genealogy.)

Rosa, 3d dau., m. Foster of Tennessee, one of whose ch. was the Senator in Congress from that State.

Another dau. of 1st Robert m. Col. John Slaughter, son of the 1st Francis of that name.

Another dau. m. Francis Slaughter, brother to the foregoing John. (See Slaughter genealogy.)

Another dau. m. a Yancey.

Lucy, another dau., m. French Strother, so long representative of Culpeper in the General Assembly and in the Convention of 1775-6, and whose oldest daughter. P. French was first wife of Capt. P. Slaughter. (See Slaughter genealogy.)

The 8th dau. of 1st. Robert m. a Crutcher, and one of their daughters m. a Foushee.

Robert Coleman in his will (1793) recorded in Culpeper, leaves legacies to his daughters Ann Clayton, Sarah Slaughter, Lucy Strother, Frances Crutcher Susanna Yancey. Philip Clayton was his executor.

THE CONWAY FAMILY.

This family has been identified with the Episcopal Church from the earliest times. You may trace the name through the vestry-books from the first settlements in the Northern Neck to the present time. I have in my possession the will of Edwin Conway, dated 19th of March, 1698. In the graveyard of Whitechapel, Lancaster County, there is a tombstone of Mary Ball, daughter of Edwin Conway, and one of James Ball, her husband, who was a near relative of Gen. Washington's grandfather, who was the son of Col. Wm. Ball, the first of the name who came from England in 1650 and settled at the mouth of Corotoman River. I transfer from the will the following clauses:—"First and PRINCIPALLY, I bequeath my soul to the God that gave it, in certain hope, notwithstanding my unworthiness, to receive pardon of all my sins, through the blessed merits of my dear Redeemer; and by no other way or means do I hope for pardon. My body I commit to be buried in my burying-ground at Lancaster, by the left side of my dear wife Sarah, in certain hope, thro' the merits aforesaid, that soul and body will have a joyful meeting at the resurrection of the just." He gives to his son Francis and to his heirs lawfully begotten 706 acres of land in Essex; to the child or children "whereof my wife now goeth withal" the crop of sweet-scented tobacco on the lower plantation. To his son Edwin all the lands in Lancaster given him by deed, with his mathematical books and instruments, and all "the cloth and stuff sent for to England." He appoints his friend Andrew Jackson, Reuben Conway and H. Thacker to be OVERSEERS of his will, desiring them to carefully advise and instruct his children in their persons and estates and to be assistants to his dear wife.

The aforesaid E. Conway married Elizabeth Thompson. Their son Francis, near Port Royal, Caroline, married Rebecca, daughter of John Catlett and Elizabeth Grimes. (This John Catlett was son of the John Catlett killed by the Indians while defending the fort at Port Royal.) Nelly, daughter of Francis and granddaughter of Edwin Conway, married James Madison, Sr., and was the mother of President Madison, who was born at Port Conway, opposite to Port Royal, where his mother was visiting, at 12 o'clock at night between the 5th and 6th of March, 1751, and was baptized the 31st of March by the Rev. Wm. Davis, and had for godfathers John Moore and Jonathan Gibson, and for godmothers Mrs. Rebecca Moore and Misses Judith and Elizabeth Catlett.

The author of this will was the great-grandfather of old Capt. Catlett Conway, of Hawfield, in Orange (now owned by Wm. Crenshaw, Esq.,) who was the father of the late Francis, Catlett, John and Henry Conway, of Orange and Madison; of Mrs. Hay Taliaferro, of Rose Hill, Orange County, and of Mrs. Fitzhugh, of Bedford, King George. Dr. Charles Conway (vestryman) is a direct descendant of the old vestryman, the first Edwin Conway of Lancaster.

THE FIELDS.

The first person of the name in the parish register is Henry Field, Sr., a member of the first vestry chosen by the freeholders and housekeepers of St. Mark's Parish, at Germanna, in January 1731. The next is Abraham Field, elected vestryman at the Great Fork Church in 1744, and served till his death in 1774, a term of thirty years. He had a son John, who represented Culpeper in the House of Burgesses in 1765. He was probably the Col. John Field who had served in Braddock's War, and who fell, fighting gallantly at the head of his regiment, at the battle of Point Pleasant. One of his daughters married

Lawrence Slaughter, an officer of the Revolution, and who was the father of John Field Slaughter, who married Miss Alexander, of Prince William. Another of Col. John Field's daughters married Col. George Slaughter, who raised one of the first companies of minute-men in Culpeper; and after the war moved to Kentucky with George Rogers Clarke, commanded a fort at the Falls of the Ohio, and was one of the founders of the city of Louisville, which was then in the State of Virginia.

Henry Field, Sr., the vestryman of 1731, served in that office and as churchwarden till 1762, a term of thirty-one years. He executed many commissions for the vestry, such as going to Williamsburg on horseback several times on their behalf, and paying quit-rents for the churches and glebes. He and Francis Slaughter and Robert Green chose a site for a chapel between Shaw's Mountain, the Devil's Run and Hazel River. He was succeeded in the vestry by Henry Field, Jr., who served till his removal from the parish of St. Mark's into Bromfield Parish, whose records are lost or we should probaly have found his name on the vestry-books there. He represented Culpeper in the Convention at Williamsburg in 1774 to consider the state of the country, in the House of Burgesses in 1775, and with French Strother in the Convention of 1776 which asserted the principle of religious liberty, declared American independence, and adopted the first Constitution. Henry Field, Jr., died in 1785, leaving six sons—Daniel, Henry, George, Joseph, Thomas and John, who were the ancestors of the families of that name. The late judge of this court, Richard H. Field, and his brothers Yancey and Stanton, were the sons of Daniel Field of what is now Madison. He (the Judge) married first Matilda, daughter of Robert Slaughter of the Grange, and second Philippa, daughter of the Hon. Philip P. Barbour. His three sons were killed in battle during the late war, and his daughter (Mrs. Norvell) is the only surviving child. Gen. James Field of the Culpeper bar, who lost a limb at the battle of Slaughter's Mountain, is a son of Yancey Field. He married Miss Cowherd of Orange.

THE FRY FAMILY.

The ancestor of the Frys who once so abounded in Culpeper, was Col. Joshua Fry, an Englishman educated at Oxford. He lived some time in Essex, was Professsor of Mathematics at William and Mary College, a member of the House of Burgesses, commissioner to run one of the lines between Virginia and North Carolina, and negotiator of the treaty of Logstown. He, with Peter Jefferson, made a map of Virginia in 1749. He commanded a regiment against the French and Indians, of which Washington was lieutenant-colonel. I am indebted to his lineal descendant Frances Fry, of Charlottesville, for a copy of his commission, from the original in Mr. Fry's possession:—

"TO JOSHUA FRYE

"His Majesty, by his royal instructions, commanded me to send a proper number of forces to erect and maintain a fort at the Monongahela and Ohio Rivers; and having a good opinion of your loyalty, conduct and ability, I do hereby institute, appoint and commission you to be Colonel and Commander-in chief of the forces now raising, to be called the Virginia Regiment, with which and the cannon, arms and ammunition, necessary provisions and stores, you are with all possible dispatch to proceed to said fork of Monongahela, and there act according to your instructions."

Col. Joshua Fry married Mrs. Hill, the daughter of Paul Micon, a French Huguenot physician. He was the father of the Rev. Henry Fry, who lived in the fork of Crooked Run and the Robinson River, and occasionally preached in the Episcopal church near Orange C. H., when they had no minister, always prefacing his sermons with the old church service, says Col. Frank Taylor, a vestryman of that church. He was one of those good and guileless men whom all Christians respected and loved. His son Reuben m. Ann dau. of Col. Jas. Slaughter, and their ch. were Judge Joseph Fry, of Wheeling, Henry, Senator of Kanawha, and Philip S., late clerk of Orange and father of Philip, present clerk, William, Thomas and Luther. Thomas W., son of Rev. H. Fry, m. 1st Mrs. Slaughter, whose maiden name was Bourn, and 2d Ann dau. of Col. Abram Maury of Madison. He with three ch. moved to Kentucky (1816). Joshua m. Miss Walker, and Mrs. Willis dau. of William Twyman. Hugh and Joshua Fry, of Richmond, were his sons. Henry m. Mildred dau. of Rev. Mat. Maury. Frank Fry, Sr., of Charlottesville, is their son. John m. Miss Heywood, of Culpeper, and lived at the Warm Springs. Mrs. Dr. Archer Strother was his dau. Wesley m. 1st Miss Walker, and 2nd a French lady, Miss Leflet, and had thirteen children. Thornton m. a dau. of Hon. Philip R. Thompson, and their ch. were Gen. Burkitt Fry, C. S. A., Dr. Frank and Mrs. Jno. L. Bacon, of Richmond. Margaret dau. of Rev. Henry m. Philip Lightfoot and moved to Kentucky. Martha m. Goodrich Lightfoot and had ten ch., of whom Edward Lightfoot, of Madison, is the only survivor. Maria m. Hugh Walker and went to Kentucky, and had many children.

Col. Joshua Fry, the head of this family in Virginia, patented 1000 acres of land on the Robinson River in 1726, and 400 acres "in the fork of the Robinson" in 1739. Charles Meriwether Fry, of the Bank of New York, who m. Miss Leigh, is the son of Belville, who was the son of Joshua, who was the son of Rev. Henry Fry.

THE GARNETT FAMILY.

The chief seat of this family in Virginia was the county of Essex, where many of this name occupied a high social position and filled many places of public trust. The Hon. James M. Garnett was a member of Congress from 1805 to 1809. The Hon. Robert S. Garnett was in Congress from 1817 to 1827. The Hon. Muscoe Garnett was also a member of Congress and of the State Convention of 1850. Dr. A. Y. P. Garnett who married the daughter of Governor Wise, has been for many years a leading medical man of Washington City. There was a General Garnett of the Confederate army who fell in battle, whose sister married Professor Williamson of the Virginia Military Institute; and there is now a Professor Garnett in the College at Annapolis, Md.

I have been disappointed in receiving the information which would have enabled me to show the connecting links between these several members of the family in Virginia. The first of the name in Culpeper was Anthony Garnett, who came from Essex, and from the names James, Muscoe and Reuben, which are common to both families, they probably sprang from the same stock. Anthony Garnett was a vestryman, churchwarden and lay reader of St. Mark's Parish from 1758. He lived at the Horse Shoe, where Joseph Wilmer, Jr., now resides, and when there was no minister of the parish, was in the habit of burying the dead with the church service. He married Mrs. Bowler (Miss Jones), and his children were Robin, who moved to Kentucky and died in his ninety-eighth year. His daughter married Stokely Towles of Madison, and their daughter married James L. Waggener of Russelville, Ky., father of Prof. Waggener of Bethel College, Ky. James, son of Anthony, was minister of Crooked Run Church. He married Miss Rowe, and was the father of Edmund, who was the father of the late Rev. James Garnett, whose sons, Joel, Absalom and Franklin, and daughter Tabitha, still survive. James, Sr., was the father of the present James, whose children are Muscoe and others. John, son of Anthony, moved to Kentucky. Thomas married Miss Hawkins. Reuben, son of Anthony, married Miss Twyman, and was the father of the venerable Miss Tabitha Garnett, who, like her namesake in the Bible, is kind to the poor. Lucy married a Tinsley. Sally married a Stepp, and Betsy married William Willis of Culpeper, the father of the late Isaac Willis, who has many descendants, among whom is the Rev. John C. Willis of Indian Town, Orange County.

THE GLASSELL FAMILY.

The Glassell (originally Glassele) family went from Poictiers, France, with Mary Queen of Scots on her return to her native country. John Glassell of Runkan, Scotland, m. Mary Coalter, a warm Covenanter, and their son Robert m. Mary Kelton and their son Andrew Glassell was born at Galway, Dumfriesshire, Scotland, near Torthorwald, "Castle of the Douglass," Oct. 8th, 1738, and emigrated to Madison County, Virginia, in 1756. He imported mechanics from Scotland, and built a large brick residence on his fine estate on the upper Robinson River, known as Torthorwald. He m. (1776) Elizabeth dau. of Erasmus Taylor of Orange County, and died July 4th, 1827, aged 89. Their children were—

1. Millie Glassell m. Reuben Smith. Issue 1. Jane m. in 1822 Hon. Jeveremiah Morton (M. C.); issue one son, died in infancy, and one daughter, Mildred m. J. J. Halsey, issue 1. Fannie M.; 2. Anne Augusta (Mrs. Alexander); 3. J. Morton m. Miss Stearns; 4. R. Ogden m. Miss Walker, and 5. Joseph J. Halsey. 2. George A. Smith (now of Bell County, Texas), m. Julia dau. of James Somerville of Culpeper Co.; issue 1. Eudora G. (Mrs. Lees); 2. Jane M. (Mrs. Ware); 3. Mary S. (Mrs. Coffee); 4. Margaret (Mrs. Russell), and several sons unmarried. 3. Dr. William R. Smith (late of Galveston), m. first Mrs. Middleton, no issue; m. second Mary Mayrant, issue John M. m. Miss Terry; and Mildred (Mrs. Crosby of New York City.)

2. John Glassell m. first Louisa Brown. Issue 1. Dr. Andrew m. Miss Downing; 2. Fanny (Mrs. Ware); 3. Mary (Mrs. Conway); 4. Louisa (Mrs. Eno of Pennsylvania). John Glassell m. second Mrs. Lee, nee Margaret Scott; issue Mildred S. (Mrs. Covell) and John m. Miss Thom. John Glassell m. third Mary Ashton, by whom no issue.

3. Mary Kelton Glassell m. Michael Wallace. Issue 1. Ellen (Mrs. Somerville); 2. Gustavus; 3. H. Nelson; 4. Elizabeth (Mrs. Wallace); 5. Louisa (Mrs. Goodwin); 6. James, and 7. Marianna (Mrs. Conway.)

4. Helen Buchan Glassell m. Daniel Grinnan. Issue 1. Robert A. m. Robertine Temple; 2. Cornelia (died 1864); 3. Andrew G. m. Georgie S. Bryan; 4. Daniella M.

5. Jane M. Glassell m. Benjamin Cave. (See Cave genealogy.)

6. Major James M. Glassell, U. S. Army, m. Eudora Swartout.

7. Andrew Glassell m. Susan Thornton. Issue 1. Andrew m. Miss Toland; 2. Capt. William S. Glassell; 3. Susan S. m. first Colonel George S. Patton (see Williams genealogy); m. second George H. Smith of California.

8. William E. Glassell m. first Margaret Somerville. Issue one child living, Margaret (Mrs. Weeks of Louisanna). M. second Harriet Scott.

John Glassell, brother of Andrew, came to Fredericksburg long before the Revolution. He was a merchant of large transactions, having branch establishments in Culpeper and Fauquier, and became very rich. He returned to Scotland before the Revolution. He married Helen Buchan, of the family of the Earl of Buchan. One of her sisters married an Erskine, and another Dalhousie and Lord Erskine and the Earl of Dalhousie were her nephews. John Glassell's only daughter, Johanna, married Lord Campbell who became Duke of Argyle, and the present Duke of Argyle is her son.

THE GREEN FAMILY.

ROBERT GREEN, son of William Green, an Englishman, emigrated from Ireland with his uncle, William Duff, a Quaker, to Virginia, and settled in King George county about the year, 1710. He was born in the year, 1695. He soon left his uncle and settled in what is now Culpeper county, near Brandy Station on the Southern Railway. He built his home near a large spring, which is on the road leading from Brandy Station to Rixeyville, and took up large tracts of land in what was, in 1712 Essex, in 1721 Spotsylvania, in 1735 Orange, and in 1749 Culpeper. His father was an officer in the body guard of William, Prince of Orange. He died in 1748, his will and inventory of his estate being recorded in the Orange county Clerk's Office. He was member of the Virginia House of Burgesses in 1736, and was one of the first vestrymen of St. Mark's Parish. When a young man, he married Eleanor Dunn, of Scotland, and had seven sons, as follows. [Note: The names in parenthesis or brackets signify the line of descent. Thus Joseph Green, [Francis, Wm., Wm., Robt.] means that Joseph Green was the son of Francis, the grand son of William, the great grandson of the first William and the great great grandson of the first Robert.]

1. William, born in Essex county; m. Miss Coleman, of Caroline county; was vestryman of St. Mark's Parish from 1749 to his death in Culpeper county in 1770. He was called Colonel Green, probably from military service against the Indians.

2. Robert, m Patty Ball, of Northumberland, and died in Culpeper.

3. Duff, m. 1st., Miss Thomas, 2nd., Anne Willis; he died in Culpeper about the beginning of the Revolution. His three youngest sons moved to Kentucky about 1779, and afterwards carried out their mother and younger sister.

4. John, m. Susanna Blackwell; was Colonel in the Revolution; succeeded William Green in the vestry of St. Mark's Parish in 1770; was member of the House of Burgesses in 1769, and died in Culpeper in 1798.

5. Nicholas, m. Elizabeth Price, dau. of Ajola Price, of Orange, whose mother was a dau. of Capt. Wm. Barbour; died in what is now Madison county, and left many children, who moved to Kentucky.

6. James, m. Elizabeth Jones, and died in Culpeper.

7. Moses, m. Mary Blackwell, sister of Susanna, and died in Culpeper.

WILLIAM GREEN, (Robert), who m. Miss Coleman had children as follows:

1. William, m. Eliza Green, dau. of Duff; died in Culpeper; his widow moved to Kentucky, near Covington.

2. Ellen, m. Peter Marye.

3. Betsy, m. H. Camp.

4. Mary or Anne, m. Geo. Thomas.

5. Milly, m. Mr. Stringer.

6. Lucy or Susan, m. Mr. Pinckard.

7. Nancy, m. Jno. Poindexter.

8. Francis Wyatt, m. Lucy Strother, dau. of Jos. Strother. They lived near Louisville, Ky., but died in Breckenridge county of that State.

ROBERT GREEN, (Robert), who m. Patty Ball, had

1. William, m. Miss Blackwell, and moved to Woodford county, Ky.

2. Armistead, m. Frances, dau. of Capt. Harry Pendleton, of Culpeper.

3. Samuel B., m. Miss Blair of Port Royal, Va.

4. Ellen, m. Aaron Lane, of Culpeper.

5. Anne, m. Dr. Joel Gustin, of Pennsylvania.

DUFF GREEN, (Robert), m. 1st. Miss Thomas, 2nd. Anne Willis, and had

1. John, of famous memory. "My Lord John" died a bachelor, possessed of much wealth; he was Captain in the Revolution, and was badly wounded.
2. Betsy, m. William, son of first William Green.
3. Willis, m. 1783 Sarah Reed and moved to Ky., near Danville. He settled on a farm called "Waveland," which is still owned by his descendants.
4. William, m. Miss Marshall, and moved to Lincoln county, Ky.
5. Henry, died single.
6. Ellen or Anne, m. Jno. Smith, and moved to Ky., had Jno., Henry and Willis.

JOHN GREEN, (Robert), m. Susanna Blackwell, had:
1. Wm., m. Lucy Williams; was Capt. of the navy, and was lost at sea on the brig Defiance.
2. John, killed at 18 in duel at Valley Forge.
3. Robert, m. Frances Edmonds, and died 1789.
4. Moses, m. Fanny Richards.
5. Thomas m. 1st Miss Miller; 2nd Lucy Peyton, and moved to Christian county, Ky.

NICHOLAS GREEN, (Robert), m. Elizabeth Price, and had:
1. Robert, d. single.
2. Jno., m. Jenny Hawkins.
3. Wm. m. and moved to Tenn. and had William and others.
4. Nicholas, left no children.
5. Mary, m. Mr. Stevens.
6. Lucy, d. single.
7. Eleanor, m. Mr. Rankin.
8. Joyce, m. Willis Ballance, and moved to Ky. Lived in Madison and Mercer counties.
9. Chas., had seven sons and two daughters.

JAMES GREEN, (Robert), m. Elizabeth Jones and had:
1. Gabriel, m. Miss Grant and moved to Green River, Ky.
2. James, m. Betsy Jones.
3. Jones, m. Miss Nevil, and moved to Hardy county, Va., and had Nevil, Jones, Nancy, Mrs. Parsons, Mary and Betsy.
4. Robt., m. Miss Edmunds, and had William, James, Thomas, Robert, Fanny, Ellen, Elizer, and Mrs. Cross.
5. John, m. Miss Catlett, of Fauquier, and moved to Henderson, Ky.
6. Dolly, m. Nimrod Farrow; no children.
7. Elizabeth, m. R. W. Peacock, and had 4 children; and died in England.
8. Lucy, m. Noah G. Glascock, and moved to Mo.
9. Polly, m. Mr. Catlett.
10. Austin, m. Miss Ball; lived and died in Hardin county, Ky. Some of his children went to Texas.

MOSES GREEN, (Robert), m. Mary Blackwell, and had:
1. Sarah, died single
2. Eleanor, m. Gen. Jas. Williams.

WILLIAM GREEN, (Wm., Robert,) m. Eliza Green, and had,
1. Wm., moved to Tenn.
2. Jno. m. Mrs. Faulk, and lived in Campbell county, Ky.; his widow m. Mr. Vickers.
3. Betsy, m. 1st. Mr. Craig, 2nd ———, 3rd. Mr. Magruder; she d. a wid. in 1850, in Covington, Ky., leaving no children.

ELLEN GREEN, (Wm., Robt.,). m. Peter Marye, and had,
1. Wm. 2. Jas., and 2 daughters, who both m. a Gordon.

BETSY GREEN, (Wm., Robt.,) m. H. Camp, and had Jas., Jno. G., Wyatt, and Betsy, who was married.

MARY, OR ANNE GREEN, (Wm., Robert), m. Geo. Thomas, and had Jas., a dau. m. Jas. Camp and 2 other m. daus. and 4 s. daus.

NANCY GREEN, [Wm., Robt.], m. Jno. Poindexter, and had Wm. G. and others.

FRANCIS WYATT GREEN, [Wm., Robt.] who m. Lucy Strother, had

1. Robt. who went to N.O. in war of 1812 ; settled and died there leaving a large family.

2. Nancy. m. Mr. Bostwick·

3. Jos., a soldier in battle of N. O. m. Susan dau. of Jno. Ball ; died 1852 in Columbus, Ky.

4. Thompson, m. Betsy Askins ; lived in Breckinridge county, Ky., no children.

5. Francis, m. and left several children.

6. Jno., m. Mary Holt ; lived in Indiana.

7. Austin, m. and left 2 children in Perry county, Indiana.

WILLIAM GREEN, [Robt.,Robt.,] m. Miss Blackwell, had Robt., Jas., Wm. S., Lucy, m. Mr. Bourne, Susan, m. Mr. Neale, Kitty, m. Mr. Blackman, Betsy, m. Mr. Bourne, Celia, m., and others ; lived in Woodford county, Ky.

ARMISTEAD GREEN, [Robt., Robt.] m. Frances Pendleton,and had : Henry, Robt., Anne, m. Jno. Ferguson, Polly, m. Slaughter, Fanny,m. Mr. Campbell, Harriett, m. Mr. Cenard, Ellen, Caroline, and

Edmund Pendleton, m. Martha Weems, and had Martha, who m. Francis W. Dickson, having Frank C., and Mattie Green, who m. Irwin Dugan

SAMUEL B. GREEN, [Robt., Robt.] m. Miss Blair, of Port Royal, and had Samuel and Sally.

ELLEN GREEN,[Robt., Robt.], m. Aaron Lane, and had Robert ; Jas.; Jno.; Peggy B., m. Wm. Bell, and had Fontaine ; Polly, m. H. Latham ; Ellen, m. Mr. Crenshaw; Nancy, m. Mr. Whiting, having Jno., Ellen and Catherine ; and

William A. m. Eliza Green, dau. of James Green.

ANNE GREEN, [Robt., Robt.], m. Dr. Joel Gustin, of Pennsylvania, and had Samuel G.; Theodosia, m; Ellen, m ; and Mary, who m. Daniel Remer.

WILLIS GREEN, [Duff, Robt.,] m. Sarah Reed, and had :

1. Dr. Duff, major in war of 1812, died 1858. m. Miss Crecy, niece of Simon Kenton. Dr. Duff's children were: Dr. Willis Duff Green, m. and lived at Mt. Vernon, Ill., having numerous children ; Judge Wm. H., of Cairo, Ill., who m. 2 sisters [Misses Hughes] and had 2 children ; and 2 daughters who m. and lived in Ill.

2. Judge John, b. 1786. d. 1838, m. 1st. Sarah Fry, 2nd Mary Keith Marshall He was at the battle of the Thames in 1812.

3. Letitia, m. Major Jas. Barbour an officer of the war of 1812.

4. Eliza, m. Dr. Ben. Edwards. bro. of Gov. Nimian and Judge Cyrus Edwards ; lived at Kirkwood, Mo.

5. Martha, m. Dr. William Craig ; home near Danville, Ky.

6. Dr. Lewis Warner Green, Pres. of Centre College, Ky., m. 1st. Eliza J. Montgomery, 2nd. Mrs. Mary Lawrence Fry, and had Julia, who m. M. T. Scott, of Bloomington, Ill., having two daus ; and Lettie, who m. Hon. A. E. Stevenson,, vice-president of the U. S., having 4 children.

WILLIAM GREEN, [Duff, Robt.] m. Miss Marshall, and had Willis, m. but left no children ; Judge William M., m. Miss Stone, lived in Russell county, Ky., and had dau. that m. Col. Spencer ; Gen. Duff, a prominent editor at

Washington in Jackson's day, who m. Lucretia, a sister of Dr. Benjamin Edwards ; Nancy m ; Betsy m. Mr. Huling ; Ellen, m. Gen. Jas. Semple ; Sarah, m. Rev. Neale, a Presbyterian minister of Glasgow, Ky., and had several children.

WILLIAM GREEN, (Jno., Robert), m. Lucy Williams, and had one son, John W. Green, Judge of the Virginia Court of Appeals.

ROBT. GREEN, (Jno., Robt.,), m. Frances Edmunds, and had Robert, and Eliza who m. Robt. Payne, and moved to Nicholas Co., Ky.

MOSES GREEN, (Jno., Robert), m. Fanny Richards, and had

1. Julia Amanda, who m. Bernard Peyton, having Jno. G., Susan, Eliza, T. Jefferson, Bernard, T. Green, M. Green, and Julia.

2. Thomas, m. 1st, Miss Lyons, 2nd. Miss Richie, 3rd. Miss Lomax, and had Mary Frances, who m. W. J. Stone, of Washington City; Isabella, who m. Mr. Ward; Emily, who married Mr. Legare; Thomas, and Bernard Peyton.

3. William, m. Miss Saunders, and had Wm., who m. Miss Bagtop; Patty, who m. Col. Williamson; and Georgie.

4. Archibald Magill, m. 2 sisters (Misses Furnish) and had Moses; Rebecca, who m. Mr. Parr; Jno., who m. Miss Lewis; and Fanny. who m. F. M. Gilkeson.

THOMAS GREEN, (Jno., Robt.), m. 1st Miss Miller, 2nd. Lucy Peyton and had:

1. Edward H., who m. 1st. Sarah Short, 2nd. Miss Ward, and had Bernard P., Anne. m. Wm. C. Green; Sarah; E. H., m. Anna Wilson, and had Jno. W.; Mary E. m. C. S. Robertson; William W., Arrie, Mattie; and Chas. Short, who m. Laura E. Kinchloe, having Jno. Rouzie, Clara C.; C. S.; B. P., Grant, Thos., Laura Lee, Mary, Sallie, Wm. S., and Edward H.

2. Anne Augusta, m. Edward Randolph, having Bathurst E., who m. Lizzie Glass; Dr. Thos. G., m. Anne Edgar.

3. Lucy Williams, who m. 1st. Daniel Henry, 2nd. Jas. C. Moore, and had Lucy Ann. m. Jno Nelson; Mary Green, m. Geo. Champlin, a lawyer at Hopkinsville, Ky.; Dr. Green, m. Kate Mansfield; Lucy W., m. Chas. Dade; Mattie P., John C., and Gustavus H.

4. Mary Peyton, who m. 1st. Thomas Edmunds, 2nd. Col. Wm. S. Moore, and had John T., m. Mollie Campbell; Jas. H.; Lucy Peyton, m. Eckstein Norton, pres. of L. & N. R. R.; Lizzie McA., m. Jno. D. Tyler; Wm. S.; Fannie Peyton; and Caroline Green.

5. Jno. Rouzie, who m. Elizabeth Nelson, and had William, m. Miss Armistead; Wallace, m. Miss Somerville; Edward, m. Miss Hartman; Lucius, m. in California; Jno. R. m. Miss Phelps; Rosalie, m. Hunter Wood, of Hopkinsville, Ky.; Lizzie, m. Nicholas Edmunds; Robert; Anne, m. Wm. T. Townes; and Nelson.

6. Moses Thomas, who m. 1st. Caroline Venable, 2nd. Mary T. Moore, had Lucy P., m. Randolph Dade; Bettie, m. Bankhead Dade; George, m. Lizzie Dade; Jno. R.; Thomas and Jas. W.

ELIZA GREEN, (Jno., Robert.), m. Jno. Hooe, of Fauquier county, and had no children.

JOHN GREEN, (Nicholas, Robt.), m. Jenny Hawkins, and had:

1. Benjamin, m. Becky Walker, and had Letitia; Lizzie, m. Mr. Evans; Morton, m. Mrs. Buckley; Coley; Nicholas; and John Willis, m. and had Benjamin, who m. Miss Parrent, and Sally, who m. Mr. Notey.

2. Willis, who m. Artemisia Lillard, of Owen county, Ky.; had John R., m. Hannah McClure; David, m. Lizzie Sale, and had Mollie, Tinnie and Nanie; and Ann Mary, m. 1st. Ben. Spencer, 2nd. Line Sale.

3. Hawkins, m. Jane Bulkly, and had Jno. W., who m. and had Fanny and others.

4. Nicholas P., of Franklin county, Ky., m. 1st. Mrs. Hawkins, 2nd. Mrs. Gaines, and had, Martha, m. Jas. Thomas; Scott, m. Helen Henry; Ruth, m. Geo. Green, and Dee, m. Colon M. Jones.

5. Morton, who m. Eliza Spencer, and had Sallie, m. Robt. Payne, whose son, Jno. J., m. Ella Landrun ; Lizzie, m. 1st. Jno. McGinnis, 2nd. Geo. Clarke of Springfield, Ill.; Jno. m. Lida McGinnis ; Susan, m. Dr. Austin.

6. Letitia, m. Willis Roberts, Owen Co., Ky., and had Willis ; and Mary, who m. Charles Samuels in Mo.

7. Betsy, m. Wm. Bower, and had John, in Mo.; Sue, m. Jas. Duncan ; Jane, m. Jno. Roberts.

8. Samuel, m. America Roberts, and had Mollie, m. Jas. Suter ; Geo. m. Ruth Green; and Wm. Joseph.

JOYCE GREEN, (Nicholas, Robt.) m. Willis Ballance, and had James L., Eliza; Chas., married, and lived at Peoria, Ill., had Jenny who m.; and Patience, Judge Bryant of Peoria, Ill.

GABRIEL GREEN, (Jas., Robt.) m. Miss Grant and had

1. Jno., who m. Martha Dixon, and had, Henry Dixon, m. Misses Lambert and Swift, having Grant, a lawyer in Ark., John, Henry Allen, Mary, Joshua and Lambert ; 2. Grant, who m. Kate Averton, having Eliza, m. Geo. B. Alexander; Grant, m. Miss Gray; Walker, Kate and John ; 3. Jno. W., who m. Miss Randolph, and had Gertrude, m. Mr. Blake; Mattie m. Mr. Willett, Mary, Nathaniel and Cornelia ; 4. Mary, who m. Mr. Hall and had Jos., Ben. and Chas.

2. Richard, m. Betsie Henry, and had Gabriel, who m. and had 2 or 3 sons.

3. William, m. Miss Andrews, and had a dau. who m. Mr. Pentrust ; William who m. Ann Green, of Hopkinsville, Ky.; and 2 other sons.

4. Gabriel, m. Mary Dixon and had Henry D., m. Sue Dixon, and left 2 children : Anne m. Rev. W. G. Allen, leaving 2 children ; and Gabriel, m. Miss Stinson, leaving son and 2 daughters.

5. Sallie, who m. Jno. Boyle, and had several children, including Dr. Hugh and Dr. Green, of Ky.; the rest lived in Ill.

6. Amelia, who m. Mr. Wilkins, and had dau. who m. Jno. W. Givens of Louisville, whose dau. m. Thos. Sugg, of Webster county, Ky.

7. Judith, m. Wilkins.

JAMES GREEN, (Jas., Robt), m. Betsy Jones, and had

1. Eliza, who m. Wm. A. Lane, and had 1. James, m. Miss Norris; 2. Julia, m. J. Jett, and had Lavinia, m. Mr. Witheroe, Ellen, m. E. McCormick, Elvira, m. B. Taylor, Wm., m. Alice Hopper, Hannah, m. Atchison Pollock, James, and Fannie, m. James W. Green, of Rappahannock; 3. Eliza, m. Phillip Slaughter, and had dau. who m. M. Slaughter ; 4. Jno., m. Helen Berry, and had Helen, who m. Rev. Johns, Wm. A., Harry B., and Lizzie; 5. Fanny, m. J. F. Scott, who had Fanny, m. Mr. Carter, Susan m. Rev. Clemens, and William ; 6. Ellen, m. Geo. B. Scott ; 7. Elvira, who m. Munroe Kilby, and had Ellen A., m. R. Carmichael, Lane, Margaret, and Lizzie.

2. J. Strother, who m. 1st. Miss Jett, 2nd. Mrs. Jones, and had 1. John, who m. Miss Crabb, of La., and had Henry, m. Miss Crab, Jno. J., m. Miss Campbell, Mary, Fanny, Jenny Douglas, Alex. Barrows, Lizzie Payne, Thomas Hunt, Delia, Robert Edwin, Eleanor Estille, and Charles Augustine ; 2. Lizzie, m. Miller Payne; 3. Duff, m. Miss Lane ; 4. Robert m. Miss Douglas ; 5. Delia, m. Ben Crump ; 6. Fanny m. Dr. Crump ; 7. Chas., m. Jessie A. Ford ; 8. Anne, m. Richard Payne.

3. Jas., who m. Miss Shackleford, and had John Shack, m. Miss Taylor, of

Norfolk; E. Gertrude m. Rev. R. S. Bell ; Margaret J., m. Andrew Aldridge ; Victorine S., m. Wm. M. Fuller ; Estelle St. Pierre, m. Chas. Lewis.

4. Fanny, who m. Geo.M. Parsons,and had Elizabeth m. Geo. Brent,of Alexandria, having Fannie, m. Robert Hunter ; Hughes, m. Miss Hutchinson; and Florence, married.

5. Duff, who m. Miss Payne, and had Marian, m. John Porter ; McDuff, m. Miss Howison ; Isabella, m. Wm. Lewis ; Jas. Lane, m. Miss Whittemore ; Charles, m. Miss Whittemore.

6. Dolly, who m. Turner Ashby, and had James, m. Miss Moncure ; Gen. Turner Ashby, killed in battle; Dolly or Dora, m. P. Moncure ; Betty m. Geo. Green ; Mary, m. Geo. Moncure.

7. Jones, who m. Miss Scott,of Fredericksburg, and had Rebecca, m. Howard Shackelford ; Betsy, m. Geo. Williamson ; James, m. Lina Hopper ; Fanny, m. Cassius Carter.

8. Charles, who m. Ann Herndon, and had Elizabeth, m. P. St. George Ambler; and James William, m. M. T. Jett.

9. Mary, who m. Sam Bailey, and had Mary E., m. William Allen ; and James P. m. Ary Ward.

10. Austin, who m. Miss Gordon, of Stafford.

JONES GREEN, (Jas., Robt.) who m. Miss Neville, moved to Hardy county, Va., and had Nevil, Jones, Nancy, Mrs Parsons, Mary and Betsy.

ROBERT GREEN, (Jas., Robt.), who m. Miss Edmunds, had William, Jas. Thomas, Robt., Sarah, m. Mr. Cross, Fanny, Ellen and Eliza.

JOHN GREEN, (Jas., Robt.), m. Miss Catlett, of Fauquier, moved to Henderson, Ky., and had

1. Jno. C. m. Miss Ruggles, and died without issue.

2. Hector, m. 1st. Louisa Ellen,widow of his bro. Jno. C.; 2nd Miss Missouri Grant, and had Chas. Catlett, m. Maggie Bell ; David Simmons, m. 1st. Mary Brown, who d. without issue, 2nd. Fannie G. Gunter ; Jno. Wm., m. Annie Amiss ; Nellie R., Winnifred, Maggie, Robt. H., Orla, Alexander and Harvey.

3. Nathaniel Peter, m. Mary Anderson, and had Winnifred, m. Fred Johnson ; Simion Catlett, m. Fannie Atkinson.

AUSTIN GREEN, (Jas., Robt.), m. Miss Ball; lived and died in Hardin county, Ky., and had Dr. Austin; a dau. m. Mr. Powell; a dau. m. Mr. Long; a dau. m. Mr. Snow; Jessee, and others, some of whom went to Texas.

ELEANOR GREEN, (Moses, Robt.), m. Gen. James Williams, and had

1. Wm. who m. Anne Stubblefield, and had, Jas., m. Rosalie Fitzhugh ; Geo. S. who went to Ky., Wm. m. Miss Pannill ; Ellen, m. Ennis Adams; Anne, m. Dr. Alfred Taliaferro ; Fannie m. Jos. Pannill ; Sarah G., m. E. S. Taliaferro; and Lucy A., m. Thos. Fitzhugh ;

2. Sally, m. Geo. French Strother, and had Jas. French, who m. Elizabeth Roberts, and had Geo. French, m. Miss Cary ; Jno. R., m. Miss Payne ; Phillip W. m. Miss Pendleton ; Jas. French, m. Miss Botts ; Wm. H. and J. Hunt, killed in battle ; W. J., m. Miss Shackelford ; Louis Harvie and Sallie.

ELIZABETH GREEN, (Jno., Wm., Wm., Robt.) m. Thomas Jones, sheriff, Campbell county, Ky.

NANNIE GREEN,(Jno., Wm., Wm., Robt.), m. Mr. Thomas, of Cincinnati, and had a dau. who m. W. D. Frazer, of Mason county, Ky.; also had a son.

JNO. A. GREEN,(Jno., Wm., Wm., Robt.), lived in Lexington, Kentucky.

JOSEPH GREEN, (Francis, Wm., Wm., Robt.), m Susan Ball, and had

1. Dr. Norvin Green, president of the Western Union Telegraph Co., who m. Martha English; and had Susy-Thornton ; Jas. Olive, m. Amy Hewitt, of

New York City ; Pinckney Frank, m. Carrie Conant, of Brooklyn ; Jno. English, m. Annie Lindenberger ; and Warren, m. Blanche Smith.

2. Neville, m. M. J. Morris.

3. Thornton, who m. Mathilda Stewart, of Carroll county, Ky., and had Daniel, m. Minnie Todd ; Joseph moved to Oregon ; Norvin m. Ida Stratton ; and Mollie, m. Will Erwin.

WILLIAM A. LANE, (Ellen, Robt., Robt.,) m. Eliza Green, and had

1. Jas. m. Miss Morris.

2. Julia, m. Jas. Jett, and had Jno., m. Belle Roberts ; Lavinia, m. Mr. Witheroe ; Ellen, m. E. McCormick ; Elvira, m. B. Taylor ; Wm., m. Alice Hopper ; Hannah, m. Atchison Pollock ; and Fannie, m. Jas. W. Green.

3. Eliza, who m. Phillip Slaughter, had Eliza, who m. Montgomery Slaughter.

4. John m. Helen Berry, and had, Helen m. Rev. Authur Jones ; Wm. A. H. B.,and Lizzie;

5. Fanny, m. J. F. Scott, and had Betty J.; Fanny, m. Mr.Carter; Susan, m. Rev. Clemons ;

6. Ellen, m. Geo. B. Scott.

7. Elvira, m. Monroe Kilby, and had Ellen A., who m. R. Carmichael ; Lane, Margaret and Lizzie.

JUDGE JOHN GREEN,(Willis, Duff, Robt.), m. Sarah Reed and had

1. Dr. Willis, m. Louisa Smith.

2. Peachy,who m. Rev. R. A. Johnstone,of Danville,Ky.; and had Mary,m. Mr. Hogutt; Alice,and Dr. Arthur.

3. Sarah Reed, who m. Jno. Barkley, and had Jno. G., of Danville, Ky.; Mary, m. Rev. W. R. Brown, near Chicago ; Jessamine, m. E. W. C. Humphreys, of Louisville ; Martha, m. W. L. Green, Jr., of Peoria, Ill.; Ada, m. Nat Lafox, of Harrodsburg, Ky.; and Wm. Craig, of Louisville.

4. Rev. Joshua Fry, m. Harriet Booker ; died in Memphis ; had Louisa, Sallie and William, who lived in Little Rock.

5. Susan who m. Jas. Weir, of Owensboro, Ky., had Jno. G., m. Lizzie Griffith; Belle, m. Clinton Griffith ; Authur, Jas., Susan, and Dora.

6. Rev. Wm. L., who m. Susan Weir, had Wm. L., m. Martha Barkeley, of Peoria.

7. Thos. M., m., 1st. Nannie Butler, 2nd. Pattie Craig, and had Jno. Allen, Bessie Logan, Pierce Butler, Lettie Craig, Wm. O. Butler, Mary Keith, Pattie Craig and Nannie Thomas.

8. Jno. Duff, who m. Ida Triplett of St. Louis.

LETITIA GREEN, (Willis, Duff, Robert), m. Maj. James Barbour, and had

1. Catherine, who m. J. Wesley Vick, of Vicksburg, and had Kate, Martha, Nannie, Amanda and Neville.

2. James, who m. Elizabeth Foster, of Maysville, Ky., had Jas. F. m. Elizabeth Taylor; and Rev. John Green Foster, a Presbyterian minister in Gillney county, Ky.

3. Martha, who m. Rev. B. M. Hobson, had Barbour and Lewis Green.

4. Rev. Lewis G., who m. Elizabeth Ford, of Richmond, Ky., and had several children.

ELIZA GREEN, (Willis, Duff, Robt.,) m. Dr. Ben Edwards, and had

1. and 2. Sarah and Julia, who both m. Col. Lewis Parsons.

3. Ellen, m. M. Whitaker and had son, Edward.

4. Peachy, m. Mr. Ostcone.

5. Martha, m. Dr. Todd, of Lexington, Mo.

6. Rev. Willis G., professor in St. Louis medical college.
7. Ben, m. Miss Midge, and died in Texas.
8. Presley, m. Miss Tunstall, of Illinois.
9. Frank, m. and left widow and child in St. Louis.
10. Cyrus, lived in Texas.

MARTHA GREEN (Willis, Duff, Robt.), m. Dr. Wm. Craig, and had
1. Eliza J.
2. Jno. J., m. Amanda Goodloe, and had Alma, Lettie and Bettie.
3. Rev. Willis G., m. Amelia Owsley of Keokuk, Ill., and had 7 children.
4. Lettie B., m. Dr. Geo. Cowen, and had son, Harry.
5. Pattie E., m. Thos. M. Green, of Maysville, Ky.

GENERAL DUFF GREEN (Wm., Duff, Robt.), m. Lucretia Edwards, and had 1. Laura, m. Shelby Reed, having 4 sons and 2 daughters; 2. Margaret, m. Andrew Calhoun, having 7 sons and 2 daughters; 3. Benjamin, m. Lizzie Waters, of Dalton, Ga.; 4. Lizzie, m. Dr. Bivings; 5. Mary, m. Mr. Maynard, having Constance, who m. Mr. Dixon, and 7 other children; 6. Duff, m. Miss Pickens, having Duff, Lizzie and Floride; 7. Jessie; 8 Constance, and 9. Florine.

JUDGE JNO. W. GREEN, (Wm., Jno., Robt.), m. 1st. Mary Browne, by whom he had
1. Wm., who m. Columbia Slaughter, and had John, killed in battle; and Bettie, m. Jas. Hayes, of Richmond, having 2 sons and several daughters.
2. Raleign B., died single.
3. Dr. Daniel S., U. S. A., m. Virginia Slaughter, and had Dr. William, of Baltimore; Samuel S., of Charleston, W. Va.; and Mollie, m. Richard Morton, of Baltimore, having one daughter and several sons.

Judge J. W. G., m. 2nd. Millian Cooke, a granddaughter of Geo. Mason, of Gunston Hall, by whom he had.
1. Jno. Cooke, m. Lucy Morton, and had two daughters, Bessie, m. Jno. Ambler Brooke; and Cooke.
2. Thos. Claiborne, Judge of the West Virginia Court of Appeals, m. Mary Naylor McDonald, and had Claiborne, m. Miss Harris; Annie. m. Jno. Porterfield; Flora, m. Kruger Smith; Kate, m. Jno. Lattimer; and Elizabeth Travers, m. Dr. Perry.
3. George, m. Bettie Ashby, and had a number of children, one of whom, Dora, m. G. M. Wallace, of Stafford county.
4. James Williams, m. Anne Sanford McDonald, and had Augus McDonald, m. Miss Taylor; Mary Mason, m. J. R. Norris; Leacy Naylor, m. J. M. Leach; Nancy Craig, m. Dr. W. W. Grant, of Denver; James Williams, m. Mamie Hill, of S. C.; Sue McDonald, m. Franklin Stearns; John Williams; and Raleigh Travers.
5. Lucy Williams, died single.

[The Green genealogy has been revised and added to by the publisher of this book, from reliable data in his possession, the work being done in December, 1899.]

COLONEL JOHN GREEN.

COLONEL JOHN GREEN (4th. son of the first Robert), was born in Culpeper county about 1730. He m. Susanna Blackwell; was chosen collector of St. Mark's Parish 1761; made churchwarden with his brother Robert in 1764. In 1776 Richard Yancey was chosen vestryman "in place of John Green, in Continental service." Colonel Green entered the military service of Virginia as Captain 1st. Va. Bat., Sept. 4, 1775. When his command was mustered into the Continental Line, he was re-elected Capt., Jan. 20, 1776, at which time he was under the command of Gen. Andrew Lewis at Williamsburg. In the fall of that year he served under Washington in New York; was engaged with his troops at Mamaroneck in the attack on Major Roberts of the British Army, Oct., 21, 1776, when he was wounded in the shoulder.

"A detachment of our men under Col. Haylet surprised Major Rogers and his regiment at Marinack last night. * * * We have two men killed and twelve wounded, among them Major Greene, of the 1st. Va. Reg't., an officer of great merit." (Force.) Col. Tench Tilghman, in his report of the action, says: "Gen. Washington detached Major Green, of Va., with 150 men of the 1st. and 3rd. Va. Reg'ts., and Colonel Haslet, of Del., with 600 men to support them. * * * We had 12 wounded, among them Major Green, in the shoulder." (Force.) In 1777 (Carrington says) "a portion of Greene's Va. Reg't. joined the garrison at Fort Mifflin," and took part in the gallant defence of that post. Col. Green was promoted by Congress Jan. 26, 1778, to be colonel of the 6th. Va. Reg't., with which command he acted with conspicuous bravery at Brandywine and Monmouth. At Gilford C. H., he covered the retreat of Gen. Greene, but to his own personal dissatisfaction. When Gen. Greene decided that his safety lay in withdrawing his troops from action, "Col. Greene of Va., was ordered to withdraw his regiment from the line, and to take a position at some distance in the rear, for the purpose of affording a rallying point to the fugitives, and of covering the retreat of the two regiments which continued in the field." (Marshall, IV. 431.) Gen. Lee, in his memoirs, describing the battle, says: "Colonel Green, one of the bravest of brave soldiers, with his regiment of Virginians, was driven off without having tasted of battle, and ordered to a given point in the rear for the security of this movement (the retreat), which was performed deliberately under cover of Col. Green."

Col. Green was much dissatisfied with the General's selection of his regiment for this service - though esteemed among the most honorable—so anxious was the veteran officer to be led at once into keen conflict. When it was announced upon the first of the retreat that the British were close advancing he became better humored, but soon the pursuit was discontinued, and his sourness returned. His friends would often console him by stating his selection as an evidence of the confidence reposed in him as a soldier. This would not satisfy the Colonel, who never failed to reply that he did not like such sort of distinction; and he hoped the Gen. would upon the next occasion attach to some other regiment the honor of covering his retreat. Getting to the General's ears he took the first opportunity of telling the Colonel, whom he much esteemed and respected, that he had heard he did not relish the part assigned to his regiment the other day. "No, that I did not," replied the old Colonel. "Well," rejoined Greene, "be patient. you shall have the first show the next time." This delighted him, and he always reckoned upon the promised boon with pleasure.—[The publishers are indebted to Rev. Horace Edwin Hayden's "Virginia Genealogies" for the above information relative to Col. Green's service in the war of the Revolution.]

Colonel Green's sons were William, m. Lucy Clayton Williams; John, killed at Valley Forge in a duel; Robert, m. Frances Edmunds; Moses m. Fanny Richards; Thomas, m. 1st. Miss Miller, 2nd. Lucy Peyton.

There has been a continuous succession of vestrymen in this family, from Robert of 1731, who was a member of the House of Burgesses, to Major J. W. Green, late a leading member of the Culpeper bar.

THE LIGHTFOOTS.

The Lightfoots were among the early colonists in Virginia. They seem to have settled originally in Gloucester and James City when the latter embraced what is now Charles City County. Colonel Philip Lightfoot was a vestryman of Petsworth Parish as early as 1683. By his last will he devised his lands to his eldest son Francis, remainder to his son Philip. Francis devised his lands to his daughter Elizabeth, who married Peter Randolph of Henrico; remainder to his brother Philip Lightfoot. The entail was docked by the House of Burgesses in 1740, and by agreement between the parties these lands were vested in Philip Lightfoot.

The present writer remembers to have seen at Sandy Point in Charles City when it was owned and occupied by Col. Robt. B. Bolling, divers portraits of the old Lightfoots. There were three William Lightfoots in succession at Sandy Point, and their tombs are still there. The first died in 1727, the second in 1809, and the third in 1810. We have in our possession now a copy of Bayles' folio dictionary, in ten volumes, with the name and coat-of-arms of William Lightfoot Tedington on each volume. Tedington was one of the four farms which composed the splendid estate of Sandy Point, between the James and Chickahominy Rivers. Three of these farms were inherited by Miss Minge (Mrs. Robert B. Bolling), and the fourth was added by Mr. Bolling.

There is a family of Lightfoots at Port Royal, Caroline, represented by the late Philip Lightfoot and his sons, Lewis Lightfoot and his brother John.

In 1726 we find the name of Major Goodrich Lightfoot as a member of the vestry of St. George's Parish, Spotsylvania, when that parish and county embraced what was afterwards the parish of St. Mark's and county of Culpeper. He was one of the lay readers at the Germanna Church, and he and Robert Slaughter were appointed to count all the tobacco plants from the mouth of the Rapidan to the mouth of Mountain Run, and up Mountain Run and across to the mouth of the Robinson River, in obedience to an Act of the Assembly limiting the number of plants to be cultivated by each planter.

At the organization of St. Mark's Parish, at Germanna in 1731, he was chosen a member of the first vestry by the freeholders and housekeepers of St. Mark's, his home being within the limits of the new parish. He served as vestryman and churchwarden till his death in 1738, and was succeeded by Captain Goodrich Lightfoot in 1741, who served till his removal from the parish in 1771. William Lightfoot was also a vestryman from 1752 to 1758, when he moved out of its bounds to the parish of Bromfield, which had been cut off from St. Mark's in 1752. William, we think, was the father of Goodrich, who married the daughter of the Rev. Henry Fry, who lived in the fork of Crooked Run and the Robinson River. Goodrich Lightfoot lived opposite to the present home of George Clark, Esq., on the Robinson River. He was the brother of the late Major Philip Lightfoot of the Culpeper bar, and of Walker Lightfoot (clerk), and he was the father of Frank Lightfoot, clerk of Culpeper, who married Miss Fielder (father of Col. Charles E. Lightfoot), and of Edward, of Madison, who married Miss Conner, and is the father of Virginia; and John, who married Miss Turner, the granddaughter of Major John Roberts of the Revolution, whose wife was the daughter of the old vestryman Captain Robert Pollard.

From the names of Philip, John, and William, which were common to these several branches of the Lightfoots, the presumption is that they sprang from the same stock.

THE MADISON FAMILY.

From the record of James Madison, Sr., the father of the President, and from the record of James Madison, Jr., the President.

The first of the name in Virginia, John Madison patented land in Gloucester county, in 1653. His son John was the father of Ambrose, who married Frances, daughter of James Taylor, Aug. 29th, 1721. Their son, James Madison, Sr., was married to Nelly, daughter of Francis Conway of Caroline, Sept. 13th, 1749. James Madison, Jr., (the President) was born at Port Conway at 12 o'clock (midnight) 6th March, 1751, was baptized by Rev. Wm. Davis, March 31st, and had for godfathers John Moore and Jonathan Gibson, and for godmothers Mrs. Rebecca Moore and Misses Judith and Elizabeth Catlett. Frances, daughter of James, Sr., born June 18th, 1753, baptized by the Rev. Mungo Marshall, July 31st; godfathers, Richard Beale and Erasmus Taylor; godmothers, Miss Milly Taylor and Mrs Frances Beale. Ambrose, son of James, Sr., born Jan. 27th, 1756, baptized by Rev. Mr. Marshall, March 2d; godfathers, James Coleman and George Taylor; godmothers, Mrs. Jane Taylor and Alice Chew. Catlett, son of James Sr., born Feb. 10th, 1758, baptized by Rev. Jas. Maury, Feb. 22d; godfathers, Col. Wm. Taliaferro and Richard Beale; godmothers, Mrs. E. Beale and Miss Milly Chew. Nelly, daughter of James, Sr., (Mrs. Hite) born Feb. 14th, 1760, baptized March 6th by Rev. Wm. Giberne: godfathers, Larkin Chew and Wm. Moore; godmothers, Miss E. Catlett and Miss C. Bowie. William Madison born May 1st, 1762, baptized May 23d by Rev. James Marye, Jr.; godfathers, William Moore and Jas. Taylor; godmothers, Miss Mary Willis and Miss Milly Chew. Sarah (Mrs. Thomas Macon), born Aug 17th, 1764, baptized Sept. 15th, by Rev. James Marye; godfathers Capt. R. J. Barbour and Andrew Shepherd; godmothers, Mrs. Sarah Taylor and Miss Mary Conway. Elizabeth Madison born Feb. 19th, 1768, baptized Feb. 22d by Rev. Thomas Martin; godfathers, Major T. Burnley and Ambrose Powell; godmothers, Miss Alice and Miss Nelly Chew. Reuben Madison born Sept. 19th, 1771, baptized Nov. 10th by Rev. Mr. Barnett; godfathers, Francis Barbour and James Chew; godmothers, Alice and Nelly Chew. Francis Taylor Madison (Mrs. Dr. Robert Rose) born Oct 9th, 1774, baptized Oct. 30th by Rev. Mr. Wingate; godfathers, Thos. Bell and Richard Taylor; godmothers Miss Frances and Miss Elizabeth Taylor. Here the old family record closes. It is a model record, which others would do well to imitate. In it we have the succession of the ministers of the parish, Wingate being the last of the colonial clergy. James Madison, Jr., was chairman of the Committee of Public Safety and an active vestryman.

The living representatives of James Madison, Sr., so far as is known by the writer, are:

1. The oldest child (Nelly) of Ambrose, eldest son of James Madison, Sr. married Dr. Willis and their living descendants are Col. John Willis of Orange and his children.

2. Of General William Madison, 2nd brother of James Madison Jr., (President) the living descendants are Wm. Madison and children of Texas, Dr. Jas Madison of Orange, and the children of Col. John Willis through their mother; the wife and children of Wm. P. Dabney of Powhatan; the children of Robert Marye; the wife and children of Dorsey Taliaferro of Texas; the children of Major John H. Lee by his second wife Fanny, daughter of Lewis Willis and Eliza Madison; Dr. Robert Madison (the son of Robert) and his children, Virginia Military Institute; the children of Daniel F. Slaughter by his first wife, Letitia Madison; and the children of Dr. Thomas T. Slaughter by his first wife.

Of Frank, third brother of the President, the representatives are the children of Alexander and Thompson Shepherd.

The eldest sister of the President, Nelly (Mrs. Hite), left a son and daughter. Her son Madison Hite, left two sons and a daughter (Mrs. Baker), all believed to be living. Her daughter Nelly married Dr. Baldwin. Miss Baldwin, the untiring Missionary in Greece, and now at Joppa, is the illustrious offspring of this marriage.

The second sister of the President, Sarah, married Thomas Macon. Of a number of children of this marriage, two only left issue. 1. Conway Macon left a son and three daughters. The son, who was killed at Manassas, left an only son, Edgar, now living. Conway Macon's daughter married Washington, Cave and Smith; the first and last of whom are living and have several children. 2. James Madison Macon's daughters, Mrs. Hite and Mrs. Knox. There was also a Thomas Macon, Jr., and that mother in Israel, the late Mrs. Reuben Conway, was a daughter of Thomas Macon, Sr., and Sarah Madison.

The youngest sister of the President, Fanny, married Dr. Robert Rose and they emigrated to Tennessee about 1822 or '23 with children, Ambrose, Hugh, James, Robert, Erasmus, Henry, Sam, Nelly, Frances and Mary. Of these, Dr. Erasmus Rose, if living, is a resident of Memphis.

James Madison, Sr., the zealous old vestryman, had a habit of making short sketches of sermons he heard. Col. John Willis had some of them. His great son, the President, left among his papers comments on the Gospels and the Acts of the Apostles. Among these are the following:—"Christ's Divinity appears in St. John, ch. xx. v. 28." On the words of Christ to St. Paul, "Arise and go into the city, and it shall be told tnee what thou shalt do," his comment is, "It is not the talking, but the walking and working person that is the true Christian." It was he that furnished a list of theological authors for the Library of the University of Virginia. There are doubtless other descendants of James Madison, Sr., but the author of this notice is unable to trace the line of their connection with him.

THE SPOTSWOOD FAMILY.

Alexander Spotswood, Governor of Virginia, and Ann Butler his wife, had four children.

1. John m. (1745) Mary dau. of Wm. Dandridge of the British Navy, ch. 1. Alexander, General in the army of the Revolution, who m. Elizabeth dau. of Gen. Wm. Augustine Washington and niece of Gen. George Washington: their ch. were 1. John, Capt. in the American Revolution, wounded at Brandywine, 2. George W., 3. William, 4. Elizabeth (Mrs. Page), 5. Mary (Mrs. Brooke), 6. Ann (Mrs. Taliaferro), 7. Henrietta (Mrs. Taliaferro), 8. Martha. Capt. John m. Sally Rowzie, ch. Mary, John, Susan, Robert. Dandridge, Norborne. Berkely, Lucy and Ann.

Ann Catherine, dau. of the Governor, m. Bernard Moore, of Chelsea, King William Co., ch. Augustine m. Sarah Rind and their dau. m. Carter Braxton; Bernard Moore, Jr., m. Lucy Ann Lieper, of Philadelphia, their ch. were Andrew, Thomas, Elizabeth and Lucy. Elizabeth, dau. of Bernard Moore, Sr., m. John Walker, of Belvoir, Albemarle Co., ch. Mildred m. Francis Kinloch, M. C., of South Carolina, and their ch. Eliza m. Judge Hugh Nelson, of Belvoir. (The tradition is that when Congress was sitting at Philadelphia, Francis Kinloch met Mildred Walker on the street as she was returning from her hairdresser, and fell in love with her at first sight and afterwards married her.)

Ann Butler Moore dau. of Bernard Moore, Sr., m. Charles Carter, of Shirley, ch. 1. Robt. m. Mary Nelson, of York, 2. Ann Hill m. Gen. Henry Lee (his second wife), ch. 1. Charles Carter, 2. Robert Edward (the great Confederate general, 3. Captain Sidney, U. S. and C. S. Navy, 4. Ann, 5. Mildred. Bernard Moore Carter, son of Charles Carter of Shirley and Anne Butler Moore, m. Lucy dau. of Governor Henry Lee and Matilda (his first wife). Catherine Spotswood Carter, m. Carter Berkley, ch. Elizabeth, Edmund and Farley. Williams Carter m. Charlotte Foushee. Lucy Carter m. Nat Burwell, of Roanoke,

Dorothea Spotswood dau. of the Governor, m. Captain Nat West Dandridge of the British Navy, ch. 1. John m. Miss Goode, 2. Robert m. Miss Allen, 3. William m. Miss Bolling, 4. Nat m. Miss Watson, 5. Mary m. Woodson Payne, 6. another daughter m. Archy Payne, 7. another m. Philip Payne, 8. Anna m. John Spotswood Moore, 9. Dorothea m. Patrick Henry, the orator (see Henry genealogy).

For other branches of this family see Spotswood genealogy by Charles Campbell, the historian, a descendant of Gov. Spotswood.

THE PRELIMINARIES OF MARRIAGE IN ANTE-REVOLUTIONARY TIMES.

The following correspondence will show how courtships were conducted by our forefathers. The patriarchal authority was recognized, and young folks did not make love until the preliminaries were arranged by their fathers. We are indebted to Mr. K. Nelson, a lineal descendant of the parties, for the original letters; as the old folks have been dead for more than a hundred years, we presume no one's delicacy will be offended by the exposition of these illustrations of a past age. In the foregoing Spotswood genealogy will be found the relations of the parties to the past and present generations.

May 27th, 1764.

DEAR SIR:—My son, Mr. John Walker, having informed me of his intention to pay his addresses to your daughter Elizabeth, if he should be agreeable to yourself, lady and daughter, it may not be amiss to inform you what I think myself able to afford for their support, in case of an union. My affairs are in an uncertain state; but I will promise one thousand pounds, to be paid in the year 1765, and one thousand pounds to be paid in the year 1766; and the further sum of two thousand pounds I promise to give him, but the uncertainty of my present affairs prevents my fixing on a time of payment:—the above sums are all to be in money or lands and other effects at the option of my said son, John Walker

I am, Sir, your humble servant,

JOHN WALKER.

COL. BERNARD MOORE, Esq.,
in King William.

28th May, 1764.

DEAR SIR:—Your son, Mr. John Walker, applied to me for leave to make his addresses to my daughter Elizabeth. I gave him leave, and told him at the same time that my affairs were in such a state that it was not in my power to pay him all the money this year that I intended to give my daughter, provided he succeeded; but would give him five hundred pounds next spring, and five hundred pounds more as soon as I could raise or get the money; which sums, you may depend, I will most punctually pay to him.

I am, Sir, your obedient servant,

BERNARD MOORE.

THE REV. JAMES STEVENSON.

The official history of Mr. Stevenson is given in the body of this work. He m. Fanny Littlepage, a sister of Gen. Lewis Littlepage, whose brief and brilliant career is delineated in this volume. He had nine children, viz:—James, Edward, Nancy, Jane, Sarah, Carter, Lewis, Robert and Andrew. 1. James (M. D.) died in New Orleans, 2. Sarah m. Rev. John Woodville, of St. Mark's, 3.

Edward was lost at sea, 4. Jane was lost in the burning of the theatre at Richmond (in 1811), 5. Nancy never married, 6. Robert m. Miss Towles and lived in Lewisburg, Va.; ch. Robert, James, Charles and Fanny Littlepage. 7. Andrew Stevenson (Speaker of Congress and Minister to England) m. first Miss White, daughter of a clergyman of South Carolina. The Hon. John White Stevenson, late Governor of Kentucky and Senator of the U. S., is their son. Governor Stevenson m. Miss Winston. Hon. Andrew Stevenson m. second Sarah, daughter of John Coles and Miss Tucker, and their only child, a daughter, died young. Hon. Andrew Stevenson m. third Mary Shaaf of Georgetown, D. C. Lewis Stevenson, brother of Andrew, m. Miss Herndon; issue, James; William, and Fanny, who m. Dr. Wellford. Carter Stevenson m. Miss Jane Herndon; issue, Fanny Arnotte (Mrs. Thompson Tyler), Isabella m. Mr. Carter, Jr. (General C. S. A.), Byrd, and Sally.

THE TAYLOR FAMILY.

The root of this family in Virginia was James Taylor, who, coming from Carlisle in England, settled on the Chesapeake Bay, and died in 1698. His daughter Mary m. first Henry Pendleton (see Pendleton genealogy,) m. second Edward Watkins. His son John m. Catharine Pendleton, and was the father of 1. Edmund m. Anne Lewis, 2. of John who m. Miss Lyne, 3. of James who m. Anne Pollard, 4. of Philip, who m. Mary Walker, 5. of William who m. Miss Anderson, 6. of Joseph, who m. Frances Anderson, 7. of Mary, who m. Mr. Penn, 8. of Catharine. who m. Penn, 9. of Isabella, who m. Samuel, father of the late Gen. Samuel Hopkins,of Henderson, Ky., 10. of Elizabeth, who m. first Mr. Lewis, m. second Mr. Bullock.

James, son of 1st James, m. Martha Thompson; issue, 1. Zachary m. Elizabeth Lee, and their son Zachary m. Alice Chew, 2. Richard m. Sarah Strother, and was the father of Gen. Zachary Taylor (President), whose daughter Sarah Knox m. Jefferson Davis (President C. S.) The present Gen. Dick Taylor is a son of the President. Another son of James 2d, George, m. Rachael Gibson and had many sons, seven of whom were Revolutionary officers; George was the ancestor of many Kentuckians, among whom Dr. Frank Taylor, Major Wm. Taylor, and Edward M. Taylor of Oldham County, Samuel Taylor of Clark County, and Dr. Gibson Taylor of Union. Another son of James 2d, Charles, m. Sarah Conway, and was the father of Harriet, who m. Catlett Conway; another daughter, Matilda, m. William Moore, and another, Evelina, m. George Morton. Erasmus, son of James 2d, m. Jane Moore, and 1. their dau. Milly m. William Morton, uncle of Hon. Jere. and Dr. George Morton. 2. Frances m. Garland Burnley, 3. Elizabeth m. Andrew Glassell (see Glassell genealogy), 4. Lucy m. Rev. Alex. Balmain, 5. John m. Ann Gilbert, 6. Jane m. C. P. Howard, 7. Robert m Frances Pendleton; issue 1. Robert m. Mary Taylor, 2. Milly m. Hay Taliaferro, father of Jaquelin, of Dr. Edmund and Mrs. B. Stanard. 3. Lucinda m. James Shepherd, 4. Jaquelin P. m. Martha Richardson, 5. Jane m. John Hart, 6. Dr. Edmund m. Mildred Turner; issue, 1. Elizabeth m. Rev. Joseph Earnest, late Rector of St. Thomas Parish, 2. Robenette m. Dr. Thomas Reeveley, 3. Edmonia, 4. Lucy Jane (deceased), 5. Erasmus m. Miss Ashby.

Alexander, son of 1st Robert m. Mildred C. Lindsay, and their daughter Sally m. Col. John M. Patton.

Frances, daughter of James 2d, m. Ambrose Madison (see Madison genealogy), Martha m. Chew, Tabitha m. Wild, Hannah m. Battaile, Milly m. a Thomas.

James, son of James and grandson of James 1st, m. Alice Thornton, and their son James m. first Ann Hubbard, m. second Sarah Taliaferro, m. third Eliza Conway and had a numerous posterity, among whom are Capt. Robert Taliaferro of Louisville, Ky., and others.

Major Frank Taylor, from whose diary we have quoted so lengthily in this volume m. Ann Craddock; issue, James, Thornton, Robert, Elizabeth, Sutton and Francis Craddock.

THE WINSTON—HENRY GENEALOGY.

RICHMOND, VIRGINIA, September 21st, 1876.

MRS. DANIEL SLAUGHTER.

Dear Madam:—I have been informed that your maiden name was Winston, and that you have a family tree. As I am very anxious to learn accurately the Winston ancestry of my grandfather, Patrick Henry, I trust you will pardon me for asking a copy of the tree, or if it is a very large one, of that part which relates to his ancestry.

I am, very respectfully,

WM. WIRT HENRY.

CULPEPER, VIRGINIA, October 10th, 1876.

DEAR SIR:

My sister, Mrs. Daniel Slaughter, has requested me to acknowledge the receipt of your letter of the 21st ultimo, and to answer it. The account of the Winston family in our possession was written for the satisfaction of her own family by my grandmother, whose maiden name was Lucy Coles, a granddaughter of Isaac Winston the emigrant; and she married her cousin Isaac Winston, a grandson of the same emigrant. I will compile a genealogy of the family from my grandmother's record, and from information of a later date derived from other sources. I have compared her record with the old wills, also in our possession, and I find it correct for two generations.

Isaac Winston, the most remote ancestor of that name that I can trace back to, was born in Yorkshire England, in 1620. A grandson of his pursued his fortunes in Wales, where he had a large family. Three of his sons emigrated to America, and settled near Richmond, Virginia, in 1704. Their names were William, Isaac and James. It is the genealogy of the descendants of Isaac, the second of these brothers, that my grandmother has written.

Isaac Winston the emigrant, married Mary Dabney, and died in Hanover County in 1760, leaving six children, William, Isaac, Anthony, Lucy, Mary Ann, and Sarah. I do not mention them in the order of their births; on the contrary, I think Sarah, the last mentioned, was the oldest.

1. William, son of Isaac Winston; the emigrant, ("He was said to have been endowed with that rare kind of magnetic eloquence which rendered his nephew, Patrick Henry, so famous."—Campbell's History of Virginia, p. 520. See also Wirt's Life of Henry), m. Sarah Dabney, issue, Elizabeth, Edmund, (Judge Winston) and Mary Ann. 1. Elizabeth m. Peter Fontaine, issue, 1. John m. Martha Henry dau. of Patrick Henry, issue, Patrick Henry (other children not known). 2. Sarah Fontaine m. Charles Rose; issue, John, Peter, Sarah and Alexander. 3. William Fontaine m. Ann Morris. 4. Mary Fontaine m. first Bowles Armstead; issue, William, Elizabeth, Mary and Peter; m. second John Lewis a nephew of General Washington; issue, Frances, Howel and Mary Ann. (The other children of Peter Fontaine and Elizabeth Winston were James, Edmund, Judith and Susanna, but their marriages are not given in the record. The Rev. William Spotswood Fontaine, now of Reidsville, N. C., and the Rev. Edward Fontaine, now of New Orleans, belong to this branch, and are grandsons of John Fontaine and his wife Martha Henry.) 2. Edmund (Judge Win-

ston) m. 1. his cousin Alice Winston; issue, 1. George m. Dorothea Henry dau. of Patrick Henry; issue, James a distinguished lawyer and politician of Mo., (died in 1852.) 2. Sarah m. Dr. George Cabell. 3. Alice m. Frederick Cabell. 4. Mary m. Mr. Jones of Buckingham. 5. Edmund m. Eliza Wyat. Judge Edmund Winston m. second the widow of Patrick Henry, no issue. His descendants are scattered in N. C., Mo., and Miss. Dr. Wm. Winston, now of Toccapola, Miss., is his great-grandson. 3. Mary Ann Winston m. Dr. John Walker; issue, Benjamin, John, Frances and Edmund.

2. Isaac, son of Isaac Winston the emigrant, m. Marianne dau. of Rev. Peter Fontaine, Rector of Westover Parish, (great-great-grandson of John de la Fontaine, martyred in France A. D. 1563, ancestor of all the Fontaines and Maurys in Virginia); issue, two sons. 1. Peter (see Valentine Supplement to this genealogy) 2. Isaac m. his cousin Lucy Coles; issue, Mrs. Garland Anderson, who left one son Alfred, who emigrated to Kentucky, Walter, Mrs. Armstead and Mrs. Dr. Beckwith; all of whom moved to Alabama years ago: Dr. Isaac Winston of Alexandria, who survived all his children and left no grandchildren, and last William A. Winston who m. Mary Wallace; issue, 1. Walter died unmarried. 2. Martha m. Dr. Payne; issue, William Henry. 3. Mary m Daniel F. Slaughter; issue, Mary, Eliza, Caroline, John and Daniel. 4. James m. in Cal. 5. Wallace. 6. Isaac (your correspondent). 7. Caroline m. John S. Hamilton; issue, Hugh and Mary. 8. Arthur, and 9. Lucien.

3. Anthony, son of Isaac Winston the emigrant, m. Alice dau. of Col. Edmund Taylor of Caroline; issue, 1. Sarah died single. 2. Anthony (whose children moved to Ala., their names were John J., Anthony, Governor of that State, Edmund and Isaac, and a daughter, Mrs. Peters.) 3. Alice m. Judge Edmund Winston. 4. Mary.

4. Lucy, dau. of Isaac Winston the emigrant, m. first William Dabney; issue, William; m. second Wm. Coles; issue, 1. Walter m. Miss Darricott; issue; Walter. 2. Lucy m. Isaac Winston (as before mentioned). 3. Mary m. John Payne of Philadelphia; issue, Walter, William Temple and Isaac (all died unmarried). 4. Dorothea or Dolly m. first John Todd; issue, John Payne and William Temple (both died unmarried); m. second James Madison (President of the U. S.), no issue. 5. Lucy m. George Washington, nephew of Gen. Washington; issue, George, William and Walter; m. second Thomas Todd of Kentuckey. 6. Anne m. Richard Cutts of Washington City; issue, Mary, Richard and James Madison Cutts, whose dau. Adele m. first Stephen A. Douglas, Senator in Congress from Illinois, m. second General Robert Williams, U. S. Army. 7. Mary m. John G. Jackson; issue, Mary, and 8. John Payne m. Clarissa Wilcox; issue, sons and daughters in Kentucky.

5. Mary Ann, dau. of Isaac Winston the emigrant, m. John Coles, brother of William Coles; issue, Walter, Isaac, Sarah, Mary and John. 1. Walter m. Mildred Lightfoot; issue, Mildred m. Col. Carrington, Sarah m. Mr. Bruce, and Isaac died unmarried. 2. Isaac (if he married, not known). 3. Sarah m. but no issue. 4. Mary m. Mr. Tucker; issue, a dau. who m. Judge Carrington. 5. John m. Miss Tucker; issue, 1. John m. Miss Shipwith. 2. Walter m. Miss Cocke. 3. Isaac m. Miss Stricker. 4. Tucker m. Miss Skipwith. 5. Edward m. Miss Roberts. 6. Mary m. Robert Carter. 7. Rebecca m. Mr. Singleton. 8. Sarah m. Andrew Stevenson (Minister to England). 9. Elizabeth never married. 10. Emily m. Mr. Rutherford.

6. Sarah, dau. of Isaac Winston the emigrant, m. first John Syme; issue John; m. second John Henry, a Scotch gentleman; issue, 1. Jane m. Samuel Meredith. 2. William m. but no issue. 3. Sarah (marriage not mentioned). 4. Patrick (Governor Henry) m. first Sarah Shelton, m. second Dorothea Dand-

ridge. 5. Lucy m. Valentine Wood. 6. Mary m. Luke Bowyer. 7. Anne m. John Christian. 8. Elizabeth m. first Gen. Campbell, m. second Gen. Russell. 9. Susanna m. Thomas Madison.

I find from this genealogy that we are relations. My great-grandfather, Isaac Winston, and your great-grandmother, Sarah Winston, were brother and sister. I annex to the genalogy a copy of the will of our common ancestor, Isaac Winston the emigrant.

Very truly yours,
ISAAC WINSTON.

WM. WIRT HENRY, Esq.,
  Richmond, Va.

Supplement to the foregoing genealogy by Wm. Wirt Henry of Richmond:

Sarah, daughter of Isaac Winston the emigrant, m. first John Syme; issue, John, member of the House of Burgesses and of the Convention of 1775, one of his daughters m. a Fleming; and John Syme, once an editor in Virginia, was his descendant. Sarah Syme m. second John Henry (a Scotchman, a nephew of Dr. Wm. Robertson, the historian, and a cousin of Lord Brougham); issue:

1. Jane Henry m. Col. Samuel Meredith, issue, 1. Samuel m. Elizabeth dau. of Gen. John Breckenridge, 2. Sarah m. Col. Wm. Armstead, 3. Jane m. Hon. David S. Garland.

2. Wm. Henry m. but died without issue.

3. Sarah Henry m. Thomas Thomas of Bristol, England.

4. Susanna Henry m. Gen. Thomas Madison. The Bowyers and Lewises of Botetourt County are descendants.

5. Mary Henry m. Mr. Bowyer.

6. Anne Henry m. Gen. Wm. Christian, killed by the Indians in Kentucky, one dau. m. Gov. Pope of Kentucky. From Mrs. Christian are descended the Warfields, Bullits, and Dickinsons of that State.

7. Elizabeth Henry m. Gen. Wm. Campbell the hero of King's Mountain; their only child Sarah m. Francis Preston; issue, 1. Wm. C. Preston, the distinguished Senator in Congress from South Carolina, 2. Eliza Preston m. Gen. Carrington of Halifax county, 3. Susan Preston m. Gov. James McDowell, 4. Sophonisba Preston m. Rev. Robt. J. Breckenridge, D. D., of Kentucky, 5. Sarah Preston m. Governor John B. Floyd, 6. Charles Campbell Preston, 7. Maria Preston m. John H. Preston, 8. Gen. John S. Preston (C. S. A..) 9. Col. Thomas L. Preston (C. S. A.), 10. Margaret Preston m. Gen. Wade Hampton of S. C. After the death of Gen. Campbell, his widow m. Gen. Wm. Russell.

8. Lucy Henry m. Valentine Wood of Goochland; issue, 1. Mary m. Major Stephen Southall of the Revolutionary army; issue, 1. Dr. Philip T. Southall, father of Professor Stephen O. Southall of the University of Virginia, 2. Valentine W. Southall, late of Charlottesville, father of William Southall, James C. Southall, V. W. Southall, Mrs. Charles Venable of the University of Va., and Mrs. Chas. Sharpe of Norfolk. By a second marriage, the widow of Major Southall had issue, Joseph Stras and several daughters. 2. Martha, daughter of Valentine and Lucy Wood, m. Judge Peter Johnston of Prince Edward, a Lieutenant in the Army of the Revolution, and a distinguished Legislator and Judge; issue, 1. John Warfield Johnston, 2. Gen. Peter Carr Johnston, 3. Hon. Charles Clement Johnston, 4. Edward William Johnston, 5. Algernon Sidney Johnston, 6. Beverly Randolph Johnston, 7. Valentine Johnston, 8. Gen. Jos. Eggleston Johnston of the late Confederate army, 9. Benjamin Johnston, 10. Jane Wood Johnston who m. Henry Michel of Washington, D. C. (The daughters of Sarah Henry were women of remarkable talents.)

Patrick Henry m. first. Sarah Shelton in 1754; issue, 1. Martha Henry m. John Fontaine; issue, Wm. Winston Fontaine, father of Rev. Wm. Spotswood Fontaine, now of Reidsville, N. C. 2. Anne Henry m. Judge Spencer Roane of the Court of Appeals; issue, 1. Wm: H. Roane, U. S. Senator, who left one child, Mrs. Edward Harrison, 2. Fayette Roane, who moved to Kentucky and died, leaving a daughter. 3. Betsy Henry m. Philip Aylett, of King William, issue: a dau. who m. Rev. Wm. Spotswood Fontaine, and a son, Gen. Aylet, father of Patrick Henry Aylett, killed in the Capitol disaster, of Col. Wm. Aylett of King William, of Pattie Aylett who m. Henry Ware of New York, and of Rosalie Aylett who m. Mr. Sampson of Brooklyn. 4. John Henry, who left one son, Edmund, who settled in Tennessee. 5. William Henry died childless Patrick Henry m. second,9th Oct. 1777, Dorothea Dandridge, granddaughter of Gov. Spotswood, the issue of this marriage were 6. Dorothea Spotswood Henry m. George D. Winston; issue, Patrick, George, Edward, Fayette, James, Edmund, Sally and Elvira. These went to North Carolina, Missouri and Mississippi. 7. Sarah Butler Henry m. first Robert Campbell, brother of Thomas Campbell the poet, no issue; m. second Alex. Scott of Fauquier; issue, 1. Henrietta m. Gen. Wm. H. Bailey of Louisanna, 2. Catherine m. Dr. Robert Scott, 3. P. H. Scott m. Mary Yancey and left six children. 8. Martha Catherine Henry m. Edward Henry of Northumberland, son of Judge James Henry, and died leaving a daughter, Dorothea Dandridge, who died unmarried. 9. Patrick Henry m. Elvira Cabell, daughter of Wm. Cabell of Union Hill, Nelson County, and had issue a dau. Elvira, who m. Wm. H. Clark of Halifax,and had issue, 1. Elvira C. m. Augustine Claiborne, 2. Nannie m. Thomas Bruce, 3, John, 4. Patrick, 5. Eliza m. Alfred Shields of Richmond, 6. Martha m. Lyle Clark, 7. Ellen m. George Lee of Richmond, 8. Rosa m. Mr. Wilkins.

10. Fayette Henry m. Miss Elcan, of Buckingham, and died childless.

11. Alexander Spotswood Henry m. Paulina Cabell dau. of Dr. Geo. Cabell of Lynchburg. Issue, 1. Geo. Fayette; 2. Patrick; 3. John Robert; 4. Lewis Cabell; 5. Sallie m. Dr. Geo. Cabell Carrington; 6. Paulina m. Mr. Jones; 7. Marion m. Sam'l. Tyree; 8. Maria Antoinette.

12. Nathaniel Henry m. Virginia Woodson. Issue, 1. Capt. P. M. Henry; 2. Lucy m. John Cardwell; 3. Mary m. Mr. Garrett; 4. Martha m. Mr. Ward; 5. Dorothea Virginia m. Beasely.

13. Richard Henry died in infancy.

14. Edward Winston Henry m. Jane Yuille. Issue, 1. Dr. Thomas Y. Henry; 2. Patrick Fayette; 3. Marie Rosalie m. Dr. Wm. B. Lewis; 4. Lucy D. m. Mr. Leighton; 5. Celine m. Robert Catlett; 6. Ada B. m. John G. Smith; 7. Edward Winston.

15. John Henry m. Elvira McClelland, granddaughter of Col. Wm. Cabell of Union Hill. Issue, 1. Margaret Anne m. Wm. A. Miller; 2. Elvira M. m. first Jesse A. Higginbotham; m. second Alexander Taylor; 3. Wm. Wirt Henry; 4. Dr. Thomas Stanhope Henry; 5. Laura m. Dr. James Carter; 6. Emma C. m. Major James B. Ferguson.

SUPPLEMENT TO THE FOREGOING WINSTON GENEALOGY BY EDWARD V. VALENTINE, (THE VIRGINIA SCULPTOR).

Peter Winston, son of Isaac Winston and Marianne Fontaine, m. Elizabeth Povall. Issue, 1, Isaac m. Miss Burton; 2. Mary Ann m. Alexander Jones; 3. Peter m. two sisters, Misses Jones; 4. Elizabeth m. Hesekiah Mosby; 5. Susanna m. Mr. Grubbs; 6. John Povall m. Miss Austin; 7. Sarah m. John Mosby; 8. William m. Martha Mosby; 9. Ann m. Benjamin Mosby.

The children of Alexander Jones and Mary Ann Winston were John Winston, Eliza and Gustavus.

John Winston Jones, (Speaker of the U. S. House of Representatives), m. Harriet Boisseau, issue, 1. Mary m. George W. Towns, (Governor of Georgia). Issue, Harriet Winston, Margaret, John, Mary Winston, Anna, Lou Morton and George W. 2. James B. Jones m. Ann Crawley Winston, dau. of Peter Winston, son of Peter; issue : Jno. Winston, Peter E., Wm. Gustavus, Louisa Winston and Augustus Drewry; 3. Alex. Jones.

2. Eliza Jones m. John Mosby. Issue John A. Mosby.

3. Gustavus Jones m. Elizabeth, dau. of Wm. Winston of Half-Sink, Henrico County, and moved to Puducah, Ky.

The children of Benjamin Mosby and Ann Winston were 1. Peter Winston, 2. Elizabeth, 3. John O., 4. Robert P., 5. Mary Ann, 6. Sarah Winston, 7. Benjamin, 8. Lucy, 9. Patrick Henry, 10. Wm. H., 11. Susanna Virginia.

Elizabeth Mosby m. Mann Valentine. Issue 1. Elizabeth Ann m. William F. Gray, 2. Mann S. m. Ann M. Gray, 3. Benjamin Batchelder, 4. Wm. Winton, 5. Robert Mosby, 6. Mary Martha m. J. W. Woods, 7. Sarah Benetta, 8. Virginia Louisa, 9. Edward Virginus Valentine m. Alice C. Robinson.

P. B. Jones of Orange County belongs to this family, but the author does not know the connecting links.

REV. JOHN WOODVILLE, RECTOR OF ST. MARK'S.

He was born in the north of England, and was the son of a captain, either in the merchant service or Royal Navy. Rev. John Woodville m. Sarah, daughter of Rev. James Stevenson. Issue James Littlepage, born 1791, who m. Miss Mary Lewis and left one son, James Littlepage, who m. Miss Breckenridge of Botetourt Co., Va. Fanny, daughter of Rev. John Woodville, born 1793, m. William Payne, and their son Dr. John J. W. Payne of Riverside, Tenn., m. first Martha V., daughter of William A. Winston, of Culpeper (see Winston genealogy), and m. second Elizabeth R., daughter of Col. Rufus K. Anderson of Alabama, a son of Col. William Anderson (U. S. Infantry), Tennessee. William Payne, who m. Fanny Woodville, and whose piety and devotion to the Church is so touchingly described by Bishop Green of Mississippi in his charge to the last Convention, was a son of the old vestryman of St. Mark's, Richard Payne of Culpeper, Va., who was the son of George Payne of Westmoreland (1716), who was the son of John Payne of Lancaster (1679) who was the son of Richard Payne of Northumberland (1633), whose father came to Virginia in 1620 (see Smith's History of Virginia, p. 52). The Rev. J. Walker Woodville (b. 1799) m. Miss Mary E. Carmach. Sarah Ann, daughter of Rev. John Woodville, (b. 1802) died single.

FAMILY OF THE REV. JOHN THOMPSON

This gentleman was born at Muckamore Abbey near Belfast in Ireland, and came to Maryland a Presbyterian minister. I am indebted to Mrs. Murray Forbes for documentary proof of this fact in the form of a letter from the Rev. Jacob Henderson (Commissary) to the Bishop of London, dated Maryland, July 30th, 1739, in which he says:—"The bearer, Mr. Jno. Thompson, has been a Preacher in the Presbyterian way at Newton, on the Eastern Shore of this Province; but was, by the distractions of the ministers and people of that persuasion, put upon considering the terms of communion in the Church of England; and I do verily believe, upon full conviction, has embraced it. He appears to be a person of great candor and sincerity. He has been intimate with the leading clergymen for some years, and your Lordship will perceive what a character they give him in their testimonials. When I was in the North of Ireland, I had a very good character given him from many people of different persuasions. He is desirous of Holy Orders, and has a nomination from the Rev. Mr. Williamson to be his assistant,and I recommend him for Holy Orders as a person not only very deserving, but one that I sincerely believe will be an ornament to our Church."

The Rev. Mr. Thompson, as we have seen, became Minister of St. Mark's Parish (1740), and married (1742) the widow of Governor Spotswood, by whom he had two children.

1. Ann (b. at Germanna 1744, d. 1815) m. Francis Thornton of the Falls. Their only son, Francis Thornton, m. Sally, daughter of Col. Innes ; children

1. Sally Innes m. Murray Forbes of Falmouth ; children, 1. Jno. M. Forbes (of the Fauquier bar) m. a daughter of Dr. Semmes. 2. Delia m. Alfred Thornton, 3. Frank m. Mercer, daughter of John Chew, 4. Dr. Wm. Smith Forbes m. in Philadelphia, 5. Alfred m. daughter of G. Bastable, 6. Kate m. G. Bastable, 7. David, 8. Mrs. Dr. Taylor, and 9. Mrs. Stevens Mason, deceased.

2. Betsy, daughter of F. Thornton and Ann Thompson m. Dunbar of Falmouth; ch. Anna. 3. Polly m. Dr. Vass of Madison County, 4. Fanny m. Dr. Horace Buckner of Culpeper, 5. Milly m. Col. Abram Maury of Madison, 6. Dolly m. Samuel Washington of Culpeper.

William, son of Rev. Jno Thompson m. Sarah, dau. of Charles Carter of Cleve by his 2nd wife Miss Byrd; children, 1. Charles Carter Byrd Thompson, Captain U. S. N., who m. in England ; no issue. 2. Gillies m. Mary Carter; children, Charles, and a daughter reared by Mrs. Judge Brooke. 3. William m. first Betsy Strother of Culpeper, m. second Caroline dau. of John, son of Rev. John; children, 1. Ann, 2. Wm. Fitzhugh Thompson, father of Mrs. Carrie Thompson Williams, of Henderson, Ky., and of William who m. Delia dau. of Frank Thompson; ch. Maria.

Rev. Jno. Thompson m. second a dau. of Philip Rootes; children, 1. Hon. Philip Rootes Thompson of Culpeper, M. C. (1801-1807), m. daughter of Burkett Davenport, vestryman of St. Mark's; ch. 1. Eliza m. Thornton Fry ; children, General Burkett Fry,C. S. A., Dr. Frank Fry,and Cornelia m. Jno. Lyddall Bacon, President of State Bank and other institutions, Richmond, Va. 2. Eleanor m. Wm. Thornton, son of Col.Wm. Thornton of Montpelier; ch. Dr. Thornton, m. Charlotte Hamilton, Mrs. Andrew Glassell Jr. Mrs. Charles Gibbs, and Philip Rootes m. Sarah Hamilton. 3. Burkett Devenport m. Miss Bostwick, 4. Philip Rootes, Jr., m. 1. dau. of Col. Wm. Thornton, 2. m. Sarah dau. of George Hamilton.

Hon. P. R. Thompson m. second a dau. of Robert Slaughter of the Grange, Culpeper; ch. 1. Dr. John Thompson m. a dau. of Dr. Geo. Thornton, 2. Hon. Robert A. Thompson, M. C. of Va., and Judge in California m. first Mary Smith, dau. of Captain P. Slaughter of Culpeper; children, Sarah E. m. Dr. Huie. 2. Mercer m. Gen. Ord, U. S. A., 3. Reginald H. Thompson C. S. A. lawyer, Louisville, Ky., m. Miss Thompson, 4. Robert m. Miss West, 5. Thomas m. (name unknown), 6. Frank m. Miss West. Robert and Thomas are editors of Sonoma Democrat, Santa Rosa, Caliafornia,and Frank, State Printer. 3. Francis, son of Philip R. Thompson, m. Caroline, dau. of Dr. George Thornton; ch. Mrs. Jno. James Williams. 4. Benjamin, who m. Elizabeth dau. of Gen. Andrew Lewis, 5. Wm. Henry, who m. Elizabeth Huie

John Thompson, son of Rev. John of Culpeper, born Oct. 2, 1764, married Miss Elizabeth Howison, daughter of Dr. Thos. and Bettie Lightfoot Howison, Feb. 15, 1784 and had the following children:

1. John Jr., born April 5, 1785, married Miss Le Chase of Louisanna; 2. Thos. Howison, born Feb. 8, 1787 m. Miss E. Hudson, of Louisanna; 3. Elizabeth, born April 3, 1788, never married; 4. Fanny, born Nov. 10, 1789, married Daniel French Strother June 1. 1813; 5. Wm. Lightfoot, born May 7, 1791, married Miss Elizabeth Massie; 6. Camilla, born Feb. 13, 1793, never married; 7. Caroline, born Aug. 20, 1795, married Wm. F. Thompson, whose first wife was Bettie Strother; 8. Malinda, born Oct. 17, 1797, married James B. Huie of Louisville; 9. Philip Rootes, born June 27, 1799, married Miss Elizabeth Tompkins; 10. Robt. Coleman, born March 30, 1801, married Miss Sarah Rigglesworth; 11. Mildred Ann, born April 17, 1803, never married; 12. Francis Thornton, born Nov. 27, , 1805, never married.

This John, son of Rev. John, moved about 1795 with his family to Jefferson County, Ky., and was afterwards U. S. Judge in Louisanna.

Mildred, daughter of Rev. John Thompson, married Capt. George Gray, Rev. Officer, who was the son of John and Mary Strother Gray, daughter of Jas. Strother and wife Margaret French dau. of Daniel French, issue of Capt. Geo. Gray, Sr.

Issue of Capt. George Gray, Sr.

1. Capt. Geo. Gray, U. S. A., married Selenah Cecilia Neal. His widow married twice. He died without children. She married second Abraham Hite, merchant of Louisville; 2. John Thompson Gray, m. Mary Ormsby, only child of Peter Benson Ormsby, and niece of Judge Stephen Ormsby of Louisville. The Ormsbys were from Sligo, Ireland. Issue below. 3. Philip Rootes Gray, m. Miss Kitty Holloway; 4. Horace Minor Gray, lived to old age. Never married; 5. Capt. John Strother Gray, U. S. A., never married; 6. French Strother Gray, m. Sarah Taylor, daughter of Rich'd. and Sarah Taylor; 7. Angereau Gray married Myra McConnell; 8. Weeden Gray died young, never married; 9. Mary (Polly) Gray m. Ambrose Camp; 10. Eliza Gray m. James McCrum; 11. Mildred Gray m. James Stewart; 12. Susan Gray m. James Stewart.

Children of John Thompson and Mary Ormsby Gray

1. Elizabeth Gray m. Dr. Norborne Galt, son of Dr. Wm. C. Galt; 2. Geo. E. H. Gray married Lucy Bate; 3. John T. Gray married first Miss Anita Anderson, second Virginia Hook, of Baltimore and third Caroline De Butts and had child or children by each; 4. Henry Weeden Gray married Miss Russell, one child, second Miss Peers; 5. Catherine Ann Mercer Gray m. Geo. Fetter; 6. Ormsby Gray married first Miss Nelson and second Miss Baker, daughter of Dr. Baker of Shelbyville, Ky.; 7. Selena Gray married first Ben Lawrence and second John Churchill. No children.

[Addenda to last but one paragraph on page 80, by Major B. S. Thompson, of Huntington W. Va.]

Issue of Philip Rootes Thompson and Second Wife, Dau. of Robert Slaughter.

1. John m. Matilda, dau. of Dr. Geo. Thornton; no issue; 2. Hon. Robt. A. m. first Mary S., dau of Capt. Philip Slaughter, second Mrs. Elizabeth Woods; 3. Helena M. m. John P. Turner, of Boston, Mass; 4. Francis m. Caroline H. dau. of Dr. Geo. Thornton; 5. Benjamin S. m. Elizabeth. dau. of Col. Charles Lewis, killed at the battle of Point Pleasant, Oct. 10, 1774, issue; I. Cameron Lewis, m. Elizabeth F. Weathers of Ky.; II. Margaret Lynn m. John I. Hurvey; issue: Cameron L., Agnes Lewis, Elizabeth Lynn, John S. and Marie Elinor. III. John S.; IV. Wm. Rootes, m. Sallie Helena Huie; 6. Wm. Henry, m. Elizabeth Huie, issue I. William m. Anselam Buckhannon, issue I. Thompson, II. Mildrid, III. Anselam, IV. Roberta.

ISSUE OF HON. ROBT. A. THOMPSON AND FIRST WIFE MISS SLAUGHTER.

1. Sarah E. m. Dr. Wm. Huie; issue: Wm. Henry, Robt. Blackburn, Elizabeth m. Geo. Flournoy, (ch: Geo. Huie,) Sallie Helena m. Wm. Rootes Thompson, Geo. Bullitt, and Edward Mercer; 2. Robt. A. Jr. m. Elizabeth West; issue: Reginald m. Miss Byson, Mary Nixon m. Paul Deady, Virginia Carter m. Allendean Whittaker, Elizabeth, and Wilmer; 3. Thomas L. m. Marion Satterlee; issue: Margaret m. Ed. L. Whipple, Frances Williams, Hugh S., Ethel, and Grace Evelyn; 4. Judge Reginald H., m. Elizabeth H. Thompson, no issue; 5. Mary Mercer m. Gen. E. O. C. Ord, U. S. A., issue: I. Capt. E. O. C. Ord m. Mollie Herton, issue: Edward, Harry, Nellie, Gurische, and Mollie; II. Roberta, m. Gen. Trivino of Monterey Mex., issue: Gerinimo; III. Lucy, m. Capt. John Mason U. S. A., issue: Mercer, Annie, Ruth, Mollie m. Mr. Hilcott; (ch: John,) Gurische, Lieut. U. S. A., killed in Cuba: 6. Frank P. m. Mary West, issue: Mary m. Jno. L. Means, (ch. Mary, Jno. L.); II. Page E. m. Dr. Westwood Baker, (ch. Westwood Sally;) III. Helen, Thomas Larkin, Roberta, Robert and John.

HON. ROBT. A. THOMPSON m. SECOND MRS. ELIZABETH WOODS; ISSUE:

7. Ruth Harrison, m. Wm. Craig, issue: Earle; Willie, Robert, Olive, Donald; 8. Helena; 9. Roberta.

HELENA M., DAU. OF (HON. P. R. THOMPSON,) m. JOHN P. TURNER; ISSUE:

1. Sarah Elizabeth; 2. Chas. Philip; 3. Matilda; 4. John P. m. Ella Taylor; ch. Francis; Helena, Garnet, Fannie, and Jas. McFarland.

FRANCIS, SON OF (HON. P. R. THOMPSON); m. CAROLINE H. THORNTON; ISSUE:

1. Fannie, m. John I. Williams; ch: Frank and Harry; 2. Geo. Philip, m. Margaret Mussie; ch: Frank, Mary m. Mr. Smith, Aylette, Maggie, Caroline; 3. Delia, m. Wm. N. Thompson; ch: Maria; 4. Mary m. James Lockhart.

Rev. John Thompson's will was recorded in Culpeper 16th Nov. 1772. Witnesses, Benjamin Johnson and Thos. Walker: executors, Fielding Lewis, Jos. Jones, Wm. and Frank Thornton. He devised to his son Wm. 1550 acres of land in Culpeper and 19 negroes. To his son John, 2000 acres and 15 negroes. To Frances Thornton and Ann his wife, 800 acres and "a negro wench Queen." To his daughter Mildred, all the money due from estate of Gov. Spotswood. To his son Philip Rootes 1079 acres on Summer Duck below Mount Poney and 12 negroes. To his wife, his mansion, his furniture, his coach, 600 acres of land and 18 negroes. To his Sister Ann Neilson, a home and support. To his sons William and John, each a lot in Fredericksburg.

Col. Wm. and Col. John Thornton were brothers of Francis Thornton of Falls, who married Ann, daughter of Rev. John Thompson. They were all sons of Francis Thornton the elder, who married Frances Gregory. Col. Wm. Thornton, who married Miss Washington, was the father of Dr. Philip Thornton, Dr. Geo. Thornton, John, Howard, and Stuart Thornton. Francis the elder had also a son George, who was the father of Reuben, who married a niece of Gen. Washington, and lived at Greenwood, near Germanna, and was the father of Charles Augustine Thornton, now of Enfield, North Carolina.

[Addenda by Mrs. Mary D. Micou, Theological Seminary, Va.]

Dr. Burkett Davenport Thompson, b. 1788 d. 1829, son of Philip Rootes Thompson and Anna Davenport, m. Mary Ann Bostwick, issue:

1. Philip Rootes, b. 1812 d. 1857, m. Henrietta Lochett. 2. Anna Davenport, m 1831 Wm. Chatfield Micou, d. 1864. 3. Susan Jane, m. Rene Brunet. 4. Wm. Thornton, m. Aglaie Lochett.

Philip Rootes, son of Burkett D. Thompson, b. 1812, graduated at West Point about 1834, was rapidly promoted in the army. During the Mexican war he was a Captain, and was breveted Major for "bravery in the battle of

Sacramento." Died with the rank of Colonel on board the U. S. Man of War, Wabash, 1857. Married Henriette Lochett of New Orleans.

Anna Davenport, dau. of Burkett D. Thompson, m. Wm. C. Micou, 1831, who become a prominent member of the New Orleans bar, he died in 1854, she, in 1864. For issue see Micou genealogy.

Philip Rootes Thompson, 2nd. son of Hon. Philip Rootes Thompson, m. 1st. Lucy Thornton, 2nd. Sarah Hamilton dau. of Capt. Geo. Hamilton, of Forest Hill, Va., Dec. 1838.

Issue of Philip Rootes Thompson and Lucy Thornton. 1. William Thornton. 2. Philip Rootes. 3. Susan, m. Archibald Blair of Va., issue: Philip and Susan. 4. Lucy Ellen m. Clinton Palmer, of S. C., issue: Edwin, Wm., and Eliza. 5. G. Howard m. Meta Fitzhugh, of Maryland, issue: Dr. Geo. H. and Meta.

Issue of Philip Rootes Thompson and Sarah Hamilton. 1. Maria Hamilton b. 1839, m. Collins Macrae, issue: Collins, Cornelia and Howard Macrae. 2. Eliza Rootes b. 1841. m. Randolph Harrison of James River, issue: William Mortimer, Lilias Edwina, Sarah Hamilton, Thos Randolph, Randolph Hammond, and Macpherson. 3. Lilias Ritchie b. 1843, m. Edwin C. Palmer, of South Carolina. 4. Ellen Thornton, b. 1845, m. Chas. R. Allen; issue: Ellen Hamilton, George Hamilton, b. 1848.

Lilias Edwina Harrison m. Lieut. John J. Knapp, U. S. N. Sarah Hamilton Harrison m. Lieut. Edward W. Eberle, U. S. N.

THE STROTHER FAMILY.

Some think this family of Scotch origin, and that it had then the prefix of Mac. Others insist that it is Saxon. Gen. Dick Taylor, son of the President, whose mother was a Strother, says, as we learn from Judge Strother of Giles, that he had visited the old burial-ground of the family in the Isle of Thanet, County of Kent, England, and seen the name in its various transitions from its original form Straathor to its present orthography. However this may be, it has long had its present form in England, for Chaucer has a facetious tale of two Strothers, the orthography being the same then as now. The earliest date to which we have traced the name in Virginia is 1734, when Anthony Strother patented a tract of land under the doubletop mountain in what was then St. Mark's Parish, and is now Bromfield in Madison. The family abounded in the county of Stafford. John Madison, clerk of Augusta, father of Bishop Madison, John Lewis, who so long represented the same county, and Gabriel Jones, "the Valley Lawyer," all married Misses Strother of Stafford. Jeremiah, who may have been the father or brother of Anthony, died in what was then Orange County, (Culpeper not being yet formed) in 1741, leaving his property to his wife Eleanor, and appointing his sons, James and William, executors. The will was attested by Francis Slaughter, G. Lightfoot and Catlett. His children were James, Wm., Francis, Lawrence, Christopher, Robert and several daughters. Francis married Miss Dabney and died 1752. He was the ancestor of Gen. Gaines, John S. Pendleton, Gen. D. Strother (Porte Crayon), Gen. Duff Green, and Capt. French Strother of Rappahannock. William married Mrs. Pannill and was the grandfather of Gen. Z. Taylor.

James, the eldest son, married Margaret, daughter of Daniel French of King George, whose son Daniel died in 1771. He gave property by deed to Jas. Strother's children, who were French, James, and Mary (Mrs. Gray). James died in 1761 and left property to his son French. French Strother, the vestryman of St. Mark's, married Lucy, daughter of Robert Coleman. He lived where Coleman Beckham now lives. He became a vestryman in 1772, and churchwarden in 1780. He made himself very popular by releasing a Baptist minister who had been imprisoned by a Justice of the Peace, by substituting his man Tom in his place and letting him out at night. That fact is stated on the authority of Capt. P. Slaughter, who married his daughter. He represented the county for nearly 30 years in the General Assembly; was a member in 1776, and of the Convention of 1788-9, and voted against the Constitution and for the famous Resolutions of 1798-99. He was solicited to oppose Mr. Madison for Congress (see Rives' Madison), but Monroe became the candidate and was badly beaten. Monroe had only 9 votes in Orange, Madison 216; Culpeper, Monroe 103, Madison 256. Col. Frank Taylor in his diary says, "Col. Pendleton of Culpeper came to my house from meeting of Sheriffs in Charlottesville, and he says Madison has 336 majority in the district." In the State papers published by Dr. Palmer there is a correspondence between him and Jefferson in 1776 which would seem to show that he had some local command, perhaps City Lieutenant. He died on his way from the Senate in Richmond, at Fredericksburg, and was buried there. His executors were Capt. P. Slaughter and his son Daniel French. His children were Daniel French, who went to Kentucky and m. Miss Thompson, a descendant of Rev. John Thompson of St. Mark's; Geo. French, who represented this district in Congress 1817-20, and moved to Missouri where he died. Hon. Geo. F. Strother m. Sally, daughter of Gen. James Williams; his son, the late James French Strother, who was a member of the Legislature (Speaker) and of Congress, m. Elizabeth, daughter of Major John Roberts; children, 1. French, late Superintendent of the Penitentiary, m. Miss Cary, of Gloucester county, no ch. 2. Capt. John R., member of Assembly many years, m. Miss Viola Payne, dau. of Dr, Payne, of Culpeper, and had I. Jas. Alexander, m. Miss Taylor, of Giles, II. Wm. Henry, III. Geo. French, IV. Ellen Payne, m. E. L. Gaines, V. Elizabeth Roberts, VI. John Hunt, VII. Philip Johnson, and VIII. Viola Williams. 3. Philip W., Judge and Representative of Giles county, m. Nannie Pendleton, of Giles county, and had I. James French, m. Miss Bondurant, II. Elvina Chapman, m. Mr. Barnes, of Tazewell, III. Elizabeth Roberts. IV. Albert Pendleton, V. Nanny Mary. VI. Sallie Viola, and VII. Lucy Williams, 4. James French, Judge of {Rappahannock county, m. Miss Mary Botts, and had I. Sallie Hunt, m. Clarence J. Miller, II. James French, III. Andrew Botts, IV. Catherine Tutt, V. Isabel Lewis, VI. Elizabeth Roberts, and VII. Eliza Harvie. 5. and 6. William Henry and John Hunt, died during the war. 7. William Johnson, m. Letitia Shackelford. 8. Sally Williams, and 9. Lewis Harvie.

Jeremiah Strother, late of Culpeper, who m. Miss Clayton, and is the grandfather of the Rev. J. P. Hansbrough, is of the same family. So also, we suppose, was Wm. Strother, of Madison, who m. Miss Medley, and whose dau. Louisa married Rev. H. Stringfellow, and is the father of Rev. Horace Stringfellow, D. D., of Montgomery, Ala., (who has also a son, Rev. James Stringfellow, in the ministry,) and 2. of Chas. S. Stringfellow, a leading member of the Petersburg bar, 3. of the wife of La Fayette Watkins, also of the Petersburg bar, and of others.

THE BROADUS FAMILY.

Another man of mark to whom Culpeper gave birth, is the Rev. John A. Broadus, D. D., Professor in the Baptist College, Greenville, South Carolina, a scholar of rare culture, and a preacher who exemplifies many of the best precepts in his excellent work on the art of preaching with power. He is a son of Edmund Broadus, who so long represented Culpeper in the General Assembly. Edmund was the son of Thomas, who was the brother of the Revolutionary officers, Ensign James and Major Wm. Broadus, vestryman and lay delegate, who married Mrs. Jones, the daughter of the first churchwarden of St. Mark's, Robert Slaughter. Their daughter Kitty married William Mills Thompson, vestryman of St. Mark's, who was the father of the Hon. Richard Wigginton Thompson, the present Secretary of the Navy. Major William Broadus married second Miss Richardson and left several children, among whom is Miss Sarah A. Broadus of Charlestown, W. Va. Major Broadus was Paymaster at Harper's Ferry when he died, about 1830.

The first Broadus of whom I find any trace in Culpeper was Edmund, who patented land in what is now Madison County in 1700. The Rev. William F. Broadus of Fredericksburg was a son of Thos.; and Jas. M. Broadus of Alex is a son of Edmund, and brother of Dr. John A. Broadus William Broadus, clerk of Culpeper, was the son of Major Wm. Broadus.

THE SLAUGHTER FAMILY.

[The Slaughter genealogy, as it was in the first edition of St. Mark's, has been revised (the work being done in April 1900) by members of the family who were in a position to know. Besides this, there is additional addenda to this genealogy, covering other branches and lines.]

It is not worth while to trace this family to the stock from whence they sprang in England. We limit our notice to two brothers, who were transplanted in this Parish early in the eighteenth century, and who by the light of later research, have been found to be the sons of Robt. Slaughter and Frances Anne Jones, his wife.

ROBERT AND FRANCIS SLAUGHTER (the two sons) were the first church wardens of St. Mark's Parish, chosen by the first vestry in 1731.

ROBERT SLAUGHTER (Robt.) m. Mary Smith, dau of Augustine Smith, in 1723, and had:

1. Robert, m. Susannah Harrison in 1750; 2. Wm., m. Miss Zimmerman, moved to Jefferson county, Ky.; 3. Thomas, m. Miss Thornton, dau. of Francis Thornton; 4. Francis, m. Miss Luggett; 5. James, m. Susan, dau. of Major Philip Clayton, 6. Lawrence, m. Field, dau. of Col. John Field; 7. George, m. Miss Field, dau. of Col. Jno. Field; 8. Elizabeth Lightfoot; and 9. Martha Jones, who m. 1st. Capt. Gabriel Jones, 2nd. Major William Broaddus.

FRANCIS SLAUGHTER (Robt.) m. Anne Lightfoot, in 1729, and had:

1. Francis, m. dau. of Robert Coleman; 2. John m. Milly Coleman; 3. Reuben, m. 4. Cadwallader, m. 5. Frances, m. Capt. Wm. Ball; 6. dau. m. Edward Thomas, and had son, Edward Slaughter Thomas, member of Ky. House of Representatives in 1793, and m. Susannah Beall, and had several children, one of them Lucinda, m. Dr. Wm. Elliott, of New Haven, Ky.

FRANCIS SLAUGHTER (Francis, Robt.) m. dau. of Robt. Coleman, on whose land Culpeper Court House was founded; had Francis, m. Miss Hollaway, and had Henry, (M. D.) who moved to the South. This same Francis (the second) moved to Ky., and settled in Hardin county about 1785, as did all of his children, except Francis, who m. Miss Hollaway.

REUBEN SLAUGHTER (Francis, Robert.) m. and had 1. Goodrich; 2. Joseph; 3. William; 4. Robert. They moved to Bedford county, Virginia, where Jos. m. and has descendants, who are Harrises.

CADWALLADER SLAUGHTER (Francis, Robt.) m. 1st. Miss Ramsdell, of Fauquier, and had, 1. Margaret, m. Chas. Morehead; 2. Matilda, m. Jno. Churchill; 3. Francis Ramsdell, m. Fanny Latham; 4. Presley, m. Martha Slaughter; and 5. Edward.

FRANCIS RAMSDELL SLAUGHTER (Cadwallader, Francis, Robt.) m. Fanny Latham, had 1. Elizabeth, died single; 2. Cadwallader, m. Francis Ann Vance, had one dau. Elizabeth, who m. Squire Bassett, of Lexington, Ky; 3. Philip, m. Mary Ann Smith; 4. Henry, died single; 5. Matilda, m. Joseph Longest.

ELIZABETH SLAUGHTER (Cadwallader, Francis, Ramsdell, Cadwallader, Francis, Robert) m. Squire Bassett, and had two daughters, who m. Messrs. Scott and Threlkeld.

JOHN SLAUGHTER(Francis, Robt.) m. Milly Coleman, dau. of Robt. Coleman, and had, 1. Robert, m. sister of Gov. Slaughter, of Ky., and had two sons Chas. and Edward, and several daughters. 2. Cadwallader, m. 1st. Miss Yancey, 2nd. Miss Hampton, and had Rich., Jno. H., Robt., Edward, Cadwallader, and several daughters. 3. and 4. Francis and Thos. K., both went to Ky. 5; John S. m. dau. of Capt. William Brown, and had thirteen children, who were:

1. Col. John Slaughter, of Culpeper, m. dau. Maj. Gabriel Long, and had four daughters, Mrs. C. C. Conner, Mrs. Gabriel Long, Mrs. George Slaughter, and Emily, died single.

2. William, m. Miss Ficklen, and had I. Franklin, m. Miss Gill, having Lawrence, Frank, Etta, and Harriet, who m. Mr. Tackett, vestryman of St. George's Church, Fredericksburg. II. Montgomery, m. Eliza Lane Slaughter, having Wm., Philip, Mary Montgomery, Fanny, Charles, and Bessie. III. J. Warren, m. Sallie Braxton.. IV. Elizabeth, m. R. Garnett. V. Sallie, m. Jno. F. Ficklen, having Kate and Harry. VI. Jennie, m. Dr. Kerfoot. VII. Matilda. VIII: Fanny.

3. Samuel, m. Allen.

4. Philip, m. 1st. Eliza, dau. of Wm. Lane, and had Eliza; m. 2nd. Mrs. Fletcher; m.3rd. Mrs. Robinson.

5. Reuben, m. Emily, dau. of R. Long, of Baltimore, having I. Albert, m. 1st. Mary Edmonia Rogers, had 1. Wm. Pendleton, m. Mollie Rea Duncan, 2. Frank;, Albert m. 2nd. Louise Cary Funston, having 1. Emily Virginia, 2. Sue Meade, 3. Jas. Albert, 4. Evelyn, 5. Homozelle, 6. Eleanor, 7. Louise Nelson. II. Frank L., m. Susan Fitzhugh Motley, of Caroline, having 1. Albert Judson, m. Virginia Jackson Daniel, 2. Gibbon Minnigerode, 3. Frank Raymond, 4. Persis Read. III. Anne Trippe, m. Dr. Boulware, of Caroline, having McCalla, who m. Ada Jackson Miller, and had 1. Jackson Darius, 2 Gideon Brown, 3 Elizabeth Trippe. IV. Maria, m. Rev. Mr. Buckner, of Caroline.

6. Thomas Jefferson, m. dau. of Capt. R. Moore, having I. Reuben, m. Miss Turner, and had 1. Lou Turner, 2. Thomas Jefferson, 3. Milton, m. Miss Wright, 4. Marcellus, 5 Anne W., 6. Herbert, 7. Anna C. II. Susan, m. Col. Coons. III. Anne, m. Lieut. Winfield, killed at Spottsylvania C. H., in 1864.

7. Albert Gallatin, Commander in the U. S. Navy, m. Miss Emily Randall, of Baltimore, having I. Josephine. II. Emily G., m. Judge Stuart, a lawyer of distinction of Baltimore, having 1. Wm. m. Miss Carter, of Fauquier, 2. Emily, m. Lieut. Macklin, U. S. Navy, 3. Kate, m. Mr. Drake, 4. Lewis.

8. James Madison, m. Miss Long, of Baltimore, and had I. Mary, m. Rev. J. G. Minnigerode.

9. Mary, m. John S. Long, of Ky.

10. Elizabeth, m. Mr. Downer, and with eleven children lived in Ky.

11. Lucy, m. 1st. Gabriel Long: 2nd. Thos. S. Long, both sons of Maj. Gabriel Long, of Culpeper.

12. Nancey, m. Reese Jury, and had I. John S., m. Miss Wolfe. II. Lewis C., m. Miss Holt, and lived in New Orleans. III. Mary, m. Edward R. Gaines, having Dr. J. M. Gaines, of Hagerstown, Md., James, surgeon in the U. S. N., Archibald, m. Freeman, Lucy, m. Crawford, Bettie and Susan. IV. a dau. m.

John Long, Ky. V. Catherine, m. J. M. Lewis. VI. Bettie m. Rev. Mr. Huff. VII. Susan. VIII. Margaret. IX. Francis.

13. Susan, m. Roberts Menefee, and moved to Missouri.

WILLIAM SLAUGHTER (Robt. Robt.) m. Miss Zimmerman, moved to Jefferson County, Ky., had:

1. Thomas, 2. William, m. Miss Brisco. 3. John, 4. Gabriel, 5. Smith, m. Miss Crane, of Jefferson County, Ky., and represented that county for many years.

THOMAS SLAUGHTER (Robt., Robt.) m. Miss Robinson, and had:

1. Robert, of the Grange, m. Miss Stanton, having I. Thomas. II. Henry. III. Stanton (High Sheriff), m. Miss Pickett. IV. Authur. V. Augustine. VI. Wm. Stanton. VII Martin, of Culpeper bar, m. Miss Bolling of Petersburg.

2. Augustine, surgeon in the Revolution.

ANNA SLAUGHTER (Stanton, Robt., Thomas, Robt., Robt.), m. Rittenhouse Stringfellow, and I. Robert Stanton, m. Miss Green, having Anna and Mary. II. Martin, m. Miss Willis. III. Rev. Frank Stringfellow, Gen. Lee's famous scout, and now Chaplain of the Woodbury Forest High School, m. Emma F. Greene, of Alexandria, having 1. Ida, m. Wm. Alex. Bar, rector of Monumental Church, Richmond, Va., had Jas. R., B. Barr, Janetta E. and Frank Stringfellow. 2. Stuart, died single. 3. Alice Lee, m. Robert W. Shultice, of Norfolk, Va. 4. Martin Slaughter, m. Lelia Palmer, of Kilmarnock, Va. 5. Frank. 6. John Stanton.

SARAH SLAUGHTER (Robert, Thos., Robert, Robt.) m. Geo. Hamilton, of Spottsylvania, and had 1. Dr. Hugh Hamilton, m. Miss Scott, 2. Sarah, m. Roots Thompson, 3. Charlotte, m. Dr. Thornton, and had Susan, and Robert, m. dau. of Judge Brooke. 4. Maria, m. Mr. Page, 5. Margaret, m. Geo. Thornton, of Ky., 6. Matilda, 7. Jane, m. Jno. L. Marye.

COL. JAMES SLAUGHTER(Robt. Robt.), who commanded a Regiment at the battle of Great Bridge, m. Susan Clayton, and had:

I. Capt. Philip, b. 1758, d. 1849, m. 1st. Peggy French Strother, 2nd. Elizabeth Towles, and had:

1. Lucy Coleman, m. Isaac H. Williams(see Williams genealogy).

2. Susan, m. Mr. McConchie.

3. Polly m. Dr. Frank Conway, having I. Susan, m. Dr. Shepherd. II. Margaret, m. Philip Clayton,. III. Dr. Philip Clayton, m. Bettie Yerby. IV. Dr. Albert.

4. Eliza French, m. Col. John B. Dade, of King George County, and had Capt. Townsend, Philip, and Margaret, m. Edward Smith, of Washington, D. C., having Edward, Thownsend, Jno. Battaile, Philip and Ofelia Ann, who m. Jas. F. Hansbrough, and had Benjamin F., Lucien, Annie, Eliza French, Pearl, and Rosalie Fitzhugh.

5. Sally, m. Judge Philip Slaughter, of Ky.

6. Daniel French, m. 1st. Letitia Madison,(see Madison genealogy), and had I. James Edwin. II. Philip Madison, m. Clementine Luzenberg of New Orleans, having Edward Luzenberg, m. Lucy Williams, and Mary Clement, m. Hugh Hamilton Jr., who had Cornelia Long and Edwin Slaughter. Daniel French, m. 2nd. Mary W. Winston, and had I. Mary Wallace. II. Eliza French. III. Caroline. IV. John M. V. Daniel Alexander, who m. Katherine Somerville, having Daniel French.

7. Thos. Towles, M. D., m. 1st. Jane, dau. of Reynolds Chapman, of Orange, and had I. Thos. Larkin. II. Reynolds Chapman, m. Louise Lake. III. Col. Philip Peyton, C. S. A., m. Emma Thompson, having Elizabeth Pendleton, who m. Lucien Smith, and had Katherine Mercer. IV. Dr. Alfred Edwin, C.

S. A., m. Jennie Taylor, and had 1. Robert Carroll, 2. Jane Chapman, m. Judge Moore, of Nelson county, and had Downer, 3. Sadie Patton, 4. Alfred Edwin. V. James Shepherd, Lieut. C. S. A. VI. Col. Mercer Slaughter, C. S. A., genealogist and literateur, m. Mary Bull, and had Mary and Vivian. VII. Richard, Lieut. C. S. N. Thos. Towles Slaughter, M. D. m. 2nd. Julia Bradford, and had Jane Chapman, and Robert Madison, M. D., who m. Fanny Innis, having Virginia Lemoine, Julia Bradford, Nanny Stricker, and Robt. Innis.

8. Rev. Philip, D. D., m. Anna Sophia Semmes, and had Mary Elizabeth, and Sophia Mercer, m. Thos. Towles Slaughter.

9. Mary, m. Robt. A. Thompson, M. C. of Virginia and Judge in California, grandson of the Rev. John Thompson, and had I. Sarah E., m. Dr. Huie, having Robt., Sadie, m. Roots Thompson, and others. II. Robert A., editor of Sonoma Democrat, and collector of customs at San Francisco, m. Elizabeth West, having Mary Nixon, m., Jennie, m. Mr. Whitaker, of Philadelphia, Andrew Glasell, Elizabeth and Wilmer. III. Thos. Larkin, M. C. from California, and minister to Brazil under Cleveland, m. Marion Satterlee, having Mary, m. Mr. Whipple, Francis, Hugh S., Edith, and Grace. IV. Reginald Heber, Judge of the City Court of Louisville for many years, m. Elizabeth Howison Thompson, dau. of Col. Lightfoot Thompson. He died, full of honors, April 2, 1899, having won for himself the title of "The Sir Galahad of the Louisville Bar." V. Frank Poulson, Superintendent of Prison Reform in Central America, where he died of yellow fever in 1898, m. Mary West, and had Mary, m. Mr. Mears, Page, m. Lieut. Cunningham, U. S. A., Helena, Thomas, John, Roberta, and Augusta. VI Mary Mercer, m. Gen. Ord, U. S. A., and had 1. Lucy, m. Lieut. Mason, U. S. A., having three daughters, of whom Mercer is the eldest. 2. Mary Mercer, 3. Roberta, 4. James, 5. Lieut. Garusha, killed in the charge at San Juan in 1898, and 6. Edward.

10. Anne Mercer, m. 1st. Edward Robertson, having Cornelia, who m. . Dr. R. K. Long, and had Mary Mercer, m. Dr. Henry Somerville, having John Wilson, Cornelia Long, Jennie, and Harry Tunstall. Anne Mercer, m, 2nd. Philip Slaughter, of Rappahannock, and had I. Dr. John Philip, m. Kate Foster, having Mary Mercer, Thos. Foster, C. E., Cornelia Long, Sophie Clayton, m. Marion Speiden, James William, and Delia Towles. II. Thos. Towles, m. S. M. Slaughter. III. Bessie, m. Dr. F. S. Hall. IV. Edward Mercer, killed at the battle of Newtown, aged seventeen.

II. Samuel, m. 1st. Miss Banks, and had I. Emily, m. S. K. Bradford, having 1. S. S. Bradford, who m. 1st. Miss Walden, and had Emily, m. Miller, and Flora, m. Travers Daniel, having Alice, Minnie and Travers. S. S. Bradford, m. 2nd. Fanny Battaile, and had Slaughter and Caroline Grandine; 2. Louisa, m. Gen. Wright, having Edward, Rosa, m. Mr. Smith, and had I. Lt. Wright Smith, U. S. A. II. Mollie, m. Mr. Wooten, and had Dr. Herbert, Harry, and Isabel, m. Dr. Richardson; 3. Robert Bruce, 4. Rose. m. Prof. Nairne, of Columbia College. N. Y., 5. Maria Champe, m. Mr. Van Schaik, and 6. Dr. Alfred. II. Col. Wm B., m. dau. of Judge Slaughter, and had Mary. III. Col. Henry Slaughter, m. Mary Tony, having Burgess. IV. Maria, m. Prof. Bailey, of West Point, and had Loving, Whittaker, and Samuel S. V. Louisa, m. Gen. Merrill, U. S. A., and had Wm. Emory, S. S., and Anne Loving. VI. Dr. Philip Clayton, m. Mary McDowell, and had Ella, John, Clayton, Wood, and Clarence. VII. Isabella, m. Col. Burbank, U. S. A., and had Sally, Fanny, and a son. VIII. Lavinia, m. Mr. Jack, of Ky., and had Matilda, Frances, Rebecca, and others. Samuel (2nd. son of Col. James) m. 2nd. Virginia Stanard (see Carter genealogy) and had 1. Columbia, m. William Green, L. L. D., of Richmond, having John, killed in battle, and Bettie, who m. Jas. H. Hayes, having John,

Columbia, m. W. J. Walker; Somerville, m. Ewing Eachins; Henrietta; Bettie; Virginia, m. Mr. McDonough; Lucy; and William. 2. Virginia, m. Dr. Daniel S. Green, having Dr. William, Samuel S., and Mary, m. Richard Morton. 3. Sally Champe, m. Rev. William F. Lockwood, of Md., having Dr. William, Bessie, Mary, and another son.4. Marcia, m. Maj. John B. Stanard (see Carter genealogy). III. Thomas Smith, Jackson elector in Ky., b. 1778, d. 1838, m. Lucy Bibb, and had 1. John m, and left three sons and two daughters. 2. Thos. Jefferson, banker in New York, m. Mary Henry, relative of Patrick Henry, and had Henry, m. Miss Wainwright, having Gertrude, and Mayhew, Julian, Clayton, Gabriel, Lucy, m. Dr.———-———, Mattie, m.————————, and Mary, m. Mr. Emmons, of Chicago.

IV. Robert, m.Margaret Pendleton, and had 1.JohnPendleton, who died in Culpeper; 2. Philip, 3. Geo. Clayton; 4. James, m. Miss Fergerson, of Culpeper, having James Burr, of Louisville, Ky., who m. 1st. dau. of Judge Carpenter, of Bardstown, 2nd. dau. of Rev. Frank Thornton.

V. George m. and died in Culpeper.

VI. Anne m. Reuben Fry,(see Fry genealogy.)

VII. Sally m. McLaughlin.

VIII.———-———m. Judge Speed.

IX. Mary m. Bell.

LAWRENCE SLAUGHTER (Robt., Robt.) killed in battle at Point Pleasant, m. a dau. of Col. John Field.

GEORGE SLAUGHTER (Robt., Robt.) m. a dau. of Col. John Field. He raised one of the first companies of "Minute Men" of Culpeper, and after the Revolution, went to Kentucky, with George Rodgers Clark, and commanded a fort at the falls of the Ohio, and was one of the founders and first trustees of the City of Louisville. Died in Columbus in 1815, leaving no issue.

JOHN SLAUGHTER (Chas., Robt., Robt., Robt.) m. Miss Armistead, and had Chas., Sarah, and Pauline. Chas. m. Miss Coleman and moved to Tennessee.

DR. ROBERT SLAUGHTER (Chas., Robt., Robt., Robt.) m. a dau. of Rice Garland, and had 1. Chas., lawyer of Lynchburg, and member of State convention, who m. Kate Garland, having Lillian, Mary, Chas. A., and Kate; 2. Dr. Samuel, m. Miss Henderson; 3. John F., lawyer, m. Miss Harker, having Chas., John F., Robt., Samuel, Edith, and Susan. 4. Austina, m. R. W. Brodnax, having Mary and Celeste.

GABRIEL SLAUGHTER (Robt., Robt., Robt.) m. 1st. Miss Slaughter, 2nd. Miss Hoard, of Caroline, and had John. He was the Governor Gabriel Slaughter of Kentucky, and the officer who was so highly recommended by General Jackson for his gallantry in the battle at New Orleans.

JESSEE SLAUGHTER (Robt., Robt., Robert.) m. Miss Slaughter.

AUGUSTINE SLAUGHTER (Robt., Robt,. Robt.) m. Fisher, and lived near Harrodsburg, Ky.

William, brother of John S., m. Lucy Brown; children, 1. William, m. Fanny Brown, and their son Alfred is Principal of Prairie Home Institute, Mo., and their son Capt. Daniel Slaughter, C. S. A., m. Miss Berry, and lives in Madison; 2. Catherine, daughter of William, m. William Armstrong: children, John, William, Ringgold, Lucien, and Edward, and a daughter Mary Ann; 3. John, son of William, m. Miss Harper, and moved to Zanesville, Ohio, Reuben, went to Tennessee, Gabriel to Missouri, George m. 1st. Miss Adams, m. 2nd. Miss Slaughter, Elizabeth (Mrs. Yates) Ellen, daughter of William, m. Benjamin Ficklin: children Slaughter W., m. Caroline Wilkins of Baltimore, Benjamin F., had an adventurous life,and died in Georgetown, D.C.,Lucy Ann (Mrs. Brockman), Elizabeth (Mrs. Dunkum); Ellen (Mrs. Dr. Brown), Susan (Mrs. Dr.

Hardesty), Lucy, daughter of William, m. W. W. Covington: children, John, Warren and William, D. C. The last was captain C. S. A. Nancy, daughter of William, m. G. W. Thomas, and their daughter, m. Fenton Henderson of Leesburg and left several children.

Of the Slaughter family of Culpeper there were seven officers of the Revolution. Col. James and Col. John were members of the Committee of Safety of Culpeper. Robert, Francis, Col. Robert, Col. James, Thomas, Robert Jr., Lawrence, Cadwallader, Samuel, William B., and Philip, Jr., were vestrymen of St. Mark's Parish.

Dr. R. Coleman Slaughter, of Evansville, Indiana, and Thomas C. Slaughter of Corydon are descendants of the 1st. Francis. Some members of the family may be interested in knowing that its chief seats in England were Lincolnshire, Gloucester, and Worcester, and that the first of the name who took up lands in Virginia were John 1620, Richard 1652- '55, '79, '89, '95, 1710; George 1710, '19, '32. Robert first churchwarden St. Mark's 1732-35.

ADDITIONAL SLAUGHTER GENEALOGY.

[Note: from John Slaughter Carpenter, of Louisville, Ky., we have the following. The figures following the name denote the generation.]

(Robt.[1] Robt.[2] Col. James.[3])

ROBERT SLAUGHTER[4] married Margaret (Peggy) Pendleton about 1783; left Culpeper about 1787 for Nelson county Ky. He was born in 1762 and died in 1803 of an accident aged 41 years, leaving three sons and four daughters. His widow m. 2nd. John Lightfoot, and had one son, Pendleton Lightfoot, who m. Caroline Crow, daughter of Judge Warner Crow, of Davies county Ky., and had two sons, Joshua Pendleton Lightfoot, and Warner Crow Lightfoot. John Lightfoot lived only about a year. After his death, his widow m. Rev. Joshua Morris, a prominent Baptist minister who had been pastor of the first Baptist Church organized in Richmond, Va. They had no children. Hon. Robert Slaughter represented Nelson county in Kentucky House of Representatives in 1798. His colleague was Hon. Ninean Edwards, who was the first Governor of Illinois, and re-elected by the people of Illinois and afterward U. S. Senator from that State.

Children of Robert and Margaret B. Slaughter, (nee) Pendleton.

I. James Pendleton Slaughter,[5] m. 1st. in Jefferson county, Ky., Sept. 30, 1805, Mary, dau. of Samuel Fergerson, formerly of Culpeper county m. 2nd. Mrs. Fenwick, of Illinois.

II. Susan Clayton Slaughter,[5] m. Capt. Matthew Duncan, U. S. A.

III. Ann Pendleton Slaughter,[5] m. John Dabney Strother in 1811; farmer of Nelson county Ky.

IV. Margaret Bowie Slaughter,[5] m Hon. Samuel Carpenter, of Bardstown, Ky. 1815.

V. Philip Clayton Slaughter,[5] m. Miss Betsy Payne, of Logan county, Ky. in 1818.

VI. John Pendleton Slaughter,[5] never m. Died in Culpeper county in 1823, at the home of his uncle Samuel Slaughter.

VII. Catherine Slaughter,[5] never m; died young.

(Robt.,[1] Robt.,[2] Col. James,[3] Robt.[4])

Children of James Pendleton Slaughter,[5] and Miss Mary (nee) Fergerson.

I. Robert Pendleton Slaughter,[6] m. Eveline Fenwick, and had several children.

II. James Burr Slaughter,[6] m. 1st. in 1837, Margaret Ann Carpenter, dau. of Judge Samuel Carpenter, of Bardstown, Ky., children James B. Jr., Margaret Cambridge, Mary, and Fanny Rawson Slaughter. Fannie m. Wm. Bolling Carter, formerly of Virginia, and they have three children: J. Slaughter, Fannie Bolling, and Margaret Virginia Carter. Mr. Slaughter m. 2nd. Mrs. Elizabeth Grant, dau of Rev. Francis Thornton. and had two children, Miss Bessie B. Slaughter, Thornton Grant Slaughter, who m. Edith, dau. of Wm. S. Parker, of Louisville, Ky.

III. Frank Slaughter,[6] m. Eulila Fenwick, and had several children.

IV. George Clayton Slaughter,[6] m. Miss Julia Redding, of Shelbyville, Ky., and had three children.

1. James Edward,[7] m. 1st Miss Frazier, of Shelbyville, and had one son, John E. Slaughter,[8] m. 2nd. Miss Florence Baker, of Louisville, and had one daughter, Elchen Slaughter.[8]

2. George Clayton Jr.,[7] m. Miss Jennie Cooper, of Nashville, and had two daughters, Belle,[8] and Mary Slaughter.[8]

3. Ella Slaughter,[7] m. Orlando V. Wilson, formerly of Louisville, now of Kansas City, Mo., and has two children, Orlando Victor Wilson, and Julia Wilson.

(Robt.,[1] Robt.,[2] Col. James,[3] Robt[4].)

ANN PENDLETON SLAUGHTER,[5] m. John Dabney Strother, and had:

I. Elizabeth Strother,[6] m. in 1834, Enoch H. Hinton, moved to Missouri.

II. Mary Strother,[6] m. in 1832, Henry Glasscock, moved to Missouri.

III. Margaret A. Strother,[6] m. Wm. H. Slaughter, of Hodgenville, Ky., son of Robert Coleman Slaughter, of Hardin county Ky., and his wife Nancy, dau. of Thos. Haynes, children :

1. Anna Slaughter, who m. Dr. Robert M. Fairleigh, of Hopkinsville, Ky., and had John, Fannie, who m. Mr. Ware, Madge, Letitia, and Robert Fairleigh.

2. Mary F. Slaughter m. Luke Kennedy, of Elizabethtown, Ky; had Lena m. Jos. Covington, of Bowling Green, Ky., Margaret, who m. Wallace McKay of Louisville, and Anna.

3 Elizabeth Slaughter.

4. Wm. H. Slaughter, Jr., farmer near Hodgensville, Ky.

5. Geo. M. Slaughter, m. ——— and had Nellie, Willie, Margaret and Sarah Bess Slaughter.

6. Emma Slaughter, m. Dr. Garrett E. Smock, of Hodgensville, Ky., and had Maggie, and Fannie Smock.

IV. Dr. Robt S. Strother[6] m. Miss Whitney, dau. of Mrs. Gen. Edmond Pendleton Gaines by first marriage.

V. Sarah Strother[6] m. Frank Bealmear of Nelson Co., Ky.

VI. Maria Strother[6] m. Wm. Howard of Lee's Summit, Mo., formerly of Jefferson Co. Ky. Issue: Anna Howard who m. Mr. Lee, and had one son Howard

VII. Dr. Wm. D. Strother[6] m. Miss Julia Sanders, dau. of Jos. Sanders of Bullitt Co. Ky. Issue:

1. Mary Elizabeth Strother m. Joseph Field, of Lee's Summit, Mo.

2. Dr Jos. Sanders m. Miss Cowherd, Belton, Mo.

3. Hon John D. Strother, Lee's Summit Mo. Atty. Represented Jackson Co. in Mo. House of Representatives.

4. Geo. Beauregard Strother, Atty. Belton Mo.

5. Howard Strother, Atty. Belton Mo.

6. Benj. F. Strother, Ins. Agt., Kansas City.

7. Sam'l C. Strother, Atty. Kansas City.

8. Juliet Strother, Lee's Summit, Mo.

VIII. Emily Strother,[6] m. Chas. J. Cowherd, Kansas City, Mo. Issue:

1. Hon. Wm. S. Cowherd, Mayor of Kansas City; now M. C; m. 1889 in Leadville, Col., Miss Jessie Kitchen.
2. Miss Sallie Cowherd.
3. Miss Fannie Cowherd, m. 1889, E. H. Graves, of Lee's Summit, Mo.
IX. Catherine Strother,[6] never married.
X. Dr. John D. Strother,[6] m. Esther Elliot, of Big Spring, Ky., Ch.; Dr. Wm. Strother, of Big Spring, Hardin county, Ky., and Zelmar Strother.
XI. Benj. Strother, of Kansas City, Mo., m. Miss Macauley, of Washington City, Ch.; Benjamin, Clement, John D., and William.

(Robt.,[1] Robt.,[2] Col. James,[3] Robt.[4])

MARGARET BOWIE SLAUGHTER,[5] m. Samuel Carpenter, of Bardstown, Ky., Att'y at Law, State Senator, Circuit Judge; children:

I. Margaret Ann Carpenter,[6] m. James Burr Strother, a resident of Louisville, for over 65 years. He died in January, 1895, in his 80th year. Prior to the civil war, Mr. Slaughter was a hardware merchant. At the time of his death he was the oldest member of the Board of Fire Underwriters, and of the First Christian Church of Louisville; children: James B. Jr., Margaret, who m. Mr. Cambridge, Mary and Fannie Rawson Slaughter, Fannie m. Wm. Bolling Carter, and has three children, James Slaughter Carter, Fannie Bolling and Margaret Virginia Carter.

II. Rebecca Delph Carpenter,[6] m. John A. Y. Humphreys, teacher and farmer, of Nelson county, formerly of Spottslyvania county, Va., children:
1. Margaret Mildred Humphreys.[7]
2. John S. Humphreys,[7] farmer.
3. Dr. Wm. T. Humphreys,[7] m. Annie B. Graham, and had one child, who died young.
4. Rev. Samuel C. Humphreys,[7] m. Mattie Thurman. Issue: Robert H. Humphreys,[8] m. Maggie Boner; John S. Humphreys,[8] A B. and A. M.. of Harvard, m. Sue Hite Maxey, and has one son, Samuel Maxey; Emily Humphreys,[8] and Brewer Humphreys.[8]
5. Thos. J. Humphreys,[7] m. Kate Summers, of Bullitt county, and has two children: Rebecca (Reba) Carpenter Humphreys,[8] who m. Robert Walter Owens, and Lucy Catherine Humphreys.[8]

III. Catherine Carpenter,[6] m. Luther Howard, Jefferson county, Issue:
1. Margaret (Rettie) Howard, m. Henry V. Sanders, Treasurer of Columbia Finance and Trust Company, Louisville. They have four children: Anna Blake Sanders, m. Alexander Thompson; Howard C. Sanders, m. Kate Berryman; John W. Sanders; and Ellen H. Sanders.
2. Ellen Howard, m. David Hardin, of Nelson county, Ky., and had one son, Rowan Hardin, a young lawyer of Louisville, who m. Anne Allen.

IV. John Slaughter Carpenter,[6] represented Louisville, in the Common Council, Board of School Trustees and the Kentucky House Representatives, m. November 21, 1850, Ellen Blake Cosby, dau. Fortunatus Cosby, editor, educator and poet, and grandaughter of Judge Fortunatus Cosby, one of the largest land owners of Louisville in early times, and great grandaughter of Capt. Aaron Fontaine, son of Rev. Peter Fontaine, Rector of Westover Parish, Va. over forty years. Issue:
1. Ellen Blake Carpenter.
2. Mary Carpenter.
3. Alice G. Carpenter, m. Wm. Henry Slaughter, son of D. Strother Slaughter and grandson of Judge Jas. Slaughter, of Nelson county, Ky., formerly of Culpeper county, Va.
4. Anna Sanders Carpenter,

5. John S. Carpenter, Jr., Paymaster U. S. Navy, m. Charlotte Clarke, dau. of Edward Clarke, Architect of the Capitol at Washington City for the past forty years, They have one child, Evelyn Fessenden Carpenter.

6. Samuel Carpenter.

7. Frank Cosby Carpenter, (Fire Insurance Agent), m. Anna Pope Smith, dau. of Thos. Floyd Smith, U. S. A., and wife Blanche, dau. of Geo. W. Weissinger, of Louisville; Ch: Floyd Smith Carpenter, and Eleanor Blake Carpenter.

V. Lucinda Carpenter[6] m. 1 L. L Able, ch: 1 Sallie m. first Ed Harris, and had one daughter, Lucie who m. Chas. D. Pennebaker, Jr., of Washington City and had six children. Sallie m. 2nd. Ludwell McKay.

2. Margaret C. Able m. James E. Callahan, of Louisville, and has five children: Mattie E., who m. Dr. Frank D. Boyd, of Texas, and has one son, Frank Douglas; Lulie May, Elliot, Emily L., and Sallie Winifred.

3. Lou Able m. Geo. M. Abell of Nelson co. and has four children, Edward, Geo. M., Robert, Lucile.

Lucinda Carpenter m. 2nd. M. Dupin.

VI. Mary Carpenter[6] m. 1. Dr. Wm. T. Winsor, of Lexington, Mo., and 2nd. Dr. James Muir, of Bardstown, Ky. children:

1. Susan L. Muir m. Nathaniel Wickliffe Halstead, Issue: Margaret, Muir, Mary, Sue, Nathaniel, Annie Dawson and Martha Porter Halstead.

2. Wm. C. P. Muir, Lt. U. S. Navy, m. Annie Dawson Beckham, of Shelbyville, Ky.

3. Dr. Sam'l C. Muir, of Bardstown.

VII. Samuel Carpenter[6] A. B. St. Joseph College, City Attorney of Memphis, Tenn., where he died 1860, m. Annie Merrill.

VIII. Susan Carpenter[6] m. Hon. John Darwin Elliott, of Nelson co., Ky., member of Kentucky Senate, County Clerk of Nelson for many years and Master Commissioner, children:

1. Mary L. Elliot m. John LeBosquet, of Desmoines, Iowa; Issue: Elliott and Henry LeBosquet.

2. Samuel Carpenter Elliott m. Miss C. Jackson, Issue: Darwin Elliott.

3. Lulie P. Elliott m. Capt. Leonard S. Miller; Issue: Susan Carpenter Miller, and Martha Porter Miller.

4. Amanda Elliott m. Wm. Newman, children: Nellie Elliott, Williams H., John E., Charles Merrill, Stanley O., Chester L., and Rockville B.

5. Charles Merrill Elliott m. Carrie Powers, of Atlanta, Ga., ch: Henry Powers Elliott.

6. John Carpenter Elliott.

7. Ellen Carpenter Elliott m. Thos. Hooge, Issue: Nellie and Lucille.

8. Nannie Elliott m. Ernest Beeler, of New Haven, Ky. ch. Ernest.

IX. Martha Carpenter[6] m. James Joseph Porter, a native of Green co., Ky., Cotton Commission Merchant of Louisville, President of Board of Trade; children:

1. William Porter.

2. Mary Porter.

3. Carrie Porter.

X. James Slaughter Carpenter[6] m. Emilie Alston Leach, dau. of Dr. Sewell J. and Elizabeth Fitts Leach, of Tuscaloosa, Ala. Mr. Carpenter is General Agent of Com. Mutual Life Ins. Co. for Ky. and Tenn., and was Captain Commissionary Dep't., C. S. A. children:

1. Lizzie Carpenter m. Geo. James, of Memphis, Tenn, ch. Emilie Carpenter, James and Edith W. James.

2. James S. Carpenter, Jr.
3. Samuel Sidney Carpenter.
4. Emilie Alston Carpenter.
5. John Darwin Carpenter.
6. Norma S. Carpenter.

(Robt1., Robt2., Col. James3, Robt4.)

PHILIP CLAYTON SLAUGHTER5, m. Miss Betsy Payne, of Russellville, Ky., 1818. Their only child, Mary, m. Cardwell Breathitt, son of Gov. John Breathitt, of Kentucky. Their descendants live in Missouri.

DESCENDANTS OF LAWRENCE SLAUGHTER.

[Note : From a descendant of Lawrence Slaughter, son of Robert, one of the two brothers, we have the following.]

Lawrence Slaughter, son of Robert 1st., Lieut. in Virginia State Line under Gen. George Rodgers Clarke in campaign in that part of Virginia which is now Illinois, m. Susanna Field, dau. of Col. John Field, (see Field genealogy page 57, St Mark's) Colonel in Virginia State Line, killed in battle of Point Pleasant, Gen. Andrew Lewis commanding. Col. Field was also member of House of Burgess from Culpeper county in 1765.

Children of Lawrence Slaughter and Susanna Field: 1st. John Field Slaughter, m. 1st. Miss Alexander, of Effingam, Prince William county, m. 2nd. Miss Slaughter, dau. of Col. Robert Slaughter, of The Grange, Culpeper county; 2nd. Anne Slaughter, m. Baylor Banks; 3rd. Mildred, m. James Marye; 4th. Robert Field, m. Sarah Bond; 5th. Mathilda, m. McCoul; 6th. George S.; 7th. Lawrence; 8th. Frances.

Children of Baylor Banks and Anne Slaughter: 1st: Elizabeth (b. 1784) m. William Barker, (1808); 2nd Ann Baylor, (b. 1784) m. L. Roberts (1806); 3rd. Dr. Wm. Tunstall, (b. 1788) m. Pamela Somerville Harris (1812); 4th. Lawrence Baylor, (b. 1790), (died 1797); 5th. John Field, (b. 1792) m. Frances Roberts; 6th. Baylor, (b. 1793) m. Mary Stern; 7th. Richard Tunstal (b. 1795) never married; 8th. Mildred (b. 1797) m. William Field (1819); 9th. Lawrence Slaughter (b. 1803) m. Margaret J. Noble (1834); 10th. George (b. 1805), (died 1808); 11th. Tunstal (b. 1807).

Children of Wm. Barker and Elizabeth Banks, 1st. Joshua (b. 1810) m. Lucy Ann Mason; 2nd. John Butler (b. 1812) never married; 3rd. Ann Baylor (b. 1815) m. William Stewart; 4th. Baylor Banks (b. 1818) m. 1st. Martha Ann Sample, 2nd. C. Penrith Ewing; 5th Fanny Britton (b. 1821) m. Col. M. C. Gallaway.

Children of Lawrence Banks and Margaret J. Noble: 1st. William Henry (b. 1834) m. Mary Stewart of Ala.; 2nd. Cyrus Aiken (b. 1836), (died 1843); 3rd. George Noble (b. 1838), (died 1842); 4th. Mildred Ann (b. 1840), (died 1842); 5th. Margaret Lawrence (b. 1842); 6th. Mary Ann (b. 1844), (died 1881); 7th―― m. John Nichols; 8th. Martha Noble (b. 1847); 9th. Lawrence Slaughter (b. 1849), (died 1884); 10th. a son, m. Emma Dial; 11th. James Baylor (b. 1851) m. Neal Payne; 12th. Mathilda White (b. 1853) m. W. R. Jones, 13th. Charles Albert (b. 1856);

Children of Dr. William Tunstal Banks, (vestryman for a number of years at Madison C. H.), and Pamela Somerville Harris his first wife: one child, Catherine J. (b. 1817), (died 1861) m. Benjamin M. Yancey, 1839. Children of second wife, Clara Foy, m. 1825, were :

1st. William Eldridge, m. Mary Willis; their children were : James W., Susan, Ida, Sally, Mollie and Florence; 2nd. Sophia, m.1st. Dr. Talley, 2nd. Mr. Allen, no children; 3rd. Clara m. Jas. B. Willis, and had Clara H., Salley, Willie, Sophia, Alice, and Tunstal; 4th. John Lawrence m. 1st. Miss Hobson, 2nd.

Bettie A. Carson, no children. Two children of first wife were: 1st. Minnie Hawes, m. Dr. Richard M. Smith, Ph. D., and had Nellie Blackwell, John Lawrence Banks, and Elizabeth; 2nd. William Tunstal.

Children of Bemjamin M. Yancey and Catherine J. Banks, his wife. 1st. Pamela Somerville, m. Capt. Joseph D. Brown; 2nd. Edward D.; 3rd. Dr. Chas. K.; 4th, Mary Crimora, m. John W. Payne; 5th. Sallie Thomas, m. John W. Payne.

Children of Capt. Joseph D. Brown and Pamela S. Yancey:

1st. Mary Catherine, m. Rufus T. Carpenter, and had Ninette Brown, Stacy Harris, Joseph Daniel, Ellie Florence, Frank Hill, and Leslie Pamela.

2nd. Lilly Banks, m. Thomas M. Henry, Att'y Princeton, N. J., and had Lucy Maxwell, Pamela Brown.

3rd. Josephine, m. J. Benjamin Flippen, of Cumberland county, and had Sue Gray, Elsie Josephine, Harry, Marjorie Pamela.

4th. Benjamin Armistead, m. Frances Todd Faunt Le Roy, of King and Queen county, and had Virginius Faunt Le Roy, Joseph Daniel, and Juliet Faunt Le Roy. 5th. Andrew Edward. 6th. Gertrude Pamela, m. John Bannister Sparrow, of Danville, Va. 7th. Florence Armistead, m. Olliver G. Flippin, of Cumberland county.

Children of John W. Payne and Crimora Yancey. 1st. Mary Catherine; 2nd. Emma Carson; 3rd. Fannie Keith; 4th. Crimora Yancey.

THE PENDLETON FAMILY.

[Revised and corrected by Mrs. Mary Dunnica Micou.]

The first of the name of Pendleton who came to the Colony of Virginia to make their home (in 1674) were two young men, Philip Pendleton, a teacher, and Nathaniel, his brother, a clergyman. The latter died very soon, unmarried; he evidently held no clerical charge in the Colony, as his name has never been given among the lists of the clergy of that time. Philip returned to England about 1680; tradition says he married a lady of high social position, but she died, and he returned to the Colony, and in 1682 married Isabella Hurt (or Hert or Hart,) and from this marriage are descended all the Pendletons of Virginia. Philip was born in Norwich, England, in 1650, son of Henry Pendleton, 3rd son of Henry Pendleton, son and heir of George Pendleton, Gentleman, who married Elizabeth Pettingall dau. of John Pettingall, Gentleman of Norwich, Eng. George Pendleton moved from Manchester to Norwich in 1613. His son and heir, Henry, probably married Susan—— because in Vol. 48 of the New England Hist. and Gen. Register, is found a copy of the will of Sir John Pettus, Knight, of Norwich, Jan. 1613, which says: "Appoint my cousin, Henry Pendleton, Supravisor of my estate." Also Thomas Pettus, of Caistree, St. Edmond's Norfolk, Oct. 1618. "To my Cousins, Henry Pendleton and Susan, his wife, annuity out of my houses &c. in Norwich." This family of Pettus is the same as the one in Va. The Pendletons were originally from Manchester, where the name was well known, some of them being in public life as early as the reign of Henry VIII. The Coat of Arms used by the Pendletons of Norwich and by the emigrant, Philip, indicate by the presence of Escallop shells and by the Cardinal's chapeau, in the Crest, a connection with Crusader traditions. The New England Pendletons, descendants of Brian Pendleton, came from Lancaster, and show a different Coat of Arms. Philip Pendleton is said to have settled in New Kent Co., but there is no record of the family on the Register of St. Peter's Parish; he probably lived always in the portion called afterwards Caroline county, the records of which were burnt during the war of '61-65. Most of his descendants settled in counties to the north of New Kent. He died in 1721, the same year his oldest son Henry died, and the same year his grandson, the eminent Judge Edmund Pendleton, was born. He had three sons and four daughters, two of his family married into the family of James Taylor, of Carlisle, Eng., and by other intermarriages, a close connection with the Taylor family has been preserved. Some of his descendants were among the founders of St Mark's Parish.

ARMS OF "PENDLETON" OF NORWICH, ENGLAND.

Gules, an inescutcheon, argent, between four escallop shells in saltire.

Or. Crest. On a chapeau gules, turned up ermine, a demi-dragon, wings inverted, or holding an escallop shell argent.

PHILIP PENDLETON, born in Norwich, England, 1650, emigrated to the Colony in 1674, visited Eng. in 1680, returning, m. in 1682 Isabella Hurt or Hart, and died in 1721. issue:

1. Henry[2] b. 1683, m. Mary, dau. of James Taylor, of Carlisle, Eng. 1701; he d. May 1721; his wife m. 2nd. Ed. Watkins, d. 1770; 2. Elizabeth[2], m. Samuel Clayton, of Caroline county; issue: Philip, of "Catalpa." 3. Rachael[2], m. John Vass. 4. Catherine[2], m. John Taylor; issue: "John Taylor of Caroline"? U. S. S. 5. John[2], b. 1691, d. 1775, m. ——Tinsley, of Madison county, removed to Amherst county. 6. Isabella[2], m. Richard Thomas. 7. Philip[2], m. Elizabeth Pollard.

HENRY PENDLETON[2], eldest son of Philip Pendleton, the emigrant, and Isabella Hart or Hurt, was born in 1683. He m. in 1701, Mary Taylor, dau. of James Taylor, of Carlisle. Eng., and his 2nd. wife Mary Gregory. Henry was 18 and Mary 13 years of age. He died in 1721, the same year his youngest son, Edmund, was born. His wife m. 2nd. Ed. Watkyns and died 1770. Of his five sons, the oldest, James, and the third, Nathaniel, were for many years Clerks of the Vestry and Lay readers at the small chapels of St. Mark's Parish; and Philip, the son of James, was Clerk in 1782, when the Vestry books closed. His two daughters married brothers, James and William Henry Gaines. His youngest son, Edmund, though without a father's care, made for himself a name which will be known and remembered as long as Virginia's sons read her history. By his large circle of nephews and neices, many of them his own age, he was loved and revered, and the tradition of his kindness and ever ready help is handed down through nearly every branch of the family. Almost all the Pendletons of Virginia trace their descent to Henry Pendleton and Mary Taylor; their issue were:

1. James[3], b. 1702, m. ——issue: James[4], Henry[4], Philip[4], Annie[4], m. Taylor.

2. Philip[3], m. Martha——and dying 1778, left 15 children (five of them daughters) who intermarried with Gaines, Barbour, Thomas, Turner, &c.

3. Nathaniel[3], b. 1715, m. his second cousin, dau. of Philip Clayton; he d. 1794, in Culpeper county, Va.

4. John[3], b. 1719; d. 1799; Burgess from King and Queen, 1795: m. 1st. Miss James; issue: Edmund[4], John[4], Elizabeth[4], and Mary[4]; m. 2nd. Sarah Madison (cousin of President James Madison); issue: Henry[4], Sarah[4], James[4], Lucy[4] and Thomas[4].

5. Edmund[3], b. Sept. 1721, d. at Richmond, Va., Oct. 1803; patriot and jurist; m. twice; 1st. 1743, Elizabeth Roy, who died the same year; 2nd. 1743 Sarah Pollard. There are on record in the Virginia Land Reg. Office grants in his name numbering nearly 10,000 acres of land.

6. Mary[3], m. James Gaines.

7. Isabella[3], m. William H. Gaines. She was the grandmother of Gen. Edmund Pendleton Gaines, U. S. A.

JAMES PENDLETON[3] eldest son of(Henry[2], Philip[1].) m. Mary Taylor Pendleton; issue: 1. James[4], 2. Henry[4], 3. Philip[4], 4. Anne[4], m.———Taylor.

JAMES PENDLETON[4], (James[3], Henry[2], Philip[1].) m. Catherine Bowie, dau. of Gov. Bowie, of Maryland; issue: 1. John[5], m.———Taylor, 2. Margaret[5], m. 1st. R. Slaughter, 2nd.———Morris; 3. Nancy[5], m. 1st.———Brown, 2nd. Valentine Johnson; 4. Catherine[5], m. Archibald Tutt; 5. James Bowie[5]; 6. Thomas[5], m.———Farmer; 7. William[5], m. Nancey, dau. of Capt. John Strother; 8. Catlett[5]; 9. Elizabeth[5], m. Henry Pendleton, her cousin.

JOHN PENDLETON[5], (James[4], James[3], Henry[2], Philip[1].);m.——— Taylor, issue: 1. James[6]; 2. John T[J].; 3. Thomas[6]; 4. Catherine[6].

NANCY PENDLETON[5], m. 1st.———Brown, 2nd. Valentine Johnson, (James[4], James[3], Henry[2], Philip[1].); issue: 1. James Bowie[6]; 2. Thomas M[6]., m Jane Farmer.

THOMAS PENDLETON[5], (James[4], James[3], Henry[2], Philip[1].) m.———Farmer, issue: 1. William[6]; 2. James[6], m.———Conner; 3. Daniel[6], m.———Simms; 4. John[6]; 5. Alexander[6]; 6. George W.[6]; 7. Anne[6], m. John Menefee: 8. Eliza[6], m.——— Haynes.

WILLIAM PENDLETON[5], (James[4], James[3], Henry[2], Philip[1].) m. Nancy Strother, issue: 1. John Strother[6], Mem. House of Del. Va., M. C; served seven years in diplomatic service, m. Lucy Ann Williams. 2. Albert Gallatin[6], House of Del., d. 1875, m. Elvira Chapman. 3. James French[6], Supt. Va. Penitentiary m. Narrisa Cecil, issue: 1. Albert G[7]., 2. John S[7]., 3. James F[7]., 4. William C[7]. and 5. Edmund[7]; 4. William[6]: 5. French[6].

ALBERT GALLATIN PENDLETON[6], (William[5], James[4], James[3], Henry[2], Philip[1].) m. Elvira Chapman, issue: 1. son d. young[7]; 2. Nannie Strother[7], m. Judge P. W. Strother; 3. Sarah Elizabeth[7], m. Van Taliaferro; 4. Alberta Fowler[7], m. S. R. Crockett.

HENRY PENDLETON[4], (James[3], Henry[2], Philip[1].) (Mem. of Culpeper Com. of Safety 1775. and of Patriot Convention 1775-6) m. Ann Thomas, issue: 1. Dau[5]. m. ———Browning, issue: dau. m. Capt. French Strother, of Missouri; 2. Dau[5]. m.———Smith; 3. Dau[5]. m.———Green, issue: Harriet, Judith, and Caroline; 4. Edward[5], m. Sarah Strother; 5. Henry[5], m. Elizabeth Pendleton, his cousin; 6. Frances[5], m.———Ward; 7. Edmund[5], m. Elizabeth Ward.

EDMUND PENDLETON[5], (Henry[4], James[3], Henry[2], Philip[1].) m. Elizabeth Ward, issue: 1. Edward[6]; 2. William[6]; 3. Daniel[6]; 4. Theoderick[6], settled in Clarke county, Va.; 5. Robert W[6]., resides in Baltimore, Md., (Pres. Valley R. R. Co.); 6. Peter[6], is Pres. of Valley R. R. Robert W., d. a merchant in 1859; 7. George W[6]., removed to Arkansas; 8. Mary Ann[6], m. Wm. Foushee; 9. Elizabeth W[6]., m. E. B. Long, of Baltimore, issue: Gertrude, m. Geo. M. Williams. (see Williams genealogy).

PHILIP PENDLETON[3], (Henry[2], Philip[1].) was born about 1704 or 1705. The record of his residence and the names of some of his children is lost; he probably lived in Caroline county, because he is mentioned in the only record of that county, 'not burnt during the Civil War, as witness in a suit in 1768 and as having travelled 30 miles to attend Court. His wife is supposed to have been named Martha———, because of a deed of sale to his stepfather, Ed. Watkyns, in Culpeper county, signed by Philip Pendleton and wife, Martha. He is said to have had 15 children, five of whom were daughters, all married, according to the records in Judge Pendleton's bible. Of these five daughters, Mary, the oldest, m. Col. Edmund Waller, second clerk of Spottsylvania. Jemina, m. her first cousin, Richard Gaines, son of Isabella Pendleton and Wm. Henry Gaines. Martha, m. Massey Thomas, of Culpeper county, the other two are said to have been named Mildred and Judith, but their record is uncertain. There was a son Henry, as is proved by deed in Orange county, land left to him to go after his decease to his sister Mary Waller, recorded in 1742. A great-grandaughter of Philip mentions sons of his: "John, Edmund, Philip, and I cannot remember all their names." Some of them probably moved West as did his daughter Martha. His youngest son Micajah, lived and died in Amherst county; Philip Pendleton died in 1778; his four children of whom we have record are as follows:

I. Mary[4], m. Col. Edmund Waller, 2nd Clerk of Spottsylvania, issue: 1. John[5]; 2. Leonard[5]; 3. Wm. Edmund[5]; 4. Benjamin[5]; 5. Ann[5], m. 1783, Geo. Mason, issue: Nancy[6], m. Henry Coleman, issue: 1. Sally[7], m. Charles B. Claiborne; 2. Emma[7], m. Henry Rose Carter, issue: Hill[8]; Nannie[8], m. Judge Redd; Edward[8]; Charles[8]; and Mary[8].

II. Jemina[4] or Germina, m. Richard Gaines, issue: 1. William[5]; 2. Lucy[5], m.———Botts; 3. Rowland;[5] 4. Germina[5], m.———Speak; 5. Benjamin[5]; 6. Nathaniel[5]; 7. James[5]; 8. Judith[5], m.———Chancellor; 9. Annie[5], m.———Crigler; 10. John Cook[5]; 11. Elizabeth[5], m———Thomas.

III. Martha[4], m. Massey Thomas, son of Massey Thomas, of Culpeper county; they moved to Varsailles, Woodford county, Kentucky, about 1811; all their children were born in Va., issue: 1. Fannie Taylor[5], b. 1788, m.——— Lewis; 2. Philadelphia Pendleton[5], b. 1789, m. James Dunnica; 3. Sallie Minor[5], b. 1791, m. William Hamilton Dunnica; 4. Granville Pendleton[5], fought under Gen. Harrison in 1813 to 1815; 6. Virginia Curtis[5], b. 1794, m.———Norwood; 6. John Price[5], b. 1794; 7. Martha Curtis[5], b. 1798, m.——Ramsey.

PHILADELPHIA PENDLETON THOMAS[5], (Martha Pendleton[4], Philip[3], Henry[2], Philip[1]) m. James Dunnica, moved to Missouri, issue: 1. Fontaine Murray[6], m. Caroline P. Harrison, issue: Leon[7], and George P[7].; 2. Martha Zerelda[6]; 3. Lewann Melvina[6]; 4. Granville Price[6], m. Mary Ann Bagley, issue: Mary[7], m. Rev. Richard W. Micou, and had Granville Price[8]; 5. America Vespucia[6], m. Isaac Cutler; 6. William Hamilton[6], (killed at Battle of Atlanta, Ga., C. S. A.); 7. John Logan[6]; 8. Fannie Sallie Virginia[6].

SALLIE MINOR THOMAS[5], (Martha Pendleton[4], Philip[3], Henry[2], Philip[1],) m. William Hamilton Dunnica, issue: Louise[6], m.———Baber; Granville Thomas[6]; Virginia[6], m.———Pollock.

JOHN PRICE THOMAS[5], (Martha Pendleton[4], Philip[3], Henry[2], Philip[1],) issue: Adelia[6], m.———Burns; James Waller[6]; William Massey[6].

IV. MICAJAH PENDLETON[4], youngest son of (Philip[3], Henry[2], Philip[1],) m. Mary Cabell Horsely, dau. of Wm. Horsely, of Amherst county, issue: 1. Martha[5], d. unmarried; 2. Edmund[5]; 3. Edna[5], m. Dabney Gooch; 4. Joseph[5]; 5. Elizabeth[5], m. Thomas Emmet, issue: Pendleton[6], and two daughters; 6. Letitia Breckenridge[5], m. Hudson Martin Garland, issue: Breckenridge C[6]., Henrietta M[6]., m. Pleasant S. Dawson; 7. Robert[5], m. Mary Taliaferro, issue: Rosa[6], m. Henly.

ELIZABETH PENDLETON[5], (Micajah[4], Philip[3], Henry[2], Philip[1],) m. Thomas Truxton Emmet, son of Lewis Emmet and Jane Barnet Gibbs, dau. of Churchill Gibbs and Judith Richardson, son of———Gibbs and———Churchill. Lewis Emmet was son of John Emmet and Mary Stephens, dau. of Maj. Peter Stephens and Miss Rittenhouse, of Philadelpha, issue: Pendelton Emmet[6], m. Alice Pringle, and has two daughters; he was Lieut. in the C. S. A.; was taken prisoner and sent to Johnson's Island until end of the War.

NATHANIEL PENDLETON[3],(Henry[2], Philip[1],). He was born 1715; m.———his second cousin, dau. of Philip Clayton: he d. 1794, in Culpeper county Va. issue:

1. Nathaniel[4] b. 1746, d. in New York, Oct. 20, 1821. Entered Rev. Army in 1775, aide-de-campe to General Greene; prominent lawyer and jurist in

New York; second of Alexander Hamilton in his duel with Aaron Burr; m. Susan Bard; 2. William[4] b. 1748, settled in Berkeley county, and was a faithful layreader of the Church of England, as was also his son, William, who was the father of the late Rev. William H. Pendleton; 3. Henry[4], b. 1750, d. in S. C., Jan, 1789. Eminent as jurist and patriot; numerous descendants in S. C.; Pendleton District in that state named in honor of him; 4. Philip[4] b. 1752, Martinsburg, Va.; 5. Mary[4], m. John Williams, no issue; 6. Elizabeth[4], m. Benjamin Tutt; 7. Susanna[4], m.——Wilson.

NATHANIEL PENDLETON[4], (Nathaniel[3], Henry[2], Philip[1],) m. Susan Bard, issue : 1. Edmund H[5]., Judge, M. C. Left no issue; 2. Nathaniel Greene[5], b. Savannah, Ga. Aug. 1793, d. June 16, 1861. Aide to Gen. Gaines 1813-16; member Ohio Senate 1825-23; M. C. 1840-2; father of Hon. George H. Pendleton; 3. John Bard[5], left no issue: 4. James M[5]., m. Margaret Jones, issue : Capt, James M. Jones; 5. Anne F[5]., m. Archibald Rogers.

PHILIP PENDLETON[4], (Nathaniel[3], Henry[2], Philip[1],) m.——Pendleton, issue : 1. Philip C[5]., (U. S. District Judge); 2. Edmund[5] (Washington, D. C.); 3. Anne[5], m.——Kennedy; 4. Sarah[5], m. 1st.——Hunter, issue : Hon. R. M. T. Hunter; m. 2nd.——Dandridge, issue : seven children; 5. Maria[5], m. John R. Cooke, (celebrated lawyer), issue: Phil. Pendleton, (poet) and John Esten, (novelist); 6. Elizabeth[5], m.——Hunter.

PHILIP C. PENDLETON[5], (Philip[4], Nathaniel[3], Henry[2], Philip[1],) issue : 1 Philip[6]; 2 Edmund[6], (Judge Circuit Court); 3. E. Boyd[6].

WILLIAM PENDLETON[4], (Nathaniel[3], Henry[2], Philip[1],) was born 1748, m. Elizabeth Daniel, of Culpeper, moved to Berkely county; had a large estate, which he left to his son, William. He was a man of classical education, and composed many sermons and essays. He had seven daughters and three sons, as follows:

1. Mary[5], m. Nicholas Orrick, issue: Cromwell, and other children; 2. Elizabeth[5], m.——Ferguson; 3. Susan[5], m.——Wigginton; 4. Ellen[5], m. 1st. James Walker, issue : William; 2nd.——Lindsay; 5. Benjamin[5], m. 5 times, issue : Catherine and James, d. young; 6. Frances[5], m. James Campbell; 7. Nathaniel[5], m. had children, moved to Ohio; 8. Emily[5], m.——Dyer, moved to Missouri; 9. William[5].

WILLIAM PENDLETON[5], (William[4], Nathaniel[3], Henry[2], Philip[1],) was b. 1789, m. 1811 Susan, dau. of Stephen Snodgrass, and his wife, Elizabeth Verdier, dau. of the Countess of Monti, who m. Francis Verdier, and being Huguenots, were forced to fly from France. Susan (Snodgrass) d. 1834. He m. 2nd. Mrs. E. A. Robinson; d. 1855, issue :

1. Anne Eliza[6], b. 1812, d. 1884, m. Amos Williamson, issue : Samuel, Susan, Benjamin, Robert, Amos, Edmund, and Annie; 2. Susan Verdier Sheperd[6], b. 1813, d. 1888, m. James Campbell Orrick; 3. Eleanor[6], b. 1815, d. 1844, m. Nathaniel Pendleton Campbell; 4. William Henry[6], b. 1817, d. 1873, m. Henrietta Randolph; 5. Nathaniel[6], b. 1820, d. 1824; 6. Robert S[6]., b. 1824, d. 1880, m. Mary Pfeiffer; 7. Philip Edmund[6], b. 1827, d. 1830; 8. Stephen James[6], b. 1831, killed at Malvern Hill; m. Emma H. Taylor, issue : Emma, Claudia, and William H.

SUSAN PENDLETON[6], (William[5], William[4], Nathaniel[3], Henry[2], Philip[1],) m. James Campbell Orrick, issue : 1. Rev. William Pendleton[7], Dean of Cathedral at Reading Pa.; 2. Charles James[7], m. Helen Marr Lewis, issue : Jesse Lewis[8], Virginia Pendleton[8], and Helen Cromwell[8].

ROBERT S. PENDLETON[6], (William[5], William[4], Nanthaniel[3], Henry[2], Philip[1],) m. Mary A. Pfieffer, issue : 1. Mary M[7].; 2. William H[7]., m. Ellen Wright; 3. J. Philip B[7]., m. Edith Hower; 4. Robert Edmund[7].

REV. J. PHILIP B. PENDLETON[7], (Robt. S[6]., William[5], William[4], Nathaniel[3], Henry[2], Philip[1].) m. Edith F. Hower. Rector of St. George's Church, Schenectady, N. Y., issue: Edith May St. George[8], Edmund Randolph[8], and Philip Clayton[8].

WILLIAM PENDLETON[6], (William[5], William[4], Nathaniel[3], Henry[2], Philip[1].) was b. 1817, d. 1873; m.Henrietta, dau. of Dr. Philip Grymes Randolph; was ordained at the Theological Seminary, 1843. Had parishes in Fauquier, Roanoke, and Bedford counties; was an eloquent preacher, and an indefatigable worker; issue: 1. Lucy Welford Randolph[7]; 2. Susie Randolph[7]; 3. Mary Randolph[7]; 4. Philip Randolph[7]; 5. Henrietta Grymes[7]; 6. Ellen Shepherd[7]; 7. Garnett Peyton[7]; 8. Rev. William H. K[7].

EDMUND PENDLETON[5], (Philip[4], Nathaniel[3], Henry[2], Philip[1].) m.——issue: Isaac Purnell[6]; 2. Serena[6], m.——Dandridge.

ANNE PENDLETON[5], (Philip[4]. Nathaniel[3], Henry[2], Philip[1].) m.——Kennedy; issue: 1. John Pendleton[6], b. in Balt. Oct. 25, 1795, d. in Newport, R. I. Aug. 18, 1870. (LL. D. H. H. 1863, author and politician, M. C., Sec. U. S. Navy 1852); 2. Andrew[6]; 3. Philip P[6].; 4. Anthony[6], U. S. Senator.

ELIZABETH PENDLETON[5], (Philip[4], Nathaniel[3], Henry[2], Philip[1].) m.—— Hunter; issue: 1. Philip Pendleton[6]; 2. David[6]; 3. Andrew[6], Charlestown, W. Va., (distinguish lawyer); 4. Edmund P[6]; 5. Elizabeth[6], m.——Strother, issue: Gen. D. H. Strother, "Porte Crayon"; 6. Mary Matthews[6]: 7. Moses H[6].; 8. Louisa Brooke[6]; 9. Nancy[6], m: Rev. John Hoge, D. D., issue: John Blair, (Circuit Judge, W. Va.)

ELIZABETH PENDLETON[4], (Nathaniel[3], Henry[2], Philip[1].) m. Benjamin Tutt; issue: 1. Mildred[5], m. Burkett Jett, of Loudon county, Va.; 2. Lucy[5], m. John Shackleford, (Commonwealth Att'y., Culpeper county, Va.); 3. Dau[5], m. Capt. John Williams; 4. Dau[5], m. William Broadus, (Clerk of Culpeper county, Va.); 5. Elizabeth[5]; 6. Annie[5], m. Robert Catlett, of Fauquier county; 7. Chas. P[5]., issue: Dau. m. Charles Bonnycastle (Prof. Univ. of Va.), Dau. m. Joshua Colston, Dau. m. Maj.——Throgmorton, of Loudon county.

LUCY TUTT[5], (Elizabeth[4], Nathaniel[3], Henry[2], Philip[1];) m. John Shackleford, issue: 1. Elizabeth[6], m. Minor Gibson of Rappahannock county, in 1818; 2. Mary[6], m. Col. Catlett Gibson, of Culpeper county; 3. Henry[6], m. Miss Ross, Culpeper county; 4. Barlow[6], m. Miss Doty, of Wisconsin; 5. St. Pierre[6], m. Elvira Gibson; 6. Muscoe Livingston[6], U. S. A., killed in Mexico; 7. Martha[6], m. Richard Spotswood; 8. John Lyne[6]; 9. Benjamin Howard[6], m. Rebecca Green, dau. of Jones Green.

ELIZABETH SHACKELFORD[6], (Lucy[5] (Tutt), Elizabeth[4], Nathaniel[3], Henry[2], Philip[1].) m. Minor Gibson; issue: 1. Lucy E[7].; 2. Mary Ellen[7], m. James Porter, M. D., Frostting, Md.; 3. Martha Irene[7]; 4. Isaac[7], (Episcopal clergyman) m. Annie Wingerd, of Georgetown, D. C., 1853; 5. Alcinda Esther[7], m. G. E. Porter, M. D., of Md.; 6. John St. Pierre[7], M. D., m. Mary Wallace, Augusta, Ga.; 7. Moses[7]; 8. James Green[7].

REV. ISAAC GIBSON[7], (Elizabeth[6] (Shackleford), Lucy[5] (Tutt), Elizabeth[4], Nathaniel[3], Henry[2], Philip[1];) m. Annie Wingerd; issue: 1. John Shackleford[8], (Episcopal clergyman), m. 1881, Ilicia Davis, dau. of Dr. J. M. Davis, Trenton, N. J.; 2. Ethel Wingerd[8]; 3. Muscoe Minor[8], (Lawyer) m. Amy Whitton, Norristown, Pa.; 4. Delia Pendleton[8].

REV. JOHN SHACKLEFORD GIBSON[8], (Rev. Isaac Gibson[7]), Elizabeth[6], (Shackleford), Lucy[5] (Tutt), Elizabeth[4], Nathaniel[3], Henry[2], Philip[1].) m. Ilicia Davis; issue: 1. Frances Bodine[9], b. Nov. 1881; 2. James Davies[9], b. Oct. 1883; 3. Anna[9], b. Sept. 1885; 4. John Shackleford[9], b. Jan. 1887; 5. Philip Pendleton[9], b. June 1890.

MUSCOE M. GIBSON[8], (Rev. Isaac Gibson[7], Elizabeth[6] (Shackleford), Lucy[5] (Tutt), Elizabeth[4], Nathaniel[3], Henry[2], Philip[1]). m. Amy Whitton; issue: 1. Anna Bertha[9]; 2. Joseph Whitton[9].

MARY E. GIBSON[7], Elizabeth[6] (Shackleford) Gibson, Lucy[5] (Tutt), Elizabeth[4], Nathaniel[3], Henry[2], Philp[1]). m. Dr. Jas. Porter; issue: 1. Lucy[8], m. in Maryland; 2. Glissen[8], m. Hattie Hollingsworth, Winchester.

ALCINDA E. GIBSON[7], (Elizabeth[6] (Shackleford), Lucy[5] (Tutt), Elizabeth[4], Nathaniel[3], Henry[2] Philip[1]). m. G. E. Porter; issue: 1. Emma[8]; 2. Frank[8], Minister M. E. Church, m. Miss Miller; 3. Muscoe[8], d. naval cadet at Annapolis; 4. Elizabeth Pendleton[8]; 5. Minor Gibson M. D[8].; 6. Alexander Shaw M. D[8]., Surgeon U. S. A., m. Miss Keen.

JOHN ST. PIERRE GIBSON[7], (Elizabeth[6] (Shackleford), Lucy[5] (Tutt), Elizabeth[4], Nathaniel[3], Henry[2], Philip[1]). m. Mary Wallace; issue: 1. Edwin Lacey[8], M. D., m. Mary Miller, Raleigh, N. C.; 2. Elizabeth Pendleton[8].

MARY SHACKLEFORD[6], (Lucy[5] (Tutt), Elizabeth[4]. Nathaniel[3], Henry[2], Philip[1]). m. Col. Jonathan Catlett Gibson; issue: 1. Mary Catlett[7], m. Milton Fitzhugh, and had Milton Catlett Fitzhugh, of California; 2. Lucy Ellen[7], m. John Strother Buckner (see issue below.); 3. Ann Eustace[7], m. James B. Welch, of Ala., died leaving Leila[8], m. A. H. Davis, Eustace, m. Sally Berry, Susan, m. James Leisure, and Thomas; 4. Wm. St. Pierre[7], Lieut. Cav. C. S. A. Killed at Westminster; 5. Jonathan Catlett[7], (enlisted as a private in the Culpeper Minute Men. Was rapidly promoted and became Colonel of the 49th. Virginia Infantry, succeeding Col. Wm ("Extra Billy") Smith. Represented Culpeper county in the Virginia House of Delegates for a number of terms). m. Mary G. Shackleford, and had Edwin H[8]., m. Janie Grigg, having Jonathan Catlett[9] and Edwin Agnew[9]; and Felix[8], died single; 6. Mildred Williams[7], died young and unmarried; 7. John Shackleford[7], died unmarried; 8. Susan[7],died young; 9. Eustace[7]. m. Mattie Lacklin, and had Pierre, Howard and Lee. Represented the Huntingdon, W. Va. district in the House of Delegates, being Speaker, and also in the U. S. House of Representatives for two terms; 10. Edwin[7], died single.

LUCY ELLEN GIBSON[7], (Mary[6] (Shackleford), Lucy[5] (Tutt), Elizabeth[4], Nathaniel[3], Henry[2], Philip[1]). m. John Strother Buckner, having 1. Mary Elizabeth[8], who m. Richard P. Spiers, of North Carolina, and had Winfield Buckner[9], Mary Dandridge[9], and Helen Strother[9]; 2. Aylette Hawes[8], who m. Anna Burt, of Ala., and had Bert[9], John Strother[9], Aylette Hawes[9], Martha Ball[9]; 3. Anne Eustace[8]; 4. Eugenie[8], who m. W. I. Winfield, of North Carolina, and had John Buckner[9], Edith Spottswood[9], Courtlandt Scott[9], Gladys Gibson[9], Richard Marshall[9], and William Meade[9]; 5. Blanche St. Pierre[8], who m. John E. Dove, and had Lucile Buckner[9].

HENRY SHACKLEFORD[6], (Lucy[5] (Tutt), Elizabeth[4], Nathaniel[3], Henry[2], Philip[1]). m. Elizabeth Ross; issue: 1. Mary George[7], m. Col. Jonathan Catlett Gibson; 2. Lucy[7], m. 1st. Judge Sinclair. 2nd. Emile Le Grande; 3. Kate[7], m. Corbin Jameson; 4. Bessie Lee[7], m. Capt. C. H. Lester, U. S. A.; 5. Shirley[7], m. Rev. W. R. Davis, and had Henry Shackleford[8].

DESCENDANTS OF JOHN PENDLETON (HENRY, PHILIP.)

John, 4th. son of Henry and Mary (Taylor) Pendleton, b. 1719, d. 1799, was in his 58th. year at the beginning of the Rev. war; he held various offices of honor and trust in the Colony of Va., and in the Senate. He was appointed by a convention of delegates of the Counties and Corporations in the Colony of Va. at Richmond Town, on Monday, July, 17th., 1775, to sign a large issue of Treasury notes. These notes were issued upon the credit, taxes and duties having been suspended to suit the distressed circumstances of the Colonists. The issue was about £350,000 and the ordinance read; "of the notes to be so issued, 50,000 shall be of the denomination of one shilling, and shall be signed by John Pendleton, Jr., Gentleman, which notes last named shall be on the best paper. John Pendleton was appointed, by the Governor of Va., Judge of her courts at a time when they were composed of the leading men of the Colony." (Taken from Henning's Statutes at large, 9th Vol). He m. 1st.———James; issue: 1. Edmund^4, b. 1758, m. 1773, Mildred Pollard; 2. John^4; 3. Elizabeth4; 4. Mary^4. m. 2nd. Sarah Madison, (cousin of Pres. Madison), issue: 1. Henry^4; 2. Sarah^4; 3. James^4; 4. Lucy^4; 5. Thomas^4.

EDMUND PENDLETON^4, (John^3, Henry^2, Philip^1). of White Plains, Caroline county, m. Mildred Pollard, youngest sister of Sarah Pollard, 2nd. wife of Judge Edmund Pendleton. Issue: 1. Edmund^5, b. 1774, m. 1794, 1st. Jane B. Page, 2nd. 1798, Lucy Nelson; 2. Mildred^5, b. 1776, m. 1798, Thomas Page; 3. John^5, m. Annie Lewis.

EDMUND PENDLETON^5, (Edmund^4, John^3 Henry^2, Philip^1). The estate called "Edmundton," was given to him by his great-uncle, Judge Edmund Pendleton. He m. 1st. Jane Burwell Page; issue: one dau. Elizabeth Page, m. John C. Sutton. Edmund m. 2nd. Lucy Nelson in May, 1798; issue: 1. Hugh Nelson^6, m. 1st. Lucy Nelson; 2nd Elizabeth Digges; 2 Mildred^6, m. Edmund A. Pendleton, of Augusta, Ga.; 3. Judith Page^6, m. Robert H. Harrison; 4. Francis Walker^6, M. D.,m. Sarah F. Turner; 5. Rev. William Nelson^6, m. Anzolette Page; 6. Robert Carter^6; 7. James L^6., m. Analethia Carter; 8. Guerdon H^6., m. Jane Byrd Page.

HUGH NELSON PENDLETON^6, (Edmund^5, Edmund^4, John^3, Henry^2, Philip^1). m. Lucy Nelson; issue: 1. Julia^7, m. James Allen, issue: Hugh Allen. He m. 2nd. Elizabeth Digges; issue: 1. Dudley Digges^7, m. Helen Boteler; 2. Robert Nelson^7, m. Fannie Gibson; 3. Kennith^7.

MILDRED PENDLETON^6, (Edmund^5, Edmund^4; John^3, Henry^2, Philip^1). m. Edmund A. Pendleton, of Augusta, Ga.; issue:
1. Edmund Lewis^7, m. Catista E. Norton; issue: Edmonia, m. F. S. Mosher
2. William^7, m. Zemula C. Walker. Has four sons.
3. John^7.
4. Hugh^7, (twin brother of John,) m. Rebecca Jones. Has two sons and two daughters.
5. Judith Page^7, m. Richard B. Williams.
6. Armistead Franklin^7, m. Isabella Garvin; issue: two daughters and one son.
7. Annie Elizabeth^7

JUDITH PAGE PENDLETON^6, (Edmund^5, Edmund^4, John^3, Henry^2, Philip^1). m. Robert H. Harrison; issue: 1. William L^7., m. Lama A. Lumpkin; issue: Robert, Rosa, Annie, Mary, and Lama; 2. Mary F^7., m. Dr. James E. Williams.

DR. FRANCIS WALKER PENDLETON^6, (Edmund^5, Edmund^4, John^3, Henry^2, Philip^1). m. Sarah F. Turner; issue: 1. Robert Carter^7; 2. Nannie F^7; 3. Mildred E^7., m. Tasker Crabbe, issue: Fannie.

REV. WILLIAM NELSON PENDLETON^6, (Edmund^5, Edmund^4, John^3, Henry^2, Philip^1). m. Anzolette Page; issue: 1. Susan^7, m. Ed. Lee; 2. Mary^7; 3. Rose^7; 4. Alexander S^7., m. Kate Corbin, d. 1864; 5. Nancy^7; 6. Lella^7.

JAMES L. PENDLETON^6, (Edmund^5, Edmund^4, John^3, Henry^2, Philip^1). m. Analethia Carter; issue: 1. Samuel H^7., m. Sallie A., dau. of Philip H. Pendleton; 2. Thomas Hugh^7; 3. Emma Walker^7, m. Robert C. Little; 4. Martha Carter^7, m. Joseph M. Furqurean; 5. William J^7., m. Mary J. Royall.

JOHN PENDLETON^5, (Edmund^4, John^3, Henry^2, Philip^1). m. Annie Lewis; issue: 1. John Lewis^6; 2. Edmund Allen^6; 3. William Armstead^6; 4. Charles Lewis^6; 5. Robert Taylor^6; 6. Benjamin Franklin^6; 7. Nathaniel Philip Henry^6; 8. Elizabeth Allen^6; 9. Eveline Mildred^6.

Edmund[4] and Mildred (Pollard) Pendleton had five daughters: one m. ——Taylor; two m. ——Turners; one m. ——Page; one m. ——Richards.

HENRY PENDLETON[4], (John[3], Henry[2], Philip[1]) He was born in 1762, d. 1822. Mem. House of Delegates Va. 1805. m. 1st. Alcey Ann Winston, 2nd. Mrs. Mary B. (Overton) Burnley. Moved to Louisa county, 1786; issue: 1. Edmund[5], m. Unity Yancey Kimbrough; 2. John Beckerton[5], b. 1788; 3. Joseph[5], m. Elizabeth Hayes Goodwin; 4. Thomas M[5]., m. Miss Jackson, b. 1804; 5. J. B[5].; 6. Matilda W[5]., m. P. Strachan Barret; 7. Henry[5], b. 1789, d. 1801; 8. Sarah Madison[5], m. Philip Winston, of Hanover county, b. 1793; 9. Barbara Overton[5], m. William Philips, b. 1795; 10. Lucy A[5]., m. John Voroles, b. 1799; 11. Catherine R[5]., m. Dr. Frank Johnson, b. 1801; 12. Elizabeth[5], b. 1806; 13. Martha T[5]., m. Capt. J. M. Trice, b. 1803; 14. Wm. James[5], m. Catherine M. Harris; 15. Alice Winston[5]; 16. Samuella[5], m. Tompkins.

COL. EDMUND PENDLETON[5], (Henry[4], John[3], Henry[2], Philip[1]). m. Unity Kimbrough, and moved to Cuckoo, Louisa county, 1823. In the war of 1812 he was Capt. of a company from his State; issue: 1. Madison[6], m. Elizabeth Barrett; 2. Joseph K[6]., m. Charlotte Harris; 3. Elizabeth[6], m Thompson Goodwin; 4. William Kimbrough[6], m. 1st. Lavinia Campbell, 2nd. Clarinda Campbell, 3rd. Catherine King; 5. Sarah[6], d. young; 6. Henry[6], d. young; 7. Philip Barbour[6], m. Jane Kimbrough Holladay.

DR. MADISON PENDLETON[6], (Col. Edmund[5], Henry[4], John[3], Henry[2], Philip[1]). m. 1829, Elizabeth Kimbrough Barrett; issue: 1. John B[7]., mem. 23rd Va. Reg. Garnett's command, at Rich Mountain, 1861; 2. Edmund S[7]., 1st. Serg. Co. F. 4th Va. cavalry, also Ass't. Surgeon, C. S. A.; 3. Charles K[7]., 2nd. Serg. 4th Va. cavalry, prisoner in Fort Delaware 14 months; 4. Wm. B[7]., Adj., of Taliaferro's brigade, lost a limb at the battle of Cedar Mountain; 5. Joseph Madison[7]; 6. Philip Henry[7], Carrington's Battery, C. S. A., killed at Spottsylvania C. H., May 1864.

DR. EDMUND S. PENDLETON[7], (Madison[6], Col. Edmund[5], Henry[4], John[3], Henry[2], Philip[1]). m. 1st. Susan M. Trice, 2nd. Sallie W. Flipps; issue: 1. Mary Unity[8]; 2. James Madison[8], d. Jan. 14, 1899; 3. John Henry[8], d. March 5, 1900; 4. Katherine Kimbrough[8]; 5. Susie Strachan[8]; 6. Edmund Littleton[8]; 7. Edmund Strachan Jr[8]; 8. Littleton Flipps[8].

JOHN HENRY PENDLETON[8], (Dr. Edmund S[7]., Madison[6], Edmund[5], Henry[4], John[3], Henry[2], Philip[1]). m. Mamie G. Porter; issue: Edmund Barton[9].

KATHERINE K. PENDLETON[8], (Dr. Edmund S[7]., Madison[6], Edmund[5], Henry[4], John[3], Henry[2], Philip[1]), m. J. W. Smith, of N. C.; issue: Virginia Pendleton[9]; John Bellamy[9].

SUSIE S. PENDLETON[8], (Dr. Edmund S[7]., Madison[6], Edmund[5], Henry[4], John[3], Henry[2], Philip[1]). m. Edward Dillon, Lexington, Va.; issue: Edward Jr[9].

JOHN B. PENDLETON[7], (Madison[6], Edmund[5], Henry[4], John[3], Henry[2], Philip[1]) m. Sallie A. Meredith; issue: Elizabeth B[8]., m. Dr. Eugene Pendleton, issue: John Barret[9], d., Eugene Barbour[8], Lewis[8], Anne[8].

CHARLES PENDLETON[7], (Madison[6], Edmund[5], Henry[4], John[3], Henry[2], Philip[1]). m. Lucy T. Chandler; issue: 1. Madison Strachan[8], b. 1876; 2. Thomas Chandler[8], b. 1878; 3. Elizabeth Kimbrough[8], b. 1879; 4. Mary Washington[8], b. 1881; 5. Charles Kimbrough[8], b. 1885; 6. Harry Leigh[8], b. 1888; 7. Brodie Herndon[8], b. 1891.

WILLIAM B. PENDLETON[7], (Madison[6], Edmund[5], Henry[4], John[3], Henry[2], Philip[1]). m. Mrs. Juliana Meredith, (nee) Pendleton; issue: 1. Phil. Henry[8], m. Charlotte Reid; isssue: Julia and Elizabeth; 2. Alice O[8]., m. Schuyler Moon; 3. Julia Madison[8]; 4. Bessie K[8]; 5. William Barret Jr[8].

WILLIAM KIMBROUGH PENDLETON[6], (Col. Edmund[5], Henry[4], John[3], Henry[2], Philip[1]). Pres. Bethany College, Mem. Constitutional Convention, W. Va.,

1872; d. 1899; m. 1st. 1840, Lavinia Campbell, 2nd. 1845, Clarinda Campbell, 3rd. 1855, Catherine Huntington King; issue:

1. Alexander C[7].; b. 1841; 2. William C[7]., b.1849, m. Helen K. Austin; issue: Austin Campbell, b. 1881; 3. Clarinda Huntington[7], b. Aug. 25, 1856, m. 1879, Joseph Rucker Lamar, of Augusta, Ga.; issue: Philip Rucker[8], William Pendleton[8], Mary[8]; 4. Huntington King[7], b. 1861, m. 1884, Martha Wellman Paxton; issue: Katherine King[8], b. 1885, Mary Whitehead[8], b. 1886, George Paxton[8], b. 1888, Frances Jean[8], b. 1889; 5. Philip Yancey[7], b. 1863, m. 1893, Ada Harvout Lloyd; issue: William Lamar[8], b. 1895, Eleanor[8], b. 1898; 6. Winston Kent[7], 1869, m. 1898, Daisy Bell Watt; issue: Stewart Watt[8]; 7. Dwight Lyman[7], b. 1871, m. 1899, Sarah Prewitt.

JOSEPH K. PENDLETON[6], (Col. Edmund[5], Henry[4], John[3], Henry[2], Philip[1]). m. Charlotte Harris; issue: 1. Dr. Lewis[7], m. Mary Kean; 2. Jane[7], m. John Hunter, Jr.; 3. Henry[7].

ELIZABETH PENDLETON[6], (Col. Edmund[5], Henry[4], John[3], Henry[2], Philip[1]). m. Thompson Goodwin; Had Edmund P. Goodwin[7], m. Lucy Chiles; issue: 1. Weir R[8]., m. Virgie Chiles; issue: Virginia and Weir Jr.; 2. Rosa Elizabeth[8]; 3.Lucy Fendal[8]; 4. Edmund P[8]., m. Beulah Maddox; issue: Inez L., William P., Beulah L., Lucy R., and Edward P.; 5. Anna Rhodes[8]; 6. Thompson W.[8], m. Martha Terry; issue: Mary; 7. Fendal[8].

DR. PHILIP BARBOUR PENDLETON[6], (Col. Edmund[5], Henry[4], John[3], Henry[2], Philip[1]). m. Jane Kimbrough Holladay; issue: 1. Madison H[7]., m. E. Mildred Davis; 2. Eugene, M. D[7]., m. Elizabeth B. Pendleton; issue: John[8], Eugene[8], and Annie[8]; 3. Louise[7], m. Rev. I. J. Spencer; issue: Jessie[8], Gale[8], Eva[8] and Julia[8]; 4. Joseph K[7]., m. Ida Kaufman; 5. William W[7]., m. Blanche Craighill; issue: Philip C[8]; 6. Ella K[7]., m. D. S. McCarthy; issue: Jennie[8], Maria[8], Edith[8], Dan[8], and Ella[8]; 7. Lizzie Y[7]., m. Percey Thornton; issue: Henry[8], Dan[8], Flora[8], Mary[8]; 8. Philip Barbour Jr[7].

DR. JOSEPH W. PENDLETON[5], (Henry[4], John[3], Henry[2], Philip[1]). m. Elizabeth Hawes Goodwin; issue: 1. Maj. Joseph H[6]., m. Margaret Ewing; 2. John O[6]., b. 1829, m. 1851, Annie L. Harris; 3. Mary B[6]., b. 1833, m. 1857, Prof. Chas. J. Kemper; issue: Charles, b. 1859, George, b. 1870, Maury, b. 1874, Graham, b. 1877; 4. Elizabeth[6], m. Dr. John Anderson, 1854: issue: Elizabeth and Mattie; Mattie, m. John L. Bowles; issue: Elizabeth, John, and Augustus; 5. Lucy[6].

JOSEPH H. PENDLETON[6], (Dr. Joseph[5], Henry[4], John[3], Henry[2], Philip[1]). b. 1827, d. 1881, m. 1848, Margaret Ewing. Mem. House of Del. Va., 1863. Brevetted Lieut. Colonel C. S. A.; issue:

1. Joseph[7], b. 1840; 2. John O[7]., b. 1857; Mem., of Congress from W. Va., 1889-90; 3. Henry H[7]., b. 1853, Consul to Southampton, Eng., 1887-89, Assist. Atty. Gen. W. Va.; 4. Elizabeth W[7]., b. 1855; 5. Ida E[7]., b. 1858, m. 1876, Frank P. Jepson; issue: Evelyn[8]; 6. Virginia C[7]., b. 1861, m. 1888, Andrew U. Wilson; issue: John Pendleton[8]; 7. Margaret J[7]., b. 1866, m. 1892 Geo. S. Hughes; issue: John Pendleton[8].

JOHN B. PENDLETON[6], (Dr. Joseph[5], Henry[4], John[3], Henry[2], Philip[1]). b. 1829, m. 1851, Annie L. Harris; issue: 1. Sarah[7], b. 1852; 2. John[7], b. 1861, m. 1883, Corrinne M. Davis; issue: Edmund C[8]., Annie L[8]., Ida D[8]., Henry H[8]., David M[8]., John S[8]., and Philip D[8].; 3. Barbara[7], b. 1864, m. 1890, John Moomaw.

THOMAS M. PENDLETON[5], (Henry[4], John[3], Henry[2], Philip[1]). m. Miss Jackson; issue: William J[6]., and Elisha[6].

DR. WILLIAM JAS. PENDLETON[5],(Henry[4], John[3], Henry[2], Philip[1]). b. 1809, d. 1872 m. 1831. Catherine M. Harris; issue: 1. Dr. David H.[6], b. 1832, d. 1859, m. 1855, Juliana Hunter; issue: 1. Hunter, A. M. Ph D. (Gottengen) m. Louise White; issue: Nancy Lewis Hillah; 2. Fred H[6].; 3. Juliana[6], m. Wm. Meredith;

issue: Kate, Lottie, William; m. 2nd. William B. Pendleton; 5. Alice[6], b. 1843, d. 1877, m. 1860, Waller Overton; issue; Kate[7], b. 1871, Susan[7], b. 1874, and William[7], b. 1876.

MATILDA W. PENDLETON[5], (Henry[4], John[3], Henry[2], Philip[1]). b. 1792, d. 1840, m. 1810, P. Strachan Barret; issue: 1. Alexander B[6]; b. 1811, d. 1861, m. 1836, Juliana Harris, issue: Alexander[7], m. Emma E. Chinnock; issue: Lily[8], Cecil[8], Virginia[8], m. Theodore K. Gibbs; 2. John Henry[6]; 3. Mary[6], m. Samuel Mallory; issue: John B., Sarah Elizabeth, m.———Wilson; 4. Sarah[6], m. 1841, Waller Holladay; 5. William Thomas[6]; 6. Caroline[6]; 7. Lucy[6].

SARAH STRACHAN BARRET[6], (Matilda[5], Henry[4], John[3], Henry[2], Philip[1]). m. Waller Holladay; issue: 1. Mary[7], m. 1862, H. Fitzhugh Dade; issue: Fitzhugh[8], Barret[8], Waller[8], Jessie[8], Lelia[8], Albert[8]; 2. Mattie[7], m 1882, Miles H. Gardner; issue: Sarah[8]; 3. Louisa[7], b. 1845, m. Wm. H. McCarthy; issue: Frank[8], Agnes[8]; 4. Frederick[7], b. 1847, Mem. House of Delegates. Va., 1855-6, m. 1st. Janet Garrett, 2nd Fannie Garrett; issue: Garrett[8], Waller[8], Frederick[8], Sallie[8], Maxwell[8], and Lizzie[8].

JOHN B. MALLORY[7], (Mary A. Barret[6], Matilda W[5]., Henry[4], John[3], Henry[2], Philip[1]). m. Sallie Glass; issue: 1. Robert[8], m. Lockie White; issue: Holladay; 2. Mary[8], m. H. F. Dade Jr.; 3. John[8]; 4. Samuel[8].

MARY HOLLADAY[7], (Sarah K. Barret[6], Matilda W[5]., Henry[4], John[3], Henry[2], Philip[1]). m. H. F. Dade; issue: 1. Henry Fitzhugh[8], m. Mary Mallory; 2. Waller Holladay[8], m. 1st. Blanche Farra, 2nd. Eliz. Rhodehainel; issue: Anna Belle[9]; 3. Jessie Conway[8], m. E. D. Scrogin; issue: Blanche[9].

JOHN HENRY BARRET[6], (Matilda W[5]., Henry[4], John[3], Henry[2], Philip[1]). m. Susan Rankin; issue: John Henry[7], Jas. Rankin[7], Susan[7].

WILLIAM THOMAS BARRET[6], (Matilda W[5]., Henry[4] John[3], Henry[2], Philip[1]). m. Elizabeth Towles; issue: Thomas[7], Strachan[7], Betty[7], Alexander[7].

SARAH MADISON PENDLETON[5], (Henry[4], John[3], Henry[2], Philip[1]). m. Philip B. Winston; issue: William Overton[6], Bickerton L[8]., John R[6]., Philip[6], Barbara[6], Edmund Thomas[6], Joseph Pendleton[6], and O. M[6].

FRANCES SAMUELA PENDLETON[5], (Henry[4], John[3], Henry[2], Philip[1]). m. W. M. Tompkin; issue: Pendleton[6], Alexander[6], John[6], Joseph Bickerton[6].

BARBARA OVERTON PENDLETON[5], (Henry[4], John[3], Henry[2], Philip[1]). m. William H. Phillips; issue: 1. Sarah Eliz[6]., m. 1st. B. F. Trice, 2nd. C. C. Branford; 2. Dr. William H[6]., b. 1819, d. 1884; 3. Catherine J[6]., b. 1826, m. ———Kyle; 4. Joseph Pendleton[6], b. 1828, d. 1892; 5. Richard S[6]., b. 1830, d. 1856, m. M. E. Christian: 2 children; 6. Patty P[6]., b. 1833, m. Dr. John G. Boatwright.

JOHN HENRY BARRET[7], (John H. Barret[6], Matilda W[5]., Henry[4], John[3], Henry[2]; Philip[1]). m. Henrietta Offitt; issue: 1. Mary[8], m. Jas. Heddino; issue: J. Barret Spencer[9]; 2. Augusta[8], m. Earl Carley; issue: John Barret[9].

JAS. RANKIN BARRET[7], (John H. Barret[6], Matilda W[5]., Henry[4], John[3], Henry[2], Philip[1]). m. Lucy Stiles; issue: Henry[8], Susan[8].

SUSAN BARRET[7], (John H. Barret[6], Matilda W[5]., Henry[4], John[3], Henry[2], Philip[1]). m. Jas. Rankin; issue: Susan[8], Ewing[8].

THOMAS F. BARRET[7], (Thomas Barret[6], Matilda W[5]., Henry[4], John[3], Henry[2], Philip[1]). m. Clara Pringle; issue: 2 sons and 3 daughters.

STRACHAN BARRET[7], (William Thomas Barret[6], Matilda W[5]., Henry[4], John[3], Henry[2], Philip[1].) m. Margaret Rudy; issue: 4 sons.

ELIZABETH BARRET[7], (Wm. Thomas Barret[6], Matilda W[5]., Henry[4], John[3], Henry[2], Philip[1]). m. Fred. Eldridge.

EDMUND PENDLETON.

Was the fifth son of Henry Pendleton and Mary Taylor. His father died before his birth. The following sketch of him is taken from Appleton's Encyclopedia of American Biography:

"Edmund Pendleton, statesman, was born in Caroline county, Va. 9th Sept., 1721. His grandfather, Philip, descended from Pendleton, of Manchester, Lancaster county, England, came from Norwich, Eng., to this country in 1674. Edmund began his career in the Clerk's office of Caroline county. He was licensed to practice law in 1744; became County Justice in 1751, and the following year was elected to the House of Burgesses. In 1764 was one of the Committee to memorialize the King. During the session of 1766, he gave the opinion 'that the stamp act was void, for want of Constitutional authority in Parliament to pass it,' and voted in the affirmative on the resolution that the 'act did not bind the inhabitants of Virginia.' He was one of the Committee of correspondence in 1763; County Lieutenant of Caroline in 1774. A member of the colonial convention, of the latter year, that was consequent on the Boston Port Bill. and was chosen by that body to the first Continental Congress. Accordingly, in company with George Washington, Peyton Randolph, Patrick Henry, Benjamin Harrison, and Richard Henry Lee, he attended in Philadelphia in 1774. As President of Virginia Convention, he was at the head of the government of the Colony from 1775 until the creation of the Virginia constitution in 1776, and was appointed President of the Committee of Safety in that year. In May, 1776, he presided again over the convention, and drew up the celebrated resolutions, by which the delegates from Virginia were instructed to propose a declaration of independence in Congress, using the words that were afterwards incorporated almost verbatim with the Declaration. As the leader of the Cavalier or Planter class, he was the opponent of Patrick Henry, and as leader of the Committee of Public Safety, he was active in the control of the military and naval operations, and of the foreign corréspondence of Virginia. On the organization of the State Government, he was chosen Speaker of the House, and appointed, with Chancellor George Wythe and Thomas Jefferson, to revise the Colonial laws. In 1777, he was crippled for life by a fall from his horse; but the same year he was re-elected Speaker of the House of Burgesses, and President of the Court of Chancery. In 1779, he became President of the Court of Appeals, holding the office until his death. He presided over the State Convention, which ratified the Constitution of the United States in 1783. His masterly advocacy of the document gained him the encomium from Jefferson that 'taken all in all, he was the ablest man in debate that I ever met with.' He received very large grants of land from the State, and having no children, was ever generous to his nieces and nephews, whose descendants still hold his memory in tender veneration. He married twice—1st. Elizabeth Roy. 2nd. Sarah Pollard. He died in 1803."

JOHN PENDLETON[2], (Philip[1]). m.----Tinsley. Had son William[3], whose will, probated in Amherst county, gives the following children by name [this correction is made by the authority of a descendant of Edmund, the 4th son, who has a copy of the will of William, dated 1775.]:

1. Benjamin[4], emigrated after Rev. War to Kentucky; 2. Isaac[4], emigrated after Rev. War to Kentucky; 3. John[4], emigrated after Rev. War to Kentucky; 4. Edmund[4], emigrated to Tennessee: issue : Benjamin[5], emigrated to Missouri, and had Edmund[6], moved to Texas, having George C. Pendleton[7], Belton, Texas; 5. Richard[4], m.------Tinsley, his first cousin; issue : William[5], Betty[5], Lucy[5], Sarah[5], James[5], Pauline[5], Reuben[5], Polly[5], Richard[5], Henry[5]; 6. Reuben[4], m. Ann Garland, of Amherst; 7. James[4], m.------Rucker; 8. William[4]; 9. Polly[4], m.------Whitten; 10. Sarah[4], m.------Mahone; 11. Frances[4], m.------ Camden; 12. Betty[4], m.------Baldock; 13. Margaret[4]. m.------Miles.

REUBEN PENDLETON[4], (William[3], John[2], Philip[1]). m. Ann Garland; issue : 1. William Garland[5], Clerk of Richmond Chancery Court, Register of State Land Office, 1814-23, member of State Council, Proctor of Uni. of Va: 2. James

85., m.——Aldridge, of Amherst county, d. in California, 1851; 3. Nancy5, m. Capt.——Ware; 4. Sophia5, m.——Powell; 5. Polly5, m. 1st.——Wills, 2nd. ——Seay, 3rd.——Nowlin; 6. Eliza5, m. Walter Scott; 7. Jane5, m.——Crow; 8. Martha5, m. 1st.——Lucas, 2nd.——Stovall; 9. Frances5, m.——Staples; 10. Harriet5; 11. Micajah5, M. D., b. 1796, d. 1861. M. D. degree from U. of New York, 1816, U. of Penn. 1819, m. 1822, Louisa Jane Davis, b. 1806, d. 1840, greatgranddaughter of Robert and——(Hughes) Davis, who settled in Amherst about 1720 upon a tract of land numbering 10,000 acres. Their descendants by marriage are connected with the Beverleys, Dudleys, Raglands, Burks, Ellises, and other prominent Virginia familes. Micajah Pendleton m. 2nd. 1844, Mary Ann Cooper.

WILLIAM GARLAND PENDLETON5, (Reuben4, William3, John2, Philip1). m. Mary G. Alexander; issue : 1. Alexander6, officer in the National Observatory; 2. Stephen Taylor6, Principal of High School, Richmond, Va.; 3. Douglas6, engineer; 4. Mary6, m.——Hightower; 5. Eliza6, m.——Reid.

JAMES SHEPERD PENDLETON5, (Reuben4, William3, John2, Philip1). m.——Aldridge; issue : 1. Robert6, Clerk of Amherst county; 2. James Sheperd6, m. ——Mills, of Richmond; 3. Nancey6, m. William H. Rose.

MACAJAH PENDLETON5, (Reuben4, William3, John2, Philip1). m. 1st. Louisa Jane Davis, 2nd. Mary Ann Cooper; issue : 1. Edmund6, m. Cornelia Morgan, of Cincinati, O., (now living at Buchanan, Botetourt county, Va); issue : William W7., Lizzie C7., and E. Morgan7; 2. Ann Garland6, m. Lewis Bough, of Amherst county; issue : Cornelia P7., m.——Clarke, of Ga., Louisa Jane7, Virginia Grove7, Alice Dudley7, Nannie Lewis7; 3. James Dudley6, (M. D.) Assistant Clerk Va. Senate, m. Clara Pulliam, dau. of William Rock, of Buchanan county; issue : William D7., R. Edmund D7.; issue of Macajah and Mary Ann Cooper 1. William6, 2. Charles6, 3. Elizabeth6, 4. Walter6, 5. Louisa6.

PHILIP PENDLETON2, (Philip1). m. Elizabeth Pollard: issue : 1. Benjamin3, m. Mary Macon; 2. Daughter3.

BENJAMIN PENDLETON3, (Philip2, Philip1). m. Mary Macon; issue : 1. Jas4., (Officer in Rev. Army.); 2. Philip4, from whom the Pendletons of King and Queen county are descended; 3. Dau4., m.——Holmes.

ELIZABETH PENDLETON2, (Philip1). m. Samuel Clayton, of Caroline county; issue : 1. Major Philip3. of "Catalpa", m. Ann Coleman; issue : Maj. Philip4, of Rev. Army, Lucy4, m. William Williams, Susan4, m. Col. James Slaughter, Dau4., m. her first cousin, Nathaniel Pendleton, Dau4., m.——Crittenden; 2. Nancy3, m. Jeremiah Strother.

LUCY CLAYTON4, (Philip (Clayton)3, Elizabeth2, Philip1). m. William Williams; issue : 1. Lucy5, m. William Green, having one child, Judge John W. Green6, of the Va. Court of Appeals (see Green genealogy); 2. John5, m. Miss Hite (see Williams genealogy); 3. Gen. James5, m. Eleanor Green (see Williams and Green genealogy); 4. Philip5, and 5. William5, m.——Croutson and —— Burwell, respectively (see Williams genealogy); 6. Mary5, m. John Stevens, son of Gen. Edward Stevens, and died childless.

ISABELLA PENDLETON2, (Philip1). m Richard Thomas; issue : 1. Mary3, m. Thomas Barbour and had Gov. James and Judge Philip Barbour; 2. Catherine3, m. Ambrose Barbour; issue : several sons.

CATHERINE PENDLETON2, (Philip1). m. John Taylor, son of James Taylor, of Carlisle, Eng. issue: 1. Edmund3, m. Annie Lewis; 2. John3, m. Miss Lynne; 3. James3, m. Anne Pollard; 4. Philip3, m. Mary Walker; 5. William3, m. Miss Anderson; 6. Joseph3, m. Frances Anderson; 7. Mary3, m. Robert Penn; issue : Gabriel4; 8. Catherine3, m. Moses Penn; issue : John4, one of the "Signers"; 9. Isabella3, m. Samuel Hopkins; 10. Elizabeth3, m. 1st.——Lewis, 2nd.——Bullock.

THE WILLIAMS FAMILY.
[By George M. Williams.]

The Williams family of Culpeper are descendants of Peere Williams, of London, Barrister at Law, and author of Reports of Decisions in the English Courts of his day.

Three brothers, James, John, and Otho, emigrated together about the year of 1698, and landed at the mouth of the Rappahannock River. They ascended the river and when they reached the Falls, where Fredericksburg now is, they separated. James went to Maryland, John remained, and Otho went to North Carolina.

John^1 m. a Miss Dixon, who, according to the family tradition, was of the same family as Roger Dixon, the first Clerk of Culpeper county—He had two children: William^2 and John^2. William^2 m. Lucy Clayton, dau. of Major Philip Clayton, "Catalpa," and had eight children : 1. John^3, who was a Major in the Revolution; 2. James^3, who was a Captain in the Revolution and General in the war of 1812, m. Eleanor Green; 3. Philip^3; 4. William C^3.; 5. Mary^3, m. John Stevens, son of Gen. Stevens, but had no children; 6. Lucy^3, m. William Green; 7. Sasannah^3, died unmarried; 8. Isabelle^3, died unmarried.

John^2, the second son of John^1, m. Mary Pendleton, and died leaving no children.

John^3, the oldest son of William^2, m. Miss Hite and had three children : 1. Isaac H^4: 2. John G^4; 3. Ellen^4.

Isaac H^4. was a distinguished lawyer, and m. Lucy Slaughter, dau. of Capt. Philip Slaughter (see Slaughter genealogy), and had seven children : 1. Ophelia^5; 2. P. French^5; 3. Eleanor^5; 4. Isaac H^5., died unmarried; 5. Eliza^5, died unmarried; 6. John James^5; 7. Lucy Ann^5.

Ophelia^5 m. Rev. George A. Smith, of Alexandria, and had seven children: 1. Isaac^6, who never married; 2. George Hugh^6, Colonel in Confederate service; 3. Mrs. Dunbar Brooke^6; 4. Eliza^6, who m. Mr. Corse, of Alexandria; 5. Henry^6; 6. Eleanor^6; 7. Belle^6.

P. French^5, the second daughter of Isaac H^4., m. John M. Patton, one of the ablest lawyers of his day, for eight years a member of Congress, and had nine children : 1. Robert W^6. who died unmarried; 2. John M^6.; 3. Isaac W^6.; 4. George S^6.; 5. W. Tazewell^6; 6. Eliza^6; 7. James French^6; 8. Hugh Mercer^6; 9. William M^6.

Eleanor^5, the daughter of Isaac H^4., m. Dr. Hite, of Amherst County, and had five children : 1. Isaac^6; 2. Edmund^6; 3. Fontaine^6; 4. Maury^6; 5. Eliza^6.

John James^5, son of Isaac H^4., m. Miss Thompson, and had three children : 1. Frank^6; 2. Henry^6; 3. Thornton^6.

John G^4., the second son of John^3, the son of William^2, m. Mary Tutt and had two children : 1. Mary Stevens^5; 2. John G. Jr^5. Mary Stevens^5 m. Henry Porter, and had several children. John G^5. m. Miss Mason, and had two children: a son and daughter living in Giles county, Virginia.

Ellen^4, the daughter of John^3, the son of William^2, m. Nimrod Long, and had three children : 1. Daughter^5, who m. Mr. Turner—She was the mother of Judge R. H. Turner^6, of the Winchester Circuit, and of S. S. Turner^6, member of Congress; 2. Daughter^5, who m. Mr. Lovell, and had one child, John T^6., who was Judge of Warren county; 3. John^5, who left no children.

James^3, the second son of William^2, m. 1st. Eleanor Green, and had three children : 1. William^4; 2. James^4; 3. Sarah^4. He m. 2nd. Elizabeth Bruce, and had six children : 1. Fanny B^4; 2. Charles B^4.; 3. William B^4; 4. Lucy Ann^4; 5. Philip^4; 6. Elizabeth^4.

William^4 m. Anne Stubblefield, and had nine children : 1. Anne^5 and 2. Ellen^5 (twins); 3. James^5; 4. Sally^5; 5. Fanny^5; 6. William^5; 7. George S^5.; 8.

Charles B. Jr⁵.; 9. Lucy⁵. Of these, Anne⁵ m. Dr. Alfred Taliaferro, and had six children : 1. Ellen Green⁶; 2. Susan Conway⁶; 3. Anne⁶, 4. Georgianna⁶; 5. William⁶; 6. Alice⁶. Ellen⁵, one of the twins, m. Ennis Adams, of New York, and died without children. James⁵, the oldest son, m. Rosalie Fitzhugh, and had four children : 1. William F⁶; 2. Charles B⁶; 3. Thomas⁶; 4. James G⁶.

Sally⁵, the 3rd. daughter, m. Edwin S. Taliaferro, and had one child : Sally⁶, who m. James Vass, and had three children.

Fanny⁵, the 4th. daughter, m. Joseph Pannill, and had seven children : 1. Lucy⁶, 2. William⁶, 3. George⁶, 4. Sallie⁶, 5. John⁶, 6. Susan⁶, 7. Fanny⁶.

William⁵, the second son of William⁴, m. Fanny Pannill, the sister of Joseph, and had two children : 1. William⁶; 2. Lucy⁶. He was married three times, but had no children by his second or third wife.

George S⁵., the 3rd. son of William⁴, moved to Kentucky; was married and had children.

Charles B⁵., the 4th son of William⁴, died unmarried.

Lucy Ann⁵, the 5th daughter of William⁴, m. Thomas Fitzhugh, and had four children : 1. Sally Roane⁶; 2. Parke⁶; 3. William⁶; 4. Nannie⁶. Sally Roane⁶ m.——O'Mohundro, left no children; Parke⁶ m. Miss Wrekham, and had one child, William⁷; Nannie⁶ m. Wash. Peace.

William F. Williams⁶ m. Margaret N. Walker, and had James A⁷., Ellen N⁷., Rosalie F⁷., Margaret Bruce⁷, and Lucy Ann⁷.

Charles Bruce Williams⁶ m. Kate Daniel, and had Inez⁷, Celeste⁷, Alpheus⁷, Chas. Bruce⁷, Bernard⁷, and Lucile⁷.

James Green Williams⁶ m. Jessie Wood, and had Annie Bell⁷, Mary⁷ and James M⁷.

James⁴, the son of James³, died unmarried.

Sarah⁴, the 1st daughter of James³, m. George F. Strother, and had one child, James French⁵. (See Strother genealogy).

Fanny B⁴., the 2nd. daughter of James³, m. Fayette Ball, son of Col. Burgess Ball, who was a cousin of General Washington, and who m. a daughter of General Washington's brother, Charles. She left no children.

Charles B⁴., the 3rd son of James³, m. Ann M. Hackley, and had eight children : 1. Ann Eliza⁵, who died in childhood; 2. Fanny⁵, who m. E. S. Taliaferry (being his second wife) and had three children :——⁶, Alfred⁶ and James⁶; 3. James Edward⁵, m. Miss Harrison, but had no children; 4. Finella⁵, died unmarried; 5. Bessie⁵, m. George H Reid, and had two children; 6. Janet Bruce⁵, m. Wm. S. Hill, but had no children; 7. Harriet⁵, m. C. D. Hill, and had one child, a daughter; 8. Charles U⁵., a prominent lawyer in Richmond, m. Miss Davenport and had five children.

William B⁴., the second son of James³, by his second wife, m. Miss Pate, but left no children.

Lucy Ann⁴, the second daughter of James³ by his second wife, m. John S. Pendleton, the brilliant orator of Culpeper, but had no children.

Philip⁴, the 3rd son of James³ by his second wife, m. Mildred Catlett, and had six children : 1. James⁵, who died in childhood; 2. Betty Bruce⁵, who never married; 3. Robert⁵, Brigadier and Adjt. Gen., U. S. Army, m. Mrs. Douglas, widow of Senator Stephen A. Douglas and had six children : Robert⁶, m. Miss Yoe, of Chicago, Ellen⁶, m. Bryson Patton, Lieut. U. S. Navy, Philip⁶, m. Miss Harrison, Adele⁶, James⁶ and Mildred⁶; 4. Anne⁵, who died in childhood; 5. George M⁵., m. Miss G. S. Long, of Baltimore, and had twelve children : I. Elizabeth⁶, m. T. Clifford Stark; II. Lucy Pendleton⁶, m. Edwin S. Slaughter; III. Mildred B⁶., IV. Ellis B⁶., V. Helen V⁶., VI. John S. P⁶., VII. George P⁶., VIII. Mary J⁶., IX. Gertrude M⁶., X. Bettie B⁶., XI. Pendleton L⁶., XII. Anne Harvey⁶; 6. Lucy Mary⁶, who died in childhood.

Elizabeth S⁴., the 3rd daughter of James³, by his second wife, m. Dr. George Morton and had eight children : 1. William J⁵., who died unmarried; 2. Geo. P⁵., who died unmarried; 3. Lucy P⁵., who m. John Cooke Green, for twenty years Commonwealth's Attorney for Culpeper county, and a distinguished lawyer (see Green genealogy); 4. Jeremiah⁵. who m. Charlotte Turner; 5. Chas. B⁵., who m. Miss Dickinson; 6. John P⁵., who died unmarried; 7. Thomas D⁵., who m. Sally Pannill; and 8. James W⁵., member of the Legislature and Judge of Orange county, m. Miss Harper.

Jeremiah⁵, who m. Miss Turner, had six children : 1. Fenton⁶, who m. Mr. Dejarnette; 2. Bessie⁶, who m. Mr. Marshall; 3. Lucy⁶; 4. Wallace⁶; 5. Kate⁶; and 6. Jeremiah⁶.

Charles B⁵., who m. Miss Dickinson, had one child : Rev. W. J. Morton⁶.

Thomas D⁵., who m. Sally Pannill, had three children : 1. Thomas⁶; 2. James⁶; 3. Fanny Bruce⁶.

James W⁵., who m. Miss Harper, had five children : 1. Walton⁶; 2. George⁶; 3. Jackson⁶; 4. Caroline⁶; and 5. Jas. Williams⁶.

Lucy³, the oldest daughter of William², m. William Green, son of Col. John Green, of the Revolution, and had one child, John Williams⁴, who was Judge of Court of Appeals, (see Green genealogy).

Philip³, the 3rd son of William², moved to Shenandoah county, of which he was clerk for fifty years, and married Miss Croutson. He had seven children : 1. Lucy⁴, m. Capt. A. P. Hill, and had no children; 2. Philip⁴; 3. Sarah⁴, m. Col. Travis Twyman, and had no children; 4. James⁴; 5. Samuel C⁴.; 6. Mary⁴; 7. Ellen⁴.

Philip⁴, m. 1st. Miss Hite, 2nd. Miss Dunbar. By his first wife he had two children : 1. Dr. Philip C⁵., of Baltimore, who m. Miss Whitridge, and had four children : I. John W⁶; II. T. Dudley⁶; III. W. Whitridge⁶; IV. a Daugter⁶; 2. Anne⁵, who m. Judge T. T. Fauntleroy, and had one child, Philip⁶. By his second wife Philip⁴, had six children : 1. Mary L. D⁵; 2. John J⁵; 3. Philipa⁵; 4. T. Clayton⁵; 5. Sally⁵; 6. Lucy⁵.

Mary L. D⁵., m. Rev. James B. Avirett and had two children : John W⁶., and P. W⁶.

John J⁵., m. Miss Gray and has several children.

James⁴, the second son of Philip³, m. Miss Ott, and had one child, a daughter, who m. Mr. Miller.

Samuel C⁴., the 3rd son of Philip³, m. Miss Otland, and had six children : 1. James H⁵., a prominent lawyer of Woodstock; 2. Samuel C. Jr⁵.; 3. William⁵; 4. Lucy⁵, who m. Judge Lovell, of Warren county; 5. Betty⁵, who m. Thomas Marshall, of Fauquier; and 6. A daughter, who m. L. Wagner, of Richmond.

Mary⁴, daughter of Philip³, m. Dr. Magruder, of Woodstock, and had several children.

Ellen⁴, daughter of Philip³, m. Rev. Dr. Boyd, and had three children : 1. Holmes⁵, prominent lawyer of Winchester; 2. Philip W⁵., merchant of Winchester; 3. Hunter⁵, Judge of District Court in Maryland.

William C³., the 4th son of William², m. Alice Burwell, of Gloucester county, and had three children : 1. John G⁴.; 2. Lewis B⁴.; 3. Lucy⁴.

John G⁴., m. Miss Cringan, of Richmond, and had six children : 1. William Clayton⁵, 2. John Jr⁵.; 3. Chauning⁵; 4. Mary Ogilvie⁵; 5. Robert F⁵; and 6. Alice⁵.

Lewis B⁴., second son of William C³., married three times; 1st. Mary Catlett, 2nd. Charlotte Blair, 3rd. Mrs. O'Bannon. By his first wife he had eight children, by his 2nd. and 3rd. none. His children were : 1. Wm. Grymes⁵, Judge of Orange county and a member of the Legislature; 2. Lewis B. Jr⁵.; 3. Mary Blair⁵; 4. Charles⁵; 5. Mildred⁵; 6. Alice⁵; 7. John G⁵; and 8. Anne⁵.

William Grymes[5], m Roberta Hansborough, and has five children : 1. Richard C[6].; 2. Wm. Clayton[6]; 3. Lewis B[6].; 4. Bessie[6]; and 5. Samuel[6].

Lewis B[5]., was Colonel of the 1st. Va. Regiment in the Civil War, and was killed in Pickett's famous charge at Gettysburg. He was never married.

Mary Blair[5], m. Mr. Leigh and has several children : 1. Charles[6], died unmarried; 2. Mildred[6], m. R. S. Booton, of Madison, and has eight children : Lucy[7], Richard[7], Susan[7], Lewis[7], Kate[7], William[7], Alice[7], and George[7].

Lucy[4], the daughter of William C[3]., m. J. A. Smith, cashier for many years of Freedman's Bank of Virginia, and had one son, Bathurst[5], who lives in Tenn.

MISCELLANEOUS ITEMS.
—ooo—

LIEUT.-GENERAL AMBROSE POWELL HILL.

Among the men of Culpeper who deserve commemoration is General Ambrose Powell Hill (one of Jackson's favorite lieutenants), who illustrated his knightly prowess on many a battle-field, sealing his patriotism at last with the blood of martyrdom. He was the son of the late Major Thomas Hill, and a lineal descendant of Capt. Ambrose Powell, the old vestryman of Bromfield Parish, Culpeper, in 1752.

THE BROWN FAMILY.

There lies before me a patent for land in the South Fork of the Gourdvine River, from Lord Fairfax, proprietor of the Northern Neck, to John Brown ; he paying every year the free rent of one shilling sterling for every 50 acres, on the Feast of St. Michael the Archangel. It is dated 22d June, in the 20th year of our Sovereign Lord George II., by the grace of God King of Great Britain, France and Ireland, and Defender of the Faith, A. D. 1749.

(Signed)   FAIRFAX.

This land was surveyed by Major Philip Clayton, and it adjoins the land of Thomas Howison and Wm. Brown. It appears in the vestry-book that Daniel Brown was sheriff and collector of the parish levy. Coleman Brown was clerk and lay reader in the church. Thomas Brown was undertaker of a chapel in the Little Fork ; and Capt. Wm. Brown was the contractor for an addition to Buck Run Church. These are the ancestors of the late Armistead and Daniel Brown and their families.

MEDICAL MEN IN CULPEPER BEFORE THE REVOLUTION.

The vestries having charge of the poor, boarded them among the planters, and furnished them with medical attention. The first physician employed by the vestries, as early as 1734, was Dr. Andrew Craig, then Dr. Thomas Howison, then Dr. James Gibbs, and in 1755 Dr. Michael Wallace, ancestor of the Winstons now living in Culpeper, and of the Wallaces of Fredericksburg and Stafford County. Dr. Michael Wallace was born in Scotland, and apprenticed in his youth at Glascow to Dr. Gustavus Brown, of Port Tobacco, Maryland, to learn medicine. The indenture is now in the possession of one of his descendants in Kentucky. That seems to have been the way (before medical schools) to make a doctor.

THE LAWYERS.

Lawyers who served as counsel to the vestries of St. Mark's were : 1st. Zachary Lewis 1731 to 1750. 2d. John Mercer 1752, 3d. John Lewis 1754, and lastly, Gabriel Jones, the eminent "Valley Lawyer," who married Miss Strother of Stafford County, sister of Mrs Madison, the mother of Bishop Madison. The present Strother Jones of Frederick is the great-grandson of Gabriel Jones the lawyer. Mercer was the author of Mercer's Abridgment of the Laws of Virginia. He was the father of Judge James Mercer, of Ch. Fenton Mercer, and of John F. Mercer, Governor of Maryland.

TOWNS IN CULPEPER.

The first town, by Act of Assembly, was Fairfax in 1759. The name has unhappily been changed to Culpeper. After the Revolution there was a furore for towns, under the impression that they would draw mechanics and increase trade.

STEVENSBURG.

Was established in 1782, on 50 acres of land where William Bradley then lived. French Strother, B. Davenport, Robert Slaughter, Robert Pollard, and Richard Waugh were the first Trustees, all vestrymen but one. In 1799 the Academy was established by Act of Assembly, and its first Trustees were Robert Slaughter, Charles Carter, David Jameson, R. Zimmerman, Wm. Gray, Gabriel Gray, Philip Latham and William C. Williams.

CLERKSBURG, NOT CLARKSBURG.

In 1798, 25 acres of James Baysy's land vested in Thomas Spilman, Henry Pendleton. Jr., Bywaters and Reid.

JEFFERSON.

On 25 acres of Joseph Coons' land, vested in John Fishback, Thomas Spilman, John Spilman, Thomas and Robert Freeman, P. Latham, F. Payne, F. F. Fergurson and John Dillard.

SPRINGFIELD.

On 25 acres of John Spilman's land, vested in John and Thomas Spilman, and Messrs. Matthews, Fletcher and Tapp. Clerksburg, Jefferson and Springfield are in the Little Fork. They yet survive, but have not realized the anticipations of their founders, whose names we have reproduced above.

JAMESTOWN.

It will be news to some that we have a Jamestown in Culpeper. 25 acres of land were set apart by the General Assembly to be called Jamestown, and Gabriel Green, A. Haynie, and Messrs. Grant, Corbin and Howe were Trustees to lay it off into convenient lots and streets. Who will recognize in Jamestown our modest James City ?

BRICK MAKING IN VIRGINIA.

The prevailing opinion that our colonial churches were built of imported brick is an error. As to those in the interior of the country, the transportation of the brick was an insuperable obstacle. It is possible that a few of the churches on tidewater may have been made of imported brick, but as to many of these there are unquestionable traces of brick-kilns very near them, in some cases within the churchyard. The following bill show that bricks were made even at Williamsburg as early as 1708 :

HENRY CARY to the Council, 1708.

150 loads of wood at 12s—£6 7 6.
Moulding and burning 70,009 bricks at 3s. 6d. per M.
Laborer's work resetting and burning 3s. 3d.

VESTRYMEN OF ST. MARK'S.

The names of the old vestrymen will all be found in order in the text. The following is an imperfect enumeration of the successors:—The last vestry under the old regime (1785) was composed of the following persons, viz. French Strother, Sam. Clayton, Rd. Yancey, William Ball, James Pendleton, Burkett Davenport, Cadwallader Slaughter, Lawrence Slaughter, James Slaughter. Then followed P. R. Thompson, P. Slaughter, Jno. Jameson, Rt. Slaughter, David Jameson, G. Jones, Wigginton, Wm. Broadus, Rd. Payne, Rt. Freeman, Thomas Freeman, John Spilman, Thos. Spilman, Peter Hansbrough, Isaac Winston, Waller Winston, Samuel Slaughter, John Thom, Geo Fitzhugh, Jno. Wharton, W. Williams, Fayette Mauzy, Dr. Thos. Barbour, Rt. A. Thompson, P. Slaughter, Jr., James Farish, Moses Green, Spilman, Rd. Randolph, Wm. Payne, S. R. Bradford, Garland Thompson, John Cooke Green, Wm. B. Slaughter, Dr. A. Taliaferro, Rd. Cunningham, T. S. Alcocke, S. S. Bradford, Frank Lightfoot, Jere. Morton, Geo Morton, P. P. Nalle, Jno. Knox, Downman, Dr. Hugh Hamilton, John Porter, Rt. Stringfellow, Jas. W. Green, Jas. Williams, L. P. Nelson, Thos. Freeman, Geo. Hamilton, Wallace Nalle, Martin Stringfellow, S. Wallis, F. B. Nalle, Rt. Davis, A. G. Taliaferro, C. C. Conway, P. B Jones, Jr., Rt. Maupin, J. P. Alexander, Jos. Wilmer, Jr., Dr. Payne, Wm. S. Peyton, E. Keerl, Burrows, J. W. Morton, Jas. Crawford, Spilman, Jas. Bowen, Jr. These names are from memory and therefore are not in exact order of time, and doubtless unintentionally omit some who have been or are vestrymen. The author has failed to received the full list, for which he asked repeatedly.

An analysis of the families of the old ministers and vestrymen of St. Mark's yields some curious results. Among their descendants were two Presidents of the United States, viz. Madison and Taylor; a Justice of the Supreme Court of the United States, viz. P. P. Barbour; several Governors of States, as Barbour of Virginia, and Slaughter, Morehead and Stevenson, of Kentucky; several United States Senators, as Barbour of Virginia, Morehead and Stevenson, of Kentucky; members of Congress, P. K. Thompson, Geo. F. Strother, John S. Barbour, John S. Pendleton, Rt. A. Thompson, Jas. F. Strother, B. Johnson Barbour, and Pendletons of Ohio; legislators and judges of circuits in great numbers, among whom Judges Pendleton, of South Carolina, of New York and Ohio, Judge Green, of the Court of Appeals of Virginia, and Judges Field, Shackleford, Williams, &c. These are but a few of the examples of this truth. It is also a curious fact that every Episcopal minister within the bounds of the original St. Mark's at this date, viz. Scott of Gordonsville, Hansbrough, of Orange, Slaughter, Minnegerode and Steptoe, of Culpeper, is a lineal descendant of the ante-revolution vestrymen, or he married one of their lineal descendants.

ADDENDA TO ST. MARK'S.
PARISH HISTORY CONTINUED.

[Rev. F. G. Ribble, the present rector of St. Mark's (Jan. 1900), has furnished the following continuation of St. Mark's History.—R. T. G.]

1878, January 1: Rev. J. G. Minnegerode resigned the rectorship of St. Mark's Parish, and took charge of Cavalry Church, Louisville, Diocese of Kentucky. At this writing, he is beginning the twenty-second year of his rectorship of that large and important work. He is a member of the Standing Committe of the Diocese, and was a delegate to the General Convention in 1878 1882.

May 1: Rev. E. Wall accepted the rectorship of the parish, coming from the Diocese of Huron, Canada. In 1880, the Church school, founded by the Rev Mr. Peterkin, was abandoned, and the building rented for a private school.

Rev. Mr. Wall resigned his rectorship January 1, 1882, going to Baltimore as assistant to the Rev. Dr. Campbell Fair. He was sometime rector of St. Matthew's Parish, Diocese of Washington. At present he has charge of Grace Church, Berryville, Diocese of Virginia. In 1881 he reported for St. Mark's Parish 111 communicants, 5 Sunday school teachers and fifty scholars.

1882-1884, September 1: Rev. H. D. Page became rector of the parish. He came as a deacon, having graduated at the Virginia Seminary the June before. He resigned March 18, 1884, to go to Japan as a missionary. After fourteen years of faithful service in that field, he returned, and is at present rector of Durham Parish, Diocese of Washington. In 1884 he reported for St. Mark's Parish 123 communicants, and 60 Sunday school teachers and scholars. During his rectorship the exterior of the church was painted and repaired.

1884-1888, August 1: Rev. W. T. Roberts accepted the call of the vestry as rector of the parish. Under the date of March 1, 1887, the following resolution was spread upon the minute book of the Vestry. "Whereas, the Rector, W. T. Roberts, having presented to the Vestry, in the name of Miss Savilla Denton, a communion service of solid silver, in memory of her sister, Miss Margaret Denton, therefore be it resolved: (1) That the Vestry hereby express their appreciation of this generous and appropriate gift, and hereby record the same in the vestry book of this Church. (2) That the Registrar be requested to furnish a copy of these resolutions to Miss Denton."

March 1, 1888: The Vestry passed a resolution to remove the galleries from the Church. This work was done, the interior of the Church being much improved thereby. About the same time a new pipe organ was placed in the Church, at the right of the chancel. On September 15, 1888, Rev. W. T. Roberts resigned his rectorship, and took charge of a parish in Essex county. After serving there for some time, he took charge of Emmanuel Church, Harrisonburg, Va. Resigning this work, he then took charge of Bruton Parish, Williamsburg, Diocese of Southern Virginia, of which he is still rector.

In 1888, he reports for St. Mark's Parish 100 communicants, and 53 Sunday school teachers and scholars.

At a meeting of the Vestry, held September 25, 1888, Mr. S. Russell Smith submitted to the Vestry a plan of improvements for the chancel and vestry room, to be a memorial to his deceased wife. The beautiful chancel window and the large and comfortable vestry room were his generous gifts to the church.

1889-1895. From September 15, 1888, to Sept 15, 1889, the parish had no rector. During this period, Mr. Eppa Rixey faithfully served the congregation as lay reader. The Vestry, with the help of the Ladies' Aid Society, painted the exterior of the church building, and put some repairs on the rectory and lecture room. Rev. S. P. Watters, of Morganton, N. C., took charge of the parish September 15, 1889. Under date of March 5, 1890, a motion was made and carried "that Mr. Eppa Rixey be appointed a committee of one to confer with Col. Bradford and make a report at the next meeting of the vestry on the present status of the war claim of this Church, said claim being for occupancy of the Church as a hospital during the war by the Federal Army." At a called meeting of the Vestry, held June 12, 1890, the following preamble and resolutions, relative to the death of Dr. Philip Slaughter, were passed and ordered to be spread upon the minutes of the Vestry. "In the death of the Rev. Philip Slaughter, D. D., Historiographer of the Church, in the Diocese of Virginia, the Church has been called to mourn the loss of an eminent son, a faithful presbyter, a learned historian, whose varied talents were adorned by a long life of devotion to the Church of Christ, and by his humble Christian life, led in imitation of the Master, full of years and full of honors, having been called from his earthly to his heavenly home. We, the Rector and Vestry of St. Stephens Church, St. Mark's Parish, desire to place on record our appreciation of his services, and our expression of the great loss the Church in Virginia has sustained; therefore be it it Resolved : (1) That in the death of the Rev. Philip Slaughter, D. D., the Church has sustained an irreparable loss, Learned, pious, and devoted to the cause of Christ, his removal from our midst will be felt with sorrow throughout the Church. (2) As Presbyter and Historiographer of the Church in Virginia, he leaves an honored name, calling forth the affection and esteem of his contemporaries. His literary works are an invaluable legacy to the Church. (3) Full of years, and full of honors, he has served his day and generation faithfully and well. Ripe for the harvest, he has been garnered by his Master, and has entered upon his eternal reward, leaving an illustrious example to future generations. (4) That the Rector and Vestry of St. Stephen's Church attend the funeral of Dr. Slaughter in a body, to be held tomorrow evening at five o'clock at Calvary Church, Culpeper county. (5) That a copy of these resolutions be sent to the family of Dr. Slaughter, as an expression of our sympathy as a body with them in their bereavement, and also to the Southern Churchman for publication.

Signed,

EPPA RIXEY,

Registrar.

February 10, 1892, the following letter, which explains itself was laid before the Vestry for consideration by the rector.

CULPEPER, VA., Jan. 30th, 1892.

MR. T. S. ALCOCKE,

Senior Warden, St. Mark's Parish.

Dear Sir: Whereas it is popularly believed in the neighborhood of "Oak Shade Church," that it has been a "Free Church" since the days of the Revolution, and whereas it is now in such a condition as to be unfit and unsafe for worship, and desiring to put it in a suitable condition for worship, we submit to you the following proposition: We, as a denomination, will raise the funds and repair the church, provided we may have the continual use of it for any one Sunday in the month we may desire, and for such special occasions as circumstances may demand. This in no wise to infringe upon your right to the use of the building for occasions that will not conflict with us.

Believing that such a movement will best subserve the interests of the entire community, we ask you to take immediate action, and, as NOMINAL CLAIMANTS of the property, unite with us in preserving the building, and at the same time retaining your right, without an outlay, to its partial occupancy.

Respectfully submitted,

GEO. H. SPOONER,
Preacher in charge of Woodville Circuit,
Virginia Conference.

W. H. BOTTS,
R. W. McDONALD,
Committee from Oak Shade Church.

This letter occasioned a careful review of the history of "Little Fork" church from 1750 to 1892, and a thorough investigation of the laws passed by the Virginia Legislature for the control of the old Colonial Churches of the State. This work was entrusted to Capt. G. G. Thompson, who performed it faithfully and well, showing conclusively that the church was not a "Free Church," and had never been a "Free Church." His historical sketch of the church, and his learned presentation of the legal aspects of the question, were ordered to be spread upon the minute book of the vestry.

The whole matter as to the right of ownership of the property known as "Little Fork Church" was finally settled by the following agreement. "Whereas, Little Fork Church, in St. Mark's Parish, Culpeper County, has been, since its erection in 1774–1775, an Episcopal Church, continuously to the present time in the possession, use and control of the minister and vestry of St. Mark's Parish, and the possession, use and control of this said church has been recognized as lawful, and has been secured to them by the laws of Virginia; and, Whereas; The Methodist congregation, living in the vicinity of this said Church, through their minister in charge, the Rev. Geo. H. Spooner, as a committee representing his congregation, have applied to the minister and vestry of St. Stephen's Church, St. Mark's Parish, to grant them their permission and consent to use the said Church on the fourth Sunday in each month of the year, and upon any other Sunday which will not conflict with the appointments of the minister of St. Stephen's Church, and on such week days in the year as their interest may require for religious worship; and the minister and vestry of St. Stephens' Church, St. Mark's Parish, in a spirit of Christian duty and brotherly love, being willing to grant such permission and consent, thereby increasing the opportunities and privileges for religious worship of all the good people living in the vicinity of said Church; Therefore, this agreement made this 21st day of March, 1892, between Thos. S. Alcocke and G. G. Thompson, wardens of St. Stephens' Church, and as such, a committee acting for and representing the minister and vestry of said Church, and the Rev. Geo. H. Spooner, minister in charge, and as such, a committee acting for and representing the Methodist congregation living in the vicinity of the said Little Fork Church, Witnesseth : That the permission and consent of the minister and vestry of St. Stephens' Church is hereby granted to the said Rev. Geo. H. Spooner and his Methodist congregation to use the said Little Fork Church for their religious services on the fourth Sunday of each month of the year, or upon any other Sunday of each month of the year which will not conflict with the appointments of the minister of St. Stephen's Church, and upon such week days during the year as their religious interest may require. Provided the days appointed for such week day services shall not be on, or conflict with the religious services that may be appointed by the minister of St. Stephen's Church; and provided further that the permission and consent hereby granted for the use of said Little Fork Church may be withdrawn and revoked whensoever, in the opinion of the minister and vestry of St. Stephen's Church, there may be reason or cause for so doing.

In testimony of the acceptance of the terms and conditions of this agreement, witness the following signatures.

THOMAS S. ALCOCKE, } Wardens of St. Stephens' Church and
G. G. THOMPSON, } Committee of the vestry of said Church.

GEO. H. SPOONER, } Minister in charge and Committee representing Methodist Congregation of Little Fork Church.

The following improvements on the property of the parish, during the years 1892-1894, are recorded in the minutes of the vestry : Little Fork Church repaired and put in a condition for use as a place for public worship; a new communion rail placed in St. Stephen's Church—the gift of Mrs. Thos. S. Alcocke; the rectory painted and repaired; the school room put in thorough repair, interior and exterior, and furnished for use as a lecture room—the work of the Young Ladies' Guild.

October, 1894, Rev. S. P. Watters resigned the rectorship of St. Mark's Parish, and accepted a parish in Florida. At present he is rector of St. Matthew's Church, Hillsboro, Diocese of North Carolina. In 1894, he reports for St. Mark's Parish 98 communicants, and 86 Sunday school teachers and scholars.

1895-1897. April 1895 : Rev. E. L. Goodwin took charge of the parish. During the following year St. Mark's Chapel was built at Rixeyville, and consecrated by Bishop Newton August 23, 1896. St. Andrew's Chapel, Inlet, was built in the spring of 1897, chiefly by the efforts of St. Mark's Chapter of the Brotherhood of St. Andrew. In 1897 the lines between St. Mark's and Ridley Parishes were altered, and were fixed by the action of the Council as follows : Beginning at the corner of Slaughter Parish, on the Orange and Culpeper road, thence by the said road to Fairview school house, thence by the old Buck Run road to its intersection with the old Fredericksburg road, about two miles south of the C. H., thence by the old Fredericksburg road to the cross-roads near the western base of Mt. Pony, and thence by an air line to the railroad crossing at Inlet station, thence northerly by a new country road to its intersection with the Chesnut Fork and Brandy road, thence by an air line to the bridge on the Warrenton road, over Muddy Run, thence with Muddy Run to the Hazel River, to the Rappahannock River.

October, 1897 : Rev. E. L. Goodwin resigned the rectorship of the parish, and accepted the position as assistant to the rector of Grace Church, Charleston, South Carolina. On the death of the rector in the summer of 1898, he succeeded to the rectorship, which position he still holds. In 1897 he reported for St. Mark's Parish 153 communicants, and 146 Sunday school teachers and scholars.

1898-1900. January 1, 1898 : Rev. F. G. Ribble, the present rector, assumed charge of the parish. In the summer of 1898, a new pipe organ was placed in the church by the Ladies' Aid Society, and the exterior of the church was painted by the Young Ladies Guild. In 1899, the rectory was repaired, and the lecture room painted. 1900 : Present status of St. Mark's Parish : Communicants 160; Sunday school teachers and scholars 120.

Vestrymen of St. Marks's Parish since 1877 : S. S. Bradford, Thos. S. Alcocke, Jas. W. Green, J. L. Burrows. G. G. Thompson, J. M. Leavel, J. W. Crawford, R. D. Keerl, Geo. Freeman, E. R. Shue, J. B. Stanard, J. W. Morton, R. C. Vass, Samuel Chilton, N. B. Meade, J. F. Rixey, L. P. Nelson, P. L. Jameson, S. Russell Smith, Eppa Rixey, Alfred Taliaferro, W. Porter Nelson, T. Carter Page, Travers Daniel, Earl English, C. B. Chilton, J. W. Smith, R. D. Luttrell, W. A. Ashby, R. B. Macoy, E. J. Brand, B. C. Macoy, and C. J. Rixey, Jr.

CALVARY CHURCH REBUILT.

On page 29 of St. Mark's Parish, in the next to the last paragraph, Dr. Slaughter speaks of the destruction of Calvary church, at the foot of Slaughter's Mountain. This church has been rebuilt through the kindness of friends at home and abroad; it was consecrated June 13, 1894, and named "All Saints," in memory of those who fell on the battlefield of Cedar Mountain, and who have "fought the good fight of faith in the daily walks of life."—Pub.

REV. A. H. LAMON.

Rev. A. H. Lamon (see page 25) was a Virginian. Married a Miss Rapley at Alexandria, Va. Moved to Evansville, Indiana. From there removed to Baton Rouge, La., and died in that city of yellow fever in 1852. His children were: Jno. H., Archibald. Sarah and Charlie Lamon. Elizabeth, his youngest child, was the daughter of his last wife, who was a Miss Toron. Rev. Frederick Du Monties Devall, of Palatka, Fla., James Wilmer Devall, cadet at West Point, Charles Kenneth Thomson, of Harrisburg, Pa., are his grandsons. Mrs. Samuel Hewett, of Washington, D. C., is a niece. Jno. G. Lamon, of Culpeper, is a nephew.

NOTES ON DR. SLAUGHTER'S ST. MARK'S PARISH.

[By Dr. Andrew Glassell Grinnan, of Madison.]

The account of the route of the Horseshoe Expedition of Gov. Spotswood is in some respects erroneous. The expedition crossed from Orange county into what is now Madison, at the old German Ford, across the Rapidan, about half a mile above its junction with the Robertson river. It is still called the German Ford. The Germans used this ford when they moved from Germanna to the head waters of the Robertson. It is at the lower end of the tract of land, bought by Dr. A. G. Grinnan in 1859, from Mr. Charles Bankhead; traces of the old road could be seen then. The expedition evidently passed by the present Woodbury Forest house. From this point is a clear view of the Swift Run Gap in the Blue Ridge, which the expedition ascended. The route was on the north side of the Rapidan river, to the Forks, turned west into Greene county, crossed Turkey Ridge, along the side of Saddle Back Mountain, to Summit of Swift Run Gap.

St. Mark's, page 57—Conway Family—Francis Conway, of Port Conway, opposite Port Royal, Va., m. Rebecca, daughter of Elizabeth Gaines (not Grymes), and Col. John Catlett, Jr. She was daughter of Col. Daniel Gaines, of Essex. After Francis Conway's death, she m. John Moore, of Caroline. She had six Conway children, one of whom was Nelly Conway, the mother of President Madison. She had two Moore children, one of whom, Jane Moore, m. Erasmus Taylor, of Orange.

St. Mark's, p. 74—The Taylor Family—This is a very large family, and cannot be noted at length for lack of space. The 1st settler, James Taylor, of Carlisle, Eng., did not settle on Chesapeake Bay. The Virginia Land office records show that he lived on the Mattaponi River, in the lower part of what is now Caroline county. He was succeeded in the ownership of this place by his oldest son in 1799, Col. James Taylor, who m. Martha Thompson (see Beverley's Hist. of Va.) Col. James Taylor, of the Horseshoe Expedition, entered large bodies of land—about 15,000 acres—in what is now Orange, about the year 1720—22. He removed to Orange and lived and died there. His widow long survived him. Dr. Charles Taylor was not a son of James (2) Taylor; he was his grandson, son of the well known Col. George Taylor, of Orange, who lived about two miles east of Orange C. H., which house is still standing. Here also lived Col. Frank Taylor, the diarist; he was another son of Col. George Taylor.

He never married, and died in 1799. His will, on record, shows that he left most of his property to his nephews, who lived in Kentucky. The diary is in possession of Dr. Andrew G. Grinnan. He was Lt.-Colonel of the Convention Guards, who had charge of the Burgoyne prisoners near Charlottesville.

St. Mark's, p. 75—Winston Family—Anthony Winston m. Alice Taylor, dau. of James (3) Taylor, of Orange, who was son of Col. James (2) Taylor and Martha Thompson. The account of Alice and her supposed husband in Campbell's History of Va. is erroneous.

St. Mark's, p. 60—Children of Helen Buchan Glassell and Daniel Grinnan, of Fredericksburg: Robert Alexander, b. 1817, d. 1884; Eliza Richards, b. 1819, d. 1846; Cornelia, b. 1821, d. 1864; Helen Mary, b. 1823; Daniel, b. 1825, d. 1826; Daniel Glassell, b. 1827; Daniella M., b. 1830, d. 1888.

St. Mark's, p. 85—Slaughter Family—The first Robert Slaughter of Culpeper m. Mary Smith, daughter of Augustine Smith, of Culpeper, an early land surveyor, who lived on the Rappahannock river. His will is on record in the first Vol. of Will records of Orange county. Augustine Smith was of the Horseshoe Expedition of Gov. Spotswood, as was also another surveyor, Col. James Taylor. Augustine Smith was the son of Col. Lawrence Smith, of Gloucester county, and York Town. Col. Smith for years was commandant of the fort at Falmouth, Va. The House of Burgesses also gave him civil jurisdiction over a section around the fort, an unusual mark of confidence, and donated to him a tract of land on the Rappahannock, three and a half miles wide by five miles long. He was once defeated in battle by Bacon, his troops deserting him. Altogether he was one of the most distinguished Virginians of his day. He laid out York Town.

In St. Mark's, page 46, it is stated that the tradition is that the organ in the Lutheran church in Madison county was paid for by subscriptions taken up in Germany and Sweden. This may be erroneous, for several years ago, an article appeared in a Northern newspaper, probably in the New York Evening Post, giving an account of John Thornburg, a German, who lived at Listy, Pennsylvania, who built an organ for the Lutheran Church of Madison in 1760, for $300.00, which he delivered to the agent of the Madison church in Philadelphia, who hauled it to Madison, Va., in a wagon. He also built one for the Lutheran Church in Winston-Salem, N. C.

ADDENDA TO PENDLETON GENEALOGY.

[To precede the last two paragraphs on page 100.]

MARTHA SHACKELFORD[6], (Lucy[5] (Tutt), Elizabeth[4], Nathaniel[3], Henry[2], Philip[1].) m. Richard Spotswood; issue : 1. Lucy[7], died in 1868; 2. Sally Bland[7], m. William Randolph Smith, and resides in Richmond, Va.; 3. Col. Muscoe L. Spotswood[7], a lawyer of Richmond, Va. Richard Spotswood was a great, great grand-son of Governor Spotswood, being the son of John Spotswood and Mary Goode, the grand-son of John Spotswood and Sally Rowsie, the great-grand-son of John Spotswood (son of Governor Alexander Spotswood) and Miss Dandridge.

BENJAMIN HOWARD SHACKELFORD[6] (Lucy[5] (Tutt), Elizabeth[4], Nathaniel[3], Henry[2], Philip[1].) m. Rebecca Green; issue : 1. Jones Green[7], m. Belle Kirk, having Howard Green[8]; 2. John Howard[7]; 3. George Scott[7], m. Virginia Minor Randolph, having Virginius Randolph[8], Nanny Holladay[8], George Scott[8], and Margaret Wilson[8]; 4. Lucy[7], m. C. C. Walker, having Rebecca[8], Reuben Lindsay[8] and C. C. Jr[8]; 5. Anne Berry[7], m. Prof. R. B. Smithey, Randolph-Macon College; 6. Muscoe Livingston[7], of Freemont, Ohio, m. Delia Taylor.

FROM AMERICAN ARCHIVES BY PETER FORCE.
[4th Series, Vol. 1, page 522.]

At a meeting of the freeholders and other inhabitants of the County of Culpeper, in Virginia, assembled, on due notice, at the Court House of the said county, on Thursday, the 7th of July, 1774, to consider of the most effectual methods to preserve the rights and liberties of America, the following resolutions were adopted.

HENRY PENDLETON, ESQ., MODERATOR.

Resolved: That we will, whenever we are called upon for that purpose maintain and defend his Majesty's right and title to the Crown of Great Britain, and all other of his Dominions thereunto belonging, to whose royal person and Government we profess all due obedience and fidelity.

Resolved: That the right to impose taxes or duties, to be paid by the inhabitants of this country, for any purpose whatsoever, is peculiar and essential to the General Assembly, in whom the Legislative authority is vested.

Resolved: That every attempt to impose taxes or duties by any other authority, is an arbitrary exercise of power, and an infringement of the constitutional and just rights and liberties of the colony, and that we will, at all times, at the risk of our lives and fortunes, oppose any act imposing taxes or duties, unless we are legally represented; and the Act of the British Parliament, imposing a duty on tea to be paid by the inhabitants of the colonies upon importation, is evidently designed to fix on the Americans those chains, forged for them by a corrupt minister.

Resolved: That the late cruel and unjust Acts of Parliament, to be executed by force upon our sister colony of the Massachusetts Bay, and the town of Boston, is a convincing proof of the unjust and corrupt influence obtained by the British Ministry in Parliament, and a fixed determination to deprive the colonies of their constitutional and just rights and liberties.

Resolved: That the town of Boston is now suffering in the common cause of the American colonies.

Resolved: That an association between all the American colonies not to import from Great Britian, or buy any goods, or commodities whatsoever, except negroes, clothes, salt, saltpetre, powder, lead, nails, and paper, ought to be entered into and by no means dissolved, until the rights and liberties of the colonies are restored to them, and the tyrannical Acts of Parliament against Boston are repealed.

Resolved: That it is our opinion, that no friend to the rights and liberties of America ought to purchase any goods whatsoever, which shall be imported from Great Britain, after a general association shall be agreed on, except such as are before excepted.

Resolved: That every kind of luxury, dissipation and extravagance, ought to be banished from amongst us.

Resolved: That the raising of sheep, hemp, flax and cotton, ought to be encouraged; likewise, all kinds of manufactures by subscriptions or any other proper means.

Resolved: That the importing of slaves and convict servants is injurious to this colony, as it obstructs the population of it with freemen and useful manufacturers, and that we will not buy any such slave or convict servant, hereafter to be imported.

Resolved: That every county in this colony ought to appoint deputies to meet upon the first day of August, in the city of Williamsburg, then and there to consult upon the most proper means for carrying these or any other resolutions, which shall be judged more expedient for obtaining peace and tranquility in America, into execution.

Resolved: That Henry Pendleton and Henry Field, Jr., Esquires are appointed upon the part of the freeholders and inhabitants of this county to meet and consult with such deputies as shall be appointed by the other counties.

Resolved: That the clerk transmit these resolves to the press, and request the printer to publish them without delay. By order of the meeting.

JOHN JAMESON, Clerk.

PART SECOND.

CULPEPER COUNTY HISTORY.

INTRODUCTORY CHAPTER.

Culpeper, named in honor of Thomas Lord Culpeper, governor of Virginia 1680—1683 (for sketch of whom see Hardesty's Encyclopaedia of Biography), was formed in 1748 from Orange county (Orange was taken from Spotsylvania, which county had been cut off from Essex). Its territory, embracing originally what is now Culpeper, Madison and Rappahannock counties, was the subject of a protracted controversy, involving the title to several million acres of land. The entire territory "within the bends of the rivers Tappahannock, alias Rappahannock, and Quiriough, or Potomac, the courses of those rivers, and the Bay of Chesapayork, &c.," was granted at different times, by King Charles I. and II., to Lord Hopton, the Earl of St. Albans, and others, and subsequently by King James to Lord Culpeper, who had purchased the rights of the other grantees. Thomas, fifth Lord Fairfax, who married Catharine, daughter of Lord Culpeper, became the proprietor of this princely domain, commonly known as the Northern Neck. From him, it descended to his son Thomas, sixth Lord Fairfax, and comprised the counties of Lancaster, Northumberland, Richmond, Westmoreland, Stafford, King George, Prince William, Fairfax, Loudoun, Fauquier, Culpeper, Madison, Page, Shenandoah, Hardy, Hampshire, Morgan, Berkeley, Jefferson and Frederick. In 1705 Edward Nott, governor of Virginia, in the name of the king, granted 1,920 acres of land to Henry Beverley, in the forks of the north and south branches of the Rappahannock. Robert Carter, commonly known from his large landed possessions as "King" Carter, who was the agent of Fairfax, objected to the grant as being within the limits of the Northern Neck grant. The question then arose whether the south (the Rapid Anne) or the north branch of the Rappahannock was the chief stream. To settle the controversy, Thomas Fairfax, the sixth Lord, and Baron Cameron, petitioned the king in 1733, to order a commission to ascertain the bounds of his patent. In consequence, commissioners were appointed severally in behalf of the crown and of Lord Fairfax These were William Byrd of "Westover"; John Robinson of "Piscataway," Essex county, and John Grymes of "Brandon," Middlesex county, on behalf of the crown; and William Beverly, William Fairfax and Charles Carter, on behalf of Fairfax. They made their report on December 14, 1736, to the council for plantation affairs, which body, on the 6th day of April, 1745, confirmed the report, which was in turn confirmed by the king, who ordered the appointment of commissioners, to run and mark the dividing line. This was done in 1746. The decision was in favor of Lord Fairfax, and made that branch of the Rapid Anne called the Conway, the head-stream of the Rappahannock river, and the southern boundary of the Northern Neck; and thus confirming to Lord Culpeper the original county of Culpeper. The original journal of the expedition kept by Major Thomas Lewis, is now in the possession of his descendant, Hon. John F. Lewis, ex-lieut. governor of Virginia. The conflicting rights of the Northern Neck patent, with those claimed by Joist Hite and others, have been the cause of innumerable law suits, which crowded the records of the State courts to a period advanced into the 19th century. There was an attempt made by the State of Maryland as late as 1832 to extend her boundary by an infraction of the Fairfax line, as above, established in 1746.

The name of Governor Alexander Spotswood, one of the ablest executives of Colonial Virginia, is prominently associated with Culpeper county, as the largest landed proprietor of that portion of Spotsylvania county (named in his honor), which subsequently formed the county of Culpeper, and as the founder in 1714 of the town of

GERMANNA,

On a peninsular of 400 acres of land on the banks of the Rapid Anne, which was settled by about four-score Germans, whom he brought thither to conduct his iron manufactories; and the town was, until the division of Spotsylvania county, its countyseat. It is thus described by Hugh Jones, in his "Present Condition of Virginia," published in 1724:

"Beyond Colonel Spotswood's furnace, above the falls of Rappahannock river, within view of the vast mountains, he (Spotswood) has founded a town called Germanna, from some Germans sent over by Queen Anne, who are now removed up further [into what is now Madison county]. Here he has servants and workmen of most handicraft trades; and he is building a church, court house, and dwelling-house for himself, and with his servants and negroes, he has cleared plantations about it, proposing great encouragement for people to come and settle in that uninhabited part of the world, lately divided into a county.

"Beyond this is seated the colony of Germans or Palatines, with allowance of good quantity of rich lands, who thrive very well and live happily, and entertain generously. These are encouraged to make wine, which by the experience (particularly) of the late Robert Beverly, who wrote the History of Virginia, was done easily, and in large quantities in those parts; not only from the cultivation of the wild grapes, which grow plentifully and naturally in all the lands thereabouts, and in the other parts of the country; but also from the Spanish, French, Italian and German wines."

THE PRESENT LIMITS OF THE COUNTY

Comprise an average length of twenty miles, with a breadth of about eighteen miles. It is drained by the Rappahannock and Rapid Anne rivers and their tributaries, the former river running along its northeast and the latter upon its southeast and southwest boundaries. According to the census of 1890, the population was 13,233. Number of acres of land 232,545. It is a good fruit county, including grapes, and is self-sustaining in all of its farm products. The grazing is excellent, including clover, timothy, orchard, Randall, Herds and blue grasses. The county is traversed by the great Southern Railway. The health of the county is excellent. Highland 75 per cent.; bottoms 25 per cent. About two-fifths of the county is in timber, consisting of walnut, ash, hickory, the oaks, locust, pine, cedar, chestnut, maple, etc. Minerals: Magnetic and hematic iron ores and gold, a mine of the latter being worked.

CULPEPER IN THE REVOLUTION.

Culpeper was distinguished in the Revolutionary war by the important service of her gallant Minute men, who, as the brilliant John Randolph of Roanoke said in the United States Senate, "were raised in a minute, armed in a minute, marched in a minute, fought in a minute and vanquished in a minute." Immediately on the breaking out of the war in 1775, Patrick Henry, then commander of the Virginia troops, sent to this section of the colony for assistance. Upon his summons, 150 men from Culpeper, 100 from Orange, and 100 from Fauquier, rendezvoused here, and encamped in a field the property of the late

Hon. John S. Barbour, half a mile west of the village of Fairfax. An old oak marked the spot. These were the first Minute Men raised in Virginia. They formed themselves into a regiment, choosing Lawrence Taliaferro of Orange, colonel; Edward Stevens of Culpeper, lieutenant colonel; and Thomas Marshall of Fauquier—father of Chief Justice John Marshall—major. The flag used by the Culpeper men bore in its center the figure of a rattlesnake coiled and in the act of striking—above which was inscribed "The Culpeper Minute Men," on either side "Liberty or Death," and beneath "Don't Tread on Me." The corps were dressed in green hunting shirts with the words "Liberty or Death" in large letters on their bosoms. A wag on seeing this, remarked it was too severe for him; but that he was willing to enlist if the words were altered to "Liberty or Be Crippled."

They wore in their hats buck-tails, and in their belts tomahawks and scalping knives. Their savage, war-like appearance excited the terror of the inhabitants as they marched through the country to Williamsburg. Shortly after their arrival at that place, about 150 of them—those armed with rifles—marched into Norfolk county, and were engaged in the battle of the Great Bridge. Among them were Chief Justice Marshall, then a lieutenant, and General Edward Stephens. In the course of the war, eight companies of eighty-four men each were formed in Culpeper for the Continental service. They were raised by the following captains: John Green (subsequently promoted to colonel, and wounded in the shoulder and crippled for life while storming a breast work. He was grandfather of Judge John Williams Green, of the court of appeals of Virginia, and great-grandfather of several distinguished jurists--the learned brothers, the late William Green, LL. D., of Richmond, the late Major James W. Green of Culpeper, and the late Thomas C. Green, judge of the supreme court of the State of West Virginia, being among them): John Thornton, George Slaughter, Gabriel Long (promoted major), Jno. Gillison, (who while gallantly leading his men to attack the enemy at Brandywine to prevent them making prisoners of the company of Captain Long, was struck in the forehead by a musket ball; the surgeon examined the wound, and then, lifting up his hands, exclaimed "Oh, captain! it is a noble wound, right in the middle of the forehead, and no harm done!" the wound soon healed and left a scar, of which any soldier might be proud).——McClannahan (Captain McClannahan was a Baptist clergyman, and at first preached to his men regularly; his recruits were principally from his own denomination and in conformity with the wishes of the legislature, who invited the members of particular religious societies, especially Baptists and Methodists, to organize themselves into separate companies, under officers of their own faith; the Baptists were among the most strenuous supporters of liberty.) and Abraham Buford. (Abraham Buford, promoted colonel, was defeated by Tarleton, May 29, 1780, at the Waxhaws, near the borders of North Carolina). John Jameson who was clerk of Culpeper county at the beginning of the Revolution, promptly joined the cause of his fellow colonists, and commanded a company that marched to Williamsburg. He was promoted to Lieutenant Colonel. John Paulding, David Williams and Isaac van Wart, the three immortal patriots who captured Andre, were in the command of Lieut. Col. Jameson, who, in turn, informed General Washington of the capture.

Among other heroes of the Revolution from Culpeper, may be named Captain Philip Slaughter, who entered the Culpeper Minute Men at the age of seventeen as a private, and marched with them to Williamsburg shortly after the seizure of the powder in March, 1775, by Dunmore. Having received a commission of lieutenant he marched to the North in the fall of 1776, with the

Eleventh Virginia Continental Regiment. Daniel Morgan then commanded this corps, and also a volunteer rifle regiment. There Slaughter remained until the commencement of the year 1780, and was in the battles of Brandywine, Germantown, Monmouth and at the storming of Stony Point. He spent the winter of 1777-8 at Valley Forge. His messmates were Lieutenant Robert (afterwards General) Porterfield, Captain Charles Porterfield, Captain Jameson and Lieutenant (afterwards Chief Justice) Marshall. There they were all reduced to great privation in the want of food and clothing. They bore their sufferings without murmur, being fortified by an undaunted patriotism. Most of the officers gave to their almost naked soldiers nearly the whole of their clothing, reserving only what they themselves had on. Slaughter was reduced to a single shirt. While this was being washed he wrapped himself in a blanket. From the breast of his only shirt he had wristbands and a collar made to complete his uniform for parade. Many of his brother officers were still worse off, having no undergarments at all; and not one soldier in five had a blanket. They all lived in rude huts, and the snow was knee deep the whole winter. Washington daily invited the officers in rotation to dine with him at his private table, but for want of decent clothing few were enabled to attend. Slaughter being so much better provided, frequently went in the place of the others, that, as he said, "his regiment might be represented." While in this starving condition, the country people brought food to camp. Often the Dutch women were seen riding in, sitting on bags on their horses' back, holding two or three bushels each of apple pies, baked sufficiently hard to be thrown across the room without breaking. These were purchased eagerly, eaten with avidity, and considered a great luxury. Slaughter performed the duties of paymaster and clothier in addition to those of a captain of the line. He was promoted to a captaincy in 1778, he being then not twenty years of age. Captain Slaughter held various civil offices, among which was that of high sheriff of Culpeper county. He married twice, first a daughter of Colonel French Strother, and secondly a daughter of Colonel Thomas Towles, having issue by the two marriages nineteen children who intermarried with the Maconickie, Conroy, Dade, Smith, Madison, Chapman, Bradford, Thompson and Semmes families, and their descendants now include many additional honored names. He died in 1849 at the advanced age of ninety-one. His ninth child the venerable and widely beloved Rev. Philip Slaughter, D. D., historiographer of the Episcopal Diocese of Virginia, an eloquent pulpit orator and a glowing and prolific writer, whose delightsome pen was tireless, before his death celebrated at his home near Mitchell's, two touching anniversaries, the semi-centennial of his ordination as a minister and his golden wedding. He had in his possession a brief journal of his honored father giving an account of the movements of the troops during the time the latter was in service, together with certificates of the faithful service of Captain Slaughter, given by Chief Justice Marshall, General Robert Porterfield and Colonel Jameson.

To the list of Culpeper worthies should be added the names of Colonel Gillison, Colonel Gabriel Jones, Colonel William Green, Colonel John Thornton, Colonel James Slaughter, Colonel John Slaughter, Colonel John Jameson, Major John Roberts, Colonel David Jameson and Colonel Philip Clayton (subsequently State Judge and member of congress from Georgia) of the Revolution; Colonel John Field, who was in the battle of Point Pleasant, October 10th, 1774; Colonel French Strother, member of Virginia assembly in 1776; his son George French Strother, member of congress, 1817-20; Philip Rootes Thompson, member of congress, 1806; John Strother Pendleton, member of congress and United States minister to Beunos Ayres; Colonel James Pendleton, Colonel Nathaniel Pendleton (who was the second of Alexander Hamilton in his lamentable duel with Aaron Burr); John Strode Barbour, sr., member of Congress; Hon. Richard W. Thompson, member of congress and secretary of the navy; Major General Edmund Pendleton Gaines, United States army, and Rev. John A. Broadus, D. D., of the Baptist Church, pulpit orator, author and educator. The distinguished William Wirt, the author of the "British Spy," was once a resident of Culpeper, having commenced the practice of law here in 1792, when only twenty years of age.

In his family burying-ground (which is now the Masonic Cemetery) half a mile north of Culpeper, the countyseat, is the tomb of a revolutionary hero with the following inscription:

"IN MEMORY OF

GENERAL EDWARD STEVENS

WHO DIED

AUGUST THE 17TH, 1820,

At his seat in Culpeper, in his 76th year of age.

This gallant officer and upright man had served his country with reputation in the field and Senate of his native State. He took an active part and had a principal share in the war of the Revolution, and acquired great distinction at the battles of Great Bridge, Brandywine, Germantown, Camden, Guilford Court House and the siege of York; and although zealous in the cause of American Freedom, his conduct was not marked with the least degree of malevolence or party spirit. Those who honestly differed with him in opinion he always treated with singular tenderness. In strict integrity, honest patriotism and immovable courage, he was surpassed by none and had few equals."

There may be added of General Stevens the following detail of services: At the commencement of the Revolution he commanded with distinction a battalion of riflemen at the battle of Great Bridge, near Norfolk, Virginia; was soon after made colonel of the 10th Virginia Regiment with which he joined Washington; and at the battle of Brandywine (September 11th, 1777,) by his gallant exertion saved a part of the army from capture, checked the enemy and secured the retreat. He also distinguished himself at Germantown, and being made a brigadier-general of Virginia militia, fought at Camden, also at Guilford Court House, where his skillful dispositions were extremely serviceable to the army, and where, though severely wounded in the thigh, he brought off his troops in good order. General Greene bestowed on him marked commendation. At Yorktown he performed important duties, and throughout the revolution possessed a large share of the respect and confidence of General Washington. He was a member of the senate of Virginia from the adoption of the State constitution until the year 1790.

GEORGE WASHINGTON, SURVEYOR.

In one of the books in the clerk's office of Culpeper is the annexed entry: 20th July, 1749 (O. S.)—GEORGE WASHINGTON GENT., produced a commission from the President and Master of William & Mary College, appointing him to be surveyor of this county, which was read, and thereupon he took the usual oaths to his majesty's person and government, and took and subscribed the abjuration oath and test, and thereupon took the oath of surveyor, according to law.

THE CULPEPER COMMITTEE OF SAFETY OF 1775.

Upon these committees were devolved the appointment of officers and other local executive functions. They were elected by the freeholders. In 1775, the committee was composed of John Jamesom, Henry Pendleton, James Slaughter, John Slaughter, and others, not certainly known to the writer. They probably were some of the following justices of the peace of that day, to-wit: Henry Field, Wm. Ball, Wm. Green, Ben. Roberts, Joseph Wood, Jno. Strother, Sam. Clayton and James Pendleton. Col. James Barbour and Henry Field represented the county in 1765, &c.—Henry Field and French Strother in '74-75-76, &c.

"CATALPA."

This name has become historical from having been the scene of the first encampment of the Minute Men and by being applied to a district in the county. It may be well, therefore, to record its origin.

The place now owned by Mr. J. C. Bell was the seat of Major Philip Clayton, in colonial times, and was named from a catalpa tree (the first in the county), transplanted by him from Essex. He married the sister of Robert Coleman, on whose land Culpeper was established in 1759, and called Fairfax, which was its legal title before the Civil war. The first trustees of the town were Nat. Pendleton, Wm. Green, Wm. Williams, Thomas Slaughter and Philip Clayton. Ben Davis had leased the land from Coleman and hence the names Davis and Coleman streets. One of the daughters of P. Clayton married Nat. Pendleton, whose son Nat. was a Minute Man of Culpeper, afterwards aid to Gen. Greene, and was the second of Alexander Hamilton in his duel with Aaron Burr. He was the ancestor of Geo. H. Pendleton, who was minister to Berlin. His brother Henry was an eminent jurist in South Carolina, after whom the Pendleton District was called. Another daughter of Clayton married Wm. Williams, the father of Gen. James, Maj. John, Philip and Wm. Clayton Williams, from whom a numerous progeny has descended. Another daughter married Col. James Slaughter, the father of Captain P. Slaughter, who was born at Catalpa, Dec. 1758. He was living with his grandfather and going to school here to Adam Goodlet, master of the first classical school ever in Culpeper to that date, when the Minute Men met in Clayton's old field (Catalpa) in 1775. Hence he had the best opportunity of knowing the facts recorded in his journal. The Minute Man, Gen. Stevens, who cast the electoral vote of this district for Washington, also married the daughter of Robert Coleman.

Hon. Thos. L. Thompson, who was once elected to Congress from California, is a lineal descendant of Philip Clayton and Philip Slaughter. The first colonel of the Minute Men of Culpeper, Laurence Taliaferro, has descendants here in the children of the late Dr. Alfred Taliaferro and Mrs. Alcocke.

FAIRFAX LODGE, NO. 43, A. F. & A. M.

The publishers are much indebted to Mr. George Dabney Gray, of the Culpeper bar, for the following extracts of an address which he delivered before the members of Fairfax Lodge on the occasion of their Centennial Anniversary, which was the 27th. day of December, 1894. The address was published in pamphlet form, at the request of the Lodge:

"At the request of Fairfax Lodge, which came to me with the force of an order, it was my pleasure to obey. I am here to speak to you on this Centennial Anniversary of our Lodge, which we meet to celebrate to-night. We meet as a band of brothers to retrim our altar fires and renew our devotion to the sacred principles of our order.

"The day itself is a proud Masonic Jubilee, hallowed by associations of the past and by traditions of the most thrilling interest to every Mason. For many hundred years our order has celebrated the 24th of June, and the 27th. of December, in honor of St. John the Baptist and St. John the Evangelist, two eminent church Patrons in Masonry. But this 27th of December, 1894, is of especial interest to the members of this Lodge.

"One hundred years ago to to-day Fairfax Lodge, No. 43, was organized at this place, under a charter from the Grand Lodge of Virginia, which was signed by Chief Justice John Marshall, then Grand Master.

"The Grand Lodge of Virginia was organized 1778, with John Blair, Master and with only five Lodges Increased rapidly so that in 1794, 16 years afterwards when this Lodge was organized there were 42 Lodges in Virginia In 1822, there were 123 Lodges

James Mercer was Second Grand Master.
Ed. Randolph, Third Grand Master.
Alex. Montgomery, Fourth Grand Master.
Thomas Mathews, Fifth Grand Master.
John Marshall, Sixth Grand Master.

"The present number of Lodges in Virginia is over 300. On the 9th of December, 1794, a charter was issued by the Grand Lodge of Virginia for the formation of Fairfax Lodge No. 43, at this place, then known as Fairfax. It was signed by Chief Justice of the U. S., John Marshall, and named the following as officers of the new Lodge: Philip Rootes Thompson, Master; Birket Davenport, S. W. and Philip Lightfoot, Jr., Warden, and at the same time a committee of three members of the Grand Lodge were appointed to install the said officers.

"On the 27th day of December, 1794, at the house of Benjamin Shackelford, in the town of Fairfax, the said officers were duly installed and the first meeting of the new Lodge was held and the following additional officers were elected and installed: Thomas Knox, Treas., John Shackelford, Secty., Thomas Jameson, S. D., Ed. Pendleton, J. D., John Hawkins, Tyler. The new Lodge and the members repaired in procession to the Court House where a sermon was preached by Rev John Woodville, Chaplain. He was the Rector of the Episcopal church at that time.

"There were twenty members at the first meeting. The little town of Fairfax was then in its infancy, having been laid out in 1734; indeed the Republic was then in its infancy. It had only been 13 years since the battle of Yorktown, which secured the independence of the American Colonies, 7 years from the adoption of the Constitution of the United States, and five years from the election of the first President, George Washington, and he was still President in 1794, having been elected for the second term in 1792. George III was still on the throne of England.

"Philip Rootes Thompson was the son of Rev. John Thompson, who was Rector of St. Mark's Parish, and in 1801-7 represented this district in Congress. Birket Davenport was the great grandfather of P. L. Jameson. Major P. Lightfoot is well known to many of you: an old bachelor whose white cravat and linen bosom were always spotless—the only man ever known who could walk from his residence to the court house without getting a stain on his shining shoes. Benj. Shackelford kept the house known as the old Bell Tavern which was a large frame building situated on the corner of the lot on which B. C. Macoy now lives. He was the father of John Shackelford, our old attorney for the Commonwealth and grand-father of the late Judge Henry Shackelford. This hotel was afterwards kept by Jerre Strother and it was burned down in the year 1845. Thomas Knox was the father of the old merchant, Thos. F. Knox, of Fredericksburg. Thomas Jameson was a nephew of Col. John Jameson an officer of the Revolution. John Jameson is the grand-father of Phillip Jameson and was Clerk of the County from 1772 to 1810. Ed. Pendleton was the son of Col. James Pendleton.

"Among the friends of this infant Lodge there was a distinguished General of the Revolutionary army. He had gained great distinction at the battle of Great Bridge and Brandywine, Germantown, Camden, Guilford C. H. and Yorktown. He had been severely wounded at Guilford. He lived in the house afterwards owned by F. T. Lightfoot (burned down). Soon after the Lodge was formed he donated to them a lot of ground for the erection of a building to be used as a Lodge room, and the Lodge by private subscription soon raised money enough to erect a building for their meetings. Gen. Stevens also devised by his will one acre of land near his own family burying ground to be used as a cemetery for the members of the Lodge and their families. He died in 1820.

"The new Lodge continued to hold its meetings at the house of Benj. Shackelford until they moved into their own Hall built upon the lot donated to them by Gen. Ed. Stevens. The last meeting held at the house of Benjamin Shackelford was June 3rd. 1797. The first meeting held in their new Hall was on July 7th. 1797. The dedication was Aug. 1st. 1797, with appropriate ceremonies. At their March meeting in 1798, a committee was appointed to wait on Genl. Stevens and express the thanks of the Lodge for his great liberality. At the meeting Dec. 27th. 1799, the following resolution was passed: Resolved, that this Lodge show a testimony of their deep regret at the decease of our late and worthy brother, Genl. George Washington, Grand Master of America, by wearing crape for the day and that the Treasurer procure the same." Washington died December 14th. 1799.

"Among the members of the old Lodge from 1820, 1836, were the following: Judge R. H. Field, distinguished Judge of the Circuit Court. Robt. G. Ward, Clerk of Circuit Court till 1851. John C. Williams, known as Capt. Jack. Jeremiah Strother, grand-father of Rev. John Hansbrough and great grand-father of Mrs. Macoy; at one time kept old Bell Tavern. Wm. M. Thompson, father of Hon. R. W. Thompson, member of Congress from Ind., and Sect. of Navy under President Hays. Jonathan C. Gibson, father of Col. J. C. Gibson, and a great lawyer. Wm. Foushee, father of Mrs. Fayette Latham, and the late Mrs. Cole. John Strother, cousin of Jeremiah Strother and law partner of Fayette Mauzy. Andrew Glassell, grand-father of Dr. A. G. Grinnan. Wm. Emison, long Commissioner of Court, &c. J. W. Denton, father of Mrs. Robert Williams. Isham B. Mason, father of Mrs. Jessie L. Burrows (built old C H. and St. Stephens church.) Rev. Herbert Marshall, father of the late George E. Marshall. Samel A. Starrow, Col. in U. S. Army, father of Mrs. Judge Bell and Mrs. Dr. Thompson. Hon. John S. Pendleton, member of Congress and Minister to Chili. Major Philip Williams, father of George M. Williams. Jeremiah Latham. St. Pierre Shackelford. Wm. G. Allan, father of J. M. and A. M. Allan. Richard Jeffries, grand-father of W. L and J. L. Jeffries. Martin Slaughter who built brick house (now jail). James B. Clayton. Thomas Bell. Thomas W. Lightfoot, Clerk from 1816 to 1831, father of Frank Lightfoot. Col. David Jameson, father of David and Washington Jameson. Col. John Thorn, of Berry Hill. Robt. N. Norris, father of Miss Bell Norris. Thos. Knox, father of the old merchant Thomas F. Knox, of Fredericksburg. Wm. Clayton Williams, father of Lewis B. Williams of Orange; was an eminent lawyer. Thos. Hall, old merchant, lived at old Hall farm. Robt. Green, son of Col. John Green, of the Revolution and brother of Genl. Moses Green. Reuben Fry, son of Rev. Henry Fry, built the house where Ed. Lightfoot died, was father of Judge Fry of West Virginia and Philip S. Fry, Clerk of Orange. Maj. John Roberts officer of Revolution and grand-father of John Strother and Dr. Johnson Strother, Past Master of this Lodge. Wm. Broadus, Clerk from 1811 to 1816. Zephaniah

Turner, and John Turner. Robert Lovell, Wm. Hurt, Jones Green, Geo. Ficklen, Wm. Conner, Nimrod Popham, Thos. Porter, Wm. Ward and Moses Samuel.

"A ball was given in this Lodge room and by the Lodge to the Marquis De La Fayette, upon his visit to this country in 1822. La Fayette was a great Mason as well as a distinguished General and was the bosom friend of George Washington.

"Culpeper was as famous then, as she has always been, for her beautiful women, and La Fayette is said to have remarked on that occasion that he had never seen prettier women.

"The Lodge continued to work under this charter of 1794 till the year 1847. But we have no record of their meetings after January, 1801. Their building was burned in the year 1846 or '47. In 1855, the Lodge was reorganized under a new charter but with the same name and number and met in the Verandah Building. The officers were F. Mauzy, Master, Dr. P. C. Slaughter, Sr. Warden, J. L. Burrows, Jr. Warden. In the year 1858 the present building was erected by the subscriptions of the members of the Lodge with such aid as could be obtained from other Masons.

"During the war between the States the work of the Lodge was suspended from 1861 to 1865. During the occupation of the town by the Federal army in the summer of 1862, under Gen. Pope, the Lodge room was broken open and the Hall was greatly damaged, the furniture all destroyed and the charter, regalia, jewels and books of the Lodge carried away. These books contained all the minutes and proceedings of the Lodge from its organization down to the year 1861. Only one of these books has been recovered and fortunately that is the one containing the minutes from the organization down to 1801, together with a copy of the charter issued by Grand Master John Marshall. This old book was sent by one Wm. J. Jenks, in 1884, just ten years ago to the Grand Lodge of Pennsylvania, and by that Lodge ordered to be sent to the Grand Lodge of Virginia, which was done and that Lodge sent it to this Lodge. No more inexcusable act of vandalism was perpetrated during the war. The damages were assessed in August, 1835, at $1,169.05 and certified to by the Federal officer then in command of what was then termed the "Sub District of Culpeper." It is hoped that the time will come when these damages will be paid by the U. S. Government as well as all other damages done to other Masonic property and to churches.

"On the 30th of August, 1865, the Lodge held its first meeting after the war under dispensation from the Grand Lodge dated 24th. of Aug. 1865. The meeting was held in the office of Dr. R. S. Lewis over Alcocke's store. The officers then were G. D. Gray, W. M., who had been Master since 1858, C. T. Crittenden, S. W., R. S. Lewis, J. W., L. C. Turner, Secty., Wm. M. Thompson, S. D., F. D. Johnson, J. D., J. L. Burrows, Tyler. The Lodge met in their Hall the 26th. of January, 1866, and G. D. Gray was requested to visit Baltimore and other places to solicit aid to purchase carpet, jewels, &c.; under this resolution he visited Baltimore and obtained money sufficient for these purposes and the Lodge passed resolutions of thanks to these Lodges on the 23rd. of Feb. 1866. The Hall had then been papered and carpeted &c..

"Fayette Mauzy, Clerk of this County from 1838-73, 35 years, was a man of rare intelligence and geniality of nature; he had a memory unsurpassed in tenacity and accuracy and enjoyed the unwavering confidence of the people and of the bar and bench. He was greatly beloved by his brethren of the Lodge, and indeed by the whole community. He was ready at all times to give information and advice to those who needed it. His most striking characteristic perhaps was his wonderful equanimity of temper. Diogenes hardly excelled him.

"When Alexander the Great was at the city of Corinth during the Persian war he was visited by many statesmen and philosophers who came to do him honor and he hoped that Diogenes would have come with them, but as he did not, Alexander went to see him and he found him lying in the sun and taking little notice of the great General. Alexander asked him how he could serve him. 'Only stand a little out of my sunshine' said Diogenes. Alexander was struck with surprise at finding himself so little regarded and saw something so great in that carelessness that while his courtiers were ridiculing the Philosopher he said: 'if I were not Alexander I would wish to be Diogenes.' Fayette Mauzy would have received a visit from Alexander or Napoleon or from a greater man than either, Robt. E. Lee, with the same composure but with more politeness than was shown by Diogenes to Alexander. He was always polite and courteous to every one and ready to serve them.

"Dr. Philip C. Slaughter was a man of great sagacity and capital sense and though somewhat reserved and peculiar he wielded great influence in the county. He was truly a zealous Mason and rarely failed to attend the meetings of the Lodge, and although for many years S. W., he was like the Ephraimites who wanted to pass over the Jordan but could not give the true Shibboleth. He could never give the true response of his office. His death on the 19th. of June, 1866, occurred at the Lodge room in this place; he was then S. W. protem and we were giving the Master's degree to J. S. Grinnan.

"What shall we say of our faithful and zealous Chaplain, John Cole, one of nature's noblemen, and one of God's highest and best gifts to man, for his life was devoted to all that was noble and good and true. No thought of wrong ever entered his mind or disturbed his high purposes. He had a virtue which no power could tempt and a courage no danger could shake, and although his face and bearing to some might seem austere, his big heart was as tender and gentle and soft as a woman's.

"Dr. Wm. M. Thompson, so long J. W., full of humor and fun and of great kindness of heart, full of sympathy for the distressed. He was a man of singularly pure and upright character, honored and respected by all who knew him. Perfectly devoted to his family and always in a good humor. His home was the place where he was most loved and by wife and children he was considered without fault. He had a way, long to be remembered, of asking assent to every proposition or opinion advanced by himself with the question "Don't you think so."

"Jesse L. Burrows, the faithful Tyler of the Lodge for more than 50 years. The sacred oracles at Delphi were not guarded with more fidelity than did this faithful sentinel guard the entrance of his Lodge. He loved his Lodge and his heart was full of charity and love for all his brethren, and he was ready to serve them at all times with alacrity and pleasure.

"Charles Ed. Lightfoot, fitted by nature to command, was one of the best Masters that ever presided over the Lodge, and was as true and Knightly a Cavalier as ever drew sword in defense of his country. In his dealings with his fellow men, no one possessed a higher sense of honor.

"Of the ante-war Masons there are not more than half a dozen left. The memory of those brethren and their deeds is gradually fading away. How forcibly these memories impress upon us the solemn lessons taught us so beautifully in the Master's Degree. 'Man that is born of a woman is of few days and full of trouble. He cometh forth as a flower and is cut down. He fleeth as a shadow and continueth not.' 'Our life is as a vapor that appeareth for a little while and then vanisheth away.' The hearts of the strongest of us are but as muffled drums beating funeral dirges to the grave."

THE CULPEPER OF TO-DAY.

To-day Culpeper, the old town of Fairfax, is a thrifty place of some 2000 people. The town contains a number of handsome residences, with large green lawns and beautiful shade trees, the delight of the Southern people. It is supplied with first class brick sidewalks, and a system of water works that is of great advantage, the natural pressure being entirely sufficient for all purposes.

The present municipal government is as follows; Mayor, John Strode Barbour; Recorder and Assessor, G. Chapin Lightfoot; Treasurer, G. W. Keerl; Councilmen, R. B. Macoy, W. A. Ashby, J. H. Traylor, J. W. Swan, David Baily and Robert F. Booton; Town Sergeant, A. P. Hill.

There is a bank, C. J Rixey, proprietor, and two weekly newspapers, the CULPEPER EXPONENT, established 1881, Raleigh T. Green, editor and proprietor; and the CULPEPER ENTERPRISE, J. T. Wampler, editor and proprietor.

There are two drug stores, Joseph B. Gorrell's, established in 1858, and R. B. Macoy's, a roller flour mill with a capacity of 125 barrels a day, Fray & Co., grain commission merchants, successors of Waite, Miller & Company, several dry goods stores, two furniture stores, two jewelry establishments, two undertakers, one marble yard, iron foundry, machine shop, two hardware stores, one Baptist, Episcopal, Catholic, Presbyterian and Methodist church. Large, modern and commodious public school buildings for both white and colored. A female seminary, &c., &c.

The resident physicians are: Drs. W. J. Strother, A. S. Rixey, E. H. Lewis and H. T. Chelf. The lawyers are Messrs. G. D. Gray, D. A. Grimsley, J. C. Gibson, W. L. Jeffries, J. L. Jeffries, J. S. Barbour, Burnett Miller, T. Edwin Grimsley, Chas. M. Waite, E. H. Gibson, C. J. Rixey Jr., D. J. F. Strother and Raleigh T. Green.

The county government is as follows: Judge of the Circuit Court, Daniel A. Grimsley; Judge of the County Court, William L. Jeffries; Attorney for the Commonwealth, Chas. M. Waite; Clerk of the County and Circuit Courts, Warren E. Coons; Treasurer, S. Russell Smith; Sheriff, A. W. Pulliam; Surveyor, J. R. P. Humphries; Commissioners of the Revenue, John A. Holtzman and Russell H. Yowell; Superintendent of Public Schools, James M. Beckham; Member of the State Senate, John L. Jeffries; Member of the House of Delegates, S. R. McClanahan; Member of Congress from this district, John F. Rixey.

Besides Culpeper, the county seat, other towns and villages are: Brandy Station, Mitchell's Station, Richardsville, Germanna, Raccoon Ford, Rapidan, Jeffersonton, Rixeyville, Homeland, Eggbornsville, Boston, Stevensburg, Lignum, Hudson's Mill, Crooked Run, Clarkson, Kelly's Ford, Winstonville, Oak Shade (the seat of Little Fork Church) and Waterloo.

The present county officers of Rappahannock county are as follows: Circuit Judge, C. E. Nicol, of Prince William county; County Judge, H. M. Dudley (succeeded J. F. Strother); Clerk, Thomas F. Haywood; Sheriff, N. J. Cropp, Jr.; Treasurer, B. J. Wood; Commonwealth's Attorney, Horace G. Moffett; Superintendent of Schools, H. M. Miller; Surveyor, J E. Sutphin; Member of House of Delegates, G. W. Settle; Member of Congress from the district, James Hay, of Madison county. The county seat is Washington. Other towns are Sperryville, Amissville, Woodville, Laurel Mills, Gaines X Roads, Slate Mills, Flint Hill and Castleton.

The county officers of Madison county are as follows: Circuit Judge, D. A. Grimsley, of Culpeper; County Judge, F. M. McMullan; Clerk, N. W. Crisler; Treasurer, H. P. Smith; Sheriff, D. M. Pattie; Commonwealth's Attorney, James E. Thrift. Madison C. H. is the county seat. Other towns and villages are: Haywood, Criglersville, Oak Park, Dulinsville, Fray, Peola Mills, Graves Mill, Rochelle, Twyman's Mill, Locust Dale, Wolftown and Nether's Mill.

CHAPTER II.

"THE CULPEPER MINUTE MEN."

The following is an address which was delivered by the late Rev. Philip Slaughter, D. D., on the occasion of the presentation on the 6th. of September, 1887, of a flag to the Culpeper Minute Men. The reply of the late Judge John W. Bell, who received the flag on behalf of the company, is also given.

"As the son of one of the original Minute Men of 1775, I naturally feel an interest in their history. And as I happen to have the only contemporary record of their first formation, I have thought it might have some interest for you. The late Captain Slaughter, of Slaughter's Mountain, left a journal of his daily life from the year 1775 (when, at the age of sixteen years, he joined Capt. John Jameson's company of Minute Men, to the year of his death), covering a period of 75 years. In this journal he recorded the first formation of the Minute Men of Culpeper, their first march to Williamsburg, and his daily marches throughout the Revolutionary War, including a minute detail of the battles of Brandywine and Germantown; of the dreadful winter at Valley Forge, near Philadelphia, where some officers were reduced to a single shirt, and had to wrap themselves in a blanket while that shirt was washed, and had to cut up the body of the shirt to make collars when they appeared on parade, until the yoke and sleeves were all that remained; and the soldiers left the print of their naked feet upon the cold snow. Some officers were better off, and he tells an anecdote of his mess mate, Lieut. John Marshall (the embryo Chief Justice) who had the only pair of silk stockings in the regiment. Just before the battle of Brandywine, Marshall wore his stockings to an evening party in the country, and slept that night in camp upon a bed of leaves. At midnight alarm guns were fired, and Marshall not being able to find his stockings in the dark, set fire to the leaves, which burned a hole in his stockings, into which he thrust his feet, and away he went in that comical costume.

"Capt. Slaughter's war journal was taken by the Federals when my house was pillaged during the Civil War. There was, however, a duplicate of the first twelve pages in the author's autograph, and it so happened that these pages contain the account of the time, place and circumstances of the organization of the Minute Men of Culpeper. Before I read some extracts from the journal it may be well to remind you of the political situation that led up to these events.

"The year 1775 was the transition era from a monarchy to a republic. When Lord Dunmore, fearing the resentment of the people for his removal of the gun-powder from the magazine at Williamsburg, had taken refuge on a man-of-war, British rule had practically ceased in what used to be called his Majesty's "Ancient Colony and Dominion of Virginia," but the republic had not been formally inaugurated. In this emergency it became necessary to take measures of self defence. The people met in convention July 17th., 1775. The convention appointed a general committee of safety for the colony and directed committees of safety to be chosen by the freeholders in each county.

Upon these committees was devolved the supreme executive authority. The military consisted of two regiments of regulars, commanded by Patrick Henry and William Woodford—and of the militia. The county lieutenant and commander-in-chief of the militia of Culpeper was James Barbour, the great-grandfather of the Hon. John S. Barbour and James Barbour, who was once a representative from this county.

"The convention also divided the colony into 16 districts, in each of which a battalion of 500 men was to be raised and disciplined to march at a moment's warning. This district was composed of the counties of Fauquier, Culpeper and Orange, and the committee of safety commissioned Lawrence Taliaferro, of Orange, to be the colonel; Edward Stevens, of Culpeper, to be the lieutenant colonel; and Thos. Marshall, of Fauquier, the father of Chief Justice Marshall, the major of this battalion. They also commissioned ten captains for the companies into which the battalion was distributed.

"Captain Slaughter only gives the name of the captain of the company to which he belonged, to-wit: John Jameson, the grandfather of your townsman, Mr. Philip Jameson, who was then clerk of the county. One of them probably was Capt. Nat. Pendleton, who was the ancestor of George H. Pendleton, once Minister at Berlin. Others may have been captain afterwards. General James Williams, who has so many descendants in the county, and Major John Williams, the ancestor of the Pattons, who were so prominent in the late war, and Captain James Pendleton, the ancestor of the Hon. John S. Pendleton, Capt. Philip Clayton and Col. James Slaughter, who were with the Minute Men in in the first battle in Virginia. The camp of the Minute Men was in Major Clayton's old field (Catalpa), and the precise spot was marked within my memory by a grand old oak, which, with all its honors, the woodman 'would not spare.' The author of the journal thus describes the meeting of the Minute Men:

'We encamped in Clayton's old field. Some had tents, and others huts of plank, &c. The whole regiment appeared according to orders in hunting shirts made of strong, brown linen, dyed the color of the leaves of the trees, and on the breast of each hunting shirt was worked in large white letters the words, 'Liberty or Death'! and all that could procure for love or money bucks' tails, wore them in their hats. Each man had a leather belt around his shoulders, with a tomahawk and scalping-knife. The flag had in the center a rattlesnake coiled in the act to strike. Below it were the words, 'Don't tread on me!' At the sides, 'Liberty or Death'! and at the top, 'The Culpeper Minute Men.'

'During our encampment an express arrived from Patrick Henry, commandant of the First Virginia Continental Regiment, by order of the committee of safety, then sitting in the city of Williamsburg, requesting the Minute Men to march immediately to that city, as Governor Dunmore had conveyed powder and military stores from the magazine to a British man-of-war, etc., etc. The Minute Men immediately made ready and marched with all possible dispatch, and in a few days reached the city of Williamsburg. Many people hearing that we were from the backwoods, near the Indians, and seeing our dress, were as much afraid of us for a few days as if we had been Indians; but finding that we were orderly and attentive in guarding the city, they treated us with great respect. We took great pride in demeaning ourselves as patriots and gentlemen. The Minute Men were chiefly armed with fowling-pieces and squirrel-guns, and Dunmore having retired to the man-of-war, one-half of the men returned home. My father remained, but insisted that I should go back to school, I not being quite seventeen years old. This, by the advice of friends,

I agreed to do. Those Minute Men who remained under the command of Col. Edward Stevens, of Culpeper, and Major Tom Marshall, of Fauquier, had the honor of being at the battle of the Great Bridge, that being the first battle fought in Virginia. They were also at Norfolk when that city was burned.

'In the spring of '76 I again left school and enlisted as a soldier in Captain John Jameson's troop of cavalry, but before the company was ready to march I was appointed by the committee of safety a lieutenant in Capt. Gabriel Long's company of riflemen. We raised the company and marched to join the army under Gen. Washington, in New York. In the spring of '77 we joined the 11th. Va. Continental Regiment, in New Jersey, which was commanded by Daniel Morgan.'

"This is all in the journal which concerns the Minute Men of Culpeper.

"So many of the Culpeper companies having been in the course of the war absorbed into the Continental regiments that, by Act of Assembly October, 1776, they were dissolved and merged in the militia. Thus, though the men were fighting on every field, the name no longer survived. When the name had been buried nearly a century and the blast of the bugle was again heard in the land, the sires rose in the persons of their sons, unfurled the old flag, disclosing its emblem ready to strike, and rattling the warning, 'Don't tread on me.' The Minute Men were reorganized, with Tazewell Patton, a graduate of the Virginia Military Institute, for their captain. In 1860 a flag was presented to them by that unique orator, John S. Pendleton, who stirred their hearts with his burning words. Captain Patton rapidly rose to be colonel of the 7th. Virginia Infantry, and after braving the battle and the breeze on many a hard-fought field, fell in that dreadful charge of Pickett's Division on the Heights of Gettysburg in 1863. His body, after lying embalmed in a vault at Baltimore, was re-interred in the Stonewall cemetery at Winchester, at dead of night, in the same grave with that of his brother George, colonel of the 22nd. Virginia Infantry, who, while commanding a brigade in the battle of Winchester, was mortally wounded by a shell in 1864. And these two gallant, loving brothers embraced each other in the dust of one grave. Three streams of Revolutionary blood met in their veins—that of the Minute Men of Culpeper, Major John Williams and Capt. P. Slaughter, and that of Gen. Mercer, the hero of Princeton.

"And this reminds me of an incident in Gen. Mercer's life, pertinent to the present occasion. When a captain under Washington, in the war against the Indians and French in 1775, his right arm being shattered by a ball, he became separated from his company, and with the Indians whooping in hot pursuit, he only escaped by hiding in a hollow tree, upon which they sat without discovering him. Having a wilderness of 100 miles to traverse he was only saved from starvation by killing a rattlesnake, upon which, and some roots, he subsisted until he reached Fort Cumberland. It was fitting that the son of a sire who had fed upon a rattlesnake should command a company whose flag was emblazoned with a picture of that animal, and which was a *fac simile* of the flag under which his ancestor marched through the wilderness to Williamsburg in 1775. There appeared in the London Morning Chronicle, of Feb. 25, 1776, a remarkable article in these words: 'The Americans have a flag with a snake with 13 rattles on it, in the attitude to strike, and with the motto, 'Don't tread on me.' It is a rule in heraldry that the worthy properties of an animal on a crest should alone be considered. The rattlesnake is an emblem of America, being found in no other part of the world. The eye excels in brightness. It has no eye-lids, and is therefore an emblem of vigilance. She never begins an attack, and never surrenders, and is therefore an emblem of magnanimity.

She never wounds until she has given warning. Her weapons are not displayed until drawn for defence. Her power of fascination resembles America—those who look steadily on her are involuntarily drawn towards, and having once approached, never leave her. She is beautiful in youth, and her beauty increases with age. Her tongue is forked as lightning.

"Captain Patton was succeeded by his lieutenant, Capt. Crittenden, who soon rose to the command of a regiment, whose flag he followed in many a bloody battle, and is with us to-day, a battle-scarred veteran, still owning the flag, all tattered and torn, presented by Pendleton to Patton in 1860. The Minute Men of Culpeper were again reorganized in 1879 by Capt. Wm. Nalle, a graduate of the Virginia Military Institute. His lot has fallen in times of peace, but if ever the occasion comes to "flash his maiden sword," he will doubtless bear himself as becomes a Minute Man of Culpeper. And this brings me to your present gallant captain (Burrows), who, though not himself derived from the Minute men of '75, his better half is; and what is better still, he has won his laurels on the field, having shed his blood at Manassas, and been captured in Picket's historic charge at Gettysburg. To him I now present this flag in memory of the men who fought our battles in council and in the field. Perhaps it may enhance your interest in it to know that it was painted for me by a maiden who is a lineal descendant of a Minute Man of '75. And now let me say to the young men who have not been promoted to the holy estate of matrimony, that when the aforesaid Minute Man was made captain in the field he wrote the name of his sweetheart upon his commission, vowing that it would never be disgraced. Having heard that a powerful rival was besieging the heart of his betrothed in his absence, and not being able to get a furlough, he sent a sergeant 500 miles to Culpeper, to make a reconnoisance of the situation, who reported that the enemy had retreated. After the war they were married. Perhaps you would like to know her name—it was Margaret French, the same as that of Col. Patton's mother, who was her grand-daughter. She was the daughter of French Strother, who represented Culpeper for thirty (30) years, and who was Senator when he died. He was a member of the Assembly of '76, which gave us our constitution, bill of rights, and act of religious freedom. His own son, Geo. French, was a member of Congress from Culpeper, as was also his grandson, James French, whose son, Captain John Strother, has served in council and in the field. He is represented here to-day in the person of Dr. Johnson Strother, who also, with Mr. George Williams and his son, represent Gen. James Williams, of the Revolution. And I may add that a grandson of this romantic marriage is here this morning, a member of the present company of Minute Men, as are also two descendants of James Barbour—the county lieutenant of 1775, whose grandson and great-grandson have represented us in Congress, and another of the same name in the General Assembly and the convention."

JUDGE BELL'S REPLY.

"Dr. Slaughter:

Rev. Sir.—It gives me the profoundest pleasure to meet and to greet you here to-day. I rejoice from the inmost depths of my heart to look upon your face again, and to see in it plainly the fading lineaments of your distinguished sire who, one hundred and eleven years ago, stood near the wide-spreading and historic oak on yonder hill, and helped form and command the first 'Culpeper Minute Men' of 1775, and who threw to the breeze their ever memorable flag with the defiant motto, 'Don't tread on me.'

"They shed lustre on themselves in the Revolution of '76, and have come down to posterity with imperishable honor! Glory and honor, and riches and fame to the illustrious old Philip Slaughter of Culpeper.

"Born and commissioned for an exalted destiny, the old Minute Men of Culpeper boldly declared, 'no taxation without representation,' and courageously adhered to the great prerogatives of Magna Charta, 'life, liberty, and the pursuit of happiness.' They will live in history and in the hearts of the people, as long as the love of American liberties survives.

"The second company of the Culpeper Minute Men was formed in April or May, 1859, just eighty-three years thereafter. Impelled by the like gallant spirit that aroused their fathers of '76, they marched out, fought and bled in defense of their personal and property rights, of their constitutional and political liberty: a cause than which, none more sacred ever enlisted the feelings and patriotism of men, or employed the strong arm and courage of soldiers.

"Glorious, valorous Minute Men of 1860! They, like their illustrious predecessors of '76, 'formed in a minute, marched in a minute, and fought in a minute.'

"Turned over to the Confederate States they were afterward merged in the distinguished and chivalrous 13th. Virginia, once commanded by the distinguished and gallant Hill, afterwards Lieutenant General of the Confederate forces, and the courageous and "bloody 49th.," then commanded by the gallant and intrepid Smith, afterwards the War Governor of Virginia. They will live in the brilliant history of the Southern Confederacy of States, as those of '76 do in that of the united colonies of North America.

"And now, soldiers, can a richer compliment be paid to the 'Minute Men' of 1879, than to receive this beautiful and lovely flag, this day presented to you by this distinguished and eloquent son of the yet more distinguished old Captain Philip Slaughter of Culpeper.

"As I behold you standing before me, I recall an incident which, if my memory does not fail me, I read in the history of the campaigns of Frederick the Great. At night-fall, after one of those sanguinary, but victorious engagements, which crowned him as the mightiest captain of his age, the shattered and bleeding remnant of one of his legions was ordered up for the roll-call. As the name of each absentee was called, a shout like the sound of a trumpet rent the air with the answer, 'dead on the field of honor'!

"Soldiers and man, if the roll-call of the 'Minute Men' of a century ago was now called, how those brave, grand words would reverberate down the lapse of years.

"You bear on your flag the fierce motto under which they marched to death—you bear their name, and though no stern alarms now dispel the peaceful quiet of your lives, the strict performance of military duty the soldierly fidelity of comrade to comrade, the sleepless vigilance by the bivouac and by the camp-fires are yours to perform.

"Bone of their bone, and flesh of their flesh, may you, soldiers, prove worthy of your illustrious predecessors; bear aloft their flag untarnished and unsoiled, and emulate their example in war and their virtues in peace.

"I accept this flag, Dr. Slaughter in the name of the 'Culpeper Minute Men' with the profoundest gratitute and pride."

CIVIL WAR ROLL.

The following is the roll of the Minute Men at the beginning of the war between the states. With some few exceptions, this is the roll of the men as they left Culpeper for Harper's Ferry, with a partial statement of those killed and wounded.

Tazewell Patton, Captain.   Chas. T. Crittenden, 1st. Lieutenant.
James H. Baughan, 2nd. Lieutenant.   B. H. Priddie, 3rd. Lieutenant.
Geo. M. Williams, 1st. Sergeant.   Ben. H. Gorrell, 2nd. Sergeant.
W. A. Ashby, 3d. Sergeant.   A. J. Stofer, 4th. Sergeant.
W. A. Coppage, Color Sergeant.   Z. T. Ross, 1st. Corporal.
P. L. Jameson, 2nd. Corporal.   J. P. Morton, 3rd. Corporal.
J. J. Utz, 4th. Corporal.

Privates—Wm. F. Anderson, killed in battle; W. C. Apperson, R. L. Apperson, J. H. Apperson, F. M. Burrows, H. W. Bell, dead: John W. Bell, dead; John Brown, dead; H. W. Carpenter, Geo. S. Carter, dead; J T. Finney, dead; Jas. Farish, dead; Bruce Farish, John Freeman, John. W. Fry, Jas. G. Field, R. Y. Field, A. F. Gaines, J. C. Gibson after serving a short while organized a company and was assigned to 49th. Va., and elected Col.; Jas. T. Grinnan, G. A. Grinnan, killed 12th. May, 1863; G. D. Gray, J. C. Green, Wm. Hill, Charles Jenkins, R. S. Jeffries, dead; C. S. Jones, dead; P. S. Jones, Jas. Keys, J. E. Lewis, T. M. Lewis, dead; J. M. Lewis, killed in battle: E. P. Long, dead; John Lee, J. W. McDaniel, J. P. Starke, J. T. Shepherd, J. W. R. Smith, Brooke Roberts, J. W. Slaughter, Clayton Slaughter, Lewis Turner, R. M. Thomas, W. A. Thompson, died soon after enlisting aged 17 years; Jas. Wood, J. M. Wood, H. C. Pendleton, Jas. H. Patton, J. R. R. Tapp, J. T. White, John Steward, dead; Dr. R. S. Lewis, Surgeon, dead; Mead Battle, Ben Battle, Jas. Vass, Geo. F. Vass, John Lawrence, Minnis Jameson, George W. Jameson, John Rivercomb, Jacob Barnes, Hugh Patton.

Lieutenant J. H. Baughan was appointed Quartermaster and Commissary by Colonel Hill in Spring of 1861; Sergeant W. A. Ashby was appointed at same time Quartermaster Sergeant of Regiment. This company was disbanded in fall of 1862, and all of its men went into service again in different branches of the services.

THE ROLL OF 1898.

The Minute Men were in the Third Virginia Regiment. The following regimental officers were from Culpeper.

Colonel William Nalle.   Charles J. Rixey, Jr., Adjutant and Lieut.
Silas L. Cooper, Quartermaster and Lieutenant.
John R. Cooper, Quartermaster Sergeant.

The Minute Men enlisted in the United States Volunteer army in the Spanish war, but did not do any service at the front. They were mustered out after about six months. The following is the roll of the members from Culpeper, Madison and Rappahannock, the ranks of the company being filled by men from other parts of the state.

Thomas E. Grimsley, Captain.
S. A. Shadrach, 1st. Lieutenant.   Frederick P. Hudgins, 2nd. Lieutenant.
Robert H. Howard, 1st. Sergeant.   J. Williams Jones, 2nd. Sergeant.
Henry O'B. Cooper, 3rd. Sergeant.   Charles E. Mosby, 4th. Sergeant.

Corporals.

Reuben N. Howard.   Charles E. Kilby.
John A. Croisant.   John E. Dennis.
Benjamin F. Estes.   James H. Filling.

William G. Johnson, Wagoner.   Franklin K. Williams, Artificer.

Privates.

Nelson Abel, Charles E. Atkins, Peyton Anderson, Otis Burgandine, James E. Brown, Ernest L. Bibb, Eugene Bowen, Alden A. Bell, Frank Barham, Samuel T. Byram, Roscoe C. Bruce, John W. Broy, Luther Brown, Charles L.

Curtis, Richard H. Dennis, Charles F. Davis, Eppa Deal, William T. Edwards, Francisco C. Elkins, dead; Joseph T. Foltz, John H. Finks, James B. Freeman, Thomas H. Freeman, John W. Green, Herbert R. Griffith, died; Egbert B. Hudson, Bailey Hawkins, Joseph C. Hawley, A. B. Hawley, Paul Hansbrough, Ernest Hansbrough, Charles F. Johnson, Joseph Johnson, John W. Jefferson, William Jefferson, William W. Kilby, William S. King, Rufus Lillard, Charles E. Lillard, Frank R. Lucas, Benjamin M. Marshall, William L. McFarland, Thomas H. Miller, William T. Nichols, Isaac B. Nicholson, Beverley Peter, John M. Patton, George W. Roach, James A. Roach, Frederick K. Sprinkel, Gustavus B. Sullivan, William W. Settle, David P. Stallard, John M. Stone, Edgar Spicer, died; William Tipton, Richard P. Thrall, Lawrence H. Thrall, James C. Williams, George W. Yates.

CHAPTER III.

CULPEPER IN THE CIVIL WAR.

It is not the intention of the publishers to give a complete history of Culpeper in the Civil War. An effort is made to give only the names and records of those men who enlisted on the side of the Confederacy.

ROSTER OF THE LITTLE FORK RANGERS.

This company was Company D. Fourth Virginia Cavalry, Stuart's Brigade, Fitz Lee's Division.

Captain Robert E. Utterback after first Battle of Manassas, was promoted to Major. Died after the war.

Captain William A. Hill.   George T. Freeman, 1st Lieutenant badly wounded at Statesville, dead.

Wilkins Coons 2nd Lieutenant, died,   O. M. Corbin 2nd. Lieutenant wounded at Aldie, dead,

A. C. Jennings 3rd. Lieutenant, died,   St. Pierre Gibson 3rd. Lieutenant killed at Westminster,

John A. Holtzman 3rd. Lieutenant wounded at Nancy's Shop,

George A. Sudduth, Orderly Sergeant,   George D. Coons, 1st. Sergeant wounded at Kellyville, dead,

John W. Bell, 2nd. Sergeant,   W. H. Cole, 3rd. Sergeant, killed at Fisher's Hill,

A. L. Stallard, 4th. Sergeant,   George W. Shaw, 1st. Corporal, wounded at Spottsylvania Court House, died,

Gideon McDonald, 2nd. Corporal, wounded at Five Forks, died,   S. M. Newhouse, 3rd. Corporal,

Dennis Kelley, 4th. Corporal, badly wounded at Spottsylvania C. H.

Privates—Amiss W. L., Amiss S. Y., Armstrong A. J., Adam John G., Adam Willie, Allen W. H., Ball Daniel F., Bugler, Browning W. L., Bywaters John E., Bywaters Addison, Bywaters Smith, taken prisoner and died; Bywaters R.

F. dead; Bray Alpheus, Cannon W. G. dead; Cannon John H. dead; Colvin W. D., Corbin Joseph R., Corbin Thomas J., Corbin Sylvester, dead; Corbin W. B., Corbin A. F. wounded at Spottsylvania, C. H., Corbin James, dead; Coughtry I. R. wounded, dead; Coons G. H. dead; Cooper Richard, dead; Compton John C., Crigler W. G., Chilton S. B., Doyle William, dead; Doyle James, badly wounded at Brandy; Doores Fred, Dulin James, badly wounded at Statesville; Dulin Edwin killed at Spottsylvania Court House; Doggett M. J., killed by lightning after the war; Embrey Fred horse killed under him by a cannon ball; Embrey Silas, Elly Thomas N., dead; Edwards I. F. dead; Freeman W. H., Ficklen Joseph, Field Charles Daniel, Hackley Joseph H., Hoffman F. E., Hoffman John, died; Hill Henry, dead; Hume Westley, Hobson Matthew, Jeffries Octavus, Jeffries Hill, Jeffries Marion, Jeffries George, Kilby James P., Kilby Walter, Kines Jack, died; Kines Thomas, Loyd A. W., deserted; Luttrell R. Thomas, died; Luttrell B. E , Luttrell M. C., wounded at Spottsylvania Court House, dead; Luttrell R D. wounded at Statesville; Lake Isaac N., Lyon, on John W. dead; Lawler Montgomery, Lear James, Lear William, killed in the valley; Newman Alex, McDonald W. M., McDonald James, McDonald John wounded at Spottsylvania Court House; McDonald L H., McDonald Coleman, died, McDonald B. W., Myers George A. horse killed under him by a cannon ball; Myers John W., dead; Myers James, Miller George B., McCormick A. W. McCormick J. T., McVeigh Harvey, Payne C. B., Payne Benjamin, dead; Parr A. W., killed at the White House; Pearson I. C., wounded and died; Perry O. P., Ross James P., Roberson Walter S., dead; Roberts Joseph, dead; Rivercomb John killed in the valley; Smith W. E., Smith John, had a horse killed under him by a shell; Smith James, Stallard Joseph H., dead; Stallard James, dead; Stallard Marcellus, Settle B. F., killed at the White House; Silvey Joseph H., dead; Scott W. H., Stuart B. P., Stuart W. B., Spindle J. M., Shaw Richard killed at Statesville; Taylor Daniel, Triplett G. S. P., Wood P., dead; Wood W. W., Wood Lewis L., dead; Wayman James W., Wayman John J., Wrenn P. M., Woodyard M. D., badly wounded at Statesville; Yates Benj., Yates Booten, badly wounded and died, Yates A. J., dead.

Explanation.—The word dead denotes those who have died since the war. The word died those who died during the war. A star could have been used against those who displayed great courage, a good and brave soldier, but it would have required discrimination.

COMPANY C, SEVENTH VIRGINIA INFANTRY.

Captain, J. C. Porter, promoted colonel.
First Lieutenant, James W. Green, promoted major and C. S.
Second Lieutenant, John R. Strother, promoted captain; discharged 1862; joined Mosby's command.
Third Lieutenant, Daniel Brown, discharged 1862.
First Sergeant, Philip Ashby, promoted captain; wounded '62 at Williamsburg.
Sergeant, William Apperson, killed 1862 at Fraziers Farm.
Sergeant, W. D. Brown, promoted lieutenant; resigned 1862.
Corporal, William H. Strother, promoted sergeant; died 1862 of fever.
Corporal, J. W. Carter.   Corporal, John Heaton.
Ashby, Dr. John W., promoted surgeon; died 1867 in Mississippi.
Apperson, William, promoted corporal; killed in seven days fight at Richmond.
Barbour, Dr. Edwin, killed May 5th, 1864, at Wilderness.
Byron, Charles, promoted sergeant; wounded '62 at second Manassas; died '63.
Bolen, Ed., killed 1862 at Fraziers Farm.
Bashaw, John, promoted second sergeant; wounded June 30, 1862, at Frazier's farm; July 3, 1863, at Gettysburg; May 16, 1864, at Drewry's Bluff; captured

April 1, 1865, at Five Forks; held at Point Lookout.
Battle, Richard, killed 1861 near Upton Hill.
Battle, Benjamin, accidentally killed August, 1861.
Bowers, R. A., promoted ensign; discharged August, 1862.
Bowers, Robert.
Beckham. A. Camp, cadet Virginia Military Institute; promoted captain; wounded September 11, 1862, at Sharpsburg; lost a leg; died June, 1888.
Beckham, Dr. H. C., promoted lieutenant Co. E, 7th Virginia Infantry, then surgeon.
Bickers, John, discharged 1862.
Burk, Frank, wounded 1861 at Upton Hill.
Brown, William H.
Brown, William D., promoted lieutenant; captured and held at Fort Warren; died 1881.
Burruss, John.   Barber, Ed.
Colvin, Gabriel, wounded July 21, 1861, at first Manassas; died September following.
Crutchfield, Peter.
Creel, J. W., captured 1863 in James City county; held at Washington.
Davis, W. A.. wounded June 30, 1862, at Fraziers farm; killed June 17, 1864, at Howlett House.
Davis, Thomas, killed July 3, 1863, at Gettysburg.
England, Robert, enlisted 1863; killed May, 1864, at Milford Station.
Eggborn, William H.   Fox, George.
Fox, Thomas F., captured April 1, 1865, at Five Forks; held at Point Lookout.
Feeley, ——, discharged 1862.
Fouchee, David, wounded June 30, 1862, at Frazier's farm; killed July 3, 1863. at Gettysburg.
Fouchee, Daniel M., killed July 3, 1863, at Gettysburg.
Gaines, John, captured 1864 at Milford; held at Point Lookout.
Garnett, Joseph, discharged 1861.   Hull, John.
Hull, Charles W., died at Lynchburg Hospital 1862.
Hacklea, ——, wounded 1862 at Williamsburg.
Heisel, John, killed 1862 at Frazier's farm.
Hill, W. H., promoted first corporal; killed July 3, 1863, at Gettysburg.
Hume, B. W., captured April 5, 1865, at Five Forks; held at Point Lookout.
Jenkins, Fountain, captured 1864 at Milford; held at Point Lookout.
Jenkins, Frank, captured 1864 at Milford, held at Point Lookout.
Kilby, Amos.
Kahl, William, enlisted 1862; wounded December 13, 1862, at Fredericksburg; never heard of since.
Lewis, William Wallace, promoted hospital steward.
Malton, James, died November 15, 1863.
Melton, James.   Melton, Robert.
Milton, James, killed.   Mathews, Joseph.
Mitchell, Henry, killed August 31, 1862, at Manassas.
Narr, Henry.   Oden, Alexander.
Pennell, Jerry, promoted second lieutenant; killed May 5, '62, at Williamsburg.
Parker, Horace H. (served in the Mexican war; detailed as engineer), died August 29, 1870.
Perry, George P., discharged September, 1862.
Perry, George, transferred to another company 1861.
Payne, Charles.

Petty, William C., enlisted February, 1864.
Bowles, Dr. B. T., captured near Richmond; held at Point Lookout.
Reed, Richard.
Read, R. S., captured at Frazier's Farm June 30, 1862; held at Fort Delaware and Governor's Island; wounded April 1, 1865, at Five Forks.
Shadrick, Abram, mortally wounded 1863 at Gettysburg.
Smith, Phil. D., wounded in arm at first Manassas.
Smith, George, promoted lieutenant; wounded and captured 1863 at Gettysburg; held at Johnson's Island.
Smith,——.
Somerville, Robert B., killed 1863 at Gettysburg.
Shotwell, John T., promoted corporal; killed June 30, 1862, at Frazier's Farm.
Shotwell, William, promoted hospital steward.
Smith, W. C., promoted sergeant.
Simms, A. Broaddus, killed May, 1864, at Milford.
Simms, T., promoted sergeant; killed in seven days fight at Richmond.
Towles, Joseph,   Turner, Frank.
Turner, B. F., died March, 1884.
Wilkes, John W., wounded at second Manassas.
Winston, Arthur, captured 1864 at Milford; held at Point Lookout.
Winston, A. W.
Willis, A. G., promoted sergeant; captured May, 1864 at Milford Station; held at Point Lookout:
Willis, Lewis, killed June 30, 1862, at Frazier's Farm.
Yowell, Thomas O., promoted sergeant; captured at Hanover Junction and Five Forks; held Point Lookout.

COMPANY E, SEVENTH VIRGINIA INFANTRY.

Beckham, H. C , lieutenant; promoted captain and assistant surgeon.
Brown, Daniel T., wounded July 3, 1863, at Gettysburg.
Brown, Thornton S., captured at Gettysburg July 3, 1863; held at Fort Delaware and Point Lookout eight months.
Byram, Charles, killed 1862.   Byram, James M.
Eggborn, William H., November, 1861, detailed as courier for General Johnston; March, 1862, detailed as chief wagon master for Major Alfred Barbour. then chief quartermaster for General Johnston's army; June, 1863, transferred to General Johnston's headquarters.
Hitt, George H.
Jones, George H., promoted sergeant; wounded July 21, 1861, at Manassas; captured June 31, 1862, at Frazier's Farm; held at Fort Delaware one month.
Legg, Alexander F , promoted sergeant; killed 1863 at Gettysburg.
Legg, John T., promoted sergeant; wounded at first Manassas, Fredericksburg and Drury's Bluff; captured June, 1862, at Chaflin's Farm, near Richmond; held at Fort Delaware.
Norman, Joseph T , wounded January 1, 1862, at Seven Pines
Smith, James K. P.   Tansill, James G., promoted captain.

COMPANY B, THIRTEENTH VIRGINIA INFANTRY.

Captain, William T. Patton, promoted colonel of 7th Virginia Infantry; killed July 3, 1863, at Gettysburg.
Apperson, W. C. transferred to Co. F. 6th Virginia Cavalry, Wickham's Brigade, Fitz Lee's Division.
Apperson, Richard, enlisted 1862; killed at Petersburg, 1862.
Beckham, J. T., promoted lieutenant; wounded at Hatcher's Run three times, in legs and arms.

Brown, Edward W., enlisted May, 1865.
Collins, J. H., captured April 1, 1865, at Richmond; held at Washington.
Collins, L. F., captured 1865 in Augusta county; held at Fort Delaware.
Colvin, W. D., enlisted March 2, 1862; promoted sergeant; captured at Gettysburg; held at Fort Delaware and Point Lookout.
Creel, Benjamin F., enlisted March, 1862.
Crittenden, C. T., first lieutenant; promoted captain, major and lieutenant-colonel; wounded three times at Cold Harbor, May 31 1862, May 3, 1864, and June 3, 1864.
Farish, B. B., transferred March, 1862, to Co. E, 9th Virginia Cavalry, Fitz Lee's Division, W. H. Lee's Brigade.
Gaines, James W., captured at Petersburg at the mine explosion.
Hudson, Champ D., enlisted September, 1864; killed February 6, 1865.
Hudson, Joel A., enlisted March, 1862; wounded September 19, 1864, at Winchester; April 1, 1865, in the trenches on the Appomattox river; captured April 3, 1865, at Richmond; held at Point Lookout; released July 3, 1865.
Hudson, N. D., enlisted March, 1862; wounded June 2, 1864, at Cold Harbor.
Hudson, Thomas J.
Jameson, W. C., captured 1862 at Culpeper; detailed as clerk in enrolling department.
Jones, Charles S., transferred 1862 to Co. H, 6th Virginia Cavalry.
Jones, John O., enlisted April, 1862; wounded June, 1864, at Richmond; wounded and captured September 19, 1864, at Winchester; held at Point Lookout.
Judd, William, wounded May 31, 1862, at Seven Pines; died from the effects.
Kilby, Andrew T., enlisted March, 1862; wounded September 19, 1864, at Winchester.
Kilby, Anslem M., enlisted April, 1865; captured April, 1865, at Petersburg; held at Point Lookout.
Kilby, Marcellus, promoted corporal; killed July, 1863, at Louisa C. H.
Kirby, William H., enlisted 1864; wounded February 6, 1865, at Hatcher's Run.
Lewis, John E., discharged October, 1861; appointed to post at Culpeper C. H. known as Culpeper Guards; served till close of war; wounded July, 1861, at Baily's Cross Roads.
Lewis, John M., killed April 2, 1865, at Petersburg.
Massey, J. P. B., enlisted April 28, 1862; promoted fourth corporal.
Nalle, W. C., detailed by Confederate States Congress as miller.
Pendleton, H. C., enlisted April 1, 1861; Co. B, 13th Virginia Infantry, Jackson's Brigade, Johnston's Division; transferred gunner in Sturtevant's Battalion; wounded November 12, 1862, at Petersburg.
Ross, T. W., promoted sergeant; captured October 19, 1864, at Fisher's Hill; held at Point Lookout; wounded at Spottsylvania C. H; died October 30, 1882.
Ross, Z. T., promoted captain; captured October 19, 1864, at Fisher's Hill; held at Fort Delaware; died February 28, 1884, in San Jacinto county, Texas.
Rowles, George W., enlisted May, 1863.
Scott, William H., captured February 14, 1864, in Culpeper county, while on detached duty; held at Fort Delaware till October 9, 1864; March 1863, joined Co. D, 4th Virginia Cavalry, known as "Little Fork Rangers;" returned to army January, 1865.
Smith, John Martin, enlisted April, 1862; wounded at Seven Pines and Cold Harbor.
Tapp, James R., wounded 1863 at Chancellorsville; detailed 1834 as courier to General R. E. Lee.
Wise, T. I., promoted corporal; captured and held at Point Lookout eighteen months.

MISCELLANEOUS SERVICE.

Amiss, Carroll., enlisted 1862, at Culpeper; Captain Utterback's Company Artillery; served over two years; killed July 2, 1864, at Petersburg.

Apperson, G. F., enlisted 1863; Co. F, 6th Virginia Cavalry, Wickham's Brigade, Fitz Lee's Division; served till close of war in ordnance department.

Banks, S. N., enlisted 1861, Co. D, 13th Virginia Infantry, Kemper's Brigade, Pickett's Division; discharged and re-enlisted 1862 in Stuart's Horse Artilery; wounded 1863 at Gettysburg; captured 1865 in North Carolina; held in hospital.

Battle, James Robert, enlisted April 17, 1861; Co. C, 13th Virginia Infantry, Pegram's Brigade, Early's Division; lost one eye at Petersburg.

Beckham, J. G., enlisted 1863; Mosby's Battalion; promoted lieutenant.

Beckham, J. M., enlisted 1861; Co. E, Wheat's Battalion, Taylor's Brigade, Ewell's Division; cadet Military Institute; promoted lieutenant.

Beckham, W. A., assigned to quartermaster's department under A. M. Barbour.

Berlin, Sanford W., enlisted March 17, 1862, in Alexander's Battery at Fort Spottswood; served till May 2, 1862; then temporarily attached to the 5th Alabama Battalion; transferred June 26, 1862, Co. M, 55th Virginia Infantry, Walker's Brigade, Hill's Division; May 6, 1864, captured in the two days fight at Wilderness; held at Point Lookout till August 10, 1864; transferred to Elmira, New York; released July 1, 1865.

Borst, John B., enlisted March, 1861: Co. K, 10th Virginia Infantry, Stuart's Brigade, Jackson's old Division; promoted regimental commissary.

Bowers, S. Carson, enlisted April, 1861; Co. E, 4th Virginia Infantry, Stonewall Brigade; promoted captain.

Bowman, William B., enlisted September, 1864; Co. H, 10th Virginia Infantry, Terry's Brigade, Gordon's Division; captured April 6, 1865, near Appomattox; held at Point Lookout four months.

Bradford, H. C., enlisted April 18, 1861; Co. B, 6th Virginia Cavalry, Pegram's Brigade, Fitz Lee's Division; captured 1864 at Culpeper; held at Old Capitol and Point Lookout.

Bragg, P. E., enlisted April 1, 1861; Co. B, 6th Virginia Cavalry, Jones' Brigade, Fitz Lee's Division; discharged October 15, 1861.

Brown, A. Hill, enlisted 1862; quartermaster's department.

Brown, Daniel, enlisted 1862; Mosby's command Cavalry; captured 1863 in Fauquier county; held at Fort Delaware.

Brown, George W., enlisted May 1, 1861; Co. F, 21st Virginia Infantry, Jones' Brigade, Johnston's Division; wounded May 5, 1864; died May 12, 1864.

Brown, James R., enlisted February, 1862. Co. F, 21st Virginia Infantry, Ewell's Brigade, Johnston's Division.

Brown, Joseph D., enlisted September, 1864; Co. F, Mosby's command; detailed to supply the army with provisions, 1862; died November 27, 1879.

Brown W. H., enlisted April 30, 1861, Co. B, 7th Virginia Infantry, Kemper's Brigade, Pickett's Division; promoted second sergeant; wounded July 3, 1863, at Gettysburg.

Burdett, James B., enlisted October, 1864; Co. A, 7th Virginia Infantry, Pickett's Division.

Burke, George F., enlisted 1862; Co. B, 6th Virginia Cavalry, Fitz Lee's Brigade, Stuart's Division; wounded July 3, 1863, at Gettysburg; captured at Cold Harbor; held at Point Lookout and died there.

Burke, James E. enlisted January 1, 1863; Co. B, 6th Virginia Cavalry, Jones', Lomax's, Poague's Brigade, Fitz Lee's Division

Burke, James Elias, enlisted July 15, 1861; Co. K, 49th Virginia Infantry, Early's Brigade, Ewell's Division; promoted orderly sergeant; wounded July, 1863, at Gettysburg; captured March 25, 1865, at Petersburg; held at Point Lookout; released June 23, 1865.

Burke, J. H., enlisted February 14, 1862; Co. B. 6th Virginia Cavalry, Fitz Lee's Brigade, Stuart's Division.

Burke, John M., enlisted 1861; Co. B, 6th Virginia Cavalry, Jones' Brigade, Hampton's Division; killed at Spotsylvania C. H.

Burke, M. N., enlisted October, 1864; Co. B, 6th Virginia Cavalry, Lomax's Brigade, Stuart's Division; wounded 1864 at Front Royal.

Burnley, Charles T., enlisted 1862; 2d Richmond Howitzer Artillery.

Burrows, H. C., enlisted April 16, 1861; Co. E, 1st Virginia Artillery; first sergeant; wounded July 18, 1861, at Blackburn's Ford; captured at Gettysburg, July 3, 1863; held at Fort Delaware and Point Lookout.

Burton, Arthur W., enlisted November. 1862; Co. L, 10th Virginia Infantry, Jackson's Brigade, Jackson's Division; wounded at second Manassas, August 27, 1862; at Chancellorsville May 2, '62; at Mine Run November 30, '63.

Bushong Isaac A., enlisted July, 1861; Co. H, 52d Virginia Infantry, Johnston's Brigade; second lieutenant; discharged May, 1862.

Carrico, William H., enlisted March, 1862; Pelham's Artillery, Fitz Lee's Division.

Chadduck, John M., enlisted 1861, at Culpeper; Co. G, 12th Virginia Cavalry; wounded 1864 at Charles City; service four years.

Christian, John T., enlisted July, 1861; Co. E, 1st Virginia Cavalry, Wickham's Brigade, Fitz Lee's Division.

Collins, E. B., enlisted 1861; 7th Virginia Infantry, Pegram's Brigade, Pickett's Division; captured 1865 at Appomattox; held at Point Lookout;

Cooper, Alexander H., enlisted April, 1861; Co. I, 6th Virginia Cavalry, Lomax's Brigade, Fitz Lee's Division.

Coppage, William, enlisted May, 1861; Co. C. 4th Virginia Cavalry, Fitz Lee's Brigade, Stuart's Division.

Corbin, Joseph R., 4th Cavalry.

Corbin, Lemuel A., enlisted 1864; Co. C, Mosby's Command Cavalry; wounded 1864 at Berryville.

Covington, Robert C., enlisted July 16, 1861; served in hospital department at Culpeper C. H., Virginia; afterwards acted as wagon master of the 7th Georgia till 1862, when discharged.

Covington. Thomas H., M. D., detailed as physician at home; captured January, 1864, in Culpeper county; held at Point Lookout.

Covington, Thomas R., enlisted April, 1862; Co. F, 9th Virginia Cavalry, Beale's Brigade, Fitz Lee's Division; wounded December, 1864, near Reame's Station.

Creel, Mathew, enlisted 1861, in the Valley of Virginia; 52d Virginia Infantry, Early's Brigade, Ewell's Division; killed August 27, '62 at second Manassas.

Cunningham, John M., enlisted September, 1861; 1st Virginia Artillery, Jackson's Division; first lieutenant; promoted captain, captured at home 1863; held at Fort Warren.

Curtis, T. O., enlisted April 10, 1861; Co. E, 13th Virginia Infantry, Walker's Brigade, Early's Division; promoted first sergeant; wounded June 6, 1862, at Cross Keys; December 13, 1862;, at Fredericksburg; May 19, 1864, at Spotsylvania C. H.; captured March 28, 1865, at Petersburg; held at Point Lookout.

Daniel, Samuel A., enlisted March 16, 1862; Purcell's Artillery, Hill's Division.

Davis, A., enlisted 1863; Co F, Mosby's command; captured July 1863, at Falls Church; held at Old Capitol; Washington, D. C., two months.

Doggett, Basil, enlisted May, 1861; Co. A—Infantry, Kemper's Brigade, Pickett's Division; wounded at Fredericksburg and Gettysburg: captured March, 1865, at Richmond; held at Point Lookout.

Doggett, James, enlisted June 1861; Horse Artillery, Fitz Lee's Division.

Doggett, Meredith J., enlisted May 1861; Co. A, 4th Virginia Cavalry, Pegram's Brigade, Pickett's Division; died August, 1880.

Doran, Francis B., enlisted April, 1862; Co E, 7th Virginia Cavalry; wounded May 5, 1864, at Wilderness.

Doran, John E., enlisted 1861; Co. A, 11th Virginia Cavalry, Garnett's Brigade, Jackson's Division; captured in Loudoun county, Virginia; held at Fort Delaware; killed.

Doolin, James A., Co. E, 7th Virginia Cavalry, Kemper's Brigade, Ewell's Division.

Duncan, R. R., enlisted August, 1861; Co. B, 6th Virginia Cavalry; promoted lieutenant and captain; wounded 1862 at second Manassas; 1864 at Trevillian's and in the Valley; captured '64 in the Valley; held at Fort Delaware.

Duncan, V. F., enlisted 1861; Co. B. 6th Virginia Cavalry, killed May 23, 1862, at Cedarville.

Embrey, L. J., enlisted April, 1861; Co. A, 9th Virginia Cavalry, Beale's Brigade, Fitz Lee's Division.

Eastham, Philip A., enlisted September, 1861; Co. B, 7th Virginia Cavalry; Jones' and Rosser's Brigade, Jackson's Division; first lieutenant.

Farish, G. G., enlisted September, 1864; Co, E, 9th Virginia Cavalry, W. H. Lee's Brigade, Fitz Lee's Division.

Farish, Robert T., enlisted in Co. E, 9th Virginia Cavalry; W. H. Lee's Brigade, Fitz Lee's Division; killed September, 1863, in Culpeper county near Cedar Mountain while scouting for General Stuart.

Fant, John S., enlisted April 17, 1861; Co. H, 4th Virginia Cavalry, Wickham's Brigade, Fitz Lee's Division; wounded at Winchester September 19, 1863.

Finks, H. W., enlisted December 1. 1862; Co. L, 10th Virginia Cavalry, Walker's Brigade, Ewell's Division; promoted first sergeant; wounded June 17, 1863, at Winchester; captured May 19, 1864, at Spotsylvania C. H., held at Fort Delaware.

Foster, Warrington D., enlisted August, 1863, Co. A, 39th Battalion Cavalry, Lee's body-guard; captured November 29, 1863 at Mine Run; held twelve months at Point Lookout.

Foster, McKidru F., enlisted April, 1861; Co. E, 6th Virginia Cavalry; '63 transferred to General Lee's body-guard.

Fouchee, Frank R., enlisted June 1, 1861; Co. A, 7th Virginia Infantry, Terry's Brigade, Pickett's Division; captured April, 7, 1865, at Farmville.

Fowles, G. R., enlisted 1853; 17th Virginia Infantry, Kemper's Brigade, Pickett's Division; killed May 16, 1864, at Drury's Bluff.

Fox, Henry, enlisted May, 1861; Co. F. 21st Virginia Infantry, Jones' Brigade, Johnston's Division; killed at Petersburg.

Fray, William H., enlisted April, 1861; Co. A, 7th Virginia Infantry, Kemper's Brigade, Pickett's Division; captured April 6, 1865, at Sailor's Creek; held at Point Lookout.

Freeman, George, enlisted 1861; Pelham's Battalion Horse Artillery; participated in all the battles of his command; captured May, 1862; held at Point Lookout.

Freeman, J. G., enlisted April, 1861; Deering's Artillery, Ewell's Brigade, Longstreet's Division; promoted commissary sergeant.

Freeman, William T., enlisted February, 1863, Deering's Artillery, Ewell's Brigade, Longstreet's Division; captured near Richmond; exchanged in a few days; died 1872.

Gaines, B. F., enlisted March 14, 1862; Co. L, 1st Virginia Reserves Artillery; captured July 3, 1863, at Gettysburg; was carried about two miles, and dodged the Federals by jumping behind an old shop and escaped.

Gaines, Henry L., enlisted April, 1862; 4th Virginia Cavalry, Wickham's Brigade, Fitz Lee's Division; killed at Williamburg, near Richmond.

Gaines, Reuben M., enlisted April 17, 1861; Co. L, 7th Virginia Infantry, Kemper's Brigade, Pickett's Division; killed at first Manassas July 21, 1861.

Garnett, John K., enlisted August, 1863; Co. C, 39th Virginia Battalion.

Gibson, Daniel W., enlisted January 1862; Crenshaw's Company, Pegram's Battalion Artillery; captured at Five Forks; held at Point Lookout two months.

Gibson, John W., enlisted January, 1862; Crenshaw's Company, Pegram's Battalion Artillery.

Gibson, Thomas C., enlisted March, 1861; Co. E, 13th Virginia Infantry, Early's Brigade, Ewell's Division; re-enlisted at Richmond, Virginia, 1862, in Crenshaw's Company, Pegram's Battalion Artillery.

Gordon, Albert S., enlisted April, 1861; Co. E, 13th Virginia Infantry; was afterwards in Jackson's Brigade; discharged August, 1861.

Godfrey, Alexander, enlisted April, 1862; Co. A, 18th Virginia Cavalry, Imboden's Brigade.

Goodwin, James H., enlisted 1864, after the burning of the Military Institute; Infantry, Breckenridge's Division; wounded at Maryland Heights.

Grimsley, Daniel A., enlisted April 17, 1861; Co. B, 6th Virginia Cavalry; Payne's Brigade, Fitz Lee's Division; promoted major.

Hackley, William, enlisted April, 1861; Co. A, 2d Virginia Infantry, Stonewall Brigade; battles, four; service two years; discharged 1863.

Hale, Daniel W., enlisted June, 1861; Co. C, 15th Virginia Infantry, Pegram's Brigade; Ewell's Division; wounded at Gaines' Mill, Hatcher's Run, and February, 1865, at Fisher's Hill.

Hall, F. S., enlisted June, 1861, first under Captain Nolan in D. H. Hill's Artillery and under Captain Braxton in A. P. Hill's Artillery; promoted assistant surgeon in Pegram's Battalion.

Holliday, W. D., enlisted April, 21, 1862; Co. A, 13th Virginia Infantry, Early's Brigade, Ewell's Division; wounded June 8, 1862, at Cross Keys in arm; September 1, 1862, at Ox Hill, in thigh; May 12,1864 at Spotsylvania, lost an arm; discharged December 7, 1864.

Hatcher, Mahlon G., enlisted 1861; Co. C. 17th Virginia Infantry, Corse's Brigade, Pickett's Division; promoted color sergeant; wounded May 5, 1862, at Williamsburg; captured 1862 in Loudoun county; escaped. Dead

Hawkins, Benjamin F., enlisted 1863; Co. B, 7th Virginia Infantry, Kemper's Brigade, Pickett's Division; conscript officer, serving as such until December 1, 1864, when he again entered the field service.

Hawkins, William L., enlisted April, 1862; Co. B, 6th Virginia Cavalry, Lomax's Brigade, Stuart's Division; wounded at the time of General Stuart's death, near Richmond.

Hawley, John A., enlisted March, 1862; Fry's Artillery, Jackson's Corps.

Hawley, M. R., enlisted April, 1, 1862; 6th Virginia Cavalry, Payne's Brigade, Fitz Lee's Division.

Hiftin, John L., enlisted February, 1864; Co. E, 13th Virginia Infantry, Kemper's Brigade, Pickett's Division.

Hill, William H., enlisted April, 1861; Co. C, under Colonel Porter, Pickett's Brigade, Longstreet's Division; promoted corporal; killed at Gettysburg July 3, 1863.

Hitt, Festus, enlisted May, 1861; Co. G, 49th Virginia Infantry, Smith's Brigade, Early's Division.

Hitt, Blewford A. enlisted May, 1861; Co. G, 7th Virginia Infantry, Kemper's Brigade, Pickett's Division; died September, 1861, at home in Culpeper county.

Hitt, James W., enlisted March 1862; Co. A, 7th Virginia Cavalry, Stuart's Brigade, captured August 6, 1863, near Brandy Station, held at Point Lookout.

Hitt, Martin L., enlisted May, 1861; Co. G, 7th Virginia Infantry, Kemper's Brigade, Pickett's Division; discharged January 4, 1865, on account of disability.

Hudgins, Albert G., enlisted April 14, 1861; midshipman on the steamer "Sumter," Confederate States Navy; promoted lieutenant.

Hoffman, F. W., enlisted July 1, 1861; Stribbling's Battery, Pickett's Division; wounded March 26, and captured April 2, 1865, at Petersburg, held at Newport News; discharged July, 1865.

Holliday, John Z., enlisted May, 1861; Co. G, 20th Virginia Infantry, Garnett's Brigade; re-enlisted in Co. A, 3d Virginia Cavalry, Fitz Lee's Brigade, Stuart's Division; captured 1861 at Rich Mountain; paroled.

Holmes, F. Wallace, enlisted April 1861; Co. F, 18th Virginia Infantry; Stonewall Brigade; wounded July 18, 1861, at Manassas; discharged July 18, 1861.

Hooe, George G., enlisted April 17, 1861; Co. G., 4th Virginia Cavalry, Wickham's Brigade, Fitz Lee's Division; captured several times, always escaped; was on general scout duty all through the war.

Howard, Thomas C., enlisted April 17, 1861; Co. A, Huger's Battalion Artillery, Jordan's Battery; promoted sergeant.

Hudson, Bruce, enlisted 1864; 4th Virginia Cavalry; killed at the Wilderness.

Hudson, James W., enlisted April 17, 1861; Co. G, 7th Virginia Infantry, Kemper's Brigade, Pickett's Division ; wounded July 3, '63 at Gettysburg.

Hudson, Samuel T., enlisted April 17, 1861; Co. G, 7th Virginia Infantry, Kemper's Brigade, Pickett's Division; captured April 3, 1865, at Richmond; held at Point Lookout.

Hudson, Thomas J., enlisted October, 1862; Camp Lee Guards, City Battalion at Richmond; served till January, 1865; re-enlisted, Co. B, 13th Virginia Infantry.

Hoffman, Moses A., enlisted March, 1861; Co. K, 7th Virginia Infantry, Pickett's Brigade, Kemper's Division.

Hume, R. E., captured and held at Point Lookout.

Janney, Ashberry, enlisted October 1861; courier for General Hill.

Jeffries, Robert S., enlisted 1863; 13th Virginia Infantry; captured 1865; held at Point Lookout.

Kibler, Ferdinand, enlisted April, 1861; Virginia Cavalry, Rosser's Brigade.

Kilby, Andrew J., enlisted May 1861; Co. G, 7th Virginia Infantry, Kemper's Brigade, Pickett's Division, wounded July 3, 1863, at Gettysburg.

Kilby, H. C., enlisted August, 1861; Co. G, 7th Virginia Infantry, Hill's, Taylor's, Kemper's Brigade, Longstreet's Division; wounded and captured at Frazier's Farm; held at Fort Delaware.

Kilby, James P., enlisted March, 1863; 4th Virginia Cavalry.

Kilby, Joseph M., enlisted 1862; 6th Virginia Cavalry, Kemper's Brigade; Pickett's Division;

Kilby, Thomas M., enlisted April 18, 1861; Co G, 7th Virginia Infantry, Kemper's Brigade, Pickett's Division; wounded slightly at Seven Pines, May 31, 1862.
Lampkin, J. W., enlisted 1861; Co. B, 38th Battalion Virginia Artillery; captured July, 1863; paroled; wounded July, 6, 1864, at Petersburg.
Lampkin, Thomas O., enlisted 1861; 13th Virginia Infantry, Walker's Brigade, Ewell's Division; discharged on account of disability.
Leavel, James W., enlisted 1861; Co. K, 7th Virginia Infantry, Kemper's Brigade, Pickett's Division; promoted orderly sergeant; wounded August 30, 1862, at second Manassas.
Leavel, William A., enlisted October, 1861; Co. E, Mosby's Battalion.
Legg, Ambrose C., enlisted 1863; 21st Virginia Infantry, Johnston's Division; killed at Spotsylvania C. H.
Legg, James W., enlisted April 1861; Co. C, 13th Virginia Infantry, Pegram's Brigade, Early's Division.
Legg, Peyton E., enlisted September, 1862; Co. C. 13th Virginia Infantry, Pegram's Brigade, Early's Division; captured October, 1864, at Culpeper; held at Washington.
Lewis, Richard, enlisted 1861; Co. H, 4th Virginia Cavalry, Fitz Lee's Brigade, Stuart's Division, captured 1862, near Ashland; held at Fort Delaware; wounded May 6. 1864, at Wilderness.
Legg, Alec, enlisted June 1861, Co. E, 7th Virginia Infantry, Kemper's Brigade; killed at Gettysburg July 3, 1862.
Legg, John, enlisted November 1861, Co. E, 7th Virginia Infantry; wounded; served 4 years.
Lee, John, enlisted Co. B. 13 Virginia Infantry, afterwards Sturdevant's Battery; served to close of war.
Lipscomb, Waddy, enlisted 1864; Co. C, 1st Virginia Reserves; Infantry, C. Lee's Division.
Long, J. F., enlisted January, 1863; Co. F, 6th Virginia Cavalry, Fitz Lee's Division.
Major, E. P., enlisted May 1861; Crane's Company of Wise's Legion; promoted adjutant; killed May 31, 1862, at Seven Pines.
Major, Langdon C., enlisted 1864; Co. E, Mosby's command.
Major, Samuel, enlisted March 17, 1863; Sturdevant's Battery, Colonel Jones' 12th Virginia Field Artillery, Anderson's corps; participated in the battles in and around Richmond.
Major, W. jr., enlisted May, 1863; Sturdevant's Battery; October 14, 1864, wounded by the explosion of the magazine.
Marsh, C. W., enlisted September, 1864; Co. F, 2d Virginia Reserves, Walker's Division.
Massey, John, enlisted April 10, 1861; Co. I, 6th Virginia Cavalry, Payne's Brigade, Fitz Lee's Division; died December 18, 1883, in Texas.
Massey, T. C., enlisted April 1, 1862; Co. I, 6th Virginia Cavalry,[1] Payne's Brigade, Fitz Lee's Division; wounded November 15, 1863, at Stevensburg, and November 1, 1864, at Winchester.
Maupin, H. A., enlisted 1862; Co. I, 7th Virginia Cavalry, Ashby's Brigade, Rosser's Division.
McConchee, William A., enlisted April, 1861; Co. I, 11th Virginia Infantry, Kemper's Brigade; promoted corporal.
Miller, Henry T., enlisted July, 1861; Co. I, 7th Virginia Cavalry, Ashby's Brigade, Jackson's Division.
Miller, Robert B., enlisted 1864; 1st Virginia Reserves; second lieutenant; captured near Richmond; held at Fort Delaware.

Milton, John W., enlisted 1862, Co. E, Mosby's Cavalry, transferred to Co. C, 13th Virginia Infantry, Pegram's Brigade, Pickett's Division.
Morgan, William B., enlisted April 1861; Co. B, 7th Virginia Infantry, Kemper's Brigade, Pickett's Division.
Nalle, G. B. W., enlisted October 12, 1863; Co. D. Cadet Corps, Virginia Military Institute, Breckinridge's Division; first sergeant.
Nolan, John. enlisted April 17, 1861; Co. C, 13th Virginia Infantry, Pegram's Brigade, Early's Division; promoted corporal; captured September 22, 1864, at Fisher's Hill; held at Point Lookout; exchanged in one month.
O'Callahan, William, enlisted 1861; Co. K, 49th Virginia Infantry, Smith's Brigade, Early's Division. promoted first sergeant; wounded 1862, at Seven Pines; captured 1862, at Sharpsburg; held at Fort Delaware; service four years; discharged at close of war.
Pattie, D. M., enlisted April 1861; Co. K, 17th Virginia Infantry, Pickett's Brigade, Longstreet's Division; promoted department marshal of Eastern Virginia under confiscation act.
Patton, Hugh M., enlisted April 18, 1861; 7th Virginia Infantry, Kemper's and Cook's Brigade, Pickett's and Heath's Division; promoted first lieutenant; wounded at second Manassas.
Patton, James, enlisted April 18, 1861; Echols' Brigade; promoted lieutenant; wounded at Giles C. H.; died March 30, 1882.
Patton, W. T., enlisted April 18, 1861; 7th Virginia Infantry, Kemper's Brigade, Pickett's Division; captain; promoted colonel; wounded at second Manassas; killed at Gettysburg.
Payne, J. W. enlisted April, 1864; Black Horse Cavalry, Co. D, Stuart's Brigade, Fitz Lee's Division; served till close of war.
Payne, Joseph F., enlisted March 9, 1862; Co. H. 4th Virginia Cavalry, Wickham's Brigade, Fitz Lee's Division; wounded and captured March, 1863, at Kellys Ford; held at Washington, D. C., "Old Capitol building," three months; exchanged and returned to company.
Payne, Robert W., enlisted 1861; Co. A, 7th Virginia Cavalry, Rosser's Brigade; Fitz Lee's Division; wounded 1862, at second Manassas; 1863, at Gettysburg; 1864, at Ream's Station, and four other times.
Pendleton, Edmund, enlisted 1862; 1st Virginia Infantry, Kemper's Brigade, Pickett's Division; died 1863.
Penick, N., enlisted May, 1861; Co. A, 38th Virginia Infantry, Smith's Brigade, Johnston's Division; lieutenant; promoted adjutant; served in Infantry till autumn 1861; entered artillery service 1862 as captain Co. A, Poague's Battalion Artillery.
Pendleton, John R., enlisted June, 1861; Co. H, 7th Virginia Cavalry, Jones' Brigade, Fitz Lee's Division; wounded at Hanover Junction and Reams' Station; captured at Mount Jackson and in Albemarle county; held at Fort Delaware seven months.
Perry, George P., enlisted August, 1861; 7th Virginia Infantry, Kemper's Brigade, Pickett's Division.
Perry, W. G., enlisted April 12, 1862; Co. G. Horse Artillery, Stuart's Brigade, Jackson's Division.
Pierce, J. M., enlisted 1862; Co. D, Gowe's Regiment Arkansas Infantry, Churchill's Brigade, Hindman's Division; wounded 1864, at Mansfield.
Pinkard, A. A., enlisted May 15, 1861: 49th Regiment, Pegram's Brigade, Early's Division; ensign; killed June 26, 1862; at Mechanicsville.
Porter, John J., enlisted September, 1861; Co. F, Mosby's command; promoted to Mosby's staff; captured in Culpeper county, October 1, 1863; held ten

days at Culpeper C. H.; discharged at Winchester, April 12, 1865.
Ratrie, Henry H., enlisted March 10, 1862; Co. K, 4th Virginia Cavalry, Jones' Brigade, Fitz Lee's Division.
Rixey, Samuel, enlisted June, 1863; under captain Taylor in conscript service till close of war.
Robinson, William A., enlisted March, 1862; Purcell's Battery, Hill's Brigade, Field's Division.
Robson, W. T., enlisted September 16, 1863; Co. G, 12th Virginia Cavalry; wounded 1864 in the Valley.
Rosson, J. W., enlisted March 1862; Co. G, 12th Virginia Cavalry, Rosser's Brigade, Fitz Lee's Division; promoted sergeant.
Rudasill, F. M., enlisted July 12, 1861; quartermaster department; then Co. C, Mosby's Rangers.
Scott, J. M., jr., enlisted April, 1861; Co. F, 10th Virginia Cavalry, Hampton's, then Chamberlain's Brigade, Fitz Lee's Division; sergeant of color guards; slightly wounded at Gettysburg and Brandy Station; captured October 11, 1863, at Brandy Station; held at Old Capitol and Point Lookout 16 months.
Shackelford, John M., enlisted February, 1863; Co. C, 4th Virginia Cavalry, Wickham's Brigade, Fitz Lee's Division; wounded at Five Forks, April 2, 1865; captured at Richmond, April 4, 1865; held there.
Shaw, Jackson N., enlisted 1864; Captain Franklin's Company, Mosby's command; lost an eye below Upperville, 1864.
Sims, William B., enlisted September 28, 1862; Co. A, 4th Virginia Cavalry, Wickham's Brigade, Fitz Lee's Division.
Slaughter, Thomas T., enlisted April, 1861; Co. B, 6th Virginia Cavalry.
Smith, Early, enlisted August 9, 1861; Co. L, 10th Virginia Infantry, Taliaferro's Brigade, Jackson's Division; captured March, 1864, at Hamilton, Loudoun county; held at Fort Delaware.
Smith, Elza, enlisted May, 1861; assigned to quartermaster department.
Smith, John W., enlisted August 9, 1861; Co. L, 10th Virginia Infantry, Taliaferro's Brigade, Jackson's Division; captured April 1, 1865, at Five Forks; held at Fort Delaware.
Smith, Joseph T., enlisted March, 1863; Co. F, 21st Virginia Infantry, Terry's Brigade, Johnston's Division.
Smith, Philip, enlisted May, 1861; Taylor's Company 7th Virginia Infantry, Kemper's Brigade, Longstreet's Division; killed at the Seven Days fight.
Smith, Thomas J., enlisted September, 1862; 21st Virginia Infantry, Stuart's Brigade; captured in Culpeper county; held at Point Lookout.
Somerville, C. B., enlisted November, 1863; Douglass' Pontoon Corps.
Somerville, J. W., enlisted May, 1861; Co. G, 20th Virginia Infantry, Pegram's Brigade, Garnett's Division; discharged July, 1861; re-enlisted 1863, 3rd Alabama Regiment, Rhoades' Brigade; wounded at Rich Mountain and Boonesboro Gap.
Somerville, Langdon, enlisted November, 1863; Douglass' Pontoon Corps; died April, 1864.
Somerville, Walter, enlisted 1862; surgeon at Yorktown; died 1863.
Somerville, R. B., enlisted May, 1861; Porter's Company, 7th Virginia Infantry, Kemper's Brigade, Pickett's Division; killed at Gettysburg.
Sparks, Champ C., enlisted May, 1861; Co. G, 7th Virginia Infantry. Kemper's Brigade, Pickett's Division; promoted corporal; wounded May 5, 1862, at Williamsburg; wounded and captured July 3, 1863, at Gettysburg; held at Fort Delaware, and died there October, 1863.
Sparks, Robert W., enlisted April, 1861; Co. A, 7th Virginia Infantry, Kem-

per's Brigade, Pickett's Division.

Spicer, James S., enlisted April, 1862; Co. E, Pioneer Corps.

Spicer, James S., promoted quartermaster sergeant.

Stallard, Randolph R., enlisted 1861; Captain Vanderslier, 49th Virginia Infantry; mortally wounded November, 1864, at Spotsylvania C. H.

Starke, A. E., enlisted August 9, 1861; Co. I, 49th Virginia Infantry, Smith's Brigade, Early's Division; promoted sergeant; 1863 transferred to Co. K, same regiment; October, 1864, wounded and captured at Cedar Creek, held at Point Lookout.

Stewart, Broaddus, enlisted January, 1862; cavalry; died 1882 in Missouri.

Stewart, James W., enlisted April 20, 1861; Co. I, 30th Virginia Infanty, Corse's Brigade, Pickett's Division; wounded June 26, 1862, at Chickahominy; died June 29, 1862.

Stewart, Joseph, enlisted May, 1861; infantry, Stuart's Brigade, Pickett's Division.

Stewart, Richard, enlisted May, 1861; cavalry; died 1868.

Stringfellow, B. W., enlisted May, 1861; Co. I, 11th Virginia Infantry, Kemper's Brigade, Pickett's Division; lieutenant; wounded May 31, 1862, at Seven Pines; captured 1862, in Orange county; paroled; captured 1864, at Petersburg; held at Old Capitol, Washington.

Stringfellow, Martin S., enlisted April 10, 1861; Co. A, 13th Virginia Infantry, Early's and Pegram's Brigade, Ewell's and Walker's Divisions; promoted first lieutenant; slightly wounded at Chantilly.

Strother, George F., enlisted March, 1863; as assistant commissary.

Strother, Philip W., enlisted April, 1861; Co. F, 13th Virginia Infantry, Early's Brigade, Ewell's Division; lieutenant; wounded May 12, 1864, at Spottsylvania C. H.; discharged same day.

Taliaferro, Alex. G., enlisted May, 1832; 13th. then 25th Virginia Infantry, Johnston's Division; promoted captain, lieutenant colonel, colonel, and brigadier general; wounded at second Manassas.

Taliaferro, John K., enlisted February, 1863; Co. H, 4th Virginia Cavalry, Wickham's Brigade, Fitz Lee's Division; wounded at Trevilian Depot; captured April 1, 1865, at Five Forks; held at Point Lookout two months.

[General Hooker took command of the army, but no advance was made; the condition of the army and the long winter were his excuses, but spring opened and but one engagement broke the long silence of the lines along the banks of the Rappahannock.

That was on the 17th of March, when a Federal Force of 3,000 crossed the river at Kelly's Ford and advanced to within six miles of Culpeper Court House, when they were engaged by the brigade of General Fitzhugh Lee. The engagement continued some hours, but at last the Federals were driven from the field after having inflicted a loss of one hundred upon the Confederates, among which was the gallant Pelham, the "boy Major."]

Tansill, G. S., enlisted 1861; 7th Virginia Infantry; sergeant major.

Tanner, John W., enlisted March, 1862; Co. E, 7th Virginia Infantry, Kemper's Brigade, Pickett's Division; wounded June 3, 1862; at Frazier's Farm; discharged July, 1862.

Thomas, G. S., enlisted March 13, 1862; Purcell's Battery; Hill's Division.

Towles, G. R., enlisted 1863; 17th Virginia Infantry, Kemper's Brigade, Pickett's Division; killed May 16, 1864, at Drury's Bluff.

Throckmorton, John A., enlisted April, 1861; 6th Virginia Cavalry; courier to
J. E. Johnston; May 1862, promoted major; discharged December 19, 1864.

Torreut, Lewis C., enlisted 1861; Co. I, 11th Virginia Infantry, Kemper's Brigade, Pickett's Division; captured 1862, at Williamsburg; held at Fort Delaware; released and discharged 1862.

Turner, T. H., enlisted 1863; Pelham's Battalion Horse Artillery; participated in the principal battles of the command.

Vaughan, Franklin D., enlisted 1863, Co. E, Mosby's Rangers.

Vaughan, Henry J., enlisted 1861; teamster; served on hospital duty, and engineers' corps, Colonel Talcott, Captain Johnson.

Vaughan, Peter, enlisted July, 1861; quartermaster department, carpenter and scout.

Wager, James P, enlisted April, 1861; Co. E, 13th Virginia Infantry, Kemper's Brigade, Pickett's Division; discharged 1862.

Waite, C., enlisted April 3, 1861; Co. B, 9th Virginia Cavalry, Fitz Lee's Division; captain; promoted major; served on General Lee's staff from May 1, 1862, till close of the war.

Walker, Thomas G., enlisted March, 1862; Crenshaw's Company, Pegram's Battalion Artillery, A. P. Hill's Division; wounded July 3, 1863, at Gettysburg; captured April, 1863, at Louisa C. H.; held at Washington one month; captured April 1865, at Five Forks; held at Point Lookout three months.

Wallace, A. Henderson, enlisted October, 1864; Co. C, 30th Virginia Infantry, Corse's Brigade, Pickett's Division.

Wayland, John W., enlisted 1861; Co. A, 7th Virginia Infantry, Kemper's Brigade, Pickett's Division; served two years in quartermaster department.

Wharton, Stanton, enlisted April, 1861; Co. E, 13th Virginia Infantry, Pegram's Brigade, Early's Division; wounded at second Manassas; captured at Petersburg in 1865; held at Point Lookout four months.

Wheatley, James G., enlisted April, 1861; 4th Virginia Cavalry, Fitz Lee's Division.

Whitlock, Martin, enlisted 1864; Co. I, 6th Virginia Infantry, Wickham's Brigade, Fitz Lee's Division; wounded 1864, at Manassas.

Winston, Arthur W., enlisted May, 1861; 7th Virginia Infantry, Kemper's Brigade, Pickett's Division.

Winston, L. D., enlisted April 18, 1861; Culpeper Minute Men, Purcell's Battery Hill's Division.

Wise, John B., enlisted 1862; wounded 1863, at Leesburg; died 1873, at Shreveport, Louisana, of yellow fever.

Wise, Louis A., enlisted 1861; Richmond Howitzer Company Artillery.

Wood, P., enlisted 1863; Co. D, 13th Virginia Infantry.

Wood, Robert W., enlisted June 6, 1861; Co. D, 23rd Virginia Infantry, Taliaferro's Brigade, Jackson's Division; lost all toes by frost; discharged February 9, 1862.

Yancey, Edwin D., enlisted 1861; artillery; promoted lieutenant.

Yowell, John, enlisted September 1, 1863; Pegram's Battalion Artillery.

Yowell, William L., enlisted September, 1863; Co. C, 4th Virginia Cavalry, Wickham's Brigade, Fitz Lee's Division.

ENGAGEMENTS IN CULPEPER COUNTY.

On June 26, 1862, General John Pope was appointed to the command of the Federal "Army of Virginia." One of his first official acts was to issue a manifesto to the soldiers and officers of this army, directing a series of depredations upon the peaceful, noncombatant residents of the country they had invaded, authorizing arbitrary arrests, ordering such as should refuse to take the oath of allegiance to be "driven from their homes, considered spies, and subjected to the extreme rigor of military law." This placing of the helpless people of an invaded country at the mercy of an unbridled and unscrupulous soldiery was keenly felt in Culpeper county where Banks, commanding Pope's second corps, had at this time a strong advance guard stationed South of Culpeper C. H., and near Gordonsville, Orange county.

Pope's object was to obtain possession of Gordonsville, where the Virginia Central and Orange & Albemarle railroads intersect, and destroy communication between the Confederate capital and the Shenandoah Valley. To effect this, Banks ordered a brigade of infantry to Culpeper C. H., July 14th, while this cavalry, under General Hatch, advanced to seize Gordonsville. But General Lee's superior strategy had enabled him to comprehend the purpose of the advance through Culpeper, and although the whole army of the Potomac menaced him before Richmond, he had not hesitated to dispatch to Gordonsville, on the 13th, his most trusted lieutenant. "Stonewall" Jackson, at the head of his own and Ewell's divisions.

Hatch fell back only too quickly from Gordonsville on finding an army of 15,000 men where he had looked to overawe non-fighting citizens. Until re-inforced, the Federals in Culpeper largely outnumbering his force, Jackson held Gordonsville, warily watching the gathering of the enemy before him. July 26th A. P. Hill's division joined him, and he determined to offer battle. "Having recieved information," says Jackson's official report "that only a part of Pope's army was at Culpeper C. H.," [Its numerical force outnumbering his force even then] "and hoping, through the blessing of Providence, to be able to defeat it before reinforcements should arrive there, Ewell's, Hill's and Jackson's divisions were moved on the 6th in the direction of the enemy from their respective encampments near Gordonsville. * * * On the 9th, as we arrived within about eight miles of Culpeper C. H., we found the enemy on our front, near Cedar Run, a short distance west and north of Slaughter [Cedar] mountain."

BATTLE OF CEDAR RUN.

Jackson was not the general to hesitate in the face of overwhelming odds, and he promptly offered battle. Ewell's division was ordered forward on his right, Timble's and Hay's brigade on the northern slope of Cedar mountain, Early's brigade on the Culpeper road; Jackson's division commanded by General Winder, was on the left; Campbell's brigade commanded by Lieutenant-Colonel Garnet, the brigade of General W. B. Taliaferro, and the famous "Stonewall" brigade in reserve. Hill's division was in reserve. The Federals were drawn up in strong position on a plateau just beyond Cedar Run, the artillery in front of the infantry, the cavalry on the flanks. Crawford's brigade of Williams' division (Federal) was the extreme right of Banks' line of battle, Geary's, Prince's and Greene's Brigade of Augur's and Bayard's divisions confronting Ewell's division, and Gordon's brigade formed the Federal reserve.

The artillery opened the battle about noon, and until 3 p. m. kept up a constant fire. General Winder was killed about 3:30 p. m., while directing the fire of some batteries. At 3 p m. Banks ordered forward his whole line. The First Virginia Battalion was struck at great disadvantage, and the Forty-Second, ordered to change front and meet a flank attack, lost its commanding officer, Major Layne. The Confederate forces met the attack with heroic obstinacy; Colonel Garnet was wounded, Lieutenant-Colonel Cunningham, of the Twenty-First Virginia was killed; the 12th Georgia held their ground, though attacked in front and rear. Jackson then ordered up the brigades of Branch, Archer and Pender—Hill's division. The Federals fell back across a wheat field and endeavored to form another line of battle, and Banks ordered Gordon's reserve into action. The fresh Confederate brigades flung themselves into action with an order against which the demoralized Federals could make no stand, and in another hour they were driven from the field, leaving the narrow valley where the infantry fought covered with their dead. One Massachusetts regiment (Second Infantry) had thirty-five per cent. of the men engaged killed.

The battle had been short, sharp and sanguinary. Jackson's official report shows: 223 killed, 1,060 wounded, 31 missing. He captured 400 prisoners, three stand of colors, and 5,302 small arms. The Federal loss was 1,661 killed and wounded, 723 missing; total 2,393. After a day spent in burying the dead, Jackson fell back toward Gordonsville, satisfied there would be no further effort to mass troops in that direction. He had won what the northern newspapers were pleased to term "a tactical victory," and it was not the first "tactical" defeat Banks had met at his hands. This battle of Cedar Run is also variously called: Cedar Mountain, Slaughter Mountain, Southwest Mountain, and Mitchell's Station

August 12th Longstreet, with his division and two brigades under General Hood, Stuart's cavalry, and the brigade from the James under R. H Anderson, were ordered to Gordonsville, which force, combined with Jackson's, Lee intended should give battle to Pope's "Army of Virginia," now in force beyond the Rapidan For once, comprehending the Confederate purpose, Pope hastily retreated across the Rappahannock, and Culpeper county was relieved of the presence of his hated troops

In the early months of 1863, General Lee initiated the movements preparatory to the invasion of Pennsylvania, and the troops for the campaign were marshalled on the Culpeper plain. Stuart, his war horse literally covered with floral offerings from the ladies who gathered to witness the display, reviewed the cavalry of the Army of Northern Virginia at Brandy Station.

THE BATTLE OF BRANDY STATION

Was an attack, June 9, 1863, on his cavalry by a portion of Pleasant's cavalry. General Hooker, the "fighting Joe Hooker" of the Northern press, was now in the command of the "Army of the Potomac," and Pleasanton was his recently appointed cavalry leader. The Federals crossed the Rappahannock at Beverlys and Kellys fords, nine thousand men and six batteries, at daybreak June 9th. Major McClellan, Stuart's adjutant-general, puts Stewart's force at nine thousand three hundred and thirty five men and twenty guns, but states that three thousand men were absent at the time of the battle, making Stuart's actual fighting force one third less than Pleasant's. The latter formed his plan of attack on the mistaken supposition that Stuart was at Culpeper C. H., and ordered his troops to rendezvous at Brandy Station. Unfortunately for his plans, Stuart's troops were concentrated at his place of rendezvous.

General Buford, commanding Pleasanton's first division, came up from Beverly Ford, met Stuart's whole force at St. James church, fought some hours, was attacked in the rear, and finally compelled to fight his way out and back to the ford. Colonel Gregg, with Pleasanton's third division, came up from Kellys Ford, and in turn received the attention of Stuart's men, now well warmed up for the work. Pleasanton's second division, commanded by Colonel Duffie, did not reach the battle field until late in the day, just as Pleasanton, informed that Confederate infantry was approaching, ordered a retreat. The Federal official report of the battle places the loss at five hundred, and Stuart's loss at seven hundred. As Stuart captured four hundred prisoners, it is safe to presume that this official statement is far from accurate—by no means an uncommon occurence.

Other engagements on the soil of Culpeper county were of minor note, chiefly as follows: A repulse of three Federal regiments of infantry and one of cavalry, raiding near Culpeper C. H., July 12, 1862; August 20, 1862, a similar experience for a body of Federal cavalry at Brandy Station; and the same next day at Kellys Ford; a skirmish at Kellys Ford, March 17, 1863; a raid of Federal cavalry through Rappahannock Station, Kellys Ford and Brandy Station, August 1–3, 1863; a cavalry raid for the "Army of the Potomac" to Brandy Station, September 6, 1863; a fight at Kellys Ford November 7, 1863.

THE BRANDY RIFLES.

A Roll of the Brandy Riflemen of Culpeper county at the time of organization in 1859.

C. H. Wager, Captain; Stockton Heth, 1st Lieutenant; John P. Wellford, 2nd Lieutenant; Thomas Faulconer 3rd Lieutenant; Thomas W. Parr, Sergeant; Thomas O. Curtis, Sergeant; George M. Wood, H. B. Milser, G. G. Thompson, F. M. Gilkeson, J. P. Wager, John D. Brown, R. O. Grayson, Albert Gordon, James W. Field, William McConkie, William Spicer, John Mallony, James Luckett, Wm. Shaw, J. T. Norman, William Green, Thomas W. Jones, J. O. Harris, P. M. Wrenn, Benjamin Yates, John Cash, Matthew Johnson, Stanton Wharton, J. C. Childs, Geo. Wheatley, R. C. Brown, J. F. Terrell, J. T. Bankhead, Lewis Yancey Sanford Berlin and William Luckett.

COMPANY B, 6TH VIRGINIA CAVALRY.

The publishers are indebted to Judge Daniel A. Grimsley for the following roll of Company B, 6th. Virginia Cavalry which was composed of men, most all of whom were from Rappahannock county. Many were from Culpeper; others from adjoining counties. The Company served from the beginning of the war to the close. The following roll gives the casualties, as far as is known.

Green, John Shackelford; Captain, Major, Lieutenant Colonel, Colonel, 6th. Va. Cavalry; twice wounded; died since the war.

Green,* James W., 1st. Lieut., resigned in 1861.

Wigginton, Benj., 1st. Lieut , 2nd. Lieut., taken prisoner in 1863. Living in Missouri.

Grimsley, Daniel A., Sergeant, 1st. Lieut., Capt., Major, 6th Va. Cavalry.

Duncan, R. R., 1st. Lieut., Capt., wounded at 2nd. Manssas, Trevillian's and Tom's Brook.

Browning, W. S., 2nd. Lieut., 1st. Lieut., killed at Cedar Creek.

Fristoe,* W. S., 2nd. Lieut., resigned in 1862.

O'Bannon.* Walter, jr., 2nd. Lieut., not re-elected at reorganization, afterwards ordnance officer 6th. Virginia Cavaly.

NON COMMISSIONED OFFICERS.

Corbin, Henry M., 1st. Sergeant, promoted in order to 2nd. Lieut. in place of Browning; wounded, killed in Maryland.

Willis, A. M., 1st. Sergeant, Capt. Co. G, 12th. Va. Cav.

Daniel, A. R., 1st. Sergt., discharged in 1861 on account of disability.

Roberts, G. B., 1st. Sergt., killed in action.

Slaughter, F. L., Sergeant.

Burke, Cornelius, Sergeant, wounded in action.

Smith, W. M., Sergeant.

Jones, E. T., regimental quartermaster Sergeant.

Justis, James F., regimental forage master.

Botts, A. T., wounded at Yellow Tavern.

Bruce,* W. S., wounded.

Carpenter, M. C., died in prison.
Duncan, B. F., killed in action.
Lillard,* W. J., promoted in order to jr. 2nd. Lieut.
Brownell,* W. H., elected Lieut. 12th. Va. Cavalry.

PRIVATES: Atkins,* Silas H., enlisted 1861, disabled in action. Armstrong, J. W., enlisted 1861, wounded twice. Atkins,* Thos. C. enlisted in 1861. Anderson, Peyton, 1861, killed in action. Wounded badly May 27, 1861. First soldier to shed his blood for the Confederacy. Discharged. Atkins, George, enlisted in 1862. Amiss, Edmond T., 1861.
Brown, Wm., 1861. Bowen, Wm., 1861. Bowen, Henry, 1861. Bragg, P. E., 1861. discharged on account of ill health. Re-enlisted Burke,* Jos., 1862. Burke, Edmund, 1862. Burke, Festus, 1862, wounded, died in prison. Burke, Mike, 1862, killed in action. Burke, (Tony) Robert, 1862. Killed in action., Burke, M. N., 1862. Burke, Robert, 1862. Brown Dallas, 1862, killed in action. Brown,* Robert C., 1863. Brown Harvey, 1863. Browning, Henry R., 1863, accidently wounded. Bywaters, Jas. E., 1862, died of disease. Bywaters,* Robert, 1863. Brooke,* Wm., 1861, prisoner. Brooke, Davis, 1861, died in 1862. Brown, Henry C., 1862, wounded. Browning, Joseph, 1862, wounded. Brown, J. Thompson, 1862, wounded; detailed to light duty in commissary department. Bruce,* Wm., 1861, wounded. Bradford. Hill C., 1862, prisoner. Brady, Albert, 1861, severely wounded. Brady,* Josephus, 1861, wounded. Butler, John, 1861.

Cannon,* Geo. W., 1861, discharged honorably. Cannon,* Elijah, 1861, twice wounded. Corbin,* Robert, 1862, detailed as teamster. Chancellor, Jas., 1861, promoted Lieut. of infantry. Crawford, Jas. M., 1862, prisoner and escaped from Elmira. Cannon, John R., 1863. Carpenter, Wm., 1862. Carpenter, Jas., 1862, died in prison. Chelf, Jas. N., 1862. Cooksey,* Jas., 1863, wounded. Clarke, Wm., 1861. Carr, Jno. O. 1863, killed in action. Curtis,* Jno., 1863, teamster. Corbin, Jas., 1862, wounded. Chewning, Robert, 1863, prisoner.

Daniel,* Wm., 1861, discharged. Deal,* Geo. W., 1862. Dwyers,* Alfred, 1863. Deatherage,* Robert R., 1863. Deatherage,† Robert, 1862. Dennis,† Newton, 1861. Dennis,† Wm., 1862.

Eastham, Robt. W., 1861, Eastham, F. Dabney, 1861, wounded and discharged. Eastham, Geo., 1863, killed in action.

Fant,† W. D., 1861, discharged. Fletcher, Geo. W., 1861, died of disease. Field, R. Y., disabled in action, detailed in quarter-master department. Fogg, Chas. E., 1862, badly wounded. Field, P. B., 1862, killed in action. Field, Wm., 1862, killed in action. Fisher, Thos., 1863, wounded.

Grimsley, Thos. F., 1861. Green,† George, 1861. Green, Robert R. 1861, wounded at Cold Harbor. Green, Jas. W., 1862, wounded at Winchester. George, Williamson C., 1864. Green,† Arthur, 1862, prisoner. Garnet,† Wm. A., 1864, wounded at Spottsylvania.

Hill,† Jas., 1861, wounded. Houghton, Jackson, 1861. Houghton, Marshall, 1861, killed in action. Houghton, Thos., 1862, twice wounded. Houghton, Wm. J., 1863, wounded. Houghton, Chas., 1864. Huff, Edward H., 1861, prisoner, Huff, Jno. 1861, teamster. Huff, Thos., 1864. Haddox, Jno., 1861, killed in action. Heaton, A. B., 1861, wounded. Hawkins, Muscoe, 1862, wounded. Hawkins, Wm., 1862, wounded at Yellow Tavern. Hawkins,† Mortimer, 1863. Hawkins,† Jno., 1863. Hisle, Lloyd, 1862, wounded at Ream's Station. Hisle, Daniel, wounded at

Brandy Station.   Hartley, Thos., 1862, wounded at Five Forks.   Hitt, Jas., 1862.   Hitt, Albert H., 1862.   Hitt, Albert, 1863, killed in action. Hitt, Jno., 1862.   Hill, Jas., 1861, wounded.   Hood, C. B., 1864.   Hawes, Wm. F., 1833.   Hand,† Eastham, 1862.   Hand, Wm., 1863.   Hambrick, Wm, 1863.   Hudson, Richard O., 1862, wounded.   Herrell, Thomas, 1861.   Huff, Jas., 1861, wounded.   Hawkins, Arthur, 1863, wounded at Newtown.

Jett, W. A. L., 1861, wounded.   Johnson, M. M., 1862.   Johnson, Henry, 1863.   Johnson, Dallas, 1864.   Jorden Robert, 1864.   Judd, Jacob, 1864, died.

Kendall, Sawarrow, 1862, killed in action,   Kendall, Braxton, 1863.   Kerfoot, Jas. F., 1863.   Kerfoot, Judson, 1863.   Kerfoot, Willie, 1833.

Miller, Eastham J., 1861, died.   Miller, Robert E., 1862.   Miller, Jno, R., 1862, wounded, prisoner.   Mason, Wm. B., 1861.   Murphy, Samuel, discharged.   Menefee, Henry St. Cyr, 1862.   McQueen, Henry C., 1862.   Millan† J. W., 1861.   Moffett, Frank, 1864, killed at Yellow Tavern.   Moore,* Jno., 1862.

Newby,† J. W. P., 1861, discharged.   Nicholson, Geo W., 1862, killed in action.

O'Bannon† Henry C. 1862.

Pullen† Jos. Sr. 1862; was over sixty years of age when enlisted and served to close of war.   Pullen, Jos. Jr., 1862, killed in action.   Pullen, Jno., 1861, wounded.   Putnam, Jno. B., 1863, wounded.   Peyton,† Hamilton, 1863.

Rudasilla, Wm. G., 1861, wounded.   Rudasilla, Kenley, 1861.   Rudasilla, Thaddeus A., 1861, wounded.   Rudasilla, Jack, 1862.   Rudasilla, Mifflin, 1862.   Rowles, Jno. F., 1861, wounded and died.   Rowles,† Jos. F., 1861, teamster.   Ritenour, T. C., 1862, wounded.   Roberts,† Robt. P., 1864.   Reagan,† Lewis, 1863.

Slaughter, P. P. 1861,* discharged.   Slaughter, T. T. 1831, wounded.   Slaughter, M. L., 1863, killed in action.   Starke, Wm., 1861, killed in action.   Scott,† Wm., 1861, discharged.   Scott, David, 1861, died.   Sheads,† Geo. M., 1863.   Scroggins, Jas. M. 1863.   Simms* Wm., 1862, wounded.   Settle, Broaddus, 1862, prisoner.   Smith, Chas. E., 1864.   Sutphin, Robt. 1863, wounded.   Spicer, Thos., 1863, wounded.   Smith, Jas., 1833, wounded.

Turner, Absolam, 1861.   Tapp,* Elijah, 1862, discharged.   Thornton, Jno., 1862.   Thornton, Frank, 1862.

Updike, B. F., 1861, wounded and taken prisoner.   Utz, Jno., 1833, taken prisoner.

Vanhorne, Robert, 1861, taken prisoner.   Vaughan, Johnson, 1863.

Walden, Turner, 1861, died.   Wood, Jas. M., 1861, severely wounded and discharged.   Willis, Albert G., 1862.   Willis, Wm., 1863.   Wright, Wm., 1863.   Wilson, Wm., 1862, taken prisoner.   Weaver, Gustavus, 1863.

Yates, Samuel S. 1861, killed in action, Yates, Robert, 1863.

There are six or eight names appearing on the original roll, marked as having deserted to the enemy, which are omitted from the above roster.

Those marked with a * or † have died since the war. This marking was done in September, 1899. It is interesting to note the large number that were living at that date.

THE BAPTISTS OF CULPEPER.

CHAPTER IV.

[The publisher is indebted to Rev. E. W. Winfrey, pastor, and to Mr. H. C. Burrows, of the Culpeper Baptist Church, for all the information contained in this chapter.]

Within the territory which originally formed the County of Culpeper, now embracing the counties of Culpeper, Madison and Rappahannock, there are at the date of this writing, (October, 1899) thirty churches or congregations, of white Baptists, with an aggregate membership of more than three thousand and seven hundred (3,700,) and we may say that nearly all of the colored people of this territory, who are members of any church, are Baptists. When the original Culpeper county was formed (1748) there was probably not a Baptist within its borders. In the year 1763 Allen Wyley, "a man of respectable standing in the county," living near Flint Hill, now Rappahannock county, having been "turned to God," but not knowing of any preacher whose teaching fully accorded with views which he had formed, "had sometimes gathered h s neighbors, read the scriptures, and exhorted them to repentance; but, being informed of the labors of Rev. David Thomas in Fauquier county, he with some of his friends traveled thither to hear him." The immediate result of this visit was that Mr. Wyley was baptised, and prevailed upon Mr. Thomas to go home with him and preach at his house. This man, David Thomas, "the first Baptist preacher that ever proclaimed the gospel" in the county, was born at London Tract, Pennsylvania, Aug. 16th. 1732, and educated at Hopewell, N. J. The degree of A. M. was conferred upon him by Rhode Island College, (Brown University.) He was in Virginia, a noble champion of religious liberty, and suffered severe persecutions. Thomas Jefferson and Patrick Henry held him in high esteem, and he highly valued them as friends of liberty. He will be long remembered as the author of a stirring poem on 'Freedom.'" (Beale's Semple, p. 21.) Eleven years after this first visit to the county, that is, in 1774, Mr. Thomas organized the Mt. Pony church, "the members coming from a church in Orange County, called Mountain Run, constituted in 1768, and dissolved in 1772." The first pastor of Mt. Poney church was Nathaniel Saunders, who professed religion under the preaching of Mr. Thomas. The name of this church was taken from the small, well-known mountain at the base of which stood the first house of worship, some two miles from the town of Culpeper, on the road to Stevensburg, but was changed to " Culpeper " April 29th, 1873. In 1833 this church removed with sixty white members to the town of Culpeper." At that time Waller R. Asher and his wife were the only white Baptists living in the town." In 1834 a house of worship was built at a cost of $1,200 on a lot purchased of Dr. Buck near Bell's Ford on Mountain Run, a part of which building still remains and constitutes the rear portion of the present residence of Mr. C. F. Chelf.

For valuable information concerning each of the churches of this denomination in the territory in question the reader is referred to the "Historical Sketch of the Shiloh Association,," published with " the Minutes of the One Hundredth Session," 1894. (See Specimen " Sketches " below). And for much profitable reading as to the lives and characters of the leading men who a century and more ago proclaimed the doctrines, planted the churches, and suffered in the service of this sect, we refer to Semple's History of the Rise and Progress of the Baptists in Virginia, (Revised and Extended by Dr. G. W. Beale in 1894), and to Dr. James B. Taylor's " Virginia Baptist Ministers."

No one thinks to-day with other feelings than those of shame and sorrow and severest disapprobation of the misguided zeal of those who blindly and vainly sought to suppress this people when they began to arise and assert themselves upon our soil. Nor can any fair minded person for a moment think to hold any individual, church, party, or sect of the present responsible for the crimes or mistakes of a generation long since departed. At the same time, the true historian cannot fail to note and all generations need to know such heroism, such devotion, such self-sacrifice as was exhibited by the pioneers of the Baptist faith in this part of Virginia. John Picket, one of these pioneers, was for about 8 months, (possibly in 1760), confined in the Fauquier prison for the " crime " (?) of preaching the gospel. Elijah Craig, who was spoken of as " a man of considerable talent," was upon one occasion arrested " at his plow," and " taken before three magistrates of Culpeper who, without hearing arguments, ordered him to jail. At court, he, with others, was arraigned." In spite of sound arguments on the part of their lawyer they were imprisoned for one month and " fed on rye bread and water, to the injury of their health." James Ireland,of whom Henry Howe in his " Virginia, Its History and Antiquities " speaks as " a worthy clergyman of the Baptist persuasion," was born in the city of Edinburgh, in 1748. While still a young man he came to America and took charge of a school in the northern part of Virginia. His was an active and versatile mind, though, his education an account of the roving disposition of his youth, was defective. He is described as being " a man of common stature, a handsome face, piercing eye, and pleasant countenance. In his youth he was spare, but he became by degrees quite corpulent, so that not long after his second marriage he wanted but nineteen pounds of weighing three hundred."

In 1769 or 1770, at a meeting in Pittsylvania County, Mr. Ireland was baptised by the Rev'd Samuel Harris, immediately returned to his home with credentials signed by eleven ministers, "and in the spirit and power of his Master devoted himself to the great work of preaching the gospel." But, his growing popularity and success excited the indignation of those who were in authority and brought down upon his head fierce persecution." Being roughly seized by order of magistrates, he was thrust into the Culpeper jail because he had dared to preach without the authority or sanction of the bishop." He was accompanied to prison amid the abuses of his persecutors, and while incarcerated in his cell not only suffered by the inclemency of the weather, but by the personal maltreatment of his foes. They attempted to blow him up with gunpowder, to suffocate him by burning brimstone, etc., at the door and window of his prison, and even to poison him. He states that he might speak of a hundred instances of cruelty which were practiced." When, subsequently, Mr. Ireland went down to Williamsburg with a petition to the governor, Lord Botetourt, for a permit to have a meeting house built in Culpeper county, he found the governor altogether kindly and affable in manner, but the clergy of the city, to whom by direction of the governor he applied for examination, were " of quite a different character:" " they appeared," he says," obstinately determined not to give me the requisite examination; every one shifted it upon another, till at last I obtained it from a country parson living 8 miles from the capital, and presented it to the governor and council, who granted me a license for those things petitioned."

The growth and success of this denomination in this, as in other sections, of the State is in no small measure due humanly speaking, to this unwise persecution : The rage of these misguided ecclesiastics was the excess of folly: They defeated their own aims: They contributed to the power and increase of those whom they esteemed enemies to the cause of truth and religion. We do not question the sincerity of their motives, but their error of judgment was, from every point of view, colossal and inexcusable.

It would be pleasant if we could here put on record suitable mention of all those zealous, noble men who built so wisely and successfully upon the foundation laid by them that suffered and toiled through the initial stage of the history of this denomination in this section. There were Nathaniel Saunders, Wm. Mason, John Churchill Gordon, J. Koontz, James Garnett, Geo. Eve, John Picket, H. Goss, Lewis Conner, W. Fristoe, Oliver Welch, A. Moffett, E. G. Ship. Robert Jones, John Hickerson, Thomas Holtzman, Daniel James, John Garnett, Thornton Stringfellow, Barnett Grimsley, A. M. Poindexter, Joshua Leather, L. L. Fox, J. N. Fox, James Fife, Champ C. Conner, Thaddeus Herndon, Richard Herndon, A. H. Spillman, James Garnett Jr., Wm. F. Broadus, Cumberland George, T. R. Miller, P. M. Carpenter, Silas Bruce, H. C. Briggs, J. A. Mansfield, W. G. Roan, Wm. A. Hill, Wm. A. Whitescarver, L. R. Steele, J. W. Brown, H. E. Hatcher, Jno. C. Willis, A. H. Bennett, B. P. Dulin, W. S. Briggs, A. M. Grimsley, Milton Robert Grimsley, and others among deceased ministers, not to mention those who are still zealously engaged in the same work, nor the many strong and influential " laymen," living and departed, who perhaps have been not less faithful nor less efficient in their less conspicuous spheres.

We cheerfully attest that the Baptists of this region are among the most peaceable, law-abiding, enterprising, industrious, frugal, and everyway valuable as well as the most numerous of our citizens. Not a few of them are prominent and influential in business, in social life, and in the various professions. It is an honor to the County, as well as to the denomination of which we now write, that so devout and scholarly, preeminently useful, a man as Dr. Jno. A. Broadus, who died but a few years ago while occupying the position of President of the Southern Baptist Theological Seminary, was a son of this old County. If space allowed, we might name others who have gone forth from among us and in various callings and walks of life have adorned the name of their native county and the traditions of their religious denomination.

The peculiarities of this people are not numerous, but are esteemed by them as of vital importance:—They have always laid great emphasis upon the doctrine of individual responsibility, and contended that it is the right and the duty of every man to study the Scriptures for himself and to worship God according to the dictates of his own conscience: They insist upon a credible profession of faith in Jesus Christ as the prerequisite to baptism,—upon immersion as essential to baptism,—upon the independence of the churches—(holding that each church is responsible only to Christ as her Head and Lawgiver, though any number of churches may combine and co-operate. in benevolent and religious enterprises,)—and upon the absolute equality of the ministry; the majority of them hold that none are entitled to the privilege of coming to the Lord's table, or participating in the observance of the Lord's

Supper, who are not consistent members of a church of regenerate and immersed believers. They are aggressive in educational and benevolent and missionary enterprises, and readily co-operate with all other Christians in all good works when they can do so without sacrificing their cardinal principles.

We append, from the " Historical Sketch " above referred to, a few extracts, or individual sketches, which contain matter of interest to many of our citizens. It will be observed that the churches named are those within the present limits of Culpeper County.

" Jeffersonton, at the village of that name, in the county of Culpeper, about 16 miles N. E. of the court house, formerly Hedgeman's River, was organized in 1773, the constituent members coming from Carter's Run in Fauquier. John Picket was pastor till 1790. His successors have been John Hickerson till 1809. Daniel James till 1811, Thornton Stringfellow till 1818, Daniel James again 1818-1822, E. G. Ship one year, Cumberland George 1823-1863, Barnett Grimsley 1863-1881, L. R. Steele 1881-1884, and M. R. Grimsley who still serves in that capacity. Her membership, since 1876 has grown from 134 to 171."

Since this was written the membership of the Jeffersonton church has increased to 204, but the pastor last named, Mr. Milton Robert Grimsley, loved, honored, and now lamented by many hundreds of our people, has entered into the everlasting rest. He is fitly spoken of as "Grimsley, the loving and beloved." A strong and useful man, just a little past 45 years of age when on June the 9th, 1899, he ceased from the joys and labors of earth. The present pastor of this church is Rev. L. R. Thornhill, D. D., who has but recently come to reside within our borders.

"CULPEPER (of which your committee have the honor to be members) situated since 1834 in the town of Culpeper, was constituted in 1774 by Elder David Thomas, 'the first Baptist preacher that ever proclaimed the gospel in Orange and Culpeper,' the constituent members coming from a church in Orange county, organized in 1768, and known as Mountain Run. Until April 29th, 1873, the Culpeper church was known as the MT. PONEY CHURCH. 'In 1791 she sent off her first colony to Gourdvine, and in 1803 her second—(72 members) to Bethel; In 1833 she dismissed a third to Stevensburg and removed with the remaining sixty white members to the town of Culpeper. At that time Waller R. Asher and his wife were the only white Baptists living in the town.'.. The pastors have been Nathaniel Saunders (as supply 1774-1777,) John Leland, Wm. Mason, Nathaniel Saunders, Wm. Mason again, John Churchill Gordon, (1822-1847,) Cumberland George, (1847-1863,) J. N. Fox and R. H. Stone until Sept. 24th, 1865, James B. Taylor, (1865-1875,) A. C. Barran, (1875-1882,) C. F. James, (1882-1889,) and E. W. Winfrey who came into the service of this church in December, 1889. The house of worship erected in 1858, at a cost of about $10,000.00, 'on the spot where stood the old jail in which James Ireland' and others were 'imprisoned for preaching the gospel' as Baptists, was destroyed by fire on the night of October 6th, 1892. The new building which takes its place, on the same historic spot, will cost about $15,000.00. This church has enjoyed frequent revivals and, at various times, large additions to her membership; But, by reason mainly of deaths and removals, the net increase in members has not been considerable for a number of years. In 1876 there were 195 members, now there are 265. Elders M. D. Jeffries and S. W. Cole were members of this church. The lamented Frank C. Johnson who had just entered the ministry and his brother Thomas A., now a promising young Baptist preacher, were both members of this church in their early boyhood."

The Rev. Jno. F. Harris, since deceased, was a son of this church and in his purposefulness and fervent zeal was laboring as the pastor of churches in another county when fatal sickness laid its hand upon him. It is proper to say also that the membership of this church has grown to be 312, and that the beautiful and substantial new house of worship memtioned in the above sketch was dedicated on the 16th day of June, 1895.

"CROOKED RUN, in Culpeper county, about 10 miles S. W. of the court house, 'is a daughter of Blue Run.' She began her career in 1777. Her pastors have been Elijah Craig 'for about two years,' James Garnett Sr. for more than fifty five years, his grandson James Garnett Jr. for about forty-six years, J. W. McCown for more than fourteen years, J. W. Bishop one year, John C. Willis (as a supply) for about 10 months, and J. E. Gwatkin whose term of service began February, 1893. The membership in 1876 was 74; it is now 73. The eloquent Elder Champ C. Conner, who subsequently removed to Tennessee, was a son of this church."

Rev. E. L. Grace is now the pastor of Crooked Run, and the membership is 89. The annual reports of contributions of this church are next to the largest of all the churches of the Shiloh Association.

"GOURDVINE, in Culpeper county, 12 miles North of the court house, was constituted March 11th, 1791—(see CULPEPER)—with Wm. Mason as pastor. He served in that capacity until Oct., 1822, and was followed by Jas. Garnett —1822-1863—Barnett Grimsley—1863-1881—T. P. Brown—(first as assistant to B. Grimsley and then as sole pastor 1881-1888,) and F. P. Berkley who assumed pastoral care of the church in February, 1890. The membership of this church in 1876 was 132; This year she reports 121—(see AMISSVILLE.) Elders A. M. Grimsley and John Roberts Moffatt were ministerial sons of this church. A brief account of Bro. Grimsley's life and labors and death will appear in your Minutes of this session. Bro. Moffatt, a great nephew of Elder Anderson Moffatt, already mentioned in this paper, had devoted himself with characteristic sincerity and enthusiasm to the cause of Temperance and become a leader of the Prohibition party in the State. In November 1892, while on his way to the opening—(night)—session of the Baptist General Association in Danville, he was met and killed by a political enemy. At that time he was the much beloved pastor of the Baptist church in North Danville, as well as Editor of the Prohibition paper—Anti-Liquor. He was a man of no small abilities, decided convictions, earnest piety, consuming zeal and unfaultering courage, and though only 34 years old had been largely useful."

The present pastor of the Gourdvine church is Rev. S. W. Cole, who also serves the New Salem church mentioned below.

"BETHEL, in Culpeper county, about 9¼ miles West of the court house, was constituted in 1803—(see Culpeper.) Her pastors have been Wm. Mason— (1803-1821)—Daniel James, as supply—August 1822-March 1823—Jas. Garnett— (1823-1874)—A. H. Spilman—(Sept. 1874—March 1875)—, and Thomas F. Grimsley since July 1875. During the past 18 years her membership has increased from 167 to 285. From this church have gone into the ministry T. P. Brown, John H. Boldridge, James R. Brown, and Wade Brown."

Rev. T. F. Grimsley is still pastor at Bethel, and the membership has come to be 310.

"Cedar Run, in Culpeper county, some 6 or 7 miles South West of the court house, was organised in April, 1830. The first house of worship was built on an island in the stream, Cedar Run, just below the point at which the railroad now crosses the same. The second, erected a few years before the war, and torn down by Federal soldiers, stood about a half-mile East of Mitchell's Station. Another by the almost unaided liberality of the pastor, Elder James Garnett, was erected on the same spot after the war between the States, but was torn down in 1878, and rebuilt on the present site. Two years ago, the church determined to erect a new house of worship; this is now nearly completed, and will probably cost about $1,400. Her pastors have been James Garnett—(1830-1874)—Dr. Wm. A. Hill—(1877-1880)—W. G. Roan—(1881-1883)—J. A. Chambliss—(June 1883—Feb. 1884)—and I. N. May, who has been serving in that capacity since 1884. The parents of Elders J. S., M. B. and H. M. Wharton were active and honored members of this church, and Elder J. S. Wharton was by her licensed to preach. Seventeen years ago her membership was 33; this year she reports 75."

Since the above was written, the membership of Cedar Run has increased to 103, the Rev. Gabriel Gray has served for a number of years as pastor, and the Rev. Hugh Goodwin has but recently taken charge.

"New Salem, in Culpeper county, about 7 miles North of the court house, on the Sperryville and Culpeper Turnpike, was constituted in January, 1834, by Wm. F. Broaddus and B. Grimsley. Her first pastor, Champ C. Conner, served from March 1834, to March, 1835, and was followed by B. Grimsley—(Oct. 1835-Oct. 1849)—, J. W. Brown—(Feb'y 1850—Oct. 1850)—, Jno. W. George—(June, '53-Feb'y '54)—Silas Bruce—(1854-1861)—A. M. Grimsley—(1865 until his death in April, 1894.) During the terrible period of the civil war, the church had no pastor. Since 1876 her membership has grown from 89 to 146 in 1894. Chas. W. Collier became pastor in August, 1894. Elders Jno. A. Broadus and J. M. Farrar went into the ministry while members of this church. Elder A. H. Lewis, now in Missouri, was for a number of years a member here. Elder R. H. Stone once held membership in this body. And, this was the church of Edmund Broadus, father of Elder John A. Broadus, and for many years a very prominent and influential member of this Association."

As noted above, Rev. Mr. Cole is now pastor at New Salem, the Rev. C. W. Collier having previously served in that capacity for a year or two.

"Stevensburg, at the village of that name in Culpeper county, 7 miles from the court house, was organized in 1833—(see Culpeper.) Thornton Stringfellow was her pastor from October, 1833 to October, 1848. Cumberland George served in that capacity one year. Then followed Jno. W. George—(1851-1861.) In 1862 the meeting house was burned, and the membership became scattered, and seems to have had no regular meetings for five or six years. In July 1868 they began to gather for worship in a small house at or near Lignum. Elder H. E. Hatcher preached for the little band several times in 1867 and 1868. Elder A. H. Bennett was pastor 1869-1871. In October 1871 the church was reorganized in the Methodist house of worship at Stevensburg by Elder James B. Taylor. From that time until his death in April 1875, Elder A. H. Spilman served as pastor. J. W. McCown was his successor—(1875-1881)—and he was succeeded—(1881)—by the present pastor, Elder T. P. Brown. In eighteen years her membership has increased from 79 to 97. For some years, during the sixties and seventies, this church appears on your Minutes under the name of Germanna."

Rev. Mr. Brown is still pastor at Stevensburg, and the membership is now 103.

"Alum Spring, in Culpeper county, 6 miles North of the court house, became a church November 16th, 1855. From that date until his death, August 25th, 1863, Cumberland George was her pastor. Her other pastors have been

John N. Fox—(June 1865—May 1878)—John H. Boldridge—(December 1878—August 1881)—and T. P. Brown from September 1881 until now. This church was one of the fruits of a prayer meeting held in the woods during the Summer of 1854. Seven of the twelve original constituent members are still in the flesh. Her membership eighteen years ago was 44; this year she reports 130. Elders B. W. N. and A. M. Simms, now preaching in Texas, went into the ministry while members of Alum Spring."

This church, still under the pastoral care of Rev. Mr. Brown, reports this year a membership of 137.

"Lael, four or five miles S. E. of the village of Stevensburg, in Culpeper county, was organized in May 1874 by Elders J. B. Taylor Jr. and R. H. Stone, with nine male and twelve female members who came from Stevensburg and Flat Run, a majority from the former. Her pastors have been R. H. Stone—(1874-1884)—and F. H. James since March 1885. Her present house of worship, a beautiful building, was erected in 1890. The 21 members with which she began 20 years ago have now become 188. In the beginning, she paid her pastor $40 00 a year for "once a month" preaching; The pastor now occupies her pulpit on two Sundays of each month, and receives a salary of $250.00 per annum. In something like this ratio she has increased her contributions to missions and other benevolent enterprises. Mr. A G. Williis, one of her best beloved and most highly honored members, has contributed much to the attainment of this prosperity and progress."

Lael, with Rev. F. H. James still serving as her pastor, reports a membership of 205.

"Brandy, at the railway village of that name in Culpeper county, was constituted in 1887, by Elders T. P. Brown, F. H. James, F. P. Robertson, and C. F. James. The twelve constituent members came from Stevensburg, Jeffersonton and Good Hope churches. Elders C. W. Brooks served as pulpit supply for one year. For 14 months F. P. Berkely was pastor. J. E. Gwatkin, who now serves in that capacity, took charge in 1891. Her membership this year is 53. This church, beginning in a school house and afterwards occupying for a time the house of worship kindly tendered by the Methodists of the place, has manifested a most praiseworthy zeal and perseverance in the erection of her own handsome building, now almost completed."

The church at Brandy Station now has a membership of 62, some of these being among the most "well-to-do" and influential people of the county, and has the pastoral services of Rev. L. H. Shuck, D. D. During the past year this church has been much afflicted in the death of Mrs. Sallie Stringfellow to whose energy and zeal the origin and progress of the church are largely due.

NOTES ETC. FOR GENEALOGISTS.

CHAPTER V.

From the early will books of Culpeper county, beginning July 20, 1749, and extending to March 19, 1821, the publisher has taken the following notes. In doing so we were guided by no set rule, but took notes of wills from which it was possible to derive any genealogical information, excepting some few, which he deemed not of sufficient importance to justify the printing of notes therefrom. Following the notes from wills we give the complete marriage record of Culpeper from the year, 1781 to January 1, 1825. Prior to 1780 the marriage record was kept by the Church authorities; an effort was made to procure the whole or a part of this record, but it could not be found.

The marriage record which follows immediately after the notes from wills etc., can be used in this way. Take the will of Spencer Butler, by which it appears, that he had a daughter, Dorcas, who married a Duncan. Now, look in the marriage record, where it can be seen that in 1797 James Duncan married Dorcas Butler.

Roger Dixon was the first clerk of the county. He was succeeded in 1772 by John Jameson. The first will recorded was that of

Elmore George, dated Sept. 1st, 1748, which was witnessed by Wm. Nash, Christopher Threlkeld and Jno. Wetherall. He speaks of his wife, Martha, of his sons, William and Thomas; also of his brother, William George.

The remainder of the notes we give in alphabetical order. Note the following explanations. First is given the testator's name, then the date the will was written; then his wife's name, where it is possible to obtain it; lastly the names of his children, and other genealogical information that might be at hand: The date last given is the probate of the will. Book "G," from April 1, 1813, to June 17, 1817, is missing, the supposition being it was lost during the war between the States.

A

Roger Abbett, Jul. 2, 1762, Ann; had daughters who married Triplett, Cummins and Jerome Rosson. Nov. 18, 1762.

Roger Abbott, Feb. 21, 1809, Anna; children were Jemina, m. McClanahan, Daniel, William, Susanna, m. Roberts, Edward, John W., Geo. W., Polly D., Elizabeth P., and Mahala. April 17, 1809.

Wm. Allen, July 12, 1799; children; Betty, m. Bartley, Judy, m. Hall, Polly, m. Gregory, Ann, m. Gideon Rees, Jas., Wm. G., and Chas. C. Sept. 16, 1799.

B

Samuel Ball, Aug. 16, 1751, speaks of his wife, Anna Catharina, and of his children, Wm., Margaret, Judith Hackley and Mary Green, and of his sons-in-law, Jno. Hackley and Robert Green. Nov. 22, 1751.

William Banks, Mar. 2, 1808, speaks of Baylor and Tunstall, sons of Baylor Banks, of Wm. F., son of Richard Banks, Miss Jane Leigh, "sister" Elizabeth R. Thornton, "brother" Tunstall Banks, "aunt" Jane Voss, "sister" Anna Banks. Nov. 16, 1812.

Jas. Barbour, Feb. 23, 1775; children: Richard, Jas., Thos., Philip, Ambrose, Betty; grandchildren: Jas. Boyd and Francis Smith. April 17, 1775.

Sarah Barbour, May 19, 1781; children: Jas., Thos., Philip, Ambrose, Mary, m. Harrison, Betty, m. Johnston; grandchildren: Mordecai, Thos. and Frances Barbour, Lucy Johnston, Lucy Todd, Sarah, Mary and Jas. Barbour. Feb. 18, 1788.

Leonard Barnes, May 1805. Children: Charles, Henry, Leonard, Rawleigh, Clara, m. Partlow, Judith, m. Dulany, Polly, m. Kirtley, Catherine, m. Hume, and another dau. who seems to have m. a Thompson Aug. 20, 1810.

Jos. Belfield, Aug. 9, 1766; had nephew Belfield Cave; speaks of his bro. Wm. Glass; his sister Elizabeth m. Benj. Cave. July 19, 1770.

Charles Benson, Sept. 23, 1805. Children; James, John, Agathy, m. Yancey, and a daughter who m. Richard Bullard. Had land on the "North River." Feb. 15, 1813.

Jno. Blakey. Dec. 30, 1781; children: Jno., Churchill, Frances, m. Bush, Martha, m. Morris, Sarah, m. Eddins, and Elizabeth, m. Daviss. Mar. 18, 1782.

Wm. Bledsoe, Dec. 27, 1769; Mary; children were: Geo., Aaron, Mille, m. Geo. Wetherall, Mary, m. Ambrose Powell, Jno., Wm., Jas., Hannah, m. Cave, and Moses. Apr. 19, 1770.

Elliott Bohannon, Apr. 1781; Ann; ch.: Ambrose, Mildred, m. Gaines, Mary, m. Herndon, Anne, m. Kirtley, Jno., and Elliott. May 21, 1781.

Jno. Bond. Apr. 17, 1756; Mary; had dau. who married Benjamin Long, who had sons, Bloomfield and John Bond Long. May 15, 1760.

Joshua Botts' estate was divided Jan. 1818. Had dau. Nancy, m. Jessee Nalle, and Susanna, m. and son Benjamin, who died leaving dau., Susanna, m. Triplett. Philip Harrison and John Minor were executors of Benj. Botts.

Andrew Bourn, Aug. 22, 1788; Jane; children: Elizabeth, m. Hawkins Ann, m. Hawkins, Sarah, m. Piece, Jane, m. Hawkins, Frances, m. Reuben Newman, Judith, m. Zimmerman, Polly, Andrew and Wm. Jan. 18, 1790.

Francis Brandum, Jan. 1, 1799; Mary. Children: Wm., Jno., Ezekiel, Lucy, Rachall, Molly and Eleanor.

Jacob A. Broil, Nov. 3, 1761; Catherine; children: Adam, Nicholas, Peter, Michal, Matthias, Cyrus, Jacob, Jno., Zacharias, Mary, Catharine Wayland and Elizabeth Wilhoite. May 19, 1763.

John Brown, Jan. 7, 1774; Elizabeth: Jno., Elizabeth, m. Dickerson, Ann, Mary, Daniel, Coleman, Thos., Wm., and Richard. Nov. 20, 1780.

John Brown, June 20, 1803. Mary. Had John, and Ann, m. Lightfoot. Sept. 21, 1807.

Thos. Brown, Aug. 16, 1758, married Eleanor, the widow of Edward Stubblefield, and had one daughter, Eleanor; he speaks of his brothers, Daniel, Coleman and Wm., and of his niece, Elizabeth Fargeson. Dec. 21, 1758.

Horace Buckner, Mar. 13, 1820; ch. Frances, Horace, Archibald. Otway, Ritchie, and Walker. Had bro. Geo. Buckner. Aug. 21, 1821.

Richard Burdyne, July 2, 1761; Catherine; leaves to his son Reginald, a tract of land on the west side of the "ragged" Mountain, adjoining the lands of Dick and Bogle; to his son, Samuel, land adjoining Jno. and Martin Nalle, Wm. and Francis Gaines, and Capt. Wm. Brown; his two daughters, Hannah and Barbara, married Shotwell and Grissom; to his son, Nathaniel, a tract of land on the north branch of the Rappahannock river, adjoining lands of Geo. Wm. Fairfax Esq., Capt. Robert Green. Capt. Cave and Edward Herndon; to his son, Jno., land on the north side of Robinson river, adjoining lands of Alexander and Daniel Campbell, and Jas. Hurt; he directs that a cow and a calf be given to each of his sons on the day of their marriage. Oct. 15, 1761.

Spencer Butler, July 20, 1818; ch. Thornton, Wm., Fielding, Willis, Landon, Joel, Dorcas, m. Duncan, Sally, m. Grimsley, Ann, m. Willey, and Polly, m. Miller. Sept. 21, 1818.

Harmon Button, April 10, 1822; ch. John, Elias, Frederick, Hannah, m. Burrell, Luttrel, Martin. Polly,Wm., and Jas.; May 20, 1820.

C

Susanna Carter, wife of Thos. Carter; ch. Wm , Landon, Thos., Jas , Abner, Robt. and Jas. June 19, 1820.

Lawrence Catlett; Mary; June. 30, 1782; children: Kemp, Thos., Geo., Mary, Sarah, Alice and Nancy. Sept. 16, 1782.

John Cole, Jan. 5, 1757, children, Richard, John, Mary Ann, Martha, who m. Wm. Reynolds; speaks of his son-in-law, Jno. Morgan, who m. Alice Jan. 15, 1757.

Margeret Conner, (widow), Mar. 4, 1744, witnessed by Mary Stokes, John and Judith Hackley, speaks of her children, Wm. Conner, Ann Kelley, Hannah Wood, Elizabeth Lynch and Sarah Balynger. May 16, 1751.

Wm. Corbin, Nov. 10, 1789; Sarah; children: Benj., Lewis, Wm., Isaiah, Caty, Jno., m. Thatcher, Ann, m. Andrew Grant, Margaret, m. Walker. April 17, 1797.

Wm. Covington, Feb. 11, 1783; children: Eleanor, m. Robt. Hensley, Guzzel, m. Cooper, Elizabeth, and Robert. Had bro. Richard; Aug. 18, 1784.

Thos. Covington, Dec. 5, 1756, who lived and owned property in the town of Culpeper, had daughters, Ann, who m. Travers, and Sarah, who m. Tutt. Jan. 15, 1767.

Christopher Crigler, Sept. 9, 1808; children: Elizabeth, m. Taylor, Wm., Lewis, et als. May 23, 1810.

D

Birkett Davenport, Feb. 20, 1813. Had four grandchildren who were Birkett Davenport Thompson, Philip Roots Thompson, Eliza Fry, and Eleanor Thornton; had dau. Elizabeth, m. Jameson. Sept. 16, 1817.

Geo. Dillard, Mar. 2, 1790; children: Major, Ann, m. Robt. Freeman, Jno., Sam'l., Jas., Elizabeth, m. Chas. Duncan, and Sarah, m. Jno. Colvin. Sept. 20, 1790,

John Dillard, Dec. 30, 1797; Ann; Left property to Priscilla Bowman, Peggy Duncan, Ann Carter, Mary Duncan, Elizabeth Duncan, Sally James Duncan, Lucinda Duncan, daus. of his sister, Lizza Duncan, Priscilla Colvin, dau. of sister, Sarah Colvin, and to Elizabeth Latham Freeman, dau. of Hezekiah Freeman. Oct. 17, 1898.

Wm. Duncan,   May 17, 1790; Rosanna; children: Wm., Jas., Frederick and Benj. Sept. 20, 1801.

Wm. Duncan,   Feb. 24, 1781; children: Chas., James, Rawley, Wm., Jno., Jos., and Anne, m. Roberts. Witnessed by Wm. Hughes, Wm. and Shadrack Browning. Oct. 15, 1781.

Robt. R. Duncan,   June 7, 1788; Ann; children, Robert, Chas., Sammy, Jos., John, Gollup or Gallup, Phillis, m. Jno. Barbee, who had dau. that m. Enoch Bradford, Ann, m. Thos. Pope, Mary, m. Jos. Hackley first, and Thos. Grinnan second, Rosey, m. Jas. Jett, Lavinia, m. Jno. Lightfoot. Oct. 21, 1793.

Jas. Duncan,   Aug. 17, 1801; Mary; children; Sally, m. Yancy, Mary; Geo., Francis, Jos., Liney, m. Johnston, Lucy, m. Threlkeld, Elizabeth, m. Rout.

James Duncan's   estate was divided in August, 1819, Geo. Duncan, Jno. D. Browning and Bryant O'Bannon being the commissioners. He lived on Thornton river. His ch. were Lewis, Michael, James, Lucy, Wm., Hiram and John.

Henry Duval,   Mar. 11, 1810. Children, Lucy, m. Seal, Polly, m. Samuel, Daniel, Henry, Charlotte, m. Ball. April 17, 1810.

Daniel Duval,   Aug. 30, 1819. Polly; ch. Wm., Jas., Isaac, Emely, Juliett Ann, and Thomas Albert; Nov. 15, 1819.

E

Wm. Edgar,   Feb. 14, 1763, had nieces, Susannah, who m. Wm. Jett, Sarah m. Allen Ranes. July 20, 1769.

Jos. Early,   Feb. 12, 1780; Jane; ch: Indiana, Paschal, Mary, Wm., Whitefield and Jos., to whom he left his lands in the "County of Kentucky." Oct. 20, 1783.

F

Saml. Fargeson,   1772; ch. were Saml., Susannah, m. Daniel, Ann, m. Francis Strother, and Lucy, m. Jno. Graves. May 10, 1772.

Jno. Faver,   Jul. 19, 1779; Isabel; children: Henrietta, m. Lewis Yancey, Wm., Jno., m. Ann, dau. of Thos. Covington and Jael, his wife. Mar. 18, 1783.

John Favers,   died in May 1789, left Rosanna, Isabella, Frances, John, and probably a dau. who m. John Apperson, who shares in the division of the estate.

Henry Field Jr.,   Mary. Nov. 7, 1785; ch: Daniel, Henry, Wm. S., Dinah, Suze, Elizabeth, Mary, Sarah, Nancy, m. Delany, Geo., Jos., Thos., and Jno. Owned large lot of land in Kentucky. Oct. 15, 1787.

Jno. Field,   Aug. 21, 1774; Anna; ch: Elizabeth, m. Lawrence Slaughter, Jno., Mary, m. George Slaughter, Larkin, Anna; refers to the fact of his son; Ezekiel, being missing, and the "certainty of his being dead or alive not known," and leaves him much property in case he is found alive. May 15, 1775.

Frederick Fishback,   Sept. 20, 1782; Eve; ch: Martin, Ann, m. Smith, Jno., Jacob, Elizabeth, m. Spilman, Catharine, m. Atwood, Sarah, m. Button, Mary and Frederick. Oct. 21, 1782.

Francis Fletcher,   Mar. 25, 1781; m. Nanny, the dau. of Thos. Collins; ch.: Jenny, Jerry White, Ann White, Billey and Sukey. Aug. 20, 1781.

John Foushee,   April 15, 1777; Aphia; lived on Cedar Run; children: Jno., Thornton, Geo., Chas., Jos., Wm., Elijah, Dan'l., Nancy, m. Jno., Tureman,

Jemimah, Hannah, Elizabeth and Benj. June 21, 1779.

Robert Freeman, May 13, 1793. Elizabeth. Children: Robert and a dau. m. Wm. Haynie. Dec. 22, 1807.

Jno. Freeman, Mar. 19, 1800; wf. Sarah; children: Jno., Elizabeth, m. Francis Miller, and Harris. Sept. 15, 1800.

Robt. Freeman, July 31, 1811; ; children: Elizabeth, m. Collins, Priscilla, m. Hawkins, Robt., Geo.. Polly, Harriet. Sept. 16, 1811.

Harris Freeman, July 25, 1821. Had nephews, Harris Read and French English, and niece, Elizabeth Ball. Aug. 20, 1821.

G

Doratha Gaines, April 24, 1786; children: Doratha, Susannah, m. Carter, Anne, m. Martin, Elizabeth, m. Yates, and Jas. June 19, 1786.

Richard Gaines, July, 27, 1802. Children: Wm., Lucy, m. Botts, Rowland, Gemima, m. Speak, Benj., Nathaniel, Jos., Judith, m. Chancellor, Anne, m. Crigler, Jno. Cook Gaines, and Elizabeth, m. Thomas. Speaks of his grandson, Travis Gaines. Feb. 18, 1805.

Jas. Gaines, Oct. 10, 1805. Children: Melinda, Clarissa, Susanna, Mary Ann, Lucy, Francis, Wm. S., Thos., Horace, Fontaine, and Mortimer. His "friend," Philip Lightfoot, was his executor. Oct. 21, 1805.

Richard Gaines, Feb. 4, 1807. Elizabeth. Children: Mary, m. Orr, Elizabeth, m. Clayton, Caty m. Rosson, Sally, m. Rucker, Richard; had granddaughter, Polly Pendleton Gaines. Feb. 16, 1807.

Wm. George, Apr. 4, 1781; ch: Mary Ann, m. Thos. Hoffer, Elizabeth m., Corder. Sept. 15, 1783.

Jas. Gillison, Feb. 5, 1759, left all his property to his brothers, John and Archibald Gillison, of Caroline county. Aug. 21, 1760.

Henry Green of Fauquier county, Sept. 6, 1782; had bros. Willis and Wm., sister, Eleanor Duff Green. His mother was Ann. Sept. 19, 1785.

Ann Green, Sept. 20, 1804. Children: Ann, m. Poindexter, Eleanor, m. Marye. Elizabeth, m. Camp. Mary, m. Thomas, Milly, m. Stringer, Lucy Coleman, m. Pinkard, Francis Wilhoite Green. Speaks of sister, Elizabeth Triplett. Oct. 15, 1804.

Jas. Green, Dec 3, 1807. Elizabeth. Ch: Gabriel, Jas., Dolly, m. Farrow, Elizabeth, m. Peacocke, Jones, Robert, Augustine, John, Lucy, Mary Bohon Green. August 23, 1809.

Wm. Grey's estate was divided Aug. 18, 1820; Wm., Wilson, Walton, Henry, Rebecca, Adaline, John and Harriet Grey, and Lucy, who m. A. Brockenborough.

Thos. Griffin, Feb. 9, 1781; Elizabeth; children: Zachariah. Elizabeth, m. Long, Mary, m. Peters and Anthony. Oct. 21, 1782.

Henry Griffin, Jun. 25, 1807; Gracey; ch: Thomas, Edward, Elizabeth and Mary. Lived near "Capt. Green's Mill." Feb. 16, 1818.

H

John Hackley, died in Oct. 1768; his four eldest daughters married Peter Taliaferro, Richard Hackley, Samuel Reeds and Jas. Jameson.

John Hackley, Mar. 16, 1799; owned land in the "Western country." Speaks of his uncle, Wm. Ball, of his bros. in law, Thos. Jameson, m. Lucy Hackley, Sam'l. Reed, m. Sarah Hackley, Richard Hackley, m. Elizabeth

Hackley, and of his sister, Ann Taliaferro, of his uncle and aunt Barrow, of his bro. Jas. Hackley, of Fanny Ball Long, dau. of Gabriel Long, and Fanny Ball Thomas, dau. of Edw. Ball Thomas, of Ky. June 15, 1801.

Jacob Hanback, Nov. 1, 1785; Mary; children: Jno., Jacob, Wm., Susannah, Elizabeth, m. Jacob Coons, Mary, m. Henry Coons, and Catherine. Owned land adjoining Jac Coons, Harmon Young and Jos. Wayman. Dec. 19, 1785.

Wm. Hansford, June 7, 1750, speaks of his daughter, Sarah Porter, who married Nicholas Porter, and had son, Benjamin, and of his sons, Wm., Salis, Chas., Jno., and his daughter Anne. Oct. 17, 1754.

Winifred Harford, May 28, 1807, had dau. who m. John Quaintance. Feb. 20, 1809.

Mathew Hawkins, May 27, 1820; Betty; ch. Job, James, Rebecca, m. Hawkins Popham, Betty, m. Humphrey Popham, Phebe, m. Thos. Popham, Susanna, m. Benj. Duncan, Mary, m. Lightfoot,& John. Grandchildren were Samuel Hawkins, Clarisa, Sarah, Virinea, Melinda and Julia Kilby. June 19, 1820.

Saml. Henning, Nov. 13, 1770; Eleanor; children: Saml., Jas., Mary, wife of Lewis Stephens Jr., of Frederick county, Joanna, Nancy, Elenor, Sally, and David. July 18, 1774.

John Hill, May 7, 1766; Betty; had daughter, Sarah, who m. Deforest. His sons were Chas., Jos. and Le Roy. Apr. 16, 1767.

Richard Hill, Nov. 12, 18_1; lived on Hedgeman River; had sons in law, Jas. Lear and Jas. Burdette.

William Hill, Jan. 25, 1809. Frances; children, Ann, m. Geo. Roberts, Russell, Armistead, Sally, Lucy, m. Nalle, Betsy, m. Daniel Brown, William, and Patsey, m. Colvin. April 20, 1812.

Jas. Hoard, Dec. 14, 1802; owned land in Spotsylvania; ch: Jas., Anne, m. Jas. Withers, Jane m. Thos. Brookes, Frances, m. Slaughter; testator m. dau. of Tenion Miller, of Spottsylvania. Dec. 17, 1803.

Jno. Hoofman, Dec. 30, 1762, wills his two bibles, in addition to his large estate, to his ten sons, "the two eldest to take them the first year, and then deliver them to the two next until they have had them around, and beginning again with the eldest and so continue as long as the bibles shall last." children were: Frederick, John, Nicholas, Michael, Jacob, Paul, William, George, Henry, Dilman, Margaret, Catherine, Elizabeth, and Mary. Aug. 17, 1772.

Thos. Hopper, Jan. 25, 1803. Mary Ann. Children: Frances, m. Blackwell, Jemima, m. William Tapp, Elizabeth, m. Vincent Tapp. Speaks of his grandson Wm. Coons, whom he appoints as one of his executors. Nov. 20, 1809.

Dr. Thos. Howison, Mar. 2, 1769; Betty; had bros. Jno. and Wm. who lived near Alloa in North Britain; another bro. was Robt. Howison. Owned land on Blue Ridge adjoining Col. Fitzhugh. Left a daughter. Jun. 16, 1769.

Henry Huffman, Apr. 5, 1767; Margaret; children: Tilman, Jno., Henry, Jos., Hermon, Elizabeth, m. Jno. Young, Catherine, Mary, Alice, Susannah and Eve. Sept. 6, 1783.

Jas. Hurt, Mar. 28, 1785; Sarah; children: Wm., Frances, m. Grayson, Anna, m. Acra Berry, Mary, m. Berry, and Sarah, m. Yowell. Jun. 15, 1789.

J

James Jeffries, June 29, 1805; children: Molly, m. McCoy, Lydda, Sally, Susanna, m. Hansbrough, Thos., Selah, m. Mason, Elizabeth, m. Yancey, Jno.,

James, Thomas and Alexander. Dec. 16, 1805.

Jno. Jett, May 6, 1763; children were Stephen, Jas., Jno., Wm., Elizabeth, m Roach, Margaret, m. Butler, and Mary, m. Tapp. Nov. 18, 1771.

Wm. Jett, Jul. 25, 1799; Susanna; children: Edgar, Milly, m. Wm. Jett, Molly, m. Wm. Williams,(and had Geo., Urban, Ezra and Tephamah,) Margaret. m. Jas. Withers Downey,(and had Jane, Edgar and Wm. Jett,) Betsy, m. Wm. Whitehead, Phebe, m. Jas. Withers Doores, Matthew, Anne, Susannah, and Dicey. Sept. 25, 1801.

John Jett. Nov. 21, 1802. Children: Wm., Stephen, Jas., Jos., Ninunt, Ann. m. Churchman. Elizabeth, m. Canady, Sarah, m. Hopper, and Abigail, m. Arnold. April 18, 1808.

David Jones, Feb. 2, 1751, speaks of his sister Mary Morris and of his bro. in law, Thos. Morris. Apl. 16, 1752.

Gabriel Jones, Sept. 3, 1776; Martha; children: Ann, Robt., Gabriel, Frances, m. Slaughter, and Mary. Testator m. Martha, dau. of Mrs. Ann Waller; had four sisters; Lucy Poindexter, Betty Green, Jane Gray and Dorothy Johnston. His widow m. Wm. Broaddus. Oct. 21, 1777.

Mary Jones, Aug. 27, 1807. Children: Ann, m. Boughan, Mary, m. McGrath, Lucy, m. Thornhill, and Thomas. Feb. 17, 1812.

Thos. Jordan, June 19, 1809. Children: Mary, Rachel, Marshall, Geo., Jno., Wm., Absolam, Sarah, m. Corley, Frances, m. Hand, and Ann, m. Geo. Johnston. Aug. 21, 1809.

K

Michael Kaffer. Dec. 28, 1762, had daughters, Elizabeth, m. Adam Garr, Barbara, m. Jno. Weaver, Mary, m. Geo. Utz, Margaret, m. Nicholas Crighter, and Doratha, m. Jno. Clore. Nov. 17, 1768.

Francis Kirtley, Nov. 22, 1762, had daughters who m. Cowherd and Collins. Mar. 1, 1763.

Samuel Kennerly, Sept. 22, 1749; Eleanor; children: Thos., Jas., Elizabeth, Coleman, Craffron Strother, Samuel, Margaret Ruddal, and Ann Namsley. Had land adjoining Thornton, Covington and Jno. Strother. Jan. 10, 1749.

Elin Kennerly, Oct. 28, 1753; children, Thomas, Elizabeth, who married Wm. Coleman, James, and Katherine who married Jeremy Strother. Sept. 16, 1756.

Wm. Knox, Feb. 6, 1805. Susannah. Children: Thos. Fitzhugh, Janet Somerville, m. Voss, Susannah Fitzhugh, m. Gordon; unmarried daughters were Sarah Stewart, Caroline, Anne Campbell, and Agnes. Other sons were William Alexander and John Somerville. April 22, 1806.

L

Thos. Latham, Mar. 6, 1778; wf. Caroline. Children: Henry, Anne, m. Jas. Gaines, and Sukey. Jan. 18, 1796.

Frances Latham, Oct. 28, 1789; children: Susannah, m. Thos. Freeman, Frances, m. Lynfield Sharpe, Robert, George and Philip. Jan. 18, 1790.

Paul Leatherer, Nov. 5, 1780; wf. Margaret; children: Michael, Nicholas, Samuel, Jno., Paul, Joshua, Susannah, Margaret, and Mary, m. Jno. Yowell. Nov. 21, 1785.

Goodrich Lightfoot, Apr. 24. 1778; children; Elizabeth, m. James, Ann, m. Grasty, Mary, m. Hubbard, Fanny, m. Hackley, Susanna, m. Brooks, Jno., Phillips, Priscilla, Martha; had four unmarried children. June 15, 1778.

Robert Lines, Jan. 16, 1749; Margaret; had several daughters who m.

Garrat, Carter, Foote, and Howell. Feb. 15, 1749.

Reuben Long, Dec. 29, 1791; wf. Mary. Children: Gabriel, Evans, Anderson, Nimrod, Fanny, m. Daniel Richardson, Peggie, m. Robert Kay, Polly, m. John Nash. June 18, 1792.

M

Mary Major, Aug. 23, 1809. Children: Wm., Mary, m. Richard Payne. Sept. 18, 1809.

Elizabeth Marshall, Apr. 17, 1779; children: Thos., Wm., Jno.. Mary, m. McClanahan, Markham, Margaret, m. Snelling; grandchildren: Thos. Smith and Wm. Lovell. May 17, 1779.

John Matthew, June 19, 1800. Children; Nancy, Polly, and Caty. all of whom m. a Shackelford. Jan. 1810.

Frances Mauzy; Dec. 30, 1816. Ch: Anne, m. Nalle, Susan, m. Triplett, having several daus. and two sons, Wm. H., and Joshua B. Triplett. Jan. 19, 1818.

Chas. Morgan, Feb. 3, 1782; children: Ann, m. Wright, and Milly, m. Cornelius. Speaks of his son-in-law, Bryant Thornhill. Feb. 18, 1782.

N

Martin Nalle, Mar. 14, 1780, left his estate to his brothers, Richard, Jno., Francis and Jas. Nov. 20, 1780.

Jno. Nalle, Sept. 16, 1780: children: Richard, Jno., Wm., Francis, Jas., Agatha, m. Russell Hill, Mary, m. Sims, Ann, m. Burke, Gressel, m. Parker, Amie, m. Wm. Morris, Elizabeth, m. Sims, and Martin, whose whereabouts were not known. Aug. 19, 1782.

Martin Nalle, Mar. 9, 1783; wf. Isabel; children: Wm., Martin, Ann, Rachel, Winny, Clary, and Milly. Caty Sparks, dau. of Humphrey Sparks, was his gran. dau. Sept. 15, 1788

Richard Nalle, Dec. 7, 1785: wf. Judah; children: Susannah, m. Burk. Was bro. of Francis Nalle. Dec. 18, 1786.

Bazel Nooe, Sept. 3, 1803. Speaks of brother, Zachiniah, sister, Sarah Watson, and his nephew, James Slaughter. April 17, 1809.

Courtney Norman, Mar. 11, 1770; Mary; dau. Amey, m. Murphy; sons were Jno., Courtney, Reuben, Benj., Wm. and Ezekiel. Aug. 20, 1770.

Jos. Norman, Nov. 20, 1783; wf. Sarah; children: Thos., Jno., Wm., Jas., Isaac, Mary, m. Dillard. Winifred, m. Bywaters, Peggy, m. Calvert. Fanny and Kisiah. Feb. 16, 1784.

O

Roger Oxford, Mar. 10, 1758, Margaret; had daughters, Hannah, who married Morgan, and Mary who married Brown. Mar. 15, 1759.

Thos. Oxford, Nov. 11, 1781; Elizabeth; children: Molley, m. Augustine Jennings. Apr. 15, 1782.

P

It appears from the records that Sarah, the widow of Wm. Pannill, married Wm. Strother.

Richard Parks, Mar. 2, 1817, Anne. Had seven children, among them being Jas., Gabriel, Peggy, m. Nalle and left children. Aug. 18, 1817.

Jas. Bendleton, * Aug. 12, 1793; wf. Catherine; children: Catlett, Jas. Bowie, Thos., Wm., Elizabeth, m. Jno. Pendleton, Ann, m. Wm. C. Brown, Peggy, m. Slaughter. Oct. 21, 1793.

Ann Pendleton, Feb. 25, 1804. Speaks of her granddaughters, Harriett, Juliette and Caroline Green. Had Henry, Edmund, and Frances, m. Ward. July 16, 1804.

Wm. Peyton, July 7, 1771; children were Wm., Chas., Jno., Benj., Ann, m. Stone, Mary, m. Smith, Judith, m. Allen, and Susannah, m. Perfect. Oct. 21, 1771.

Jno. Pickett, July 9, 1803. Hannah. Children: John, Wm., Caty, m. Hume, Elizabeth, m. Settle, Polly, m. James, Sally, Judith, Nancy. Hannah and Lucy. Owned land in Ky. Sept. 17, 1803.

Benj. Powell, 1768, children: Benjamin, Jas., Wm., Sarah, Ann and Betty Munford. Had brother Ambrose, and brother-in-law, Geo. Wetheral. Feb. 16, 1769.

Ambrose Powell, Jan. 6, 1782; wf. Mary; children : Robert, Wm., Anne, m. Henry Hill, Fanny, m. Sutton (children were John, Mary and Bledsoe.) Devised "warrant for 2,000 acres of land as an officer in the last war." Oct. 20, 1788.

Jane Pritchard, July 14, 1781; children: Isabella, wife of John Hill, Elizabeth, m. Page, Sarah, m. Cook, Ann, m. Treany. Aug. 20, 1781.

Q

Darby Quinn, Dec. 21, 1754. Son, Richard, and dau., Elizabeth, who m. a Bruce. Sept. 16, 1756,

R

John Read, Aug. 17, 1755, Winifred, had dau. Mary who m. Jos. Norman, Elizabeth, who m. Stephen Jett, and Ann, who m. Hugh Freeman. Sept. 19, 1763.

Jno. Read, Sept. 21, 1819. ch. Samuel, Elizabeth, m. Carter, Mary m. Hufman, Griffin, Tabitha, m. Chewning, Rebekah, m. Freeman, Theophilus, Robert Coleman, and Ann, m. Robson. June 19, 1820.

Martha Richards, June 7, 1805; children: Thos., Ann, m. Wm. Robinson, Rebecca, Lucy, Richard, Martha and Elizabeth. Dec. 16, 1805.

Richard Rixey, June 25. 1808. Elizabeth; Children: John, Richard, Samuel, Presley, Charles, Wm., and dau. who m. Chancellor. Sept. 19, 1808.

John Rixey, Sept. 9, 1820. Elizabeth. Ch: Elizabeth, m. Francis Fargeson, Jane m. Chas. Jones, Frances, Richard and Kitty; witnessed by Sam'l., Presley and Wm. Rixey, and Benj. Fargeson. Other ch. Chas., Wm., John, Presley and Samuel. Oct. 16, 1820.

Benj. Roberts, Feb. 14, 1782; children: Benj., Jos., Hannah, m. Dan'l. Field, Mary, m. Dulany, and Anne, m. Field. Mar. 18, 1782

Wm. Robertson, July 24, 1794; ch: Wm. and Elizabeth; speaks of his grandson, Andrew Bourn as living in his family. Apr. 20, 1801.

Wm. Roebuck, Oct. 30, 1780; Mary children: Rawleigh, Elizabeth, Millie and Lucy. Jan. 21, 1781.

Jerome Rosson, Mar. 2, 1794; children: Wm., Jos., Jas., Reuben, Daniel, Lucy, m. Jas. Butler, Susannah, m. Jno. King, and Ann. Sept. 19, 1796.

Sarah Russel, widow, Apr. 20, 1756, speaks of her daughters, Sarah, Elizabeth and Mary, who respectively married Read, Roberts and Wright. Oct. 20, 1757.

S

Jno. Sanford, April 10, 1804. Betsy. Children : Alexander, John,

Fanny Murphy, Julia Horner, Betsy and Kitty.   July 17, 1809.

Jno. Sanders,   Nov. 2, 1818 Ch: Isabella, Mildred, Nathaniel, Mary, m. Sims, Wm., Elizabeth, m. Sims, Robt., and James. Lived near Stone House Mountain. Jan. 18, 1819.

Anthony Scott,   Jan. 7, 1754, Jane; had children, Thos., Frances, who married Abraham Cooper, Elizabeth, who m. Rawley Corbin, and Ann, who m. Burk. May 17, 1764.

John Simpson,   July 2, 1776; Elizabeth; children: Wm. Jas., Alexander, Jno., Anne, Elizabeth, m. Berry; Mary, m. Burke, Eleanor, m. Booton, and Jane. Dec. 16, 1776.

Richard Sims,   April 16, 1809. Mary. Children: Robert Terrill Sims, Richard Miclin, Edmund, Joseph T., Henry, Sally Butler, Avel Collins, Nancy Tucker, and Mary Foster Sims. June 19, 1809.

Robt. Slaughter,   Nov. 3, 1769; Mary; children were: Robt., Thos., Wm., Jas., Francis, Lawrence, Geo., Susannah, m. Lightfoot. Dec. 21, 1769.

Francis Slaughter,   Sept. 2, 1765, had daughters, Frances, who m. a Ball, His sons were Francis, Reuben, John and Cadwallader. May, 1766.

Wm. Smith,   July 29, 1811. Children: James, Wm., Winney, who was married, Leana, Laura, m. Cooper. Sept. 16, 1811.

Wm. K. Spilman,   May 15. 1819. Had bros. John and Conway. nephew, John A. Spilman, and niece, Elizabeth Frances Armstrong. May 19, 1819.

Walter Stallard,   July 13, 1803. Hannah. Children: Eliza, m. Cavender, David, Samuel, Walter, Randolph, Peggy, m. Clore, Rachael, m. Luttrell, Mary Ann, m. Scott, Fanny, m. Shumate. Apr. 20, 1807.

Diana Stanton,   dau. of Henry Field Sr., Sept. 26, 1794. Children: William and a daughter, who m. a Slaughter, having son, Stanton Slaughter. Dec. 16, 1811.

Edward Stevens   (Gen. Stevens) June 1, 1820. Gilly. Had daughter in law, Polly (wife of John Stevens, who d. before his father). Left Kentucky land to James Scanland, Wm. Edmondson, Richard Chandler, Mr. Bland (who m. Nancy Edmundson), Edward Evans, James Edmondson, Betsy Emery, (late Betsy Edmondson) and Jno. Edmondson; Had sister Patty, who m. Edmondson. Aug. 24, 1820.

Jas. Stevenson,   who m. Frances Arnott. Feb. 24, 1805. Children. Robert, Sarah, m. Woodville, Jas., Carter and Andrew, Oct. 16, 1809.

Wm. Steward,   Dec. 13, 1802. Elizabeth. Children: Charles, Joseph, Humphrey, John, Elizabeth, Lucy, Sarah, m. Smith, and Grannan (a daughter). Owned land in King George county. Speaks of land he bought of Capt. Jas. Thomas, Philip Slaughter and Robt. Patton. Dec. 17, 1804.

Francis Strother,   Apr. 17, 1751, Speaks of his wife Susanna, and of his children, John, George, Anthony, Frances, Robert, Mary, Behethaland, Elizabeth and Susanna. He refers to his failure to get from Lord Fairfax's office a deed for land which he had purchased and afterwards sold to John Minor. Apr. 16, 1752.

James Strother,   who was dead on the 16th of December, 1761, left children: French, James, and Mary, who married George Gray.

Geo. Strother,   June 20, 1767, Mary, leaves 100 acres on Kennerly's Mountain to his daughter, Margaret, directs land on Little Pass mountain to be sold. John and George were his sons. Aug. 20, 1767.

Jno. Strother, Mar. 29, 1795; wf. Mary; children: Ann, m. Strother, Susanna, m. Lawlor, Mary, m. Browning, Lucy. m. Covington, Elizabeth, m. Browning, Mildred, m. Covington, John, Jos., Sarah, m. Hughes. Apr. 20, 1795.

Robt. Stuart, May 14, 1770; wf. Mary; children: Lucy, m. Pulliam, Nancy, m. Strother, and Robert. Sept. 21, 1789.

Edward Stubblefield, Oct. 19, 1750; Elener; Lewis Davis Yancey was his brother-in-law; his widow m. Thos. Brown. Mar. 21, 1750.

T

Harry Taliaferro, Jan. 1, 1803; Elizabeth. Children were John, Harry, Lindsey, Caty, Judith, Lucy, and Melinda. Sept. 19, 1803.

Martha Tannahill, Mar. 19, 1821. Ch. Wm., Nancy, Keziah, Geo., Elizabeth, m. Lewis Moore, Mariann, m. Baker, and two daus. who m. Wm. Carter and Anson Dearing. Mar. 19, 1821.

Wm. Tapp, June 27, 1780; wf. Christian; children: Vincent, Ann, m. Jno. Cunningham, Alice, m. Jno. Graham, Elizabeth, m. Green, Sarah m. Jno. Jett, Wm., Lewis, and Mary, m. Yates. Jan. 27, 1791.

Massey Thomas, who was dead in Aug. 1776, had wife Elizabeth. ch. Jno., Wm., Reuben, Massey, Jessee and Susannah.

Jno. Thomas, Apr. 29, 1782; children: Benj., Jno., Wm., Massey, Margaret, m. Robert McKey, Sarah m. Wm. Powell, and Ann, m. Jeremiah Kirk. Feb. 21, 1785.

Geo. Thompson, Catherine; July 11, 1755; had children, Elizabeth, who married Henderson, Winnifred, Geo., Jno., and David. Aug. 16, 1764.

Constance Major, Nov. 6, 1764, speaks of his grandson, Philip Major, who was the son of Samuel, her son, John, and her daughters, Jane, who m. Loggins, and Precilla, who m. George Dillard. Apr. 18, 1765.

Jno. Thompson, Feb. 3, 1771; chil. were Wm., Jno., Phillip Roots, Ann, m. Francis Thornton, and Mildred had sister Ann Neilson. Nov. 16, 1772.

Bryant Thornhill, Dec. 8, 1779; Thomson; children: Jos., John, Reuben, Wm., Bryant, and Elizabeth. Apr. 17, 1780.

Geo. A. Thornton. Nov. 30, 1818, a physician of Alexandria, speaks of his wife "Frances G. Thornton," of his kinsmen, Aylett Hawes, Geo. Washington Thornton, and Stewart G. Thornton.

Stokley Towles, Jan. 15, 1757, speaks of his children, Joseph, Henry, Mary and John; also of having sent to Liverpool for goods by Capt. Gayworth. Dec. 15, 1757.

Jas. Tutt, Jan. 20, 1786; wf. Ann. Children: Benj., Mille, m. Lynch, Elizabeth, m. Sanders, Richard, Mary, m. Tutt, Lewis, Gabriel, Hansford, and Ann, m. Paul Williams. Sept. 21, 1789.

Jno. Tutt, May 8, 1812. Children. Benjamin, Jno., Elizabeth, m. Taliaferro, Gabriel, Nancy, m. Taliaferro, Philip, Richard Johnston. June 15, 1812.

U

Geo. Utz, June 28, 1758. had daughters, Margaret, Barbaba, who m. Blakenbaker. His sons were Geo. and Michael; lived on Robinson river. Aug. 21, 1766.

V

Robert B. Voss, of "Mountain Prospect, Culpeper county." July 12,

1811. Children: Susan F., Benjamin F., Robert S., and Wm. Edward. Oct. 21, 1811. Samuel Gordon, of Falmouth, executor.

W

Thos. Wallace, Jan. 1814. Owned land in Madison county, Kentucky and Ohio. Had James, Caroline et als. Had nephew, G. B. Wallace, and bro. John Wallace. Sept. 21, 1818.

Edward Watkins, Jan. 6, 1787; wf. Sarah ; his nieces were Sarah Watkins Cowne, Elizabeth Tutt, and nephew, James Broaddus. Sept. 17, 1787.

Thos. Watts, Jan. 25, 1760, Eliza; speaks of his bro. Wm. Watts, his sons Richard and Wm. Watts, and his dau. Elinor Cox. Apr. 13, 1763.

Joel Watts, July 17, 1781; Isabel; Ch: Lettie m. Brown, Barbara, m. Thomas, Joauna, m. Stewart, Frederick. Aug. 20, 1781.

Peter Weaver, Mar. 27, 1763, Elizabeth; had daughters, Margret, Barbary, who m. Carpenter, Catharina and Hannah, Aug. 18, 1763.

Jas. Whitehead, Sept. 23, 1806, Margaret. Children: John, Sarah, m. McGuinn, Jas., Nelson, Frances, William and Margaret, m. Daniel Duval. Oct. 20, 1806.

Michael Wilhoite, Aug. 10, 1803. Children: Elizabeth, m. Spicer, Gabriel, Jas., Michael, Agnes, m. Coginhill, Frances, m. Lucas, Ann, m. Hawkins, Sarah, m. Green. July 16, 1804.

Y

Nicholas Yager, Sept. 12, 1779; Susanna; children: Nicholas, Frederick, Cornelius, Beggee, Rosanna and Susanna, (twins), Absolam, Benj., Elijah, and Jessee. Aug. 20, 1781.

Lewis Davis Yancey, Apr. 17, 1778; wf. Winifred. Children; Chas., Lewis, Richard, John Philemon, Ann, m. Nalle, Winifred, m. Nalle, Jas. and Robert. Apr. 22, 1788.

Chas. Yancey, Mar. 10, 1805. Elizabeth. Children: Ann, m. Doggett, William, Thomas, Keziah, m. Freeman, and Major; had grandson., Chas. Lee Yancey. Apr. 15, 1805.

Geo. Yates, Mar. 13, 1788; wf. Mary. Children: Laurence Catlett; was bro. in law of Kemp Catlett, and a grandson of Geo Yates, of Caroline county. June 16, 1788.

NOTE: See will of Constance Major in the Ts, which was put there by mistake.

MARRIAGE RECORD.
[Note: The year of marriage only is given. From 1781 to 1825.]

Jno. Abbot, m. Eliz. Heaton, 1805;
Jno. Abel, m. Frances Fennell, 1785;
Thos. Adams m. Anne Houton, 1797;
Thos. Adams m. Anne Houton, 1796;
Jno. Adams m, Marg. Calvert, 1794;
Ephraim Adams m. Mary Moore, 1820;
Am. Adkins, Frankie Marrifield, 1784;
Jno. Adle m. Nancy Yates, 1803;
Wm. Alexander, Frankie Rucker '82;
Jas. Aines m. Winnie McGuinn, '95;
Wes Allen m. Susannah Gaines, 1800;
Jas. Allen m. Mary Hunt, 1792;
Jas. Allen m. Bettie Chilton, 1799;
Jas. Allen m. Sarah Chapman, 1788;
Churchhill Allen m. Peg. Walden '14;
Newman Allen m. Peggie White 1812;
Benj. Allan m. Eliz. Caul 1815;
Newman Allen, Mary A. Brown, 1819;
Presley Allen m. Nancy Walden 1817;
Jas. Allen m. Eliza C. White, 1806;
Jno. Almand m. Jane Bingham, 1814;
P. Amiss m. Anne Tapp, Feb. 22, 1786;
Philip Amiss, Anne Tapp Sept. 4 '86;
Jas. Amiss m. Nancy Dennis 1815;

Aug. Anderson, Annie Underwood, '86;
Josiah Anderson, Eliz. Richerson, '92;
Edmund Anderson, Fannie Turner '16
Elijah Anderson m. Mary Priest 1804;
Aaron Antram, Charlotte King, 1799;
Jno. Appleby m. Mary Long 1793;
Turner Ashby, Dorathea Green '20;
Wm. Ashby, Wilhimina Strother, '05;
Jno. Asher, Betsey Burbridge 1802;
Benj. Askins m. Lucy Settle 1802;
Jno. Athe m. Dorcas Cullen 1785;
Spencer Atkins, Mildred Brandam '18;
Mich. Aylor m. Sarah Boughhorn '95;

Jno. Anderson m. Lucy Sutton, '86;
Geo. Anderson m. Berkley Clarke, '89;
Jno. Anderson m. Nancy Little, '00;
Thos. Antram m. Esther Sharp 1799;
Geo. Apperson m. Mary S. Yancey '19;
Ed. Archer m. Susannah Pener 1788;
Thompson Ashby, Anne L. Menefee '08;
Wm. Asher m. Eliz. Sharp 1797;
Waller R. Asher, Eliza Shannon 1805;
Wm. Askins m. Catherine Jones 1798.
Elias Atkins m. Eliz. Atkens 1816;
Cornelius Austin m. Eleanor Butler '92;
Lewis Aylor m. Nancy Creel 1810.

B

Jno. Bachelder m. Sarah Pup 1799;
Jas. Baines m. Frances Thompson '91;
Jacob Baker m. Eliza Lawrence 1819;
Philip Baker, Kittie Lawrence 1820;
Solomon Baker, B—— Herrington, '21;
Peter Balden m. Amy Smith, 1815;
Ezra Ball m. Anne Dillen, 1799;
Willis Ballance m. Joyce Green, 1796;
Curtis Ballard m. Esther Gaines, 1781;
Wm. Ballenger m. Eliz. Hughes 1806;
Jas. Balwick, Elizabeth Bryan, 1817;
Mich. Barmer, Frances Brown, 1795;
Wm. Barbour m. Eliz. White, 1796;
Geo. Barger m. Hannah Boon, 1789;
Ephraim Barlow m. A. Carter, 1789;
Martin Barnes m. Rhode Sampson '87;
Jas. Barnes m. Polly Hill, 1792;
Benj. Barnes, Eleanor Stapleman, '94;
Dan. Barnett, Ruthy Magruder, 1795;
Law. Barnett, Cath. Vass or Voss;——
Elias Bartlett m. Mary Brown, 1819;
Henry Basye m. Eliz. James, 1786;
Wm. Bates Sr., Mary Harris, 1781;
Wm. Batson m. Aggie Lawrence, 1820;
Mordecai Baughn, Mary Tineman, 1801;
Abner Baughan, Priscilla Hume, 1817;
Wm. Bayley m. Catharine Smith——
Henry Bazel m. Lucy Brandon——
Geo. Bean m. Nancy Petty, 1788;
Jno. Beckham m. Rebecca Gray. 1813;
Jno. Beam m. Patsy Partlow, 1815;
Wm. Bennett m. Patty Carder, 1792;
Jno. Bennett m. Caty Carder. 1800;
Jessee Berry m. Anna Miller, 1790;
Wm. Berry, Jemima Weakley, 1798.
Anthony Berry m. Peggy Ward, 1797;
Reuben Berry, Millie Reusens, 1815;
Chris. Biofey m. Clara Horton, 1804;

Jno. Bailey m. Alice Patton 1802;
Jacob Baker m. Lydia Trimble 1799;
Archibald Baker m. Eliz. Massie 1819;
Philip Baker m. Catherine Baker '21;
Jos. Balden m. Betsey Dillard '03;
Jno. Ball m. Pollie Gibbs, 1792.
Sam'l Ball m. Anne Thud, 1807;
Larkin Ballard m. Eliz. Gaines, 1786;
Johnson Ballard, Bettie Eastham, 1791;
Jno. Ballesu m. Anne Cooke, 1791:
Jessee Banley m. Ellen Bosan, 1822,
Wm. Barbee m. Fannie Curtis, 1808;
Jno. Barger m. Anne Swindler, 1793;
Joshua Barler m. Rhode Thomas, 1789;
Zach. Barner m. G. Roberts, 1797;
Shadrach Barnes, Fran. Mozingo 1786;
Wm. Barnes m. Eliz. Marshall, 1790;
Rich. Barnett Sarah Utterback; 1794;
Wm. Barnett m. Sarah Matthews, '97;
Wm. Barron m. Lucy Stwentiman '91;
Jno. Basye m. Catherine Basye, 1793;
Edmund Basye m. Caty Thomas, 1808;
Wm. Bates Jr. m. Eliz. Harris, 1781;
Abraham Baughan, Mary Weaver, '97;
Moses Baughan m. Sarah Yowell, '12;
Jno. Bayless m. Fannie Porter, 1809;
Jno. Bayne m. Sarah Hawkins, 1793;
Geo. Beale m. Susannah Brooke, 1817.
Osborn Beatty m. Anue Willis, 1819;
Jno. Beem m. Nancy Bowen, 1818;
Wm. Bennett, Sarah Clatterbuck, 1786;
Geo. Bennett m. Mary Holloway, '99;
Geo. Bennett m. Peggy Dodson——
Simpson Berry, Jemima Jennett, 1790;
Wm. Brooks m. Fannie Lloyd, 1792
Wm. Berry m. Lucy Berry, 1807;
Jno. Bigbee m. Sallie Wheatley, 1799;
Thos. Bingham m. Nancy Norman, 1793;

Josiah Bishop, Susannah Inskeep, '84; Thos. Bishop m. Eliz. Morris, 1794 ;
Jno. Bishop m. Anne Stokes, 1798 ; Jonathan Bishop, Nancy Kobler, 1805 ;
Churchhill Blakey, Mary Clark, 1781; Jos. Blackwell m. Frances Hopper, 1798;
Wm. Blackwell, Rach. Tompkins;—— Jas. Blair m. Eleanor Vaughan, 1784 ;
Wm. Blakey m. Polly Gaines, 1799 ; Wm. Blair m. Polly McQueen, 1810 ;
Jas. Blake m. Sarah Asher, 1808 ; Jno. Blake m. Lucy Atkins, 1809 ;
Jas. Blankenbaker, Eliz. Carpenter, '90; Jac. Blankenbaker m. Han. Weaver, '91
S. Blankenbaker, Charl. Leatherer, '91; Jas. Bledsoe m Judith Ward, '85;
Thos. Bohannan, Frances Dicken, '89; Joel Bolling m. Anne Gaines, 1792;
Wm. Bonnifield, Eliz. Wilson, 1792 ; Jno. Booker m. Kitty Taliaferro, 1804.
Jno. Booton m. Frances Clarke, 1786 ; Wm. Botts m. Anne Gaines, 1791;
Jos. B. Botts m. Nancy Fristoe, 1796 ; Henry Baughan m. Eliz. Walle, 1793;
Francis Bowen m. Millie Yates, 1788 ; Jos. Bowen m. Nannie Gibson, 1797 ;
Jas. Bowen m. Anne Foushee, 1814; Jas. Bowen m. Amelia Pollard, 1815;
Peter B. Bowen, Sarah Fishback, 1815; Jos. Bowen m. Sarah Nalle, 1816 ;
Wm. Bowen m. Polly Partlow, 1815; Jessee Bowlin m. Nancy Kelly, 1788 ;
Geo. Bowlin m. Eliz. Priest, 1810; Henry Bowyer, Rebecca Bennett, 1810;
Wm. Barford m. Nancy Fry, 1806; Sam. K. Bradford, Emily Slaughter, '16 ;
Aug. Bradley m. Frankie Hurt, 1788 ; Aug. Bradley m. Polly Lillard, 1805;
Abso. Bradley, Rebec. Rambottom, '24; Jno. Bradley, m. Rosamond Botts '99;
Ben. Bragg, Polly Twentiman, 1735; Gabe Bragg, m. Polly Estes 1800;
Ezek. Bragg, m. Nancy Estes 1802; Evans Bragg, m. Polly Hudson 1809;
Thos. Bragg, m. Eliz. Jones 1816 ; Jno. Branham m. Sallie Boswell, 1789;
Wm. Branham m. Eliz. Yates, 1784; Jas. Branham m. Bettie Doggett, 1784 ;
Jas. Branham, Marg. Lindsey, 1806; Nimrod Branham, Peggy Marshall, '97;
Rich. Branham, Marg. Threlkeld, '98; Reub. Branham m. Becca Farley, '98;
Dan. Brannan, Eliz. Canady, 1806; Vinson Branson m. Anna Dodson, 1807 ;
Jas. Brany, Charity Humphrey, 1808; Wm. Breedline m. Marg. Wright, '02 ;
Ananias Breedwell m. Celey Daniel, '93; Cuthbert Breedwell m. Mary Hilton, '96;
Jas. Briant m. Susannah Jollett, 1782 ; Jas. Bright m. Dinah Johnston, 1797 ;
Jno. Britton m. Polly Bragg, 1815 ; Thos. Broadus, Susannah White, 1792;
Wm. Brooke m. Fannie Loyd, 1792; Armistead Brown, Peggy Collins, 1792 ;
Garfield Brown m. Nancy Long, 1784 ; Ezekiel Brown m. Sarah Long, 1786;
Jas. Brown m. Eliz. Gore, 1788; Dan. Brown m. Peggy Covington, 1794 ;
Wm. Brown m. Lucy Campbell, 1786; Jno. Brown m. Phoebe Brown, 1787 ;
Thos. Brown, Eleanor Weatheral, 1796 ; Chas. Brown m. Nanny Hall, 1794;
Jno. Brown, m. Polly Norman, 1795 ; Henry P. Brown m. Hannah Butler, '98;
Jas. Brown , Sukey Zimmerman, 1791; Nich. Brown m. Nancy Cardwell, 1799;
Wm. Brown m. Mary C———, 1797; Evans Brown, Mary Anne Williams, 1802
Braxton Brown m. Lucy Carder, 1804 ; Jas. Brown m. Sallie Jett, 1803;
Dan. Brown, Penelope Collins, 1809 ; Wm. Brown m. Mary Griffin, 1807 ;
Jno. F. Brown, Susannah Dulaney, '09; Jas. Brown m. Mary Smith, 1804;
Jas. Brown, Cassendia Menefee, 1808; Jno. Brown m. Caty Ramey, 1804;
Jno. Brown Jr., Lucy Hughes, '12; Jno. Pow. Brown, Isabel. Thompson, '11;
Wm. Brown m Tab. R. Menefee, 1814; Enoch Brown m. Sallie Yates, 1800;
Thos. C. Brown, Frances Griffin, 1814 ; Norman Brown m. Gracy Reesee, '18;
Daniel Brown m. Lucy Powell, 1818; Jas. Brown m. Kitty Morris, 1814;
Presley Brown, Anne M. Popham, '21; Robertson Brown m Nancy Bishop, '22;
Robertson Brown, Sarah Bishop, 1817 ; Wm. Brown m. Sarah Ficklin, 1816;
Rich. Brown m. Frances M. Hill, 1822; Thos. Browning m. Eliz. Sewright, 1793;
Thos. Browning, Eliz. Bywaters, 1793; Caleb Browning m Anne Moor ——;
Jas. Browning, Jane Whitledge, 1789; Shadrach Browning m. Peg. Routt, '94.
Jno. Browning m. Fran. Pendleton, '98; Wm. Browning m. Lu. McClannahan '92.

Wm. Browning m. Nancy Stone, '93;
Frances Browning, Polly Farmer, '93;
Nich. Browning, Lucy Browning '00;
Willis Browning, Caroline Menefee, '17;
Jno. Brumley, Martha Hopper, 1793;
Jyuashus Bruce, Sarah Johnston, '99;
Thos. Bryan m. Mary Stanton, 1783;
Jno. Bryan m. Nancy Lillard, 1807;
Jno. Henry Buck, Lucy Colvin, 1794;
Bailey Buckner m. Mild. Strother, '14;
Jno. Burdyne m. Jemima Clarke, 1788;
Joshua Birkland, Frances Harden '96;
Wm. Burke m. Nancy Weaver, 1802;
Thos. Burrows m. Polly Meade, 1803;
Towson Butler m. Cath. Blackwell ——
Aaron Butler m. Sarah Simms, 1801;
Jno. Butler m. Nancy Butler, 1805;
Wm. Butler m. Bertha Little, 1805;
Chas. Butler, Susannah Neale, 1809;
Wm. Butler m. Eliz. Green, 1796;
Thos. N. Butt, Caty G. Broadus, 1806;
Jas. Butterfield, Polly Ballinger, 1793;

Taliaferro Browning, Mary Id '92;
Francis Browning m. Polly Yates, '02;
Geo. Browning Millian Covington, '09;
Jas. Broyles m. Anne Wilhoite, '21;
Benj. Bruce m. Mary Crisal, 1789;
Elijah Bruce m. Malinda Browning, '10;
Jas. Bryan m. Lottie Kennard, 1804;
Reub. Burley, Jeannetta Delaney, '99.
Jno. Buchannon m. Sarah Jones, 1797;
Chas. Bullard, Martha W. Herndon '13;
Alex. Burgess m Agnes Reece, 1815.
Edmund Burke m. Fran. Weaver, '97;
Jno. Burke m. Betsy Berry, 1805;
Harris Burriss m. Nancy Hudson, 1812;
Benj. Butler m. Mary Edwards, 1790;
Armistead Butler, Mary Wheatley, '01;
Taliaferro Butler, Janny Grimsley, '04;
Elijah Butler m. Catharine Watts, 1798;
Taliaferro Butler m. Polly Miller,——;
Jno. Butt m. Eliz. Norris, 1800;
Sam'l. Butt m. Nancy Oder, 1803;
Martin Button m. Cath. Matthews '12;

C

Jno. Calvert m. Anne Askins, 1804;
Jessee Calvert m. Sericy Rea 1810;
Danl. Cameron m. Sallie Oliver, 1811;
Jno. Camner m. Esther Olive, 1805;
Marshall Camp, Lucy Wilkerson, '05 ;
Willis Camp m. Nancy Colvin, 1798 ;
Morgan Campbell, Mary Huffman, '07;
Elias Campbell m. Chloe Swindler, 1796;
Pat. Campbell m. Lydia Hill, 1789 ;
Silas Campbell m. Nancy Turner, 1791;
Elijah Campbell m. Eliz. Cannon, 1799;
Jno. Camper, Susannah Huffman, 1792 ;
Sam. Compton m. Eliz. Harper, 1790 ;
Leroy Canady m. Sarah Leavel, 1782 ;
Jas. Cannon m. Sarah Scott, 1812 ;
And'w Carpenter m. Eliz. Konslar, '92;
Joshua Carpenter m. Sarah Smith, '90;
Benj. Carpenter m. Susanna Burkes, '00;
Archibald Carnal m. Eliz. Oder, 1819;
Jno. G. Carson m. Lucy Hall, 1802;
Geo. Carder m. Anne Hume, 1806;
Wm. Carter m. Mary Chester, 1789;
Chas. Carter m. Susannah Tapp, 1797;
Geo. Carder m. Lilly Brown, 1799;
Thos. Carter m. Marg. Green, 1803;
Wm. Carder, Keziah Tannahill, 1812;
Landon Carter m. Polly Lillard, 1815;
Jno. Cason m. Judith Roebuck, 1788;
Reuben Cave m. Anne Jenkins, 1782;

Ralls Calvert m. Polly Strother, 1709;
Geo. Calvert m. Nancy Norman, 1809;
Owen Campbell m. Jemima Lear, 1787;
Antram Camp m. Nancy Pierce, 1803;
Ambrose Camp m. Eliz. Conner, '95;
Geo. H. Camp m. Handy Bohen, 1816;
Jno. Campbell m. Frances Green, '98;
Jos. Campbell m. Su. Shackelford, '93;
Robt. Campbell. Lucy Campbell, 1794.
Wm. Campbell m. Anne Howard, 1800;
Reub. Campbell m. Mary Cannon, 1801;
Joel Camper m. Anna Coons, 1792;
Ed. Compton m. Rebecca Murphy, '09;
Jno. Carnegie m. Frances Jones, 1802;
Jno. Cannon, Jr., Judith Monroe, 1813;
Sam. Carpenter, Peg. Blankenbaker, '93
And'w Carpenter m. Anna Wayland,' 91;
Dav. Carmichael m. Nan. Anderson, '93;
Garland Carr m. Mary Philips, 1783;
Burkett Carder m. Nancy Hawkins; '05
Wm. Carder m. Lythia Yowell, 1807;
Wm. Carter m. Susannah George, 1795;
Benj. Carder m. Polly Carder, 1796;
Fred. Carter m. Nancy Jenkins, 1797;
Randolph Carder, Fannie Pierce, 1812;
Wm. Carder Jr. m. Eliz. Holland, '15;
Abner Carter m. Martha Moore, 1816;
Hemp Catlett m. Sallie Pierce, 1791;
Jos. Cave m. Mary Jenkins, 1791;

Wm. Cave m. Susannah Fincham, 1801; Jno. Caynor m. Lucy Caynor, 1824;
Edw. Cason m. Sallie Muse Cave, '89; Erasmus Chapman m. Nancy Lewis, '85;
Jno. Chapman m. Eliz. Menefee, '97; Cadwallader Chapman, Pol. Morris, 98;
Henry Chapman m. Eliz. Morris, 1800; Zach. Chappalior m. Sinney Settle, '99;
Elijah Cheek m. Millie Horton, 1806; Geo. Cheek m. Elizabeth Williams, '93;
Francis Cheek m. Nancy Gaines, 1801; Jas. Cheek m. Nancy Horton, 1809;
Luke Cheek m. Sallie Crouch, 1823; Elias Chelf m. Eliz. Weaver, 1787;
Jno. Chewning m Tabi. Reed, 1792; Geo. Chilton, Eleanor Zimmerman, '07;
Stephen Chilton, Frances Norman, '90; Rich. Chilton m. Sarah Short, '96;
Geo. Chilton m. Sallie Asher, 1809: Wm. Chisham, Delphia Raines, 1791;
Jno. Christian m. Anne Powell, 1803; Robt. Chewning m. Mildred Walker, '90;
Jere Chrisel m. Mary Bruce, 1791; Julian Christler m. Eliz. Souther, 1792;
Abra. Christler, Mary Harvey, '92; Jno. Clark m. Millie Gibbs, 1788;
Wm. Clark m. Lucretia Clark, 1791; Josiah Clark m. Jane Adams, 1798:
Robt. Clark m. Joannah Jones, 1791; Thos. Clark m. Towsey Powell, 1801;
Wm. Clark m. Judy Jenkins, 1813; Landon Clatterbuck, Nelly Rose, 1809;
Jas. Clatterbuck m. Eliz. Hurt, 1786; Wm. Clatterbuck, Dicey Turner, 1792:
Gab. Clatterbuck, Nan. Richardson, '99; Thos. Clayton m. Sar. Cunningham, '07
Geo. Clayton m. Eliz. Gaines, 1798; Aaron Clements, Lucy Shackelford, '99;
Jas. Colvin m. Polly Hill, 1806; Philip Calender, Malinda Yancey, '05;
Philip Cline m. Polly Turner, 1789; Sam'l. Clore, Frances Christopher, 1792;
Benj. Clore, Anne Christopher, 1790; Aaron Clore m. Susan Swindle, 1790:
Fred. Cobler, Anne Threlkeld, 1792; Wm. Cochran m. Charity Spencer, 1791;
Henry Cocke m. Susannah Mills, 1796; Thos. Cocke m. Nancy Hume, 1816;
Mat. Cardwell m. Betty Hisle, 1803; Jno. Coghill m. Eleanor Butts, 1795;
Josiah Colbert, Susannah Spiller, 1797; Jno. Colbert m. Sarah Adams, 1799;
Cecilius Colbert, Nancy Colbert, 1797; Wm. Colvert m. Harriett Weeden,——;
Farish Coleman m. Eliz. Camp, 1798; Jere. Colen m. Mary Shepherd, 1798;
Wm. Collins m. Arie Simms, 1807; Jno. Collins, Charlotte Wortham 1793:
Andrew Collins m. Eliz. Freeman, 1795: Andrew Collins m. Polly Morris, 1813;
Jno. Colsolsoror m. Anna Blair, 1812. Jere. Colvin m. Sallie Smith, 1806;
Benj. Colvin m. Nancy Coleman, 1793; Mason Colvin m. Eliz. Hawkins, 1788;
Jno. Colvin m. Eliz. Colvin, 1789; Gab. Colvin m. Polly Roberts, 1801;
Robt. Colvin m. Hattie Yeager, 1815; Dan. Compton m. Betsey Yates, 1800;
Wm. Compton m. Hannah Hay, 1812. Stephen Compton, Eleanor Duker, '02.
Mat. Compton m. Nancy Vaughan, '06. Howard Compton m. Eliz. Yates, 1800.
Walker Compton, Eliz. Adams, 1798. Uriel Conner m. Nancy Nalle 1796.
Jno. Conner, Nancy Higginton 1796. Lewis Conner m. Marg. Farrow 1816.
Fran. L. Conner, Mary L. Withers, '22. Wm. Coons m. Eliz. Freeman, 1808.
Thornton P. Cooke m. Anne Ward, '04. Thos. Cooke m. Marg. Debourd, 1732.
Lewis Cooke m. Mary Yager 1793. Geo. Cooke m. Eliz. Stipe, 1794.
Jno. Cooke m. Martha Powell, 1790. Philip Cooke m. Sallie Doggett, 1799.
Alf. Cooke m. Susannah Corbin, 1815. Fred. Coons, Mary Ann Matthews, '83.
Jno. Coons m. Anne Coons, 1792. Jas. Coons m. Anne Atwood, 1781.
Jessee Coons m. Lucy Withers ——— Wm. Cooper m. Laura Smith, 1808.
Rob. Cooper m. Nancy Triplett, 1809. Jos. Corbin m. Hannah Menefee 1799.
Benj. Corbin m. Anne Corbin, 1786. Martin Corbin m. Nancy Scott, 1787.
Chas. Corbin, Nancy Jones, 1793. Fielding Corbin, Susannah Collins, '0 0.
Mich. Corbin, Nancy Bywaters, 1811. Thos. Corbin m. Eliz. Johnston, 1811.
Seneson Corbin, Mary N. Mason, '12. Geo. Corbin m. Sallie Monroe, 1814.
Nelson Corbin m. Sallie Garnett, 1819. Jas. Corder m. Sallie George, 1792.
Elias Corder m. Anne Tapp, 1793. Thos. Cown m. Lucy Gaines, 1803.
Wm. Cornelius, Betsey Plunkett, 1786. Geo. Cornelius m. Judith Mason, 1797.

Chas. Cornelius, Eliz. Jennings, 1794.
Jas. Courtney m Amy Johnston, '93.
Wm. Covington, Lucy Slaughter, 1816.
Jno. Cowgill m. Polly Huans, 1801.
Aug. Cowne m Frances Yancey, 1789.
Benj. Craig m Betsey Green, 1808.
Henry Crank, Maryan Haywood, '94.
Jos. Crawford m Mag. Utterback, '06.
Aaron Crawford, Ruth Threlkeld, '89.
Wm. Crigler m Kitty Brown, 1808.
Chris. Crigler, Frances Botts, 1793.
Jas. Crigler, Susan W. Gaines, 1812.
Jas. Crisdenberry, Eliz. Threlkeld, '99.
Wm. Crouch m Mary Crawford, 1793.
Jno. Cunningham, Janney Haddox '91.
Elijah Curtis m Hepsaba Guinn, 1806.

Chris. Courtney, Mary A. Johnston, '94.
Jno. Covington m Eliz. Griffin, 1819.
Isaac Cowgill m Eliz. Stokesberry, 1797.
Thos. Cowgill m. Sarah Antram 1800.
David J. Cox m Anne Calvert, 1799.
David Crane m Rebecca Young——
Geo. Craver m Jane Calvert, 1804.
Oliver Crawford m Lucy Alexander,'86.
Jno. Creal m Fannie Kilby, 1811.
Jas. Crigler m. Sallie Triplett, 1810.
Jno. Crigler m. Sallie Hume, 1789.
Kufley Crigler m. Leanah Sudduth, '09.
Robt. Crook m. Nancy Campbell, 1806.
Coleman Crutcher, Eliz. Pierce, 1798.
Thos. B. Cer—— m Dinah Wood, 1815.

D

Thos. Daniel m Marg. Rosson, 1793.
Wm. Daniel, Anne G. Calvert, 1821.
Jno. Davis m Polly Threlkeld, 1807.
Jno. Daviss m Frances Ham—— 1787.
Benj. Dawnes m Eliz. Slaughter, 1804.
Jno. Dawson m Lucy Cosney, 1799.
Chas. Day m. Susan Threlkeld 1801.
Peter Deale m. Mary Viscarver, 1800.
Wm. R. Dearing m. Eliz. Keith, 1819.
Wm. Deatherage, Mary Maddox, 1789.
Wm. Deatherage, Mary Covington,'17.
Jno. Dulany m Anne Walle, 1794.
Leroy Dulaney m Anne Routt 1792.
Levy Derry, Hannah Rainbottom, '15.
Edw. Dickenson, Eliz. Landrum, '02,
Jas. Dillard, Jane Edrington, 1800.
Thos. Dobbs m Sarah Johnston, 1785.
Jas. Dodson, Marg. Woodard, 1803.
Stephen Dodson, Cath. Chilton, '93.
Wm. Dodson, Judith Chilton, 1801.
Jas. Doggett, Anne Brown, 1788.
Thos. B. Doggett m Sallie Ward, '95.
Thos. Doggett, Sarah Harden, 1802.
Nehemiah Dowd m Eliz. Goodman,'82.
Rich. Duke m. Eliz. M. Doyle, 1799.
Elias Dulaney m Fannie McQueen,'03.
Isaac Dunnaway, Milly Kinnard, 1794.
Uriel Dunnaway, Eliz. Hammows, '23.
Gallop Duncan, Lucy Covington, 1805.
Jas. Duncan, Dorcas Butler, 1797.
Fred. Duncan, Sarah Stallard, '97.
Edmund Duncan, Harriet Dulaney '12.
Benj. Duval, Lucy Jennings 1793.

Elijah Daniel, Nancy Cunningham, '97.
Jno. Davenport, Eliz. Pierce, 1785.
Chas. Davis m. Hannah Gaines, 1733.
Jno. Davis m. Anne Smith, 1815.
Thos. Dawson m Eliz. Foushee, 1709.
Thos. Day m Ellis Duval, 1796.
Horatio Day m Rebecca Pettinger 1813.
Jno. Deale m. Sallie Ordor, 1802.
Anson Dearing m Anne Tannahill, 1817.
Geo. Deatherage, Cath. Waters, 1816.
Wm. Debbs, Anne Marshall, 1818.
Abijah Dulany m Nancy Burke, 1792.
Jno. Denton m Eliz. Hendrick, 1809.
Chris. Dickens m Mary Pullam, 1791.
Thos. C. Dickenson m Eliz. Amiss, '83.
Asa Dillen m Lydia Bigbee, 1805.
Thos. Dobbs m Nancy Clatterbuck,'14.
Joel Dodson, Polly Fincham, 1805.
David Dodson m Lucy Hisle, 1791.
Henry Dogan m Eliz. Hilton 1814.
Rich. J. Doggett, Mariah Ward, 1807.
Wm. Doggett m Mildred Brown, 1819.
Quarles Dorsett m Lavinia Sisk, 1809.
Fran. P. Drake, Mar'h A. Washington,'24
Gab. Dulaney m Patsy Leathers, 1805.
Gabriel Dulaney, Polly Leathers, 1805.
Wm. Dunnaway, Jane Hopkins, 1814.
Geo. Duncan, Hannah Brown, 1810.
Nimrod Duncan, Lucy Browning, 1797.
Benj. Duncan, Eliz. Browning, 1793.
Wm. Duncan, Lucy Bywaters, 1789.
Wm. C. Duncan, Cath. Hughes, 1823.
David Dyke, Polly Thaver, 1808.

E

Reub. Earthen, m. Eliz. Johnston, '90.
Philip Eastham, Polly Farrow, 1810.

Benj. Eddings, Fannie Etherton, 1808.
Jno. Eddins, Millie Dulaney, 1789.
Wm. Edgar, Martha Lightfoot, 1785.
Owen Ellis, Marg. McKelbin, 1803.
Thos. Ellis, Amelia Jenkins, 1810.
Wm. Embry, Hannah Patton, 1808.
Jos. Emry, Isabel Butler, 1802.
Peter Estes, Sallie Yates, 1792.
Absolam Estes, Gilly Simms, 1816.
Jos. Etherton, Eliz. T. Simms, 1811.
Jno. Etherington, Frances Yancey, '99.
Wm. Evans, Betsey Wood, 1786.
Frosty English, Nancy Razor, 1820.
Churchhill Eddins, Marg. Harvey, '91.
Philip Edwards, Easter Corbin, 1789.
Peyton R. Eldridge, Polly Guinn, 1800·
Aug. Ellis, Mildred Slaughter, 1804.
Hiram Ellis, Polly Chappaliar, 1816.
Chas. Emory, Winney Peyton, 1799.
Jno. Estes, Susannah Butler, 1807.
Sam. Estes, Mary Peyton——
Reub. Etherton, Eleanor McDonald, '04.
Jas. Ethrington, Martha Blackburn,'04.
Jas. Ethrington, Hannah Dulaney, '00·
Jno. Evans, Gilly C. Strother, 1800.
Abraham Early, Phoebe Peyton, 1802.

F

Thos. Falconer, Sallie Winston, 1795.
Dan. Farmer, Eliz. Dulaney, 1814.
Jno. Fayer, Roda Gaines, 1803.
Wm. Fincham, Polly Kebbon, 1815.
Jno Ferguson, Anne Green, 1795.
Mason Fewell, Sarah Fiddle, 1806.
Benj. Fewell, Nancy Walle, 1789.
Benj. Ficklin, Susannah Foushee, '87.
Wm. Fincham, Bettie McAllister, '04.
Jno. Fincham, Millie Simms, 1818.
Elijah Finks, Eliz. Foster, 1800.
Chas. Finnell, Lucy Finnell, 1786.
Jacob Fishback, Hannah Huffman, '88.
Geo. Fisher, Dolly Alsop, 1804.
Jno. Flemming, Mary Walle, 1799.
Rawleigh Fletcher, Polly Estes, 1801.
Jas. Fletcher, Edy Bywaters, 1798.
Jno. Fletcher, Polly Jeffries, 1819.
Thos. Flint, Mollie Ballard, 1788.
Ben. Ford, Eliz. F. Leavel, 1803.
Joshua Ford, Nancy Terrell, 1791.
Wm. P. Ford, Gilly Marshall, 1822.
Rich. C. Foushee, Nancy Martin, 1817.
Jno. Foushee, Sallie Crutcher,1788.
Edwin Fox, Betsey Higgason, 1814.
Wm. Franklin, Agnes Oder, 1821.
Fred. Frazier, Marg. Whale, 1821.
Jno. Freeman, Lydia Edge, 1792.
Jno. H. Freemen, Sarah Grinnan, '21.
Ephraim Fry, Mary Huffman, 1786.
Enoch Furr, Susannah Waters, 1813.
Thos. Furniss, Francis Dulaney, 1785.
Jno. Farmer, Jemima Grant, 1784.
Wm. Farrow, Lydia Wiley, 1806.
Jno. Feedlow, Marg. Oder, 1808.
Benj. Fincham, Susannah Smith, 1809.
Jno. Ferguson, Eliz. Burton, 1811.
Benj. Fewell, Amy Coghill, 1798.
Jas. Fewell, Lucy Zimmerman, 1801.
Ben. Ficklin, Eleanor Slaughter, 1816.
Wm. Fincham, Eliz. Clatterbuck, 1796.
Fielding Finks, Frances B. Triplett,'17.
Abner Finnell, Nancy Dowling, 1793.
Morgan Finnell, Eliz. Sisson, 1791.
Jno. Fishback, Eliz. Norman, 1818.
Wm. Fisher, Polly Hand, 1803.
Zach. Fleshman, Phoebe Leather, 1791.
Vinson Fletcher, Sallie Barnes, 1803.
Stephen Fletcher, Mary Barnes, 1793.
Jno. Flint, Sallie Porter, 1788.
Wm. Flint, Eliz. Ballard, 1788.
Reub. Ford, Eliz. Belly, 1806.
Jno. Ford, Rosey Norman, 1738.
Robt. Foster, Eliz. Finks, 1805.
Geo. Foushee, Susan Foushee, 1819.
Wm. Fox, Caty Woodard, 1809.
Jonathan Franklin, Milly Tinsley, '88.
Henry Frazier, Nancy Bredlove, 1795.
Wm. Freeman, Nancy Hughes, 1806.
Garnett Freeman, Nancy Foster, 1813.
Archibald Freeman, Marg. Welch, 1819.
Thos. W. Fry, Eliz. Slaughter 1795.
Sam. Furnis, Sarah Roberts, 1782.
David Fulks, Eliz. Huffman, 1788.

G

Lawrence Gaar, Rosannah Broyles, '90.
Thos. Gaines, Nancy Fryer, 1805.
Geo. Gaines, Susannah Graves, 1788.
Rich. Gaines, Frances Jolly, 1789.
Jno. Gaines, Peggy Wise, 1792.
Abraham Gaar, Dinah Weaver, 1791.
David Gaines, Peggy Mitchell, 1790.
Humphrey Gaines, Eliz. Warren, 1789.
Edw. W. Gaines, Nancy Yowell, 1796.
Reub. Gaines, Emma Lewis 1818.

Jno. P. Gaines, Frances Mason, 1821.
Lunsford Gant, Sarah Ratcliffe, 1785.
Edmund Garner, Susannah Turner, '07.
Jno. Garriott, Eliz. Kinnard, 1791.
Jos. Garriott, Caty Hudson, 1802.
Henry Gateshill, Anne Lightfoot, '84.
Geo. Garnett, Sarah Butler, 1791.
Jas. Garnett, Polly Jones, 1795.
Jas. Garnett, Nancy Clarke, 1791.
Samuel Garnett, Sallie Fucks, 1799.
Jas. Garnett, Eliz. Garnett, 1816.
Robt. George, Duncan Tussey, 1801.
Zach. Gibbs, Lucy Clarke, 1789.
Jno. Gibson, Eliz. Norman, 1801.
Sam. Giddings, Sarah Mason, 1787.
Lawrence Gin, Sarah Leavel, 1785.
Jas. Ginn, Eliz. Butt, 1789.
Wm. Goss, Mary Simms, 1799.
Ben. Gosney, Sarah Applebee, 1789.
Wm. Gore, Mary Simms, 1799.
Wm. Gordon, Eliz. Smede, 1810.
Jas. A. Gordon, Anne G. Gaines, 1814.
Dan. Good, Eliz. Lipp, 1791.
Thos. Godfrey, Polly Settle, 1798.
Geo. Glore, Eliz. Mauck, 1783.
Rob. Godney, Eliz. Wills, 1819,
Jas. Glasscock, Susannah Kilby, '24.
Wm. Gray, Jennie Manuel, 1823.
Leonard Graves, Rebecca Bingham,'94.
Jno. Graves, Eliz. Eddins, 1788.
Thos. Graves, Mary Mason. 1795.
Jno. T. Green, Lavinia Jett, 1812.
Thos. Green, Mary Hawkins ———.

Jno. Gallahue, Anne Rowe, 1793.
Jos. Garring, Patsy Smith 1823.
Jas. Garriott, Susannah Campbell, '92.
Jas. Garrett, Lydia Haynes, 1800.
Levy Garwood, Sarah Inskeep, 1795.
Chas. D. Gaunt, Rachael Lillard, 1824.
Edmund Garnett, Sarah Graves, 1787.
Rob. Garnett, Eleanor Cochran. 1790.
Elijah Garnett, Nancy Branham. 1799.
Larkin Garnett, Eliz. Garnett, 1812.
Jas. Garnett, Anne Hilton, 1823.
Burnett George, Sarah Starke, 1816.
Thos. Gibson, Nancy Feaganes, 1807.
Minor W. Gibson, Eliza Shackelford,'19.
Law'ce Gillock, Betsey Twenteman,'88.
Thos. Ginn, Eliz. Brady, 1786.
Thos. Ginn, Mary Threlkeld, 1789.
Geo. Grady, Fannie Bredlove, 1795.
Rich. Gosney, Fannie Rowe, 1800.
Joshua Gore, Eliz. Rountree, 1816.
Mungo M. Gordon, Mildred Marye, 1809.
Alex. Gordon, Jr., Eleanor C. Ball, '15.
Rich. Goodall, Eliz. Merry, 1785.
Enoch Golden, Lucy Googe, 1807.
Rich. Glovier, Milly Shackelford, 1795.
Eli Glasscock, Susan. Bumgardner, '98.
Jos. Gray, Lydia Stout, 1796.
Hezekia Gray, Anne Dyke, 1811.
Philip Graves, Eliz. Jones, 1785.
Dan. Graves, Eleanor Grady, 1792.
Jos. Graves, Nellie Branham, 1800.
Rich. Green, Eliz. Hanve, 1811.
Francis Gaines, Lucy Hughes, 1805.

H

Walter Hackley, Chloe Clarke, 1799.
Fred. Hagert, Mary Davis, 1791.
Jno. Haleys, Rachael Fleshman, 1787.
Jere. Hall, Judy Allan, 1792.
Henry Halley, Eliz. Reed, 1816.
R. Ham, E. Pemberton or Pendleton,'90.
Nimrod Hambrick, Mariah Adams, '16.
Thos. Hand, Anne Eastham, 1818.
Martin Harden, Jane Aynes, 1792.
Jas. Hardy, Pattie Ballance, 1784.
Rob. Harden, Eliz. Oder, 1808.
Jno. Horford, Pattie Fennell, 1792.
Jos. Harper, Eliza Anne Greenway, '11.
Jessee Harris, Mollie Clatterbuck, '87.
Geo. Harrison, Nancy Duff, 1784.
Elijah Harvey, Mary Jarrell, 1785.
Achilles Hawkins, Leaty Yowell, 1807.
Wm. Hawkins, Dolly Gaines, 1786.

Wal. Hackley, Winnif. Chancellor, '17.
Carlysle Hanes, Dorcas Williams, 1798.
Thos. Hall, Amy Nalle, 1803.
Jas. Hall, Jane Willey, 1813.
Stephen Ham, Rhoda Coffer, 1782.
Jno. Hambrick, Eliz. Spencer, 1810.
Wm. Hamilton, Sarah Hume, 1805.
Moses Harbinson, Anne Barler, 1789.
Wm. Harden, Eliz. Doggett, 1822.
Jacob Hardman, Nancy Collins, 1788.
Jno. Harmond, Mary Haney, 1808.
Wm. Harper, Anna Suliman, 1793.
Geo. Harrold, Nancy Horsley, 1786.
Jas. Harris, Mary Brady, 1788.
Obed Harrison, Frances Lewis, 1793.
Elijah Harkins, Polly Kelly, 1805.
Wm. Hawkins, Anne B. Smith, 1785.
Jno. Hawkins, Nancy Jones, 1787.

Jno. Hawkins, Mahala Randolph, '95. Jas. Hawkins, Sarah Jones, 1797.
Math. Hawkins,NancyWilhoite,——— Thos. R. Hawkins, Matilda Pinkard,'2 3·
Jas. J. Haydon, Cath. Branham, 1783. Ezekiel Hanes, Anne Hopkins, 1801.
Geo. Hanes, Anne S. Smith, 1794. Jasper Hanes, Eliz. Roberts, 1790.
Jas. Hanes, Sarah Jackson, 1786. Geo. Hanes, Eliz. Smith, 1793.
Anthony Haynie, Sarah Williams, 1787. Jno. Haton, Sarah Calvert, 1803.
Benj. Head, Milly Long, 1785. Wm. Head, Sallie Oliver, 1792.
Patterson Heaton, Polly Bridwell, '13. Jos. Heaton, Anne Antram, 1799.
Wm. Helm, Susan S. Cowne, 1819. Alex. Henderson, Eliz. Roebuck, 1789.
Jno.Henderson,NancyHansbrough,'21. Wm. Henry, Eleanor Yancey, 1795.
Benson Henry, Keziah Manwell, 1792. Wm. Henslee, Eliz. Corbin, 1792.
Enoch Hensley, Jane Nicolson, 1789. Enoch Hensley, Sallie Boling, 1800.
Wm. Henton, Hannah Heaton, 1805. Thos. Herford, Sarah Heaton, 1796.
Thos. Herford, Sarah Heaton,1797. Reu. Herndon, Betsey Marshall, 1806.
Elliott Herndon, Sallie Carter, 1791. Ben. Herndon, Susan Chart, 1787.
Edw. Herndon, Nancy Rucker, 1791. Wm. Hermon, Polly Ferguson———.
Geo. Hesser, Emily Evans, 1824. Jacob Hessong, Charity Duke, 1793.
Jas. Heaton, Sallie Evans, 1804. Wm. Hickerson, Judith Ball, 1814.
Silas. Hickerson, Polly Tutt, 1811. Jno. Hill, Mary Finch, 1804.
Wm. Hill, Sallie Ballinger, 1791. Rob. Hill, Nancy Sutton, 1785.
Wm. Hill, Frances Fennell, 1786. Wm. Hill Jr., Isabel Parson, 1797.
Jno. Hill, Nancy Palmer, 1792. Jos. Hill, Rhoda Marshall, 1796.
Humphrey Hill, Anne Myrtle, 1798. Reub. Hill, Fannie Samuel, 1797.
Joel Hill, Nancy Vaughan, 1820. Jno. Hill, Eliz. Naughan, 1822.
Jno. Kennon Hill, Grace Jenkins, '17. Jno. Hilman, Dorotha Garnett, 1798.
Sam. Hinsley, Rosanna Pierce, 1786. Wm. Hisle, Nancy Woodard, 1803.
Leonard Hisle, Ramey Jasper, 1804. Rob. Hisle, Lydia Jenkins, 1789.
Jno. Hisle, Polly Hisle, 1797. Wm. Hisle, Jane Willis, 1796.
Strother Hisle, Eliz. Smith, 1809. Wm. Hitcher, Hannah Hurt, 1781.
Jas. Hitt, Frances Reynolds, 1822. Rich. Hisle, Nancy Neathers, 1795.
Stephen Hogg, Sarah Williams, 1800. Wm. Holdway, Eliz. Thornhill, 1794.
Jno. Holland, Catharine Coghill, '88. Eph. Hollaway,Susannah Garwood,'21.
Jno. Hopper, Sarah Jett, 1785. Sam. Horner, Julia Sanford, 1804.
Jas. Y. Horner, Polly Ferguson, 1815. Job. Houghton, Lucy Simms, 1818.
Elijah Houghton, Caty Norman, 1818. Matthias House, Susannah Floyd, 1792.
Mich. House, Nancy Zimmerman, '89. Thos. Howell, Marg. White, 1790.
Jos. Huans, Rhoda Pinkard, 1803. Thos. Hubbard, Sallie Strother, 1794.
Taliaferro Hubbard, Abbie Gibson, '97. Arm. Hubbard, Beacheth Strother,'92.
Alex. Hudson, Polly Jones, 1804. Joel Hudson, Fannie Yager, 1809.
Walter Hudson, Eliz. Mason, 1810. Martin Hudson, Synthia Newton, 1794.
Jno. Hudson, Jane Appleby, 1799. Moses Hudson, Mary Clark, 1789.
Reub. Hudson, Polly Garnett, 1798. Ezekiel Hudson, Polly Mason, 1800.
Abner Hudson, Betsey Mason, 1800. Wm. Hudson. Eliz. Cheek, 18·1.
Ambrose Hudson,Mary AnneSmith, '19. Jos. Huffman, Rosannah Deale, 1793.
Jacob Huffman, Mary Floyd, 1786. Ephraim Huffman, Mary Ward, 1787.
Rub. Huffman, Caty Huffman, 1787. Nathan Huffman, Mary Stonesiffer, '92.
Sam. Huffman, Eve Huffman, 1792. Jno. Huffman, Eliz. Huffman, 1794.
Jos. Huffman, Frances Payne, 1790. Rob. Huffman, Eliz. Bruce———.
Jos. Huffman, Frances Payne, 1791. Jas. Huffman, Letty Arnold, 1795.
Mich. Huffman, Eliz. Huffman, 1791. Dan. Huffman. Marg. Bingard, 1790.
Henry Huffman, Lucy Reed, 1799. Aaron Huffman, Betsey Hume, 1817.
Rob. Hughes, Eliz. Strother, 1794. Anthony Hughes, Eliz. Adams, 1799.
Jno. Hughes, Anne Waggoner, 1785. Jno. Hughes, Eliz. Brown, 1798.

Rob. Hudson, Eliz. Jones, 1803.
Chas. Hume, Lizzie Banks, 1785.
Jno. Hume, Anna Crigler, 1792.
Armistead Hume, Priscilla Colvin, '98.
Wm. Humphrey, Mille Carder, 1805.
Geo. Humphrey, Polly Lawler, 1787.
Julius Hunt, Mary Brown, 1791.
Thos. Hurleigh, Nellie Harrison, '88.
Rob. Hysle, Eliz. Pulliam, 1796.
Wm. Hume, Sarah Baker, 1782.
Jas. Hume, Eliz. Powell, 1784.
Jas. Hume, Caty Barnes, 1797.
Humphrey Hume, Peggy Lowen, 1800.
Jesse Humphreys, Eliz. Diffle, 1791.
Jno. Hundley, Ibby Turner, 1822.
Wm. Harrew, Lucy Collins, 1818.
Jno. Hysle, Frances Pulliam, 1796.

I

Wm. Ingram, Susannah Lawler, 1802.
Dan. Inskeep, Rachel Pusey, 1797.
Job Inskeep, Patiner Bishop, 1801.
Jno. Inskeep, Esther Garwood, 1804.
Jas. Inskeep, Deliah Dulaney 1797.

J

Wm. Jackson, Sarah Horton, 1808.
Jno. Jackson, Sallie Simms, 1815.
Jno. D. James, Peggy F. Brown, 1808.
Dan. James, Nancy Graves, 1787.
Jere. Jarrell, Sarah Simms 1788.
Alex. Jeffries, Frances Faver, 1794.
Jno. Jeffries, Rosamond Faver, 1800,
Zach. Jenkins, Ellen Jenkins, 1805.
Nathan Jenkins, Betsey Weakley, '93.
Abraham Jenkins, Nancy Weakley, '89.
Philip Jenkins, Rebecca Jenkins, 1793.
Dan. Jenkins, Sarah Jenkins, 1793.
Dan. Jenkins, Sarah Jenkins, 1800.
Roland Jenkins, Nancy Robins, 1818.
Hedgman Jenkins, Nancy Hensley,'14.
Jno. Jesse, Susannah Carpenter, 1792.
Daniel Jett, Lucinda Jones, 1798.
Jos. Johnson, Susannah Reed, 1802.
Allan Johnston, Seney Duncan, 1793.
Jas. Jollett, Nancy Walker, 1787.
Jno. R. Jones, Gilly Marshall, 1809.
Garden Jones, Senie Browning, 1789.
Thos. Jones, Agnes Pulliam, 1785.
Standley Jones, Nancy Garnett, 1797.
Lewis Jones, Nancy Borst, 1795.
Theo. Jones, Fran. Shackelford, 1797.
Thos. Janes, Polly Butler, ———.
Tim. Jones, Sarah Cocke, 1799.
Jas. Jones, Nancy Turner, 1800.
Jno. Jones, Judy Doggett, 1813.
Jno. Jones, Mary Hisle, 1813.
Stephen Jones, Millie Kennard, 1814.
Robt. Jones, Sallie Crigler, 1815.
Inbey Jones, Lucy Johnston, 1817.
David Jones, Lucinda Foushee, 1812.
Jno. Jordan, Caty Wilson, 1791.
Geo. Jury, Damsel Holland, 1811.
Moses Jackson, Sallie Lampkin, 1781.
Henry Jackson Anne Lampkin '91.
Thos. Jacobs, Eliz. Burgess, 1806.
Sam. James, Frances Bates, 1783.
Wm. Jarrell, Eliz. Jarrell, 1787.
Dan. Jasper, Millie Cheek. 1807.
Thos. Jeffries, Thiza Kegg, 1797.
Jno. Jennings, Fannie Hurt, 1801.
Irvine Jenkins, Peggy Jenkins 1808.
Dan. Jenkins, Agatha Jenkins, 1789.
Timothy Jenkins, Eliz. Smith, 1794.
Jere. Jenkins, Anne McKensey, 1791.
Timothy Jenkins, Nancy Weakley, '97.
Amb. Jenkins, Susannah Weakley, '09.
Anthony Jenkins, Milly Sisk, 1812.
Amiss Janny, Barbara Gregory, 1797.
Jesse Jett, Nancy Chandler, 1804.
Jas. Jett, Julia Anne Lane, 1821.
Wm. Johnston, Mary Yancey, 1806.
Valentine Johnston, Anne Brown, 1816.
Gabe. Jones, Patsey Yates, 1800.
Ambrose Jones, Mary Waggoner, 1784.
Moses Jones, Mary Florence, 1789.
Rob. Jones, Susannah Bahanghan, '87.
Francis Jones, Esther Cowne, 1795.
Jno. Jones, Dolly Petty, 1793.
Henry Jones, Mildred Grigsby, 1792.
Bailey Jones, Lucy Corbin, 1791.
Elisha Jones, Eliz. Freeman, 1799.
Thos. Jones, Mary Underwood, 1798.
Jas. Jones, Rebecca Dyke, ———.
Chas. Jones, Lavinia Glass, 1815.
Chas. Jones, Jane Rixey, 1819.
Jos. Jones, Nancy Yates, 1815.
Jas. Jones, Lucinda Walden, 1822.
Absalom Jordan, Eliza Eastham, 1806.
Wm. Jordan, Anne Clark, 1791.
Reese Jury, Anne Slaughter, 1811.
Elijah Jones, Sarah Freeman, 1793.

K

Gab. Key, Sarah Waggoner, 1802.
Geo. Kelley, Jane Field, 1803.
Jas. Kelly, Frances Wright, 1805.
Edw. Kelly, Barbara Yates, 1784.
Wm. Kelly, Nancy Terry, 1790.
Jas. Kemper, Sallie Walker, 1822.
Jacob Kendrick, Susannah Jett, 1805.
Reub. Kendrick, Effie Rich, 1795.
David Kennard, Polly Yates, 1809.
Amos Keys, Anna Fennell, 1802.
Adam Kibler, Eliza Brandon, 1822.
Armistead Kilby, Sarah Hawkins, '94.
Thos. Kilby, Matilda Hawkins, 1817.
Benj. King, Walter Haywood, 1794
Philip S. King, Martha Grant, 1821.
Wm. Kirtley, Sarah Lewis, 1805.
John Klugg, Nancy Nelson Graves '90.
Geo. Kootz, Mary Threlkeld, 1800.

Jas. Kay, Fannie Waggoner, 1802.
Thos. Kelley, Kesiah Norman, 1806.
Jacob Kelly, Peggy Gore, 1790.
Wm. Kelly, Eliz. Poulton, 1786.
Jno. Kelly, Susannah Hill, 1797.
Jas. Kendall, Eliz. Threlkeld, 1819.
Benoni Kendrick, Mary Warner, 1789.
Geo. Kennard, Frances Yates, 1800.
Reub. Kenneday, Ursula Falconer, '11.
Wash. Keys, Marg. Strother, 1812.
Wm. Kidwell, Susannah Jett, 1806.
Jos. Kilby, Celia Jenkins, 1801.
Leroy Kilby, Eleanor Mary, 1820.
Thos. King, Eliz. King, ———.
Pleasant Kirtley, Thompson Barnes,'04.
Ephraim Klugg, Eliz. Major, 1792.
Jos. Koonly, Judy Snyder, 1809.

L

Aaron Lacy m. Eliz. Reins, 1788.
Jno. Lampkin, Jemima Lemmon, '17.
Wm. Lansdown, Triphene Settle, '97.
Wm. Lansdown m. Lucy Spiller, 1798.
Philip Latham m. Dolly Gray, 1792.
Walter Lawrence m. Polly Butler,'04.
David Lear m. Lucy Duval' 1791.
Nathan Lear m. Nancy Spicer, 1818.
Rob. Leavel m. Eliz. Harden, 1788.
Wm. Lee m. Mollie Burns, 1788.
Archelus Lewis, Jemimah Norman '93.
Thadeus Lewis m. Eliz. Garnett, 1796.
Jas. Lewis, Kitty Anne Pendleton,'16.
Edw. Lightfoot, Arthur Eldridge, 1793.
Jno. Lillard m. Rachel Garrott, 1733.
Benj. Lillard m. Eliz. Browning, 1819.
Benj. Lillard m. Lucy Brown, 1799.
Jno. Lindsey m. Ruth Bryan 1789.
Zach. Little and Mary Staunton, 1792.
Gabriel Long, Lucinda Slaughter, '05.
Thomas Long m. Nancy Shipp, 1797.
Jno. Long m. Azubah Hawkins, 1793.
Thos. Long m. Polly Wharton, 1799.
Jno. Lovell, Frances Beckham, 1815.
Francis Lowin m. Lucy Brown, 1784.
Jno. Lucas m. Polly Brown, 1810.
Geo. Lucas m. Fannie Kilby, 1816.

Jno. Lampkin m Eliz. Wily, 1799.
Mark Landram m. Nancy Tapp, 1786.
Wm. A. Lane m. Elizabeth Green, 1798.
Wm. Latham m. Malinda Gaines, 1805
John T. Latham Kitty Manzy, 1824.
Sam. Leadman, Susan. Stokesberry,'01.
James Lear m. Nancy Hill, 1787.
Joshua Leather m. Eliz. Ferguson, 1790
Benj. Leavell m. Eliz. Willis, 1811.
Jas. Lee m. Mary Callahan, 1793.
James Lewis m. Jemimah Roberts, '86.
Benj. Lewis m. Nancy Mitchell, 1815.
Thos. B. Lewis m. Cath. A. Gaines, '15.
Rob. Lightfoot. Johannah Dulany,'94.
Absolom Lillard, Nancy Holland, 1816.
Absolam Lillard m. Fannie Hisle, 1810.
Jno. Lingram m. Betsy Waggoner, 1802
Jacob Lip m. Marg. Zimmerman, 1787.
Jno. Lockhart m. Mary Wily, 1799.
Bloomfield Long m. Letty Roach, 1787.
Wm. Long m. Mary Faulconer, 1797.
Benj. Long m. Polly Garratt, 1792.
Wm. Loucry m. Anne Colly, 1799.
Dan. Lowery m. Mary Cox, 1797.
Wm. Lowry m. Anne Colly, 1799.
Thomas Lucas, Fannie Wilhoite, 1785.
Wm. Lucas m. Anne Moore, 1815.

M

Jno. Maar m. Eliz. Whitley, 1799.
Jacob Maggert, Mary Huffman, 1787.
Wm. Major m. Eliz. Corbin, 1795.
Jno. Margrave m. Abigail Moore, 1789.

Jno. Macaboy m. Mary Houghty, 1817.
Jno. Major m. Ursee Sleet, 1787.
John MacMann m. Nancy Johnson, '14.
James Markham m. Betsey Porter, '04.

Jno. W. Marshall, Paulina Moore, '07.
Thos. Marshall, Malinda Wallace 1806.
Jno. Marsten m. Rachael Spicer, 1788.
Jno. Martin m. Nelly Nicholson, 1788.
Jno. Martin m. Mary Long, 1791.
Elijah Mason m. Annie Wood, 1805.
Joel Mason m. Sallie Brown, 1791.
Silas Mason m. Patsey Garnett, 1815.
Daniel Mason m. Sarah Porter, 1819.
Jno. Mathoney m. Betsy Smith, 1802.
Jos. Mattock, Matilda Cornett, 1809.
Jno Mauzy m. Frances Long, 1803.
Alexander McBee, Harriet Borst, 1795.
Jas. McDaniel m Anne King, 1792.
Jno. McDonald, Frances Putman,'85.
Osborne McDonald, Eliz. Murphy, 1798.
Jas. McFarlen m. Nancy Wise,1797.
Nath. Magruder,Jemi. Sutherland, '99.
Robt. McKiffin m. Fannie Boswell, '98.
Strother McQueen, Lucy Yates, 1808.
May B. Medley m. Maria Payne, 1819.
Jonas Menefee m. Polly Yancy, 1808.
Jno. Menefee m. Eliza Hughes, 1795.
Wm. Menefee m. Mary Strother,1790.
Wm. Menefee m Cath. Partlow, 1811.
Jno. Menefee m. Sallie Brown, 1814.
Jno. Menefee, Anne T. Pendleton, '16.
Benj. Mershong m. Anne Jett, '99.
Michael Miller, Rebecca Carpenter, 93.
Jno. Miller, Alice Wright, 1800.
Jesse Miller m. Frances Corbin, 1816.
Jno. A. Mitchell, Cath. Hanson,1808.
Wm. Mitchell m. Lucy Garnett, 1783.
Fisher Mitchell, Mollie Gosny, 1790.
Jno. Mitchell, Margaret Yager, 1818.
Geo. Monday m. Isabel Myrtle, 1785.
Wm. Monny m. Sarah Walker 1781.
Elinthan Moor m. Polly Scott, 1788.
Wm. Morehead m. Polly Triplett,1790.
Thos. Morris m. Sallie Kinnard, 1795.
Caleb Morrison,Sallie Browning, '08.
Timothy Moore m. Mary Gully 1789.
Anthony Moore, Jane Adams, 1799.
Thos. Moore m. Polly Hughes,——
Elisha Moss m. Mary Groves, 1809.
Benj. Mozengo m. Mary Little ,1795.
Jno. Murphy m. Sallie Sedwicke, 1805.
Thos. Murphy, Eliz. Edrington, 1801.
Jac. Myers m. Mariah Calvert, 1808.

Thomas Marshall m. Mary Bishop, 1805
Rob. Marshall m. Mary Dobbs, 1813.
Willis Martin m. Agatha Gaunt 1806.
Wm. Martin m Lucy Sanford, 1796.
Enoch Mason m. Fannie Ramey,1806.
Nelson Mason m. Mary Newlon. 1806.
Jas. Mason m. Susannah Tapp, 1793.
Benson Mason m. Margaret Fox, 1820.
Lewis D. Massie m. Eliz. Adams, 1822.
James Matthews m. Sallie Stuart, 1794.
Abraham Maury m. Eliz. Wilhoite, 1810.
Wm. McBee m. Sarah McDugley, 1798.
Dan. McCarty m. Sallie Whorton, 1792.
Geo. McDonald m. Marg. Wayland, '91.
Mathias McDonald, Eleanor Jarrell,'91.
Wm. McDonald m. Mary Donald, 1794.
Dan. McGowan m. Frances Corley,1820
Jas.McKiffin m. Anne Reed Taylor, '10.
Wm. McKoy m. Nancy Turner, 1800.
Dan. McQueen m. Caty Lammon, 1818.
Rob. Menefee m. Polly Waggoner, 1806.
Jno. Menefee m. Lucy Partlow, 1808.
Larkin Menefee m. Lucy Yancey.
Henry Menefee m. Nancy Hughes,'97.
Henry Menefee m. Phila. Yancey, 1811.
Jarred Menefee m. Fannie Hopkins,'15.
Wolery Meng m. Esther Morris, 1794.
Jas. Middleton m. Lucy Jenkins, 1814.
Adam Miller, Polly Wilhoite, 1790.
Sam Miller m. Delena Bywaters, 1815.
Waller Minor, Mary Cowen, 1789.
Wm. Mitchell m. Sarah Mitchell, 1787.
Mark Mitchell m. Mary Rider, 1787.
Jno. Mitchell m. Janet Newton, 1801.
James Mobly m. Eliz, Hurrin, 1792.
Roger Moody m. Anne ——— 1797.
Abraham Moor, Eliz. Cinnie, 1786.
Daniel Morgan, Sarah Thomas, 1800.
Walter Moreland m. Rach. Drake, 1804.
Edm. Morress m. Sallie Reynolds, 1801.
Jno. Morrison m. Esther Douglass,1797.
Harbin Moore m. Anne Tutt, 1793.
David Moore Hannah Woodward, 1813.
Elijah Moss m. Susannah Carroll 1797.
Wm. Motherhead m. Lucy Long, 1788.
Dennis Murphy m. Sallie Marshall, '03.
Martin Murphy m. Sarah Glass, 1786.
Wm. L. Munday, Anne Porter, 1811.
Ben. Myrtle, Fran. Broyles, 1787.

N

Jas. Nalle, Peggy Parks, 1792.
Wm. Nalle, Nancy Berry, 1817.

Jno. Nalle, Lucy Hill, 1785.
Hezekiah Nally, Susannah Bourne, '08.

Larkin Nash, Eliz. Hyne, 1793.
Rob. C. Newby, Georgiana Ward, '08.
W. H. Newman, Josemeah Tucker,'04.
And. Newman, Mary AnneFennell, '89.
Jas. Newman, Mary Early, 1789.
Jas. Nickens, Mary Berden, 1793.
Geo. Nicol, Hester Haines, 1811.
Jno. Nicolson, Phoebe Jenkins, 1790.
Zepheniah Nooe, Sarah Kirtley, 1803.
Courtney Norman, Alice Jett, 1793.
Isaac Norman, Sallie Watts, 1799.

Henry Nash, Ester Dyke, 1818.
Benj. Newlon, Nancy Kirtley, 1803.
Robt. Newman, Eliz. Latham, 1789.
Geo. Newlon, Polly Bourne, 1790.
Jos. Nichlins, Eliz. Calvert, 1802.
Mich. Nicols, Sallie Miller, 1801.
Ben. Nicolson, Eliz. Shackelford, 1792.
Jno. Nethers, Esther Dyke, 1802.
Jos. Norman, Mary Davis, 1806.
Thos. Norman, Sallie Utterback, 1796.

O

Manyard Oakes, Sukey Rosson, 1797.
Barnet O'Neil, Sallie Embrey, 1807.
Jno. O'Neil, Judy Settle, 1794.
Jere. O'Dell, Polly Menefee, 1804.
Gab. Oder, Mariah Monroe, 1805.
Joel Oder, Jane Fletcher, 1795.
Willis Overter, SusannahSturman, '91.
Harrison Owen, Lucy Vaughan, 1808.
Rich. Parks,Anne Faver, 1796.
Jas. Parsons, Lucy Myrtle, 1789.

Dan. O'Neil, Sarah Jennings, 1807.
Jno. O'Neil, Eliz. Embrey, 1808.
Jno. O'Neil, Phoebe Scott, 1789.
Thos. C. Oden, Nancy Mason, 1822.
Jno. Oder, Nancy Jenkins, 1807.
Wm. Orr, Polly Gaines, 1789.
Obadiah Overter, Ellender Crow, 1788.
Dan. Palmer, Susannah Henseley, '88.
Elisah Partlow, Frances Menefee, 1808

P

Thos. Patton, Betsey Moss, 1804.
Bennett Payne, Polly McKenzie, 1801.
Wm. Payne, Avee Garnett, 1793.
Jas. Peek, Charlotte Clatterbuck,'93.
Jno. Pemmington, Cath. Vint. 1797.
Thos. Pendleton, Jane Farmer, 1794.
Chas. Perry, Anne Washington, 1808.
Jno. Perry, Susannah Utterback,'97.
Jos. Peyton. Nancy Estes 1800.
Jno. Payne, Polly Butler, 1805.
Thos. Peyton, Anne Lambkin, 1792.
Isaac Peyton, Nancy Grimsley, 1809.
Wm. Pewis, Jane Burke, 1792.
Geo. Petty, Patsy Hansbrough,'08.
Polly Petty, Frances Hill, 1799.
Geo. Phillips, Eliz. Hershberger,'08.
Solo. Phillips, Anna Huffman, 1789.
Jas. Pierce, Eliz. Crawford, 1782.
Jno. Pierce, Nancy McGuinn, 1786.
Shadrach Pierson, Rach. Clinch, 1781.
Thos. Piner, Eliz. Swindler, 1791.
Jno. Pitcher, Lucy Thornhill, 1790.
John Pitts, Priscilla Utterback, 1793.
Jas. Pollard, Amelia Tutt, 1812.
Francis Poo, Mary Allen, 1805.
Gerard Popham, Kesiah Boughan, '95.
Hawkins Popham, Reb'ca Hawkins, '17.
Reub. Porch, Nancy Asher, 1792.
Jno. Porter, Lydia Rees, 1821.

Wm. Paul, Jane Grewis, 1821.
Rich. Payne, Mary Major, 1795.
Elefas Payne, Nancy Curtis, 1813.
Foushee Pellett, Fannie Vaughan, 1808.
Edw. Pendleton, Sarah Strother, 1794.
Edmund Pendleton, Eliz. Ward, 1800.
Pierce Perry, Ellen Corbin, 1810.
Peter Peters, Mary Simms, 1786.
Geo. Peyton, Susannah Cogell, 1792.
James Peyton, Bet. Saunders, 1808.
Isaaiah Peyton, Millie Campbell, 1800.
Benj. Peyton, Henrietta Swindler, '15.
Larkin Petty, Polly Fore, 1807.
Jas. Pettle, Polly Alsopp, 1797.
Thornton F. Petty, Eliz. Grinnan, '20.
Jno. Phillips, Eleanor Casey, 1786.
Jno. Pickett, Polly Samuel, 1796.
Jno. Pierce, Sallie Jeffries, 1786.
Reub. Pierce, Mariah Simms, 1819.
Spencer Pinkard, Betsey Marshall, '99.
Wm. R. Pennell, Anna Murphy, 1799.
Jacob Petit, Hally Fryar, 1800.
Elijah Pollard, Cath. Garner, 1797.
Rob. Pompkins, Polly Gray, 1798.
Humphrey Popham, Bet Hawkins, '88.
Jno. Popham, Eliz. Brown, 1795.

Wm. Porter, Ellen Morton, 1791.
Sam. Porter, Aisley Withers, 1824.

Wm. Poulter, Nancy Marder, 1788.
Scott Pound, Patsey W. Faulconer,'98.
Ambrose Powell, Fran. Payne, 1810.
Micajah Powell, Mary Wilhoite, 1788.
Joshua Pratt m. Mary Beckham, 1789.
Geo. Pritchell m. Eliz. Compton, 1815.
Sam. Pritchard, Rebecca Anderson,'93
Rob. Pulliam, Dilly Bumgardner, '92.
Wm. Polter, Jane Willis, 1788.
Wm. Powell, Betsey B. Simms, 1810.
Benj. Powell, Eliz. Greene, 1786.
Thos. Pratt, Eliz. Smith, 1796.
Jesse Pratt, Milly Johnson, 1818.
Wm. Pritchard, Nellie Dodson, 1791.
Thos. Pulliam m. Kesiah Brown, 1786.
Jno. Purley m. Sarah Doggett, 1824.

Q

Ed. Quesenberry, Nancy Threlkeld,'09.

R

Moses Race, Mary Tomlin, 1802.
Dan. Railsback, Rocany Clore, 1788.
Jacob Ramey, Mary Latham, 1803.
Jed. Randolph, Nancy Jennings, 1793.
Chris. Rassor, Sarah Simms, 1780.
Laban Razer, Harriet Sims, 1818.
Wm. F. Reed, Emily Ballard,——
Mark Reed, Eliza A. Ficklin, 1820.
Jac. Reaser, Martha Simms, 1818.
Reub. Redman, Millie Redman, 1804.
Gid. Rees, Anna Allan, 1795.
Edw. Reynolds, Sarah Fewel, 1786.
Ezekiel Rice, Fannie Garnett, 1808.
Benj. Rice, Eliz. Tinsley, 1790.
Thomas Richards, Nancy Howen, 1806.
Thos. Richardson, Polly M. Carder,'15
Jno. Rider, Patsy Lillard, 1806.
Jac. Riffler, Millard Burris, 1785.
Jno. Roberson, Bettie Rakestraw, 1815.
Wm. Roberts, Eliza Field, 1824.
Henry Roberts, Eliz. Maddox, 1792.
Wm. Robertson, Anne Grinnan, 1795.
Wm. Robertson, Anne Cooper, 1817.
Geo. Rodgers, Mary Turner, 1811.
Burgess Rogers, Sophia Miller, 1792.
Jno. Rogers, Sarah Kirtley, 1791.
Moses Rollins, Mary Smith, 1787.
Rob. Roman, Polly Smith, 1794.
Jno. Rose, Sallie Marshall, 1807
Wm. Ross, Jane O'Neal, 1784.
Wm. L. Rosson, Polly Collins, 1816.
Olly N. Rosson, Fran. Colvin, 1824.
John Routt jr., Eliz. Duncan, 1794.
Wm. Routt, Peggy Mitchell, 1812.
Benj. Rowe, Mary Powell, 1791.
Robt. Rucker, Sallie Gaines. 1806.
Jas. Rucker, Mary Terrill, 1782.
Jno. Rudacilla, Eliz. Vaughan, 1795.
Wm. Rudacilla, Kesiah Baugher, 1797.
Wm. Rumsey, Mary Gaines, 1790.
Jno. Race, Ellen Williams, 1803.
Geo. Raison, Franky Major, 1789.
Wm. Rambottom, Clara Jenkins. 1798.
James Randolph, Susannah Duval, '90.
Jac. Raxor, Susannah Snyder, 1787.
Phil. Reed, Eliz. Chewning, 1792.
Griffin Reed, Eliz. Chewning, 1792.
Jno. Reason, Mary Moss, 1804.
Dan. Rector, Eliz. Coons, 1792.
Morris Redman, Sukey Redman, 1824.
Rob. Reynolds, Mary Taliaferro, 1790.
Elijah Rice, Jallah Garnett, 1806.
Jno. Rice, Lucy Jones 1791.
James B. Rice, Susannah Wallis, 1800.
Jno. Richardson, Su. Clatterbuck, 1801.
Sanard Ricketts, Eliz. Compton, 1801.
Arch. Rider, Peggy Gaines, 1787.
Jno. Rivercomb. Polly Jenkins, 1812.
Jas. Roberts, Betsy Roberts, 1792.
Jno. Roberts, Susannah Abbott, 1801.
Geo. Roberts, Anne Hitt, 1791.
Sam. Robertson, Rachel Ricketts, 1824.
Spencer Robinson, Mary Utterback,'97.
Joseph Rogers,'—— Wallard, 1796.
Aaron Rogers, Eliz. Bumgardner, 1798.
Jno. Rollins, Mary Monroe, 1808.
Wm. Rollins, Nancy Golden, 1815.
Leven Rose, Susannah Bawsell, 1802.
Reub. Ross, Sallie Terrill, 1791.
Gab. Rosson, Polly Pinkard, 1800.
Benj. Rosson, Sarah Collins, 1821.
David Rosson, Caty Gaines, 1801.
John Routt, Sarah Tutt, 1794.
Wm. Rowe, Sallie Towles, 1787.
Wm. Ruch, Nancy Crain, 1787.
Reub. Rucker, Mildred Tinsley, 1785.
Joel Rucker, Amey Young, 1791.
Phillip Rudacilla, Mary Vaughan, 1792.
Lawson Rudacilla, Harriet Oder, 1821.
Ephraim Rush, Eliz. Moore, 1790.

Ephraim Rush, Eliz. Marshall, 1828.
Wm. Rutter, Polly Creal, 1809.
Thos. Pratt, Celia Golden, 1805.

Jno. Russell, Jane Reynolds, 1788.
Dan. Rynor, Eliz. Fleshman, 1786.

S

Jones Safer, Mary Dunaway, 1794.
Wm. Sampson, Sallie Coleman, 1784.
Jno. Sanord, Amelia Horner, 1809.
Jno. Sanders, Sallie Williams, 1796.
Nath. Saunders, P. F. McQuinn, 1815.
Reub. Scott, Susannah Petty, 1789.
Young Scott, Sallie Tapp, 1800.
Abner Settle, Nancy Pennel, 1804.
Abra. Settle, Abigail Cummings, '08.
Meriman Settle, Mary Dell, 1787.
Joseph Settle, Eliz. Miller, 1809.
Gaden Settle, Cath. Humphrey, 1821.
Dud. Shackelford, Win. Waterspon, '84.
Jno. Shackelford, Peggy Newby, 1794.
Mallo. Shackelford, Mary Coleman, '02.
Jas. Shackelford, Cath. Beasy, 1813
Jac. Shank, Rebecca Tobin, 1804.
Thos. Shevers, Anna L. Pendleton, '12.
Ambrose Shipp, Nellie Barnes, 1789.
Mich. Short, Esther Province, 1800.
Thos. Shelton, Mild. Zimmerman, '03.
Larkin Sims, Mary Anne Swindler, '17.
Jas. Sims, Jemimah Tucker, 1820.
Elias C. Simms, Sophia Cheek, 1824.
Jas. L. Sims, Eliz. Pratt, 1817.
Jno. Sims, Peggy Baxter, 1797.
Caleb Sims, Eleanor Poulter, ——
Abner Sims, Mary Saunders, 1789.
Reub. Sims, Sarah Tatum, 1787.
Jerry Sims, Eliz. Sanders, 1794.
Henry Sims, Peggy Marshall, 1809.
Edm. Sims, Lavinia Tucker, 1809.
Thos. Standley, Susannah Smith, 1781.
Jas. Starting, Polly Norman, 1793.
Jas. Stevenson, Susan. Hanback, '89.
Jas. Sleet, Rach. White, 1791.
Rob. Stevens, Fran. Rosson, 1793.
Rob. Steal, Alice Taylor, 1798.
Jno. Stuart, Caty Campbell, 1793.
Henry Stipes, Betsy Hampkin, 1800.
Jno. Stonesiffer, Mary Huffman, 1790.
Jno. Stokesburn, Sarah Cowgill, 1804.
Wm. Stokes, Nancy Shaw, 1791.
Fran. Story, Susannah Kelly, 1791.
Wm. Story, Eliz. Yowell, 1790.
Russell Story, Eliz. Rivercomb, 1812.
Elijah Stout, Eliz. Tumham, 1798.
Jac. Stout, Mildred Bellenger, 1796.

Jos. Sampson, Polly Coleman, 1784.
Moses Samuel, Rosan. Zimmerman, '88.
Jno. Sampson, Ellen Button, 1816.
Jas. Saunders, Eliz. Camp, 1806.
Chas. Scroggins, Lucy Fergerson, 1799.
Moore Scott, Rachael Popham, 1786.
Zadoch Sedwick, Eliz. Murphy, 1802.
Wm. Settle, Nancy Pickett, 1804.
Calvert Settle, Sallie Turner, 1806.
Jas. Settle, Eliz. Spilman, 1799.
Jos. Settle, Rach. Jordon, 1811.
Jno. Shackelford, Sallie Coleman, 1808.
Wm. Shackelford, Sallie Suddith, '08.
Charles Shackelford, Poly Menifee, 1798.
Zach. Shackelford, Fran, Lillard, 1811.
Caleb Shackelford, Lu. McDonald, ——
Rob. Shelton, Alpha Vawter, 1790.
Jon. Singleton, Isabell Jett, 1796.
Edw. G. Shipp, Harriett Mauzy, 1821.
Jas. Shotwell, Polly Crain, 1788.
Manson Simmons, Eliz. Newton, 1802.
Jno. W. Simms, Nancy Dulaney, 1824.
Jno. W. Sims, Nancy B. Dulaney, 1824.
Rob. Sims, Eliz. Tatum, 1822.
Geo. W. Sims, Judith N. Dulaney, 1816.
Benj. Sims, Anne Butler, ——
Jas. Sims, Jane Towles, 1790.
Wm. Sims, Mildred Baxter, 1787.
Jas. Sims, Pattie Smith, 1794.
Jno. Sims, Peggy Baxter, 1796.
Rob. Sims, Polly Marston, 1791.
Martin Sims Polly Wilhoite, 1805.
Alex. Stanford, Mary Adams, 1803.
James Stevenson, Sarah Harden, 1786.
Sam. Stephenson, Eliz. Pierce, 1795.
Wm. Steptoe, Eliz. Cral, 1808.
Wm. Stevens, Caty Core, 1799.
Jos. Steward, Sarah Roberts, 1796.
Chas. Stuard, Lucy Collins, 1822.
Sam. Storrow, Eliz. Carter, 1819.
Ephraim Stonesiffer, Julia Wihoite, '92.
David Stokesberry, Fran. Cocke, 1801.
Phil. Stockdell, Sall. Sampson, 1788.
Jno. Story, Nancy Creal, 1783.
Jas. Story, Lucy Johnston, 1797.
Reub. Stout, Mary Van Dyke, 1784.
Peter Stout, Mary Sherwood, 1798.
Jas. Stout, Abigail Holloway, 1799.

Jas. Stringfellow, Kitty Nalle, 1818.
Wm. Strother, Milly Medley, 1790.
French Strother, Mary A. Browning, '13.
Bailey Sudduth, Nan. Shackelford, '10.
Wm. Sullivan, Eliz. Brown. 1801.
Geo. Swindle, Catharine Rasor, 1786.
Jno. Swindler, Rach. Fryer, 1787.
Clayton Swindler, Sallie Bryant, 1810.
Hendley Simpson, Eliz. Farrow, 1812.
Allen Sisk, Patsy Jenkins, 1805.
Geo. Sisk, Nancy Chishom, 1795.
Bartlett Sisk, Mary Campbell, 1787.
Chas. Sisk, Nelly Chilton, 1799.
Benj. Sisson, Eliz. Brown, 1807.
Wm. Sisson, Pollie Brown, 1798.
Wm. Skinner, Betsey Trenton, 1802.
Steed Skinner, Elener Brandorn, 1802.
Jno. Slaughter, Sallie Hopper, 1811.
Wm. Slaughter, Harriet Ficklin, 1813.
Fielding Sleet, Rebecca West, 1798.
Jno. Smith, Sallie Rush, 1808.
Hedgman Smith, Betsey Carper, 1808.
Benj. Smith, Eliz. Rogers' 1784.
Dan. Smith, Jerusha Scott, 1791.
Joel Smith, Cath. Carper, 1764.
Dan. Smith, Mary Colvin, 1796.
Wm. Smith, Dinah Yager, 1792.
Jno. Smith, Eliz. Fry, 1798.
Wm. Smith, Susannah Wickoff, 1793.
Mich. Smith, Rosannah Yager, 1791.
Isaac Smith Sr., Susannah Smith, '91.
Aug. Smith, Anne Carper, 1802.
Weedon Smith, Lucy Browning, 1814.
John Smith. Petia Hangue, 1810.
Wm. W. Smith, Mary Bishop, 1813.
Jno. Smither, Mary Greenway, 1808.
Jno. Smoot, Anne Cannaday. 1798.
Wm. Smoot, Susannah Haden, 1795.
Aquilla Snailing, Eliz. Shotwell, 1791.
Jos. Snyder, Mary Christopher, 1788.
Jno. Snyder, Winnifred Campbell, '83.
Jno. W. Somersall, Fran. Stevens, 17.
Ben. Spicer, Mary Towels, 1787.
Absolom Spicer, Mahala Moore, '19.
Robt. B. Spilman, Lucy G. Payne, '22.
Alex. Spilman, Adeline Allan, 1824.

Jno. Strother, Sallie Pendleton, 1804.
Geo. Strother, Mary Duncan, 1798.
Jno. Strother, Eliz. Brown, 1814.
Hezekiah Soutter, Eliz. Brown, 1804.
Elijah Suttle, Aggy Miller, 1795.
Geo. Swindle, Hannah Cornelius, 1790.
Henry Swindler, Peggy Boston, ——
Alex. Simson, Anne Harrison, 1783.
John Sine, Phoebe Sine, 1802.
Richard Sisk, Clara Jenkins, 1806.
Benj. Sick, Eliz. McAllister, 1786.
Pluright Sisk, Ruth Boone, 1790.
Jno. Sisk, Eliz. Fincham, 1813.
Torpley Sisson, Mollie Pound, 1798.
Hugh Skinner, Sarah Jasper, 1812.
Elijah Skinner, Eliz. Jackson, 1788.
R. Y. Slaughter, Mary G. Green, 1799.
Wm. Slaughter, Frances H. Brown, '11.
Thos. Slaughter, Martha Moore, 1824
Jno. Smith, Nancy Finks, 1803.
Joel Smith, Sarah Fincham, 1803.
Jno. Smith, Patea Hayne, 1816.
Jno. Smith, Eliz. Bowry, 1793.
Wm. Smith, Lucy Wright, 1786.
Jno. Smith, Nancy Porter, 1788.
Owen Smith, Agnes Hill, 1793.
Rob. Smith Jr., Sallie Watts, 1791.
Brisco Smith, Jane Pratt, 1800.
Jesse Smith, Joannah Pendleton, 1796.
Martin Smith, Fannie Roberts, 1792.
Caleb Smith, Jennie Scott, 1799.
Isacher Smith, Anne S. Calvert, 1811.
Pres. N. Smith, Nancy Conner 1819.
Adam T. Smith, Sarah Colvin, 1820.
Gab. Smither, Gilly Calvert, 1801.
Leo. Smoot, Abigail Heaton, 1799.
Alex. Smoot, Anne Hawkins, 1798.
Benj. Smoot, Pamelia Mills, 1818.
Fielding Sneed, Eliz. Crutcher, 1794.
David Snyder, Martha Bryan, 1788.
Jos. Snyder, Sallie Campbell, 1809.
Cain Spicer, Eliz. Lucas, 1805.
Moses Spicer, Polly Moore, 1798.
Wm. Spiller Nancy Sullivan, 1809.
Conway Spilman, Nancy Mason, 1815.

T

Jno. Taliaferro, Alice Lukie, 1795.
Wm. Taliaferro, Nancy Tutt, 1811.
Jacob Tanner, Mary Collins, 1823.
Cornelius Tanner, Su. Collins, 1812.
Wm. Tate, Anne West, 1787.

Henry Taliaferro, Eliz. Lovell. 1800.
Wm. Tannahill, Henrietta Fogg, 1814.
John Tanner, Irene Collins, 1813.
Jno Tanner, Susannah Good, 1791.
Johan Taten, Susannah Bayne, 1818.

Wm. Tatum, Polly Lucus, 1797.
Geo. Taylor, Sallie Fishback, 1799.
Jas. Taylor, Eliz. Atkins, 1798.
Henry Telph, Anne Powell, 1782.
Thos. Thatcher, Jane Menefee, 1797.
Joel Terrill, Lucy Marshall, 1806.
Wm. Terrell, Lydia Coffman, 1814.
Elisha Thomas, Leana Zigler, 1788.
Nesley Thomas, Mary Hughes, 1808.
John Thompson, Nancy Pierce, '21.
Martin Thompson, Rebecca Foster, '13.
Jno. Thompson, Mild. Raines, 1790.
Jos. Thompson, Johanah Hall, 1793.
Jos. Thornhill, Eliz. Butler, 1812.
Jos. Thornhill, Sallie Westall, 1802.
Jno. Thornton, Nancy Shannon, 1822.
Jas. Threlkeld, Eliz. Garner, 1794.
Jas. Threlkeld, Polly Cosper, 1789.
Dan. Threlkeld, Lucy Duncan, 1799.
Catlett Tiffer, Fran. Asher, 1804.
Wm. Tinsley, Fran. Rogers, 1782.
Nath. Tobin, Marg. Cammeral, 1809.
Rob. Toombs, Sallie Catlett, 1798.
Jno. Tompkin, Mary Gibson, 1816.
Geo. Towels, Eliz. Bowers, 1815.
Wm. Towles, Damsel Lucas, 1816.
Henry Towles, Uphias Tucker, 1792.
Sanford Triplett, Mary Flinn, 1821.
Dan. Triplett, Susannah Botts, 1791.
Jas. Trigger, Polly Green, 1798.
Littleton Tucker, Rach. Threlkeld, '01.
Jno. Tucker, Nancy Tobin, 1798.
Wm. Tucker, Jemimah Lewis, 1798.
Allan Tucker, Polly Mawrey, 1810.
Zeph. Turner, Susannah Tutt, 1816.
Dan. Turner, Billy Bryan, 1815.
Rich. Turner, Fran. Hume, 1802.
Zeph. Turner, Sallie M. Conifer, 1800.
Sam. Turner, Abigail Haines, 1793.
Jas. Turner, Delphia Garner, 1807.
Jas. Turner, Betsey, Turner, 1805.
Larkin Turner, Peggy Kline, 1803.
Jas. Tutt, Lucinda Colvin, 1816.
Gab. Tutt, Millie Menefee, 1812.
Wm. Tutt, Winnie Pulliam, 1792.
Ben. Twisdell, Eliz. Zimmerman, '16.
Wm. B. Tyler, Emily Hurt, 1819.

Spencer Tavel, Lucy Morgan, 1805.
John Taylor, Cath. Harmey, 1815.
Edmund Taylor, Eliz. Utz, 1791.
Nath. Thead, Nellie Campbell, 1812.
Phil. Tettason, Eliz. Day, 1817.
Jno. Terrill, Rebecca Cornelius, 1789.
Ben. Thomas, Eliz. Gaines, 1799.
Massey Thomas Eliz. Barbour, 1785.
Elijah Thomas, Nancy Hughes, 1803.
Wm.A. Thompson,Mild. T.Norman,'18.
Walter Thompson, Isabel Brown, 1802.
Thos. Thompson, Frances Ross, 1794.
Bryant Thornhill, Fran. Jones, 1817.
Reub. Thornhill, Sallie Shingleton,'96.
Benj. Thornton, Anne Poner, 1791.
Jas. Thornton, Sallie Hawkins, 1796.
Jas. Threlkeld, Anne Kelly, 1784.
Moses Threlkeld, Sarah Whitehead,'95.
John Threlkeld, Patsy Furguson, 1811.
Mecajaole Tinel, Charlotte Appleby,'05.
Isaac Tobin, Winnie Shackelford, 1811.
Nathan Tobin, Sallie Coudy, 1801.
Christine Tomlin, Lucy Wright, 1801.
Wm. Tomlin, Sarah Wright, 1801.
Oliver Towles, Eleanor Wilhoite, 1816.
Jos. Towles, Polly Wetherall, 1786.
Geo. Towles, Fran. Mason, 1809.
Alf. Triplett, Anne Oder, 1814.
Hedgman Triplett, M.McClannahan,'88.
John Tucker, Clarissa B. Smith, 1812.
Stephen Tucker, Eliz. Crawley, 1801.
Moses Tucker, Uyly Goodman, 1793.
Thos. Tucker, Nancy Simms, 1808.
Jno. Tuckwiller, Polly Edwards, 1812.
Rob. Turner, Nancy Wise. 1816.
Leonard Turner, Sallie Campbell, 1800.
Armistead Turner, Mollie Kennedy,'99.
Benj. Turner, Agatha Watts, 1789.
Joshua Turner, Mary Corley, 1792.
Martin Turner, Hannah Marshall, 1806.
Rawley Turner, Nancy Hopper, 1803.
Thos. Tutt, Sallie Parks, 1787.
Rich. Elsie Tutt, Malinda Royster, '12.
Jas. L. Tutt, Lucy Finks, 1800.
Rich. J. Tutt, Millie Conner, 1795.
Geo. Twyman, Anne Twyman, 1790.
Jas. Tye, Frankie Collins, 1801.

U

Jos. Underwood, Winnie Henderson, '82.
Amiss Updyke, Sarah Updyke, 1821.
Jno. Utz, Eliz. Christler, 1788.

Dan. Updyke, Ruth Heaton, 1799.
Lewis Utz, Mary Carpenter, 1790.
Thompson Utterback, Bet. Vaughan,'.09

V

Jere. Vaughan, May Green, 1809.
Russell Vaughan, Eliz. Hill, 1791.
Peter Vandike, Anne Stout, 1791.
Jesse Vaughter, Eliz. Watts, 1791.
Fred. VisCarver, Fran. Browning, '03.

Jno. Vaughan, Peggy Tobin, 1807.
Olion Vaughan, Lilly Brown, 1821.
Jesse VanHorn, Eliz. Pulliam, 1814.
Anthony Vermon, Fran. Quinn, 1796.

W

Wm. Waddle, Eliz. Haywood, 1792.
Greensly Waggoner, Sarah Mitchell, '86.
Thos. Walden, Lucy Hughes, 1794.
John Waldridge, Millie Hendrick, '05.
————Walker, Polly Perry, 1808.
John Walker, Jr., Eliz. Parsons, 1820.
Robt. Wall, Fannie Parsons, 1787.
Wm. Wall, Mary Wall, ————.
Wm. Wallace, Eliz. Yates, 1806.
Wm. Wallis, Mildred Walker, 1791.
Wm. Ward, Polly W. Strother, 1805.
Jacob Ward, Sallie Quinn, 1788.
Wm. Ward, Marg. Keys, 1816.
Moses Washburn, Agatha Ethenton, '92.
Rob. Watts, Susannah Lewis, 1788.
Adam Wayland, Judah Burke, 1803.
Joshua Wayland, Anne Ward, 1792.
Fran. Weakley, Mary Berry, 1804.
Mathias Weaver, Eleanor Wayland, '91.
Caleb Webb, Fannie Gosney, 1799.
Aug. Weedeh, Eliz. Farmer, 1795.
Jas. Wetherspon, Mary Gin, 1788.
Jno. Wharton, Nancy Butler, 1805.
Jno. Wharton, Eliza Colvin, 1823.
Dan. Wheatley, Susannah Cooper, '00.
John Wheeler, Alice Hawford, 1792.
Reuben White, Polly Parsons, 1807.
Galen White, Mildred Alexander, 1783.
Jno. White, Lucy Waggoner, 1795.
Jno. Whitehead, Marg. Peyton, 1801.
Jno. Whitehead, Eliz. Routt, 1794.
Cor. Whitescarver, Eliz. Browning, '04.
Jno. Whitesides, Katie Coons, 1789.
Wm. Whyly, Nancy Pulham, 1787.
Jno. Wigginton, Mary M. Bell, 1795.
Reynolds Wilhoite, Lucy Towles, 1815.
Wm. Wilhoite, Anna Clore, 1787.
Mich. Wilhoite, Jemimah Lucas, 1789.
Wm. Wilks, Anne Adams, 1794.
Thos. R. Williams, Marian Brown, '99.
Thos. Williams, Mary Mozingo, 1806.
Jno. Willis, Edna Bragg, 1802.
Jno. Willis, Jane Dogan, 1786.
Edward Willis, Frances Towles, 1787.
Rob. Willis, Emily Hudson, 1824.

Thos. Waggoner, Mary Garnett, 1786.
Geo. Waite, Mary Haynes, 1787.
Peter Waldridge, Fannie Blackwell, '07.
Lawson Wale, Lucy Thornton, 1791.
Jas. Walker, Jemimah Yager, 1793.
Benj. Wall, Lucy Pinnell, 1792.
Wm. Wall, Katy Margin, 1798.
Rich. Wall, Sukie Vermon, 1790.
Oliver Wallis, Anna Wright, 1795.
Elias Walters, Sallie Gaunt, 1799.
Wm. Ward, Sarah Vermon, 1782.
Jas. Ward, Fran. Jenkins, 1789.
Geo. W. Ward, Susan W. Fishback, '20.
Wm. Waters, Mary Brown, 1787.
Jno. Watts, Sallie Sebree, 1788.
Joshua Wayland, Rachel Utz, 1781.
Harman Wayman, Fran. Clore, 1792.
Wm. Weakley, Susan Sisk, 1814.
Lewis Webb, Nellie Threlkeld, 1807.
Aug. Webb, Lucy Crittenden, 1788.
Isaiah Welch, Agnes Hawkins, 1795.
Bev. Wharton, Judith Clatterbuck, '04.
Jno. Wharton, Eliz. Smith, ————.
Wm. Wheatley, Susannah Grigsby, '92.
Thornton Wheatley, Sallie Miller, 1817.
Geo. Wheeler, Lydia Calvert, 1794.
Jas. White, Anne Buckhan, 1810.
Thos. White, Mildred Graves, 1788.
Jere. White, Rachel Herndon, 1790.
Vincent Whitehead, Eliz. Clifton, 1791.
Nelson Whitehead, Eliz. Coleman, '92.
Rob. Whitescarver, Sallie Browning, '09.
Perrin Whitney, Mary Whitehead, '16.
Wm. Wiatt, Fran. Levell, 1811.
Wm. Wilhoite, Eliz. Weaver, 1806.
Lewis Wilhoite, R. Blankenbaker, '87.
Jno. Wilhoite, Jennie Story, 1794.
Moses Wilhoite, Anne Hume, 1789.
Alex. Williams, Nancy Price, 1809.
Jos. Williams, Eliz. Settle, 1795.
Elijah Williams, Mary Holland, 1821.
Moses Willis, Susannah White, 1791.
Chas. Willis, Lucy Shelton, 1794.
Thos. Willis, Mary Wood, 1818.
Joshua Willis, Arcy Willis, 1815.

Isaac Wilson, Eliz. Cooke, 1793.
Isaac Wilson, Anna Garnett, 1798.
Thos. Winsor, Lydia Hasby, 1802.
Jas. Wise, Sallie Ethrington, 1806.
Manning Wise, Eliz. Barbour, 1793.
Cuthbert Wise, Mary Thornton, 1816.
Peter Witham, Mary Dicken, 1790.
Mathias Withers, Cath. Spencer, 1794.
Peter Womack, Cresser Utterback,'86.
Wm. Wood, Frances Browning, 1802.
Jos. Woodard, Belvey Bowling, 1808.
Wm. Woodard, Susannah Hisle, 1791.
Geo. Woodard, Nancy Chilton, 1810.
Chas. Woodard, Sallie Hisle, 1811.
Chas. Woodard, Nancy Frazier, 1815.
Rich. Wright, Anne Story, 1793.
Rich. Wright, Anne Smith, 1799.
Nath. Wright, Clary Baldick, 1813.

Sam. Wilson, Nancy Sutherland, 1790.
Pres. Wilson, Eliz. Mason, 1817.
Wm. Winnard, Rebecca Eleason, 1821.
Jno. Wise, Dolly Morriss, 1797.
Wm. Wise, Lucy Etherton, 1816.
Alex. Wisher, Eliz. Doores, 1816.
Jno. Weatherall, Eliz. Chapman, 1788.
Elijah Withers, Jemimah Hudnell, '99.
Alex. Womax, Jemijah Steptoe, 1808.
Wm. Wood, Mary Anne Clarke, 1790.
Wm. Woodward, Dusilla Jenkens, 1824.
Wm. Woodard, Anne Barnhisle, 1793.
Jas. Woodard, Anne Young, 1800.
Jno. Woodard, Polly Martin, 1815.
Jno. Wright, Fresey Corbin, 1809.
Chas. Wright, Polly Holmes, 1796.
Chas. D. Wright, Lucy Mason, 1801.

Y

Jos. Yager, Sallie Chich, 1806.
John Yager, Marg. Wilhoite, 1791.
Elisha Yager, Eliz. Yager, 1786.
Adam Yager, Anne Dicken, 1792.
Nich. Yager, Jemimah Yager, 1790.
Nath. Yager, Betsey Hudson, 1789.
Lud. Yancey, Eliz. Jeffries, 1792
Geo. Yates, Polly Browning, 1800.
Ben. Yates, Alice Fennell, 1803.
Abner Yates, Clara Smith, 1795.
Warner Yates, Eliz. Baxter, 1789.
Wm. Yates, Eliz. Lillard, 1813.
Ben. Yates, Eliz. Jury, 1817.
Benj. Young, Sarah Williams, 1809.
Chas. Young, Sallie Mayer, 1791.
—— Yowell, Sallie Chilton, 1808.
Wm. Yowell, SemphroniaWilhoite, '21.
Benj. Yager, Anna Chistler, 1790.

Jno. Yager, Anna Cabler, 1809.
Nich. Yager, Anne Wayland, 1785.
Jno. Yager, Hannah Yager, 1786.
John Yager, Anne Carpenter, 1790.
Ephraim Yager, Sarah Rodeheifer, '91.
Birkett D. Yancey, Mil. Menefee, 1803.
Jas. Yates, Polly Browning, 1812.
Geo. Yates, Eliz. Browning, 1793.
Wm. Yates, Isabella Gaines, 1786.
Fran. Yates, Peggy Hughes, 1798.
Boswell P. Yates, C. A. Gaines, 1813.
Garnet Yates, Fran. Yates, 1815.
Warner Yates, Mild. J. Menefee, 1819.
Sam. Young, Marg. Rogers, 1789.
Sam. Young, Mary Coons, 1786.
Wm. Yowell, Lucy Shipp, 1791.
Wesley Yowell, Jatsey Tucker, 1824.

Z

Wm. Zachary, Anne Rice, 1787.
John Zimmerman, Eliz. Fewel, 1791.
Mich. Zimmerman, Eliz. Huffman, '91.

Reub. Zimmerman, Eliz. Zigler, 1785.
Dan. Zimmerman, Mary Carter, 1794.

FAMILY GENEALOGIES.

CHAPTER VI.

From various sources, all of which we consider most reliable and accurate, the publishers have gathered the following information, which is appended in a condensed form. We have endeavored to give all the possible data that could be obtained, in which Culpeper people, or descendants of Culpeper people, might be interested.

THE DESCENDANTS OF PAUL MICOU.
1700 to 1896.

Paul Micou, b. 1658, d. 1736, a Huguenot, left his home at Nantes soon after the revocation of the Edict of Nantes (1685.)

After some years of exile, probably in England, he finally settled on the Rappahannock River, in Essex Co., before 1695. His wife (maiden name supposed, but without evidence, to be Margaret Roy or LeRoy) and his children accompanied him. Accounts vary as to his profession; judging from this clause in his will: "I give my friend, Dr. Mungo Roy, all my physick books and a gold ring," he was a physician. On the other hand, the fact that he was a Justice of the Peace as early as 1700, seems to point to his having some knowledge of law. The author of "The Huguenot Emigration to Virginia," in the Va. Hist. Collections, states that he was educated to the Bar. He served as Justice of the Peace in Essex county, from 1700 to 1720; his son, Paul, from 1740 to 1760; and his grandson, Paul, from 1780 to 1799. He judiciously invested in land and slaves, owning at the time of his death, in addition to the Port Micou estate, large tracts of land in King George Co., in Pewmansand, and 800 acres in Spotsylvania County.

Bishop Meade, in his "Old Churches, Ministers and Families of Virginia," mentions Rev. Wm. Giberne, who became minister of Lunenburg Parish, Richmond county, in 1762, and adds "he married a daughter of Moore Faunt LeRoy and Margaret Micou. Her father was Paul Micou, a Huguenot who fled from Nantes before 1700." "At the old Port Micou estate on the Rappahannock, may still be seen the large, heavy ironstone or black marble headstone of this Paul Micou, the first of the name who came into this country. By reason of its weight and the lightness of the soil, it sinks every few years somewhat beneath the earth but is raised up again." Rev. P. Slaughter, in his "Memoirs of Col. Joshua Fry," says "Col. Fry married the widow of Col. Hill, a large landed proprietor on the Rappahannock River. Her maiden name was Mary Micou, and she was a daughter of Paul Micou, physician and surgeon, a Huguenot exile from France. Another of his daughters married Lunsford Lomax, the grandfather of Judge John F. Lomax of Fredericksburg, Va. Another daughter married Moore Faunt LeRoy, a man of mark in his day, and the ancestor of the family of that name in Virginia." PAUL MICOU'S children were as follows:

1. Paul Micou, who inherited the Homestead, Justice of the Peace for Essex county, from 1741 to 1760. He died a bachelor. 2. John Micou, m. Catherine

Walker. Died 1754. 3. James Micou. 4. Henry Micou. 5. Mary Micou, m. 1st. Col. John Hill, 2nd Col. Joshua Fry. 6. Margaret Micou, m. Moore Faunt LeRoy. 7. Judith Micou, m. Lunsford Lomax. 8. Daughter, m. —— Scott, issue: Paul and Margaret. 9. Daughter m. Rev. Mr. Waddell, the blind Preacher.

SECOND GENERATION.

[Note: The names in parenthesis or brackets denote the line of descent.]
JOHN MICOU (Paul), m. Catherine Walker. Died 1754. Left issue:

1. Paul m. Jeanne Roy. 2. John. 3. Richard m. Anne Boutwell. 4. Henry m. Anne Hill. 5. William. 6. Clara m. ———— Brooke. 7. Margaret. 8. Catherine m. Dr. Mungo Roy. 9. James.

THIRD GENERATION.

PAUL MICOU (John, Paul), m. Jeanne Roy died 1799, issue:

1. Paul m. Mary Lee. 2. Catherine. 3. John m. Sarah Brooke. 4. Jeanne Roy, m. Walker Roy. 5. James Roy, m. Fanny Mathews.

RICHARD MICOU, (John, Paul), settled in Caroline Co., Va. He m. Anne Boutwell, issue:

1. William m. Martha Ann Chatfield. 2. Henry. 3. John. 4. Samuel. 5. Catherine, m. John Garrett. 6. Margaret m. Thos. M. Barnett. 7. Anna m. Mr. Hudson. 8. Richard.

HENRY MICOU, (John, Paul), m. Anne Hill, issue: 1. Henry. 2. Beatrix. 3. Eleanor.

FOURTH GENERATION.

PAUL MICOU, (Paul, John, Paul), m. Mary Lee. On the death of Paul Micou (4th) the Port Micou estate was sold out of the family. He died in 1821, issue:

1. Albert Roy m. Bettie M. Micou, dau. of Jas. Roy Micou. 2. Paul m. Fanny M. Micou, dau. of Jas. Roy Micou. 3. John H. m. C. C. Wood. 4. Maria m. Rev. John Micou, son of John and Sarah (Brooke) Micou. 5. Felicia, m. ——Tupman. 6. Susan. 7. Betsy.

JOHN MICOU, (Paul, John, Paul), m. Sarah Brooke of "Farmers' Hall," 1789, died 1848. He moved to Winsten county, Mississippi, issue:

1. John m. Maria Micou, dau. of Paul and Mary (Lee) Micou. 2. Wm. F. m. Betsy Denholm. 3. Maria. 4. Susan m. Eugene Ferris. 5. Lucy m. Eugene Ferris. 6. Harriet m. Eugene Ferris.

JAMES ROY MICOU, (Paul, John, Paul), and Jeanne Micou m. Fanny Mathews, issue:

1. James Roy m. Ellen H. Jones. 2. Wm. F. m. Fannie McClanahan. 3. Maria. 4. Fannie m. Paul Micou, son of Paul and Mary (Lee) Micou. 5. Betty m. Albert Roy Micou son of Mary (Lee) Micou. 6. Jeanne. 7. John P. 8. Eleanor R. 9. Ann O. L.

WILLIAM MICOU, (Richard, John, Paul,) and Anne (Boutwell) Micou, was born in Caroline county, 1774. Left Virginia in 1795 and settled at Augusta, Ga. He died there in 1834. He married there, Martha Ann Chatfield, 1804. Her parents were from New Haven, Conn. Issue:

1. Caroline Margaret, b. 1803. 2. Wm. Chatfield, b. 1807, m. Annie Davenport Thompson (Burkett Davenport Thompson, Hon. Philip Rootes Thompson, Rev. John Thompson). 3. Matilda Ann, b. 1809 m. Geo. W. Morgan. 4. Margaret Camilla, b. 1810 m. Abner Standish Washburn. 5. Ellen Harriet, b. 1812, m. Andrew G. Bull. 6. Henry Oswell b. 1814, m. Martha M. Taliaferro. 7.

Geo. Washington b. 1816, d. 1828. 8. Chas. Edwin, b. 1818, d. 1840. 9. Catherine Adeline, b. 1819, m. Frederick W. Jordan in 1836. 10. Clara Elizabeth, b 1821, m. her cousin, Thomas M. Barnett, in 1845. 11. Martha Augusta, b. 1828, m. 1st. Wheaton Baker 1851, 2nd. Burkett D. Fry of Virginia, at San Francisco, Cal., July 1853. He was the son of Thornton Fry (Rev. Henry Fry, Col. Joshua Fry), and Eliza Thompson, (Hon. Philip Rootes Thompson, Rev. John Thompson). 12. Benjamin Hall, b. 1825, m. 1st Lucy Barnett, 2nd Mary J. C. Sims. 13. George b. 1828, d. 1836. 14. Isaac Mix, b. 1830 m. Sarah V. Roberts.

HENRY MICOU, (Richard, John, Paul), and Annie (Boutwell) Micou, wife's name unknown; issue:

1. William Henry m. Caroline Cheathem. 2. Richard. 3. Jane, m. Green Gilliam.

FIFTH GENERATION.

ALBERT ROY MICOU, (Paul, Paul, John, Paul,) and Mary (Lee) Micou, m. Bettie, dau. of James Roy and Fannie M. Micou. Issue:

1. Albert Roy, Editor of "Tidewater Times," Md. Has two children. 2. Nannie B. m. —— Davies. 3. William.

PAUL MICOU, (Paul, Paul, John, Paul,) and Mary (Lee) Micou, m. Fannie, dau. of James Roy and Fannie M. Micou. Issue:

1. Frances m Geo. Stark. 2. Stella. 3. James.

JOHN H. MICOU, (Paul, Paul, John, Paul), Mary L. Micou, m. C. C. Woods. Issue:

1. Edgar. 2. M. E. Micou, m. —— Bougham. 3. Olympia. 4. Kate Carter, m. John Micou, son of John and Sarah Micou. 5. Maria m. John Micou, son of John and Sarah Micou.

JOHN MICOU, (John, Paul, John, Paul,) and Sarah (Brooke) Micou, m. his cousin Maria, dau. of Paul and Mary Lee Micou. Issue:

1. Eliza. 2. Ellen. 3. Rebecca. 4. Mary, moved to Mississippi.

WILLIAM F. MICOU, (John, Paul, John, Paul,) and Sarah Brooke Micou, m. Betsy Denholm. Issue.

1. Susan Lee m. Dr. L. Reese. 2. Wm. D. 3. Thos. B. m. Julia Mosely. 4. John. 5. Margaret.

JAMES ROY MICOU, (James Roy, Paul, John, Paul,) b. 1807, m. Ellen H. Jones and settled in Essex Co., where he was clerk for 57 years. Died in 1892.

1. James Roy, died. 2. Fannie B. m. Tom Roy of Spottsylvania Co. 3. Philip. 4. Nannie. 5. Susan. 6. Ellen. 7. Rosa G., m. G. D. Nicolson. 8. James Roy, m. Roberta Morrison, dau. of Prof. Morrison, of William and Mary College. James Roy Micou is now Professor in Washington College, Chestertown Md.

WILLIAM CHATFIELD MICOU, b. 1807, (William, Richard, John, Paul,) m. Anna Davenport Thompson (Burkett Davenport, Hon. Philip Rootes. Rev. John Thompson) Feb. 1831. He was educated at the U. of Ga., studied law, and in 1835 removed to New Orleans, where he rose rapidly in his profession, becoming one of the most eminent members of the New Orleans Bar. He died in 1854. Issue:

1. Thompson, b. 1833, d. 1889. 2. Susan Virginia, b. 1836, m. 1st George P. Ring, issue: Willie and Rita, m. 2nd her cousin Andrew Glassell, of California. Died 1895. 3. William, b. 1838 d. young. 4. Augustine S., b. 1841, d. 1888. 5. Wille Annie, b. 1843, m. I. Tharpe. 6. Philip Rootes, b. 1845, d. 1858. 7. Richard Wilde, 1848, m. Mary Dunnica in 1872. 8. Henry, died young. 9. William Henry, b. 1853, m. Susan Turrentin.

HENRY OSWELL MICOU, (William, Richard, John, Paul) m. Martha M. Taliaferro 1835. Issue:

1. Mary m. Dr. Geo. W. McDade. 2. David F. 3. Wm. Henry, m. Mary Phinizy, issue: Augusta Louise. 4. Emily Augusta.

BENJAMIN HALL MICOU, (William, Richard, John, Paul,) settled in Tallassee, Ala., where his uncle, Thos. M. Barnett, and his cousin and brother-in-law, Thomas M. Barnett Jr., had developed the water power on the Tallapoosa River. He became identified with them in the establishment of large cotton mills. He died 1887. He m. 1st his cousin, Lucy A. Barnett. Issue of first marriage:
1. Clara E. m. Frank S. Boykin, issue: Marshall Boykin. 2. Lucy B. m. Edward F. Noble, issue: two sons.
He married 2nd Mary J. C. Sims, issue:
1. Benjamin, m. Ella Herbert, dau. of Col. Hillary Herbert.

ISAAC MIX MICOU, (William, Richard, John, Paul,) m. Sarah V. Roberts. 1. Benjamin. 2. Ruth A. m. Joel Barnett. 3. Paul Isaac.

WILLIAM HENRY MICOU, (Henry, Richard, John, Paul), m. Caroline Cheathem. Issue:
1. John. 2. Geo. Robert. 3. Caroline m. Mr. Clark. 4. Frank.

FIFTH GENERATION.

RICHARD WILDE MICOU,(William C., William, Richard, John, Paul,) was born in New Orleans in 1848. He was educated at the Universities of Georgia and Alabama. After the war he went abroad, and studied at the Universities of Erlangen, Bavaria, and of Edinburg, Scotland. He was ordained to the diaconate in 1870. Was advanced to the priesthood in his first parish at Franklin, La. 1872. In 1874 he took charge of St. Paul's Church, Kittanning Penn., and in 1877 accepted a call to Trinity Church. Waterbury, Conn. In 1892, Mr. Micou accepted a call to the Chair of Systematic Divinity, in the Philadelphia Divinity School. While there he received the degree of Doctor of Divinity, From Kenyon College, Ohio. In 1898, he was called to the same Chair in the Theological Seminary, Alexandria, Va., and removed there the same year. In 1872 he married Mary Dunnica, dau. of Granville Price Dunnica and Mary Ann Bagley; issue: 1. Granville R. born 1876, graduated at the University of Pennsylvania with honors in 1896. Graduated at the Virginia Theological Seminary in 1899. Ordained Deacon 1899 Ordained Priest 1900 by Bishop Nelson of Ga., in whose Diocese he is Missionary. 2. Richard Dunnica, b. 1882; 3. Paul, born 1885; 4. Margaret, born 1886.

WM. HENRY MICOU, (Wm. C., William, Richard, John, Paul,) educated at the Uni. of the South, is now Secretary and Treasurer of the Tallassee Falls Mfg. Co., Montgomery, Ala, He married in 1879, Susie E. Turrentine ; issue : 1. Morgan Turrentine, born, 1879. 2. William Chatfield, born 1883.

WM. HENRY MICOU, (Henry O., William, Richard, John, Paul,) m. Mary Phinizy; issue: Augusta Louise, born 1876.

BENJ. MICOU, (Benj. H., William, Richard, John, Paul,) after graduating at the University of the South, and taking a law course at the University of Va., was admitted to the Bar. For a time he was City Attorney of Anniston, Ala. About 1893, he was appointed Chief Clerk of the Navy Dept. He is now in the law firm of Herbert & Micou, Washington.

He married Ella Herbert, dau. of Col. Hillary Herbert, Sec. of the .Navy, issue : Hillary Herbert, Benjamin, Cresswell.

GEO. ROBERT MICOU, (William H., Henry, Richard, John, Paul,) issue George Robert, born 1886, Frank Lamar, born 1888, and several daughters.

CATHERINE ADELINE MICOU, (William, Richard, John, Paul,) m. Fred. W. Jordan, 1836. Iss: 1. Annie Eliza m. Dr. Phillips; 2. Martha; 3. George, m. Lizzie Rambo; 4. Reuben, m. Lucy Barnett; 5. Henry ; 6. William; 7. Fred. 8. Kate m. Dr. Phillips ; 9. Walter; 10. Burkett Fry; 11. Mary Ellen, m W. N. Hampton; 12. Clara m. B. P. Richards.

THE GRINNAN FAMILY.

Daniel Grinnan, Sr., b. Accomac County, Va., 1739; removed to Culpeper and settled on Cedar Run, near Mitchell's Sta. He served in the Revolutionary war under Gen. Edward Stevens, in a Virginia brigade. His eldest son, John, was in the quartermaster's department of the same brigade. His other children were Daniel Jr., and Sally.

John Grinnan m. Stuart, and had William, who m. 1st. Shepherd, of Orange; 2nd Elizabeth Welch, and had James Shepherd, Welch, Archibald, C. S. A., Oswald, d. in Ala., and Elizabeth, m. Lewis Porter Nelson, of Culpeper.

Daniel Grinnan Jr., m. Helen Buchan Glassell, of " Torthowald," Madison County, who was his second wife, he having m. Eliza Richards Green, dau. of Timothy Green, who came from the North and settled at Fredericksburg. By his second marriage he had 1. Robert Alexander who m. Robertine Temple, and had Robert Temple, Helen Glassell and Walter Alexander, 2. Andrew Glassell. who m. Georgia Screven Bryan, and had Randolph Bryan, m. Louisa Arlena Leet, Daniel, Elizabeth Coalter, Cornelia Stuart, Andrew Glassell, St. Geo. Tucker, Jno. Coalter and Georgia Bryan; 3. Daniel Morton ; 4. Eliza Richards ; 5. Cornelia ; 6. Helen Mary; 7. Daniel.

James Grinnan, son of William, m. Belle Ham, lived in Texas, and had Jas. Frederick, Lewis Porter, Libbie, Lucile, Helen, Belle, Kate and Nelson.

William Welch, bro. of above Jas., m. Ann Wheatley, of Culpeper, and had Howell, m. Tamar Gibbs, of Tyler, Texas; Mandeley, Archibald, Mary, Elizabeth, m. Alexander Kelly, of Fauquier; Nannie; Margaret, m. Horace Chilton, U. S. Senator from Texas ; Kate and Belle.

Mary Elizabeth, dau. of William, m. Lewis Porter Nelson, and had Claude, William Porter, Henry Blackwell, George Archibald, Arthur Braxton, Lewis Porter, Lizzie Edmondson, m. R. G. Pace, of Danville; Kate Davis, m. Shelton F. Leake, of Texas; Maggie Belle, m. W. G. Neal, of Richmond ; and Lucille.

THE SOMERVILLE FAMILY.

The first of the name who came to Va., was Jas. Somerville, b. Glasgow, Feb. 23,1742; located at Fredericksburg, and became a wealthy merchant; d. at Port Royal, April 25, 1798, having no heir of his body, and leaving his estate to his nephew James, son of Walter and Mary (Gray) Somerville, of Scotland, who was b. in Glasgow in 1777; d. Aug. 29, 1858. He came to Virginia in 1795, and took possession of his inheritance, settling at " Somervilla," on the Rapidan, in 1810; he m. Mary Atwell, of Fauquier, who d. Feb. 14, 1845.

BALL—MASON—COOKE.

Col. Wm. Ball, b. 1615, d. 1680, m. Hannah Atherold, in London, 1638, and had among others, Joseph, who m. 1st. Elizabeth Romney, 2nd. Mrs. Mary Johnson.

Joseph Ball, of "Epping Forest," by his marriage with Elizabeth Romney, had, among others, Hannah, m. Raleigh Travers; by his marriage with Mrs. Johnson ; he had Mary, who m. Augustine Washington, and was the mother of Gen. Geo. Washington.

Raleigh Travers m. Hannah Ball, and had Elizabeth, who m. John Cooke.

Travers Cooke, son of John, m. Mary, dau. of Mottram Doniphan, and had Col. John Cooke, of "West Farms," Stafford, who m. Mary Thompson, dau. of George Mason, of " Gunston Hall." Million, dau. of Col. Jno. Cooke, of "West Farms," m. Hon. John W. Green, of Culpeper, of the Virginia Court of Appeals, and had Jno. Cooke, m. Morton; Thomas Claiborne, m. McDonald; Jas. Williams, m. McDonald; George Mason, m. 1st. Ashby, 2nd. Lockwood ; and Lucy Williams, died single.

Sarah Mason, dau. of Col. John Cooke, of "West Farms," m. 1st. Cary Selden; 2nd Dr. Robert O. Grayson, by whom she had Dr. John Cooke Grayson, of Stevensburg, Culpeper county, and Robert O. Grayson, of Culpeper.

Gen. Geo. Mason Cooke, son of John and Mary Thompson (Mason) Cooke. m. Agatha Eliza Eustace, and had, among others, Tabitha Virginia, who m. John T. Grasty, of Orange county.

Capt. Wm. Ball, son of Col. Wm., m. Miss Harris (she being his second wife—he married 3 times), of Northumberland, and had James, who m. Mary Conway Dangerfield, widow of John Dangerfield. Jeduthun, son of James, m. Elizabeth Burgess, dau. of Charles Burgess, of England, and had Col. Burgess Ball, of Spottsylvania and Loudon counties, who was a Lt. Col. in the Continental Army. Col. Burgess Ball m. Frances Washington, dau. of Col. Charles and Mildred Thornton Washington, and a niece of Gen. Washington. Martha Dandridge, dau. of Col. Burgess Ball, was the first wife of Col. Jonathan Catlett Gibson, of Culpeper, and is buried in St. Stephen's Episcopal church yard, Her two daughters were Frances Ann and Martha Dandridge Gibson. Col. Gibson's second wife was Mary Williams Shackelford.

Frances Ann, daughter of Col. Jonathan Catlett Gibson and Martha Dandridge Ball, m. J. C. Burt having Anna, who m. Aylette Hawes Buckner who now lives in Rappahannock county.

Mildred Thornton Ball, dau. of Col. Burgess Ball, m. Wm. Mills Thompson, a vestryman of St. Mark's Parish, and was the mother of Hon. Richard W. Thompson, Secretary of the Navy under Pres. Hayes.

THE ASHBY FAMILY.

Captain John Ashby, of 3rd. Va. Reg., Continental line, 1775—1783, b. Fauquier about 1750, m. Miss Turner; had Samuel, who m. dau. of Col. Clarkson, and had 1. John Henry, 2. Jamison, m. —— Adams, having Luther, Henry and Scott, all living in; Fauquier in 1889; 3. Wm. Clarkson; and five daus., Wm Clarkson Ashby m. Miss Strother and has descendants in Culpeper

John Ashby, son of Capt. John, m. Miss Smith, and had William, Shirley and Wirt. Nimrod, son of Capt. John, m. Miss Adams, and had Albert, died single; Nimrod, has children in Fauquier; and Samuel T., who m. Miss Chinn and had Bernard, Hunter, Norman, Mrs. Grace Houck, Mrs. Mackall, Mrs. Lambert, Mrs. Johnson, Mrs. Birney, and Samuel T.

Capt. John Ashby was the son of Col. John Ashby, b. 1707, d. 1797, and Jean Combs, whom he m. May, 11, 1741. Col. A. , was :captain 2nd. Co. Va. Rangers, Oct. 21, 1755. Gen. Daniel Morgan was a private in his company. He was with Washington during the Braddock Campaign. "He bore Washington's dispatches, containing the news of Braddock's defeat, from Winchester to Williamsburg, and returned with Gov. Dinwiddie's reply before the English commander supposed he had started on his journey. A letter from Williamsburg, June 2, 1774, says that at the battle of Pt. Pleasant the Indians had killed the noted Capt. Ashby, who, in the last war, brought the first account of Braddock's defeat to this city with amazing expedition."

THE YANCEY FAMILY.

The first trace we have of this family is that four Welchmen, Charles, William, Joel and Robert Yancey, who came to Virginia, in 1642, with Sir Wm. Berkley, afterwards Governor, and settled in the James River region and prospered. From one of the original four was descended Lewis Davis Yancey, who settled in Culpeper county about 1710; married Mildred, daughter of Charles Kavanaugh, of Irish parentage, who owned a large land estate of 40,000 acres in said county. This tract extended westward and above the Beverly line up Muddy Run to Judge Field's Mills, across by Poor Town to Gibson's Mill on Mountain Run. A portion of this land he bequeathed to his daughter Mildred, which portion has never been out of the Yancey family, and is still owned by Benjamin M. Yancey, a great grandson of Lewis Davis and by Jas. Wm. Yancey, a great great grandson. Lewis Davis lived and was buried on the estate of the latter, "Arlington." From the "Crawford Book" we have, "John Yancey came from Wales about the middle of the 17th century;" then there must have been another brother.

Ch. of John Yancey: 1. Charles m. Mlle. Dumas, 2. Leighton moved to Rockingham county, 3. Bartlett to N. C.

Charles m. Mlle. Dumas. Ch: 1. Capt Charles (1741, 1841) of Louisa county, m. Mary Crawford; 2. Rev. Robert (was ordained by the Bishop of London at his palace in Fulham in Middlesex, 25th July, 1768 as an Episcopal Priest, there being no Bishop in this country under the colonial Government. On his return from England he accepted the Parishes of Tillotston and Trinity in his native country, 1774. He was the first who preached in that section of the country the doctrine of universal redemption.) He married Ann Crawford, dau. of David Crawford.

Ch. of Capt. Chas. and Mary Crawford Yancey: 1. Ann, 2. Elizabeth m. Jos. Kimbrough, 3. Unity, 4. Louisa Temperance, 5. Robert, 6. Mary, 7. Rhoda m. Rev. Wm. Crawford, 8. Joel Crawford, 9. David, 10. Wm. Crawford.

Ch. of Jos. Kimbrough and Elizabeth Yancey; 1. Dr. Wm. 2. Unity m. Col. Edmund Pendleton, 3. Sarah m. Peter S. Barrett, 4. Maria D. m. Bickerton Winston, removed to Ky., 5. Capt. Chas. Y. m. Mary P. Honeyman, 6. Elizabeth m. Dr. L. M. Ligm, 7. Susan H. m. Robt. H. Anderson.

Ch. of Rev. Robert and Ann Crawford Yancey: 1. Betsey 1775, 2. Charles 1770—1857.

Maj. Charles, son of Rev. Robert and Ann Yancey, born 1770 in Trinity Parish, Louisa county, Va., removed to Buckingham county. He was known throughout the State as the "Wheel Horse of Democracy," and also had the sobriquet of "Duke of Buckingham." He married Nancy Spencer and had 1. Mary Chambers m. Col. John Horsley, of Nelson county, 2. Francis Westbrook, 3. Elizabeth Ann m. 1st. Robt. Williams, of N. Y., 2nd. Richard Morris of Gloucester, Va.

Lewis Davis Yancey, a son of one of the original four, as stated above m. Mildred Kavanaugh and had nine children, John, Richard, Charles, Philip, Robert, James, Lewis, Nancy, and another daughter.

1. John settled in Rockingham county, ch: 1. Layton (was Lieut in "First Continental Dragoons in Revolutionary War") m. Fanny Lewis, 2. Ludwell, 3. John, 4. Fanny, 5. Polly.

Ch. of Layton and Fanny Lewis Yancey are 1. Layton, 2. Col. Wm. Burbridge, 3. Charles, 4. John, 5. Albert, 6. Thomas, 7. Fannie, 8. Clarissa, 9. Maria, and 10. Louisa.

Col. Wm. Burbridge m. 1st. Mary Smith, 2nd. Mary Gibbons, ch. 1. Diana

Smith m. Geo. Oliver Conrad (Harrisonburg), 2. Capt. Thomas L. m. Margaret Newman, 3. Edward S. m. Fannie Mauzy, 4. Wm. Burbridge, (Capt. of Peaked Mountain Greys, Civil war,) m. Victoria Winsborough, 5. Chas. Albert m. Julia Morrison, of Cumberland, Md., 6. Mary Frances, 7. Margaret J. m. Jos. N. Mauzy, 8. Dr. Layton B. m. Virginia Hopkins, (McGaheysville, Va.), 9. John Gibbons m. Bennett Bradley, (Harrisonburg).

Ch. of Chas. (son of Layton), and Lucinda Moyers, 1. Charles, 2. Elizabeth m. Hudson, 3. Ann m. Thos. K. Hamsberger, 4. Columbia, 5. Fountain Taliaferro.

Fannie (Layton,) m. Wm. Price (Standardsville); Clarissa (Layton) m. Wm. Rhodes (Albemarle Co); Maria (Layton) m. Grans; Louisa (Layton) m. Thos. Garth.

II. Richard (Lewis Davis), ch. 1. Henry, 2. Elizabeth m. Mr. Story, 3. Judith m. Daniel Field, 4. Agatha m. Benj. Pendleton.

III. Charles (Lewis Davis) m. Miss Powers (1740) of Eastern Va., ch: 1. Kesia m. Geo. Freeman (Ky.), 2. Ann m. Geo. Doggett, (N. C.), 3. William m. Miss Stone, 4. Thomas m. Sarah Mitchell, 1799, 5. Charles, major, 1774—1849, m. Susan Mitchell. 6. Jas.

Ch. of Thomas and Sarah (Mitchell) Yancey m. 1800. 1. Charles 1801—1867 m. Miss Withers and removed to Tennessee; 2. John William 1803—1894, m, 1834 Jane Terrell, ch: Wm. T., m. Nannie Stevenson, ch. William; 3. Elizabeth 1806 —1841 m. Wm. Wigginton, ch. Sallie, Edmonia m. Henry Field, Benjamin m. ——————— removed to Missouri; Susan E., 4. James Powers 1804—1884 m. 1845, Mary Coons, and had Jas. Wm., m. Florence Miller, ch. Ethel, James and Wm. 5. Benjamin b. 1809 m. 1839 Catherine Banks, dau. of Dr. Wm. Tunstal Banks, of Madison C. H., 6. Kesia Ann (1812—1881) m. Edward Lightfoot, 7. Susan.

Ch. of Benj. Mitchell Yancey and Catherine (Banks Yancey).

1. Pamela Somerville m. Capt. Joseph D. Brown, ch: 1. Mary Catherine m. Rufus T. Carpenter, and had Stacy Harris, Joseph Daniel, Ellie Florence, Frank Hill and Leslie Pamela. 2. Lily Banks m. Thomas M. Henry, Atty. at Pittsburg, and had Lucy Maxwell, Pamela Brown, 3. Josephene m. J. Benj. Flippen, (Cumberland Co.) and had Sue Gray, Elise Josephene, Marjorie Pamela, 4. Benjamin Armistead m. Frances Todd Faunt LeRoy, King and Queen county, and had Virginius Faunt Le Roy, Joseph Daniel, Juliet Faunt LeRoy, 4. Andrew Edward, 6. Gertrude Pamela m. John Bannister Sparrow, of Danville Va., 7. Florence Armistead m. Oliver G. Flippen (Cumberland county.)

2. Edward Duke.

3. Dr. Chas. Kavanaugh, U. S. N.

4. Mary Crimora m. Jno. W. Payne ch. Mary Catherine, Emma Carson, Fannie Keith, Crimora Yancey.

5. Sallie Thomas m. Jno. W. Payne.

IV. Philip (Lewis Davis) ch: 1. Lewis, 2. Philip, 3. Richard, 4. Jechanias, 5. Achilles, 6. Robert, 7. Kavanaugh, 8. Polly m. Jones Menefee. 9. Delpha m. Henry Menefee, 10. Mary Ann m. Wm. Johnson.

V. Robert (Lewis Davis) m. Miss Holliday. He was a Captain in the Revolutionary War.

VI. James (Lewis Davis) was a Maj. in Gen. Greene's army in the Revolutionary War, and after the War he settled in Western South Carolina, and practised law; he m. a Miss Cudworth, of Charleston, and had Benj. Cudworth Yancey m. Caroline Bird, dau. of Col. Wm. Bird, of the "Ariary," Warren Co. Ga., having Wm. Lowndes, (the "Orator of Secession," the "fire eater" as he was termed in the invective of those days), and Benjamin Cudworth

Wm. Lowndes Yancey m. Sarah Caroline Earle, dau. of Geo. Washington Earle, of Ga., and had 1. Col. Wm. Earle m. ——— ch: Virginia m. Mr. Besson; 2. Ellen m. Hon. W. H. Skaggs; 3. Mary m. Claude Preston Lewis; 4. Martha; 5. Eva Cubet; 6. Wm. Lowndes; 7. Benjamin Cudworth; 8. Dalton Huger; 9. Goodloe Harper, 10. ———, wife of Jno. L. Harrett.

VII. Lewis (Lewis Davis) ch. Geo., Garland, Mary m. Thompson Tutt, Ibly m. Lewis Tutt

VIII. Nancy, (Lewis Davis) m. Nalle.

IX. daughter, (Lewis Davis) m. Nalle.

THE BROWN FAMILY.

John Brown m. Elizabeth Brown,)his cousin; her mother was a Miss Coleman), and had: I. John married 1st. Sallie Gibbs 2nd. Phoebia Brown II. Capt. Daniel, received pension for services in Revolutionary war and was High Sheriff, m. Elizabeth Hill, dau. of Wm. Hill, and Miss Wood, his wife, and g. dau. of Russell Hill and Miss Towles, his wife, of Middlesex Co. III. Thomas m. Susan Powell, of Prince Edward County. IV. Wm. m. Miss Vaughan and moved to Tennessee.

Children of Daniel Brown and Elizabeth Hill, his wife: I. William m. Mary Griffin. II. John m. Sarah Hill, ch.: 1. Wm. 2. Dr. Mordica m. Nancy Henry Hill. 3. Adaline m. Rev. Dudley, and had 1. Sallie m. H.L. Staples, 4. Jane m. Col. Hamlin, Dinwiddie county, dau. Ella m. Henry Lovitt, ch. John, Harry, Jane. 5. Armistead. 6. Sarah m. Bernard Todd, dau. Sarah m. Banks, Baltimore. ch. Ed. and Sarah. 7. Robert m. Sallie Walker, lives in Dinwiddie Co.

III. Armistead m. Mary Ann Russell Meredith, of Middlesex County, dau. of Jos. Meredith and Mary Baptist, his wife, and had

1. Capt. Joseph Daniel m. Pamela Somerville Yancey, ch. Mary Catherine m. Rufus T. Carpenter. ch : Stacy Harris, Joseph Daniel, Ellie Florence, Frank Hill, Leslie Pamela. 2. Lily Banks m. Thomas M. Henry, Attorney, Pittsburg, ch. Lucy Maxwell, Pamela Brown. 3. Josephine m. J. Benj. Flippen, clerk, Cumberland Co. ch.: Sue Gray, Elise Josephine, Marjorie Pamela. 4. Benjamin Armistead m. Frances Todd Faunt Le Roy, of King and Queen County. ch: Virginius Faunt Le Roy, Joseph Daniel, Juliet Faunt Le Roy. 5. Andrew Edward. 6. Gertrude Pamela, m. John Bannister Sparrow. 7. Florence Armistead m. Oliver G. Flippen, Treas. Cumb. Co.

2nd. John Armistead, 3rd. Wm. Russell, 4th. Andrew J.

5th. Caroline Elizabeth m. John James Porter, artist of Beaver, Pa. ch. 1. Wm. Armistead m. Nannie Francisco, ch.: Robt. Francisco. 2. Mary Eliza m. C. Louis Dohme, Chemist, Baltimore, ch.: Carolyn Louise. 3. Frederick Eugene. 4. Ernest Clifton. 5. John James. 6. Eva Byron.

IV. Thomas Coleman m. Frances Griffin. ch: 1. Virginia Ann. 2. Martha m. Wm. Lewis. 3. Emily m. Madison Duncan, ch.: Martha Hill, Edwina, Mary Catherine, Julia, Ella, John, Bettie, Virginia, Olivia, Fannie, Edward, Franklin. 4. Jno. Wm. m. Miss Rector of Texas. 5. Julia Frances m. Robt. Covington. 6. Betsy Coleman. 7. Burgess m. Miss Lewis. 8. Mary Russell m. Rev. A. H. Spilman; ch.: 1. Hamilton. 2. Nellie m. Prof. R.W. Tinsley. 3. Coleman.

V. Daniel m. Lucy Powell, of Prince Edward Co., and had. 1. Sarah Bumbrey; 2. Robert m. Susan Coons, ch.: Sallie Bumbrey, Charles m. Miss Button, Ryland, Roberta m. Smith, Jennie m. Henry Coons, Wm. Hill m. Daisy Hoff, 3. Elizabeth Ann m. Jas. O. Harris, lived in Atlanta, ch.: Dr. Nathan, Clem m. Miss Dick, Dan. m. Miss Tucker, 4. Dr. Walter A. m. Jane Allen, 5. Armistead Hill m. Mit Chapman.

VI. Russell.

VII. Frances m. Wm. Slaughter, ch: 1. Lucy m. Washington Pendleton; 2. Elizabeth m. Mason Bohannon; 3. Daniel m. Mary Berry, 4. Frances m. Wm. Robson, ch. Wm., John, James, Annie, 5. Catherine m. Wm. Armistead, ch. John Ringold, Luther, Annie, Edward, 6. Albert m. Miss Abbott.

VIII. Mary Ann m. Newman Allen, ch: 1. Jane m. Dr. Walter Brown, 2. Elizabeth m. Edward Burgess, ch. Armistead, and Mary Catherine m. W. H. Eggborn, having Jackson m. Robert Jones, Armistead, Bessie m. Thomas Q. Thompson, 3. Walter m. Carrie Quaintance, ch. Carroll, Bessie, May, Reva, 4. Edward m. Lula Butler, of Baltimore, two children, 5. Jennie m. Gen. A. S. Roberts ch. Allen, 6. Ida m. Jacob S. Eggborn, ch. George, Elizabeth.

THE THOM FAMILY.

The first member of the Thom family, of whom we can trace any definite record was Alexander Thom, a native of Scotland, and of the Clan of Cameron in Invernesshire.

He was born about 1720, and died in Westmoreland county, Va., 1788.

He was an officer of rank and served under the ill starred banner of the the Royal Prince, Chas. Edward Stuart, at the fatal field of Colloden moore, April 16th, 1746.

After that dreadful disaster to the cause he was a refugee and came, as so many others, to America, where he settled in Westmoreland Co., Va., where he afterwards married Miss Annie Triplett about 1768; to them were born nine sons: John, Reuben, Geo., Allen and others.

John Thom was born about 1770 in the county of Westmoreland; he removed to Culpeper county, where he resided till his death.

He was Col. of a regiment of Culpeper troops and commanded it during the second war of Independence 1812—1815. He served the State two or more terms in the General Assembly. He died 1855 (?) in the quiet of his home at Berry Hill, at the ripe age of 85. He left a large estate which was devised by will mostly to his children.

Col. John Thom was twice married; first to Miss Lucy Lewis, of Essex Co., Va.; to them were born John Catesby, who m. Miss Ada Dormman, and issue two sons: John (who died young), and William Taylor Thom.

Lucy, the daughter of Col. John Thom and his wife Miss Lucy Lewis, married Mr. Wm. Taylor, of Point Conpa Parish, Louisiana, where they lived and died childless in 186—.

The second wife of Col. John Thom was Miss Abigail DeHart Mayo, third daughter of Col. William Mayo, of Powhatan seat, Henrico county, and his his wife Elizabeth Poythress. By this marriage he had: Elizabeth Mayo, who m. Mr. Wm. Buckner Ross, of Bel Pre, Culpeper; they had five children, Dr. George Ross, of Richmond, Col. John DeHart, of Lexington, Lieut. Wm. Alexander, who was killed in the front of battle, leading a charge in 1864, Judge Erskine Mayo now a U. S. Circuit Judge in the State of California, and Mary Cameron m. and lives in Richmond.

Janet Marion Thom, born 1818, married Mr. Bartholomew Labuzan, of Mobile, Ala.; issue; Charles, Catesby, Pembroke, Anna and Elizabeth; they all reside in the far South.

Wm. Alexander Thom, born 1820, graduated in 1841 from the Medical College of Virginia. He was surgeon to the 39th Va. Infantry in 1861, and later was on the staff of the Jackson Hospital, in Richmond, during the war. He married Miss Annie Parker, of Northampton Co.; and had 1. Wm., who married —————————— and died in 1894 leaving a widow and three children; 2. Alfred, who m. ———— and has a son, Alfred Jr., 3. Marion E.

Cameron Erskine, born 1825, married three times: first Miss Beach, second Miss Henrietta Hathwell, third, her sister Miss Belle Hathwell. He moved to California early in life, where he served that State in her legislature and other capacities. Of his children little is known in the East.

Joseph Pembroke Thom, born 1828, graduated in Medicine from the University of Virginia. He served in the Mexican war, 1846, under General Wingfield Scott; he was afterwards surgeon in the U. S. Navy. At the outbreak of hostilities in 1861 he volunteered his services to his native State. While in temporary command of Wheat's batallion at the battle of Kernstown he was struck over the left breast by a minie ball, but as he was carrying a small testament in his side pocket, the force was received on it, which saved his life.

For many years he has been a resident of Baltimore, where he has been one of the Aldermen, also in the State Legislature, where he was Speaker in 1884. He married 1. Miss Ella Wright, second Mrs. Catherine Reynolds, and had several children. Abby Mayo Thom, the youngest of the family of Col. John and Abigail DeHart (Mayo), was born December 23d, 1830, at Berry Hill, Culpeper. On June 13th, 1849, she married Mr. George Warren Fitzhugh, of Fauquier, She died Nov. 21, 1859. Issue:—1. William DeHart, March 11, 1850; 2. Thomas Cameron, Nov. 27, 1851; 3. Elizabeth Bland, May 26, 1853 ; 4. John Alexander, Dec. 4, 1854; 5. Annie Blanche, Oct. 25, 1856 ; 6. Eugene Mayo, Nov. 16, 1857 ; and 7. Henry Thom, Nov. 20, 1859.

Of these William DeHart married Miss Elizabeth Carter Grayson, Oct. 18, 1871. Issue:—1. Annie Blanche, m. H. E. Hanes ; 2. Roberta Alexander, m. W. C. Boswell ; 3. Mary Lee, m. J. C. Martin ; 4. Pembroke Thom ; 5. Lena G.; 6. Wm. DeHart ; 7. John Grayson ; 8. Mayo McGill ; 9. Bessie Catlett ; 10. E. P.; 11. Abby T. Thomas Cameron, lost at sea, 1871 ; Elizabeth Bland ; John Alexander, married Miss Agnes Allen Somerby, July 11, 1889, and had Marion Stuart, June 10, 1890, (died Dec. 23, 1893); Lena Grayson, Oct. 4., 1801 ; Beulah Thornton, June 25, 1895.

THE HILL FAMILY.

The first we know of the Hill family in this county were Russell and Needless Hill, two brothers, who came from Middlesex county. Russell m. Miss Towles, of Middlesex, having Col. Harry, William and Fannie.

I. Col. Harry m. Miss Powell, having : 1. Col. Robt., m. Judy Chapman and had Wm., m. Sallie Tutt ; Robt., m. Miss Hume ; Ann, m. —— Booton, Polly ; Fannie, m. —— Thompson, of Albemarle ; 2. William, died young ; 3. Col. Harry, m. Matilda Payne, and had John P., m. Miss Terrell ; Col. Henry, m. Miss McChesney ; Andrew, m. Miss Tatum ; Thomas ; Eliza, m. A. Twyman; and Anson ; 4. John ; 5. Ambrose Powell, m. Fannie Twyman, and had Jas., Thos., m. first his cousin, Margaret Hill, second Miss Ficklin ; Dr. William A., m. Fannie Booton, having Major Booton, Anna Lee, Julia, Irvine, and Hugh ; Sara, m. Cowherd ; Eliza, m. Flint ; Frances, m. Wm. Twyman ; Henry, m. his cousin, Evelyn. 6. Maj. Thos., m. Fannie Baptist, dau. of —— Baptist and Isabell Stearns Baptist, and had James ; Theopholus ; Edward B., m. Mildred Turner; Gen. Ambrose Powell, m. a sister of Gen. John Morgan ; Margaret A., m. her cousin, Thos. Hill; Evelyn m. her cousin Henry ; Lucy m. Carter A. Saunders; 7. Fannie m Henry Field and had Henry, m. Russell Colvin ; John ; James ; Eliza, m. W. A. Roberts; Nancy m. John P. Kelly; Diana. 8. Nancy.

II. William, m. Miss Wood, having 1. Armistead, m. Miss Tazewell, and had Nancy Henry, m. Dr. Mordicai Brown ; Sallie, m. Nelson. 2. William, m. Miss Parsons. 3. Russell, m. Peggie Baptist, and had Martha, m. Mr. Wallace, and lived in Petersburg; Sara, m. Mr. Fischer, and lived in Petersburg; 4. Elizabeth, m. Capt. Daniel Brown, and had John, m. Sara Hill, having John, William,

Armistead, Adaline, m. Rev. Dudley, Jane, m., Col. Hamblin and Sara, m. Bernard Todd; William, m. Miss Griffin; Major Armistead, m. Mary A. Russell Meredith (dau. of Jos. and Mary Baptist Meredith, and grand-daughter of ——Baptist and Isabell S. Baptist), having Capt. Joseph Daniel, m. Paemla S. Yancey (see Yancey genealogy); Thos. C., m. Miss Griffin; Russell Daniel; m. Lucy Powell; Fannie, m. Wm. Slaughter; Mary Ann, m. Newman Allen. 5. Lucy, m. John Nalle, and had William, m. Miss Colvin. having William D., Armistead, and John R., m. Tetitia Wharton; Francis; Eliza: Katherine; Martha m. Alfred Lewis having Jane; Polly Russell, m. Henry Field; 6. Nancy, m. Geo. Roberts, having a son who married Eliza Field.

III. Fannie, m. William Booton, and had John, m. Ann P. Hill, having Richard; William; Harry; Sinclair, m. Mary Field; Martha m. ——Kirtley; Fannie, m. —— Lipscomb.

THE THOMPSON FAMILY.

[By Judge John W. Jones, of Bowling Green, Ky., June, 1900.]

The oldest Thompson of whom anything is accurately and definitely known was William, who moved from England to the United States, and settled in Hanover county, Va. somewhere near the middle of the eighteenth century. January 29, 1771, he married Frances Mills, by whom he had the following children: 1. Peggy, born February 6. 1772; 2. Charles, born March 7, 1773; 3. William Mills, born January 11, 1775; 4. Anne, born June 18, 1777; 5. Sarah Mills, born Dec. 15, 1779; 6. Mary Anne, born Dec. 1, 1732; 7. Frances J., born Dec. 29, 1784; 8. Edmond, born April 11, 1787; 9. Nathaniel, born August 25. 1789.

With the exception of William Mills Thompson and his descendants, but little is known of the other children of William Thompson and his wife, Frances Mills.

William Mills Thompson was married twice: First to Catherine (Kitty) W. Broaddus; second to Mildred T. Ball, a grand-niece of George Washington. By his first wife he had the following children: 1. Richard Wigginton Thompson, born June 9, 1809; 2d. Mary Juliet Thompson, born Dec. 14, 1811; 3. Martha Frances Thompson, born Dec. 8, 1814; 4. William Mills Thompson, born Dec. 6, 1816.

By his second wife, William Mills Thompson had the following children: 1. Catherine Mildred Thompson, born Aug. 9, 1822; 2. George Washington Thompson, born Jan. 7, 1825; 3. Margaret Anne Thompson, born July 25, 1827.

May 5, 1836, Richard W. Thompson married Harriet E. Gardiner, a cultured and most estimable lady, of Columbus, Ohio, who bore him six children, as follows: 1. Mary Gardiner Thompson; 2. Frederick S. Thompson: 3. Richard W. Thompson; 4. Charles Thompson; 5. Harry G. Thompson; 6. Virginia Thompson; all living except Charles who died several years ago. Frederick Thompson married Rachel Durham. They have one child, a boy named William Mills. Richard W. Thompson, Jr., married Mrs. Mary A. Barry. They have no children. Virginia Thompson married Judge David W. Henry, and has two children, Harriett and Richard W. Mary G. and Harry are unmarried.

Mary Juliet Thompson, the second child of William Mills and Kitty W. Thompson, married Anthony Addison. Their children were as follows: 1. John F.; 2. Sallie C.; 3. Mollie A.; 4. Murray; 5. Arthur; 6. Olivia; 7. Anthony C.; 8. Keturah L. John F. joined the Confederate States' army and was killed at Williamsburg, Va. He never married. Sallie C. married twice; first Capt. Clement C. West, U. S. A., by whom she had one child, Mollie A. After the death of her first husband, Mrs. West married Capt. George A. Mitchell, U. S. A. They had no children. Her daughter by her first marriage married Capt. Cornelius Wilcox, U. S. A., and had no children.

Mollie A., daughter of Anthony and Mary T. Addison, married Rev. T. O. Ingle, and had a number of children, all of whom are dead except three, Maria, James A., and Mary. Maria married Randall Webb and has one child, Mary. James A. is also married, and has one child. Mary, daughter of T. G. and M. A. Ingle is unmarried. Murray Addison, son of Anthony and Mary T. Addison, married Clara Gantt. They have no children. Arthur, son of Anthony and and Mary T. Addison, married Carrie Steel, and has no children. Olivia C. Addison has never married. Anthony C. Addison is unmarried. Keturah L., the youngest child of Anthony and Mary T. Addison, married, Capt. R. E. Cobb, U. S. A., and has three children, Elsie, Zodie and Murray.

Martha Frances Thompson, third child of William Mills and Kitty Wigginton Thompson, married Samuel Campbell, cashier of the Leesburg, Virginia, bank. Nearly fifty years ago they moved to Louisville, Ky. They have had six children : William T., Mary C., Antionette A., Phillip S., Robert G., and Fanny C.; all of whom are living except William T., who died soon after the removal of his parents to Louisville. Mary has never married. Antionette A. married Edgar Lyttleton, and has four children, Frank C., Edgar L., Richard C., and Samuel C., all single. Phillip S. married Lizzie Milton. They had two children : Laura and Phillip S. Jr., the former of whom is dead. Robert G. married twice : First, Nannie Browder ; second, Pattie Robb. His first wife died childless.. His second wife left two children, Anite and Granville. Fanny C., the youngest child of Samuel and Martha Frances Campbell, married George A. Newman. of Louisville, Ky. They have four children, Martha C., Charlotte, Ethel and George. With the exception of the latter, all are single. He married Mabel Payne. They have one child, George Alexander.

William Mills Thompson Jr., the fourth child of William Mills and Kitty W. Thompson, married Mary T. Barker, of Baltimore, Md. They had four children: Margaret H., Catherine. (Kitty) B., John B., and William M. Margaret H. married Johnson V. Middleton, and had no children. Catherine, (Kitty) B., m. Francis E. Storm, and had one child, Kate B.; John B. Thompson married Ida McClery. They have two children, Morven, and William M. Morven is unmarried. William M. married Evangeline Munson. They have one child.

As has been already stated, the second wife of William Mills Thompson was Mildred Ball. By this marriage he had three children : Kitty, George W., and Margaret. Kitty married Richard Lyttleton, of Loudoun county, Va., and had no children. George married Sarah Bryant, daughter of Judge W. T. Bryant, of Rockville, Ind., and had two children : Margaret A., and George L. Margaret A. married Dr. W. N. Wirt, and has no children. Geo. L. married Nettie Clark. They have no children. Margaret Sr., married F. S. T. Ronald, of Louisville, Ky.. and died childless.

Of the many who have borne the name of Thompson, RICHARD WIGGINTON THOMPSON, like Saul among his people, stands forth pre-eminently. His life was so long, his honors so many, his ability so great, his person so handsome, and his manners so winning, that, even in a genealogical history like this, he demands more than a mere passing notice.

Born in Culpeper county, Va., June 9th, 1809, he received the usual education, in the schools of that early day. When about twenty years old, he made a trip to Kentucky, to look after some lands located in the Southern portion of the state, in which the Ball heirs, one of whom was the second wife of his father, had an interest. Having attended to this, he went to Louisville, where he obtained a situation as clerk in a dry goods store, which he retained a little more than a year, when he gave it up and left for Bedford, Ind., where he secured a similar position, and borrowing some books from a friend, commenced reading law at night and during such leisure moments in the day as he could snatch from his regular vocation.

In 1834 he obtained a license, and began the practice of his profession. The same year, and the following one he was elected to the lower branch of the Indiana Legislature. In 1836 he was elected to the State Senate. In the exciting Log Cabin and Hard Cider campaign of 1840, he was a Presidential elector on the Whig ticket, and made a number of speeches in support of Harrison and Tyler, in which he displayed no little oratorical ability. The same year he was elected to Congress, and re-elected in 1847, declining the nomination in 1850. He also declined the Mission to Austria tendered him by President Taylor the following year. When Mr. Fillmore, by the death of General Taylor, became President, Col. Thompson was offered the position of Commissioner of the General Land Office, which he also declined.

In 1877 he was tendered the position of Secretary of the Navy by President Hayes, which he accepted, and continued to discharge the duties of the office for nearly four years, when he resigned to accept the position of Vice-President of the Panama Canal Company, receiving for his services the handsome salary of $25,000 per annum. This place he held nearly eight years. Col. Thompson also held other positions of trust and profit, among them that of Circuit Judge, the duties of which office he discharged for a number of years. Besides the public positions held and declined by Col. Thompson, and his attractiveness and eloquence as a public speaker, he was also a forceful and graceful writer, having during his life written and published a number of works; of the list, one against Catholicism, another on the tariff, and still another containing his recollections of the Presidents and other public men, one of the most attractive and readable books issued from the press for years.

In politics as already intimated, Col. Thompson was originally an "Old Line Whig," and in addition to his canvass in support of Harrison, in 1840, took an active and prominent part in that of the "Great Commoner" in 1844.

Upon the disbandment of the Whig party, Col. Thompson united with the Republicans, with whom he continued to act as long as he lived, attending their conventions, framing many of their platforms and supporting their nominees in speeches of great force and eloquence. At the regular meetings of the party every four years to nominate a candidate for President, few men attracted more attention than Col. Thompson; his snow-white head, his brilliant, black eye, his easy and graceful carriage, united with a bright and sunny smile, never failing to make him one of the men of mark in those great assemblies.

In private life, Col. Thompson's character was as pure and spotless as his public life was distinguished and honorable. An affectionate husband, a kind and indulgent father, a true and constant friend, a liberal and public spirited citizen, he commanded the respect and esteem of all classes and conditions of people.

If one wishes to know who a man is, read the newspapers. If one desires to ascertain WHAT he is, ask those with whom he is thrown from day to day—his friends and neighbors. It does not always follow that a man's reputation from home and his character at home go hand in hand. This, however, was literally true of Col. Thompson. Popular as he was with strangers, he was no less honored and esteemed by his own people—the people of Terre Haute, where he had so long lived, and where he so recently died at the advanced age of ninety, crowned with years and honors, and presenting the anomaly of having known and conversed with more Presidents than any one living, and of having outlived all his colleagues in the Congress of 1841.

The Rev. William Taliaferro Thompson, of Charleston, S. C., grandson of Merriwether Thompson and Martha S. (Patsy) Broaddus, a sister of Kitty W. Broaddus, who married William Mills Thompson, Sr., furnishes the following concerning the descendants of his grandfather, who was a cousin of William Mills Thompson.

"Merriwether Thompson and Martha S. Broaddus were married 14th. Oct., 1815, at Maj. Wm. Broaddus' residence in Culpeper county, Va., by the Rev. John Woodville; issue :
1. William Broaddus Thompson, b. 8th. of Aug., 1816, m. Catherine M. Stribling; 2. Martha Ann Thompson, b. 31st of July, 1818; 3. Juliet Elizabeth Kitty Thompson, b. 26th July, 1820, m. John J. Abell; 4. Mary Harriet Thompson, b. 10th July, 1822; 5. Sarah Woodville Thompson, b. 3rd April, 1824; 6. Merriwether Thompson, Jr., (Gen. of Confed. fame) b. 22nd Jan. 1826, at Harper's Ferry, Va; 7. Charles Montgomery Thompson, b. 12th Oct., 1830, at Harper's Ferry, Va.
William Broaddus Thompson married Miss Catherine M. Stribling, dau. of Taliaferro Stribling and Mary Tate, and had three children : 1. William Taliaferro Thompson; 2. Martha Thompson; 3. Magnus Stribling Thompson."

THE JONES FAMILY.
[By Judge John W. Jones—June, 1900.]

It is no easy task to write the genealogical history of any family with any degree of accuracy. To write that of the Smiths or Joneses, if carried any distance into the past, is an impossibility. There are so many different families of these names, in no way related to each other, that a person who attempts a sketch of any special one, will meet with the same difficulty encountered by a traveller in a strange section when coming to a number of roads leading in the same direction, yet none of them containing a finger-board to inform him which particular one he should take, in order to reach his point of destination.

When the particular Jones family with which this sketch has to deal first came to the United States, where it located, and what was its origin, whether English or Welsh, is not certainly known. It is believed, however, that it is of English extraction, and settled in Essex county, Virginia, somewhere near the beginning of the 18th. century, if not earlier; some of its members moving thence to Culpeper about the time of the organization of that county in 1748. At any rate, the records of Culpeper show that Gabriel Jones commanded one of the eight companies, furnished by the county for the war of the Revolution; that previous to its commencement, he had twice married, first Ann Waller, who bore him one child, a daughter named Ann, who married William Scott, and moved to Lynchburg, Virginia. They had four children : Gabriel, Robert, Waller and Hugh. The records also show that Capt. Jones' second wife was Martha Slaughter, daughter of Robert Slaughter, the elder, the first Church Warden of St. Marks' Parish, by whom he had four children : Robert, Francis, Gabriel and Mary.

Robert and Francis emigrated to Kentucky, about the year 1820, the former locating in Adair county, and the latter in Warren county, near Bowling Green. Of Roberts' descendants, little or nothing is known.

Francis married Hetty Coons and left several daughters and two sons, William and Cuthbert. William married Mary Mooklar, by whom he had four children : Maria, Sarah E., Mary B., and Frank A. Maria married James E. Harney; Sarah E. married Temple Smith; Mary B. married John T. Johnson; and Frank married Adda Hall. Cuthbert studied medicine; married Eliza R. Treat, and moved to Chester, Illinois, many years ago. They had eleven children, as follows : 1. Francis S.; 2. Mary E.; 3. William C.; 4. Robert S.; 5. Llewellyn Powell; 6. Eliza R. T.; 7. Edward R.; 8. James P.; 9. Peyton C.; 10. Susan T.; 11. Herbert C.

The most of these children died young and without issue; only one of them, Judge William C. Jones, of St. Louis, Mo., marrying and having any descendants. Nov. 20th, 1850, Judge Jones married Mary A. Chester. They had ten children, of whom only four are living, viz: Fannie S., who married Walter S. Watson, Julia M., who married Joseph P. Goodman, James C. and Giles F., who are unmarried.

Gabriel Jones, the third son of Captain Gabriel of the Revolution, married Jane Wigginton. They had seven children: Emily, William Wigginton, Gabriel Scott, Seth Slaughter, Eliza Ann, John Wigginton and Martha Slaughter. Emily married George W. Ronald, son of William Ronald, a leading member of the Richmond, Virginia, bar in its early days, who was of counsel for the British creditors holding claims against persons residing in the United States prior to the Revolution. The children of George W. and Emily Ronald were as follows: Francis S. J., William A., Sarah J., Gabriel J., Richard W., Emily, Ann E., George W., Seth S., Mary M., John N., Harriet M., and Balsora J.

Francis S. J. Ronald, the first child of George W. and Emily Ronald, when quite a young man, left the parental home in Warren county, Ky., and settled in Louisville, where through his indomitable energy and close attention to business, he became one of its leading citizens, having during his life been Deputy Sheriff, Postmaster under Buchanan's administration, and proprietor of one of the largest and most popular tobacco warehouses in the city. He was married twice; his first wife being Mary Decantillon, and his second Margaret Thompson. By his first marriage he had three children: William A., Emma and Mary D. His second wife died childless. William A. married Lucy Grotjan, who had three children, Grotjan, Decantillon and William. Decantillon married Harding Williams and has one child: Harding. Grotjan and William are unmarried. Mary D. married D. M. Lawson, and has two children: Frankie and Cary. Frankie married William Garvin, and has one child: Volney L. Cary is still single. Emma, second child of F. S. J. and Mary Decantillon Ronald, died a number of years ago, having never married.

William A. Ronald, second child of George W. and Emily Ronald, like his brother Frank, located in Louisville some time previous to his having reached his majority, and like him, through his energy and business habits, he so far acquired the respect and confidence of the people as to be elected successively marshall of the city, sheriff of the county, and for many years held the position of stock agent of the Louisville and Nashville railroad. He married Mary J. Marshall, who bore him four children: Kate, Rose, Lee and Sue. Kate died young and unmarried. Rose married William Shane, and left one child: William. Lee married Benjamin E. Webb, and has three children: William, Marshall and Hugh. Sue married Andrew T. Kirby, and has one child: Mary.

Gabriel, the third child of George W. and Emily Ronald, married Lucy Moss, by whom he had three children: Ellen M., Richard, and George. Ellen M. married Columbus Smith and has four children: Clyde, Lizzie, Frederick, and Varna. Richard married Cora Shrader, and had three children: Earl, Elma, and Lee. George died young and unmarried.

Sarah J., the fourth child of George W. and Emily Ronald, died soon after reaching womanhood, having never married.

Richard W. Ronald, the fifth child of George W. and Emily Ronald, was a man of much amiability of character and excellent business capacity. For many years he was a partner of his brother Frank in Louisville's Ninth Street Tobacco Warehouse, and was a member of the firm at the time of his death. He never married.

Ann Eliza, the sixth child of George W. and Emily Ronald, married Vance Smith, and died childless.

Emily, the seventh child of George W. and Emily Ronald, never married.

George W., the eighth child of George W. and Emily Ronald, like his brothers, Frank, William, Richard and Seth, moved from Warren county, Kentucky, to Louisville when young. Not long after his arrival he commenced the study of medicine, graduating in the old medical school of that city in 1849, when he at once opened an office and commenced the practice of his profession. By assidious attention to his duties, and success in their performance, in the course of time he built up a large and lucrative business, and, although he has been in the harness for more than half a century, and is a man of fortune, he continues to practice, insisting that "it is better to wear out than to rust out." He married Laura Glover, daughter of William R. Glover, a prominent and wealthy citizen of Louisville. Doctor and Mrs. Ronald have but one child, Albert G., who is a graduate of the Louisville city schools, and also of the University of Virginia. By profession he is a lawyer, and a partner of his father-in-law, Judge A. E. Richards, having married his daughter, Jessie, several years ago. Albert G. and Jessie Ronald have two children: George and Mary T.

Mary M., the ninth child of George W. and Emily Ronald, married twice. First: Thomas B. Dent, by whom she had one child: Thomas B. Dent, Jr. Her present husband is Edwin Talbutt, a man of quiet and unobtrusive habits, but of good intellect and extensive reading. They have no children. Thomas B. Dent, Jr., married Laura Smith. They have four children: William, Lucien, Paul and Percy.

Seth S., the tenth child of George W. and Emily Ronald, married twice. First: Lizzie Herbert; secondly: Amelia Forsyth. His first wife bore him seven children: George, Herbert, Laura, Mollie, Florence S., Lavinia, and Frank. George, Herbert, Laura and Lavinia are dead. Mollie married Joseph C. Barclay, and has one child: Florence. Florence S. married William F. Owsley, a grandson of one of the Governors of Kentucky. William F. and Florence S. Owsley had five children: Erasmus B., Herbert R., Elizabeth B., William B., and Frank. Herbert R. is the only one living. Lavinia, third child of S. S. and Elizabeth Ronald, died single. Frank, their youngest child, has never married. Amelia, the second wife of Seth S. Ronald, left one child, who died in infancy.

Harriet M., the eleventh child of George W. and Emily Ronald, married Alexander C. Stevenson, and has two children: Emily and William. Emily married Thomas Berger, and has no children. William married Ophelia Ellis, and has five children: Frank L., J. H., Lena P., Eula B., and H. Ronald.

John N. the twelfth child of George W. and Emily Ronald, married Elizabeth Still. They have an only child: James.

Balsora J., the thirteenth child of George W. and Emily R. Ronald, married Thomas Rockwell, and has six children: Eula, Herbert, Ronald, Ida, Thomas and Laura D. Ronald married Ida Campbell. They have five children: Herbert, Ronald, Ruby D., William, and Thomas. Ida married Charles R. Ousley, and has no children. Laura married Judson L. Price, and is childless.

William Wigginton Jones, the second child of Gabriel Jones and Jane Wigginton, was born August 20, 1795, married Elizabeth Farish October 31, 1822, and died March 11, 1855, leaving seven children. In 1812, when the war between the United States and Great Britain commenced, Mr. Jones enlisted as a soldier, and his widow drew a pension up to the time of her death, November 16, 1882. His children were as follows: John William, Robert Henry, Thomas Wigginton, James Farish, Strother Seth, Gabriel Scott, and Mildred Jane.

John William, the first child of William W. and Elizabeth Jones, left Culpeper county for Louisville, Kentucky, when only fifteen years of age, and for three years served as clerk in the hardware store of his uncle, John Wigginton Jones. He then returned to Virginia and attended school for several years. Returning to Louisville, he began the study of law, graduating in 1851 at the law school of that city. The following year he commenced the practice of his profession at Rockville, Indiana, where he remained for two years, when he removed to Terre Haute, of which city and the county of Vigo, he was elected Common Pleas Judge in 1856. For the last twenty years he has resided at Bowling Green, Kentucky, where he has been engaged in newspaper work in the capacity of editorial writer.

Robert Henry, the second son of William Wigginton and Elizabeth Jones, was a private in the Confederate army, and was killed in Missouri in 1862.

Thomas Wigginton, third son of William Wigginton and Elizabeth Jones, is a farmer and has also served as Commissioner of the Revenue. October 16, 1851, he married Mildred D. Hansbrough, by whom he had the following children: William Wigginton, John Wesley, Mary Long, Thomas Benjamin, Emma Stevens, William Wigginton, Hervey Slaughter, and Annie Howard. William W., John W., Mary L., and Annie Howard are dead. Hervey S. married Bessie Irvine. They have one child: John Irvine. Thomas B., Emma S., and William W. are all unmarried.

James Farish, the fourth son of William Wigginton and Elizabeth Jones, was by profession a physician, graduating at the old medical school in Louisville in 1855. When the war between the States commenced, he volunteered as a private in the Brandy Rifles. In 1863 he was captured and sent to Point Lookout, where he remained until he was exchanged as a sick prisoner. At the time of his exchange his health was so poor that he could get no further than Richmond, where he died April 26, 1864.

Strother S., the fifth son of William Wigginton and Elizabeth Jones, has at different periods of his life been a farmer, school teacher, Commissioner of the Revenue, and soldier. When the war commenced he enlisted as a private in the Black Horse company, and was present at the first and last battles of that long and bloody struggle. He married Lucy Stewart, and has three chilchildren: Betty, Susan, and Mary. Betty married Arthur Hart, and has five children: Meta R., Alexander, Bessie, Susan, and Strother H. Susan married James Matthews, and has two children: Seth and Stewart. Mary is unmarried.

Gabriel Scott, the sixth son of William Wigginton and Elizabeth Jones, was, by profession, a lawyer, graduating at the Louisville Law School in 1854. He commenced the practice in Rockville, Indiana, moving thence to Terre Haute, and thence to Dubuque, Iowa, where he was residing when the war began. Coming to Culpeper he joined the Brandy Rifles as a private in the ranks, and continued in service until the surrender. In 1866 he resumed the practice of his profession, locating at Rodney, Mississippi, where he remained a few years, removing thence to Texas, and died at Beaumont, in that State, March 23, 1899.

Mildred Jane, the seventh child and only daughter of William Wigginton and Elizabeth Jones, resided with her mother until the death of the latter, which occurred at Culpeper Court House November 16, 1882.

Of the seven children of William Wigginton and Elizabeth Jones, only two, Thomas and Strother, ever married.

Eliza Ann, the third child of Gabriel and Jane Jones, died unmarried in Warren county, Kentucky, in 1847.

Seth Slaughter, the fourth child of Gabriel and Jane Jones, moved from Culpeper county, Virginia, to Warren county, Kentucky, about 1836, and settled on a farm near Bowling Green. He was a man of much amiability of character and popular with all classes of people. He married Elizabeth Briggs, and had two children: William Henry and Mary M. William Henry began his business life as a clerk in a store in Bowling Green. He also served as clerk of the common council of that city for a number of years. In 1885, when Charles H. Thomas was appointed United States Circuit Judge of South Dakota, he received the appointment of clerk of that court, and removed to Deadwood in that territory, returning to Bowling Green at the expiration of Judge Thomas' term of office. In 1897 he was elected clerk of the Circuit Court of Warren county for six years, the duties of which office he is now discharging. He married Mattie Robinson and has two children: Elsie and William Henry. Mary married John Turpin, and has three children: Redford T., William H., and Perrin Slaughter.

Gabriel Scott, the fifth child of Gabriel and Jane Jones, soon after reaching his majority, moved from Culpeper county, Virginia, to Louisville, Kentucky, where he continued to reside until his death. During the greater part of his life, he held some office under the city, generally that of constable or collector of taxes. He married Hetty Camp. They had four children: William Edward, Gabriel Ambrose, Robert C., and Eliza.

William Edward, the first child of Gabriel Scott and Hetty Jones, was a Lieutenant in the Mexican War, and a Captain in the Confederate army. In 1862, while leading his company in a charge through the streets of Glasgow, Kentucky, he was killed. He married Kate Franklin, of Louisville, and left several children, whose names are unknown.

Gabriel Ambrose, the second child of Gabriel Scott and Hetty Jones, commenced the discharge of the active duties of life as a constable. He afterwards engaged in the livery business in which he was engaged at the time of his death in 1898. He married Lottie Ellis, who bore him five children: Frank, Hugh, Ellis, Norton and Mary Lee, all of whom are living, except Ellis.

Robert Camp Jones, the third child of Gabriel Scott and Hetty Jones, was for a number of years, and at the time of his death, an excellent and popular teacher in the public schools of the city of Louisville. He was twice married. The name of his first wife was Anna Barrel. The name of his second, Anna Kirby. Each had one child. The name of the child of the first wife is May Esther. That of the second wife, Bertie.

Eliza, the fourth child of Gabriel Scott and Hetty Jones, married William Ellis, and had three children: Jessie, William T., and Fay.

John Wigginton, the sixth child of Gabriel and Jane Jones, before arriving of age, left Culpeper county and located at Louisville, Kentucky, where he obtained a situation in a dry goods store. In 1838 he purchased a stock of hardware and commenced business for himself, which he conducted for a few years, when he returned to Virginia, and married Mary Eliza Valentine, a most estimable lady, the daughter of Edward Valentine, of Staunton, Virginia, and his only child. The fruit of this marriage was six children: Susan Archer, Sally Anderson, Edward Valentine, Ella Jane, Mary Eliza, and Anna Rosa. Edward Valentine is an Episcopal minister and has charge of two churches, one in Albemarle county, the other in the county of Louisa. He married Mary Smith Ruffin, and has four children: Edward Valentine, Edmund Ruffin, Mary Ruffin, and Susan. Ella Jane married Richard B. Richardson, and has no children. None of the other daughters have married.

His first wife having died, John Wigginton Jones married Marion Stuart Alexander, who bore him five children: Julia Manderville, John Stuart, Martha Slaughter, Gustavus Alexander, and Ashton Blair. Of the children two are married: Julia Manderville and Alexander Augustus, the former having married Charles Stuart Mayo, who died without issue, and the latter Mary E. Scott, who has two children: Elvira Scott and Gustavus Alexander.

Martha Slaughter, the seventh and youngest child of Gabriel and Jane Jones, married Wesley H. Perkins, who died from cholera in 1849. They had no children.

Mary, the only daughter of the Revolutionary soldier, Captain Gabriel Jones, and his wife, Martha Slaughter, was a woman of many excellent qualities, both of mind and heart. Marrying, early in life, Richard Young Wigginton, a man of considerable fortune, who died childless soon after their marriage, having no children of her own, she was enabled to become a mother to the children of others. How well she discharged this self imposed duty is well attested by the care and attention she bestowed upon a number of her half neices and nephews, grandchildren of her mother, Martha Jones, and her second husband, William Broadus, two of whom, William H. Ward, and Martha F. Thompson, she adopted and educated, the former living with her as long as she lived, and the latter until her marriage, which took place at her home. Besides these two, there were several others, whose mothers bore the name of Broaddus, among them the late R. W. Thompson, who, after the death of their mothers, always found a home at this kind hearted old lady's residence, and received substantial legacies from her at her death.

Stern and exacting, where principle was involved, this excellent old woman, in what she regarded as the non-essentials, was yielding and indulgent. Not only was she kind and generous to her relations, but a good and true friend to the poor, and one who sympathized with them in their trials and misfortunes, and at all times stood ready, with willing hand and open purse, to minister to their comforts, and relieve their wants. Years ago she went to her eternal reward, and her body is interred in the old family graveyard, near the homestead where she so long and so well performed her deeds of thoughtful and unpretentious generosity and kindness. The old house too, which was once the scene of the performance of so many good deeds, is also gone, and another and more modern one occupies its place, but the fragrance of the memory of its inmate and owner, is still fresh in the minds of the few who are left to recall and relate the story of her many virtues and excellencies. The old Wigginton place is now owned and occupied by Mr. S. W. Thompson.

AMBROSE POWELL HILL,
LIEUTENANT—GENERAL, CONFEDERATE STATES ARMY.

Ambrose Powell Hill, a lineal descendant of Captain Ambrose Powell, a vestryman of Bromfield parish in 1752, and the son of Maj. Thomas Hill, was born in Culpeper county November 9, 1825. He entered West Point Academy July 1, 1842, and graduated thence July 1, 1847, the fifteenth in merit in a class of thirty-six, among whom were Generals John S. Mason, O. B. Wilcox, H. G. Gibson, A. E. Burnside, John Gibbon, R. B. Ayers, Charles Griffin, Thomas H. Neill, W. W. Barnes, E. L. Viele, and L. C. Hunt, of the United States Army, and General Harry Heth, of the Confederate Army. Entering the First Artillery as Brevet Second Lieutenant, Hill became First Lieutenant September 4, 1851. He was engaged during the Mexican war at Huamantla the 9th of October, and at Atlixas the 12th of October, 1847, and in Florida against the Seminole Indians in 1849—50, and from 1852 to 1855. He was an assistant on the coast survey from November, 1855, until March 1, 1861, when he resigned his commission. Upon the breaking out of hostilities between the North and South, he was chosen Colonel of the Thirteenth Virginia Regiment, which, at the first battle of Manassas, with the remainder of the command of General Joseph E. Johnston, arrived on the field just in time to secure and complete the victory of that memorable day. Colonel Hill was promoted February 26, 1862, to the rank of Brigadier-General, and by his signal gallantry at the battle of Williamsburg, in May, drew the eyes of the public upon him. He greatly distinguished himself in the sanguinary seven days battles around Richmond, commencing on the 26th of June, in command of one of the largest divisions of the Army of Richmond, and which was composed of the brigades of Anderson, Branch, Pender, Gregg, Field and Archer. At Meadow Bridge, with only a portion of his command, he made the first attack upon McClellan, and in a terrible conflict encouraged his troops by a fearless intrepidity which constantly exposed him to the fiercest fire of the enemy. Successful at this point, General Hill was placed first in the line of advance and bore the brunt of the action at Frazier's Farm, where, with his own division and one brigade of that of Longstreet, he fought and overcame a largely superior force which broke the spirit of the enemy and achieved final victory.

In this series of battles the division of Hill lost 3870 men killed and wounded Immediately after this battle General Hill was promoted, July 14, 1862, to the rank of Major-General. In the campaign of Northern Virginia the division of A. P. Hill was sent to reinforce Stonewall Jackson, who had been dispatched to check the advance of Pope. At the battle of Cedar Run, Hill gallantly sustained the prestige he had won. He also bore a conspicuous part in subsequent operations, marching with Jackson in his flank movement towards the Rappahannock and Manassas. At the second battle of Manassas he repeated a similar exhibition of valor to that of Frazier's Farm, and with dauntless abandon met and repulsed at the point of the bayonet six distinct and separate assaults of the enemy, a majority of the men a portion of the time being without cartridges. The next day (August 30, 1862), his division was again engaged, and late in the evening drove the enemy before them, capturing two batteries, many prisoners, and resting at night on Bull Run. At Sharpsburg the accomplishment of A. P. Hill was in brilliancy not surpassed by any other recorded during the war. With three brigades, numbering scarce 2,000 men, he drove back Burnside's Corps, 15,000 strong.

After the battle of Sharpsburg, when General Lee determined to withdraw from Maryland, Hill was directed with his division to cover the retreat of the army, and in the performance of this duty at Botlers Ford, on the 20th of September, 1862, was enacted one of the most terrible episodes of the war. Lee's army was well across the Potomac when it was found that some brigades of the enemy had ventured to cross during the preceeding night and were making preparations to hold their position. General Jackson at once ordered A. P. Hill to drive the enemy back. After some preliminary movements a simultaneous charge was made by Hill, and the enemy forced in a confused mass into the river. "Then writes General Hill, describing the action with graphic horror, "commenced the most terrible slaughter this war has yet witnessed. The broad surface of the Potomac WAS BLUE WITH THE FLOATING CORPSES OF OUR FOE. But few escaped to tell the tale. By their own account they lost 3,000 men killed and drowned from one brigade alone. In this battle Hill did not use a piece of artillery; but relying upon the musket and bayonet, he punished the enemy beyond precedent. At the battle of Fredericksburg, Hill's Division formed the right of Jackson's force, at Chancellorsville the center, and participated in the flank movement that crushed Hooker.

The death of the illustrious Jackson devolved the command upon Hill, and he was soon after wounded. Upon the reorganization of Lee's army he was made, May 24, 1863, a Lieutenant-General, and placed in command of the third of the three corps into which it was divided. His was the first corps in action at Gettysburg. In Lee's flank movement of the same to get between Meade and Washington City, A. P. Hill sustained the only reverse of his career. Having fallen upon a superior force of the enemy at Bristoe Station, concealed by a railroad embankment, in a vain effort to dislodge it he lost several hundred in killed and wounded, and five pieces of artillery. In the momentous campaign of 1864 General Hill was again conspicuous, his corps, with that of Ewell, opening the action in the Wilderness. A few days thereafter his feeble health so gave away that he was unable to remain on duty, when Jubal A. Early was assigned to the command of his corps. After the scenes of Spotsylvania Court House, General Hill reported for duty, resumed command of his corps, and fought with it to the last day in front of Petersburg. August 25, 1864, at Reames Station, he attacked the enemy in his entrenchments and carried his entire lines, capturing seven stand of colors, 2,000 prisoners and nine pieces of artillery.

At the final attack on the Southside Railroad and the defense of Petersburg, he was restlessly active in his exertions to repel the Federal attack. On the morning of April 2, 1865, desiring to obtain a nearer view of a portion of the line of the enemy, he left his staff behind him in a place of safety, rode forward accompanied by a single orderly, and soon came upon a squad of Federals who had advanced along a ravine far beyond their lines. He immediately ordered them to surrender, which they were on the point of doing, under the supposition that a column of troops was just behind him. But soon discovering that he was slightly attended, they fired upon him, and he fell, pierced through the heart by a rifle ball.. The following night his body was hastily buried in the cemetery at Petersburg, but was subsequently reinterred in Hollywood Cemetery, Richmond, where his remains are marked by the words, "Lt-Gen. A. P. Hill," cut into the granite curbing in front of the grave. The trust reposed in A. P. Hill by the illustrious chieftains, Lee and Jackson, found solemnly impressive exemplification in the dying ejaculations of each, which, too, are remarkable for their semblance. "Tell A. P. Hill to prepare for action," were amongst the words of Stonewall Jackson. "Tell Hill he must come up," were the last words of the peerless Lee. What more honorable tribute?

CULPEPER AS A BATTLE GROUND.

IN THE WAR BETWEEN THE STATES.
CHAPTER VII.
[By Judge D. A. Grimsley.]

[Daniel Amon Grimsley, son of Rev. Barnett Grimsley and Ruth U. Grimsley, was born April 3rd, 1840, in Culpeper, now Rappahannock county, near Washington. When about twenty years old Judge Grimsley enlisted as a private in the Rappahannock cavalry, which was first commanded by Captain John Shackelford Green, and was appointed orderly sergeant soon after the company went into active service. Was elected first lieutenant upon the reorganization of the company in the spring of 1862, and within a few days thereafter became captain upon the promotion of Capt. Green, and afterwards major and lieutenant colonel of the sixth Virginia cavalry, to which the Rappahannock company belonged. He served through the entire war from April, 1861, to the surrender at Appomattox. Major Grimsley, although he had several horses shot under him, was never wounded, sick, or on furlough for more than a day or two at a time, and was in command of his regiment a greater portion of the time during the latter years of the war. Major Grimsley has an accurate memory, which, together with his thorough knowledge of military affairs, virtually renders him an oracle, and he is always sought out by those in search of information along these lines.

After the war, Judge Grimsley studied law under a private tutor, Mr. H. G. Moffett, in Rappahannock, and upon obtaining his license, began the practice of his profession at Culpeper in 1867. He was elected to the State Senate in 1869, of which body he remained a member until 1879. In 1880 he was appointed by Gov. Holliday judge of the sixth judicial circuit to fill a vacancy caused by the death of Judge Henry Shackelford. The readjuster party obtaining control of the State in 1872, he was defeated in the election for that office. In 1885 he was elected to the House of Delegates to represent Culpeper county, and in 1886 he was elected judge of the sixth judicial circuit, which position he still occupies.

In 1866, Judge Grimsley married Bettie N., daughter of William L. Browning, and has six living children, who are: Margaret, married George Drewey, Virginia, Thomas Edwin, married Mary Edelin, Mary B., married John Strode Barbour, Fanny G., and Elizabeth Barnett. Their younger child, Ethel, died a few years since of typhoid fever.—R. T. G.]

Brandy Station was the great battle ground between the cavalry of the armies of Northern Virginia, and of the Potomac, during the war between the States. It was the scene of quite a half dozen pitched battles, in which thousands of horsemen met in the rude shock of conflict.

Brandy Station was directly on the line of advance and retreat of the armies, between Washington and Richmond. A station on the Southern railway (then the Orange and Alexandria), which either army, occupying Culpeper, used for the purpose of supply. It was a point from which the road south diverged eastward to Fredericksburg, to the Wilderness and the lower Rapidan, and westward to Madison and Orange; going north, they diverged westward towards Warrenton and upper Fauquier, and eastward towards Kellyville and the lower Potomac. So it was an objective point in the movements of either army, in either direction. The country around about the Station was admirably adapted to cavalry movements. It was a broad, open, undulating plain, without forest or other serious obstruction to the movements of large bodies of troops, but sufficiently rolling to furnish select positions for the use of artillery.

In the early part of the war the country was well fenced, occasionally by a hedge and ditch, which offered serious obstruction to the movements of cavalry, and was not unfrequently, both in charge and retreat, the occasion of serious mishap to the bold cavalier, being especially disastrous in retreat. However, the fences soon disappeared, and the hedge rows were leveled to the earth, and it became an ideal locality for cavalry.

It was occupied for a time by Gen. Stuart in the spring of 1862, on the retreat of the Confederate Army from Manassas, and some little skirmishing then took place, between the videttes and pickets along the banks of the Rappahannock. No serious engagement, however, occurred until the 20th of August, 1862, when Lee advanced on Pope, then occupying Culpeper, just previous to the second battle of Manassas.

After the defeat of McClellan, before Richmond, it will be remembered, General Lee quietly transferred his army to Orange county, and massed it behind Clarke's Mountain, from which point he designed to hurl his veteran battalions on the flank and rear of Pope, in Culpeper. Lieut-Colonel Henderson, of the English Army, who is at present [Jan. 1900.] a staff officer of Lord Roberts in the South African war, in his life of Jackson, gives the following beautiful description of the landscape, as seen from Clarke's Mountain, where Jackson had established a signal station.

"The view from the summit embraced an extended landscape. The ravages of war had not yet effaced its tranquil beauty, nor had the names of its bright rivers and thriving villages become household words. It was still unknown to history; a peaceful and pastoral district, remote from beaten tracks of trade, and inhabited by a quiet and industrious people. To day, few regions can boast of sterner or more heroic memories. To the right, rolling away in light and shadow, for a score of miles, is the great forest of Spotsylvania, within whose gloomy depths lie the fields of Chancellorsville, where the breastworks of the Wilderness can still be traced, and on the eastern verge of which stand the grass grown batteries of Fredericksburg. Northward, and beyond the woods which hide the Rapidan, the eye ranges over the wide and fertile plains of Culpeper, with the green crest of Slaughter's Mountain overlooking Cedar Run, and the dim levels of Brandy Station, the scene of the great cavalry battle, just visible beyond. Far away to the northeast, the faint outline of a range of hills marks the source of Bull Run and the Manassas plateau, and to the west, the long ramparts of the Blue Ridge, softened by the distance, stand high above the Virginia plains."

This movement was designed to be begun on the 18th day of August, but by reason of the delay of the cavalry, in reaching Orange from the Peninsula, it was not begun until about 3 o'clock on the morning of the 20th. General Pope, having in the meantime, learned of Lee's meditated attack, began his retreat on the morning of the 19th, and had reached the south bank of the Rappahannock before Gen. Lee left Orange. The Confederate Army crossed the Rapidan at Raccoon and Morton's Fords, and moved towards the towns of Culpeper and Brandy Station, preceded by Robertson's brigade of cavalry, consisting of the second, sixth, seventh, eleventh and twelfth Virginia Regiments, White's battalion, and Fitz Lee's brigade, consisting at that time of the 1st. Maryland, 3rd, 4th and 5th regiments. Gen. Fitz Lee took the road by Madden's towards Kellysville, and Gen. Robertson the road by Stevensburg to Brandy Station, Gen. Stuart moving in person with Robertson's brigade. Gen. Bayard, of the Federal Army, was directed with his brigade, then at Brandy Station, and consisting of the 1st. Pa., 1st. N. Y., 1st. R. I., 1st. Mass., and 2nd. N. Y., to protect the flank and rear of the retreating army in the direction of Stevensburg. At that time, if the writer remembers rightly, for some distance out of Brandy Station, on the Stevensburg road, there were woods on both sides of the road, and on the east side they extended beyond the point where the Culpeper road now turns off from the Stevensburg road, and in those woods, the Federal cavalry, their rearguard having been driven back from Stevensburg, made their first determined stand against the advance of the Confederate cavalry. By dismounting a portion of his force, armed with carbines, and judiciously posted in these woods, Gen Bayard was enabled to hold in check the advance of the Confederates for some time. After the contest here had been waged for quite a while, Gen. Robertson moved some portion of his command, around by the Wise house in the direction of the Barbour hill, and thus turning the flank and reaching for the rear of the Federal commander, forced him from his position in the woods in front of Brandy. Falling back from this position, he made a stand on Fleetwood Heights in solid columns of squadron, with mounted skirmishers in front and flank. The Confederates moved up rapidly, and attacked the Federals in this new position with great dash and spirit. Gen. Stuart, in his report of this engagement at this point, says: " Robertson's regiments were hurled in rapid succession, in columns of four, upon the main body of the enemy's cavalry, and before the clash of the sabres they took fright and fled, taking refuge close to the river, under protection of their batteries on the other side." He always paid a high compliment to this command, which, he says: "had been brought to the stability of veterans by the discipline, organization and drill of the brigade commander." Gen. Bayard, in his report, says: "that the sudden charge and yells of the enemy seemed to strike terror to his men, and they soon began running;" that they were rallied, however, and retreated quietly to the Rappahannock. Fitz Lee, on this same occasion, had a spirited engagement with the Federal cavalry on the road from Madden's to Kelley's Ford.

Fleetwood Heights is a beautiful location. Being an elevated ridge, which extends eastward at right angles to the elevation extending south from Welford's, and jutting out into the plains, it commands the country and roads leading north and south from Brandy Station. On this occasion it received its baptism of fire, and thereafter, there was no movement of troops across the borders of Culpeper that artillery did not blaze from its summits, and charging squadrons, on its slopes and around its base, did not contend for supremacy.

The day after this engagement the cavalry, followed by the whole army, moved westward along the south banks of the Rappahannock into the Little Fork and finally swinging around through Thoroughfare Gap, debouched on the plains of Manassas, to win, for a second time, a victory on the same field. The writer has a most pleasant recollection of the kindness on this occasion of one of the most worthy and respected citizens of the town of Culpeper. He (the writer) was on picket duty the night before, at Rapidan Station, with a squadron of cavalry, and was ordered to join his regiment the next day at Brandy. This put his line of march through the town of Culpeper, and he entered it on the heels of the retreating enemy. When he had arrived on Main street, at a point opposite the store of Dr. Gorrell, he found that that gentleman, in anticipation of the coming of the Confederates, had prepared a huge tub of lemonade to refresh the tired soldiers. Just think of it! Ice cold lemonade, with plenty of lemon in it to make it sour, and plenty of sugar to make it sweet, and ice to make it cold, to a tired, weary, dirty, dusty Confederate soldier, on a hot day in August. I think of it now, and, although it is winter time, I thirst for that lemonade to-day, and would enjoy so much a draught of it from a clean, shining tin cup. We thank him for it still. May he live long and prosper.

KELLEYVILLE.

Perhaps we might have heretofore referred to the first incursions of Federal troops in the county and village of Culpeper on the morning of the 5th of May, 1862. Major D. Porter Stowell, commanding the 1st Mass. Cavalry, crossed the Rappahannock river at Beverly's Ford on the night of the 4th, and after refreshing men and animals on the farm and at the house of Mr. Richard Cunningham, came on to the village the following morning. It seems to have been the irony of fate, that the soil of Culpeper should have been first invaded by the sons of New England. Nearly a hundred years previous, when Massachusetts was threatened with invasion and oppression from the mother country, among the first to take up arms in defense of her cause, as well as the common cause of the colonies, were the gallant "Minute Men" of Culpeper. Now, the first to appear, as armed invaders of her soil, were the sons of those, with whom they had stood shoulder to shoulder a hundred years before, and this in the sacred names of union, liberty and freedom. Well may we say with Madame Roland: "Oh liberty! What crimes have been committed in thy name."

The officer in command of the expedition says he found on the farm of Mr. Cunningham abundant forage for his horses, and that the overseer, a Mr. Wiltshire, was very kind to him, furnishing forage and opening the mansion house for occupancy by his command. He speaks of it as an elegant old mansion, handsomely furnished, and says that he and his soldiers enjoyed their repose on sofas, couches, beds, lounges and on the parlor floors. He was evidently a gentleman, and understood, even in war, the laws of property rights, for he says, notwithstanding it had been the headquarters of the Confederate generals, and the absence of the owner, yet nothing in the house, or about the premises, was taken or injured by his men. Leaving Cunningham's, he followed the ridge road, passing the brick house of Dr. Huntington (Dr. Dan'l. Green's), and came out by the Barbour house to Brandy Station. He gives, in his report, a very interesting account of his trip, of the route pursued, of the beauty and fertility of the country, and the temper of the people with whom he met. He speaks of the country as lovely in its appearance, well cultivated, and filled with supplies of all sorts, for man and beast. That most of the farmers had left their homes in charge of their overseers, but that their farming work was going on as usual.

At this time there were no Confederate troops north of Gordonsville, save two companies of cavalry of the 2nd. Va. Reg., encamped on the Greenwood estate, and engaged in picketing the roads north of Culpeper. The officer reported that he encountered the Confederate pickets some three miles north of Culpeper, who retired upon his approach, and that he sent forward an advance squadron, which pursued them rapidly into the village. He further says, that just before he reached town, he met a young man, by the name of "Bedsham," who said "he lived five or six miles north of the village; that he was in town when the news of their approach was received, and that it produced great fright and consternation among the citizens as well as the soldiers encamped near. That he was a good Union man, and that when the Confederates passed through, they wanted him and his father to go with them, but they would not do it, and that their horses were much better than the Confederates." This must have been Beverly Beckham. Was he not "soft soldering" the commanding officer, and did he not take it in beautifully? They remained but a short time in the village, and took back with them, as they reported, eight prisoners. Thomas Lewis, of the Piedmont Hotel, Col. Ned Freeman, Judge Henry Shackelford, and David P. Stallard, were four of them. Who were the others? Were they citizens or soldiers? Do any of our people remember? Upon the approach of the Confederate cavalry, a few shots were exchanged, and the Federals retired.

A few days thereafter, the writer, who was at that time captain of Co. B (Rappahannock Cavalry,) 6th Reg., was sent from the valley, with his company, to reinforce the cavalry, stationed near Culpeper. He also encamped on the Greenwood estate, and picketed the road leading north of Culpeper. We remained in this neighborhood until the morning of the 21st of May, when orders were received to join Jackson in the valley, in his advance on Banks at Winchester. As we moved through the town of Culpeper on that morning, we halted for a short while in the streets, and the men dismounted. Mr. John Turner, a highly intelligent old gentleman, a former resident of Rappahannock, but then residing in Culpeper, came to the command, mingled freely with the boys, and greeted them all warmly, for he either knew them personally, or knew their fathers. When the command to mount was given he said good bye to many, and took his position on the side walk, and as we moved off, we left him standing there gazing, tenderly and earnestly, at the column as it moved along, with the tears rolling down his furrowed cheeks. He was a very quiet, passive, undemonstrative man, and the writer was deeply impressed with the feeling and emotion which he exhibited on that occasion. All of Culpeper might have joined the old man in his feelings on that occasion, and could they have lifted the veil of the future, and seen but a few days in advance, they would have unquestionably done so, for there marched in the ranks of that company, three of Culpeper's noblest young men, who, a few days thereafter, laid down their lives for their country, and for their country's cause. We refer to Sergeant Frank Duncan, William Field and Phillip Field, sons of Judge Richard H. Field. The first was a soldier of a year's experience, a model one submissive and obedient to orders himself, he exacted obedience of others. He was bold and fearless in danger, and was actuated, at all times, by a high sense of duty to his country. The last two had but recently joined the cavalry service. At the outbreak of the war they were students at the University of Virginia, but they laid aside their books, and joined the "Culpeper Minute Men," 3rd. Va. infantry, in which they served till discharged in the spring of 1862. The elder, William, was a young man of some twenty-two or twenty-three years of age, tall and well developed, with a bright and cheery disposition, and altogether, one of the handsomest young men we ever knew. The younger, Philip, was a tall, slender boy of some eighteen years, with a face as delicate, as gentle, and as refined as a woman's, but with a shade of sadness which but added to the attractiveness of his expression.

Two days thereafter, Duncan and Philip Field were killed, and a few days following, William was also slain on the battlefield. Their bodies were sent to their homes, and buried in the family burying ground, where they sleep with their ancestors of many generations. There names are worthy to be remembered and cherished by the people of Culpeper among their heroic dead. The death of his two promising sons broke the heart of the father, Judge Field, who soon sank into a premature grave.

The Confederate army went into quarters for the winter of 1862-3 on the south side of the Rappahannock river, from the Wilderness to Port Royal, with the cavalry brigade of Fitz Lee on its left, in Orange and Culpeper counties, guarding the Rappahannock. The Federal army occupied the counties of King George, Stafford, and lower Fauquier on the north bank of the Rappahannock, with its cavalry on its right. In the early spring of 1863, Gen. Stoneman, then in command of the cavalry corps of the Federal army, ordered Gen. Averill, of the 2nd. cavalry division, to take a force of about three thousand, with six pieces of artillery, across the Rappahannock river at or near Kelleyville, and to rout and destroy the Confederate cavalry brigade of Fitz Lee, then occupying Culpeper, and encamped in the neighbood of Brandy Station and Stevensburg. Gen. Lee's brigade at that time consisted of the 1st., 2nd., 3rd., 4th. and 5th. Va. regiments, and one battery of horse artillery, commanded by one of the most gallant and promising artillery officers in the service, Major John Pelham, of Alabama. Lee's brigade numbered perhaps 1200 in all. Averill's command was about 2100, after making details for scouts, pickets and couriers. It seems from the records that Gen. R. E. Lee first learned of this reconnoisance by the Federal cavalry, and as early as 11 A. M. on the 16th, notified Fitz Lee of the movement. But it was unknown what point the enemy would select for crossing the river. Early on the morning of the 17th, the Federal cavalry appeared at Kelley's Ford, at which point the Confederates had a strong picket force, commanded by Captain White, and by its resistance, and the obstruction which had previously been placed about the ford, the crossing of the Federals was delayed for an hour or more After a spirited picket fight at the river, resulting in some loss on both sides, the Federals effected a crossing, and, so soon as their purpose to cross at that point, with their entire force, was made apparent, Lee hurried his whole command in that direction, and at once the battle was joined with great spirit, dash and courage on both sides. The Federals first took a position half a mile or more south of the ford, and south of the point where the Stevensburg road turns to the left. The 4th., 3rd. and 16th. Penn., the 1st. and 5th. U. S., the 4th. N. J., and 2nd. Ohio constituted the line of battle, with Baker's brigade in reserve near the mill. The position of the Federals was a strong one, protected by woods and and a stone fence in front. It was, however, repeatedly charged by the Southern cavalry, the 3rd. Virginia leading in the advance, but they were unable to dislodge the Federals from the position which they occupied. After repeated efforts in this direction, the Confederates slowly retired to a position a mile or two in the rear, where the battle raged with great fury. "From the time the battle was first joined," says Fitz Lee, in his report, "it was a series of gallant charges by the different regiments, and once by the whole brigade in line. My men, some times unable to cross the fences or ditches in their front, behind which the Federals were protected, wheeled about, delivering their fire in the very faces of the enemy, and reformed again under a heavy fire from their artillery and small arms." Lieut. Holtzman, of Co. D., 4th. Virginia cavalry, who kept a diary of all the movements of his command, tells me that he has it recorded, that on more than one occasion, when the charging squadrons of Confederate cavalry would encounter fences, they would deliberately halt, dismount, and, under fire of the Federal batteries with grape and cannister, as well as small arms, pull aside the fences at the corners, to enable them to pass through. The battle continued until late in the evening, when the Federals, unable to accomplish the purpose, for which they had crossed the river, retired. The Confederates were perfectly willing that they should go, and were unable to inflict any serious loss upon them in their retreat.

Considering the superiority in numbers, the result was a splendid achievement for the Confederates, and became the subject of congratulatory orders on the part of Gen. Lee to his brigade. But it was not without serious loss in both men and animals; about 170 horses were killed, and an equal number of men killed and wounded. A peculiarity of the wounds in this engagement, was that they were nearly all made with the saber, showing that the battle was fought at close quarters, and with great obstinacy. The Culpeper company, (Capt. Hill) of the 4th. regiment, was in the thickest of the fight, from morning till the enemy retired. The Confederate loss was much greater than that of the Federals, especially in officers, among the latter were the gallant Maj. Puller, of the 5th. cavalry, and Lieut. Harris, of the 4th.,and the splendid and much beloved Pelham, of the Horse Artillery. The record of this latter officer had been bright and spotless, and he had endeared himself to the whole army. He was a modest, gentle, unassuming boy, scarcely twenty-one years old, and yet he had the coolness of a veteran on the field, and gave great promise of future achievements; a genius for war that was brilliant and attractive. He was struck on the head with a fragment of a shell, and his skull crushed, but before life was extinct, he was brought to the house of Judge Shackleford, in the town of Culpeper, where he expired amidst weeping friends and comrades. His death cast a gloom over the entire corps, and the usual badge of military mourning was worn for him for thirty days.*

Again on April 30th., Brandy Station and Culpeper were the scenes of another cavalry engagement, though not of as much consequence as some others. Just preceding the movement of the Union army for Chancellorsville, Stoneman, with his cavalry corps, crossed the river at Kellyville, for a raid on the Central Railroad, about Louisa C. H., the James river, Kanawha Canal, and other points in rear of the Confederate army. After crossing the river, Averill, with his division, was sent in the direction of Brandy Station and Culpeper, with instructions to destroy the cavalry force that he might encounter, while Stoneman, with the residue of his command, moved lower down, and crossing the river at Raccoon Ford, proceeded towards Louisa C. H. Averill encountered William H. F. Lee about Brandy Station, and they had some pretty lively skirmishing between that point and the Rapidan, towards which Gen Lee slowly retreated, keeping Averill well in check. Averill had consumed so much time in pressing back William H. F. Lee's command, that he was unable to join the raid, and, from Rapidan, was recalled to the army at Ely's Ford, and, soon thereafter, removed from his command, because of his failure to break up and destroy William H. F. Lee.

LEE'S CAVALRY REVIEW.

But it was on the 8th. of June, 1863, that a most interesting cavalry display took place near Brandy Station. It was interesting, attractive and brilliant, to be followed, however, on the next day, by one more attractive and inspiring, and which occupied a much more prominent place in the history of the times. We refer to the great cavalry review of the 8th. of June, 1863, when Stuart's whole command passed in review before the commanding general, Robert E. Lee.

The army, at this time, was on the move for Gettysburg. Some portions of Longstreet's corps was about Culpeper C. H. Stuart's cavalry was, at this time, perhaps, more efficient in number, drill, discipline, and equipment, than at any other period of the war. He had called together his whole command, save, perhaps, the brigade of Jenkins, then in the valley of Virginia. The corps consisted of Fitz Lee's brigade of five regiments, Hampton's brigade of six regiments, William H. F. Lee's brigade of five regiments, William D. Jones' brigade of four regiments, and Robertson's brigade of two regiments; twenty-two in all, aggregating, perhaps, 8000 men.

The review took place on what is known as the "Auburn" estate. A furrow was made with a plow, beginning at a point not far from the dividing line between the "Auburn" estate and the Hall estate, and about three hundred yards west of the railroad, on the land now owned by Mr. Schlosser, and extending, in a line parallel with the railroad, along by the broadspreading elm tree that stood in the flat in rear of the grave yard, on the Ross estate, quite to the run. Along this long straight furrow the twenty two regiments of cavalry were formed in two ranks, facing the railroad, extending nearly or quite its whole length. The horse artillery, of four batteries (sixteen guns), Captains Breathit, Chew, McGregor and Moorman, the whole commanded by Major Beckham, was formed in batteries along the ridge in the rear of, and on the west side of the branch. It was a splendid military parade; Stuart's eyes gleamed with peculiar brightness as he glanced along this line of cavalry in battle array, with men and horses groomed at their best, and the command arrayed with military precision, with colors flying, bugles sounding, bands playing, and with regimental and brigade officers in proper positions. Gen. Lee occupied a little hillock, immediately on the west side of the railroad, and some three or four hundred yards north of the station at Inlet. The review brought together a large number of citizens, ladies and gentlemen, young and old, from Culpeper, and the adjoining counties; many were the sly glances cast by the soldier boys at the country lassies, as they passed along their front in the columns of review. An engine brought down a train of flat cars from Culpeper, filled with soldiers and civilians, to witness the review. Gen Lee, with his staff, first rode rapidly along the front of the line, around the left flank, then along the rear, around the right flank to his position on the hill in the front. At the sound of the bugle, taken up and repeated along the line, the corps of horsemen broke by right wheel into columns of squadron, and moving south for a short distance, the head of the column was turned to the left, and again to the left, moving in this new direction, whence it passed immediately in front of the commanding general. It was a splendid military pageant, and an inspiring scene, such as this continent never before witnessed, as this long line of horsemen, in columns of squadron, with nearly ten thousand sabres flashing in the sun light, with salvos of artillery on the hills beyond, passed in review before the greatest soldier of modern times Who, that was present, will ever forget the swelling of the soul, which he experienced, as he passed the position occupied by the reviewing officers, and knew that the eyes of the great Robert E. Lee were upon him. The column moved at a walk until it came within some fifty or one hundred paces of the position occupied by the reviewing general, when squadron by squadron would take up first the trot, then the gallop, until they had passed some distance beyond, when again they would pull down to the walk. After passing in review, the several brigades were brought again to the position which they occupied in the line, whence they were dismissed, one by one, to their respective camps, to be rudely awakened early the next morning by the Federal cavalry, who crossed the Rappahannock, determined, for the first time, to measure swords with the Southerners, beyond the protection of their infantry.

BRANDY STATION, JUNE 9, 1863.

After the great review, Hampton's brigade went into camp on the south of Brandy Station, picketing the lower ford of the Rappahannock, Robertson's N. C. brigade to the right of the station, Jones' brigade near St. James' church, picketing the river from Rappahannock bridge to the confluence of the Hazel and Rappahannock rivers, while Wm. H. F. Lee's and Fitz Lee's brigades were thrown further forward, in the neighborhood of Oak Shade, guarding the river to Waterloo, and scouting the country beyond, to protect the flank of the Confederate army, en route to Gettysburg, by way of Gourdvine, Gaines X Cross, Winchester, and so on.

This was, substantially, the position of the Southern cavalry when the Federals, under Gen. Pleasanton, crossed the river on the morning of the 9th of June, to drive back the Southerners, and ascertain the object and purpose of the movement of the army under Lee. The Federal cavalry crossed the river in two columns, one at Beverly's Ford, consisting of the 1st division, and Merritt's brigade of regular cavalry, and a brigade of infantry under the command of Gen. Ames, the whole under the command of Gen. Buford. This column numbered 3,918 cavalry, 1,500 infantry and two batteries of U. S. artillery (eight guns). The other column crossed the river at Kelleyville, and consisted of the 2nd and 3rd divisions of cavalry (3,973 strong), and 1,500 infantry under Gen. Russell, and a battery of six guns, the whole under the command of Gen. Gregg. Beverly's Ford was immediately in front of Jones' camp, Co. A. (Capt. Gibson), being the picket guard at that point, and Co. B. (Capt. Grimsley), of the 6th Va. cavalry, at the railroad bridge. The Federals charged the ford at Beverly's about day-break, driving the picket guard before them, and pressed with great vigor their advance along the road towards the church. However, their progress was resisted with equal pluck, courage, and tenacity, by the reserve picket force, and their advance delayed until some portion of Jones' command could be gotten in position for battle. When the alarm was given of the advance of the Federals, the horses of the cavalry, and of the horse artillery, were grazing in the fields near the church, and at one time they were in great danger of being captured. The 6th and 7th regiments were the first to secure their horses, and move to the relief of the reserve picket. They were hurried forward, the one on the right, and the other on the left of the road leading from the church to the river, and along which the Federals were advancing, to assist in holding the attacking party's columns in check. As these two regiments rushed forward, they met the enemy's columns in the woods, beyond the church, and a hand to hand conflict ensued. The advance brigade of the Federals, consisting of the 8th N. Y., 8th Ill., and 3rd Ind. regiments, were held in check by the charge of the Virginia regiments, and its commander, Col. Davis, of the 8th N. Y., killed in an heroic effort to hold his command ready to resist the onset of the Confederates. Maj. Beckham, of the horse artillery, a Culpeper boy, a gallant soldier and a brilliant officer, had, in the mean time, succeeded in having his horses harnessed and hitched, and one or more pieces in position on the elevated knoll near the church. But before this, while some of his men were securing the horses, the others were serving the guns with all the efficacy that an unfavorable position could attain. The remaining regiments of Jones' brigade, the 11th and 12th, and also Hampton's brigade, were soon mounted, and ready for action, the latter joining on to the right of Jones and Wm. H.F. Lee, coming in on their left, near to and in front of the Thompson and Dr. Green houses. The Federals put their infantry in position, in the woods, on both sides of the road to the river, with their cavalry extending to the right and left, opposite the positions occupied by Hampton and Lee. The battle was fought here for some hours with great fury. The dismounted men on the Confederate side engaging the infantry on the Union side, and charge and counter charge was made, time and again, along the whole line, with mounted and dismounted men. The line of battle swayed back and forth from the woods, in front, towards the church, now advancing, now receding. The Federals occupied the large body of woods, from which the Confederates were unable to drive them, and from which they were unable to advance. In the meantime, the column that had crossed at Kelleyville first pressed up in the direction of Brandy by the route leading by Elkwood, and Robertson, with his N. C. brigade, was sent down on that road to arrest its progress. This body of the Federals engaged Robertson in a sharp skirmish for a time, but, so soon as the route to Brandy, by the Thom place, was uncovered, the Federal commander eluded Robertson, and moving by his left flank, pressed on rapidly in the direction of Brandy. The second division of cavalry was first across the river at Kelleyville, and, so soon as the route was opened, pressed on to Stevensburg, via Carrico's mill. A squadron of this division, which had been hurried forward in the direction of Stevensburg, reached that point in advance of the Confederate troops sent by Gen. Stuart.

Gen. Stuart, having learned early in the morning, through Gen. Robertson, as well as by information given by the captain of the picket guard at Rappahannock, that some portion of the forces that had crossed at Kelleyville, was moving in the direction of Stevensburg, detached the 2nd S. C. regiment, under Col. Butler, to that point, with instructions to picket the roads from Brandy to Carrico's mill, and to Stevensburg. Later in the day, he sent the 4th Va. regiment, under Col. Wickham, to that point to support Col. Butler. A section of artillery was also sent with this regiment. The 4th regiment, after crossing Mountain Run, moved across the field to the left of the village, and joined a portion of the S. C. regiment, under Lt. Col. Hampton, at or near the Doggett house, beyond Stevensburg. By the time a line of skirmishers deployed, extending round toward the Hansbrough house, the Federals were in their front in force, and rapidly hurled the advance regiments (the 1st Mass., 1st R. I., and 6th O.) on Butler and Wickham, and drove them back in great confusion. The Union cavalry followed up their advantage, charging into and beyond the village, to the Barbour house, in pursuit of the fugitives. The gallant Col. Hampton, son of Gen. Hampton, was mortally wounded in the fights near the village, and quite a number of others wounded or taken prisoners. After awhile, Cols. Wickham and Butler succeeded in rallying the most of their commands, and reformed on the north side of Mountain Run, on the Beckham farm. The section of artillery was put in position, and the Federals moved down towards the mill, on both sides of the Brandy road. The Federals also put their artillery in position, and a lively artillery duel was in progress, when the Federals were ordered to retire from Stevensburg by the same route that they advanced by, and join the main body at Brandy. Why this was done must ever remain a mystery. Why this column, when within three miles of Brandy, and almost immediately in rear of the Confederate position should have been withdrawn by a route twice as long, consuming twice the time, must ever remain a riddle in military affairs; but so it was. We doubt not but that the life of the Confederacy was greatly prolonged by the mistakes of its enemies. Gen. Butler lost his leg in this artillery fight at Norman's Mill, and Capt. Farley, of South Carolinia, a volunteer on General Stuart's staff, lost his life by the same shell that took off Gen. Butler's leg. Capt Farley was a noble, gallant, chivalrous man. His body was buried in the Citizens' Cemetery at Culpeper, and his relatives and friends, of South Carolina, have recently erected a suitabe shaft to mark the spot and commemorate his memory.

It was now, perhaps, mid-day. The 3rd. division of cavalry had, by this time, driven in the pickets on the Carrico road leading from Brandy, and was rapidly approaching the station. Col. Percy Wyndham, a gallant, dashing Englishman, who was making war for the love of it, and who, but a little time before, had been captured by Ashby's command, and exchanged, was in command of the advance brigade, consisting of the 1st. Maryland, 1st. N. Y., 1st. Penn., dashed into the station, and dispersed a small Confederate force that was found there. He made some captures of wagons and ambulances, and then turned his command towards Fleetwood Heights, which had been Gen. Stuart's headquarters; but all his papers, and everything else pertaining to his quarters, had been removed, save a single tent. A piece of artillery was stationed there, and some few orderlies, loungers and camp followers were also lingering about the hill. Gen. Kilpatrick, commanding the second brigade, consisting of the Harris Light Horse, the 10th. N. Y., and 1st. Maine, turned to the right, before reaching the station, and moved diagonally across the fields towards Fleetwood, to the assistance of Col. Wyndham, who, having moved down the road from Brandy, had charged the heights and taken them. Kilpatrick had hurried up his artillery, and put it in position, on the east of the railroad, so as to command Fleetwood hill. Col. Wyndham's victory was short lived; he had hardly gained possession of the hill, before he was met by Hampton, at the head of the Cobbs Legion, 1st. S. C., and 6th Va., which had been hurriedly withdrawn from the field at St. James church, upon the appearance of the Federals at Brandy. Gen. Stuart also accompanied this column, and as it approached Fleetwood, seeing the hill in possession of the enemy, he put the command at a gallop, and when it was in striking distance, called out, in that clear ringing voice that could be heard above the uproar of battle, "give them the sabre, boys." Then nearly a thousand sabres leaped from their scabbards, and with one wild shout, the Confederates rushed in furious onset against the Federal cavalry occupying the hill, and hurled it back in confusion and disorder. But Kilpatrick came, with his squadrons, to the relief of Wyndham, and succeeded in regaining a portion of the elevated ground on the west of the railroad, but the Jeff Davis Legion and 1st. N. C. was by this time on the ground, and placed on the east of the railroad, while the 11th. and 12th. Va. regiments, and White's battery, also withdrawn from St. James, in a gallant charge across the hill, drove back the Federals, who were struggling to regain it after their first reverse. The numbers at this point, were now about the same, some six or seven regiments on either side, but we presume the Federal regiments were numerically stronger than the Confederates; and then, for an hour or more, there was a fierce struggle for the hill, which seemed to have been regarded as the key to the situation. This point was taken, and retaken once, and perhaps several times; each side would be in possession for a time, and plant its batteries there, when by a successful charge it would pass into the possession of the other side, and so it continued until victory finally dwelt with the Confederates, and the Federals seem to realize their inability to hold it. They slowly and sullenly retired, leaving several guns in the possession of the Confederates, with a number of prisoners, and their dead and wounded in the hands of their enemy.

The second and third divisions of Union cavalry that were in front of Brandy, after their defeat on Fleetwood hill, swung round to their right, and moving just in front of the Stringfellow house, joined on to Buford, who as soon as the pressure from his front was relieved, advanced cautiously in the direction of Brandy Station. The Confederates re-arranged their line of battle, after getting rid of Gregg at Fleetwood. It will be remembered, in that struggle, the Confederates were facing south and the Federals north. As Gregg swung around to Buford, the direction of his line was changed, facing south, and the Confederates made the corresponding change. Hampton's brigade was placed on the right of the railroad, looking north, supported by Robertson's brigade. The greater portion of the Confederate artillery was placed on Fleetwood Heights, supported by Jones' brigade, whilst a strong line of dismounted men and infantry skirmishers from the 13th. Va. regiment, were thrown forward a little in advance of the crown of the hill, extending westward nearly to the road leading to Dr. Welford's. The fighting in the evening was principally between the artillery and dismounted men and infantry in the woods, which, according to our recollection, at that time extended from the Brandy road nearly to the summit of the ridge. Late in the evening the Federal cavalry made a last effort to break and force back the Confederate lines. This occurred on the extreme left of the Confederate line, on the summit of the hill near the road to Dr. Welford's. A column of cavalry pressed on up the road referred to and at this point made a gallant and dashing charge on the 9th. and 10th. Va. regiments of Wm. H. F. Lee's brigade, supported by one of Jones' regiments. This charge was met with great spirit and courage, and the result wavered long in the balance. Gen. R. E. Lee looked on this struggle from the cupalo of the Barbour house, and is said to have expressed great admiration of the grit and courage manifested by the soldiers on both sides. Finally, the Federals gave away, and victory once more favored the Confederates. In this charge, apparently by consent, both sides used the pistol and the lines approached within a few feet, and the men emptied their pistols in each others' faces. To those of us who were not actually engaged, but who witnessed the combat at a distance, and heard the fusilade of pistols, it seemed impossibe almost, that any should have escaped injury, and that the loss of life could be so small, but after it was all over, and results inquired into, and the dead and wounded looked after, it was found that little damage had been done. Never after this, if it could be avoided, did the Confederate officers allow a charge to be made or resisted with the pistol, but always ordered the sabre to be used as much more effective. After this attack on the left, the Federals slowly retreated and and recrossed the river that evening at Beverley's, and at the railroad bridge.

Gen. Wm. H. F. Lee was seriously wounded early in the action, and the command of his brigade devolved on Col. Davis, of the 10th regiment. Neither Fitz Lee's or Robertson's brigades participated very actively in the fight. The former was withdrawn from the Little Fork section, and the 2nd. regiment was slightly engaged on the left, while the 4th. had been detached and sent to Stevensburg. The loss of the Federal side was over 900 killed, wounded and missing; on the Confederate side 485. The Confederates captured three pieces of artillery, more than a hundred horses, and quite a large number of small arms, such as pistols and carbines etc. And thus ended the first great cavalry battle of the war. The Confederates pushed on into Fauquier, on the right flank of our advancing army, with full confidence in their ability to meet and vanquish their enemy on anything like equal terms. Upon the whole, the battle at Brandy Station was a great victory for the Confederates. It ought to have been won by the Federals. They were greatly superior in numbers in their cavalry force, besides being strongly supported by infantry. There was no fault in the plan of battle, as conceived by the Federal commander, and if it had been strictly pursued, it would have resulted in a great victory for him, but there seemed to be a want of promptness, enterprise and spirit in the movement of the two columns. Buford's force, at St. James' church, was greatly superior in numbers to the Confederates who opposed him, and yet he made but little headway against them, consisting of parts of three brigades. Gregg had outgeneraled Robertson on the Kelleyville road, eluding him and reaching Brandy in his rear. Stuart played the same trick on Buford at St. James. For when Gregg appeared at Brandy, Stuart withdrew the greater part of his force in front of Buford, and hurled it upon Gregg, and drove him from Fleetwood. If, when Stuart withdrew from Buford's front at St. James, Buford had pressed immediately on his heels, he would have caught Stuart at Fleetwood, between him and Gregg, and he, Stuart, would have been roughly handled. As it was, Buford moved slowly, and allowed Gregg to be defeated by the same troops that had been holding him at bay. We presume that Buford found his infantry both a help and a drawback. A help in enabling him to hold his position in front of St. James, for without it, he would have been driven back across the the river before Gregg reached Brandy; but a drawback to him when he should have followed Hampton rapidly, as he was unwilling to leave it in his rear unprotected. He moved towards Brandy at the same time his infantry moved, and allowed Gregg to be beaten before he got there, and Robertson, with his North Carolina troops, who had been cut off on the Kelleyville road, to return by Elkwood, between the converging columns of Buford and Gregg, almost within a stone's throw of each other. But while the victory was with the Confederates, the moral effect of the battle was of great value to the Federal cavalry. Up to that point of the war the Union cavalry had been of but little service. The Federal generals did not begin to know how to organize or use their cavalry, or to appreciate its value. The Confederates, on the other hand, had from the very beginning of the war, used their cavalry to the greatest advantage. This branch of the service seemed to suit the genius and spirit of our people, and it was brought to a state of efficiency with wonderful rapidity. The victories which crowned the Confederate arms for the first years of the war, were due, in a great measure, to the skillful manner in which the Confederate generals, Stuart and Ashby, maneuvered their cavalry, and concealed the movements of the Confederate army, thus bringing about a condition which made those great victories possible.

The Federals had been for some time organizing a select body of men for cavalry service. By promotion from the infantry, for special merit and otherwise, and by organization, drill, and discipline, they were bringing that body up to a high state of efficiency. The Confederates had always held themselves as greatly superior to the Federals in this branch of the service, and this seemed to have been conceded by them. At Brandy, for the first time, in an open field, with fair fight, with anything like equality of numbers, had they been able to maintain themselves against the superior dash and horsemanship of the Southrons. But, when a few days thereafter, they met again at Aldie, Middleburg, and Upperville, it was apparent to the Confederates that the Federals had gained in moral, as well as in numbers and discipline.

CULPEPER, FROM AUG. 1ST. TO OCT. 1ST. 1863.

The Confederate army returned sullenly and slowly from the disastrous campaign of Gettysburg to its old encampments in Culpeper; beaten and bleeding at every pore, but not dispirited, and with its confidence in its immortal leader still unshaken. Now and then, in its slow retreat, it would turn on its antagonist, like an animal driven to bay, and exhibit a spirit and willingness to suffer annihilation, rather than acknowledge defeat.

About the last of July, 1863, Longstreet's corps was encamped in the rear of Mt. Pony hills, about the village of Culpeper. Ewell, who had made a detour further south in his retreat from the valley, crossing the mountains at Milan's Gap, was encamped in Madison and Orange counties. Jones' brigade of cavalry was in the neighborhood of Rixeyville, Hampton's about Brandy Station, Wm. H. F. Lee's toward Rappahannock, while Fitz Lee's was on the right, in the vicinity of Fredericksburg. On the second of August the Federal commander, General Meade, then occupying the north bank of the Rappahannock river, directed General Buford, commanding the 1st. division of cavalry, to make a reconnoissance to the town of Culpeper, and ascertain, if possible, the location of the Confederate army. He accordingly crossed the river at Beverly's Ford, and at the railroad bridge encountered Hampton's brigade, reinforced in a short time by a portion of Jones', and they joined battle on the same ground over which they had fought on the ninth of June. The Federals were greatly superior in numbers to Hampton, having a division to a brigade, and gradually pressed him back to about where Inlet Station now is. The greater portion of Jones' brigade was on the Rixeyville road and had not, to this time, been much engaged; but leaving this road at Chestnut Fork, it moved across the Rixey and the Bradford farms, and was joined on to Hampton's left in this position, just in advance of the Bell farm. At this point, a division of infantry from Hill's corps also came on the field and the Federals begun to retire. General Stuart was present, and personally conducted the movements of his troops, and when he saw the enemy was in retreat, he pressed him with great vigor, and sought to convert his retreat into a route by hurling his squadrons, with great force and impetuosity, upon his rear, but, however, with no very great success. The Federal general conducted his retreat with great skill, protecting his rear with a strong line of mounted skirmishers, which effectually warded off the blows aimed at his main column. The area between the Auburn house and the railroad was one vast corn field, in which the corn was then fully grown. This was filled with the dismounted men of the Federals and held by them with great tenacity, notwithstanding it was swept by the Confederate artillery, and penetrated by a strong line of dismounted men. In passing through this field afterwards, it did not appear that a single stalk of corn had escaped the destructive missiles. The Federals had rebuilt the railroad bridge at Rappahannock, where Buford halted on the south bank, and held a tete de pont on the south side, extending his right flank to Welford's Ford on the west, and his left to Kelleyville on the east, protected by a line of videttes extending around in this semi-circle and located about a hundred yards apart. Immediately in front of Fleetwood, this line of videttes extended across the country from about the Stringfellow house to St. James church.

On the evening of the fourth of August, General Stuart, anxious to ascertain what the Federals were doing at Rappahannock, and why it was that they seemed anxious to hold this small area on the south of the river, with Hampton's brigade, and a portion of some other commands, attacked the Federals near what is now the station of Elkwood, and drove them back some distance towards the river so as to uncover the forces on the south side, and develop the objects of the Federal commander. It was a very sharp hand to hand fight for a time between Buford and Hampton, and was conducted with a rush on the part of the Confederates. On the day following (the 5th of August), a reconnoissance was sent out by General Gregg, commanding the second cavalry division, encamped at Waterloo, towards Rixeyville, which resulted in a sharp skirmish between the 11th Va. regiment, Jones' command, and this scouting party, in the vicinity of Rixeyville and Muddy Run. The Federal column crossed the river at Hill's mill, and then turned to Rixeyville, and from thence moved towards Muddy Run, sending out scouting parties towards Alum Spring church. Colonel Taylor, of the first Pennsylvania cavalry, was in command of the scouts, and says in his report, that finding himself being flanked at the run by the skirmishers of the 11th Va. cavalry, concluded it was prudent to retire. Again, on the 8th and 9th of August, the Federals advanced and drove back the Confederate pickets in front of Brandy, and there was a right smart skirmish for an hour or two. The writer recalls an incident, illustrative of the accurate information which the Confederates had of the Federal movements and he supposes the Federals had information equally as accurate. The reserve picket force of the Confederates was held at a spring at the foot of Fleetwood hill, on the road to Elkwood, and the lines of pickets stretched across the country a short distance in front. Gen. Stuart rode down to the picket reserves one evening, and addressing the captain of the guard, said: "Captain, what is going on with those folks over there," pointing to the Yankee picket line. "Nothing;" replied the captain. "Well," said he, "look out, they will be on you in the morning about daylight." True enough, next morning as the first grey streaks of dawn began to light up the horizon, we could see a commotion among them and they called out: "Look out Johnnies, we are coming," and begun to fire and advance.

Scouting parties from the cavalry constantly harassed the right flank of the Federals, resting in the Little Fork, with their picket line extending from Hill's mill back towards Amissville. Captain McDonald, of the 11th cavalry, crossed the river at Rixey's Ford on the night of the 2nd of September, and captured the picket force at Waterford, consisting of an officer and fifteen men. After the first of September the Federal army remained comparatively quiet, resting till the 13th of the month, when their whole army moved south of the Rappahannock and occupied Culpeper. The Federals advanced in three columns. Buford, with his 1st division, directly towards Brandy; Kilpatrick, with the third division, crossed at Kelleyville, while Gregg crossed the Hazel river at Stark's Ford. Buford, who was immediately in front of Brandy, made a demonstration early in the morning, and then seemed to turn his columns to the right, as though he were going on the Rixeyville road, along which the principal advance would be made. We presume now it was but to protect Gregg in crossing the fords of the Hazel. At any rate, it caused the withdrawal of all the Confederate cavalry from Brandy to the Rixeyville road, excepting two regiments, the 5th and 6th Va. Two or three hours were consumed in maneuvering, and about 10.30 a. m., Buford, with the whole of his and Kilpatrick's divisions, appeared on the plains of Brandy in front of these two regiments, supported by a section of artillery. In a contest so unequal, there was nothing to do but retreat, and while it was a rapid one, it was not disorderly. The retreating Confederates kept a strong line of mounted skirmishers in their rear, and withdrew by regiments, always keeping one regiment and one gun facing their adversaries. An amusing incident occurred at Jonas's run, near the railroad crossing. In attempting to get the guns across at that point, one of them got stuck in the soft muddy banks. Soldiers were dismounted and required to take hold to extricate the piece; among them, was a man by the name of Roe, of the 5th cavalry, a man who stammered very badly. And as these soldiers were laboring and tugging at the wheels, the enemy, pressing on in the rear, took in the situation, and concentrated their fire upon the poor fellows at this work, and made it very hot for them. The bullets were striking all around : zip—zip. Roe stood it for awhile, but, after a time, it got too hot for him, and he raised up from his work, and addressing his captain in an earnest pathetic manner said: " C-p-p, Cap, Captain, le-le-let's throw in, and pay for the d— - —d thing, and leave it here." One more tug at the wheel brought it safely out to be lost at Culpeper. The Confederates had considerable commissary and ordnance supplies at the depot in Culpeper, and a freight train had been sent down from Orange to remove them, and they were being hurriedly loaded on when the Federals appeared in sight of the village. The presence of the train, seemed to impress them with the idea that supports had been sent down from Orange, and they were slow and cautious in entering the village. The Confederates had but parts of two regiments, with two pieces of artillery, while the Federals had the whole of Buford's division, with a part of Kilpatrick's and Warren's corps of infantry, but a short distance in the rear. The Confederates posted their guns on the hill, between Capt Vinal's and Mr. Chelf's, supported by two squadrons of mounted men, while the fifth cavalry were dismounted at Bell's Ford in order to hold that position, and a portion of the 6th dismounted at the railroad ford. The Federal force moved forward very cautiously, forming their line of battle on the hill about the George house, extending round to the left, in front of the Wallach house, with two or three batteries stationed at intervals along this line. Their batteries were turned principally upon the town and the train loading at the depot, with an occasional shot at the guns on the hill. At no time during the war, were the citizens of the village exposed to such an ordeal as they were that Sunday morning, the 13th of September. The day had begun calm and tranquil; early in the morning a single gun was heard in the neighborhood of Brandy, but as that was not followed up by others, the alarm occasioned by it soon subsided, and the people had assembled for worship in the Baptist church, where the Rev. Barnett Grimsley, of Rappahannock, was to preach. The services were begun, but before they were concluded the Federals were in front of the village, and were sending shells screaming through the town. The congregation was hurriedly dismissed, the minister mounting his horse, and taking his departure. There was considerable damage done to the property and some casualties among the citizens. Mrs. Stone, the wife of the Rev. Richard Stone, who had recently returned from Africa, was seriously wounded, and perhaps others. After the departure of the train, which escaped without injury, taking off all the stores, the Federals showed a purpose to force an entrance into the village, and for this purpose, sent forward a brigade from the centre of their lines to charge Bell's Ford and get possession of the crossing. They came down the road, in columns of fours, in beautiful order, and looked as though they would sweep every thing before them, but they met at the ford a fire from our dismounted men, protected by the large trees, that at that time were about that point, which emptied many a saddle, broke up their organization, and drove them back in disorder. They, however, rallied, and crossing the fields to the east side of the railroad, the embankment of which protected them from the fire of the guns on the hill, dismounted some of their men, who engaged the dismounted Confederates at the bridge, drove them back and opened the way for their mounted men. They charged up the hill and made for the guns. They were here met by the mounted squadrons, supporting the guns, and driven back under the hill. The guns limbered up to retire, one coming back directly towards the depot, the other going down to the road in front of Mr. Lathams'. The 5th regiment had in the meantime, retired from Bell's Ford, and the gun came in on the road in the rear of this regiment, the Federal cavalry overtaking it at that point and making a capture of it. The Federals pressed the retreating Confederates vigorously through the town. On the hill, about where now stands the house of Walter West, and again on the slope of the hill towards Greenwood, a hand to hand conflict took place in which the saber was for the most part exclusively used. These two regiments, the 5th and 6th, lost a number of men at these places, who were never afterwards heard of; their bodies were left on the field, and we presume they are among the unknown dead of our cemetery.

Before reaching Culpeper, the 3rd division, under Kilpatrick, had turned across the country from Brandy to the Stevensburg road, and was having a close fight with Hampton's brigade in the valley, at the foot of Mt. Pony, while Jones was tussling with Gregg on the Rixeyville road with the advantages on his side. Hampton had not been so fortunate in his unequal contest with Kilpatrick, who was reinforced by some portion of Buford's command, sent across Mountain Run, by way of the Hudson farm. Hampton lost two guns, and suffered severely in men and horses, inflicting, however severe punishment on his adversary. From the Greenwood hill, the tussle between Hampton and Kilpatrick was plainly visible. The entire force on either side was in full view. The lines of battle, the advancing squadrons, the charging columns, the blazing batteries, the close grip of the skirmishers, made the scene, notwithstanding our own close quarters, as inspiring as any that we ever witnessed. This will be remembered as the occasion on which Mr. Curtis, living near Georgetown, sought safety from the shells of the Federal guns, by taking refuge in the basement of Mr. Jas. Inskeep's house. He had scarcely reached his supposed place of safety before a shell entered the house, penetrated the basement, exploded and killed him. An illustration of the soldier's maxim "that one place was as safe as another in battle." Jones, retiring by the Rixeyville road, and finding the town occupied by Buford's troops, made a detour by way of Catalpa and Thos. Rixey's, and joined the forces that had passed through the village on the hill south of Greenwood at the intersection of the Orange and Stevensburg roads. Just before Jones came up, the Federal cavalry, then occupying the Greenwood hill, made an effort to capture the remaining gun left with the Confederates at this point. It was posted in the road, just in advance of the intersection of the roads above referred to, supported by a squadron of cavalry. The Confederates had dismounted the most of their forces here, and concealed them in the pines that grew on the west side of the road, in advance of the gun. From their position near the Greenwood house, the Federals started a column to charge and capture the gun. They came down the road and were soon protected by the descent, from the fire of the gun on the hill.

They ascended the hill, near the gun, in fine style, and dashed for it with the confidence of certain capture, but as they passed these pines and exposed the flank of column, they received a deadly fire at short range from the dismounted men, which emptied many saddles and scattered the remainder in confusion over the fields. All the Confederate forces had now gotten together, and occupied a line from the Ward or Thompson hill to the foot of Mt. Pony till about night, the Federals drawing off and the fight ceasing. About dark the Confederates begun to retreat, and fell back that night to the Rapidan at Raccoon Ford, and Rapidan Station. Hampton taking position at the former, and Jones at the latter place. The Confederates occupied the hills about the Taliaferro and Nalle houses on the north side of the river, and also some points lower down the river about the Robertson house, and perhaps other places.

The next day, Sept. 14th, the Federal cavalry appeared in front of the station, and an artillery duel took place between the batteries of the Confederates on the Nalle hill and the Federal guns posted just in advance of the woods, on the road to Culpeper, which continued nearly all day. Towards evening, the Federals advanced their cavalry with a strong skirmish line in front, which movement was met by a corresponding action on the part of the Confederates, and a very pretty little fight was on; first with the skirmishers, afterwards with the mounted men, in which sabers and pistols were freely used, and a number on both sides came out of the fight with sore heads and punched backs. Lower down the river, about the Robertson house, the Confederates held the north side of the river till the 19th, at which time the Federals, by a strong advance of the infantry and artillery, compelled the Confederates to retire to the south side of the river. The Rapidan then became the line between the contending armies, and for nearly a month the sharp crack of the rifle of the picket, along the banks of the stream, was heard from morning till night, and it never died away till the armies were on the move again.

CULPEPER, OCTOBER 10TH AND 11TH.

On the 9th of October 1863, Gen. Lee, with a view of bringing Gen. Meade, then encamped in Culpeper, to an engagement, or forcing him back towards Washington, broke up his camp in Orange, and moved towards the right flank of the Federal army, by way of Madison, C. H., and along the south bank of the Hazel river. This movement was preceded by Hampton's division of cavalry, while two brigades of infantry, one at Rapidan Station, and the other near Raccoon Ford, with Fitz Lee's division of cavalry, were left on the Rapidan to guard the right and rear of Lee's advancing army.

About the middle of September the cavalry corps was re-organized. The number of regiments to a brigade were reduced to four, thus creating two new brigades, of which Lomax and Rosser were given command, and Butler and Gordon made brigadiers, to take the place of Robertson and Jones, sent to other localities. The cavalry corps was made up of two divisions, of three brigades each, of which Hampton, being made a major general, was given command of one, and Fitz Lee, also promoted, of the other. Hampton was still absent on account of wounds received at Gettysburg, and Stuart moved with his division and directed its movement. On the 10th of October he encountered the Federal pickets at Russell's Ford on the Robertson river, and drove them back rapidly till he reached James City, where he found Kilpatrick, with the third division of cavalry and a division of infantry under Gen. ———. A severe engagement took place between these forces, in which the artillery and dismounted men were principally engaged. The Federals made their stand at James City, but were driven back across Crooked Run, and took position on the hills of the Culpeper side. The Confederate artillery was posted at or near the village, and the property of the citizens of the little hamlet, being directly in the line of fire from the Federal guns, suffered severely therefrom. After having fallen back to the Culpeper side of the stream, the Federals crossed over a mounted column and attempted to capture a battery of Confederate guns, placed in front of the village. The guns were handled with such skill, and the charging Federals received with such a destructive fire from the Confederate carbiners, posted behind fences, that they precipitately retreated with great loss. Without attempting to dislodge them from the position last taken, Gen. Stuart, leaving one brigade in their front, pushed on towards the turn-pike with the residue of the division, and late in the evening came into that road at or near Griffinsburg, where he encamped for the night. The next morning, Oct. 11th, he moved down the turn-pike in the direction of Culpeper, and finding that he had passed on his right, in the neighborhood of Stone House Mountain, a Federal regiment of infantry that had been left on picket, as Meade's army retired, sent Capt. Bayler, a gallant officer of the 13th Va. cavalry, to the right of the turn-pike to capture this command. He soon came in contact with it, and at once charged into their midst; after making a short but firm resistance, they laid down their arms. Gen. Stuart, in his report, speaks of this as the second occasion, in the last two preceding days, in which he had hurled his mounted squadrons on infantry columns with entire success. Stuart pressed on down the turn-pike towards Culpeper, driving the enemy's rear guard before him, till he reached the hills on the west, overlooking the town. Kilpatrick had, in the meantime, fallen back from Brown's Store and had massed his cavalry and artillery on the hills about the George house, holding the town and the crossings at Mountain Run with his dismounted men. Stuart posted his artillery on the hill east of the Citizen's Cemetery, and opened a rapid fire on the Federal position, which was responded to with equal vigor, and for an hour or more the screaming shells passed each other in the heavens in rapid succession over the valley of Mountain Run, exploding in the ranks of their adversaries, tearing to pieces men, horses, gun carriages, and all the implements of warfare. Col. Ferebee, of the 4th N. C. cavalry, with the 5th as his support, was sent forward to drive the Federals from the crossings of Mountain Run, and to gain possession of the town; after a most stubborn fight in the streets of Culpeper, and along the banks of the stream, he succeeded in getting possession of the town, and driving the Federals from the crossings. In this little fight, in the town of Culpeper, the North Carolinians suffered severely. Col. Ferebee himself, together with Lieut. Moorehead, Lieut. Barbour, Lieut. Porter, and many others were wounded. Gen. Stuart, after keeping up the demonstration at this point for some time, withdrew the greater portion of his forces, and moving by the left flank, took the route by way of Chestnut Fork, with the view of getting possession of the high ground about the Barbour house, near Brandy, in the rear of Kilpatrick.

On the morning of the 10th, Gen. Meade, having ascertained that the Confederate army was in motion towards his right flank, directed Gen. Buford to cross the Rapidan river at Germanna Ford with his division of cavalry, move up the south bank of the river, and uncover the fords at Morton's and the one known as Raccoon, at which point he would be met by the first corps of infantry under Gen. Newton, and thus ascertain the extent and purpose of the movement of the Confederate army. Buford effected a crossing on the morning of the 10th at Germanna, and succeeded in capturing the pickets at that point, and at the other fords up the river towards Morton's, but before reaching the latter point he encountered the the 5th Va., cavalry, under Col. Pate, and his movements were retarded by the presence of this force in his front. He succeeded, however, in reaching the vicinity of Morton's Ford that night, and gaining possession of some of the little earth works that had previously been thrown up in that locality. The first corps, however, did not reach that point as was anticipated, but had been ordered to retire towards the Rappahannock. Early on the morning of the 11th Buford was attacked at Morton's Ford by the brigades of Lomax and Wm. H. F. Lee, fighting dismounted, and by them he was driven from the earth works which he occupied at that point. At the same time, Wickham's brigade of Fitz Lee's division and Johnson's brigade of infantry crossed the Rapidan river at Raccoon Ford to the Culpeper side, and moved down to assail Buford in his flank and rear. Chapman's brigade, of Buford's division was the first to cross the river at Morton's Ford, and it was sent to meet Wickham, who was bearing down on the rear. Between these two forces, about equally matched in numbers, occurred one of the hardest fought battles of the war. The Federals were in line of battle near the Stringfellow (now Spindle house), with one battery in action. The Confederates determined to capture these guns if possible, and for this purpose the 1st. and 3rd. Virginia regiments were ordered forward to the charge; this column, the second and fourth were placed in line as their support. Capt. Breathit, of the horse artillery, as was his wont, when a cavalry charge was to be made, rushed his battery up at a gallop with the charging column till he reached close quarters, and then, double shotted with grape and cannister, let drive with all his might. Before the charge was completed it was ascertained that the Federal position was protected by a ditch, impassable for mounted troops, and the order to charge, after the movement was well under way, was countermanded. In changing front in an endeaver to withdraw, some confusion arose in these commands. Finding that the Federals could not be reached by a mounted charge, the men were at once dismounted for this purpose, but before they were gotten well in line, the Federal dismounted men advanced at a charge. The 4th. regiment, dismounted, already in line, was ordered forward to resist this charge, and did so with such courage, gallantry and success, as to win the admiration of its comrades, and the encomium of the commanding officers; but the regiment suffered severely. Among those who fell were Capts. Newton and Williams, two of the most intelligent, gallant and useful officers of the cavalry corps. The Federals, having by this time withdrawn their whole force to the north side of the Rapidan, began to retreat rapidly towards Stevensburg, pressed at every point by the pursuing Confederates. The dismounted men moved in line of battle at a double quick from Raccoon Ford to Stevensburg, where Buford made a short stand, to protect some some of his moving trains.

May we be pardoned for making here a digression from the general purpose of this writing, and call attention to a fact, illustrative of the great sacrifice made by the Southern people for the cause which they believed to be just and righteous. In the little cemetery at Louisa C. H., there is a monument which marks three graves. On one side of the base is the following inscription: " To the memory of Robt. C. Towles, Co. " A," 4th Va. Cavalry, born Sept. 6, 1843, killed in battle June 16, 1864." On another side is this : " To the memory of J. Vivian Towles, private Company " A," 4th Va. Cavalry, born Feb. 11th, 1839, killed at Raccoon Ford October 11th, 1863." On another side is this inscription : " To the memory of Jas. H. Towles, private Co. " A," 4th Va. Cavalry, killed at Spottsylvania C. H., May 9th, 1864, born Oct. 19th, 1845;" and on the remaining side is the following: " The only sons of the Rev. John Towles." As the writer a few years ago was wandering through this country cemetery, he came across these graves, and reading the inscriptions on the shaft, there came into and over his soul a swelling tide of emotions, which it is vain for him to attempt to describe.

After a spirited fight at Stevensburg, in which the 2nd, 3rd and 4th regiments were hurled in successive charges upon the position held by the Federals, their lines were broken, beaten back, and they retreated rapidly towards Brandy Station, halting for a time at Norman's Mill, from which position they were driven by a rapid fire, and taking position on Fleetwood

Heights, with their artillery admirably posted, so as to command all the country in their front. The dismounted men of Lomax's brigade, principally the 1st Maryland regiment and the 4th regiment of Markham's brigade occupied the woods at that time extending up to Brandy Station, facing towards Fleetwood, whilst the 9th and 10th regiments of William H. F. Lee's brigade, thrown forward across the railroad, charged and dispersed a body of Federal cavalry occupying a position a little west of the station. But just as the battle was being well joined between Buford and Fitz Lee at the station, Kilpatrick, anticipating Stuart's purpose in leaving his front at Culpeper, retreated from that point, came rushing down towards Brandy, and planting his battery on both sides of the railroad between the Kennedy and the Wise houses, opened a raking fire on the flank of Fitz Lee's division engaging Buford. But Kilpatrick had scarcely gotten into this position and ready for effective work, before Stuart, coming down by the Botts house with two brigades of Hampton's division, appeared on Kilpatrick's left flank, and forced him to change front to meet his new adversary. Wickham's brigade, except the 4th regiment of Fitz Lee's division, was also sent forward from the station to resist Kilpatrick, who at once withdrew all his force to the west side of the railroad to meet this new danger. Stuart hurled his regiments, one after another, in rapid succession, upon the flanks of Kilpatrick's columns, breaking up in confusion some portions of his line, and in turn being broken by counter charges. Buford, seeing the straight to which Kilpatrick was put, pressed forward to his support and between him and the Confederate brigades at the station there was a fearful clash of arms. There was charge and counter charge, some regiments charging four or five times, and sometimes the whole brigade at a time, now giving away, now rallying and rushing again to the combat. At one time the Confederate dismounted men were surrounded by the Federal cavalry, but undismayed, they continued to fight till their charging comrades brought them relief. Brandy Station certainly never before, or since, that time, had such a wild waking up. There were charging squadrons in every direction. The booming of the cannon from every little billock; the clear ringing of steel, the sharp crack of the carbine; but above all, and over all, was heard the wild shout of battle from the lips of those gallant horsemen as they rushed to the conflict. The Federals finally succeeded in getting all their forces together, and rapidly retreated to and across the Rappahannock that evening. The Confederates encamped that night along the south bank about Beverly's and Milford's fords. The losses in this day's fight were serious on both sides, but especially so to Confederates in officers. Among others that might be mentioned, we recall Col. Julian Harrison, of the 6th, Maj. Gillette, of the 13th Va., Waller of the 9th., as seriously wounded. The cavalry corps, in the Bristoe Station campaign, lost in killed, wounded and missing 1336, the greater portion of which was in this day's fighting. The Federal losses during the same time were 1251.

The Confederate hospitals were established at the house of Mrs. Wise—Belle 'Pre. The mansion was soon filled, and when there was no longer room therein, comfortable places in outhouses, and in the yard, were found for suffering humanity, and all night long did this good woman and her daughters, like angels of mercy, minister to the sufferings of the wounded that were brought there, many of them to die before the morning sun arose. Providence has dealt kindly with this good woman, and led her gently along the pathway of life, even down to old age, perhaps in answer to the prayers of those who survived their sufferings and have ever held her and hers in grateful remembrance, and invoked the kindliest benediction of heaven upon them.

Oh! that the present generation could only appreciate and realize all that their mothers suffered, endured and sacrificed for the cause of the South. I would that their heroic patriotism might be written in letters of light that would glow forever, and burn into the very souls of their daughters and those who succeed them, for all time to come.

Gregg's division of cavalry was not engaged on the 11th. He had retreated on the Rixeyville road, having passed beyond Chestnut Fork before Stuart reached that point. He encamped at the Fauquier Sulphur Springs for the night, leaving a strong picket force at Jeffersonton, guarding the Hazel river as far up as the Monumental mills.

Col. Funsten, commanding Rosser's brigade, was sent from Brandy to Rixeyville to move in front of Ewell's corps, advancing by that road. Col. Ball, commanding the 11th Va. regiment, was sent forward to drive in the enemy's pickets which he found at Rixey's ford, and to follow them rapidly on their retreat. When he reached Jeffersonton, he found the 13th Pa. cavalry, posted near the church, to dispute his progress. The dismounted men of the Federals were placed about the Baptist church, behind the stone walls and fences which centered to that point, while the mounted men were kept as a support a short distance in the rear. Col. Ball dismounted his command and attacked the Federals in their position, but after considerable loss, was compelled to retire. The Federals were re-enforced by the 4th Pa., and the Confederates by the 7th and 12th Va. regiments. Col. Funsten sent the 12th regiment by a circuitous route to the right of the village, and reached the Springs road about a mile south of the river. The 7th regiment was sent to the left of the village, with instructions to move around in rear of the academy building, and attack the force at the church on its right and rear, while a portion of the 11th was mounted and passed around to the right of the church to attack them on their left, and at the same time the dismounted men were again advanced in the front. This movement on the part of the Southerners was eminently successful, and they caught the Federals on the slope of the hill, in rear of the church, between these two converging columns, and, in a gallant charge, routed and drove them back in great confusion. In the meantime, the 12th regiment had reached the Springs road some distance north of Jeffersonton, and met on the road, in the Beaver Dam woods, the Federal columns retreating from Jeffersonton. The Federals caught here between their pursuers and the 12th regiment, were charged front and rear, and dispersing through the woods, made their escape as best they could; many, however, were made prisoners.

The Confederate column then pressed on towards the Springs. They found the ford of the river strongly guarded with cavalry and artillery, and so soon as the Confederates came in sight, the batteries of the Federals, posted on the hills about the Springs, opened a terrific fire upon them; but, nothing daunted, they charged the ford of the river with a rush, crossed over, drove the enemy away and obtained a foot hold on the north bank. Fitz Lee's division crossed the river at Foxville, where they had quite a little fight with the Federal cavalry occupying the north bank. The greater portion of the Southern army crossed the river that night, and thus the tide of war once more rolled away from the shores of Culpeper, but to come again at its ebb on the 20th of October, when the Southern army re-crossed to the south bank of the Rappahannock, and occupied Culpeper after the failure of Gen. Lee, in the Bristoe Station campaign, to bring Gen. Meade to a general engagement.

The infantry, encamped near the river, extended from Welford's on the west, to Kelleyville on the right, and back towards Brandy and Stevensburg.

At Rappahannock Station the Confederates had a pontoon bridge and held a tete de pont on the north side of the fortified hill overlooking the station. Ewell's corps was encamped in the rear of Kelleyville, Rhodes' division occupying a position nearest the river and guarding the crossing in its front. About mid-day on the 7th of November the Federals appeared, in heavy columns, in front of Rappahannock and Kelleyville, and at the latter place effected a crossing during the day. The 2nd N. C. regiment, of Ramseers' brigade, numbering about 250 men, was on picket duty at Kelleyville, Wheatley's and Steven's fords. Rifle pits had been constructed near the river at Kelleyville, commanding the ford and the site of the old pontoon bridge, but these defences were commanded by the hills on the north side, which closed into the river rather in the form of a semi-circle. The Federals put three or four batteries in position on the north side of the of the river, and opened a terrific fire on the picket force along the river at Kellyville, and soon drove them to seek such shelter as they could find. Massie's Confederate battery was put in position on the south side about a half mile from the river, and engaged the enemy's battery, but the latter was so much superior in numbers, and in metal, that the Confederate guns were soon either silenced or driven to change their positions so frequently that they were of little service. An effort to re-enforce the pickets at the river also proved unavailing, because of the exposed nature of the ground, over which the re-enforcements attempted to pass, to the Federal batteries on the other side. So it was that the Federals, under the protection of their guns, succeeded in forcing the passage of the river, and capturing nearly all of the Confederate pickets at that point. Rhodes' division and perhaps parts of Ewell's corps, was formed in line of battle a mile or more in rear of the river, and so remained till after night, but the enemy made no further movement than to effect a lodgement on the South bank of the river. During the night of the 7th the Federals massed a heavy column in front of the tete de pont at Rappahannock Station, charged the position held by the Confederates on the north bank of the river, and succeeded in taking possession of the same, and capturing the greater part of Hays' and Hokes' brigade, together with a number of guns and other materials of war. The Confederate army fell back that night, and took up a position in advance of Culpeper, where it awaited during the next day the attack of the Federals. The line of battle, selected by Gen. Lee, extended from the foot of Mt. Pony, a little south of the Massie house on the right, across Mountain Run, along southward of the Hudson house, and north of the Williams house to the high ground on the Brandy road between the Bell and the Hall farm, thence along in front of where Mr. Daniel now lives and the Cleveland estate, to the road from Chestnut Fork to Brandy Station, with Hampton's ton's division of cavalry on the right beyond Stevensburg, and Fitz Lee on the left in the direction of Rixeyville. An admirable line; certainly the best that military skill and wisdom could have selected in this locality. Here Gen. Lee remained in line of battle all the day of the 8th., inviting an attack from Gen. Meade, but for some reason, he did not join battle with the Confederate chieftain at this time. There was more or less skirmishing going on all day between the skirmish lines, attended perhaps with some little loss to both sides. The Confederates lost the day before at Kelleyville some 20 or 30 men, killed and wounded, and about 200 taken prisoners. On the night of the 8th Gen. Lee fell back to his old encampment in Orange, south of the Rapidan; his army retired leisurely without any collision with the Federal advance, even between the cavalry, and the last serious fighting on Culpeper's soil was at an end.

From this time till May, 1864, when Grant moved south of the Rapidan river for his great campaign in the Wilderness, more than a hundred thousand Federal soldiers were encamped within the limits of the county. But during his time the right flank of his army was much harrassed by scouting parties of Southern cavalry that were wintering in Madison, Rappahannock and Fauquier counties, and also by Mosby's command found in the same locality. The left of Grant's emcampment was protected and guarded by a line of pickets extending from Crooked Run, near Brown's Store, across the turnpike, a little west of Stonehouse Mountain, by Apperson's gate on the Eldorado road, thence to Muddy Run about Coon's, to the river. Scarcely a night passed that this line was not disturbed at one or more points by dismounted cavalrymen, who were looking for a remount, and a number of good horses were suppled by Uncle Sam to do service for the Confederates during the next summer campaign. Many of these adventures were perilous in the extreme, but they were performed with a coolness and audacity that was indeed marvelous. Confederate soldiers, whose homes were within the Federal lines, made frequent visits to old Culpeper, to see the loved ones at home, the girl they left behind them, and made hair breadth escapes from capture. All these incidents are worth recording as a part of the history of the times. But of course the particulars of but few of them are known to the writer. We recall an incident of this character, which we will venture to put upon record. On November 24th, 1863, Capt. R. R. Duncan, a typical soldier, brave and fearless as Julius Caesar, a splendid horseman, an excellent swordsman and a good shot, stout, active, alert and atheletic, and of great wisdom, sagacity and cool judgement in times of danger, was with some 15 or 20 men of his company, scouting along the flanks of Meade's army. Finding the picket post on the turnpike not far in advance of Stonehouse Mountain, he sent forward a few men and by a dexterous movement to their rear, succeeded in capturing the two soldiers on the post. Feeling assured that the enemy would send out a scouting party to ascertain what had become of their pickets, and what force was prowling about their front, he concealed his little band in the woods near Salem church. Soon thereafter, about a company of Federal soldiers appeared, moving up the turnpike. He maintained his position till they had passed his front; he then came in on their rear, and immediately charged them, capturing the most of them and dispersing the residue. But immediately in their rear came the 3rd W. Va. cavalry, under Maj. Conger, to their support. With a number of prisoners, captured horses, and arms on his hands, it became a very difficult matter for Capt. Duncan to make good his escape, but he so skillfully and boldly managed his little force, now using them as mounted skirmishers, and again charging with them on the advance guard of the pursuing columns, that, after being pursued for several miles, he succeeded in getting off with all his captured, both men and animals, without loss to his command, but inflicting considerable loss to the Federals. One officer was killed, two others wounded, and other casualties among the enlisted men. Permit us to also put on record another incident in which a citizen of Culpeper county was the principal actor. About the latter part of December, 1864, a column of Federal cavalry, under the command of Gen. Torbett, passed through Culpeper, returning from a raid in the direction of Charlottesville. As it passed along the road in the neighborhood of Rixeyville, some four or five stragglers made their way to the home of Mr. J. W. Timberlake, who lived about a mile west of the main road. Mr. Timberlake was very kind to them, and gave them of what he had. After getting something to eat and rummaging through the lower parts of the house and taking what they chose, all left, except one, who seemed determined to explore every nook and corner about the building and appropriate to himself everything that suited his fancy. In his search he had gone into the upper rooms, Mr. Timberlake following him. In one of the upper rooms he found a bureau or some article of furniture of that kind, which he immediately begun to examine, emptying the contents of the drawers on the floor and putting some of the articles in his haversack. Mr. Timberlake stood it very patiently, until he began to scatter on the floor the articles of clothing which belonged to his dead wife, and which had been packed away there. This was too much for him, and stepping back to the fire place he grasped a heavy wrought iron shovel, and striking him with all his might on the head with this heavy instrument, felled him to the floor. In a moment he saw that he had killed him, and what was to be done? Looking from his window he saw a squad of Yankees approaching his house, and there he was with the dead soldier in his house and the horse tied to the rack.

He had a son, Edward, then about twelve years of age, whom he directed to mount the horse and make for his life to the woods in the rear. The Yankees seeing him, and thinking that he was a Confederate, made pursuit and passed beyond his house. While they were gone in pursuit of the boy, Mr. Timberlake and his daughter, Miss Senie, managed to get the dead soldier from the upper room to the basement and put him in one of the lower rooms. When the soldiers returned and asked who it was that they were pursuing he informed them that it was a half witted boy, the son of one of his neighbors, who seeing them approach, became frightened and fled, and thus he quieted their apprehension. They dismounted, and he gave them something to eat and they sat at the table and ate their meal in a room adjoining that in which was the body of their dead comrade. The old gentleman, in speaking of this years after the war, said " that when he put the soldier in the basement he was not quite dead, and kicked a little as he carried him down the steps, and while his comrades sat at the table eating their meals he was very much afraid that he would kick up a row in the cellar room adjoining. His body remained in the house until midnight or after, when Mr. Timberlake and his daughter took it therefrom and placing it in an ox cart, hauled it to the woods and buried it. And he rests not only in an unknown, but a dishonored grave.

BATTLE OF CEDAR RUN, OR SLAUGHTER'S MOUNTAIN.

On the 26th of June, 1862, the Federal Government organized what was called the Army of Va., consisting of three corps, of which the first was commanded by Gen. Sigel, the second by Gen. Banks, and the third by Gen. McDowell. Gen. John Pope, who had earned some reputation as a fighter, was given command of this army, and made himself ridiculous in the eyes of military men on both sides "by issuing" his bombastic order, upon assuming command, of "Head Quarters in the Saddle."

McClellan, having been defeated in front of Richmond by Lee, had sought shelter on the banks of the James River, under the protection of his gunboats, and had been so battered, bruised and broken in his seven days contest, that he concluded he would be unable to resume the offensive without fifty thousand additional troops, which his government, at that time, was unable to supply, without exposing the Capitol to attack. It was thought best in the Federal military councils, in this condition of affairs, to move upon Gordonsville with the army of Va., and thus threaten Lee's left and rear at Richmond. This army, with this object in view, took position to threaten Gordonsville and Charlottesville. Bank's corps was in Rappahannock, Sigel's about Waterloo and Jeffersonton, and a division of McDowell's was in Culpeper, with the remainder at Fredericksburg. A brigade of Federal cavalry, under Buford, was at Madison Ct. House, while another, under Bayard, was near Crooked Run church. During the months of July and August, the cavalry of Pope's army was very active and enterprising. It several times crossed the Rapidan on reconnoissance, and made its way to and beyond Orange C. H. towards Gordonsville.

Ashby's brigade of Confederate cavalry, now under the command of B. H. Robertson, which had been left in the valley, to conceal Jackson's movement towards Richmond, was withdrawn, and placed in position between Gordonsville and Orange, to watch the Rapidan, whilst Ewell's, Hill's and Winder's, or Jackson's old division, all under the command of Jackson, were quietly withdrawn from Lee's army below Richmond, and placed in camp in rear of Gordonsville. Jackson conceived the idea of defeating Pope by a rapid movement to Culpeper, thrusting himself between the wings of his army, and defeating them in succession. Jackson had 22,000 men, of which 1,200 was cavalry. Pope had 46,000, of which 6,500 was cavalry, but his army was scattered over a large area. On the evening of the 7th of Aug., Jackson began his movement towards Culpeper. Ewell's division moved from its camp near Gordonsville, towards Liberty Mills, whilst Winder's and Hill's divisions moved towards and encamped for the night, near Orange C. H.

Jackson expected to reach Culpeper early the next day, being only 18 miles distant. On the morning of the 8th, the cavalry crossed the river at Barnett's Ford, and drove back the enemy's cavalry towards Madison C. H. and Locust Dale. Ewell came down from Liberty Mills, on the north bank of the river, and came into the Culpeper road, south of Locust Dale. The Federal cavalry was very active, and was handled with great ability. The march of the Confederate columns was greatly impeded by the threatened incursions of this cavalry on the Confederate trains from the direction of Madison C. H. Jackson was too feeble in this arm of the service for an advancing army, and his small force had to be divided to protect his train and to press back the enemy's cavalry in front. It was hardly sufficient for both purposes and made but slow progress. This, together with the intense heat and dust of the day, the confusion in which the columns of Winder's and Hill's divisions had fallen, in respect to the order of their march, and the intermingling of their trains, blocked the road and made the progress on the 18th remarkably slow. Ewell's division reached Locust Dale, and whilst the Confederate cavalry gained possession of the fords at Robertson's river and Crooked Run, encamped for the night north of the latter stream. Winder's division had crossed the river at Barnett's ford, but Hill was still on the south side of the river. Jackson communicated with Gen. Lee from Locust Dale on the evening of the 8th, and stated that he feared the enterprise would be a failure, by reason of the day's delay. Gen. Pope, it seems, was aware of the movement of Gen. Jackson early on the 7th, and immediately ordered his forces to concentrate at Culpeper. Banks began his movement from the Rappahannock on the morning of the 8th, and encamped that night at Hazel river, on the Sperryville turn-pike. Rickett's division, of McDowell's corps, that had been encamped north of Culpeper, was moved forward on the 8th, and took position near Colvin's old tavern on the Madison road, to resist the movement of the Confederates, reported by Buford to be moving by way of Madison C. H. During the 9th Bank's corps passed through Culpeper, and was thrown forward on the Orange road, in the neighborhood of Cedar Run. Crawford's brigade of William's div'n, consisting of the 28th N. Y., 46th Pa., 10th Me., and 5th

Conn., with two batteries of artillery, was sent forward on the 8th to support Bayard's cavalry, and took position behind the hills immediately south of Cedar Run, and there remained during the night of the 8th., whilst Bayard's cavalry was kept well to the front. Early on the morning of the 9th the Confederate army, with Ewell's division in front, was again put in motion, but its movements were slow. The day, as the one before, was intensely hot and the road was a narrow one; the force of Confederate cavalry in front was insufficient to drive back, with rapidity, the Federal cavalry. At the extreme south end of Cedar or Slaughter's Mountain, Hay's brigade, of Ewell's division, consisting of 5th, 6th, 7th, 8th and 19th La. regiments, deflected from the main road, and passing across the fields to the base of the mountain, east of James Garnett's house, hugged the mountain closely and advanced along its base, under cover of the woods. Trimble's brigade, of the same division, consisting of the 12th Ga., 21st N. C., and 15th Ala., also left the Culpeper road at a point a little further north, and passing to the right by a cluster of pines, a little south of the Major house, reached the base of the mountain about where the road crosses it.

In the meantime, the Federal cavalry had been massed in the valley, on the south branch of Cedar Run, north of the Major house, and south of the Crittenden house and the one regiment of Confederate cavalry, the 6th Va., then with the advance of Ewell's division, was unable to dislodge it, without the aid of the Confederate infantry and artillery. Early's brigade, of Ewell's civison, consisting of the 13th, 25th, 31st, 52nd and 58th Va. regiments, which was marching in front, had, in the meantime, reached the intersection of the Waylandsburg and Culpeper roads. Maj. Courtney, chief of artillery of Ewell's division, posted two batteries, Capt. Dement's and Capt. Brown's of Maryland, on a small knoll on which there were growing pines, a short distance south of the Major house, whilst Capt. Lattimer's, and a section of Johnson's batteries, were sent forward with the advancing columns of Trimble and Hay, until they reached a position well up on the mountain side, not far below the Slaughter house. With a view of closing in on the rear of the Federal cavalry, massed in the valley, as before stated, Early's brigade moved from its position, at the intersection of the roads, and bearing well to the left of the road, under cover of the hills, so as to keep out of sight, reached the Culpeper road, and crossed it to the east at a point about one-half of a mile south of the Crittenden gate, and bore well down on the flank and rear of the cavalry in the valley. When his skirmishers engaged those of the cavalry, the batteries, posted by Maj. Courtney, also opened on their ranks. They broke and fled up the valley by the Crittenden house, but were rallied and reformed near the centre of the Federal lines on the main road.

Early then advanced his brigade and took position, first in line of battle along the road leading from the Crittenden house, which he occupied for a short time, then advanced his lines towards the summit of the hill overlooking the valley between the Crittenden house and where now stands the Smoot house. Three guns of Brown's and Dement's batteries were moved forward, and took position on the knoll of cedars a little north and west of the Crittenden house as did also several guns of Dement's and D'Arquin's batteries, at a point little nearer to, and north east of the Crittenden house. Ewell, with the residue of his division, had reached a position at the extreme north end of Slaughter's Mountain, keeping his infantry well under cover. The Federal commander, Gen. Banks, had, in the meantime, been busy organizing his line of battle, to meet the advance of the Confederates.

McGilvery's battery of six guns, and Robertson's and Gary's of four guns, were placed in position on the north side of the Mitchell's Station road, in front of the Hudson house pointing southeast, commanding the valley of the south branch of Cedar Run, and fronting the Confederate batteries on the slope of the mountain. Best's, Beamer's, and Knapp's batteries, of four guns each, were placed in position in the angle of the Mitchell's Station and Culpeper roads, and Mullensburg's battery of four guns was placed on the west side of the Culpeper road, on the high ground just in advance of the point where the road to Mrs. Brown's house leaves the Culpeper road. Gen. Prince's brigade, of Gen. Augur's division, supported by the brigade of Gen. Greene, occupied the extreme left of the Federal line of battle; it was placed astride of the Mitchell's Station road, with the 102nd N.Y. on the left, on the north of the road, and swinging round to the south and west in the angle of the road, were placed the following regiments, in the following order: the 109th Pa., the 3rd Md., and 11th Pa. Then came Gen Gary's brigade, of the same division, continuing the line of battle in the following order: the 5th O. on his left, connecting with Prince, then the 6th Ohio, 7th Ohio, and 29th. Ohio regiments. Crawford's brigade, of William's division, came next in order of battle, with the 5th Conn. on the east side of the main road, and the 28th N. Y., 46th Pa. and 10th Maine in the order named, their right being thrown back considerable to the rear. Still to the right of this was Gordon's brigade, of the same division, in two lines, with the 2nd Mass and 3rd Wis. in the first, and the 27th Ind. in the second line. The cavalry of the Federal army was massed about the centre of the line, near the main road, and behind the range of hills on the west. Winder's division, of the Confederate army, was now coming on the field, and four guns of Carpenter's and Poague's batteries were placed in position in the open field, in front of the Crittenden gate, on the east side of the main road, and shortly afterwards five rifle pieces of Hill's division, belonging to Caskie's, Fleet's and Pegram's batteries, were, by direction of Col. Walker, chief of artillery of Hill's division, placed along the ridge in front of Early's brigade, and but a short distance from the Federal skirmish line, extending across the corn field.

These dispositions for battle made by the two armies, consumed some time, and it was not till half past three o'clock that the battle opened, with nearly the whole of the artillery on either side in position; twenty-six of the best guns on the Confederate side, and twenty-eight on the Federal side were engaged; and for two hours they thundered at each other across this narrow valley, whilst further disposition was being made for the struggle between the infantry at closer quarters.

Garnett's brigade, consisting of the 21st, 48th, 47th and 1st Va. regiments, was ordered to move to the left through the woods, over the ground which is now the cleared ground about the Throgmorton house, and, if possible, reach the right of the Federal line, turn it, charge and capture the battery posted on the west side of the road. Upon reconnoitering the situation, it was found impracticable to execute this order. It was found that the right batteries, on the Federal line, were supported by infantry, posted in and in rear of the woods on the high ground, on what is now the Cooper farm, and the greater portion of the cavalry was also massed under the protection of the same hill. This brigade was then placed in line of battle, along the crest of the hill, in the rear of the wheat field, which lay between the two lines of battle, with its right consisting of the 48th and 21st regiments, thrown back along the road and facing north east, with a view of protecting the batteries in this field from an approach in front, whilst the 42nd regiment and 1st Va.

battalion were in line fronting the wheat-field. The 1st. Va. was on the extreme left, and an interval existed between that and the next regiment in line. About this time Gen. Jackson appeared on this part of the field. He at once saw that the exposed condition of his left flank invited an attack, and that the nature of the ground was exceedingly favorable for such a movement on the part of his adversary. He directed Gen. Garnett to look well to his left, and to request his division commander to reinforce him. Gen. Taliaferro's brigade, consisting of the 10th, 23rd, 37th and 47th Va. regiments, and the 48th Ala., having arrived on the field, was placed in line of battle along the road leading to the Crittenden house, in support of the Confederate batteries and connecting with Gen. Early on the right. About this time Gen. Winder was killed by a fragment of an exploded shell. He is said to have fallen in the main road, a short distance south of the Crittenden gate, and about where the fence of the Throgmorton land now comes to the road. There was some delay in reinforcing Garnett, owing to Winder's death and the change of division commanders on the field, and before it was done, Gen. Banks, contrary to the orders of his superior, perhaps, advanced his whole line of battle to the attack, although numerically weaker than Gen. Jackson.

The two brigades of Augur's division, with a battalion of the 8th and 12th U. S. regulars, under Capt. Pitcher, thrown forward as skirmishers, advanced in the centre, through the corn field on what is now the Smoot farm, and assailed Early vigorously. He was sorely pressed by these two brigades of Geary and Prince for a time, but being reinforced by Taliaferro's brigade on the left, and a portion of Thomas' Georgia brigade, of Hill's division, on the right, the progress of the Federal advance was soon arrested. The Federal line was also reinforced, by Greene's brigade, which was put in on the left as a support to Prince. The contest in, and in front of this corn field, was, for a time, stubborn and sanguinary. The Federal loss was very serious for the numbers engaged and the time the engagement lasted. Gen. Prince, in an effort to rally his broken command, was taken prisoner in this field by a private of the 23rd Va. regiment, surrendering his sword, however, to Gen. Taliaferro. But the Confederates were not so fortunate on their left. Before this portion of their line could be extended and reinforced, the Federals advanced. The two brigades of Crawford and Gordon, constituting the right wing of the forces engaged, the former in advance and about seventeen hundred strong, the latter in support, and still further to the right, were moved forward from their position behind the wooded hill to the assault on the left flank of the Confederate army. They moved from their position across the wheat field, in splendid order, with banners flying and confident step, and entered the woods on the south of the wheat field, overlapping and enveloping the left of the Confederate lines, breaking and routing the major part, if not the whole of Garnett's brigade, leaving the way open to the Confederate rear. The Federals pressed rapidly forward, and swinging around to their left, passed over the ground about where now stands the Throgmorton house, and well nigh gained the main road. Taliaferro, whose brigade was engaged with the Federals in the corn field, attempted to change front to meet this advance on his flank and rear. Some of his regiments, then for the first time under fire, becoming panic stricken by this destructive fire on their flank, broke and fled in utter rout. The artillery on the extreme left was withdrawn to escape capture. The whole left wing of the Confederate army seeming, for a time, to be broken and shattered, suffered great loss. Every field officer in Garnett's brigade had been killed or wounded. It was for a time a scene of great confusion. Officers were in the melee, trying in vain to rally their troops. Jackson, himself, appeared upon the scene, and drawing his sword, as it is said, for the first and only time during the war, commanded his men to rally and follow him against the advancing columns of the enemy. He remained with his discomfited troops, till reminded by Gen. Taliaferro that it was hardly a proper place for the chief officer in command.

Just at this juncture the Stonewall brigade, consisting of the 2nd, 4th, 5th, 27th, and 33rd Va. regiments, under the command of Col. Roland, appeared on the field. These regiments had been greatly reduced in numbers by the valley campaign and the seven days battle in front of Richmond, but they were staunch veterans of more than a dozen conflicts, and were not easily discomfited. This brigade was rapidly deployed in line in the woods on the west of the road, with its right extended, and left thrown back, and opening its ranks to allow the fugitives to pass through, boldly moved forward and opened a destructive fire on their enemies. Unfortunately for the Federals, especially Crawford's brigade, they had advanced too far from their supports, and suffered their line to become broken up in their rapid advance, and were not in a condition to receive the attack of this fresh Confederate brigade. They halted, attempted to reform their lines to meet their fresh antagonists, but with little avail. They were swept away before the onset of the Stonewall brigade as chaff before the wind, with frightful loss. The battle was at once renewed with great vigor. Jackson ordered an advance of the whole line. Ewell on the right, deploying his Alabama regiment as skirmishers, moved down from the mountain slope and extending his right brigade, under Trimble, reached Cedar Run and essayed to strike the Federal rear on the north side of the stream, but was prevented from crossing by the obstruction of an old millpond. The 2nd. and 6th, Va. cavalry (the 12th. having been detached to guard the left towards Thoroughfare Mountain, and the 7th. sent to Madison Courthouse), moved down the valley of the south branch of Cedar Run, and occupied the space between Early and Ewell. Ewell, finding that he could not cross the run, turned Trimble's brigade on the Federal batteries on the left of their line. The valley, immediately in their front, was so completely swept by the Confederate batteries on the slope of the mountain, that Trimble's troops could not pass over it till a staff officer had been dispatched to order a cessation of their fire. In the meantime the Federal batteries had been withdrawn, and the left was in retreat. Gen. Branch, coming on the field with his splendid brigade of North Carolinians about the time of the Confederate advance, was ordered to the support of the Stonewall brigade, and formed his line in the woods on its left at right angles to the road, followed by Pender's brigade, moving in column still further to the left. Taliaferro's brigade was quickly rallied on the right. Many of Garnett's men came back to the field, and fell in with the Stonewall brigade, which, with Branch's brigade, moved rapidly forward through the woods, and entering the wheat field, passed over the high ground, closing in towards the road, and by well directed volleys, crushed in and routed the Federal right with great loss of life, especially in Crawford's brigade, which, in killed, wounded and missing, lost more than half their number: 867 out of 1,670 taken into battle; Gordon's brigade also suffered severely.

The Federals attempted to retrieve the fortunes of the hour by a charge of cavalry on the Confederate lines as they emerged from the woods into the wheat field. Maj. Falls, with two squadrons of the 14th. Penn. cavalry, passing from behind the high ground on the west of the road, formed his command in column of squadrons, and charged down the little valley in the wheatfield on the Confederate line just as it had crossed the branch and entered the field. But they were met with such a well directed fire in front, as well as from the troops in the field on the east of the road (Thirteenth Virginia regiment), and Branch's brigade, which, at that time, was sweeping obliquely across the wheat field, and had reached the high grounds, that their ranks were broken before reaching their objective point. These squadrons lost in this charge 71, out of 164 men. The entire Confederate line was now pressing rapidly forward and the Federals were in hasty retreat, with William's division completely broken and routed. But it was now dark and the pursuit ceased for a time. Several pieces of artillery were placed in position on the high points south of the run, and the woods on the north side and the country beyond were subjected to a vigorous shelling to ascertain the position of the Federals. Rickett's division, of McDowell's corps, that had been left on the Madison road, leading from Colvin's Tavern, was ordered forward to the support of Bank's right, and took position on the north side of Cedar Run with his right, consisting of Tower's brigade, supported by Hartsuff's brigade, and two batteries of artilery—Lippen's and Matthew's—extending out to the range of hills near the Brown house, and his left, consisting of Carroll's and Duryea's brigades, resting on the Culpeper road, near the woods in the rear of the Hudson house, and Hall's battery posted on a little eminence on the west of the road, and Thompson's on the east. But, before this disposition had been entirely completed, the Confederate lines were advanced to the north side of the run. Fields' brigade, of Hill's division, crossing the run, moved in line of battle on the left of the road. Spofford's brigade, of the same division, on the right, whilst Pegram's battery and the 6th. Virginia cavalry moved in column in the road, and the 7th Va., cavalry moved on the right of Spofford's brigade. The advance of the Confederates was slow, cautious and quiet, until they reached the north skirt of the woods, where they halted and Pegram took position with his battery on a little knoll just west of the road. The line of the Federals could be distinctly seen by the little fires they had built, around which they were brewing their coffee. Pegram's batteries opened on them with grape and cannister, and threw them into great confusion. They could be distinctly seen, by the light of their fires, rushing headlong to the rear. Milroy, who was just arriving on the field with his brigade, threw it in line across the road in their rear and stopped their flight. Order in a short time was restored, and Hall's battery, on the right of the road, and Thompson's on the left, concentrated their fire on Pegram, and killed and wounded a number of his men and horses. Our esteemed former countyman, Gen. J. G. Field, then a staff officer of Gen. Hill, lost his leg in the road near Pegram's battery. This artillery duel, with some skirmishing between the infantry, continued for an hour or more, when it gradually subsided and finally ceased. The cavalry was withdrawn and went into camp in the wheat field, but the infantry and artillery remained in position during the night. The next morning a brisk skirmish was begun, and there was every indication of a renewal of the battle. It lasted till perhaps 12 o'clock, when Jackson having ascertained that nearly the whole of Pope's army was concentrated in his front, to use his own language, concluded that "it was not prudent to attack," and withdrew his lines to the position he at first occupied. On the morning of the 10th Gen. Stuart, having arrived on a tour of inspection, gathered together the Confederate cavalry, moved east to the railroad, which he followed nearly to the Stevensburg road leading from Culpeper, in the rear of the Federal army, having first sent forward a detachment to Mt. Pony to capture the signal corps there stationed. Stuart ascertained, from prisoners captured and other sources, that the remaining division of McDowell's corps was hourly expected to arrive from Fredericksburg, so that it became apparent that, if not already on the field, the whole of Pope's army was in supporting distance, and no decided victory could be reasonably expected against such odds.

The next day, the 11th, the Federal commander asked for a truce to bury his dead, and all that day the Federal and Confederate soldiers mingled freely together, engaged in the pious work of burying their dead and caring for their wounded. The Federals lost in the engagement, in killed, wounded and missing 2,381, and the Confederates 1,276. On the 12th, Jackson slowly withdrew his command to the south side of the Rapidan, unmolested by the Federal advance.

PENSIONERS OF THE REVOLUTION.

CHAPTER VIII.

From the census of pensioners of the Revolutionary Army, as published in 1841, by authority of Act of Congress, under the direction of the Secretary of the Navy, we take the following, who are put down as "Culpeper County, Va." pensioners.

Name of Pensioner.	Age.	Head of family with whom Pensioner resided in 1840.
Catherine Allen,	79.	Catherine Allen.
Nancy Bailey,	75.	Armstead Bailey.
John Creel,	—.	John Creel.
Sarah Colvin,	78.	Sarah Colvin.
John Cannady,	77.	John Cannady.
Lucy Pettit,	78.	John L. Conner.
Elizabeth Edwards,	90.	Elizabeth Edwards.
John Freeman,	83.	John Freeman.
Zachariah Griffin,	79.	Zachariah Griffin.
Gabriel Gray,	77.	Gabriel Gray.
Humphrey Hill,	77.	Humphrey Hill.
Julius Hunt,	78.	Julius Hunt.
John Hall,	79.	John Hall.
William Jett,	77.	William Jett.
William Lewis,	77.	William Lewis.
Mary Lampkin,	78.	Mary Lampkin.
Hannah Clark,	87.	Madden Willis.
Amber Newman,	85.	Amber Newman.
Richard Payne, Sr.,	77.	Richard Payne, Sr.
Reuben Rosson,	87	Reuben Rosson.
Randolph Stallard,	83.	Randolph Stallard.
Philip Slaughter,	82.	Philip C. Slaughter.
Peter Triplett,	88.	Peter Triplett.
Almond Vaughn,	84.	Almond Vaughn.
Isaiah Welsh,	—.	Isaiah Welsh.

NOTE.—This list is copied just as printed. It is supposed the females are widows of deceased soldiers, living either in their own homes, or with married daughter, and some of the old soldiers with the sons or daughters.

CULPEPER COUNTY, VIRGINIA, PENSION ROLL, AS PUBLISHED IN 1865, BY ORDER OF THE SECRETARY OF NAVY, UNDER AN ACT OF CONGRESS PASSED 1834.

NAME.	Description of Service.	When placed on Pension roll.	Commencement of Pension.	Age.	Laws under which Inscribed, Increased And reduced
Wm. Burke, 2nd.	Virginia Line.	June 14, 1819.	July, 20, 1818.	83.	
William Briley.	Virginia Line.	Sept. 20, 1819.	October 8, 1818.	60.	Died June 28, 1832.
Francis Bundy.	Virginia Line.	Sept. 25, 1819.	April, 21, 1818.	82.	
William Clark.	Virginia Line.	Dec. 18, 1818.	April 1, 1818.	72.	Died Dec. 8, 1827.
John Deane.	Virginia Line.	April 22, 1818.	April 1, 1818.	80.	Dropped under act of May 1, 1820.
John Dean.	Virginia Line.	Jan. 27, 1819.	May 4, 1818.	80.	Died July 29, 1828.
Spencer Edwards.	Virginia Line.	May 9, 1819.	May 28, 1818.	74.	
Daniel Flin.	Virginia Line.	July 25, 1818.	April 24, 1818.	92.	
John Freeman.	Virginia Line.	April 28, 1826.	May. 10, 1826.	78.	
Andrew Green.	Virginia Line.	Nov. 24, 1818.	June, 23, 1818.	73.	
John Hull.	New Hampshire Line.	Jan. 28, 1819.	April 1, 1818.	72.	Died December 26, 1832.
Clement Heatey.	Virginia Line.	Jan. 30, 1819.	July 3, 1818.	64.	Died February 26, 1821.
Robert Horton.	Virginia Line.	April, 20, 1819.	April, 10, 1818.	68.	Suspended under act of May 1, 1820.
Benjamin Hisle.	Virginia Line.	March 24, 1832.	March 10, 1832.	72.	
John Lambkin.	Virginia State.	March 24, 1832.	April 2, 1818.	—.	Dropped September 4, 1819.
Newman Landman.	Virginia Line.	April 19, 1819.	April 24, 1809.	75.	April 27, 1810; invalid relinquished
Peter Triplett.	Virginia State Troops.	March 24, 1832.	April 6, 1818.	79.	Dropped Sept. 4, 1819, [for benefit of act restored] of March 18, 1818.
Samuel Young.	Virginia Line Continental.	March 2, 1827.	March 2, 1827.	79.	
Samuel Young.	Virginia Line Continental.	Jan. 7, 1832.	January 2, 1832.	74.	February 22, 1830]

REVOLUTIONARY ARMY.

See Executive Document No. 37, 32nd Congress, Feb. 28, 1852, rejected or suspended applications for want of sufficient proof, made to the United States Senate, Feb. 10, 1852, in obedience to a resolution of the Senate, Sept. 16, 1856.

1. Zachariah Dulaney's Heirs; he died before the 1836 act was passed.
2. Frederick Natts; served less than 6 months. ["Natts" is probably "Nalls."]
3. Susannah Murry; widow of James, applied under the act of July 4, 1836.
4. Margaret Hazel; widow of Elisha, applied under the act of 1836.
5. Eleanor Shepherd; widow of John.

PAY ROLL

Of Capt. Benjamin Cole's Company of Virginia Militia, 5th Regiment, of Culpeper County, first at Camp Randolph, and then at Camp Holly, under the command of Major Wm. Armstead, and then of Col. John H. Cocke, from the 29th of March to the 19th of August 1813.

NAMES.	RANK.	MONTHS.	DAYS.
Benj. Cole.	Captain.	3	22.
Thompson Ashby.	First Lieutenant.	3	22.
George Thom.	Second Lieutenant.	3	22.
Bailey Buckner.	Sergeant.	3	22.
Wm. F. Thompson.	Sergeant.	3	22.
Catlett Pendleton.	Sergeant.	3	22.
Robert Green.	Sergeant.	3	22.
Edward Green.	Sergeant.	3	22.
Richard C. Grimes.	Corporal.	3	22.
William B. Thornton.	Corporal.	3	22.
Robert Waggoner.	Corporal.	3	22.
Richard Pettigrew.	Corporal.	3	22.
William Gaines.	Drummer.	3	22.
William Wise.	Fifer.	3	22.
Nimrod Apperson.	Private.	3	22.
Joseph Bowen.	Private.	3	22.
Willis Camp.	Private.	3	22.
George Camp.	Private.	3	22.
Thomas Charlton.	Private.	3	22.
John Dobbs.	Private.	3	22.
Payton R. Eldridge.	Private.	3	22.
George Green.	Private.	3	22.
Benjamin Hawkins.	Private.	3	22.
Silas Hawkins.	Private.	3	22.
Nicholas Hart.	Private.	3	22.
Lawson Jones.	Private.	3	22.
John Miles.	Private.	3	22.
Jesse Pratt.	Private.	3	22.
Dudley Patty.	Private.	3	22.
Thomas C. Powell.	Private.	3	22.
Abbott Rosson.	Private.	3	22.
Larkin Rosson.	Private.	3	22.
Mosses Revell.	Private.	3	22.
Robert Rowe.	Private.	3	22.
James Saunders.	Private.	3	22.
Nathaniel Saunders.	Private.	3	22.
Oliver Sims.	Private.	3	22.
John Smith.	Private.	3	22.
Henry Smith.	Private.	3	22.
Samuel Stout.	Private.	3	22.
Gustavus Summerrall.	Private.	3	22.
Larkin Turner.	Prrvate.	3	22.
Ignatious Wheeler.	Private.	3	22.
James Wise.	Private.	3	22.

Pay roll for the traveling expenses of a detachment of the 3rd Virginia Regiment that was discharged from the camp at Valley Forge, to their different counties, Feb. 15, 1776.

NAME.	Rank.	County.	Distance.	Lb.	S.	Pence.
Armstead White.	Sergeant.	Culpeper.	230 miles	1	18.	

NOTE: This is taken from the original Pay Roll as above. Heading copied correctly; signed by Lieut. Thomas Hungerford, 3rd Virginia Regiment.

CULPEPER'S PROTEST AGAINST THE STAMP ACT.

At a court held for the county of Culpeper on Monday, the 21st day of October, 1765, the sixteen justices of the peace for Culpeper county, drew up and signed a protest to Governor Fauquier against the imposition of the stamp act, emphasizing their protest by resigning their commissions. The address, which is given in full, is recorded in the Culpeper clerk's office, in deed book "E," on page 138, and is attested by Roger Dixon, who was the first clerk of the county. The address is as follows :

"To The Honorable Francis Fauquier, Esquire, his Majesty's Lieutenant. Governor, and Commander-in-Chief, of the Colony and Dominion of Virginia. The humble address of the Justices of the Peace of the County of Culpeper.

"Sir: At a time when his majesty's subjects in America are so universally alarmed on account of the late proceedings of the British Parliament, and the enemies of America employed in representing its colonies in an odious light to our most gracious Sovereign, and his ministers, by the most ungenerous interpretation of our behavior, we beg leave to take this method to assure your Honour of our inviolable attachment to, and affection for, the sacred person of his Majesty, and the whole Royal family.

"And, from your Honour's well known candor, and benevolent disposition, we are persuaded that we shall at the same time be permitted to lay before your Honour those reasons which have determined us to resign the Commission of the Peace, under which we have been sworn to act as magistrates in this county.

"It seems to be the unanimous opinion of the people of America (and of a few in England), that the late acts of Parliament, by which a stamp duty is imposed on the Americans, and a court of vice-admiralty appointed ultimately to determine all controversies, which may arise, concerning the execution of the said act, is unconstitutional, and a high infringement of our most valuable privileges as British subjects, who, we humbly apprehend, cannot constitutionally be taxed without the consent of our representatives, or our lives or properties be affected in any suit, or criminal causes, whatsoever, without first being tried by our peers.

"And, as the execution of the said act does, in some measure, depend on the county courts, we cannot, if consistent with the duty which we owe our country, be, in the smallest degree, instrumental in enforcing a law which concieves, as in itself, shaking at the very foundation of our liberties, and, if carried into execution, must render our posterity unhappy, and ourselves contemptible. In the opinion of all men who are the least acquainted with a British constitution, as we shall, in that case, no longer be free, but merely the property of those whom we formerly looked upon only as our fellow subjects.

"Permit us, Sir, to add that we still hope his Majesty and Parliament will change their measures and suffer us to enjoy our ancient privileges, and if we should incur the displeasure of our Sovereign by thus endeavoring to assert our rights, we should look upon it as one of the greatest misfortunes which could befall us.

"We do heartily and sincerely wish his Majesty a long and happy reign over us, and that there never may be wanting a Prince, of the illustrious House of Hanover, to succeed him in his dominions, that your Honour may continue to enjoy the favor of our Sovereign, long govern the people of this ancient and loyal colony, and that the people may again be as happy under your mild and gentle administration as they have formerly been, is what we most devoutly pray for.
(Signed.)

N. Pendleton,	William Williams,	Wm. Green,
Robert Green,	John Strother,	Thomas Scott,
John Slaughter,	Henry Pendleton,	Benj. Roberts,
W. Eastham,	Geo. Wetherall,	Dan'l Brown,
Ambrose Powell,	Wm. Brown,	Henry Field, Jr.,
	Joseph Wood."	

FAMILY GENEALOGIES.

CHAPTER IX.

DESCENDANTS OF WILLIAM RICE.

Among the early settlers of what is now Culpeper county, was William Rice, who came some time before the county was organized. In volume 17, of the patent records in Richmond, page 120, is a deed from George II etc., to William Rice, for four hundred acres of land in the forks of the Rapid Ann, in the county of Orange, beginning at four pines on a point on a branch of Dark Run. This deed is dated July 29, 1736, and is signed by William Gooch.

Orange county, at that time, included all of what is now Culpeper. From it Culpeper was formed in 1748. William Rice was a son of Thomas Rice, who came to America in the latter part of the 17th century, and who is mentioned in the following manner, in the memoirs of Rev. David Rice, published by Thomas T. Skillman, Lexington, Ky., 1824, pp. 420.

"Thomas Rice was an Englishman by birth, of Welsh extraction. He was an early adventurer into Virginia; where he spent the first part of his life is not certainly known. In the latter part of his life he owned a small plantation in the lower part of what is now (1824) called Hanover county. Here he left his wife, with nine sons and three daughters, and went to England to receive a considerable estate which had been left him, but returned no more. The sailors reported that he died at sea. It is supposed that he was assassinated. No return was ever made of the property after which he had gone, and his family were left destitute in a strange land." * * * * * *. "The family being left without an earthly father, were distressed, but they were, in the good providence of God, provided for. The greater part moved about thirty miles farther up the country, where they procured a small plantation, on which they raised numerous families; four or five of them became serious professors of religion, and were succeeded in their religious profession by a considerable number of their children."—pp. 13 and 14. His wife, "was esteemed truly a religious woman," pp. 33. Among those descendants, who moved North, was William Rice, of Culpeper.

In Patent Book 8 of the same Records, page 261, is recorded a patent from Sir Edmond Andros, Kt., their Majesty's Lieutenant and Governor General etc.," to Thomas Rice for land lying in "Kingston Parish, in Gloucester county, said land being due unto said Thomas Rice by and for the importation of one person into this colony." Dated the 29th day of April, 1693. This Thomas Rice was probably the one who was father of William Rice, of Culpeper. In the same records, vol. 17, pp. 132, is recorded a deed from George II, King, etc., to Thomas Rice, for 1200 acres of land in Hanover county, on both sides of Cub Creek and Dirty Swamp, bounded by the lands of Col. David Meriwether, David and William Meriwether, James Goodall, and Richard Brooks. This is probably the place where this Thomas Rice lived in the latter part of his life.

The last will and testament of William Rice was probated and recorded in Culpeper county the 17th day of April, 1780. It was dated the 9th day of February, 1780. He divided his property about equally between his children, Richard, John, Benajah, Hannah Rice, Ann Graves, wife of John Graves, and Sarah Graves, wife of Edward Graves. In his will is the following provision, "I lend to my beloved wife, Sarah Rice, one-half of my estate during her natural life." After that it was to be divided equally between his children. He appointed Benajah, John, and Richard Rice, his sons, and John Graves, his son-in-law, his executors. Among the property inventoried are slaves, horses, cattle, sheep, hogs, plantation tools, six spinning wheels, two looms, one copper still, a desk, warming pan, books of sundry kinds, valued at £70, money scales, cash in metal £7, 13s. 9d., cash in paper £55, 8s., punch bowls, valued at £16. He gave the copper still to his unmarried daughter. Perhaps he thought she would be less likely to misuse it. The fact that "money scales" were considered a part of the equipment of a plantation would seem to indicate that coin, or metal money, as it is called in this inventory, was valued according to its weight in those days.

John Rice, one of the sons of William Rice, removed to the valley of Shenandoah. He obtained there a large tract of land about six miles long. Built a log cabin upon it, and there went back. He married Mary Finney. Upon his marriage his father made the newly married couple a wedding present of a set of silver spoons, marked W. R., the initials of the donor. If they were marked on purpose for the occasion it shows a different custom in marking wedding presents from that which now prevails. These spoons are still in the possession of some of their descendants. After marrying, he returned to Rockingham county, lived and died there, and his will was admitted to probate there A. D. 1804. He willed all of his land and slaves to his wife during her life, to be divided, at her death, amonst his children, except his daughter, who had married James Snaden, and gone to Bourbon county, Ky. He had probably given her her share when she went to Kentucky. John Rice, shortly after his return to Rockingham county, and about the year 1776 to 1779, built his new house, which is still standing, and is in good order and occupied. The roof is a little steeper than 45 degrees. The first roof was on the house seventy-one years. It was made of yellow pine shingles, about three quarters of an inch thick, pinned on with locust pins. There is a cellar under the whole house, part of which was used as a kitchen, and part of it for a store-room, for bacon and whiskey. Almost every large plantation, in those days, had its own distillery and made the whiskey for the use of the plantation, and, according to modern standards, they used too much. The cellar walls and fireplaces were built of brick, which was not usual at that time. The house is a frame one. It is weather-boarded with siding, 6 inches wide, and little more than half an inch thick, of yellow pine. All the lumber in the house was sawed out by hand with whip-saws. Every one of the weather-boards has a bead run on the edge for ornament. The siding is nailed on with wrought iron nails, which still show the mark of the blacksmith's hammer. The doors are six panel doors, and the window blinds are made the same way. All the hinges are wrought iron, made by hand, and also show the marks of the blacksmith's hammer. There is a profusion of moulding all through the house. It was the first frame house lathed, plastered and weather-boarded and painted in all that region. It is in good order now, much better than Thomas Jefferson's, which was built sixteen years later. This house was called "The Painted House," and that part of the country was called "The Painted House Neighborhood," houses painted on the outside being so rare. The neighborhood is sometimes known yet among the old settlers, as "The Painted House Neighborhood," though this house lost all its paint long ago, and has not received a new application lately. The Rices of Rockingham county are buried in the Dayton burying ground, commencing at the South side of the graveyard and extending Northward. First is old Mrs. Finney, who came over from Accomac county, or Culpeper, to live with her daughter, Mary, and son-in-law, John Rice. Next to her is John Rice; then Mary, his daughter; then Ursula Gaines Rice; then Mary Finney Rice, the wife of John; then three or four children; then William Rice, John's oldest son, who is the first one who has a lettered tombstone. The rest have just plain stones from the creek. William's gravestone is marked as follows: "William Rice, born July 27th, 1779, and departed this life August 2nd, 1838. Aged 59 years and 6 days." Benajah Rice, brother of John Rice, also obtained land in the same county, and adjoining John. He never lived there himself, but some of his children did, and some of his descendants are living there now. The Mary Finney, whom this John Rice married, belonged to the family of Finneys who have lived, for the last 250 years or more, in Accomac county, on the eastern shore of Virginia. There is a place now, called "Finney," and a place called "Finney's Wharf." Honorable Louis C. H. Finney was a member of the Virginia Senate a few years ago, and was well versed in the history of the Finney family. It is probable that William Rice was an Episcopalian; also his son, John Rice, and probably his daughter-in-law, were. An old negro slave, called "Lark," was born on the property of this John Rice, and was baptized, as all the other slaves born on the plantation were, after the fashion of the patriarch, Abraham, who baptized his whole family, including all his servants. This old negro was made free by Ann Hopkins Rice, a daughter-in-law of John Rice, who inherited him, and he died in Illinois about 1863, living with one of John Rice's grandsons. Except these, nearly all of the Rice family, including even the descendants of these, were, and are, Presbyterians.

David Rice, who was sometimes called the "Apostle of Kentucky," and who was instrumental in the founding of Hampden and Sidney College, Virginia, and of the Transylvania University, Kentucky, and the Danville Theological Seminary, Kentucky, was the first moderator of the first Presbytery, and the first moderator of the first Synod of Kentucky, and a member of the first constitutional convention of Kentucky, was a nephew of William Rice, of Culpeper. Benjamin Rice, David's brother, was a lawyer, of Bedford county, Virginia, whose son, John Holt Rice, D. D., was the first pastor of Richmond Memorial church, and first Professor of Christian Theology in Union Theological Seminary, Virginia, and once moderator of the Presbyterian General Assembly. Another son, Benjamin Holt Rice, was a professor in Princeton, and was once moderator of the Presbyterian General Assembly. Nathan Lewis Rice, D. D., also one of the descendants of this Thomas Rice, was once a moderator of the General Assembly, and was a theological professor. Quite a large per cent of the Rice family have been, and are lawyers, ministers of the Gospel, or doctors of medicine.

The Rices, when living in Wales, had a Coat of Arms, of which the widow of Izard Bacon Rice long ago had a copy. The widow of John Holt Rice, D. D., who died in 1831, also had a copy. Mrs. Sara A. Pryor, a prominent member of the Daughters of the American Revolution, wife of General Roger A. Pryor, late Justice of the Supreme Court, New York, now has a copy. Mrs. Pryor is a descendant of Thomas Rice, of Hanover.

The Rice motto was "Fides Non Timet." In the old days, when written in Welsh, the name was spelled "Rhys," though even then, when written in English, it was often spelled, as now, "Rice."

THE BARBOUR FAMILY GENEALOGY.
By John Strode Barbour.

[The following genealogy of the Barbour family was received too late to be placed in St. Mark's proper, in which Dr. Slaughter's sketch of the Barbour family is printed.—R. T. G.]

There is some confusion as to the name of the first emigrant and founder of the Barbour family in Virginia, or rather who was the emigrant of this particular family. All traditions seem to give their extraction as Scotch, and the time of coming to this country as about the middle of the 17th century. Some traditions give William Barbour, who was said to have been a younger son of the Baron of Mulderg, and who was County Lieutenant of York in 1656, and also one of the commission appointed by the governor, Sir William Berkley, in 1660, to superintend the erection of the State house at Jamestown, as the first emigrant (See Hardesty's Historical and Geographical Encyclopedia [1884] p. 358), while others give James Barbour, a Scotch merchant. One tradition, in connection with this last theory, is that, on arriving in Virginia, James Barbour established a home on a plantation, since famous as the seat, for generations, of another distinguished Virginia family. That he there married a Miss Taliaferro, and died, leaving an infant son, James, and a widow. That the widow re-married, and by some means the issue of this second marriage, who was almost an imbecile, became the owner of the entire Barbour property. He was a great gambler, and soon squandered it. The only form of gambling he had intellect sufficient to engage in was "push pins", and he is reported to have lost the homestead upon the issue of a single game. However true this tradition may be, the son, James, left the home of his childhood after his father's death, and came to Culpeper near the end of the first quarter of the 18th century, and settled finally in Culpeper county. It was here that he lived, and died, and was buried. The tombstone marking his grave is still standing at Smith's Cottage, the old homestead, now in Madison county. This second James, spoken of by Dr. Slaughter as the first, was a vestryman of St. Mark's Parish at its organization in 1731. Probably the most authentic account of the founder of the Virginia family, now attainable, is the following extract from the bible of Governor James Barbour, entered therein in his own handwriting, under date of June 6th, 1806. It will be observed that he makes no reference to William Barbour, and no claim to descent from titled ancestors, but seems rather to emphasize the fact that his ancestors were "farmers or yeomen". It will be observed also that he refers to the defeat of the expectations of the second James, by reason of the re-marriage of his mother. He says: "The farthest back that I have been able to trace, with any certainty, is my great grandfather, who came over to this country from Scotland, in the 17th century. He came in the character of a merchant, and was wrecked on his first adventure. His friends, as stated by tradition, being rich, furnished him with a new cargo, which he turned to a profitable account in (I believe) the county of King and Queen. He had issue, only one son, whom he called after himself, James, who intermarried with Sarah Todd, of a most respectable family. My grandfather's prospects in life were considerably blasted by the second marriage of his mother, an usual concomitant of such connections with the wreck of his expectations. He was either the first or second settler in this country; I mean the South West Mountains. I am certain he was the first inhabitant of this neighborhood, which was at first about the plantation now in the occupancy of the Newman family, that being the place of residence from which he moved to a place nearer the river that belonged to William Johnson. He had issue, five sons, and three daughters   *   *   *. My father Thomas, as well as his father, were farmers or yeomen." In the obituary notice of his distinguished great grandson, Judge Philip Pendleton Barbour, published in Vol. 16, Peters' U. S. Supreme Court reports, it is said : "His (Judge Barbour's) great grandfather was a merchant of Scotland, who emigrated to this country. His grandfather (the second James) was the founder and first settler of the country lying between the eastern base of the Blue Ridge and the South West Mountains." While it is possible that the first James, instead of being the emigrant, was a son of a grand son of the William Barbour, above mentioned, in the following chart this James Barbour is treated as the founder of the family.

[In order that any errors or omissions, found in this account of the Barbour family, may be corrected in any future editions, the publisher requests that any such may be reported to John S. Barbour, Culpeper, Va. The names in parenthesis denote the line of descent. Thus : "Gabriel Barbour (Thos., Jas., Jas., Jas.,) signifies that Gabriel Barbour was the son of Thomas, the grandson of James, and so on.—R. T. G.].

JAMES BARBOUR emigrated from Scotland in the 17th. century; settled in King and Queen, or in Gloucester county; married Miss Taliaferro, and had but one son, James, erroneously called James, the first, by Dr. Slaughter, who was "defeated of his expectancy" by the second marriage of his mother.

JAMES BARBOUR (James.) m. twice; first Elizabeth Todd, by whom he had one son, Richard, who never married. His second wife was Sarah Todd, probably a sister of the first. He was presiding justice of the Culpeper county court in 1764, and died in 1775 in Culpeper county. His widow, Sarah, died in 1781. Their wills are both recorded in Culpeper county, and show them both to have been posessed of large estates. There were by the second marriage five sons: James, Thomas, Philip, Ambrose, and William, and four daughters, as follows : Mary, Fanny, Betty, and———,who m. James Boyd.

JAMES BARBOUR (James, James.) m. Frances Throckmorton, of Gloucester county. He was a member of the House of Burgesses from Culpeper in 1764, County Lieutenant of the militia of Culpeper county in 1775, an officer in the revolutionary army, and was also a judge of the first court ever held in Kentucky, being the head of a commission appointed by the Legislature of Virginia to settle disputed land titles. His children were 1. Mordecai, who m. Elizabeth Strode; 2. James who died unmarried; 3. Thomas, m. Mary Taylor; 4. Richard, m. Mary Moore; 5. Gabriel; 6. Philip, m. 1st. Lucy Taylor, 2nd. Eliza Hopkins; 7. Frances, m. John Moore; 8. Sarah, m. Col. John (or James) Harrison; 9. Mary, m. Col. David Walker, who was for years a member of Congress; 10. Lucy, m. Wythe Baylor.

AMBROSE BARBOUR (James, James.) lived in Orange county, where he married Catherine Thomas, a sister of Mary Pendleton Thomas, who married his brother, Thomas Barbour. They afterwards moved to Kentucky. Their children were : 1. Philip, who died in Richmond, Virginia, in 1794 unmarried; 2. Major James Barbour, of Kentucky, m. Letitia Green; 3. Lucinda, m. Benj. Hardin; 4. Richard Barbour, of Kentucky; and 5. Lucy m. Mr. Davis, and went South. Major James Barbour was an officer in the war of 1812. His wife, Letitia Green, was a daughter of Willis Green (Duff, Robert). Their children were : 1. Catherine, m. J. Wesley Vick, of Vicksburg, and had Kate, Martha, Nannie, Amanda; 2. James Barbour, a banker of Maysville, Kentucky, who m. Elizabeth Foster, of Maysville, and had James F. Barbour, who m. Elizabeth Taylor, and Rev. John Green Foster Barbour, a Presbyterian minister of Gillery county, Kentucky; 3. Martha, m. Rev. B. M. Hobson, having Barbour and Lewis Green; 4. Rev. Lewis Green Barbour, m. Elizabeth Ford, of Richmond, Kentucky, and had several children. He is the author of a poem, entitled "The End of Time," which has attracted a good deal of favorable criticism. Lucinda and Benjamin Hardin had a daughter, Mary, who m.——Letcher. Their descendants, as well as those of this Richard, and of Lucy, who married Davis, are unknown.

THOMAS BARBOUR (James, James.) m. Mary Pendleton Thomas, of Orange, (a sister of Catherine Thomas, who married his brother Ambrose). Their children were: 1. Richard; 2. James; 3. Thomas. (Richard and Thomas both died in their youth). 4. Lucy T.; 5. Phillip P.; 6. Nelly; 7. Mary, or Polly; 8. Sally. Nelly died unmarried in 1798. He was a member of the House of Burgesses from Orange county, and signed the non-importation act, of 1769, between this country and Great Britain, and after the formation of the union, was a member of the Legislature. Richard Henry Lee, in a letter to his brother, Arthur Lee, wrote that he was glad that Thomas Barbour was in our State Councils, "for he was a truly intelligent and patriotic man."

PHILIP BARBOUR (James, James.) m. and left one child, name unknown.

MARY BARBOUR (James, James.) m. John Harrison. They had one daughter, who married a Mason, and their son, James Barbour Mason, at one time represented Garrard county in the Kentucky Legislature. He married a daughter of Hugh Logan, and their son, James B. Mason, was clerk of Garrard county, Kentucky, and now (1899) lives in Lancaster.

FANNY BARBOUR (James, James.) m——Smith. Of this family was Geo. A. Smith, who sold the old Barbour homestead, Smith's Cottage, and moved to Texas before the Civil War. His older brother was Dr. Cam R. Smith, of Galveston, Texas. Mrs. Jeremiah Morton was their sister. Their mother was Mildred Glassel. Mildred, the only child of Mrs. Jeremiah Morton, m. J. J. Halsey, a prominent lawyer of Orange county. R. Ogden Halsey, and J. Morton Halsey, of Orange, are her children.

BETTY BARBOUR (James, James.) m. Benjamin Johnson. They had two daughters: Lucy, m. her first cousin, James Barbour (Thomas, James, James), and Frances Todd Johnson, m. his brother, Philip Pendleton Barbour.

——BARBOUR (James, James,) m. James Boyd. They had a son, James Boyd, whose descendants, if any, are unknown.

MORDECAI BARBOUR (James, James, James.) m. Elizabeth Strode, a daughter of John Strode, of "Fleetwood" in Culpeper county. John Strode was master of the gun factory near Falmouth, Virginia, which was largely instrumental in supplying arms to the Virginia troops in the revolutionary war. The Strodes are said to have been of French Huguenot extraction. John Strode came to Culpeper from King George county. Mordecai Barbour was in the Revolutionary army, and drew a pension for military services therein. The children of Mordecai Barbour, and Elizabeth Strode, were: 1. John Strode Barbour, m. Eliza A. Byrne; 2. Frances, m. Judge Henry Minor, of Alabama; 3. Ann, or Nancy, m. Dr. Thomas Gist, of Kentucky; 4. Maria, m. Col. Tillinghast, of South Carolina, and afterwards married Col. J. B. Hogan, who was collector of the port of Mobile, Alabama; 6. Mordecai, who died unmarried. After the death of his wife, Elizabeth, Mordecai Barbour married Sally Byrne (nee Haskell), who was the widow of James Byrne, of Petersburg, and the mother of Eliza A. Byrne, the wife of his son, John S. Barbour. Mordecai Barbour died at the home of his daughter, Mrs. Minor, of Alabama, Jan. 4th. 1846, in his 82nd. year.

THOMAS BARBOUR (James, James, James.) m. Mary Taylor, a daughter of Capt. James Taylor, Clerk of Orange county, March 22nd, 1787. This James Taylor was the oldest son of the well known Col. George Taylor, of Orange, who was commissioned Colonel by Governor Dinwiddie in 1755, and who had nine sons in the revolutionary army, and had himself been a Burgess and a member of of the convention of 1776. Captain Taylor moved to Kentucky about 1798 or '99, giving up his clerkship to a half brother. Thomas Barbour and his wife also moved to Kentucky about the same time, and had seven children : 1. James. 2. Gabriel; 3. Nathaniel; 4. Ann; 5. Lucy; 6. Fanny; and 7. Edwin.

PHILIP BARBOUR (James, James, James.) Was a colonel in the war of 1812, m. 1st. Lucy Taylor, no issue : m. 2nd. Elizabeth Hopkins, of Henderson City, Kentucky, a daughter of General Samuel Hopkins. Issue, five children : 1. Lucy, m. Dr. Glass, of Henderson, Ky; 2. Elizabeth, m. Wm. L. Jones, of Memphis; 3. Major Philip Norborne Barbour; 4. Samuel Barbour, m. Miss Clay, and left no issue; 5. James Mordecai Barbour, m. Miss Lydia A. Scott.

RICHARD BARBOUR (James, James, James.) m. Mary, daughter of Major Wm. Moore, of Orange. They had the following children : 1. Maria, m. Jack Taylor; 2. Eliza, m. Robert M. Taylor; 3. Lucy, m. Col. Alexander; 4. James, who died single.

FRANCES BARBOUR (James, James, James.) m. John Moore, of Orange, son of Major William Moore, and Mary Throckmorton, August 1st. 1798. Issue : James Barbour, b. March 8th., 1800; 2. William Catlett, b. February 13th., 1802, m. Matilda R. Taylor; 3. John Throckmorton b. 1807, m. Mary Crutchfield; 4. Gabriel Barbour, b. December 10th., 1810; 5. Richard Barbour, b. March 28th., 1814, m. 1st.——Mallory, m. 2nd. Susan Crump; 6. Frances Throckmorton, b. December 25th., 1816, m. A. G. Crutchfield.

LUCY BARBOUR (James, James, James.) m. Wythe Baylor, had a daughter Lucy, who m. Gabriel Barbour, son of Thomas Barbour (James, James).

SARAH BARBOUR (James, James, James.) m. Col. John (James) Harrison, and had two children : James, m. Miss Talbot, having five children, names not known, and Lucy, m.——-Davis.

MARY BARBOUR (James, James, James.) m. Col. David Walker, who was a member of Congress from Kentucky for years. They left seven children : 1. Mary, m. Col. R. K. Meade; 2. Fannie, m Humphrey Gwynn; 3. Helen m.———Browder; 4. James Volney; 5. Jefferson Walker; 6. George Walker; and 7. David Walker. The two latter were leading lawyers of Tallahassee, Fla., and both left families. James and Jefferson died without issue.

JAMES BARBOUR (Thomas, James, James.) m. Lucy, daughter of Benjamin Johnson and Bettie Barbour. Resided in Orange county, Virginia. Was a representative in Congress from Virginia from 1815 until he resigned in 1825. Was Secretary of War, and Minister to England under John Quincy Adams' administration, and Governor of Virginia during the war of 1812. His children were : 1. Benjamin Johnson, died in 1820 at 20 years of age; 2. James, who died in 1857 without issue; 3. Benjamin Johnson, b. 1821, m. Caroline Watson; 4. Lucy, m John Seymour Taliaferro; 5. Frances Cornelia, m. Wm. Handy Collins, of Baltimore.

PHILIP PENDLETON BARBOUR (Thomas, James, James.) was a brother of Governor James Barbour, and married a sister of his wife, Frances Todd Johnson, and earned equal distinction with his distinguished brother. He was born May 25th., 1783; was a member of the Virginia Assembly in 1812. In 1814 was elected to Congress, and continued therein until 1825, and was chosen speaker of the House in 1821. He was a lawyer of great distinction; was offered the professorship of law at the University of Virginia by Mr. Jefferson, but declined it, and was appointed a judge of the General Court of Virginia. In 1827 he resigned, and was re-eleeted to Congress without opposition. In 1829 he, together with ex-President Madison, represented Orange county in the

Constitutional Convention of that year, and on the death of ex-President Monroe, succeeded him as president of that distinguished body. In 1830 he was appointed U. S. District Judge for the Eastern District of Virginia. He declined the post of Attorney General, and refused nominations for a seat on the Court of Appeals of Virginia, for the gubernatorial chair, and the Senate of the United States, but in 1836 accepted an appointment as a Justice of the Supreme Court of the United States, and held this position until his death in 1842 (16 Peters). His children were: 1. Philippa, m. Judge R. H. Field; 2. Elizabeth, m. J. J. Ambler; 3. Dr. Thomas; 4. Edmund Pendleton; 5. Quintus; 6. Sextus; 7. Septimus, died without issue.

RICHARD BARBOUR (Thomas, James, James) Issue unknown.

MARY BARBOUR (Thomas, James, James.) m. Daniel Bryan, of Harrisonburg, Virginia. Issue: 1. Mary Anna, m.———Lathrop; 2. Caroline, m. Judge Wylie, of Washinton; 3. Sally, m.———Brown: 4. Thomas; 5. William.

LUCY BARBOUR (Thomas, James, James.) m. Thomas Newman, of Orange county. Issue: 1. Veranda, m. Nathaniel Welch; 2. Lucetta, m. James Madison Macon; 3. James B., m. Sallie Battle Fitzhugh.

NELLY M. BARBOUR (Thomas, James, James.) m. Martin Nalle, Issue: 1. Philip P., m. Elizabeth Wallace, of King George, and had the following children: G. B. W., m. Nannie Porter, P. P. Jr., Robert Mason, Fanny, m. C. Y. Steptoe, and Mary Fenton, wife of Douglas G. Somerville, all of whom reside in Culpeper county, except Mason, who lives in Washington D. C.; 2. Cordelia U. T., m. Joseph Hiden, father of Rev. J. C. Hiden, D. D., (Baptist), and Philip B. Hiden, of Fluvanna. J. C. Hiden m. Bessie Chewning, of Fluvanna, and has four children as follows: Anna, wife of Ira F. Davis, of Charleston, W. Va., Joseph H. Hiden, m. Nellie Battle, of Accomac, Robert C. Hiden, managing Editor of the Richmond Times, and Grace, wife of Edward Wilkinson, of Birmingham, Alabama. P. B. Hiden m. Bettie H. Goodwin, of Louisa, and has six children as follows: George C. Hiden, of Brandy Station, Philip W. Hiden, of Newport News, Nannie M., Elizabeth, Martin Barbour, and William Conway; 3. Edmonia Nalle, m. William Major, the father of William Major, who m. Laura M. Spindle, Samuel Major, who m., and Philip Major, m. Anna L. Hill of Culpeper; 4. Fanny Nalle, m. John C. Hansborough, a prominent lawyer, whose children are: Bettie C. Hansborough, of Upper Marlboro, Md., and Nellie Hansborough, of Virginia; 5. Martinet Nalle, m. Blucher W. Hansborough, of "Cole's Hill," where she still lives; 6. Lucetta Nalle, who m. George Booton, of Madison. He represented Madison in the Virginia Legislature, and left but one child, Mollie, who m. W. J. Cave, for years treasurer of Madison county. Their children are: Belle, Mary, m. Lucio Hill, Eloise, George, Norma, Roy, Herbert; 7. Jane Nalle, m. Edward M. Clarke, of Washington, D. C., and had Edwin M. Clarke, Jas. Clarke, and Florence, who m.———Haldiman, of the Louisville Courier Journal; 8. Dr. Richard Thomas Nalle, m. Miss Hooe, of Fauquier. Their children were: Jas., Edmund P., m. 1st. Miss Wallace, who left one child, m. 2nd. Kate Robertson of Culpeper, by whom there are four or five children, and Mary D., m. James Belt, of Upper Marlboro, Md., and Bettie Rice, m. C. C. Magruder, of Maryland; 9. Sarah Ellen Nalle, m. Col. Garrett Scott, father of Rev. F. G. Scott, of Gordensville, Nellie Scott. J. M. Scott, Edward Scott, Thomas Scott, and W. W. Scott, the present State Librarian; 10. Mary Nalle, m. Richard H. Willis, having Byrd Willis, who m. a daughter of John Willis, Philip Willis, of Mississippi, Fanny, wife of Dr. Madison, of Orange, Rosa Willis, wife of Benton Willis, of Mississippi, Elizabeth, m.———, Lucy Willis, who died unmarried, Barbour Willis, who m. a Miss Hunton, of Fauquier, and died in Dakota, Richard

H. Willis, who m. Elizabeth Hall of Syracuse, N. Y., having Richard L. and Katherine Murat, who died 1899, and Nellie M. who m. Martin Stringfellow, having Rittenhouse, Byrd, Willis, R. Stanton, Anne S., m.——Taylor, Champe, C., m.——Taylor; 11. B. Johnson Nalle; 12. James Barbour Nalle, neither of whom ever married.

SALLY BARBOUR (Thomas, James, James.) m. Gabriel Gray, of Culpeper, issue: 1. Rebecca, wife of Shelton F. Leake, a distinguished lawyer and debater, and the father of Shelton F. Leake, of Tyler, Texas, who m. Kate Nelson, a daughter of Mr. Lewis P. Nelson, of Culpeper; 2. Martha, m. Wm. L. Anderson, who was killed at the battle of Seven Pines. Their children were: John R., of the University of Virginia, and Richard, who died at Charlottesville in 1899, leaving two infant children; 3. Philippa, m. R. W. Anderson. Their children are Rev. John Gray (Presbyterian), of Tampa, Florida, Lucy, who lives with him, and Martha; 4. Lucy, m. James B. Cowles. She died about 1881, leaving one daughter, Florence; 5. Dr. John Gray, who died at Brentsville, unmarried, in 1851.

JOHN S. BARBOUR (Mordecai, James, James, James.) m. Elizabeth Byrne, of Petersburg. Was a lawyer and orator of distinction, and represented Virginia in the U. S. House of Representatives from about 1821 to 1831. Was a member of the constitutional convention of 1829, and presided over the Democratic National Convention that nominated Franklin Pierce for the presidency. His children were: 1. Sally, who never married; 2. John S. Barbour, for years president of the O. & A. R. R. Co., afterwards the Virginia Midland, a representative in congress from Virginia; conducted the campaigns that crushed the power of the coalition between the Republican and Readjuster parties in Virginia, and was afterwards elected to the U. S. Senate, of which body he was a member at the time of his death, in May, 1892. His wife was Susan Dangerfield, of Alexandria. They had no children; 3. James Barbour, m. Fanny T., a daughter of Coleman C. Beckham, of Culpeper. He represented Culpeper repeatedly in the Legislature. Was a member of the constitutional convention of 1849, and of the secession convention. He was also a member of the Peace Commission. During the civil war he was for a time Adjutant General on General Ewell's staff, but was compelled to resign by reason of health. He died in 1895, leaving seven children, as follows: Ellie B., wife of Hon. John F. Rixey, at present a representative in Congress from Virginia; Mary B., wife of Prof. Clarence B. Wallace, of Nashville, Tenn., James Barbour, of San Joaquin Co., Cal., John S. Barbour, a lawyer of Culpeper, who m. Mary, daughter of Judge D. A. Grimsley, of Culpeper, Edwin Barbour, of St. Louis, Mo., who m. Josie, daughter of Alex. McDonald, ex-senator from Arkansas, A. Floyd Barbour, of Nashville, Tenn., and Fanny C., wife of B. Collins Beckham, of Culpeper county; 4. Major Alfred M. Barbour, who was commandant of the Arsenal at Harper's Ferry at the time of the John Brown raid, a member of the secession convention, and was Gen. Joseph E. Johnston's Quartermaster General during the war. He died at Montgomery, Ala., in 1866. His wife was Kate Daniel, of Jefferson county, Virginia. His children died in infancy; 5. Eliza B., the wife of Capt. George G. Thompson, of Culpeper; she died in 1887, leaving the following children: J. S. B. Thompson, a prominent general officer of the Southern Ry. Co., with headquarters at Atlanta, Ga., who m. Mary, daughter of Col. Morton Marye, Auditor of Virginia, Lelia Thompson, Annie, the wife of Rev. J. G. Minnegerode, rector of Calvary Episcopal church, Louisville, Ky., Richard C. Thompson, lawyer, of Washington, D. C., Eliza B., of Culpeper, George G. Thompson, Jr., also prominent among the So. Ry., officials, at Raleigh, N. C., and Ruth, the wife of John Hanckle, of Roanoke, Virginia; 6. Edwin Barbour, who died unmarried in 1892.

FRANCES BARBOUR (Mordecai, James, James, James.) m. at Petersburg, Virginia, Sept. 14th., 1809, Judge Henry Minor, who was a judge of the Supreme Court of Alabama; issue: 1. Henry, b. July 7th, 1810, d. at sea November 25th., 1839; 2. Mordecai, d. in infancy; 3. Ann Virginia, b. August 23rd., 1814, m. John Gilliam Friend, of Mobile, Alabama, d. March 5th., 1884 Issue: Fanny Friend, of Mobile, Alabama, Eliza, who died in 1898, Maria, who died in 1878, Virginia Friend, of Mobile, Henry Minor Friend, of Mobile, m. Amanda Moore, Mary Minge Friend, m. James D. Harwell, and lives at Meridian, Mississippi, John Gilliam Friend, m. Lulu H. Dunn, died in 1890, and Alice Friend, who died in 1854, 4. Eliza Barbour, b. December 12th., 1816, died in 1842, unmarried; 5. Frances Cosby, b. Jan. 16th., 1819, died March 4th., 1846; 6. Maria, b. July 23rd., 1820, m. Dr. Ezra F. Bouchelle, having Fanny Minor, Maria Barbour, Ezra Fiske, m. Sally Gould, Philip Minor, Henry Minor, Benjamin Rush, Lucy, Amanda, John Friend, and Henry Tutwiler, m. Innes Gould. Ezra Fiske Bouchelle and Sallie Gould, his wife, have issue: Delia T., Maria Minor, Annie B., Sallie G., Fannie M., Ezra T., Jessie C., and Bessie Innes. Henry Tutwiler Bouchelle, and Innes Gould, his wife, have issue as follows: Delia F., Henry T., John McK. G., and Lucy Minor. The Bouchelles and Goulds reside in Boligee, Green county, Ala.; 7. Louisa, b. September 22nd., 1822, m. ———; 8. Mordecai Lafayette, b. April 22nd., 1824, m. Hattie Fleming, died at Elmira, N. Y., a prisoner after the close of the civil war. Left one son, John Launcelot Minor; 9. John Launcelot, b. June 3rd., 1826, died in Mobile, Ala., in 1855; 10. Philip P. B., b. Jan. 23rd., 1828, m. Eliza Perry, died June, 1884. Their issue were: Lucy Barbour, Fannie Friend, m. Dr. E. P. Riggs, a prominent physician of Birmingham, Ala., Mary Perry, Caro Boddie, m. Rev. J. Y. Penn, Philip Barbour, of Eutaw, Ala., and Elsie; 11 Lucy Landon Barbour, m. Dr. Joseph C. Hamilton. Their issue were: Joseph Courten, Henry Minor, Frances Barbour, who m. Richard B. Shepherd, of Mt. Vernon, Alabama, and Charlotte Anna, who m. Isaac B. Swift. The children of Henry M. Friend and Amanda Moore, are: Anne Virginia and Henry Minor. John Gilliam Friend and Loula Dunn Friend left one child, Ellen Trabue Friend. Fannie Minor, who m. Dr. E. P. Riggs, has three children: Philip Minor Riggs, Elise Riggs, and Fannie Minor Riggs. Caro Boddie Minor, who m. J. V. Penn, has one child, Sallie Bouchelle Penn, Frances B. Hamilton, who m. Richard B. Shepherd, has seven children: Frederick, Joseph H., Richard, William, Lucian M., Frances B., and Tazewell.

MARIA BARBOUR (Mordecai, James, James, James.) m. Col. Tillinghast, of South Carolina, and after his death m. Col. J. B. Hogan, of Mobile, Alabama, who was at one time collector of that port. She died without issue.

GABRIEL BARBOUR (Thomas, James, James, James.) m. Lucy Baylor, daughter of Wythe Baylor. They had one child, Winona, who m. Judge Cullen, of Richmond, Virginia, having two children: George Appleton Cullen, of Chicago, Ill., and Barbour Cullen. Mrs. Winona Cullen survives her husband, and lives in Chicago.

JAMES BARBOUR (Thomas, James, James. James.) died single.

NATHANIEL BARBOUR (Thomas, James, James, James.) m. Miss Bowles, of Jefferson county, Ky., and had three children: Frank Barbour, Medona, who died single, and Mary Bethel, who m.———.

LUCY BARBOUR (Thomas, James, James, James.) m. James Locke, and left no children.

SALLIE BRYAN (Mary, Thomas, James, James.) m. ———Brown, of Kentucky, had six children, of whom only the name of one, Frank Brown, is known. After her death, her husband married a daughter of Bishop Meade, by whom he also had several children.

FANNY BARBOUR (Thomas, James, James, James.) died single.

ANN BARBOUR (Thomas, James, James, James.) m. Charles M. Taylor, of Louisville, and had four children; Mary, Dr. Thomas W., Nathaniel, and Alfred. Nathaniel and Alfred died single. Mary m. Col. D. R. Burbank. Only one of their six children ever married, David R. Burbank, who married a daughter of Archibald Dixon, of Henderson. They had two children: Sue and Charlie.

LUCY BARBOUR (Philip, James, James, James.) m. Dr. Glass, of Henderson, Kentucky, had one son, Owen, who never married. He was in the Confederate army, and was detected while scouting near Henderson, Ky., and was killed in his attempt to escape capture.

ELIZABETH BARBOUR (Philip, James, James, James.) m. Wm. L. Jones, and removed to Memphis, Tenn., where she still lives. Her husband died many years ago. Issue: 1. Alice, m. Henry Garth, of New York City; 2. Philip B., m. Eliza Garth. They live in Memphis; 3. Wm., m. Mattie Crump, and resides at Vicksburg, Miss.; 4. Eugene, unmarried; 5. Norborne, unmarried; 6. Lucy, m. Wm. Clapp, all of Memphis. Mrs. Horace Garth has two children, Granville and Lena. Lena m. ——Garth, and has two children.

PHILIP NORBORNE BARBOUR (Philip, James, James, James.) m. his first cousin, Martha, daughter of Jacob Hopkins. They left no issue. He was a West Point graduate, and a major in the regular army. Distinguished himself in the Mexican war, and fell in the charge at Monterey. His remains are buried at Frankfort, Ky., and a monument, erected by the State, marks his resting place.

SAMUEL BARBOUR (Philip, James, James, James.) m. ——Clay. They lived and died in Henderson county, Ky. Had two sons, who entered the Confederate army as boys, and both were killed in the service. Neither ever married.

JAMES MORDECAI BARBOUR (Philip, James, James, James.) m. Lydia A. Scott, and both died at Henderson, Kentucky. They left one child, Anna Mordecai, m. Thomas F. Cheney, of Henderson, Ky. He died in 1898, she in 1892. They left six children as follows: Alice C., wife of Alfred McDaniel, of Tampa, Florida, Ruth C., wife of Jas. M. Ringo, of Clinton, Kentucky, Miss Edith B., of Henderson, Kentucky, Philip B., m. George Lee Allen, and resides in St. Louis, Mo., Harry T., of Princeton, Ky., and Robert B., of Henderson, Ky.

MARIA BARBOUR (Richard, James, James, James.) m. Jack Taylor.

ELIZA BARBOUR (Richard, James, James.) m. J. P. Taylor (Robert M.), and had two children: Alonzo, and Robert T. They had no descendants.

LUCY BARBOUR (Richard, James, James, James.) m. Col. ——Alexander. They had no issue.

JAMES B. MOORE (Frances, James, James, James.) died single in 1871.

WILLIAM CATLETT MOORE (Frances, James, James, James.) m. Matilda R. Taylor, a daughter of Dr. Charles Taylor, of Orange, and a surgeon in the Revolution. Issue: Charles Catlett, Fauny Barbour, Sarah Barbour, James Mordecai, m. a Miss Andrews, and lives at Orange, C. H., John W., and Mary Evelina.

JOHN THROCKMORTON MOORE (Frances, James, James, James.) m. Ann P. Crutchfield, and had nine children.

GABRIEL BARBOUR MOORE (Frances, James, James, James.) m. Miss Reynolds, of Clarke county, Kentucky, and had nine children.

RICHARD BARBOUR MOORE (Frances, James, James, James.) m. 1st. Mallory, and 2nd. Susan Crump, who is still living.

FRANCES THROCKMORTON MOORE (Frances, James, James, James.) m. A. G. Crutchfield. She is now living at Evansville, Indiana, in the eighty fourth year of her age, in the full posession of her health, bodily and mentally, and has recently rendered the writer most valuable assistance in tracing the various branches of the Barbour family. She has a daughter, the wife of William Field, of Evansville, Indiana, and a son, A. G. Crutchfield, of Smith's Mills, Kentucky.

LUCY BARBOUR BAYLOR (Lucy, James, James, James.) m. Gabriel Barbour, (Thomas, James, James, James).

JAMES HARRISON (Sarah, James, James, James.) m. Miss Talbot, They had five children, all of whom are now dead, and their descendants, if any, are unknown.

BENJAMIN JOHNSON BARBOUR (James, Thomas, James, James.) b. 1821, m. Caroline H., daughter of the eminent Dr. George Watson, of Richmond, November 17th., 1844. He represented Orange in the State Legislature, and in 1865 was elected a representative in the Congress of the United States; was not permitted to take his seat, Virginia not having been sufficiently reconstructed. He was an orator of distinction, and a scholar of rare culture, and was for years Rector of the Board of Visitors of the University of Virginia. He died about 1897, leaving the following children : George W. Barbour, Thomas Barbour, Caroline, the wife of Dr. J. H. Ellis, Elise, the wife of James Graves, and F. Cornelia, the wife of Prof. Wm. G. Christian, of the University of Virginia.

LUCY BARBOUR (Thomas, James, James, James.) m. John Seymour Taliaferro, who was drowned in 1880. Issue: 1. James Barbour, died in his 18th year; 2. Lucy Maria, who died unmarried; 3. Frances Cornelia, unmarried, lives with her sister, Mrs. Waters; 4. Ann B., died unmarried; 5. Lindsey T., m. Wm. Smith Waters, July 21st, 1863. He died September 7th, 1873, leaving has widow and two children, John Seymour Taliaferro Waters, lawyer of Baltimore, who m. Mary Town Donaldson, and Lucy Maria Barbour Waters, who m. Charles F. Penniman, September 6th, 1892. He died November 13th, 1898. leaving one child, Wm. S. W. Penniman. Mrs. Wm. S. Waters is living at 225, West Lanvale st., Baltimore, and the writer is indebted to her for much of the information embodied in this sketch.

FRANCES CORNELIA BARBOUR (James, Thomas, James, James.) m. William Handy Collins, a distinguished lawyer of Baltimore. They left no issue.

PHILIPPA BARBOUR (Philip P., Thomas, James, James.) m. Judge R. H. Field, who succeeded her distinguished father as judge of the General Court of Virginia. She was his third wife. Their children were: 1. Philip Field, who was a gallant soldier in the civil war, and was killed May 23rd., at Cedarville, Virginia; 2. Fanny Field, who m. Charles Norville, of Lynchburg, Va.

ELIZABETH BARBOUR (Philip P., Thomas, James, James.) m. J. J. Ambler. Their children were: 1. John J., m,. Bessie B. Davis; 2. Prof. Philip B., m. Willie H. Nicholas, of Seven Islands. They had one son, Prof. Nicholas Ambler, of Roanoke College; 3. Ella Cary, m. John Nicholas, of Lynchburg, having six children: Ambler, Philip, Lillie, Harry, J. Ellis, and Nannie Nicholas.

THOMAS BARBOUR (Philip P., Thomas, James, James.) m. Catharine Strother. He was a physician, and died in St. Louis, in 1849, of cholera incurred in the course of his profession. His children were: Thomas and John, of Missouri, Fanny Todd, m.———Gray, of Louisville, Kentucky, and Chalmers Barbour.

EDMUND PENDLETON BARBOUR (Philip P., Thomas, James, James.) m. Harriet, daughter of Col. John Stewart, of King George. He died in 1851. His children are: Philippa, Mary Conway, and Edmonia, who m. Rene de Payen des Bellisle, who was a professor in the University of Chicago. He left one child, who bears his name.

QUINTUS BARBOUR (Philip P., Thomas, James, James.) m. Mary, daughter of James Somerville, of Culpeper. Their children are: 1. Capt. Philip P., unmarried, a prominent lawyer of Gordonsville; 2. Fanny T., m. Rev. D. B. Ewing, who is now dead. She resides in Alexandria, Virginia, and has the following children: Wm., Lucy, Mary Belle, Jennie and Fannie; 3. Cornelia C., 4. James Somerville, of Mississippi; 5. Jane F., unmarried.

SEXTUS BARBOUR (Philip P., Thomas, James, James.) died unmarried in St. Louis, Mo., of cholera in 1849, with his brother, Dr. Thomas Barbour.

MARY ANN BRYAN (Mary, Thomas, James, James.) m.——Lathrop, of Washington. Issue: Florence who married, 1st.——Field, of Chicago, and 2nd. Thomas Nelson Page, the distinguished author. She has several children by her first marriage.

CAROLINE BRYAN (Mary, Thomas, James, James.) m. Judge —— Wylie, for years a judge of the Supreme Court of the District of Columbia. Issue: Horace Wylie, of Washington, D. C.

THOMAS BARBOUR BRYAN (Mary, Thomas, James, James.) m.——Page, a daughter of Rev. Charles Page, of the well known Virginia family of that name. Their children are: Charles Page Bryan, at present U. S. Minister to Brazil, and Virginia Bryan.

WILLIAM BRYAN (Mary, Thomas, James, James.) Issue unknown.

VERANDA NEWMAN (Lucy, Thomas, James, James.) m. Nathaniel Welch, Issue : 1. Thomas N. Welch, m. Lucy Dew, of Caroline. Was a State Senator from Madison, and Judge of Caroline county. Lives in Caroline county. He has no children; 2. James Barbour, m. Ann Gibson, a sister of Col. J. C. Gibson, of Culpeper. Issue : Lelia, who m. Alexander H. Davis, and Eustace B. Welch, who m. Sallie Berry; 3. John, m. his cousin, Laura, daughter of James B. Newman, and left one child, Sallie. who m. Wm. Parrin, of Orange; 4. Lucy, m. Reuben Newman, and had three children : Nathaniel, who m. Miss Taylor, Bettie who m. Col. Stoven, of Orange, having two children, William and Lula, and Florence, who m.——Henshaw, of Kentucky; 5. Wilhelmina, m. Dr. Graves. She lives at Orange C. H., Virginia, and has one child, Etta Graves.

JAMES BARBOUR NEWMAN (Lucy, Thomas, James, James.) m. Sallie Battle Fitzhugh. They had six children : Julia, m. Jessie H. Goss, of Georgia. Their only child, Julia, m.——Birdsong; 2. Laura, m. John Welch, (see descendants of Veranda Newman and Nathaniel Welch, supra); 3. Rosa, died unmarried; 4. Thomas H., killed at Aldie, Virginia, during the civil war; 5. Barbour, m. Tabitha, daughter of William Gordon, of Fredericksburg. They have two children : Alice and Lillie; 6. Conway, m. Elnora Taylor, and has nine children : Rosa, who m.——Fitz Patrick, of Orange county, Eugenia, Conway, Laura, and five others. Mr. James Barbour Newman lived to be ninety eight years of age, and died but a few month ago.

LUCETTA NEWMAN (Lucy, Thomas, James, James.) m. James Madison Macon, and had six children: 1. Thomas N., who died unmarried; 2. Conway Ella, m. Dr. John Knox, of Richmond. They had three children: John C., who m. Miss Yancy, of Richmond, Lucetta Madison Knox and Conway Macon Knox, both of Richmond; 3. Edgar Barbour, m. Virginia Caison, of Princess Ann, and has eight children: William M., Sallie, who married John Maupin, of Portsmouth, having two children, Mary and Augusta, Barbour Macon, of

Brambleton, Virginia, who maried Miss Maulbury, and has five children,——— Nathaniel Macon, who married, ———, Henry Macon, who married ———, and has one child, Lucetta, who m. Rev. John Cormick, of Westover, and has three children, and Bessie Macon; 4. Sarah F., m. Thomas Hill, of Culpeper. and has two children : A. P. Hill, who m. Anna G. Parsons, of St. Louis, Mo., and Corrie B. M. Hill; 5. James Madison, m. Miss Bridge, of New Orleans, and has three children, Conway Etta, Edward Adams, and James Madison; 6. Conway, of Orange, who m. Emma Riley, of Winchester, and has seven children : Emma, who m.———Stair, of York, Pa., Kate, who m. Frank Polson, of Pittsburg, Pa., Kenneth, Lattimer, Conway, Riley, and Eva.

ADDENDA.

It was stated on page 136 that James Barbour (James) had a son William, who married Elizabeth Bailey. Further research since that statement was printed shows it to be erroneous, but it has brought out the probability that he was related to the Culpeper family of Barbours through a more remote ancestor than any named above, viz : Gabriel Barbour, said to have been a London merchant, and a member of the London Virginia Company, and who gave 1000 pounds to establish a fund to christianize the Indians, though it has been impossible to prosecute the inquires necessary to conclusively establish this line of descent in time for incorporation in this sketch. The William Barbour, above mentioned, instead of being a son of James (James), was probably the son or grandson of Capt. William Barbour, of Richmond county, whose daughter married Ajola Price, as mentioned in the Green genealogy (p 61, part first). He had a brother, Samuel and they came to Culpeper county together, and settled before the revolution. His descendants are : William Barbour and Travers Barbour, both of whom moved to North Carolina about 1800; their descendants are unknown; and Frances, m. Thomas Taylor (Charles, of Orange county), October 4th., 1800, having Pannill Taylor, b. 1801, m. Millie Brown; Elizabeth, b. 1803, died single; Patsey Taylor, b. 1805, m. A. Ford, and moved to Mississippi; Sarah Jane, b. 1806, m. M. Burke; Nancey, b. 1808, m. M. Wise; John Barbour Taylor, b. 1811, m.———and moved to Louisiana; Thos. E. Taylor, b. 1814, m. Miss Henshaw. and went West; Margaret, b. 1820, and died single; and Arthur, b. 1823, m. Miss Murray, and left one son, R. O. Taylor. Pannil Taylor, the oldest son of Thomas Taylor, and Frances Barbour, above noted, m. 1st. Nellie Brown, a daughter of Joel Brown and Nellie Terrill, and left two children : Dr. John W. Taylor, and Mildred Frances, m. Dr. H. W. Gordon, of Madison county. Pannil Taylor m. 2nd. a Miss Weaver, of Mississippi, and left from this marriage : Jas. R., Luck, Buckhannon, Maggie, Shaw and two other daughters. John W., his son by his first marriage, m. Rebecca Crawford, and has four children : T. C. Taylor, of Madison county, who m. Ruby, a daughter of Col. F. H. Hill, of Madison; G. H. Taylor m. Sallie Lewis, and is at present Deputy Clerk of Madison county; W. S. Taylor, of Madison C. H., m. Lizzie Yager; and Blanche, m. John Hunton.

———:ooo:———

THE BROADDUS FAMILY.

[Judge John W. Jones has furnished the following more extended sketch of the Broaddus family than the one which appears in the original History of St. Mark's Parish, but the copy was received too late to be in the first part of this book.—R. T. G.]

The late distinguished Rev. John A. Broaddus, writing of his family a few years previous to his death, says that the name Broaddus was originally Broadhurst. Although of Anglo-Saxon origin, those who bear it, tradition says, came to the United States from Wales. The progenitor of the family in this country was Edward Broaddus, who settled on Gwynn's Island in the Piankitank river, near its junction with the Rappahannock. The exact time of his coming is not known, but it must have been as early as the early part of the 18th century, as, in 1715, he moved to Caroline county, then King and Queen, where he continued to reside up to the time of his death. Edward Broaddus was twice married. The name of his first wife is unknown. That of his second was Mary Shipley. The name of his children, by his first wife, are: Thomas, Richard and Dolly. Those of his second wife were: John, William, James, Shipley, Robin, and Elizabeth. These children of Edward Broaddus, and his two wives, have left a large number of descendants in Caroline and Culpeper counties, and in other portions of Virginia, and elsewhere throughout the United States, some of whom have become men of prominence and distinction, especially as educators and ministers of the gospel. Among these, Andrew, the first of the name, Andrew, his son, both of whom were born, and died, in Caroline county, Edmund, William F., his brother, and John A., son of Edmund, all three natives of Culpeper, may be notably mentioned.

While it is conceded that John A. was the most accomplished and scholarly man, who ever bore the name of Broaddus, even before he was born, his Caroline kinsman, Andrew, had begun to establish a reputation as an orator of no mean order, notwithstanding his early education was very limited, having attended school only nine months altogether. Uniting with the Baptist church while quite young, he had barely become of age when he was ordained as a minister of that denomination, and so strong was his intellect, so studious his habits, so winning his deportment, so musical his voice, so captivating the style of his eloquence, that he soon became one of the most popular pulpit orators of his day, and his services were sought by his Baptist brethren all over the State, especially at campmeetings, so common at that early time, where his presence never failed to draw an immense crowd of interested and eager listeners whenever it was known that he was to fill the pulpit. Although Mr. Broaddus, during his long and popular ministry, except for a few months while in Richmond, Va., never had charge of any other than a country church, it was not because his services were not appreciated in some of the largest cities of the United States, among them Baltimore, New York, Philadelphia, and Boston, from all of which he had calls at different times, none of which he accepted, probably from a love for a retired and quiet life, and a natural shrinking timidity which he possessed, and could never entirely overcome. Besides his popularity as a preacher, Mr. Broaddus was also a writer of much force and eloquence. During his life he wrote a number of works, among others, a "History of the Bible." which was received with much favor by the religious public. Mr. Broaddus was married four times, and left a number of children, to only one of whom, his son, Andrew Jr., will the limits of this sketch allow any reference to be made.

Andrew Broaddus, Jr., like his father, Andrew the elder, was a Baptist minister, and, like him, of much ability, both as a speaker and a writer.

While his style of oratory was hardly as attractive as that of his father, still, at times, when his mind was fully aroused to the importance of the subject under investigation, and he took a personal interest in it, his thoughts would be clothed in words of impassioned and burning eloquence. As a writer, Mr. Broaddus was terse, clear and forcible. Besides having been a contributor to the Religious Herald, and other religious papers for many years, he was the author of a history of the Broaddus family, a work requiring much time, patience and labor, to which the writer of this sketch is indebted for much that it contains. Like his father, Mr. Broaddus lived to be quite old. Both lived and died in the same county where they were born, leaving the remarkable record of having, for three generations, extending over the space of a century, father, son and grandson, successfully occupied the same pulpit and preached to the same people and and their descendants, a record that exists no where else in Virginia, or the United States, if indeed in the world, one of which any family might well be proud, and complimentary alike to pastor and people. With this brief and imperfect notice of the two leading members of the Caroline Broddus', let us now proceed to the more immediate purpose of this sketch, the genealogy of the Culpeper branch of the family.

So far as is known the name of the first Broaddus to settle in Culpeper county was William, the second son of Edward, the progenitor of the family in this country, and his second wife, Mary Shipley. William Broaddus married a Miss Gaines, who bore him three children: William, Thomas and James. His first son, William, was a major in the Revolutionary army, and was twice married, first to Mrs. Martha Jones, widow of Capt. Gabriel Jones, the Revolutionary soldier; they had four children: Kitty Wigginton, Juliet, Patsey and William. Kitty married William Mills Thompson. The names of their descendants will be found in the Thompson genealogy, pages 86-7 of part second; Juliet married Col. Henry Ward. They had two children: William H., and Woodville. William H., married Jane Roberts, a daughter of Major John Roberts, of the Revolution, and had no children. Woodville moved to Mississippi many years ago, and never married. Patsy married Merriwether Thompson. Such of their descendants, as are known, will be found in the Thompson genealogy, page 89 of second part.

The second wife of Major William Broaddus was Martha Richardson. They had four children: Sarah Ann, Lavinia, Maria and Mary. In addition to serving his country as a soldier, Major Broaddus was for many years clerk of Culpeper county. Somewhat late in life he moved to Harper's Ferry, where he filled some Federal office, paymaster in the army, it is believed, and died there.

William, the only son of William Broaddus and the widow of Capt. Gabriel Jones, married Ann Tutt, who bore him two children: Juliet Ann and William A. Juliet Ann married Edward Herndon. They had only one child, a daughter, named Mary Eleanor, who married John Roberts. William A. never married. Mr. Broaddus succeeded his father as clerk of Culpeper county.

Thomas, the second son of William Broaddus, and brother of the first clerk of Culpeper county, of that name, married Mrs. Susannah White. They had three sons: Edmund, William F., and Andrew, and two daughters, Lucy and Maria. Edmund, the first son of Thomas, and Susannah Broaddus, was twice married. His first wife was Nancy Sims. His second was Somerville Ward. By his first wife he had the following children: James M., Martha A., Caroline M., and John A. His second wife died childless.

Of the many men of prominence that Culpeper county has furnished, few have possessed more merit and ability than Edmund Broaddus. Born at a time when schools were scarce and the most of them that existed, of the "Old Field" order, he received only an ordinary education, yet so superior his intellect, and studious his habits, that, even while comparatively a young man, as a thinker and debater he took a prominent stand among the leading men of his day. By vocation Mr. Broaddus was a farmer. He also taught a country school for several years. In politics he was originally a Democrat, but left that party upon the "Removal of the Deposits" by Gen. Jackson, and afterwards became an "Old Line Whig," and a great admirer and earnest supporter of Henry Clay. Mr. Broaddus was a man of modest demeanor, excellent judgment, and rare insight into the character and motives of men. To the latter, united with his ability as a speaker, and the thorough confidence of his constituents, in his integrity, may be attributed the fact that, for twenty years—with one or two exceptions, when he declined to be a candidate—he represented the county of Culpeper in the House of Delegates, and was never defeated in any race he made before the people. During his several terms of office no member served his constituents more faithfully and efficiently, and none more thoroughly commanded the respect of his fellow members, and exerted a greater influence over them. Like the most of his name, Mr. Broaddus was a Baptist, and at the associations, and other general meetings of that denomination, always took a prominent and leading part in their deliberations, thus becoming an important factor in shaping the proceedings of these bodies. He died in Charlottesville, Virginia, whither he had gone several years prior thereto, mainly for the purpose of educating his son, the great and good John A.

As before stated, it is conceded that the most accomplished and scholarly man ever produced by Culpeper county, and the greatest who ever bore the Broaddus name, was the Rev. John Albert Broaddus, youngest child of Edmund Broaddus and Fanny Sims. His early education was conducted mainly by his father, and his sister Martha. Afterwards he became a pupil of that excellent scholar and teacher, Albert G. Sims, who, for many years, taught a highly popular boarding school near Culpeper C. H. In 1846 Mr. Broaddus entered the University of Virginia, and four years thereafter was graduated with the highest honor of that noted institution. He was twice married. His first wife was Maria Carter Harrison, daughter of Dr. Gessner Harrison, one of the professors of his Alma Mater. His second wife was Charlotte E. Sinclair, of Albemarle county. His children, by his first wife, were: Eliza Somerville, Annie Harrison, and Maria Louisa. His children, by his second wife, were: Samuel Sinclair, Caroline, Alice Virginia, Ella Thomas and Boyce. Mr. Broaddus commenced preaching in 1849, and was ordained in 1853. From 1851 to 1853 he was assistant instructor of Latin and Greek in the University, and at the same time pastor of the Charlottesville Baptist church. For two years, 1855 and 1856, he acted as chaplain to the University. In 1859 he became Professor in the Southern Baptist Theological Seminary, then established at Greenville, South Carolina. For some months in 1863, Mr. Broaddus preached as a missionary in Gen. Lee's army, but the exposure of camp life was too great for the delicate state of his health, and he gave up the work and became Corresponding Secretary to the Sunday School Board of the Southern Baptist Convention, then established at Greenville to supply destitute schools. The foregoing is the substance of a condensed sketch of Mr. Broaddus' life, down to the time it was written, prepared by himself for the Rev. Andrew's book, "The Broaddus Family," and reproduced here. It is only necessary to add that when the Theological Seminary was moved from Greenville, South Carolina, to Louisville, Kentucky, in 1877, Mr. Broaddus continued to retain the same chair in that institution formerly occupied by him, and was afterwards chosen as its President, the duties of which he continued to discharge as long as he lived. Few men ever commenced the battles of life better prepared for the struggle than John A. Broaddus. So splended was his intellect, so excellent his early training, so thorough his collegiate course, so unexceptionable his habits, and perfect his character, in a word so admirable and complete his general equipment, that when he was graduated, with the highest honors, by one of the first, if not the very first, literary institutions in the country, it seemed that, with ordinary application and industry, failure would be almost impossible. How manfully and successfully he met the issue is fully attested by the splended record which he left behind him. A finished scholar, an able and successful teacher, a chaste and beautiful writer, an eloquent and convincing speaker, a good neighbor, a true friend, a faithful and loving husband, an affectionate father, a sincere and devoted Christian, he lived a life that, in its rounded completeness few have equalled, very few excelled, and, when the end came, peacefully passed to his great reward, leaving a name that will live as long as the institution, of which he was the honored head, if not the church itself, whose doctrines he so ably and eloquently expounded. How much he was lamented by the people of Louisville, where he died, is shown by the deep feeling which was manifested on that occasion; all classes, conditions, and creeds uniting with each other in paying honor to his memory, one of the ablest and most touching tributes being an address by the Jewish Rabbi of that city, while the newspapers there, and in other portions of Kentucky, and throughout the country generally, were full of eulogistic notices of him as a Christian and a man.

William F., the second son of Thomas and Susannah Broaddus, like his brother Edmund, received a very limited early education, but like him, so strong was his intellect, so industrious his habits, and so eager his desire to excel, that, through his own unaided efforts, he not only acquired a good knowledge of books and their contents, but became a highly popular and successful school teacher, both in Virginia and Kentucky. Like the most of his name, he joined the Baptist church when young, and like quite a number, not long afterwards was ordained a minister, teaching and preaching at the same time. Commencing preaching and teaching in Virginia, where he had a school and church at Middleburg, and other places at different times. Wm. F. Broaddus afterwards moved to Kentucky and taught and preached in Lexington and Shelbyville. Leaving Kentucky and returning to Virginia, he resumed his former vocation of teaching and preaching, which he continued until he became somewhat advanced in years. Mr. Broaddus was twice married. His first wife was Mary A. Farrow. His second wife being Mrs. Lucy E. Fleet. The children of his first wife were : Edmund S., Amanda F., William H. C., Mary L., Thomas E., and John F. His second wife had only one child, a daughter, named Lucy Maria.

James, the third son of William Broaddus, and his wife, Miss Gaines, and brother of William, the first clerk of the name of Culpeper county, was an ensign in the Revolution. He married Mary A. Ferguson. Their children were: Elizabeth, Catherine, William D., Sarah W., James G., and Susan C.

In conclusion it may be stated that while a few branches of the family have, for convenience in writing, dropped one of the "d's" in spelling the name, the most of them continue to spell it with two, as it was originally written, and that whether spelled with one or two, all who bear it are of the same blood, all being the descendants of Edmund Broaddus, the first settler and progenitor of the family in this country.

———:ooo:———

THE BRYAN—LILLARD FAMILY.
[By Judge D. A. Grimsley.]

Joseph Bryan settled in the county of Culpeper in 1752. He came from King George county, and is supposed to have been the father of William Bryan, who was the great grand father of William Jennings Bryan now (1900) for the second time the nominee of the Democrats for the presidency.

William Bryan lived near the town of Sperryville, now Rappahannock, then Culpeper county, and was a large landowner. He died in 1806, leaving the following children : 1. James; 2. John, m. Nancy Lillard; 3. William; 4. Aquilla; 5. Lucy, m. Dunnaway; 6. Elizabeth, m. Baldeck.

The year following William Bryan's death, his lands were divided among his children, and to his son, John, was allotted that portion lying near the town of Sperryville The old Bryan house, on this tract, still stands in a good state of preservation.

Nancy Lillard Bryan, the wife of John Bryan, was the daughter of John Lillard, a soldier in the Revolutionary army, who lived in the Bryan neighborhood.

Between 1810 and 1825 the Bryan family sold out their ancestral estates, and moved west to Kentucky, Tennessee, and Ohio.

John Bryan, the grand father of Williams Jennings, left Virginia in 1826. Silas Lillard Bryan, the father of Williams Jennings, was, at that time, four years of age. John settled on the banks of the Ohio, near the mouth of the Big Kanawha, where he and his wife, Nancy Lillard, died, the one in 1830, and the other in 1835. After their death the family moved further West to Illinois and Missouri. In 1840, Silas Lillard Bryan, the father of William Jennings, went to live with an older brother in Missouri, who had before settled in that state. From his home he attended school for a time, then went to Marion county, Ill., where he taught school for a year or so, then went to college, studied law, and began its practice in 1852, and soon rose to prominence in the profession. He was a member of the constitutional convention, and of the senate of the State of Illinois, and a circuit judge for a number of years. He was the Democratic nominee for congress in 1862, but was defeated. He was a man of ability and high character, a devout Christian, and an uncompromising Democrat. He died about 1880, having the following children: 1. Fanny, m.———Baird; 2. Williams Jennings, m.———Baird, having Ruth, William Jennings and Grace; 3. Charles, m.———; 4. Mamie, m.———Allen; 5. Nanny, unmarried.

John Lillard, the father of Nancy Lillard Bryan, m. Miss Garrett, and besides Nancy, had: 1. Silas Lillard, who went to Mississippi, became a wealthy planter, and died without issue; 2. Capt. Benjaman Lillard, m. Elizabeth Browning, d. 1867; 3. Malinda, m. Early Corbin, and died without issue; 4. A daughter, m.———Stone; 5. A daughter, m———Yates; 6. A daughter, m.——— Shackelford, all three of whom went West.

Benjamin Lillard, who m. Elizabeth Browning, a daughter of Nicholas Browning, had issue as follows: 1. Chas. H., moved to Miss., and m.———Gurley; 2. Lucy M., m. 1st James O'Bannon, having P. H. O'Bannon, m. Josephine Miller, and Roberta J., m. Silas L. Cooper. Lucy M., m. 2nd Cornelius Smith, by whom there were no children; 3. Margaret, m. William L. Browning, having Bettie A., m. Maj. D. A. Grimsley, Annie M., m. B. F. Bywaters, Benjamin W., m. Ella Rixey, Lucy C., m. Capt. R. R. Duncan, Silas H., m. Lizzie Simms, and Elocia, m. William Timberlake; 4. Silas B., m. Mildred Duncan, having Laura, m. S. R. Browning, Lizzie, m. Geo. F. Pulliam, Lucy, m. James Miller; 5. Virginia, died single; 6. William J., m. Virginia Browning, daughter of Mason R. Browning, having Benjamin, Silas, Vernon, m. Frank Jolliffe, Lena, m.———Harrison, Roberta, m.———Funk; 7. Edwina C., m. Richard H. Browning, having Ophelia, m. William Lillard, Edward, m. and lives in Missouri, Sally, m. George Harrison, Frank, m.———Denton and lives in Missouri, Lessie, Jane, m. Richard Duncan, Robert Lee, Eva, and Lucy.

Note. All the Lillards of Culpeper and Rappahannoek are probably related, and thus, through the Lillard family, related to the Bryans.

THE BROWNING FAMILY.
[By Judge D. A. Grimsley.]

John Browning, b. in England in 1594, came to Virginia in 1622 in ship "Abigail," and served in the House of Burgesses in 1629.

William Browning came to Virginia about 1623 in ship "Bona Nova." See Hatton's list of American emigrants.

It is supposed that the Virginia Brownings descended from one, or both, of the above, but the line of descent cannot be directly traced.

The Brownings appeared in Virginia soon after the settlement of the Colony. One of them, as appears from Henning's Statutes, was a member of the House of Burgesses, but whether the Culpeper family is a descendant of this man is not definitely known.

Francis Browning settled near Gaines X Roads, now Rappahannock, in 1735. He is supposed to have come from Caroline county. One Thomas Browning also came to Culpeper about that time, but returned to Caroline.

The wife of Francis Browning was a Miss. Lloyd, of Maryland, and they had the following children : 1. Francis, m. Frances Norman; 2. Nicholas, m. Sarah Washburn; 3. John, m. Miss Demorest; 4. Jacob, m. Elizabeth Bywaters; 5. Mary, m. Courtney Norman; 6. Ruth, m. William Duncan; 7. a daughter m. ———Turner.

FRANCIS BROWNING (Francis.) m. Frances Norman, and had 1. Shadrach, m. Polly Route; 2. Charles, m. Mollie Strother; 3. William, m. Milly Roberts; 4. James, m. Miss Deane, and moved to Ky; 5. Reuben, m. Ann Hickman, and went to Ky; 6. John, m. Elizabeth Strother; 7. Isaac, m. a daughter of Joshua Browning, Captain in the Virginia State Line; 8. Francis, died in Revolutionary army; 9. Molly, m. James Duncan; 10. Sarah, m.———Duncan; 11. Asenith, m. Benjamin Duncan

NICHOLAS BROWNING (Francis.) m. Sarah Washburn, and had 1. Nicholas, m. Miss Sloane; 2. Charles, m. Miss Wright; 3. A son who went to South Carolina.

JACOB BROWNING (Francis.) m. Elizabeth Bywaters, and had 1. Samuel, m. Miss Dunn, and went to Ky; 2. George, m. Elizabeth Browning, and went to N. C.; 3. Edmund, m. Sarah Allan, and went to Ill.; 4. Jacob, m. and went to Missouri. Was a Baptist preacher; 5. Lloyd, m. Elizabeth Allan, and went to Mo.; 6. Mary, m. Capt William Norman, and was maternal grandmother of Rev. Barnett Grimsley; 7. Senie, m. Edward King, and went to Ky.; 8. Delilah, m. Joseph Tanner, and went to Ky.; 9. Bettie, m. Elijah Anthony, and went to Ky.

JOHN BROWNING (Francis.) m. Miss Demorest, and had: 1. James, m. Miss Hickman, sister of Gen. Hickman, and went to Ky; 2. Joshua, m. Ann Scott, and went to Ky. He was the father of Thomas Browning, m. Elizabeth Lewright, who was the father of Robert Lewright Browning, Lieut. in the U. S. Navy, was drowned in Trinidad bay, and was the father of Chas. H. Browning, the founder of the order of "Runnemede," and author of "Magna Charta Barons, and their Descendants;" 3. Francis went to Russell county, Va., as did his brother, Enos.

SHADRACH BROWNING (Francis, Francis.) m. Polly Route, and had: 1. Preston, died unmarried; 2. Route, m. Miss Browning and went to Mo.; 3. Francis, m. Mrs. Moore, and went to Ky.; 4. Somerville, m. Lloyd Browning.

CHARLES BROWNING (Francis, Francis.) m. Mollie Strother, and had 1. Lloyd. m. Somerville Browning; 2. Willis, m. 1st. Caroline Menefee, 2nd. Elizabeth White; 3. Joseph, went to Ky.; 4. William, m. Lucy McClanahan, and went to Ky.; 5. Francis, m. Miss Yates, and went to Mo.; 6. Charles, died single; 7. John, m. Miss Pendleton, and went West; 8. Sarah, m.———Morrison, and went to Ky.; 9. Mary m. Col. Gates Yates, of Ky.; 10. Lucy, m. Weedon Smith, and went West: 12. Ann, m. Ashley, and went to Ky.

WILLIAM BROWNING (Francis, Francis.) m. Millie Roberts, and had 1. Henry, m. Mrs. Newell; 2. James, m.———; 3. William, m 1st. Miss Funkhouser, 2nd. Mrs. Hines; 4. Robert, m. Miss Duncan; 5. John, m. Kitty Duncan; 6. Daniel, m.———. and went to Ky; 7. Charles, m. Hines, and went to Mo.; 8. Samuel, m. -———, and went to Mo.; 9. Mason, m. Kitty Stover; 10. Lucy, m. Nicholas Browning; 11. Margaret, m. Eldridge Duncan; 12. and 13.. James and Elizabeth, died single. There are said to have been nineteen children in this family, the names of the last six not being known.

JOHN BROWNING (Francis, Francis.) m. Elizabeth Strother, and had 1. George, m. Miss Covington, and went to Ky.; 2. John D., m. 1st. Miss Dulaney, 2nd. Miss Haney; 3. Charles, m. 1st. Miss Moore, 2nd, Miss Bumgarner, and went to Mo.; 4. Strother, m. Miss Reid, and went to Ill.; 5. Oliver. m. Miss Bowyer, and went to Ohio; 6. Betsy, m. ———Whitescarver, and went to Ky,; 7. Fanny, m. Frederick Whitescarver; 8. Millie, m. Elijah Bruce, and went West; 9. Polly, m. George Yates, and went West.

CHARLES BROWNING (Nicholas, Francis.) m. Miss Wright, and had 1. Chas., died single; 2. Thomas, m. Miss Bywaters; 3. Nicholas, m. Lucy Browning (William).

JAMES BROWNING (John, Francis.) m.———, and had 1. James, of Clarke county, Ky.; 2. Caleb, m. Miss Pendleton; 3. Micajah, m.———, and went to Ky. Was the father of O. H. Browning, United States Senator from Illinois, and a member of Lincoln's cabinet; 4. Polly, m. Taliaferro Browning; 5. Anne, m.———Overall, and went West.

JOSHUA BROWNING (John, Francis,) m———, and had 1. John, m. Miss Pendleton; 2. James, went to Ky.; 3. Edmund, went to Ky.; 4. Jacob, went West; 5. Polly, m. William Grant, and went West; 6. Annie, m. Wm. Pendleton; 7. Elizabeth m. Capt. Isaac Browning.

LLOYD BROWNING (Charles, Francis, Francis.) m. Somerville Browning, and had 1. Margaret, m. Thos. Deatherage; 2. Amanda, m. Carnot Walden; 3. Martha, m. Puller A. Hughes; 4. Jane, m. A. F. Menefee.

WILLIS BROWNING (Charles, Francis, Francis.) m. 1st. Menefee, 2nd. Miss White, and had 1. John A., m. Miss Willis; 2. Chas. H., died single; 3. Cassandra, died single.

WILLIAM BROWNING (William, Francis, Francis.) m. 1st. Funkhouser, 2nd. Mrs. Hines, and had 1. James H., m. 1st. Margaret Duncan, 2nd. Maria Corbin; 2. William L., m. Margaret Lillard; 3. Eliza, Samuel Baker, and went to Mo.; 4. Lucy, m. Isaac Baker, and went to Mo.

JOHN BROWNING (William, Francis, Francis.) m. Kitty Duncan, and had 1. Lafayette, m. Susan Stallard; 2. Richard H., m. Edwina Lillard; 3. Jane, m. Walker Campbell.

MASON BROWNING (William, Francis, Francis.) m. Kitty Hines, and had 1. William S., Lieut. Co. B., 6th. Va. Cav., killed at Cedar Creek, Va.; 2. Henry R., m. Fletcher; 3. David, m. Rudacilla; 4. Regina, m. Richard Coates; 5. Virginia, m. Wm. J. Lillard; 6. Lucy, m. Wm. Stickley; 7. Route, m. Miss Priest.

NICHOLAS BROWNING (Chas., Nicholas, Francis, Francis.) m. Lucy Browning, and had 1. William H., m. 1st. Kitty Rixey, 2nd. Lucy Ellen Eastham; 2. Jas. A., m. 1st. Jane Cheek, 2nd. Mary Utterback; 3. Chas., d. single; 4. Elizabeth, m. Benjamin Lillard; 5. Tabitha, m. Cornelius Smith; 6. Cassandra, m. Johnson McQueen, and went to Illinois; 7. Anne, m. Jas. Kinsey; 8. Mildred, m. Charles Smith.

MARGARET BROWNING (William, Francis, Francis.) m. Eldridge Duncan, and had 1.Chas. H., died single. Was Lieut-Col. 16th. Miss. Inf., C. S. A.; 2. Robert R., m. 1st. Louisa Kerfoot, 2nd. Lucy Browning. Was Captain of Co. B., 6th. Va. Cav., C. S. A., losing an arm at Tom's Brook; 3. Benjamin F., killed at Cedarville, member of Co. B., 6th. Va. Cav.; 4. Olivia, m. Jas. F. Kerfoot, and lives in Clarke county, Va.; 5. Mildred, m. Silas B. Lillard; 6. Margaret, unmarried.

JOHN D. BROWNING (John, Francis, Francis.) m. 1st Miss Dulaney, 2nd Miss Haney and had 1. Margaret, m. John Carr; 2. Eliza, m. B. F. Eastham; 3. Sarah, m. B. F. Miller; 4. Mark A. H., m. Miss Kendrick, and went to Texas; 5. Dr. John S., m. 1st Miss Deatherage, 2nd Miss Roberts; 6. G. Judson, m. Miss Thomas. Was a member of the Va. Legislature; 7. Fanny, m.—— Mayberry, of Mo.; 8. Sophronia, m. Wm. S. Wood.

FRANCES BROWNING (John, Francis, Francis.) m. Frederick Whitescarver, and had 1. John S., m. Miss Griffin; 2. Harmon, m. Miss Latham; 3. Winston, m. Miss Bragg; 4. Chas., m². —— and went to W. Va.; 5. Conner, m. —— and lives in Rockingham county, Va; 6. Franklin, died single, Mexican war veteran; 7. William, m. 1st Miss Harrison, 2nd Miss ——. Was a Baptist preacher; 8. Robert, m. Miss Burgess; 9. Joseph, m.—— and lives in Iowa; 10. Cornelius, m.—— and lives in Iowa; 11. Addison, m. Miss Browning, and lives in Mo. 12. Bethany, m. 1st Jack Johnson, 2nd Mathias Weaver.

MARGARET BROWNING (Lloyd, Chas., Francis, Francis.) m. Thomas Deatherage, and had: Allie, m. Wm. N. Smith, having Thomas.

JANE BROWNING (Lloyd, Chas., Francis, Francis.) m. A. F. Menefee, and had: 1. Mollie, m. Samuel Spindle, and went to Texas; 2. Henry, m. Roberta Holland, and had Lloyd and others; 3. Robert, m. Miss Miller, and had issue.

JOHN A. BROWNING (Willis, Chas., Francis, Francis.) m. Miss Willis, and had: 1. Charles, died single; 2. Bessie, m. W. G. Wood; 3. John; 4. George; 5 Willis; 6. Belle, m. Dangerfield Lewis; 7. Fanny.

JAMES H. BROWNING (William, William, Francis, Francis.) m. 1st Miss Duncan, 2nd Miss Corbin, and had: 1. Thomas, m. Miss Chappellear; 2. Susan, m. Wm. Duncan; 3. Isaiah, died single: 4. Preston, m. Miss Fletcher; 5. Lizzie, m. John Wood; 6. Fanny, m. Joseph Brown; 7. Charles, m. Botts; 8. Ada, m. Mr. Luttrell; 9. Ella; 10. Ernest; 11. Mason; 12. Lucy.

WILLIAM L. BROWNING (William, William, Francis, Francis.) m. Margaret Lillard, and had: 1. Bettie A., m. D. A. Grimsley, major 6th Va. Cav., C. S. A., and judge of Circuit Court of Virginia; 2. Annie M., m. B. F. Bywaters; 3. Benj. W., m. Ella Rixey; 4. Silas H., m. Lizzie Simms; 5. Elocia, m. Willie Timberlake; 6. Lucy, m. Capt. R. R. Duncan.

LAFAYETTE BROWNING (John, William, Francis, Francis.) m. Susan Stallard, and had 1. John, m. and lives in Richmond, Va.; 2. S. R., m. Laura Lillard; 3. Mollie, m. Geo. Burgess; 4. Ella, m. Jno. Fraley.

RICHARD H. BROWNING (John, William, Francis, Francis.) m. Edwina Lillard, and had 1. Ophelia, m. Wm. Lillard; 2. Edward, lives in Mo; 3. Sallie, m. Mr. Harrison; 4. Frank, lives in Mo; 5. Lessie; 6. Jane, m. Richard Duncan; 7. Robert; 8. Eva; 9. Lucy.

JANE BROWNING (John, William, Francis, Francis.) m. Walker Campbell, and had 1. Delia, m. Robert Bywaters; 2. Mary, m. Thomas Bywaters; 3. Scott, m. Miss Strother.

DAVID BROWNING (Mason, William, Francis, Francis.) m. Miss Rudicilla, and had 1. William; 2. Blanche; 3. Ida; 4. Fanny.

VIRGINIA BROWNING (Mason, William, Francis, Francis.) m. William Lillard, and had 1. Benjamin; 2. Vernon, m.———Jolliffe; 3. Silas; 4. Lena, m. Wm. Harrison; 5. Roberta, m.———Funk.

LUCY BROWNING (Mason, William, Francis, Francis.) m. Wm. Stickley, and had 1. Mason; 2. Browning.

ROUTE BROWNING (Mason, William, Francis, Francis.) m. Miss Priest, and had Luther, William, Regina, Ada, Frank, Russell, Lillian, and Louise.

WILLIAM H. BROWNING (Nicholas, Chas., Nicholas, Francis.) m. 1st Kitty Rixey, 2nd Lucy Ellen Rixey, and had Lucy, m. J. E. B. S. Leavel.

JAS. A. BROWNING (Nicholas, Chas., Nicholas, Francis.) m. 1st Jane Cheek, and had 1. Alice; 2. Montgomery; 3. Myrtis, m. A. J. Yates; 4. Mollie, m. George Rosson; 5. Dora, m. Chas. Jolliffe; 6. Caroline; 7. George.

ELIZABETH BROWNING (Nicholas, Chas., Nicholas, Francis.) m. Benj. Lillard, and had 1. Chas. H., m. Miss Gurley, of Miss; 2. Lucy M., m. 1st. Jas. M. O'Bannon, 2nd Cornelius Smith. By her first marriage she had Roberta J., m. S. L. Cooper, and P. H, m. Josephine Miller; 3. Margaret, m. Wm. L. Browning (see supra); 4. Silas B., m. Mildred Duncan, having Laura, m. S. R. Browning, Lizzie m. Geo. Pulliam, and Lucy, m. Jas. Miller; 5. Wm. J., m. Virginia Browning, (see supra); 6. Edwina C., m. Richard H. Browning, (see supra); 7. Virginia; 8. Sarah.

TABITHA BROWNING (Nicholas, Chas., Nicholas, Francis.) m. Cornelius Smith and had 1. Wm. N. Smith, m. Allie Deatherage (see supra); 2. Lucy A., m. H. A. Wood; 3. Rebecca, m. John B. Miller; 4. Hugh M., m. Mollie O'Bannon; 5. S. Russell, m. 1st. Frankie English, 2nd. Mrs. Mary Taunt.

ANNE BROWNING (Nicholas, Chas., Nicholas, Francis.) m. Jas. Kinsey, and had 1. Eliza, m. Wm. Smith; and others who live in the West.

MILDRED BROWNING (Nicholas, Chas., Nicholas, Francis.) m. Chas. Smith, and had 1. Lucy M., m. Matthew Carpenter; 2. Annie M., m. R. Y. Field; 3. Chas. E., m. Katherine Duncan; 4. Jennie; 5. Austin.

R. R. DUNCAN (Margaret, William, Francis, Francis.) m. 1st. Miss Kerfoot, and had 1. Blanche, m. John R. Duncan; Robert L., m. Miss Meade; 3. Ada, m. ———Napier, lives in Ga. He m. 2nd. Lucy Browning, and had : Maude, m. Jno. Button, Rosa, Frank, and Lucy Russell.

ELIZA BROWNING (John D., John, Francis, Francis.) m. B. F. Eastham, and had 1. Robert W., m. Miss Read; 2. F. Dabney, m. Miss Eastham. Was a Confederate soldier and was badly wounded; 3. Emma C.; 4. Philp B.; 5. Wm. B.; 6. John R.; 7. Edwin L.; 8. Annie M.; 9. Ada V., m. Jas. Miller; 10. Geo. B; 11. Chas. C.; m. Eva Alexander.

SARAH BROWNING (John D., John, Francis, Francis.) m. B. F. Miller, and had 1. Annie C., m. Hampson Keyser; 2. Laura F., m. Rev. J. F., Kemper, of Mo.; 3. Alice; 4. John J., m. 1st. Miss Taylor, 2nd. Miss Tyler; 5. Cora C., m. Andrew Botts; 6. Ella B., m. Ringgold Armstrong; 7. Ada F., m. John N. Keyser, of Mo.; 8. Florence, m. J. W. Yancey; 9. Rosa L., m. Wm. Benton.

G. JUDSON BROWNING (John D., John, Francis, Francis.) m. Miss Thomas, and had 1. Alexander; 2. Robert; 3. Judson.

DR. JOHN S. BROWNING (John D., John, Francis, Francis.) m. 1st. Miss Deatherage, and had 1. Robert; 2. Judson, m. Miss Deatherage. He m. 2nd. Miss Roberts, and had : Dr. Edgar Browning, m. Miss Turner.

SOPHRONIA BROWNING (John D., John, Francis, Francis.) m. W. S. Wood, and had 1. Flora, m. Eugene Brooking; 2. Emma; 3. John.

HARMON WHITESCARVER (Fanny, John D., John, Francis, Francis.) m. Miss Latham, and had 1. son, killed in C. S. A.; 2. George, lives in W. Va.

WINSTON WHITESCARVER (Fanny, John D., John, Francis, Francis.) m. Miss Bragg, and had 1. William, died in C. S. A.; 2. Lucy, m. Jas. M. Chelf.

WILLIAM WHITESCARVER (Fanny, John D., John, Francis, Francis.) m. 1st. Harrison, 2nd. Miss———, and had 1. A son who m. a daughter of Gen. J. G. Field; 2. Annie, m. Rev. Mr. Hume.

BETHANY WHITESCARVER (Fanny, John D., John, Francis, Francis.) m. 1st.———Johnston. and had 1. George, m.———; 2. Charles, died in Union army; 3. Joseph, m. Johnson; 4. Elizabeth, m. Mr. Bayne, and lives in W. Va. Married 2nd.———Weaver, and had 1. Taylor, m. and lives in W. Va.; 2. Mark, m. Miss Burke.

In compiling the genealogy of the Browning family no effort has been made to give the names and marriages of the present generation, nor has been followed the line of descent of those who emigrated from this county to the West, the descendants of whom are very numerous, and live in various States. It is quite possible that some may have been overlooked, who died unmarried, or emigrated previous to their marriage.

THE THOMAS FAMILY.
[By Mrs. Mary Dunnica Micou.]

Without doubt the Thomas family of Orange county, and also that of Culpeper county, are descended from the earliest emigrant of that name, who came to Essex county, or rather the one who patented land from Elizabeth county, to Essex, from 1437 to 1665, in all, about 3,400 acres. He is mentioned first as William Ap. Thomas, and most of his grants are given to him for bringing to this country, William Thomas and als, presumably his sons, as William Thomas, aged 22, and Robert Thomas, aged 20, came to Virginia, in June 1635, and John, aged 19, in July 1635. The way in which land patents are taken out by these young men indicate that they were sons of William Ap. Thomas, all being granted to them in the same neighborhood. Robert m. a Miss Massie, and settled in Essex, having a son, Edward, m. Catherine Williamson, (dau. of Henry Williamson). He established the Essex county family, and lived at Thomas Neck, on the Rappahannock River; was Justice of Peace in 1695, and High Sheriff in 1696; died in 1699. William Thomas, aged 22, in 1635, took out land in Northumberland county, and is called "William of Yeocomoco." He was Justice of Northumberland county in 1656, and Burgess of Surry county in 1652; he had land patents in every county from Surry to Essex county. He probably brought his wife from England, as he is granted land in Lancaster county, for transporting William Thomas and wife from England. Her name was Rebecca, and she survived him, as she takes out letters of administration in 1635. His son, John, was then 17 years of age, showing that he was born in 1648. He died in 1710, leaving wife, Elizabeth, ch.: Richard, William, Peter, John, Elizabeth, Jane, Richard, who is mentioned as son and heir of John Thomas, is undoubtedly the Richard Thomas who m, Isabella Pendleton, dau. of Philip Pendleton, the emigrant. Richard and Isabella Thomas both took out land in King and Queen and Spotsylvania counties in 1728. Richard Thomas died in 1748, and his widow, Isabella, went to live in Drysdale Parish, Caroline county. Their children are uncertain as to number and name. There is a Rowland Thomas and a Joseph Thomas mentioned with her in deeds of land, but the relationship is not defined. It is certain, though, that her daughter, Mary, m. Col. Thomas Barbour, and another, Catherine, m. Ambrose Barbour. Her son, Richard, m. in 1753 Mildred Taylor, of Orange county; their children were : Richard, George, James, Sarah, and Mildred, m. John Piper. James Thomas m. in 1781 Elizabeth, dau. of Henry Pendleton.

John Thomas, youngest son of (John, William, William Ap Thomas.) and brother of Richard, was born about 1690; he bought land in King William, Spotsylvania, Hanover, Orange and King George counties, between 1725 and 1739. In 1776 he was living in Bromfield Parish, Culpeper county. He died in 1782, a very old man, having survived two of his sons, and having several great grand children. He mentions in his will the following children: Benjamin, John, Massey, William, Margaret McKey, Sarah Powell, and Ann Kirk. His son, Benjamin. succeeded to his property in King George county, and died 1782. His son, William, made his will in 1776 in Maryland. His son, Massey Thomas, died in 1776, leaving wife, Elizabeth, children : Reuben, John, William, Massey, Jesse, and Susannah. Massey Thomas Jr. served in the Revolutionary Army from 1776 to 1779 in the 10th. Va. Regiment, Col. John Green. He m. 1st. Elizabeth Barlow, 2nd Martha Pendleton, dau. of Philip, 2nd. son of Henry and Mary (Taylor) Pendleton. Thus, the great nephew of Richard Thomas m. the great neice of Isabella Pendleton, his wife. The children of Massey Thomas and Martha Pendleton were : 1. Frances Taylor, b. 1788, m. ——Lewis; 2. Philadelphia Pendleton, b. 1789, m. James Dunnica; 3. Sallie Minor, b. 1791, m. Wm. H. Dunnica; 4. Granville Pendleton, b. 17——; 5. Virginia Curtis, b. 1794, m.——Norwood; 6. John Price, b. 1796; 7. Martha Curtis, b. 1798, m.——Ramsey. Massey Thomas moved to Woodford county, Ky., before 1812 and died there. His son, Granville Pendleton Thomas, fought in the war of 1812 to 1815, in the 2nd. Kentucky Regiment. The mother, Martha (Pendleton) Thomas, moved, after her husband's death, to Missouri with her two sons-in-law, James and William H. Dunnica, and died there in 1824. The Thomas family of Culpeper county goes back to the emigrant in the following order : Massey (6), Massey (5), John (4), John (3), William (2), William Ap Thomas.

MISCELLANEOUS.

CHAPTER X.
GEN. LA FAYETTE IN CULPEPER.

Next to Washington, as a Revolutionary patriot the memory of La Fayette is cherished and honored by Virginians.

The Marquis, Gilbert Mottier De La Fayette, was born on the 6th of September, 1757, at Charagnac, in the ancient province of Auvergne. He was the son of Col. La Fayette who was killed in the battle of Minden two months before the birth of La Fayette. His mother did not long survive her husband's death, leaving La Fayette an infant, the heir to immense estates. By his guardian, he was sent, at the age of twelve, to college in Paris; at eighteen years of age he married his wife, who was two years younger than himself, which marriage proved to be a happy co-partnership, the wife being truly a helpmeet and promoter of the independent views and plans of the husband—a worker for mankind and individual liberty.

La Fayette was the founder of the national guard at Paris. On account of this he encountered the opposition of the Royalists. He was in favor of

constitutional government, consequently he became the target of the Jacobins, being arrested and tried for treason. At that time he saw, from afar, the struggle our Colonies were making against the greedy encroachments of England; being unable to help his own people, he determined to join forces with America, and help to achieve her independence. When the news came, and was hailed with joy by the Colonists, Lord Cornwallis spoke with contempt, of his advent, calling him, in his dispatches to the Queen, a boy who could easily be put down. But the prophesy was refuted by the surrender of Cornwallis at York Town. For this "boy" took a prominent part in the final overthrow of the English commander.

La Fayette made four separate visits to America; first in 1777; then in 1780, after which he returned to bring money and men to aid the Colonists. His third visit was in 1784 to enjoy the conclusion of peace. The last in 1825, when he accepted the invitation of Congress to become the guest of the Nation. It was during this visit that he was the guest of Culpeper. The town of Culpeper sent a committee, composed of La Fayette's old comrades in arms, Col. Gabriel Long and Capt. Philip Slaughter, to convey to him their invitation, he being, at the time, at Monticello, the home of Jefferson, where he was meeting his old friends, Madison, Monroe, William Wirt, and others. That evening he journeyed, with Mr. Madison, to Montpelier, where the Culpeper committee found him and delivered their invitation, which was accepted.

The next morning, with this committee, he took up his line of journey, throughout which he received ovations from all classes of people, men, women, and children coming out to greet him as he passed along. His journey was near to the old Marquis road, which had been constructed by his troops when on their way to York Town, and on which stood the historic La Fayette Oak, which had been his shelter in '76. This tree was located near what is now Rhodesville, and known as La Fayette Station on the railroad from Orange to Fredericksburg. A piece of this La Fayette Oak was recently made into a plaque and sent to the unveiling of the La Fayette monument in Paris, as a souvenir, presented by Mrs. Anne S. Green, of Culpeper, she having procured a portion of the historical old tree from the Rev. R. R. Howison, historian, of Virginia. A representation of this testimonial from Culpeper accompanies this description of La Fayette's visit.

The party reached Crooked Run at about 10 o'clock on the 22nd. of August, 1825, where they were met by a company of horsemen, under the command of Col. Jonathan Catlett Gibson, ladies in carriages, and citizens on foot. The next stop was made at Greenwood, the home of Judge John W. Green, of the Court of Appeals of Virginia. The guests went into the house and partook of some refreshments, attended by Mrs. Green, Mrs. Patton, Mrs. Slaughter, and others, after which, the escort having dismounted and arranged themselves in a double line at their horses' heads, La Fayette, at his own request, was introduced to each man individually, Judge Green refreshing the entire party with cool drinks of iced today, which was a favorite Virginia beverage in those days. Resuming their march, the party reached Culpeper before two o'clock and stopped at the Episcopal rectory, the home of the Rev. Alonzo Welton, remaining there an hour, when they were escorted to the Masonic Hall, where Mr. John Shackelford eloquently addressed the multitude that had assembled to greet the distinguished guest. After the address La Fayette received the old soldiers, who were the veterans of '76, and who had come from far and near to see him—from the hills and valleys of Culpeper and Orange, many of whom had been members of the old Minute Men of Culpeper, who were among the earliest to enlist in the fight for liberty and country.

After this came the great dinner, which was prepared under the direction of Jere Strother, at the old Bell Tavern, the great bell in its front giving it its name. No dining hall was spacious enough to accommodate the guests, so the banquet was held under a tent in the garden, which required five hundred yards of brown linen to construct. And under this grand canopy the La Fayette banquet was held. Meats were barbecued in every style—in pits and on spits. There were roasted pigs, ducks, turkies, hams, and everything else to correspond. Thirty toasts were drank. Lovely maidens, in white, were the waitresses, one of them, Miss Sallie Barbour. reciting a poem. Mrs. Geraldine Lightfoot, Misses Sarah and Ann Norris were also among them. Years ago Miss Sarah Norris gave the writer an account of this event, in which she recalled the dessert of nuts, etc., and the filbert that La Fayette put in his mouth, which, proving a nut that he could not crack, he laid beside his plate, and was secured by her as a souvenir of the hero. A ball at night in the Masonic Hall wound up the day, La Fayette leaving next morning for Warrenton, having many citizens and military as his escort, among whom were Cols. Gibson and Storrow, Judge Green and others. On his visit to Culpeper Gen. La Fayette was accompanied by ex-President Monroe.

THE PRESBYTERIANS OF CULPEPER.
[By G. D. Gray.]

The Presbyterian church of Culpeper was organized in 1813, consisting then of 24 members.

On the 14th of April, 1815, Samuel Davies Hoge, father of the late Dr. Moses D. Hoge, of Richmond, was installed as the first pastor. He had been supplying the pulpit for about two years previous to that time. He continued to be the pastor for several years. Who succeeded him as pastor, or stated supply, is not known, but in 1832, Rev. A. D. Pollock became their stated supply, and continued to be such till some time in 1837, when Rev. John J. Royall became their stated supply. The church, at that time, comprised the counties of Culpeper, Madison, Orange, Spotsylvania and Rappahannock, and had over 50 members. Among them were the following:

Elders: William Kemper, father of Governor Kemper, John Glassell. Members: Elizabeth Slaughter, Lucy Ashby, Mary Somerville, Maria Kemper, Irena P. Green, Sarah Freeman, Lucy Gordon, Betsy Gordon, M. G. Spotswood, Hannah Grymes, Betsy Shackleford, Anne Robertson, Mildred Smith, Cecilia Wallace, Sarah C. Barbour, Mary H. Somerville, Mrs. Susan Thornton, Fanny Shackleford, William Glassell, Walter Somerville, John Ashby, William Ashby, Miss Duncanson, Marion Glassell, Elizabeth Lee, Louisa B. Glassell, Elizabeth Ashby, Emily Ashby, Mary Anne Wallace, Mrs. Martin Slaughter, Mrs. H. Strother, Mrs. Mary Ann Strother, Harriet P. Strother, Henry Strother, Aylette Buckner, Mary Rolls, Robert Deatherage, Mrs. Deatherage, George Thom, Jane Nelson, Susan Nelson, Elizabeth Nelson, Harriet P. Spotswood, Mary Frances Thornton, Elizabeth Thornton, Mrs. Nancy Shivers, Miss Calvert, Mrs. Jett, Mrs. Sally Grimes, Miss Sally Grymes, Mrs. Nellie Skinker, Miss Agnes Kemper, and Miss Sarah Kemper.

Mr. Royall continued to supply the pulpit of this church till the month of December, 1855, when Rev. A. D. Pollock again became the stated supply, and continued this relation with the church till the year 1867, when he resigned, and, at his request, Rev. Robert L. McMurran was invited to take his place. The house of worship, situated at the northern end of Main street, had been destroyed during the war between the States, the lot sold, and money invested in the lot on which the present building was erected, which was built in the year 1868. The congregation occupied their new church building in March, 1869, for the first time. Rev. Mr. McMurran continued to occupy the position of stated supply till some time in the year 1870, when Rev. R. T. Berry took his place and occupied the pulpit till September, 1871.

The church was without a pastor or stated supply till January, 1874, when Rev. W. W. Reese became the supply which position he held till January, 1876, when he was elected and installed pastor, which office he held till September, 1876. In 1877 Rev. Samuel K. Winn was elected and installed pastor, and he continued as such till April, 1879, when he resigned to accept a call to Petersburg. The church pulpit was again vacant till May, 1881, when Rev. J. P. Strider was installed pastor, which position he filled till October, 1883, when he resigned to accept a call to Savannah, Ga. The church was left again without any stated ministry till April, 1886, when Rev. Edward Eells was elected and installed pastor, which office he held till October 1887. From October, 1887, to May, 1889, the pulpit was again vacant. From May, 1889, to March, 1894, Rev. R. R. Howison supplied the pulpit From October, 1894 to October, 1895, the pulpit was filled by Rev. T. R. Sampson, D. D., after which time there was no stated supply till April, 1896, when Rev. J. Louis McClung was elected pastor. Mr. McClung declined the call as pastor but has continued to supply the pulpit to the present time, November, 1900. The present number of members is 40.

REGARDING THE GERMANNA SETTLEMENT.

[Mr. Willis M. Kemper, of Cincinnati, Ohio, author of the "Kemper Genealogy," has recently (Sept., 1900) been on a visit to Germany, and has furnished the following concerning the old settlement of Germanna.—R. T. G.]

Several years prior to 1714 Gov. Spotswood discovered deposits of iron ore on the large tracts of land he had entered, where Germanna was afterwards located, in Spotsylvania (now Orange) county. He spent much time arranging his plans to work this one, and in getting the Queen's (Ann) permission, and in having the royal share determined. After these matters were adjusted he needed iron miners and iron workers, to mine the ore, and build furnaces and run them, and there were none in Virginia. When the Baron de Graffenreid was in Virginia after his escape from the North Carolina Indian massacre, he arranged with Spotswood to get miners for him from Germany, and with this in view de Graffenried wrote to miners with whom he was acquainted in Germany, and arranged for their coming to Virginia. The colony was gathered from the neighborhood of the village of Musen in the province of Nassau—Siegen, in Westphalia, some ten miles Northeast of the old city of Seigen. This is a mining country, and at Musen is one of the most celebrated iron mines in Germany, which has been worked since early in the 14th century. The colony, as it reached Virginia, was composed of twelve heads of families, viz: John Kemper, Jacob Holtzclaw, John and Harman Fishback, John Hoffman, Harmon Utterback, Tillman Weaver (Webber), John Joseph Martin, (Merdten), Peter Hitt (Heide), Jacob Coons (Countz), ——— Wayman and ——— Handback. The colony may have been larger when it left Germany, for it spent the greater part of the fall of the year 1713, and January, 1714, in London, and some names are mentioned which do not appear in Virgina. There also came, either with them or very shortly after them, their pastor, John Henry Hager, a very learned man, who had been pastor of the reformed church at Ober Fishback, in the neighborhood of Musen. This was the first German colony that came to Virginia, and they were settled by Gov. Spotswood at Germanna in April, 1714, where cabins and a block house were built for them. They went to mining ore for the governor, and built the blast furnace, the remains of which are to be seen in the neighborhood. Here they remained for several years, when, owing to some dissatisfaction with the governor's treatment of them, they removed, about 1720, to Germantown, in what is now Fanquier county, where they leased large tracts of lands and went to farming. By this time other German colonies had come to Virginia, some of which had to pay their passage by working for the governor. The reformed part of these emigrants, with their old pastor, went to Germantown, Fauquier, while the Lutheran part of the colonists went a little later to Robinson's river. A recent visit to Musen shows it a prettily situated village of about 2,000 people in a narrow valley. It has grown up around the old mine, still worked. The parish was cut off from the neighboring parish of Ferndorf, in the wider valley nearer Siegen, in 1727. The little reformed church, built about that time, was destroyed, in the 30 years war, with all of its records. The church was rebuilt and the new records begin 1649. The church was again destroyed by fire in 1892, but the records were saved. The entire village attends this church; there is not a Catholic in the town. The villages of Fishback and Holtzclaw are a few miles to the West of Musen. No doubt the families, in the colony, of those names came from these villages. The records of the Kemper family is to be found in the church records at Musen. There is no one by the name at Musen today. Utterbacks and Webbers are still living in Musen. The names of Hoffman, Merdten and Countz are still to be found in the neighborhood. The name Heide is still to be found in the meadows about Ferndorf. No doubt old records of some of these families can be found at Ferdorf. Siegen is the large town in this part of the country, and is a picturesque old place, with its old castle high on a hill, its steep narrow winding streets, and high gabled, overhanging houses, and is a thrifty place of some 25,000 people, largely engaged in iron manufacturing. The Westphalian country is one of the most thrifty in Germany. Musen is a clean little town, with neat houses, intelligent people, and a respectable air about it. These German farmers soon made the wilderness about Germantown to blossom as the rose, and Germantown was for years the center of the German people, and known far and wide.

THE CULPEPER OF TO-DAY.

[To be read in conjunction with page 11, of Part II, which was written in April, 1899.]

Now (October, 1900.) the municipal goverment is : Mayor, Alden Bell; Recorder and Assessor, G. Chapin Lightfoot; Treasurer, G. W. Keerl; Councilmen, R. F. Booton, David Bailey, Samuel Diener, A. M. Allan, J. S. Covington and C. E. Smith.

Instead of one bank, there are now three, viz : The Culpeper National Bank, S. Russell Smith, President; The Farmers' and Merchants' Bank, C. J. Rixey, proprietor; and the Second National Bank, C. J. Rixey, President.

Among the lawyers D. J. F. Strother has removed to West Virginia, and Messrs. Alden Bell and E. S. Perry are now members of the Culpeper bar. S. M. Newhouse, having succeeded S. R. McClanahan, is now the Culpeper member of the House of Delegates.

THE FIRST COUNTY COURT.

The earliest county court held for Culpeper county, as shown by the deed books, the first minute book having been lost, was on the 18th day of May, 1749, without the place being mentioned. On another of the first pages of the first deed book it appears that court was held on Thursday, June 15, 1749, at the residence of Robert Coleman.

The clerks of the County Court, from 1749 to the present time, with their respective periods of service, are : 1. Roger Dixon, 1749 to 1772, 23 years; 2. John Jameson, 1772 to 1810, 38 years; 3. William Broaddus, 1810 to 1811 (died); 4. William Broaddus, Jr., 1811 to 1816, 5 years; 5. Thos. W. Lightfoot, 1816 to 1831, 15 years; 6. F. T. Lightfoot, 1831, to 1838, 7 years; 7. Fayette Mauzy, 1838 to 1873, 35 years; 8. W. M. Mauzy, 1873 to 1874, 1 year; 9. Charles B. Payne, 1874 to 1893, 18 years; 10. Warren F. Coons, 1893 (still serving).

The deed books of the county are intact from 1749. Three of the will books "G," from April 1, 1813, to June 17, 1817, "L," and "M," from 1827 to 1833, were lost during the war beween the States, as were also several of the County Court Minute books.

TOWN OF CULPEPER LAID OUT.

Pursuant to an act of the General Assembly, passed at a session held in Williamsburg on the 22nd. of Feburary, 1759, the town of Fairfax (Culpeper's original name) was laid off on 27 acres of the land of Robert Coleman, the Court House being located on lot No. 24 (which is now the corner of Davis and Main [or Coleman] streets, where stands the store building of Joseph Messinger), the prison and stocks on lot No. 14 (opposite corner, on which is now Joseph B. Gorrell's building). The Town was laid off by William Green, Philip Slaughter, Nathaniel Pendleton, and William Williams, the plan being submitted to the County Court on Thursday, June 21, 1759, and ordered to be recorded.

INDEX TO MARRIAGE RECORD.

The marriage record, beginning on page 56 of the second part, and ending on page 74, is printed in alphabetical order, according to the name of the husband. Owing to its great length the reverse was not printed, but the names of the wives are given in the following index. The following omissions were inadvertently made in the record :

Leroy Cooper m. Harriet Byron Vaughn in 1808.
Daniel Grimsley m. Frances Estes in 1796.
William Grimsley m. Agnes Norman in 1807.

[In looking up names in the following index, please note that where a name appears more than once on a page, it is only indexed once, hence it will be well to always look through the entire page. The names are printed exactly as they appear in the record, but in a number of instances it can be seen that they are wrongly spelled, and in a majority of cases, can be detected.]

A

Abbott, 69
Adams, 60, 63, 64, 67, 70, 73
Allan, 63, 69, 71
Allen, 68
Alexander, 61, 73
Alsop, 62, 68
Amiss, 61
Anderson, 59, 69
Antram, 61, 64
Appleby, 64, 72
Arnold, 64
Asher, 58, 60, 68, 72
Askins, 59
Atkins, 57, 58, 72
Atwood, 60
Aynes, 63

B

Babangham, 65
Baker, 57, 65
Baldick, 74
Ball, 63, 64
Ballance, 63
Ballard, 62, 69
Ballinger, 59, 64, 70
Banks, 65
Barbour, 72, 74
Barler, 63
Barnes, 62, 65, 66, 70
Barnhisle, 74
Basye, 57
Bates, 65
Baugher, 69
Bawsell, 69
Baxter, 70, 74
Bayne, 71
Beasy, 70
Beckham, 66, 69, 73
Bell, 73
Belly, 62
Bennett, 58
Berden, 68
Berry, 57, 59, 67, 73
Bigbee, 61
Bingard, 64
Bingham, 56, 63
Bishop, 58, 65, 67, 71
Blackburn, 62
Blackwell, 59, 73
Blair, 60
Blankenbaker, 59, 73
Bohen, 59
Boone, 57, 71
Borst, 65, 67
Bosan, 57
Boston, 71
Boswell, 58, 67
Botts, 58, 61, 72
Boughan, 68
Boughorn, 57
Bourne, 67, 68
Bowen, 57
Bowers, 72
Bowling, 74
Bowry, 71
Brady, 63
Bragg, 58, 73
Brandam, 57
Brandon, 57, 66, 71
Branham, 63, 64
Bredlove, 62, 63
Bridwell, 64
Broadus, 59
Brooke, 57
Brown, 56, 57, 58, 59, 61, 64, 65, 66, 67, 68, 69, 71, 72, 73,
Browning, 59, 61, 65, 66, 67, 71, 73, 74
Broyles, 62, 67
Bruce, 60, 64
Bryan, 57, 66, 71, 72
Bryant, 71
Buingardner, 63, 69
Burbridge, 57
Burgess, 65
Burke, 59, 61, 68, 73
Burns, 66
Burris, 69
Burton, 62
Butler, 57, 58, 59, 61, 62, 63, 65, 66, 68, 72, 73
Butt, 63
Button, 70
Bywaters 58, 60, 61, 62, 67

C

Cabler, 74
Callahan, 66
Calvert, 56, 58, 61, 64, 67, 71, 73
Camp, 60, 70
Campbell, 58, 59, 61, 63, 68, 70, 71, 72
Cammeral, 72
Canady, 58, 71
Cannon, 59
Carder, 57, 58, 59, 65, 69
Cardwell, 58
Carpenter, 58, 65, 67, 72, 74
Carper, 71
Carroll, 67
Carter, 57, 64, 70, 74
Casey, 68
Catlett, 72
Caul, 56
Cave, 60
Caynor, 60
Chancellor, 63
Chandler, 65

II

Chapman, 56, 74
Chappaliar, 62
Chart, 64
Cheek, 64, 65, 70
Chester, 59
Chewning, 69
Chich, 74
Chilton, 56, 61, 71, 74
Chisholm, 71
Christler, 72, 74
Christopher, 60, 71
Cinnie, 67
Clark, 57, 58, 59, 60, 63, 64, 65, 74
Clatterbuck, 57, 61, 62, 63, 68, 69, 73
Clifton, 73
Clinch, 58
Clore, 69, 73
Cochran, 63
Cocke, 65, 70
Coffer, 63
Coffman, 72
Cogell, 68
Coghill, 62, 64
Colbert, 60
Coleman, 60, 70, 73
Collins, 58, 60, 63, 65, 69, 70, 71, 72
Colvin, 59, 60, 65, 69, 71, 72, 73
Colly, 66
Compton, 69
Conner, 59, 71, 72
Cooke, 57, 74
Coons, 59, 60, 69, 73, 74
Cooper, 69, 73
Corbin, 60, 62, 65, 66, 67, 68, 74
Core, 70
Corley, 67, 72
Cornelius, 71, 72
Cornett, 67
Cosney, 61
Cosper, 72
Condy, 72
Covington, 58, 59, 61
Cowen, 67
Cowgill, 70
Cowne, 64, 65
Cox, 66
Cral, 70
Chain, 69, 70
Crawford, 61, 68
Crawley, 72
Creal, 57, 70
Crigler, 64
Crisal, 59
Crittenden, 73
Crouch, 60
Crow, 68
Crutcher, 62, 70
Cullen, 57
Cummings, 70
Cunningham, 60, 61
Curtis, 57, 68

D

Daniel, 58
David, 58
Davis, 63, 68
Day, 72
Deale, 64
Debourd, 60
Delany, 59
Dell, 70
Dennis, 56
Dicken, 58, 74
Diffee, 65
Dillard, 57
Dillen, 57
Dobbs, 67
Dodson, 57, 58, 69
Dogan, 73
Doggett, 58, 60, 63, 65, 69
Doores, 74
Donald, 67
Dowling, 62
Doyle, 61
Drake, 67
Duff, 63
Duke, 64
Dulaney, 58, 61, 62, 65, 66, 70
Dunaway 70
Duncan, 65, 69, 71, 72
Duval, 61, 66, 69
Dyke, 63, 65, 68, 70

E

Early, 68
Eastham, 57, 63, 65
Eddins, 63
Edge, 62
Edrington, 61, 67
Edwards, 59, 72
Eldridge, 66
Eleason, 74
Embrey, 68
Estes, 58, 62, 68
Etherington, 71
Etherton, 62, 73, 72
Evans, 64

F

Farley, 58
Farmer, 69, 68, 73
Farrow, 60, 61, 71
Faulconer, 66, 69
Faver, 65, 68
Feaganes, 63
Fennell, 56, 63, 64, 66, 68, 74
Fergerson, 64, 66, 70
Fewel, 69, 74
Ficklin, 58, 69, 71
Fiddle, 62
Field, 66, 69
Finch, 64
Fincham, 60, 61, 71
Finks, 62, 71, 72
Finnell, 62
Fishback, 58, 72, 73
Fleshman, 63, 70
Fletcher, 68

Flinn, 72
Florence, 65
Floyd, 64
Fogg, 71
Fore, 68
Foster, 62, 72
Foushee, 58, 61, 62, 65
Fox, 67
Frazier, 74
Freeman, 60, 65
Fristoe, 58
Fry, 58, 71
Fryer, 62, 68, 71
Fucks, 63
Furguson, 72

G

Gaines, 56, 57, 58, 60, 61, 62, 63, 66, 68, 69, 72, 74
Garner, 68, 72
Garnett, 60, 63, 64, 65, 66, 67, 68, 69, 73, 74
Garratt, 66
Garrott, 66
Garwood, 64, 65
Gaunt, 67, 73
George, 59, 60
Gibbs, 57, 60
Gibson, 58, 64, 72
Gin, 73
Glass, 65, 67
Golden, 69, 70
Good, 71
Goodman, 61, 72
Googe, 63
Gore, 58, 66
Gosney, 67, 73
Grady, 63
Grant, 62, 66
Graves, 62, 63, 65, 66, 73
Gray, 57, 66, 68
Green, 57, 59, 61, 62, 66, 69, 71, 72, 73
Greenway, 63, 71
Gregory, 65
Grewis, 68
Griffin, 58, 61
Grimsley, 59, 68
Grinnan, 62, 68, 69
Grisby, 65, 73
Groves, 67
Guinn, 61, 62
Gully, 67

H

Haden, 71
Haines, 68, 72
Hall, 58, 59, 72
Ham—, 61
Hammons, 61
Hampkin, 70
Hand, 62
Handback, 70
Haddox, 61
Haney, 63
Hangue, 71
Hansbrough, 64, 68

III

Hanson, 67
Hanye, 63
Harden 58, 59, 61, 66, 70
Harney, 72
Harper, 59
Harris, 57
Harrison, 65, 71
Harvey, 60, 62
Hasby, 74
Hay, 60
Haynes, 63, 71, 73
Haywood, 61, 66, 73
Hawford, 73
Hawkins 57, 59, 60, 63, 66, 68, 71, 72, 73
Holland, 59, 65, 66, 73
Holloway, 57, 70
Holmes, 74
Hopkins, 61, 64, 67
Hoffer, 58, 59, 71, 72
Horner, 70
Horsely, 63
Horton, 57, 60, 65
Houghty, 66
Houton, 56
Howard, 59
Howen, 69
Higgason, 62
Higginton, 60
Hill, 57, 58, 60, 66, 68, 71, 73
Hilton, 58, 61, 63
Hisle, 60, 61, 64, 6 , 74
Hitt, 69
Heaton, 56, 64, 71, 72
Henderson, 72
Hendrick, 61, 73
Hensley, 65, 68
Herndon, 59, 73
Herrington, 57
Hershberger, 68
Huans, 61
Hudnell, 74
Hudson, 58, 59, 63, 73, 74
Huffman, 59, 62, 64, 66, 68, 70, 74
Hughes, 57, 58, 61, 62, 63, 67, 72, 73, 74
Hume, 57, 59, 60, 61, 63, 64, 72, 73
Humphrey, 58, 70
Hunt, 56
Hurrin, 67
Hurt 58, 60, 64, 65, 72
Hyne, 68

I

Inskeep, 58, 63

J

Jackson, 71
James, 57
Jarrell, 63, 65, 67
Jasper, 64, 71
Jeffries, 62, 68, 74
Jenkins, 59, 60, 62, 64, 65, 66, 67, 68, 69, 71, 73, 74

Jennett, 57
Jennings, 61, 68, 69
Jett, 58, 63, 64, 66, 67, 68, 70
Johnson, 69
Johnston, 58, 59, 60. 61, 6 , 66, 70
Jollett, 58
Jolley, 62
Jones, 57, 58, 59, 60, 63, 64, 65, 69, 72
Jordon, 70
Jury, 74

K

Kegg, 65
Keith, 61
Kelly, 58, 63, 70
Kennard, 59, 65
Kennedy, 72
Keys, 73
Kibbon, 62
Kilby, 61, 63, 66
King, 57, 66, 67
Kinnard, 61, 63, 67
Kirtley, 68, 69
Kline, 72
Kobler, 58
Konslar, 59

L

Lambkin, 68
Lammon, 67
Lampkin, 65
Landrum, 61
Lane, 65
Latham, 68, 69
Lawler, 65
Lawrence, 57
Lear, 59
Leather, 62
Leatherer, 58
Leathers, 61
Leavel, 59, 62, 63, 73
Lemmon, 66
Lewis, 60, 62, 63, 66, 72, 73
Lightfoot, 62, 63
Lillard, 58, 59, 63, 69, 70, 74
Lindsay, 58
Lipp, 63
Little, 57, 59, 67
Lloyd, 57, 58
Long, 57, 58, 64, 67
Lovell, 71
Lowen, 65
Lucas, 71, 72, 73
Lukie, 71

M

Maddox, 61, 69
Magruder, 57
Major, 66, 68, 69
Manuel, 63
Manwell, 64
Marder, 69
Margin, 73
Marrifield, 56

Marye, 63
Marshall, 57, 58, 61, 62, 64, 65, 67, 68, 69, 70, 72
Marston, 70
Massie, 57
Mason, 60, 63, 64, 66, 68, 71, 74
Martin, 62, 74
Mary, 66
Matthews, 57, 59, 60
Mauck, 63
Mauzy, 66, 70
Mawrey, 72
Mayer, 74
McAllister, 62, 71
McClanahan, 58, 72
McDonald, 62, 70
McDugley, 67
McGuinn, 56, 68
McKelbin, 62
McKensie, 68
McQueen, 58, 61
McQuinn, 70
Meade, 59
Medley, 71
Menefee, 57, 58, 59, 60, 68, 70, 72, 74
Merry, 63
Miller, 57, 59, 68, 69, 70, 71, 73
Mills, 60
Mitchell, 62, 66, 67, 69, 73
Monroe, 59, 60, 68, 69
Moore, 56, 58, 59, 66, 67, 69, 71
Morgan, 72
Morris, 58, 60, 67, 74
Morton, 68
Moss, 68, 69
Mozingo, 57, 73
Murphy, 59, 67, 70
Myrtle, 64, 67, 68

N

Nalle, 58, 60, 63, 71
Naughan, 64
Neale, 59
Neathers, 64
Newby, 70
Newton, 64, 67, 70
Nicolson, 64, 66
Norman, 57, 58, 59, 60, 62, 63, 64, 66, 70, 72
Norris, 59

O

Oder, 59, 62, 63, 69, 72
Olive, 59
Oliver, 59, 64
O'Neal, 69
Ordor, 61

P

Palmer, 64
Parks, 67, 72
Parsons, 64, 73
Partlow, 57, 58, 67
Patton, 57, 62

IV

Payne, 64, 67, 69, 71	Rose, 60,	Stuart, 68
Pemberton, 63	Ross, 72	Sturman, 68
Pendleton, 58, 63, 66, 67, 70, 71	Rosson, 61, 68, 70	Suddith, 61, 70
	Rountree, 63	Suliman, 63
Pener, 57	Routt, 58, 61, 73	Sullivan, 71
Perry, 73	Rowe, 63	Sutherland, 67, 74
Pettinger, 61	Royster, 72	Sutton, 57, 64
Petty, 57, 65, 70	Rucker, 56, 64	Swindler, 57, 60, 68, 70
Peyton, 62, 73	Rush, 71	
Philips, 59		**T**
Pickett, 70	**S**	Taliaferro, 58, 69
Pierce, 59, 61, 64, 70, 72	Sampson, 57, 70	Tannahill, 59, 61
Pinkard, 64, 69	Samuel, 64, 68	Tapp, 56, 59, 60, 66, 67, 70
Pinnell, 70, 73	Sanders, 70	Tatum, 67
Plunkett, 60	Sanford, 64, 67	Taylor, 67, 70
Pollard, 58	Saunders, 68, 70	Terrill, 62, 69
Poner, 72	Scott, 59, 60, 67, 68, 71	Terry, 66
Popham, 58, 70	Sedwicke, 67	Thaver, 61
Porter, 57, 62, 66, 67, 71	Seebree, 73	Thomas, 57, 67
Poulter, 70	Settle, 57, 60, 63, 66, 68, 73	Thompkins, 58
Poulton, 66	Sewright, 58	Thompson, 57, 58
Pound, 60	Shackelford, 59, 60, 63, 65, 68, 71, 72,	Thornhill, 64, 68
Powell, 58, 60, 65, 69, 72		Thornton, 73, 74
Pratt, 70, 71	Shannon, 57, 72	Thud, 57
Price, 73	Sharp, 57	Tineman, 57
Priest, 57, 58	Shaw, 70	Tinsley, 62, 69
Province, 70	Shelton, 73	Tobin, 70, 72, 73
Pulham, 73	Shepherd, 60	Tomlin, 69
Pulliam, 61, 65, 72, 73	Sherwood, 70	Towles, 69, 70, 71, 73
Pup, 57	Shingleton, 72	Threlkeld, 58, 60, 61, 63, 66, 69, 72, 73
Pusey, 65	Shipp, 66, 74	
Putnam, 67	Short, 60	Trenton, 71
	Shotwell, 71	Trimble, 57
Q	Simms, 59, 60, 62, 63, 64, 65, 68, 69, 72	Triplett, 60, 61, 62, 67
Quinn, 73		Tucker, 68, 70, 72, 74
	Sine, 71	Tumham, 70
R	Sisk, 61, 65, 73	Turner, 57, 60, 63, 65, 67, 69, 70, 72
Raines, 60, 72	Sisson, 62	
Rakestraw, 69	Slaughter, 58, 61, 62, 65, 66	Tussey, 63
Rambottom, 58, 61		Tutt, 64, 67, 68, 69, 71, 72
Ramey, 58, 67	Sleet, 66	Twentiman, 57, 58, 63
Randolph, 64	Smede, 68	Twyman, 72
Rasor, 62, 71	Smith 57, 58, 59, 60, 61, 62, 63, 64, 65, 67, 69, 70, 71, 72, 73, 74	**U**
Ratcliffe, 63		Underwood, 57, 65
Red, 59		Updyke, 72
Redman, 60		Utterback, 57, 61, 68, 69, 74
Reece, 59		
Reed, 60, 63, 64, 65	Snyder, 66, 69	
Rees, 68	Souther, 60	Utz, 72, 73
Reesee, 58	Spencer, 60, 63, 74	**V**
Reins, 66	Spicer, 66, 67	Van Dyke, 70
Reusens, 57	Spiller, 60, 66	Vass or Voss, 57
Reynolds, 64, 67, 70	Spilman, 70	Vaughan, 58, 60, 64, 68, 69, 72
Rice, 74	Stallard, 61	
Rich, 66	Stapleman, 57	Vawter, 70
Richardson, 60	Stanton, 59, 66	Vernon, 73
Richerson, 57	Starke, 63	Vint, 68
Ricketts, 69	Steptoe, 74	Viscarver, 61
Rider, 67	Stevens, 71	Voss or Vass, 57
Rivercomb, 70	Stipe, 60	**W**
Rixey, 65	Stokes, 58	
Roach, 66	Stokesberry, 61, 66	Waggoner, 64, 65, 66, 67, 73
Roberts, 57, 60, 62, 64, 66, 69, 70, 71	Stone, 59	
	Stonesiffer, 64	Walden, 56, 65
Robins, 65	Story, 73, 74	Walker, 60, 65, 66, 67, 73
Rodeheifer, 74	Stout, 63, 73	Wall, 58, 61, 62, 73
Roebuck, 59, 64	Strother, 57, 59, 62, 64, 66, 67, 68, 73	Wallace, 67
Rogers, 71, 72, 74		Wallard, 69

V

Wallis,	69.	White, 56, 57, 58, 70, 73.	Woodward, 67.
Ward, 57, 58, 60, 61, 64, 68, 73.		Whitehead, 72, 73	Wortham, 60.
		Whitledge, 58.	Wright, 58, 66, 67, 71, 72, 73.
Warren,	62.	Whitley, 66.	**Y**
Washington,	61, 68.	Whorton, 67.	Yager, 60, 64, 67, 71, 73, 74.
Waters,	61, 62.	Wickoff, 71.	
Waterspon,	70.	Wiley, 62, 63, 66.	Yancey, 57, 60, 61, 62, 65, 67.
Watts, 59, 68, 71, 72, 73.		Wilhoite, 59, 66, 67, 69, 70, 72, 74.	
Wayland, 59, 67, 73, 74.			Yates, 56, 58, 59, 60, 62, 65, 66, 67, 73, 74.
Weakley,	57, 65.	Wilkerson, 59	
Weatherall,	58, 72.	Williams, 58, 60, 63, 64, 69, 70, 74.	Yeager, 60, 64, 67, 71, 73, 74.
Weaver, 57, 58, 59, 60, 62, 73.			
		Willis, 57, 64, 66, 69, 73.	Young, 61, 69, 74.
Weeden,	60.	Wills, 63.	Yowell, 57, 59, 62, 63, 70.
Welch,	62.	Wilson, 58, 65.	**Z**
West,	71.	Winston, 62.	
Westall,	72.	Wise, 62, 67, 72.	Zigler, 72, 74.
Whale,	62.	Withers, 60, 68.	Zimmerman 58, 60, 64, 66, 70, 72.
Wharton,	66.	Wood, 61, 62, 67, 73.	
Wheatley,	57, 59.	Woodard, 61, 62, 64.	Zimmerson, 62.

———:ooo:———

INDEX TO NAMES.

When a name appears more than once on a page, it is only indexed once, consequently it will always be well to look through the entire page when in search of a name. All surnames are indexed. The names appearing in the marriage record are not included in this index, as the record itself is arranged in alphabetical order, according to the names of the husbands, and the names of the wives are given in a separate index. Where there is great similarity in the spelling of a name, only one way is given in the index. For instance both "Stark" and "Starke" are indexed under the head of "Starke." The word "will" following a name in the index signifies that notes from a will, or wills, can be found on the page specified. "I" signifies Part First; "II" signifies Part Second. Where figures appear thus: "123-128," it signifies that the name specified appears on pages 123, 124, 125, 126, 127, and 128.

A

Abbett, II, will 45.
Abbott, II, will 45, 84.
Abel, or Abell, I, 93; II, 17, 89.
Able, I, 93.
Adams, I, 66, 89, 109; II, 18, 80, 138, 145.
Addison, II, 86, 87.
Agnew, I, 101.
Aiken, I, 94.
Alcocke, I, 33, 34, 113, 115-117; II, 69.
Aldridge, I, 66, 107.
Alexander, I, 33, 58, 60, 65, 94, 107, 113, 119; II, 23, 51, 85, 94, 138, 142, 154.
Allan, II, 8, 151, 160.
Allen, I, 65-67, 73, 86, 94, 102; II, 18, will 45, 53, 83, 84, 86, 128, 142, 150.

Alston, I, 93, 94.
Ambler, I, 52, 66; II, 139, 143.
Ambrose, II, 85.
Ames, II, 105.
Amiss, I, 66; II, 18, 23, 36.
Anderson, I, 53, 66, 74, 76, 79, 81, 104, 107; II, 17, 34, 36, 81, 95, 140.
Andre, II, 3.
Andrews, I, 65.
Andros, II, 132.
Anthony, II, 49, 151.
Apperson, II, 17, 19, 21, 23, 48, 120, 130.
Appleton, I, 105; II, 141.
Archer, II, 33, 95.
Archibald, II, 79.
Argyle, I, 60.
Armistead, I, 19, 53, 64, 75, 77, 89, 95, 102; II, 82-84, 86, 130.

VI

Armstrong, I, 89; II, 18, 36, 54, 154.
Arnold, II, 51.
Arnotte, I, 74; II, 54.
ASHBY FAMILY, II, 80.
Ashby, I, 66, 68, 74, 117; II, 11, 17, 19, 80, 107, 109, 122, 130, 158.
Asher, II, 38, 41.
Ashley, I, 6; II, 152.
Ashton, I, 60.
Askins, I, 63.
Atherold, II, 79.
Atchison, I, 67.
Atkins, II, 17, 36.
Atkinson, I, 66.
Atterbury, I, 35.
Atwell, II, 79.
Atwood, II, 48.
Augur, II, 83, 124, 125.
Austin, I, 65, 78, 104.
Averill, II, 102, 103.
Averton, I, 65.
Avirett, I, 110.
Ayers, II, 94.
Aylette, I, 78, 101; II, 55, 80.

B

Baber, I, 98.
Bacon, I, 59, 80, 119; II, 134.
Bagg, I, 51.
Bagley, I, 98; II, 78.
Bagtop, I, 64.
Bailey, I, 66, 88; II, 11, 128, 145, 160.
Baird, II, 150.
Baker, I, 72, 81, 82, 91; II, 55, 77, 102, 152.
Baldeck, II, 150.
Baldock, I, 106.
Baldwin, I, 72.
Ball, I, 6, 13, 15, 18, 57, 61, 62, 66, 85, 101, 109, 113; II, 6, 18, will 46, 48, 49, 50, 54, 79, 80, 86, 87, 118.
Ballance, I, 62, 65.
Balmain, I, 74.
Bankhead, I, 118; II, 35.
Banks, I, 46, 88, 94, 95; II, 23, 33, will 46, 82, 83, 101, 121, 122, 123, 125, 127.
Bannister, II, 82, 83.
Baptist, II, 83, 85.
Barbee, II, 48.
Barber, II, 20.
BARBOUR FAMILY, I, 52, 53; II, 135—145.

Barbour, I, 6-8, 20, 32-34, 36, 38, 46, 54, 58, 61, 63, 67, 71, 96, 103, 104, 107, 113; II, 3, 5, 6, 11, 13, 15, 19, 21, 23, will 46, 97, 100, 106, 108, 115, 156, 158.
Barclay, II, 91.
Bard, I, 99.
Barham, II, 19.
Barker, I, 94; II, 87.
Barkley, I, 67.
Barlow, II, 156.
Barnes, I, 84; II, 17, will 46, 94.
Barnett, I, 71; II, 76, 77-79, 151.
Barr, I, 87.
Barran, II, 41.
Barrel, II, 93.
Barrett, I, 103, 105; II, 81.
Barrow, II, 49.
Barry, II, 86.
Bartlett, II, 81.
Bartley, II, 45.
Barton, I, 2, 103.
Bashaw, II, 19.
Bassett, I, 86.
Bastable, I, 80.
Bate, I, 81.
Bathurst, I, 111.
Battaile, I, 74, 88.
Battle, II, 17, 20, 23, 139, 144.
Baughan, II, 17.
Bayard, II, 38, 99, 122.
Bayles, I, 70.
Baylor, I, 94; II, 115, 136, 138, 141, 143.
Bayne, II, 155.
Baysy, I, 112.
Beach, II, 85.
Beale, I, 36, 71; II, 39.
Beall, I, 85.
Bealmear, I, 91.
Beamer, II, 124.
Beasely, I, 78.
Beauregard, I, 91.
Becket, I, 7, 8.
Beckham, I, 52, 93; II, 11, 20, 21, 23, 101, 104-106, 140.
Beckwith, I, 76.
Bedsham, II, 101.
Beeler, I, 93.
Beggee, II, 56.
Beirne, I, 52.
Belfield, I, 55; II, will 46.
Bell, I, 33, 34, 54, 55, 63, 66, 89; II, 6, 8, 12, 15, 17, 18, 110, 112, 113, 119, 160.

Bellamy, I, 103.
Bellisle, II, 144.
Belmaine, I, 32.
Belt, II, 139.
Benger, I, 2, 5, 10.
Bennett, II, 40, 43.
Benson, I, 81; II, will 46.
Benton, II, 154.
Berger, II, 91.
Berkley, I, 11; II, 42, 44, 81, 135.
Berlin, II, 23, 35.
Bernard, I, 73, 109; II, 80, 83.
Berry, I, 65, 67, 89, 101, 119; II, 50, 54, 84, 144, 159.
Berryman, I, 92.
Besson, II, 83.
Best, II, 124.
Beverley, I, 11, 36-39, 41, 107, 118; II, 1, 2.
Bibb, I, 89; II, 17.
Bickers, II, 20.
Bickerton, I, 103, 105; II, 81.
Bird, II, 82.
Birdsong, II, 144.
Birket, II, 7.
Birney, II, 80.
Bishop, II, 42.
Bivings, I, 68.
Blackburn, I, 82; II, 24.
Blackman, I, 63.
Blackwell, I, 61-63, 68, 95; II, 50, 79.
Blair, I, 23, 34, 61, 63, 83, 100, 110, 111; II, 7, 94.
Blake, I, 65, 92, 93.
Blakey, II, will 46.
Blanca, I, 50.
Bland, I, 119; II, 54, 85.
Blankenbaker, II, 55.
Bledsoe, I, 54; II, will 46.
Blenheim, I, 53, 54,
Bloodsworth, I, 13.
Boatwright, I, 105.
Boddie, II, 141.
Bodine, I, 100.
Boggs, I, 33.
Bohannon, II, will 46, 84.
Boisseau, I, 79.
Bolding, I, 87.
Boldridge, II, 42, 44.
Bolen, II, 19.
Bolling, I, 70, 73, 91, 92.
Bolney, II, 138.
Bond, I, 94; II, will 46.
Bondurant, I, 84.
Boner, I, 92.

Bonnycastle, I, 100.
Booker, I, 67.
Booton, I, 58, 111; II, 11, 54, 85, 86, 139, 160.
Borst, II, 23.
Bostwick, I, 63, 80, 82.
Boswell, II, 85.
Boteler, I, 102.
Botetourt, II, 39.
Bott, I, 42.
Botts, I, 66, 84, 98, 116; II, 35, will 46, 49, 117, 153, 154.
Bouchelle, II, 141.
Bough, I, 107.
Bougham, II, 51, 77.
Boulware, I, 86.
Bourn, I, 59, 63; II, will 46, 53.
Boutwell, II, 76, 77.
Bowen, I, 113; II, 17, 36, 130.
Bower, I, 65.
Bowers, II, 20, 23.
Bowie, I, 71, 90, 92, 97.
Bowler, I, 59.
Bowles, I, 75, 104; II, 21, 141.
Bowman, I, 17, 18; II, 23, 47.
Bowyer, I, 77; II, 152.
Boyce, II, 148.
Boyd, I, 93, 99, 110; II, 46, 136, 137.
Boykin, II, 78.
Boyle, I, 65.
Braddock, I, 57.
Bradford, I, 28, 53, 88, 113, 115, 117; II, 4, 23, 36, 48, 110.
Bradley, I, 19, 112; II, 82.
Brady, II, 36.
Bragg, II, 23, 36, 153, 155.
Branch, II, 33, 95, 126, 127.
Brand, I, 117.
Brandum, II, will 46.
Branford, I, 105.
Braxton, I, 72, 86; II, 26, 37, 79.
Bray, II, 19.
Brayne, I, 2.
Breathitt, I, 94; II, 104, 116.
Breckenridge, I, 77, 79, 98.
Brent, I, 65.
Brewer, I, 92.
Bridge, II, 145.
Briggs, II, 40, 93.
Briley, II, 129.
Brisco, I, 87.
Britton, I, 94.
BROADDUS FAMILY, I, 84, 85; II, 146-149.

Broaddus, I, 22, 24, 100, 113; II, 5, 8, 40, 43, 51, 86, 88, 89, 94, 160.
Brock, I, 10.
Brockenborough, II, 49.
Brockman, I, 89.
Brodnax, I, 89.
Broil, II, will 46.
Brooke, I, 38, 42, 68, 72, 80, 87, 100, 110; II, 36, 76, 77.
Brooken, I, 32.
Brooking, I, 38; II, 155.
Brooks, II, 44, 50, 51, 132.
Broughton, I, 46.
Brougham, I, 77.
Browder, II, 87, 138.
BROWN FAMILY, I, 111; II, 83, 84.
Brown, I, 10, 13, 14, 16, 20, 27, 36, 53, 55, 60, 66-68, 86, 89, 95, 97; II, 17, 19-23, 35, 36, 40, 42-44, will 46, 47, 50, 52, 55, 56, 82, 83-85, 123, 124, 127, 131, 139-141, 145, 153.
Brownell, II, 36.
BROWNING FAMILY, II, 151-155.
Browning, I, 97; II, 18, 35, 36, 48, 54, 97, 150.
Broy, II, 17.
Bruce, I, 31, 52, 76, 78, 88, 108-110; II, 17, 35, 36, 40, 43, 53, 152.
Brunet, I, 82.
BRYAN FAMILY, II, 150, 151.
Bryan, I, 2, 53, 60; II, 79, 139.
Bryant, I, 65; II, 87.
Bryson, I, 109.
Buchan, I, 60; II, 79.
Buck, I, 34; II, 38.
Buckhannon, I, 23, 81.
Buckley, I, 64.
Buckner, I, 80, 86, 101; II, will 47, 80, 84, 130, 158.
Buffington, I, 53.
Buford, I, 19; II, 3, 34, 105, 107-113, 115-117, 122.
Bulkly. I, 64.
Bull, I, 88; II, 76.
Bullard, II, 46.
Bullits, I, 77, 82.
Bullock I, 74, 107.
Bumbrey, II, 83.
Bumgarner, II, 152.
Bundy, II, 129.
Burbank, II, 142.
Burbridge, II, 81, 82.
Burdett, II, 23.

Burdyne II, will 47.
Burgandine, II, 17.
Burgess, I, 88, 109; II, 80, 83, 84, 153.
Burgoyne, I, 119.
Burk, I, 107; II, 20, 23, 24, 35, 36, 52, 54, 129, 145, 155.
Burkett, I, 80, 82, 83; II, 76, 77, 79.
Burkitt, I, 59.
Burnett, I, 32, 34.
Burnley, I, 33, 34, 71, 74, 103; II, 24.
Burns, I, 98.
Burnside, II, 94.
Burr, I, 89, 92, 99; II, 5, 6.
Burrell, II, 47.
Burrows, I, 113, 117; II, 8-10, 15, 17, 24, 38.
Burruss, II, 20.
Burt, I, 101; II, 80.
Burton, I, 36, 78; II, 24.
Burwell, I, 73, 102, 107, 110.
Bush, II, 49.
Bushong, II, 24.
Butler, I, 2, 67, 72, 73, 94; II, 36, 45, will 47, 51, 53, 84, 106, 114.
Button, II, will 47, 48, 83, 154.
Byram, II, 17, 21.
Byrd, I, 2, 4, 6, 11, 42, 45, 74, 80, 102; II, 1.
Byrne, II, 137, 140, 144.
Byron, II, 19, 83.
Bywaters, I, 112; II, 18, 36, 52, 150-154.

C

Cabell, I, 76, 78.
Cadwallader, I, 85, 86.
Caison, II, 144.
Calhoun, I, 68.
Callahan, I, 93.
Calvert, II, 52, 158.
Cameron, I, 81; II, 1, 84, 85.
Cambridge, I, 90, 92.
Camden, I, 106.
Camp, I, 61, 63, 81; II, 49, 93, 130.
Campbell, I, 1, 2, 10, 38, 42, 60, 63-65, 73, 75, 77, 78, 99, 103, 104, 114; II, 33, 47, 51, 87, 91, 152, 154.
Canady, II, 51, 128.
Cannon, II, 19, 36.
Carder, I, 7.
Cardwell, I, 78, 94.
Carley, I, 105.
Carmach, I, 79.
Carmichael, I, 65, 67.

Carnager, I, 14.
Carpenter, I, 36, 46, 89, 90, 92-95; II, 17, 36, 40, 56, 82, 83, 124, 154.
Carr, II, 36, 153,
Carrico, II, 24.
Carrington, I, 69 76-78, 103.
Carroll, I, 88: II, 127.
Carson, I, 33, 95; II, 82.
CARTER FAMILY, I, 53, 54.
Carter, I, 3, 10-12. 17, 22, 65-67, 72-74, 76, 78, 80, 82, 86, 88, 89, 91, 92, 98, 102, 112; II, 1, 17, 19, will 47, 49, 52, 53, 55, 85, 148.
Caruthers, I, 36.
Cary, I, 66, 84, 112; II, 80, 90, 143.
Cash, II, 35.
Caskie, II, 124.
Cassine, I, 55.
Catesby, II, 84.
Catlett, I, 8, 10, 16, 33, 57, 62, 66, 71, 78, 83, 100, 109, 110, 118; II. will 47, 56, 80, 85, 138, 142.
CAVE FAMILY, I, 54, 55.
Cave, I, 6-8, 32, 36, 60, 72; II, will 46, 47, 139.
Cavender, II, 54.
Cenard, I, 63.
Chadduck, II, 24.
Chalmers, II, 143.
Chambers, I, 7; II, 81.
Chambliss, II, 43.
Champe, I, 53, 88, 89.
Champlin, I, 64.
Chancellor, I, 98; II, 36, 49, 53.
Chandler, I, 103; II, 54.
Channing, I, 110.
Chapman, I, 87, 88, 97; II, 4, 83, 85.
Chappellear, II, 153.
Charlton, II, 130.
Chatfield, I, 82; II, 76-78.
Cheatham, II, 77, 78.
Cheek, II, 153, 154.
Chelf, II, 11, 36, 38, 112, 155.
Cheney, II, 142.
Chester, II, 90.
Chew, I, 33, 71, 74, 80; II, 104.
Chewning, II, 36, 53, 139.
Childs, II, 35.
Chiles, I, 104.
Chilton, I, 117; II, 19, 79.
Chinn, II, 80.
Chinnock, I, 105.
Christian, I, 77, 105; II, 24, 143.
Christy, I, 55.

Churchill, I, 81, 85, 98; II, 40.
Churchman, II, 57.
Claiborne, I, 68, 78, 98; II, 80.
Clapp, II, 142.
Clarke, I, 38, 53, 58, 65, 78, 89, 93, 94, 107; II, 36, 78, 87, 128, 129, 139.
Clarkson, II, 80.
Clay, II, 142, 148.
CLAYTON FAMILY, I, 55, 56.
Clayton, I, 10, 13-16, 18, 19, 35, 43, 46, 47, 69, 84, 85, 87-91, 94, 96, 95, 100, 107, 108, 110, 111, 113; II, 4, 6, 8, 13, 49.
Clemens, 65, 67.
Cleveland, I, 88.
Clifford, I, 109.
Clonder, I, 38, 41.
Clore, II, 51, 54.
Coalter, I, 60; II, 79.
Coates, II, 152.
Cobb, II, 87, 107.
Cocke, I, 76; II, 130.
Coffee, I, 60.
Coginhill, II, 56.
Cole, I, 27-30, 36, 53, 74-76; II, 8, 10, 18, 41-43, will 47, 130.
COLEMAN FAMILY, I, 56.
Coleman, I, 14, 19, 34, 55, 61, 71, 81, 83, 85, 86, 89, 91, 98, 107, 111, II, 6, 51, 83, 160.
Collier, II, 43.
Collins, I, 53, 83; II, 22, 24, 48, 49, 51, 138, 140, 143.
Colston, I, 100.
Colvin, II, 19, 20, 22, 47, 50, 85, 86, 122, 128.
Combs, II, 80.
Compton, II, 19.
Conant, I, 67.
Conger, II, 120.
Conner, I, 70, 86, 97; II, 9, 42, 43, 46, will 47, 128.
Conrad, I, 28; II, 82.
CONWAY FAMILY, I, 57.
Conway, I, 30, 33-36, 60, 71, 72, 74, 75, 87, 105, 109, 113, 118; II, 4, 80, 139, 144, 145.
Cooke, I, 46, 50, 68, 98, 99, 110; II, 53, 79, 80.
Cooksey, II, 36.
Coons, I, 45, 86, 112; II, 11, 18, 19, 50, 82, 88, 89, 120, 159, 160.
Cooper, I, 91, 107; II, 17, 19, 24, 47, 54, 124, 150, 154.

X

Coppage, II, 17, 24.
Corbin, I, 101, 102; II, 18, 19, 24, 35, 36, will 47, 54, 150, 152, 153.
Corder, II, 49.
Corley, II, 51.
Cormick, II, 145.
Cornelius, II, 52.
Cornwallis, I, 2; II, 157.
Corse, I, 110.
Cosby, I, 92, 98; II, 141.
Coughty, II, 19.
Countz, II, 159, 160.
Courtney, II, 123.
Covell, I, 60.
Covington, I, 14, 15, 90, 91; II, 24, will 47, 48, 51, 55, 83, 152, 160.
Cowen, I, 68.
Cowherd, I, 58, 91, 92; II, 51, 85.
Cowles, I, 53; II, 140.
Cowne, II, 56.
Cox, II, 56.
Crabb, I, 65.
Crable, I, 102.
Craddock, I, 75.
Craig, I, 62, 63, 67, 68, 82, 111; II, 39, 42.
Craighill, I, 104.
Crane, I, 87.
Crawford, I, 86, 113, 117; II, 33, 36, 81, 122, 124-126, 145.
Crawley, I, 79.
Crecy, I, 63.
Creel, II, 20, 22, 24, 128.
Crenshaw, I, 57, 63.
Cresswell, II, 78.
Crighter, II, 51.
Crigler, I, 98; II, 19, will 47, 49.
Cringan, I, 110.
Crisler, II, 11.
Crittenden, I, 56, 107; II, 9, 15, 17, 22, 123-125.
Croisant, II, 17.
Cromwell, I, 99.
Cropp, II, 11.
Crosby, I, 60.
Cross, I, 62, 66.
Croutson, I, 107, 110.
Crow, I, 90, 107.
Crump, I, 65; II, 138, 142.
Crutcher, I, 56.
Crutchfield, I, 34; II, 20, 138, 142, 143.
Cubet, II, 83.
Cudworth, II, 82, 83.
Cullen, II, 141.
Culpeper, I, 10, 11; II, 1.

Cumberland, II, 40.
Cummins, II, 45.
Cunningham, I, 28, 88, 113; II, 24, 33, 55, 100.
Curtis, I, 98; II, 18, 24, 35, 36, 113, 156.
Cutts, I, 76.

D

Dabney, I, 71, 75, 76, 83, 90, 91; II, 6, 154.
Dade, I, 33, 34, 64, 87, 105; II, 4.
Dalhosie, I 60.
Dallas, II, 36.
Dalrymple, I, 29,
Dalton, II, 83.
Dandridge, I, 3, 10, 72, 73, 76, 78, 99-101, 119; II, 80.
Dangerfield, I, 52; II, 80, 140, 153.
Daniel, I, 86, 88, 99, 109, 117; II, 24, 35, 36, 48, 83, 86, 119, 140.
Darby, I, 34.
D'Arquin, II, 123.
Darricott, I, 76.
Darwin, I, 93, 94.
Davenport, I, 19, 80, 82, 83, 109, 112, 113; II, 7, will 47, 76, 77.
Davies, I, 100; II, 77, 158.
Davis, I, 14, 22, 33, 57, 71, 74, 101, 104, 107, 113; II, 6, 18, 20, 25, 46, 81-83, 105, 107, 108, 136-139, 143, 144.
Dawson, I, 93, 98.
Day, I, 22.
Deady, I, 82.
Deal, II, 18, 36.
Deane, II, 129, 151.
Dearing, II, 55.
Deatherage, II, 36, 152-154, 158.
De Butts, I, 6, 7, 81.
Decantillon, II, 90.
De Cuillon, I, 48, 50.
Deforest, II, 50.
De Graffenreid, I, 43; II, 159.
De Hart, II, 84, 85.
Dejarnette, I, 110.
Delaney, II, 48.
De Ligne, I, 50.
Dement, II, 123.
Demorest, II, 151.
Denholm, II, 76, 77.
Dennis, II, 17, 18, 36.
Dent, II, 91.
Denton, I, 114; II, 8, 151.
Devall, I, 118.
Dial, I, 94.

XI

Dick, II, 83.
Dickerson, I, 54; II, 46.
Dickinson, I, 77, 110.
Dickson, I, 63.
Diener, II, 160.
Digges, I, 102.
Dillard, I, 10, 112; II, will 47, 52, 55.
Dillon, I, 103.
Dinwiddie, II, 80, 137.
Dixon, I, 46, 55, 65, 68, 108; II, 45, 131, 142, 160.
Dobbs, II, 130.
Doggett, II, 19, 25, 56, 82, 106.
Dohme, II, 83.
Donaldson, 11, 143.
Doniphan, II, 80.
Doolin, II, 25.
Doores, II, 19, 51.
Doran, II, 25.
Dorniman, II, 84.
Dorsey, I, 71.
Doty, I, 100.
Douglas, I, 65, 76, 93, 109.
Dove, I, 101.
Downer, I, 86.
Downey, II, 51.
Downing, I, 60.
Downman, I, 26, 113.
Doyle, II, 19.
Drake, 86.
Drewry, I, 79; II, 97.
Dudley, I, 102, 107, 110; II, 11, 83, 86.
Duff, I, 61.
Duffle, II, 84.
Dugan, I, 63.
Duke, I, 54.
Dulaney, II, 46, 53, 129, 152, 153.
Dulin, II, 19, 40.
Dumas, II, 81.
Dunbar, I, 3, 80, 108, 110.
Duncan, I, 13, 65, 86, 90; II, 25, 35, 36, 45, 47, will 48, 50, 83, 101, 102, 120, 150-154.
Duncanson, II, 158.
Dunkum, I, 89.
Dunmore, I, 47; II, 3, 12.
Dunn, I, 61; II, 141, 151.
Dunnaway, II, 150.
Dunnica, I, 95, 98; II, 77, 78, 155.
Dupin, I, 93.
Durham, II, 86.
Duryea, II, 127.
Duval, II, will 48, 56.

Dwight, I, 104.
Dwyers, II, 86.
Dyer, I, 99.

E

Eachins, I, 89.
Earle, II, 83.
Early, II, 23, 24, 33, will 48, 123-126.
Earnest, I, 7, 23, 33, 36, 74.
Eastham, I, 13, 14; II, 25, 36, 131, 154.
Eberle, I, 83.
Eddins, II, 46.
Edelin, II, 97.
Edgar, I, 64; II, will 48.
Edmunds, I, 62, 64, 66, 69.
Edmondson, II, 54, 79.
Edwards, I, 63, 64, 67, 68, 90; II, 18, 19, 128, 129.
Eells, II, 159.
Eggborn, II, 20, 21, 84.
Elcan, I, 78.
Eldridge, I, 105; II, 130.
Elkins, II, 18.
Elliott, I, 1, 85, 92, 93.
Ellis, I, 107; II, 91, 93, 143.
Elly, II, 19.
Embrey, II, 19, 25.
Emery, II, 54.
Emison, II, 8.
Emmet, I, 98.
Emmons, I, 89.
Emory, I, 88.
England, II, 20.
English, I, 66, 67, 117; II, 49, 154.
Eno, I, 60.
Erskine, I, 90; II, 84, 85.
Erwin, I, 67.
Estes, II, 17.
Eustace, I, 101; II, 80.
Evans, I, 64; II, 54.
Eve, I, 10; II, 40.
Ewell, II, 23, 24, 33, 110, 118, 119, 122, 123, 126, 140.
Ewing, I, 94, 104, 105; II, 144.

F

Fair, I, 114.
Fairfax, I, 8, 10-12, 55, 111; II, 1, 47, 54.
Fairleigh, I, 91.
Falls, II, 126.
Fant, II, 25, 36.
Fargeson, II, 46, will 48, 53.
Ferguson, I, 63.
Farish, I, 26, 28, 64, 113; II, 17, 22, 25, 91, 92.

Farley, I, 54; II, 106.
Farmer, I, 97.
Farra, I, 105.
Farrar, II, 43.
Farrow, I, 62; II, 49, 149.
Faulconer, II, 85.
Faulk, I, 62.
Faunt Le Roy, I, 95, 110; II, 75, 76, 82, 83.
Fauquier, II, 131.
Favers, II, will 48.
Fayette, I, 78, 109; II, 8.
Feathershaugh, I, 37.
Feeley, II, 20.
Fendal, I, 104,
Fenton, II, 189.
Fenwick, I, 90, 91.
Ferebee, II, 115.
Fergerson, I, 89, 90.
Fergurson, I, 78, 99, 112; II, 149.
Ferris, II, 76.
Fetter, I, 81.
Ficklen, I, 86, 89; II, 9, 19, 85.
FIELD FAMILY, I, 57.
Field, I, 6, 8, 10, 13-16, 19, 35, 52, 85, 89, 91, 94, 113, 120; II, 4, 6, 8, 17,19, 35, 36, will 48, 53, 81, 82, 85, 86, 95, 101, 102, 127, 131, 139, 143, 144, 154, 155.
Fielder, I, 70.
Fielding, I, 82.
Fife, II, 40.
Filling, II, 17.
Fillmore, II, 88.
Finks, II, 18, 25.
Finlason, I, 6, 7, 10.
Finney, II, 17, 133, 134.
Fishback, I, 45, 112; II, will 48, 159, 160.
Fisher, I, 89; II, 36, 85.
Fiske, II, 141.
Fitts, I, 93.
Fitzhugh, I, 34, 57, 66, 80, 101, 105, 109, 113; II, 50, 51, 85, 139, 144.
Fitzpatrick, II, 144.
Fleet, II, 124, 149.
Fleming, I, 77; II, 141.
Fletcher, I, 86, 112; II, 36, will 48, 152, 153.
Flinn, II, 129.
Flint, II, 85.
Flippen, I, 95; II, 82, 83.
Flipps, I, 103.
Flournoy, I, 82.
Floyd, I, 77, 93.

Fogg, II, 36.
Foltz, II, 18.
Fontaine, I, 36-39, 41, 43, 55, 75, 76, 78, 92.
Foote, II, 52.
Forbes, I, 9, 79, 80.
Force, I, 120.
Ford, I, 65, 67; II, 136, 145.
Forsyth, II, 91.
Foster, I, 56, 67, 88; II, 25, 136.
Fountain, II, 82.
Foushee, I, 30, 56, 73, 97; II, 8, 20, 25, will 48.
Fowler, I, 97.
Fowles, II, 25.
Fox, I, 2; II, 20, 25, 40, 41, 44.
Foy, I, 94.
Fraley, II, 153.
Francisco, II, 83.
Franklin, I, 2, 48, 102; II, 30, 93.
Fray, II, 25.
Frazier, I, 66, 91; II, 95.
Freeman, I, 13, 17, 26, 35, 86, 112, 113, 117; II, 17-19, 25, 26, 47, will 49, 51, 53, 56, 82, 101, 128, 129, 158.
French, I, 5, 81, 97, 108; II, 15.
Friend, II, 141.
Fristoe, II; 35, 40.
FRY FAMILY, I, 58, 59.
Fry, I, 32, 34, 63, 67, 70, 80, 89; II, 8, 17, 47, 75-77, 79.
Fuller, I, 66.
Funk, II, 154.
Funkhouser, II, 152.
Funston, I, 86; II, 118.
Furqurean, I, 102.

G

Gaines, I, 14, 18, 33, 36, 65, 83, 84, 86, 91, 96-99, 118; II, 5, 17, 20, 22, 26, 46, 47, will 49, 51, 130, 134, 147, 149.
Gale, I, 104.
Gallaway, I, 94,
Galt, I, 81.
Gantt, II, 87.
Garden, I, 62; II, 144.
Gardiner, I, 105; II, 86.
Garland, I, 77, 89, 98, 106, 107.
GARNETT FAMILY, I, 59, 60.
Garnett, I, 14, 86, 100, 103; II, 20, 26, 33, 36, 40, 42, 43, 123-126.
Garr, II, 51.
Garratt, II, 52.

Garrett, I, 78, 105; II, 76, 150.
Garth, II, 82, 142.
Garusha, I, 88.
Garvin, I, 102; II, 90.
Gary, II, 124.
Gayworth, II, 55.
Geary, II, 33, 125.
George, II, 40, 41, 43, will 45, 49, 112, 115.
Gibbons, II, 81, 82, 94.
Gibbs, I, 10, 36, 80, 98, 105, 111; II, 79, 83.
Giberne, I, 32, 71; II, 75.
Gibson, I, 33, 34, 36, 54, 57, 74, 100, 101; II, 8, 11, 17, 18, 80, 81, 94, 105, 144, 157, 158.
Gilbert, I, 33, 74.
Gilkeson, I, 64, II, 35.
Gill, I, 86.
Gillette, II, 117.
Gilliam, II, 77, 141.
Gillison, I, 19; II, 3, 4, will 49.
Gist, II, 137.
Givens, I, 65.
Glass, I, 64, 105; II, 46, 138, 142.
Glasscock, I, 62, 91.
GLASSELL FAMILY, I, 60.
Glassell, I, 16, 33, 34, 55, 74, 80, 88, 119; II, 8, 77, 79, 137, 158.
Glissen, I, 101.
Glover, II, 91.
Godfrey, II, 26.
Gooch, I, 54, 98; II, 132.
Goodall, II, 132.
Goode, I, 73, 119.
Goodlet, I, 34, 47; II, 6.
Goodloe, I, 68; II, 83.
Goodman, II, 90.
Goodrich, I, 70.
Goodwin, I, 60, 103, 104, 117; II, 26, 43, 139.
Gordon, I, 7, 34, 66; II, 23, 26, 33, 35, 40, 41, 51, 55, 114, 124-126, 145, 158.
Gorrell, II, 11, 17, 100, 160.
Goss, 40, 144.
Gould, II, 141.
Grace, II, 43.
Graeme, I, 5, 11.
Graham, I, 104; II, 55.
Grant, I, 62, 65, 66, 68, 91, 112; II, 47, 120, 152.
Grasty, II, 51, 80.

Graves, I, 92; II, 48, 133, 143, 144.
Gray, I, 16, 17, 19, 53, 55, 65, 79, 81, 83, 110; II, 6, 9, 11, 17, 43, will 49, 51, 54, 79, 83, 128, 140, 143, 158.
Grayson, I, 17; II, 35, 50, 80, 85.
GREEN FAMILY, I, 61-69.
Green, I, 6, 8, 12, 15-19, 26, 46, 50, 53, 54, 56, 58, 79, 83, 87-89, 97, 100, 107-110, 112, 113, 117, 119; II, 3, 4, 6, 8, 9, 11, 17-19, 35, 36, 46, 47, will 49, 51, 53, 55, 56, 77, 79, 97, 100, 105, 129-131, 136, 156-158, 160.
Greene, I, 69, 87, 98, 99; II, 5, 6, 33, 82, 124, 125.
Gregg, II, 34, 95, 105, 108-111, 113, 118.
Gregory, I, 82, 96; II, 45.
Griffith, I, 67; II, 18.
Griffin, II, will 49, 83, 86, 94, 128, 153.
Grigg. I, 101.
Grimsley, II, 11, 17, 26, 35, 36, 40-43, 47, 97, 105, 112, 140, 150, 151, 153.
GRINNAN FAMILY, II, 79,
Grinnan I, 46, 60, 118, 119; II, 8, 10, 17, 48.
Grissom, II, 47.
Grotjan, II, 90.
Grove, I, 107.
Grubbs, I, 78.
Grymes, I, 7, 11, 57, 100, 110, 111, 118; II, 1, 130, 158.
Gunter, I, 66.
Gurley, II, 150, 154.
Gustin I, 61, 63.
Gwatkin, I, 34; II, 43, 44.
Gwynn, II, 138.

H

Hacklea, II, 20.
Hackley, I, 109; II, 19, 26, 46-48, will 49, 51.
Haddox, II, 36.
Haeger, I, 5, 44; II, 159.
Haldiman, II, 139.
Hale, II, 26.
Hall, I, 65, 88; II, 8, 26, 45, 77, 89, 104, 119, 127, 128, 140.
Halsey, I, 38, 60; II, 137.
Halstead, I, 93.
Ham, II, 79.
Hamblin, II, 86.
Hambrick, II, 37.

Hamilton, I, 26, 28, 76, 80, 88, 87, 98, 99, 113; II, 5, 6, 141.
Hamlin, II, 83.
Hammond, I, 83.
Hampton, I, 77, 86; II, 79, 104-106, 108-110, 113, 114, 117, 119.
Hamsberger, II, 82.
Handback, II, will 50, 159.
Hanckle, II, 140.
Hand, II, 37, 51.
Handy, II, 143.
Hanes, II, 85.
Haney, II, 152, 153.
Hansborough, I, 17, 22, 24, 33, 34, 53, 55, 84, 87, 111, 113; II, 8, 18, 50, 92, 106, 139.
Hansford, II, will 50.
Hardesty, I, 90; II, 1, 135.
Hardin, I, 92; II, 136, 137.
Harding, II, 90.
Harford, II, will 50.
Harker, I, 89.
Harney, II, 89.
Harper, I, 89, 110; II, 83.
Harriet, II, 83.
Harris, I, 68, 85, 93-95, 103-105; II, 35, 39, 42, 80, 83, 103, 107.
Harrison, I, 34, 35, 78, 82, 83, 85, 98, 102, 106, 109; II, 46, 88, 117, 136, 137, 143, 148, 151, 153-155.
Harrow, I, 22.
Hart, I, 74, 95; II, 92, 130.
Hartley, II, 37.
Hartman, I, 64.
Hartsuff, II, 127.
Harvey, I, 109.
Harvout, I, 104.
Harwell, II, 141.
Haskell, II, 137.
Haslet, I, 69.
Hatch, II, 33.
Hatcher, II, 26, 40, 43.
Hathwell, II, 85.
Hawes, I, 95, 101, 103, 104; II, 37, 55, 80.
Hawkins, I, 59, 62, 64, 65; II, 7, 18, 26, 36, 37, 46, 49, will 50, 56, 130.
Hawks, I, 6, 30.
Hawley, I, 22-24; II, 18, 26.
Hay, II, 11, 33, 123.
Hayden, I, 69.
Hayes, I, 68, 88; II, 8, 80, 119.
Haylet, I, 69.
Haynes, I, 91, 97.

Haynie, I, 112; II, will 49.
Haywood, II, 11.
Hazel, II, 129.
Heaton, II, 19, 36.
Heddino, I, 105.
Heide, II, 159, 160.
Heisel, II, 20.
Henderson, I, 46, 79, 89, 90; II, 98.
Henley, I, 98.
Henning, I, 12, 16; II, will 50.
HENRY FAMILY, I, 75-79.
Henry, I, 47, 64, 65, 89, 95, 106; II, 2, 13, 38, 82, 83, 86.
Henshaw, II, 144, 145.
Hensley, II, 47.
Herbert, II, 78, 91.
Herdman, I, 35.
Herndon, I, 33, 66, 74, 103; II, 40, 46, 47, 147.
Herrell, II, 37.
Hert, I, 95.
Herton, I, 82.
Hesty, II, 129.
Heth, II, 35, 94.
Hewitt, I, 66, 118.
Heywood, I, 59.
Hickerson, II, 40, 41.
Hickman, II, 151.
Hiden, I, 53; II, 139.
Hiftin, II, 26.
Higginbotham, I, 78.
Hightower, I, 107.
Hilcott, I, 82.
HILL FAMILY, II, 85.
Hill, I, 53, 54, 58, 68, 72, 95, 109, 111; II, 11, 16-20, 23, 27, 33, 36, 37, 40, 43, will 50, 52, 53, 75, 76, 83, 86, 94-96, 103, 110, 111, 122, 124, 125, 127, 128, 139, 145.
Hillah, I, 104.
Hillary, II, 78.
Hines, II, 152.
Hinton, I, 91.
Hisle, II, 36, 129.
Hite, I, 71, 72, 81, 92, 107, 108, 110; II, 1.
Hitt, I, 45; II, 21, 27, 37, 159.
Hoard, I, 89; II, will 50.
Hobson, I, 67, 94; II, 136.
Hodge, I, 23.
Hoff, II, 83.
Hoffer, II, 49.
Hoffman, I, 45; II, 19, 27, 159, 160.
Hogan, II, 137, 141.
Hoge, I, 24, 100; II, 158.

XV

Hogutt, I, 67.
Hokes, II, 119.
Holladay, I, 48, 50, 103-105, 119; II, 26, 27, 82, 97.
Holland, II, 153.
Hollingsworth, I, 101.
Holloway, I, 81, 85.
Holman, I, 21.
Holmes, I, 107, 110; II, 27.
Holt, I, 63, 86; II, 134.
Holtzclaw, I, 45; II, 159, 160.
Holtzman, II, 11, 18, 40, 102.
Honeyman, II, 81.
Hood, II, 34, 37.
Hooe, I, 53, 64; II, 27, 139.
Hoofman, II, will 50.
Hooge, I, 93.
Hooker, II, 81, 34, 95.
Hopkins, I, 74, 107; II, 82, 134, 136, 138, 142.
Hopper, I, 65-67; II, will 50, 51.
Hopton, I, 11; II, 1.
Horner, II, 54.
Horsely, I, 98; II, 81.
Horton, II, 129.
Houck, II, 80.
Houghton, II, 36.
Howard, I, 74, 91, 92, 119; II, 17, 27.
Howe, I, 50, 112; II, 39.
Howell, II, 52.
Hower, I, 99.
Howison, I, 13, 66, 80, 81, 88, 111; II, will 50, 157, 159.
Hubbard, I, 75; II, 51.
Hudgins, II, 17, 27.
Hudson, I, 81; II, 18, 22, 27, 37, 76, 82, 113, 119, 124, 127.
Huff I, 87; II, 36, 37.
Huffman, II, will 50, 53.
Huger, II, 83.
Hughes, I, 63, 104, 107; II, 48, 55, 152.
Hule, I, 80-82, 88.
Huling, I, 64.
Hull, II, 20, 129.
Hume, I, 11, 18; II, 19, 20, 27, 46, 53, 85, 155.
Humphreys, I, 67, 92; II, 11.
Hungerford, II, 130.
Hunt, I, 66, 84; II, 94, 128.
Hunter, I, 66, 99, 100, 104, 110; II, 80.
Huntington, I, 104; II, 100.
Hunton, II, 139, 145.
Hurt, I, 95, 96; II, 9, 47, will 50.
Hurvey, I, 81.

Hutchens, I, 14.
Hutchinson, I, 66.
Hyson, I, 82.

I

Ingle, II, 87.
Innes, I, 80, 88; II, 141.
Inskeep, II, 113.
Iredell, I, 85.
Ireland, II, 39, 41.
Irwin, I, 55; II, 92.
Isham, II, 8.

J

Jack, I, 88.
Jackson, I, 57, 64, 76, 89, 93, 103, 104, 111; II, 28, 33, 34, 95, 96, 98, 101, 122, 125-128, 148.
James, I, 45, 93, 96, 103; II, 40-42, 44, 51, 53.
Jameson, I, 19, 22, 47, 101, 112, 113, 117, 120; II, 3, 4, 6-8, 12-14, 17, 22, 45, 47, 49, 80, 160.
Janney, II, 27.
Jay, I, 48.
Jean, I, 104.
Jefferson, I, 58, 84, 89, 106; II, 18, 38, 133, 138, 157.
Jeffries, II, 8, 11, 17, 19, 27, 41, will 50.
Jenkins, II, 17, 20, 104.
Jenks, II, 9.
Jennings, II, 18, 52, 150.
Jepson, I, 104.
Jett, I, 19, 65-67, 100; II, 37, 48, will 51, 53, 55, 128, 158.
John, II, 50.
Johnson, I, 34, 47, 52, 54, 55, 66, 82, 97, 103; II, 9, 18, 35, 37, 41, 79, 80, 89, 120, 123, 135, 137, 138, 140, 143, 153, 155.
Johnston, I, 67, 77; II, 21, 28, 32, 46, 48, 51, 55, 95, 155.
Johns, I, 23, 29-31, 65.
Jolliffe, II, 151, 154.
JONES FAMILY, II, 89-94.
Jones, I, 4, 13, 17, 19, 33, 36, 45, 46, 55, 59, 61, 62, 65-67, 76, 78, 79, 82, 83, 85, 94, 102, 112, 113; II, 2, 4, 17, 21-23, 28, 35, 40, will 51, 53, 76, 77, 84, 86, 89, 94, 104, 105, 108, 110, 111, 113, 114, 130, 138, 142, 146, 147.
Jordan, II, 37, will 51, 77, 78.
Judd, II, 22, 37.
Jury, I, 86.
Justis, II, 35.

K

Kaffer, II, will 51.
Kahl, II, 20.
Kaufman, I, 104.
Kavanaugh, II, 81, 82.
Kay, II, 52.
Keeley, II, 18, 79, 85.
Keene, I, 101, 104.
Keerl, 113, 117; II, 11, 160.
Keith, I, 67, 95; II, 82.
Kelton, I, 60.
Kemper, I, 45, 46, 55, 104; II, 23, 154, 158-160.
Kendall, II, 37.
Kendrick, II, 153.
Kennedy, I, 91, 99, 100; II, 117.
Kennerly, II, will 51.
Kent, I, 104.
Kenton, I, 63.
Kerfoot, I, 86; II, 37, 153, 154.
Keys, II, 17.
Keyser, II, 154.
Kibler, II, 27.
Kilby, I, 65, 67; II, 17-20, 22, 27, 28, 50.
Kilpatrick, II, 107, 111-115, 117.
Kimbrough, I, 103, 104; II, 81.
Kincaid, I, 10.
Kinchlow, I, 64.
Kines, II, 19.
King, I, 46, 103, 104; II, 18, 53.
Kinloch, I, 72.
Kinsey, II, 153, 154.
Kirby, II, 22, 90, 98.
Kirk, I, 119; II, 55, 156.
Kirtley, I, 6, 10, 50; II, 46, will 51, 86.
Kitchen, I, 92.
Knapp, I, 83; II, 124.
Knox, I, 72, 74, 113; II, 7, 8, will 51, 144.
Koontz, II, 40.
Kosciusko, I, 49.

L

Labuzan, II, 84.
Lacey, I, 101.
Lacklin, I, 101.
La Fayette, I, 84; II, 9, 141, 156-158.
Lafox, I, 67.
Lake, I, 87; II, 19.
Lamar, I, 104; II, 78.
Lamb, I, 50.
Lambert, I, 65; II, 80.
Lambkin, II, 28, 128, 129.
Lamon, I, 25, 36, 118.
Landon, I, 54; II, 141.
Landrum, I, 65.
Lane, I, 61, 63, 65-67, 86.
Larkin, I, 82, 88.
Latham, I, 19, 63, 85, 112; II, 8, will 51, 113, 153, 155.
Lathrop, I, 53; II, 139, 144.
Lattimer, I, 68; II, 123, 145.
Lawler, II, 19, 55.
Lawrence, I, 81, 94; II, 17.
Lawrie, I, 28.
Lawson, I, 46; II, 90.
Layman, I, 118.
Layne, II, 33.
Layton, II, 81, 82.
Leach, I, 68, 98.
Leake, I, 53; II, 79, 140.
Lear, II, 19.
Leatherer, II, will 51.
Leathers, I, 33; II, 40.
Leavel, I, 18, 36, 117; II, 28, 154.
Le Bosquet, I, 98.
Le Chase, I, 81.
Lee, I, 3, 33, 60, 69, 71-74, 78, 87, 101, 102, 106; II, 10, 17, 21-24, 28, 32-34, 56, 76, 77, 95, 96, 98, 99, 102, 106, 108, 110, 114-120, 122, 137, 148, 158.
Leet, II, 79.
Leflet, I, 59.
Legare, I, 64.
Legg, II, 21, 28.
Le Grande, I, 101.
Leigh, I, 59, 108, 111; II, 46.
Leighton, I, 78; II, 81.
Leisure, I, 101.
Lemoine, I, 88.
Lester, I, 101.
Letcher, II, 137.
Lewis, I, 7, 36, 46, 64, 66, 69, 74, 75, 77-84, 87, 94, 99, 102, 107, 112; II, 1, 9, 11, 17, 20, 22, 28, 43, 81-84, 86, 101, 128, 134, 153.
Lewright, II, 151.
Lieper, I, 72.
LIGHTFOOT, FAMILY, I, 70.
Lightfoot, I, 6-8, 10, 14-16, 32, 50, 56, 59, 76, 80, 81, 83, 85, 88, 90, 113; II, 7, 8, 10, 11, 46, 48-50, will 51, 54, 82, 158, 160.
Ligm, II, 81.
LILLARD-BRYAN FAMILY, II, 150, 151.
Lillard, I, 64; II, 18, 36, 152-154.
Lincoln, II, 152.
Lindenberger, I, 67.
Lindsay, I, 74, 99, 119; II, 143.

XVII

Lines, II, will 51.
Lippen, II, 127.
Lipscomb, II, 28, 86.
Little, I, 102.
Littlepage I, 21, 26, 48, 50, 73, 74, 79.
Littleton, I, 103; II, 87.
Livingston, I, 100, 119.
Lloyd, I, 104; II, 19, 151.
Lochett, I, 82, 83.
Locke, II, 141.
Lockhart, I, 83.
Lockwood, I, 53, 89; II, 80.
Logan, I, 67, 98; II, 137.
Loggins, II, 55.
Lomax, I, 64; II, 23, 75, 76, 114,115, 117.
Long, I, 14, 19, 47, 66, 86-88, 97, 108, 109;
    II, 3, 14, 17, 28, 46, 50, will 52, 157.
Longest, I, 86.
Longstreet, II, 34, 95, 104, 110.
Lovell, I, 54, 108, 110; II, 9, 52.
Loving, I, 88.
Lovitt, II, 83.
Lowndes, II, 82, 83.
Lucas, I, 107; II, 18, 56.
Luckett, II, 85.
Ludlowe, I, 53.
Ludwell, II, 81.
Luggett, I, 85.
Lumpkin, I, 102.
Lunsford, II, 75, 76.
Luther, II, 80.
Luttrell I, 117; II, 19, 54, 153.
Luzenberg, I, 57.
Lydall, I, 80.
Lyman, I, 104.
Lynch, II, 55.
Lyne, I, 74, 81, 107.
Lyons, I, 64; II, 19.

M

Macall, II, 80.
Macauley, I, 92.
Machonichie, II, 4.
Macklin, I, 86.
Macon, I, 34, 53, 71, 72, 107; II, 139, 144, 145.
Macoy, I, 35, 117; II, 8, 11, 50.
Macrae, I, 83.
Madalinski, I, 49.
Madden, II, 99.
Maddox, I, 14, 104.
MADISON FAMILY, I, 71, 72.
Madison, I, 22, 23, 32-34, 57, 74, 76, 77,
    83, 84, 87, 88, 96, 102, 103,
    105, 112, 113, 118; II, 4, 83,
    138, 139, 144, 145, 157.

Magruder, I, 62, 110; II, 139.
Mahlon, II, 26.
Major, I, 53; II, 28, will 52, will 55, 123, 139.
Malbury, II, 145.
Mallony, II, 35.
Mallory, I, 34, 54, 105; II, 138, 142.
Malton, II, 20.
Mandeley, II, 79.
Manderville, II, 94.
Mann, I, 79.
Mansfield, I, 64; II, 40.
Marlborough, I, 1.
Markham, II, 117.
Marr, I, 99.
Marsh, II, 28.
Marshall, I, 24, 32, 47, 62, 63, 71 ,110; II,
    3, 4, 7-9, 12-14, 18, will 52,
    78, 90.
Martin, I, 32, 71; II, 49, 52, 85, 159.
Marye, I, 32, 61, 62, 71, 87, 94; II, 49, 140.
Mason, I, 38, 68, 80, 82, 88, 94, 98, 108; II,
    8, 37, 40-42, 50, 79, 80, 84, 94,
    137, 139.
Massey, I, 81; II, 22, 28, 119, 155.
Matthews, I, 100, 112; II, 7, 19, 20, will
    52, 76, 92, 127.
Maupin, I, 113; II, 28, 144.
Maurice, I, 90.
Maury, I, 32, 59, 71, 76, 80, 104.
Mauzy, I, 113; II, 8-10, will 52, 82, 160.
Maxey, I, 92.
Maxwell, I, 105; II, 82, 83.
May, II, 43.
Mayberry, II, 153.
Maynard, I, 68.
Mayo, 1, 12; II, 84, 85, 94.
Mayrant, I, 60.
McCarthy, I, 104, 105.
McChesney, II, 85.
McClanahan, I, 19; II, 3, 11, 45, 52, 76, 152, 160.
McClelland, I, 78; II, 34, 95, 98, 121.
McClerry, II, 87.
McClung, II, 159.
McClure, I, 65.
McConchie, I, 87; II, 28, 35.
McConnell, I, 81.
McCormick, I, 65, 67; II, 19.
McCoul, I, 94.
McCown, II, 42, 43.
McCrum, I, 81.
McDade, II, 78.
McDaniel, I, 8; II, 17, 142.

XVIII

McDonald, I, 68, 116; II, 18, 19, 80, 111, 140.
McDonough, I, 89.
McDowell, I, 77, 88; II, 121, 122, 128, 137.
McFarland, I, 82; II, 18.
McGilvery, II, 124.
McGinnis, I, 65.
McGrath, II, 51.
McGregor, II, 104.
McGuinn, II, 56.
McKay, I, 91, 93; II, 53, 156.
McKidru, II, 25.
McLaughlin, I, 89.
McMullan, II, 11.
McMurran, II, 158, 159.
McMurth, I, 7.
McPherson, I, 83.
McQueen, II, 37, 153.
McVeigh, II, 19.
Meade, I, 2, 6, 7, 10, 13, 17, 23-25, 28, 80, 85, 117; II, 75, 110, 114, 115, 118-120, 138, 141, 154.
Means, I, 82.
Mears, I, 88.
Medley, I, 84.
Melton, II, 20.
Menefee, I, 87, 97; II, 37, 152, 153.
Menzies, I, 34.
Mercer, I, 88, 108, 112; II, 7, 14.
Merdton, II, 159, 160.
Meredith, I, 76, 77, 103, 104; II, 83, 86.
Merrill, I, 88, 93.
Merritt, II, 105.
Merriwether, II, 88, 89, 132.
Messinger, II, 160.
Michel, I, 77.
Micou Family, II, 75-79.
Micou, I, 58, 85, 88, 95, 98; II, 155.
Middleton, I, 60; II, 87.
Midge, I, 68.
Miles, I, 106; II, 130.
Millan, II, 37.
Miller, I, 62, 64, 69, 78, 84, 86, 88, 93, 101, 110; II, 11, 18, 19, 28, 37, 40, 47, 49, 50, 82, 150, 153, 154.
Mills, I, 85, 107; II, 80, 86-88.
Milroy, II, 127.
Milser, II, 35.
Milton, II, 20, 29, 87.
Minge, I, 70; II, 141.
Minnegerode, I, 31, 36, 86, 113, 114; II, 140.
Minor, I, 2, 5, 81, 98, 100, 101, 119; II, 46, 54, 137, 141, 156.

Mitchell, II, 20, 82, 86.
Mix, II, 77, 78.
Moffet, II, 11, 37, 40, 42, 97.
Moncure, I, 66.
Monroe, I, 84; II, 157, 158.
Montgomery, I, 63, 67; II, 7, 89.
Monti, I, 99.
Montjoy, I, 12.
Mooklar, II, 89.
Moomaw, I, 104.
Moon, I, 103.
Moore, I, 3, 10, 13, 23, 24, 27, 30, 32-34, 57, 64, 71-74, 86, 88, 118; II, 37, 55, 75, 136, 138, 141, 142, 152.
Moorehead, I, 85, 113; II, 115.
Moorman, II, 104.
Mordicai, II, 83, 85.
Morgan, I, 14, 47, 107; II, 4, 14, 29, 47, will 52, 76, 78, 80, 85.
Morris, I, 67, 75, 97; II, 46, 52, 81.
Morrison, II, 77, 152.
Mortimer, I, 28, 83; II, 36.
Morton, I, 33, 36, 60, 68, 74, 89, 110, 113, 117; II, 17, 79, 80, 115, 137, 140.
Mosby, I, 78, 79; II, 17, 23, 120.
Mosely, II, 77.
Mosher, I, 102.
Moss, II, 90.
Motley, I, 86.
Mott, I, 12.
Mottram, II, 80.
Moyers, II, 82.
Muir, I, 93.
Mulderg, II, 135.
Mullensburg, II, 121.
Mungo, II, 75, 76.
Munson, II, 87.
Murat, II, 140.
Murphy, II, 37, 52, 54.
Murray, I, 79, 98; II, 129, 145.
Mussie, I, 82.
Myers, II, 19.

N

Nairne, I, 54, 88.
Nalle, I, 14, 15, 28, 35, 53, 113; II, 15, 17, 22, 29, 46, 47, 50, will 52, 56, 83, 86, 113, 114, 139, 140.
Nalls, II, 129.
Namsley, II, 51.
Napier, II, 154.
Narr, II, 20.

Nash, II, 45, 52.
Nathan, II, 88.
Natts, II, 129.
Naylor, I, 68.
Neale, I, 63, 64, 81; II, 79, 94.
Neilson, I, 82; II, 55.
Nelson, I, 30, 60, 64, 72, 73, 81, 102, 113, 117; II, 78, 79, 85, 140, 144, 158.
Nevil, I, 62, 66,
Newby, 37.
Newell, II, 152.
Newhouse, II, 18, 160.
Newman, I, 14, 34, 53, 93; II, 19, 46, 82, 84, 87, 128, 135, 144.
Newton, I, 117; II, 115, 116.
Nicholas, II, 143.
Nichols, I, 94; II, 18.
Nicholson, II, 18, 37, 77.
Nicol, II, 11.
Nixon, I, 82, 88.
Noble, I, 94; II, 78.
Nolan, II, 26, 29.
Nooe, II, will 52.
Norborne, I, 72, 81; II, 138.
Norman, II, 21, 35, will 52, 53, 80, 151.
Norris, I, 65, 68; II, 8, 158.
Norton, I, 27, 64, 102.
Norvell, I, 58; II, 143.
Norwood, I, 98; II, 156.
Nott, I, 11; II, 1.
Noty, I, 64.
Nowlin, I, 107.

O

O'Bannon, I, 110; II, 35, 37, 48, 150, 154.
O'Callahan, II, 29.
Oden, II, 20.
Offitt, I, 105.
Ogilvie, I, 110.
O'Neil, I, 33-36.
Ord, I, 80, 82, 88.
Ormond, I, 2.
Ormsby, I, 81.
Orr, II, 49.
Orrick, I, 99.
Ostcone, I, 67.
Oswald, II, 79.
Oswell, II, 77.
Otland, I, 110.
Ott, I, 110.
Ousley, II, 91.
Overall, II, 153.
Overton, I, 103, 105.

Owens, I, 92; II, 143.
Owsley, I, 68; II, 91.
Oxford, II, will 52.

P

Pace, II, 79.
Page, I, 72, 87, 102, 114, 117; II, 15, 144.
Palmer, I, 83, 84, 87.
Pannill, I, 36, 66, 83, 109, 110; II, 52, 145.
Parke, I, 109.
Parker, I, 91; II, 20, 52, 84.
Parks, I, 14; II, will 52.
Parr, I, 64; II, 19, 35.
Parrent, I, 64,
Parrin, II, 144.
Parsons, I, 62, 66, 67; II, 85, 145.
Partlow, II, 46.
Pate, I, 109; II, 115.
Pattie, II, 11, 29, 130.
Patton, I, 60, 74, 88, 108, 109; II, 13-15, 17, 18, 21, 29, 54, 157.
Paulding, II, 3.
Paxton, I, 104.
Payne, I, 21, 25, 26, 48, 50, 64-66, 73, 76, 79, 84, 90, 94, 95, 112, 113; II; 19, 20, 29, 52, 82, 85, 87, 128, 160.
Peace, I, 109.
Peacocke, I, 62; II, 49.
Pearson, II, 19.
Peers, I, 81.
Pegram, II, 23, 124, 127.
Pelham, II, 24, 81, 102, 108.
Pembroke, II, 84, 85.
Pender, II, 33, 95, 126.
PENDLETON FAMILY, I, 95-107, 119.
Pendleton, I, 2, 10, 13-20, 33, 34, 36, 52, 56, 61, 63, 66, 74, 83, 84, 89-91, 108, 109, 112, 113, 119, 120; II, 4-8, 13-15, 17, 22, 29, 49, will 52, 53, 81, 82, 84, 130, 131, 136, 137, 139, 152, 155, 156, 160.
Penick, II, 29.
Penn, I, 74, 107; II, 141.
Pennebaker, I, 93.
Pennell, II, 20.
Penniman. II, 143,
Pentrust, I, 65.
Percy, I, 104.
Perfect, II, 53.
Perkins, II, 94.
Perrin, II, 93.
Perry I, 68; II, 19, 20, 29, 141, 160.
Peter, I, 66, 76; II, 18, 49.

Peterkin, I, 30, 31, 114.
Pettigrew, II, 130.
Pettingall, I, 95.
Pettit, II, 128.
Pettus, I, 95.
Petty, II, 21.
Peyton, I, 6, 7, 10, 13, 14, 16, 62, 64, 69, 100, 113; II, 37, will 53.
Pfeiffer, I, 99.
Phelps, I, 64.
Philemon, II, 56.
Philips, I, 7, 105; II, 78, 79.
Phinizy, II, 78.
Pickens, I, 68.
Pickett, I, 26, 87, 111; II, 15, 23, 39, 40, 41, will 53.
Pierce, II, 29, 46, 140.
Pinckney, I, 67.
Pinkard, I, 61, II, 29, 49.
Piper, II, 156.
Pitcher, II, 125.
Pleasant, II, 34.
Pleasanton, II, 34, 105.
Poague, II, 23, 124.
Poindexter, I, 61, 63; II, 40, 49, 51.
Pollard, I, 15, 19, 70, 74, 96, 102, 103, 106, 107, 112.
Pollock, I, 65, 67, 98; II, 158.
Polson, II, 145.
Poniatoski, I, 49.
Pope, I, 77, 93; II, 9, 32-34, 48, 95, 98, 121, 122, 127, 128.
Popham, II, 9, 50.
Porter, I, 26, 33, 34, 45, 55, 66, 93, 100, 101, 103, 108, 113; II, 9, 19, 27, 29, 50, 79, 83, 115, 139.
Porterfield, I, 47, 68; II, 4.
Potemkin, I, 49.
Poulson, I, 88.
Povall, I, 78.
Powell, I, 15, 35, 66, 71, 107, 111; II, 46, will 53, 55, 83, 85, 86, 94, 130, 131, 156.
Powers, I, 93; II, 82.
Poythress, II, 84.
Pratt, II, 130.
Preston, I, 77; II, 83.
Prewitt, I, 104.
Price, I, 61, 62, 98; II, 78, 82, 91, 145, 156.
Priddie, II, 17.
Priest, II, 152, 154.
Prince, II, 33, 124, 125.
Pringle, I, 98, 105.
Pritchard, II, 53.
Pryor, II, 134.
Pullen, II, 37.
Puller, II, 103.
Pulliam, I, 107; II, 11, 55, 150, 154.
Purit, I, 6.
Purnell, I, 100.
Putnam, II, 37.

Q

Quaintance, II, 50, 84.
Quin, II, will 53.

R

Ragland, I, 107.
Rambo, II, 79.
Ramsdell, I, 85, 86.
Ramseers, II, 119.
Ramsey, I, 98; II, 156.
Randall, I, 86.
Randolph, I, 64, 65, 70, 83, 99, 100, 106, 113, 119; II, 2, 7.
Rankin, I, 62, 105.
Ratrie, II, 30.
Rawson, I, 90, 92.
Read, I, 62, 63, 67, 68; II, 21, 49, will 53, 154.
Reagan, II, 37.
Rector, 1, 45; II, 83.
Redd, I, 98.
Redding, 1, 91.
Rees, II, 45, 77, 159.
Reevely, I, 74.
Reid, I, 103, 107, 109, 112; II, 152.
Remer, I, 63.
Revell, II, 130.
Reynolds, II, 47, 85, 142.
Rhodehamel, I, 105.
Rhodes, I, 104; II, 82, 119.
Ribble, I, 114, 117.
RICE FAMILY, II, 132, 133.
Rice, II, 134, 139.
Richards, I, 62, 64, 69, 119; II, will 53, 79, 91.
Richardson, I, 74, 85, 88, 98; II, 52, 93, 147.
Ricketts, II, 122, 127.
Riggs, II, 141.
Rigglesworth, I, 81.
Riley, II, 145.
Rind, I, 72.
Ringo, II, 142.
Ringold, II, 84.
Ritenour, II, 37.
Rittenhouse, I, 87, 98; II, 140.
Rivercomb, II, 17, 19.

XXI

Rixey, I, 46, 115, 117; II, 11, 17, 30, will 53, 110, 113, 118, 140, 150, 153, 154, 160.
Roane, I, 78, 109; II, 40, 43.
Roach, II, 18, 51.
Robb, II, 87.
Roberts, I, 10, 14-16, 18, 19, 65-67, 69, 76, 84, 114; II, 4, 6, 8, 17, 19, 35, 37, 45, 48, 50, will 53, 77, 78, 84-86, 98, 131, 147, 151-154.
Robertson, I, 14, 24, 38, 40, 64, 77, 88; II, 19, 44, will 53, 99, 104-106, 108, 109, 114, 122, 124, 139, 158.
Robinson, I, 11, 79, 86, 87, 99; II, 1, 30, 53, 93.
Robson, II, 30, 53, 84.
Rock, I, 107.
Rockwell, II, 91.
Rodgers, I, 58, 69, 86, 99.
Roe, II, 111, 112.
Roebuck, II, will 53.
Roland, II, 104, 126.
Rolls, II, 158.
Romney, II, 79.
Ronald, II, 87, 90, 91.
Rootes, I, 14, 17, 56, 80-83; II, 4, 7, 76, 77.
Rose, I, 10, 71, 72, 75, 107.
Ross, I, 100, 101; II, 17, 19, 22, 84, 104.
Rosser, II, 114, 118.
Rosson, II, 30, 45, 49, will 53, 128, 130, 154.
Rousee, I, 8.
Rout, II, 48, 151, 152.
Rowe, I, 59; II, 130.
Rowland, II, 155.
Rowles, II, 22, 36.
Rowzie, I, 64, 72, 119.
Roy, I, 96, 106; II, 75-77.
Royall, I, 102; II, 158.
Rucker, I, 7, 104, 106; II, 49.
Rudacilla, II, 30, 37, 154.
Ruddal, II, 51.
Rudy, I, 105.
Ruffin, II, 93.
Ruggles, I, 66.
Rush, II, 141.
Russell, I, 8, 12, 14, 60, 77, 81; II, will 53, 83, 105.
Rutherford, I, 76.
Rys, II, 134.

S

Sale, I, 64.
Sample, I, 94.
Sampson, I, 78; II, 159.
Samuel, II, 9, 48.
Sanders, I, 91, 92; II, will 54, 55.
Sanford, I, 33, 68; II, 23, 35, will 53.
Satterlee, I, 82, 88.
Saunders, I, 56, 64; II, 38, 40, 41, 85, 130.
Scanland, II, 54.
Schlosser, II, 104.
Schuyler, I, 103.
Scott, I, 1, 26, 34, 35, 53, 60, 63, 65-67, 78, 86, 87, 101, 107, 113, 119; II, 19, 22, 30, 37, will 54, 76, 80, 85, 89, 90, 92-94, 131, 138, 139, 142, 151, 154.
Screven, II, 79.
Scroggins, I, 105; II, 37.
Seal, II, 48.
Seay, I. 107.
Secker, I, 35.
Selden, II, 80.
Semmes, I, 80, 88; II, 4.
Semple, I, 64.
Settle, II, 11, 18, 19, 37, 53.
Seymour, II, 138, 143.
Shaaf, I, 74.
Shackelford, I, 55, 65, 66, 84, 100, 101, 113, 119; II, 7, 8, 30, 35, 52, 80, 97, 101, 103, 150, 157, 158.
Shadrach, II, 17, 21, 152.
Shane, II, 90.
Sharpe, I, 77; II, 51.
Shaw, I, 101; II, 18, 19, 30, 35.
Sheads, II, 37.
Shelton, I, 76, 78; II, 79, 140.
Shepherd, I, 33, 34, 71, 72, 74, 87, 88, 99, 100, 107; II, 17, 79, 129, 141.
Sherlock, I, 35.
Shield, I, 2, 36, 78.
Ship, II, 40, 41.
Shipley, II, 146, 147.
Shirley, II, 80.
Shivers, II, 158.
Short, I, 64.
Shotwell, II, 21, 47.
Shrader, II, 90.
Shuck, II, 44.
Shumate, II, 54.
Shue, I, 117.
Shultice, I, 87.

XXII

Sidney, I, 73.
Sigel, II, 121, 122.
Silvey, II, 19.
Simmons, I, 66.
Simms, I, 97; II, 21, 30, 37, 44, 52, will 54, 77, 78, 130, 147, 148, 150, 153.
Simpson, II, will 54.
Sinclair, I, 101; II, 148.
Singleton, I, 76.
Skaggs, II, 83.
Skillman, II, 132.
Skinker, II, 158.
Skipwith, I, 76.
SLAUGHTER FAMILY, I, 85-95.
Slaughter, I, 6, 8, 10, 13-17, 19-26, 29, 31, 35, 46-48, 50, 53, 54, 56, 58, 59, 63, 65, 67, 68, 70, 71, 75, 76, 80, 82, 108, 112, 113, 115, 118, 119; II, 3, 4, 6, 8-10, 12-17, 30, 35, 37, 48, 50-52, will 54, 75, 84, 86, 89, 90, 93, 94, 123, 128, 131, 135, 136, 157, 158, 160.
Sloane, I, 19; II, 151.
Smith, I, 7, 24, 33, 34, 38, 39, 41, 44, 46, 55, 56, 60, 62, 67, 68, 72, 78, 80, 82, 85-87, 93, 95, 97, 101, 103, 108, 111, 114, 117, 119; II, 4, 11, 17-19, 21, 22, 30, 35, 37, 46, 48, 52, 53, will 54, 80, 81, 83, 89-91, 130, 135, 137, 143, 150, 152-154, 158, 160.
Smithey, I, 119.
Smock, I, 91.
Smoot, II, 123, 125.
Snaden, II, 133.
Snelling, II, 52.
Snodgrass, I, 99.
Snow, I, 66.
Somerby, II, 85.
SOMERVILLE FAMILY, II, 79.
Somerville, I, 38, 52, 60, 64, 87-89, 94, 95; II, 21, 30, 51, 82, 83, 139, 144, 148, 152, 158.
Southall, I, 77.
Sparks, II, 30, 52.
Sparrow, I, 95; II, 82, 83.
Speak, I, 98; II, 49.
Speed, I, 89.
Speiden, I, 88.
Spencer, I, 63-65, 78, 104, 105; II, 81.
Spicer, II, 18, 31, 35, 37, 56.
Spiers, I, 101.

Spillman, I, 14, 26, 45, 112, 113; II, 40, 42, 43, 48, will 54, 83.
Spindle, II, 19, 116, 139, 153.
Spofford, II, 127.
Spooner, I, 116, 117.
SPOTSWOOD FAMILY, I, 72, 73.
Spotswood, I, 1-5, 7-13, 17, 26, 33-38, 41-46, 55, 73, 78, 80, 82, 100, 101, 118, 119; II, 2, 158, 159.
Sprinkel, II, 18.
Stair, II, 145.
St. Albans, I, 11; II, 1.
Stallard, II, 18, 19, 31, will 54, 101, 128, 152, 153.
Stanard, I, 30, 53, 74, 89, 88, 117.
Standish, II, 76.
Stanton, I, 6, 10, 19, 58, 87; II, will 54, 140.
Staples, I, 107; II, 83.
Starke, I, 109; II, 17, 31, 37, 77, 111.
Starrow, I, 54; II, 8, 158.
Stearns, I, 60, 68; II, 85.
Steel, II, 40, 87.
Stepp, I, 60.
Steptoe, I, 30, 31, 53, 113; II, 139.
Stern, I, 94.
Stevens, I, 32, 34, 38, 47, 56, 62, 80, 98, 107, 108; II, 3, 5, 6, 8, 13, 14, 50, will 54, 79.
STEVENSON FAMILY, I, 73, 74.
Stevenson, I, 7, 19-22, 25-27, 34, 48, 63, 76, 79; II, will 54, 82, 91.
Steward, II, 17, will 54.
Stewart, I, 67, 81, 94, 104; II, 31, 51, 55, 56, 92, 144.
Stickler, II, 154.
Stickley, II, 152.
Stiles, I, 105.
Still, II, 91.
Stinson, I, 65.
Stofer, II, 17.
Stokeley, II, 55.
Stokes, II, 47.
Stone, I, 63, 64; II, 18, 41, 43, 44, 53, 82, 112, 150.
Stoneman, II, 102, 103.
Storm, II, 87.
Story, II, 82.
Stout, II, 130.
Stovall, I, 107.
Stoven, II, 144.
Stover, II, 152.
Stowell, II, 100.

XXIII

St. Pierre, I, 100, 101.
Strachan, I, 103, 105.
Stratton, 1, 67.
Stribling, II, 89.
Stricker, I, 76, 88.
Strider, II, 159.
Stringer, I, 61; II, 49.
Stringfellow, I, 14, 84, 87; II, 31, 40, 41, 43, 44, 107, 110, 116, 140.
Strode, I, 34, 52; II, 135-137.
STROTHER FAMILY, I, 83, 84.
Strother, I, 13, 14, 19, 34, 36, 52, 54, 55, 59, 61, 63, 66, 80, 81, 87, 91, 92, 97, 100, 101, 107, 109, 112, 113; II, 4, 6-8, 11, 15, 19, 31, 48, 51, 54, will 54, will 55, 80, 91, 92, 100, 131, 143, 151, 152, 154, 158.
Stuart, I, 52, 86; II, 19, 23, 24, 34, 79, 84, 85, 94, 98, 99, 103, 104, 106, 107, 109-111, 114, 115, 117, 118, 127, 128.
Stubblefield, I, 14, 66, 108; II, 46, will 55.
Sturtevant, II, 22.
Sudduth, II, 18.
Sugg, I, 65.
Suggett, I, 54.
Sullivan, II, 18.
Summerall, II, 130.
Summers, I, 92.
Suter, I, 65.
Sutphin, II, 11, 37.
Sutton, I, 102; II, 53.
Suwarrow, II, 37.
Swan, II, 11.
Swartout, I, 60.
Swift, I, 65; II, 141.
Syme, I, 76, 77.

T

Tackett, I, 14, 86.
Talbot, II, 91, 138, 143.
Taliaferro, I, 7, 10, 12, 32, 33, 35, 44, 47, 53-55, 57, 66, 71, 72, 74, 75, 97, 98, 103, 109, 113, 117; II, 3, 6, 13, 31, 33, 49. will 55, 76, 77, 82, 88, 89, 113, 125, 126, 136, 138, 143, 152.
Talley, I, 94.
Tannahill, II, will 55.
Tanner, II, 31, 151.
Tansil, II, 21, 31.
Tapp, I, 112; II, 17, 22, 37, 50, 51, will 55.

Tarleton, II, 3.
Tasker, I, 102.
Tate, II, 89.
Tatum, II, 85.
Taunt, II, 154.
TAYLOR FAMILY, I, 74, 75.
Taylor, I, 20, 22, 32, 34, 40, 47, 58, 60, 65, 67, 68, 71, 76, 78, 80-84, 88, 96-99, 101, 102, 105, 107, 113, 118, 119; II, 19, 23, 30, 39, 41, 43, 44, 47, 84, 88, 111, 136-138, 140, 142, 144, 145, 154, 156.
Tazewell, I, 108; II, 14, 85.
Tedington, I, 70.
Temple, I, 76; II, 79, 89.
Tench, I, 69.
Tennant, I, 10, 13, 35.
Terrick, I, 21.
Terrill, I, 19, 34, 54; II, 35, 82, 85, 145.
Terry, I, 60, 104; II, 23.
Thacker, I, 57.
Tharpe, II, 77.
Thatcher, II, 47.
Thaurman, I, 92.
THOM FAMILY, II, 84, 85.
Thom, I, 22, 34, 60, 113; II, 106, 130, 158.
THOMAS FAMILY, II, 155, 156.
Thomas, I, 11, 24, 52, 53, 61, 63-66, 74, 77, 85, 90, 95-98, 105, 107; II, 17, 31, 38, 41, 49-51, 54, will 55, 56, 93, 125, 136, 137, 153, 154.
THOMPSON FAMILY, I, 79-83; II, 86-89.
Thompson, I, 2, 8-10, 14-17, 22, 24, 30, 52-57, 74, 84, 85, 87, 88, 92, 103, 104, 108, 113, 116-118; II, 4-10, 17, 35, 46, 47, will 55, 76, 77, 80, 83-85, 90, 94, 105, 113, 127, 130, 140, 147.
Thorn, II, 8,
Thornburg, I, 119.
Thornhill, II, 41, 51, 52, will 55.
Thornton, I, 7, 12, 17, 19, 35, 36, 59, 60, 66, 74, 80-83, 85, 87, 89, 91, 104, 108; II, 3, 4, 37, 46, 47, 51, will 55, 77, 80, 85, 130, 158.
Thrall, II, 18.
Threlkeld, I, 86; II, 45, 48.
Thrift, II, 11.
Throckmorton, I, 33, 100; II, 32, 124, 125, 136, 138, 143.
Tilghman, I, 69.
Tillinghast, II, 137, 141.

Timberlake, II, 120, 121, 150, 153.
Tinsley, I, 60, 96, 106; II, 83.
Tipton, II, 18.
Todd, I, 34, 38, 39, 52, 67, 76, 95; II, 46, 82, 83, 86, 135, 136, 138, 142
Toland, I, 60.
Tompkins, I, 81, 103, 105.
Toney, I, 88.
Torbett, II, 120.
Toron, I, 118.
Torrent, II, 32.
Tower, II, 127.
Towles, I, 34, 59, 74, 87, 88, 105; II, 4, 21, 31, will 55, 83, 85, 116.
Townes, I, 64, 79.
Townsend, I, 87.
Trabue, II, 141.
Travers, I, 68, 110; II, 47, 79, 80, 145.
Traylor, II, 11.
Treany, II, 53.
Treat, II, 89.
Trice, I, 103, 105.
Trimble, II, 33, 123, 126.
Triplett, I, 8, 10, 67; II, 19, 45, 46, 49, 52, 84, 128, 129.
Trivino, I, 81.
Trueman, II, 48.
Tucker, I, 74, 76; II, 83.
Tunstall, I, 68, 88, 94, 95; II, 82.
Tupman, II, 76.
Turner, I, 7, 34, 46, 70, 74, 81, 82, 86, 96, 102, 108, 110; II, 9, 17, 21, 32, 37, 80, 85, 101, 130, 151, 154.
Turpin, II, 93.
Turrentine, II, 77, 78.
Tutt, I, 34, 84, 97, 99, 100, 101, 108, 119; II, 47, will 55, 56, 83, 85, 147.
Tutwiler, II, 141.
Twyman I, 59, 60, 110; II, 85.
Tyler, I, 64, 74; II, 7, 9, 154.
Tyng, I, 23.
Tyree, I, 78.

U

Updike, II, 37.
Utterback, II, 18, 23, 153, 159, 160.
Utz, II, 17, 37, 51, will 55.

V

Valentine, I, 76, 78, 79; II, 83.
Vance, I, 86; II, 90.
Vanderslier, II, 31.
Vanhorn, II, 37.
Van Shaik, I, 54, 88.

Van Wart, II, 3.
Vass, I, 18, 80, 96, 109, 117; II, 17.
Vaughan, II, 32, 37, 83, 128.
Vawter, I, 36.
Veill, II, 94.
Venable, I, 64, 77.
Verdier, I, 99.
Vick, I, 67; II, 136.
Vickers, I, 62.
Vinal, II, 112.
Volney, II, 90.
Voroles, I, 103.
Voss, II, 40, 51, will 55.

W

Waddell, I, 32, 34; II, 76.
Wager, I, 16, II, 32, 35.
Waggoner, I, 59; II, 17, 130.
Wagner, I, 110.
Wainwright, I, 89.
Waite, II, 11, 32.
Walden, I, 88; II, 37, 152.
Waldridge, I, 55.
Walker, I, 33, 34, 59, 60, 64, 72-74, 76, 82, 89, 99, 102, 107, 109, 119; II, 23, 32, 47, 76, 83, 124, 136, 138.
Wall, I, 114.
Wallace, I, 14, 53, 55, 60, 68, 76, 100, 101, 111; II, 32, will 56, 85, 139, 140, 158.
Wallach, II, 112.
Waller, I, 7, 46, 97, 98, 105; II, 38, 51, 89, 117.
Wallis, I, 113.
Wampler, II, 11.
Ward, I, 64, 66, 78, 97; II, 8, 9, 53, 94, 113, 147.
Ware, I, 60, 78, 107.
Warfields, I, 77.
Warren, II, 85, 112.
Washburn, II, 76, 151.
Washington, I, 2, 3, 12, 13, 47, 57, 58, 69, 72, 75, 80, 82, 103, 106, 109; II, 3, 5, 7, 8, 14, 55, 77, 79, 80, 83, 84, 86, 156.
Waters, I, 68, 115, 117; II, 143.
Watkins, I, 33, 74, 84, 96, 97; II, will 56.
Watson, I, 48, 52, 73; II, 52, 90, 138, 143.
Watts, I, 104; II, will 56.
Waugh, I, 16, 33, 112.
Wayland, I, 35; II, 32, 46.
Wayman, II, 19, 50, 159.

XXV

Weathers, I, 81.
Weaver, I, 45; II, 37, 51, will 56, 145, 153, 155, 159.
Webb, II, 87, 90.
Webber, II, 159, 160.
Weedon, I, 81; II, 152.
Weeks, I, 60.
Weems, I, 63.
Weir, I, 67, 104.
Welch, I, 53, 54, 101; II, 40, 79, 139, 144.
Wellford, I, 74, 100; II, 35, 108, 110, 118.
Wellman, I, 104.
Welsh, II, 128.
Welton, II, 157.
West, I, 80, 82, 88; II, 86, 113.
Westbrook, II, 81.
Weston, I, 54.
Westwood, I, 82.
Wetherall, II, 45, 46, 53, 131.
Wharton, I, 113; II, 32, 35, 43, 86.
Wheat, II, 23, 85.
Wheatley, I, 29-31; II, 32, 35, 79.
Wheaton, II, 77.
Wheeler, II, 130.
Whipple, I, 82, 88.
Whitaker, I, 67, 82, 88.
White, I, 26, 55, 74, 94, 104, 105; II, 17, 99, 102, 107, 130, 147, 152.
Whitehead, I, 104; II, 51, will 56.
Whitescarver, II, 40, 152, 153, 155.
Whiting, I, 63.
Whitlock, II, 32.
Whitney, I, 91.
Whitridge, I, 110.
Whittemore, I, 66.
Whitten, I, 100, 101, 106.
Wickham, II, 21, 23, 106, 116, 117.
Wickliffe, I, 93.
Wigginton, I, 26, 46, 85, 99, 113; II, 35, 82, 86, 87, 90, 91-94, 147.
Wilcox, I, 76; II, 86, 94.
Wilde, I, 74; II, 77, 78.
Wilhoite, II, 46, will 56.
Wilkes, II, 21.
Wilkins, I, 65, 78, 89.
Wilkinson, II, 139.
Willey, II, 47.
Willett, I, 65.
WILLIAMS FAMILY, I, 108-111.

Williams, I, 14, 15, 17, 19, 33, 34, 55, 56, 60, 62, 64, 66, 69, 76, 80, 82, 84, 87, 97, 99 102, 107, 112, 113; II, 3, 6, 8, 13-15, 17, 18, 51, 55, 80, 81, 90, 116, 119, 122, 124, 127, 131, 160.
Williamson, I, 34, 59, 66, 80, 99; II, 36, 155.
Willis, I, 11, 33, 38, 58, 59, 60, 61, 67, 71, 72, 87, 94; II, 21, 35, 37, 40, 42, 44, 128, 139, 140, 152, 153.
Willoughby, I, 30.
Wills, I, 107.
Wilmer, I, 31, 59, 113, 118.
Wiltshire, II, 100.
Wilson, I, 34, 64, 88, 91, 99, 104, 105, 119; II, 37.
Winder, II, 53, 122, 124, 125.
Winfield, I, 101.
Winfrey, II, 38, 41.
Wingate, I, 32, 71.
Wingerd, I, 100.
Wingfield, I, 86; II, 85.
Winn, II, 159.
Winsborough, II, 82.
Winslow, I, 34.
Winsor, I, 93.
WINSTON FAMILY, I, 75-79.
Winston, I, 22, 24, 25, 28, 74, 87, 103-105, 111, 113, 119; II, 21, 32, 81, 155.
Wirt, I, 32, 34, 56, 75; II, 5, 80, 87, 157.
Wise, I, 59; II, 22, 32, 99, 117, 130, 145.
Witheroe, I, 65, 67.
Withers, I, 26; II, 50, 51, 82.
Wolfe, I, 86.
Wood, I, 33, 34, 64, 77, 109; II, 6, 11, 17, 19, 32, 35, 37, 76, 83, 85, 131, 153-155.
Woodford, II, 13.
Woodmason, I, 17.
Woods, I, 79, 81, 82; II, 77.
Woodson, I, 78.
WOODVILLE FAMILY, I, 79.
Woodville, I, 7, 16, 19, 21, 22, 24-28, 36, 73; II, 7, 54, 89, 149.
Woodyard, II, 19.
Wooten, I, 88.
Woots, I, 46, 50.
Wrekham, I, 109.
Wrenn, II, 19, 35.
Wright, I, 7, 14, 54, 86, 88, 99; II, 37, 52, 53, 85, 151.
Wroth, I, 36.

XXVI

Wyatt, I, 61, 63, 76.
Wylie, I, 53; II, 38, 139, 144.
Wyndham, II, 107.
Wythe, I, 106; II, 136, 138, 141.

Y

Yager, I, 13, 14; II, will 56, 145.
YANCEY FAMILY, II, 81-83.
Yancey, I, 14, 15, 18, 19, 56, 58, 68, 78, 86, 94, 95, 103, 104, 113; II, 32, 35, 46, 48, 50, 55, will 56, 81, 83, 86, 144.
Yates, I, 89; II, 18, 19, 35, 37, 49, 55, will 56, 150, 152, 154.
Yerby, I, 87.
Yoe, I, 109.
Young, I, 14, 16; II, 50, 129.
Yowell, II, 11, 21, 32, 50, 51.
Yuille, I, 78.

Z

Zemula, I, 102.
Zimmerman, I, 15, 53, 85, 87, 112; II, 46.
Zollicoffer, I, 44.

Errata.

————:ooo:————

PART FIRST.

The name "Spotswood" is properly spelt with only one "t."

Page 6, second paragraph, 12th. line, read Kirtley. instead of "Kirtly." On next line read Stanton for "Staunton."

Page 17, 4th. line, read owned instead of "tenanted." In 7th. line read Spotswood for "Spootswood." On same page, in 5th. line from bottom read Robert for "Robort."

Page 24, last paragraph, 7th, line, read wielded for "yielded."

Page 26, second paragraph, 11th. line, read Downman for "Dowman."

Page 41, next to last line of second paragraph, read pistole for "pistol."

Page 50, in 5th. souvenir, read Count for "Court."

Page 58, first line of last paragraph, read Micou for "Micon."

Page 64, 11th. line read Ritchie for "Richie." In 16th. line of same page, read Farish for "Furnish."

Page 68, 32nd. line, read Cruger for "Kruger." In 26th. line, read Angus for "Augus."

Page 86, 2nd. line, read Frances for "Francis." In 5th. line, read Francis Ramsdell for "Francis, Ramsdell." In 39th. line, read Orie C., for "Anna C." In 40th line, read Wingfield for "Winfield."

Page 90, 30th. line, read Ninean for "Ninean."

Page 114, 2nd. line of 2nd. paragraph, read Calvary for "Cavalry."

PART SECOND.

Page 3, second paragraph, 7th. line, read Stevens for "Stephens."

Page 4, 31st. line. read Conway for "Conroy."

Page 6, 2nd line, read Jameson for "Jamesom."

Page 15, 12th. line, read flesh for "flash."

Page 35, 5th. line from bottom, read W. N. Smith for "W. M. Smith." In 3rd. line from bottom, read James L. Justice for " James F. Justis."

Page 36, 7th. line, leave out words "killed in action." In 9th. line, read Edmond L. Amiss for "Edmond T. Amiss."

Page 37, 28th. line, read J. P. Slaughter for "P. P. Slaughter." In 29th. line read E. M. Slaughter, for "M. L. Slaughter."

Page 44, 20th. line read Willis for "Williis."

Page 59, 1st. line, 2nd column, read Mary Browning for "Mary id."

Page 72, 15th. line, read Milly Bryan for " Billy Bryan."

Page 83, 5th. line from bottom, read Hooff for "Hoff."

Page 97, 13th. line from bottom, read 1882 for "1872." In 9th. line from bottom, read Bettie A. for "Bettie N."

Page 131, the expression: "the sixteen justices of the peace for Culpeper county," is used, giving the impression that at that time those sixteen were all of the justices of Culpeper county. From later research it has become quite evident that they were not all, but that there were others who did not join in the protest against the stamp act.

Page 160, 15th. line, read Ferndorf for "Ferdorf."

www.ingramcontent.com/pod-product-compliance
Lightning Source LLC
Chambersburg PA
CBHW071955220426
43662CB00009B/1138